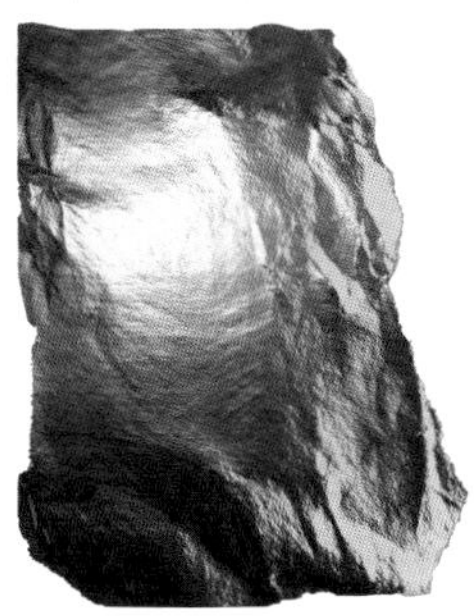

Impossible and Hyper-Real Elements of Architecture

Exercises, provocations, and theories of digital representation.

CARL LOSTRITTO

WITH CONTRIBUTIONS BY VIOLA AGO, JULIE KRESS, AND HANS TURSACK

a r +d
APPLIED RESEARCH +DESIGN PUBLISHING

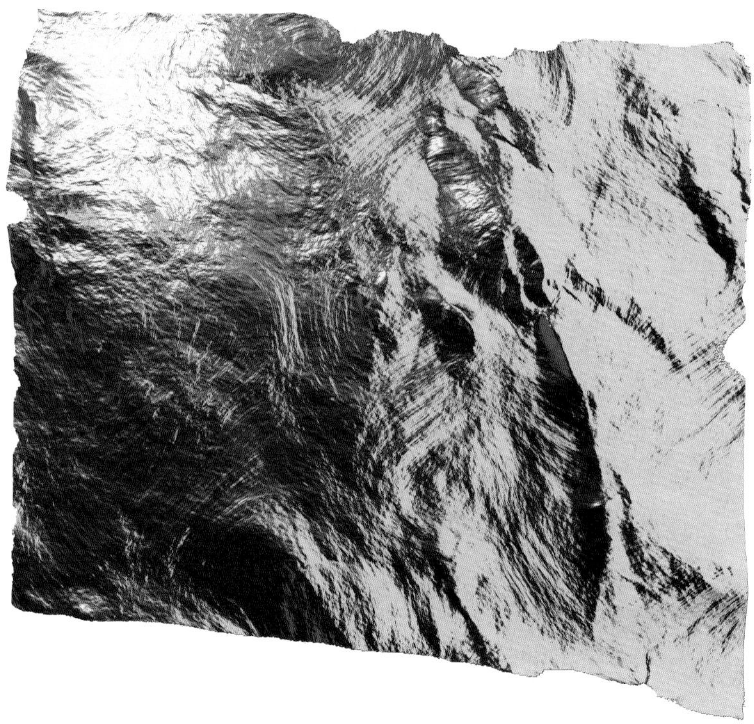

Dedicated to the memory of Lucia,
who wasn't a big reader,
but who affected my reality.

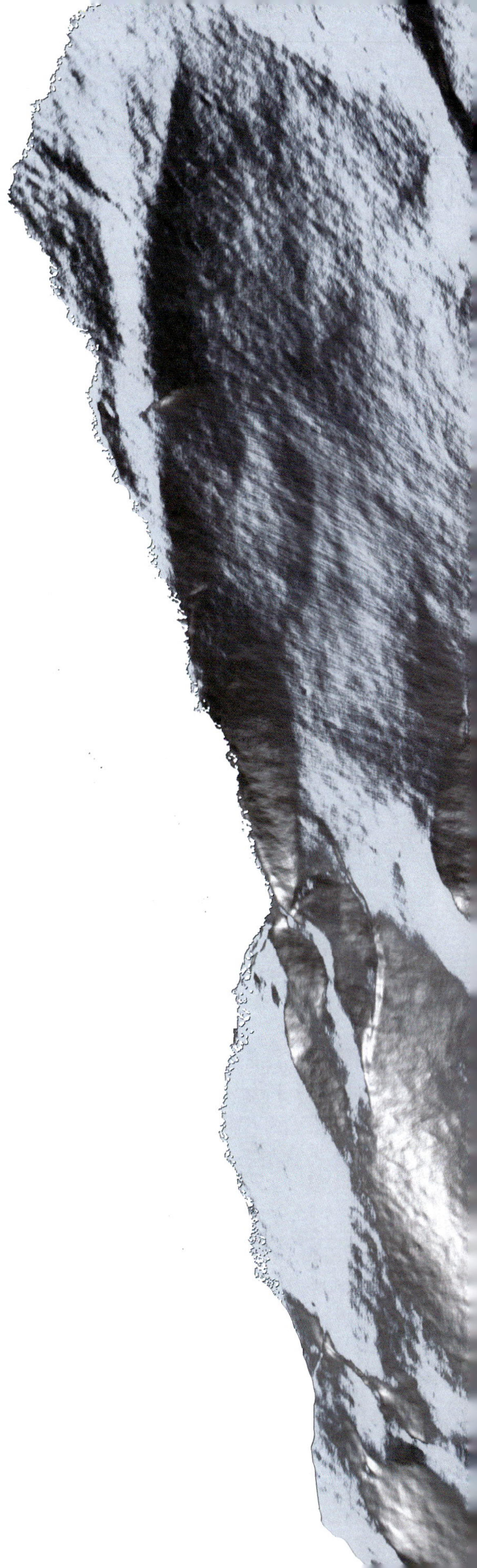

Contents

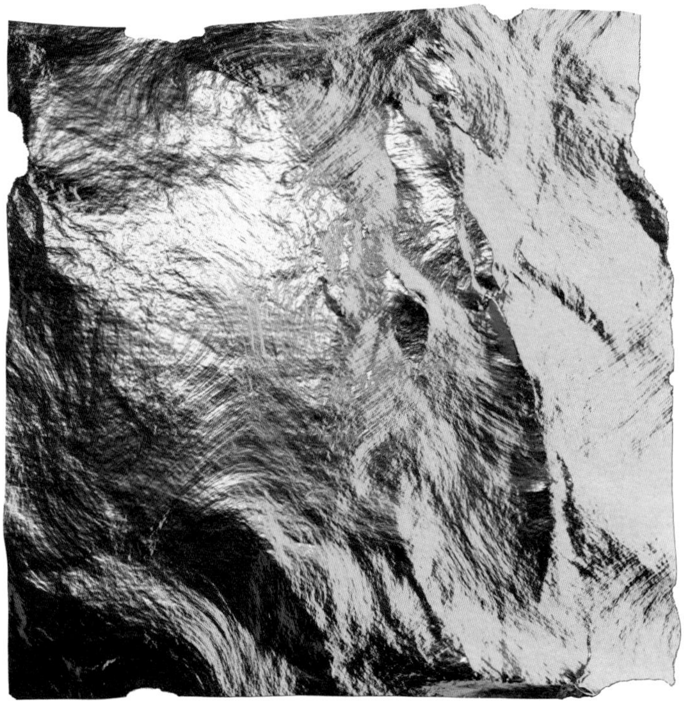

Acknowledgments

First, I want to thank Viola Ago, Julie Kress, and Hans Tursack for trusting this project in its early stages. Each signed on with barely a project brief in hand. I had the privilege of seeing it all come together including the significant extent to which their work influenced the direction of the whole project. We've never all been in the same room at the same time, and I hope that can soon change. When we do convene, our guest of honor will certainly be Chelsea Limbird, who influenced this project as our reader and my most trusted advisor. Her curious candor has always been precious to me. She edits with empathy and intensity. I also note that some of our email threads resemble a book.

For the last few years, I've taught a series of studio courses to RISD architecture students. They've heard me say almost all of what's written here. Their reactions, creatively and discursively, advanced my thinking about representation and digital media. Their surprising, critical, and exciting work regularly impressed on me that learning while creating work of an unusual and critical nature is possible. Thank you to the students who enrolled in *All That is Solid Melts Into Air* (2019), *Eggshell Digital* (2020), and *Uncanny Realism* (2021).

This is the second book project working with Managing Editor Jake Anderson at Applied Research and Design Publishing. Books are hard, but Jake makes it look easy. I'm thankful for Jake and the AR+D team, especially Publisher Gordon Goff, whose early enthusiasm to support this project and faith in our first collaborative endeavor, *Computational Drawing*, cemented what I hope will be a longstanding partnership. Pablo Mandel of CircularStudio designed and typeset both books. I did not make his job easy. I'm profoundly thankful for a creative collaborator who can get excited about strange constraints and self-imposed design prompts. Our early conversations influenced the structure of this book and throughout it was a joy to collaborate.

This project was supported by a RISD Professional Development Fund grant.

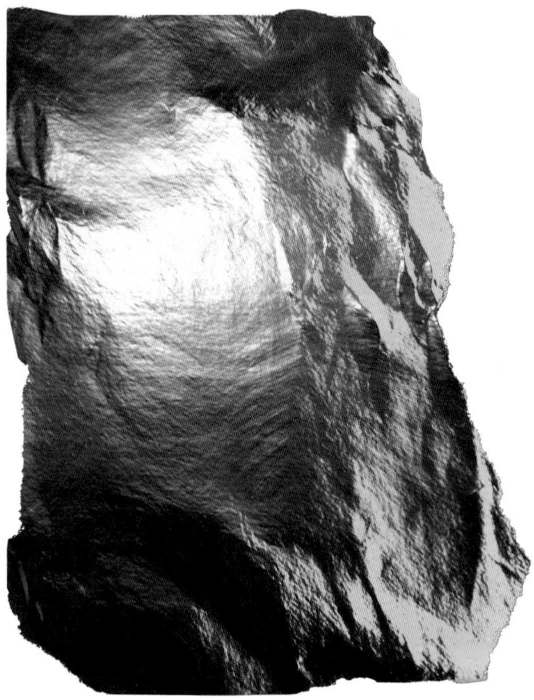

Introduction

Most often, to render is to engage a thick software interface, to accept a photographic framework of variables and effects, and to assume an unquestioned posture that involves articulating material, mass, and color. But like drawing, rendering can be an interdisciplinary, algorithmic, historically rooted cultural practice as much as it is a digital vocation. Today, rendering is so intertwined with the digital that any serious inquiry into the cultural and technical implications of representing reality must also involve inquiry into what it means to operate with and within digital images, digital interfaces, and digital formats. Despite (and maybe even because) the presence of the digital is a given in our creative practices, it's important to note that in the discourse that follows, digitality is itself rich with conflict and contradiction. For example, rendering consumes and produces digital images. Likewise, rendering requires mastery of the digital to subvert digital aesthetics. Throughout this book we'll return to a reoccurring pattern: given some reality (often a digital reality), rendering captures it, yes, but also changes it. Sometimes that change is aesthetic. Sometimes that change is structural. But sometimes, that change becomes so disruptive that it affects our sense of reality. We'll explore, for example, renderings in which the method becomes the subject or in which the rendered image can't be seen as a consumable product and is instead positioned as a rhetorical performance. Said another way: this book proposes that rendering and many of the affiliated techniques can be interesting and relevant in a way that is more complicated, more critical, and more challenging than one might find in a computer graphics textbook or a theoretical analysis of rendering cultures.

Will this book tell you how to make a rendering?

No, not exactly. But don't stop reading if you are interested in learning! The authors of this book *do* want to teach you, and this book *is* designed to help your creative practice directly. As authors we think about readers like our colleagues and students at the institutions we teach. We want to get into the details of how we make (and how you might make) with you, but we are writing for a reader who doesn't want to be led by the hand to make what we've preconceived for you. We want to transmit knowledge and ideas, not tutorials to follow. Therefore, this isn't a manual or a textbook. However, this isn't a volume of pure theory or criticism either. This book is written for the reader who wants to make and theorize at the same time. In that spirit, authors aim to provoke and demystify at the same time.

As is the case with *Computational Drawing, From Foundational Exercises to Theories of Representation*, this book aims to use creative work to open up representation as a field of discourse. Yes, you will find new access to new skills and ideas within these pages, but that knowledge takes the form of prompts and provocations. You'll notice that the exercises throughout the book stand out. Like the prompts in the studios we teach, you can take them literally. You can sit with this book and do the exercises. But you don't have to. We hope the exercises also can work as rhetorical "what if?" statements that can be read in parallel to the other texts. Throughout, we hope you'll find value from our perspective as creators who want to influence and enable others to create. We do this by setting the stage for discourse with a series of elements that have a slippery way of existing in new or varied forms of reality.

Onto the Elements

So, what are these elements? That's complicated. Each author has a slightly different conception, but it can be said that the elements generally grow in complexity beginning in Chapter 1 with an inquiry into the most primitive of elements, the pixel. Because these elements are intertwined with (and sometimes created wholly through) the representational media that convey them, the act of unpacking, explaining, and sharing these elements is itself a project. Our methods are exposed, including (and especially) those that are strange, weird, messy, extravagant, and obscene. Ultimately though, our interest in elements reflects an obsession and discomfort with representation. Representation can often be misunderstood as merely a matter of visual communication. We posit, however, that representation is speculative, and that speculation is more than a matter of depicting proposals. It's about how we see, affect, live, and exist in the world.

Various conceptions of realism are first order matters for architects, artists, and designers. Realism is tantalizingly powerful, but there is good reason to be skeptical of default realism. Let's pause for a moment and pose a self-defeating question, "what is realism?" There is no answer without representation, but even then, software defaults, perceptual assumptions, or cultural aesthetic trends are all forces that conspire to reduce realism to a convergent aesthetic. Things look real because we've been conditioned to associate certain qualities with realism. It still doesn't address what it means to confront the concept of reality in what we make. Further complicating the matter is the fact is that realism can also be problematic—a kind of jump to conclusion that leaves necessary abstraction and open-endedness off the table. Even worse, realism can be exclusive, requiring a shared and privileged understanding of reality to be "in" on the discourse. One contemporary tendency is to take a modest approach to rendering by making images that are self-aware of their limits by reining in or editing out the realism cues. Another approach is to withhold realism until after the design process, when it comes time to sell or market the project. This work does neither and instead comes at realism from the other side: that which is too real, over-real, extra real or "hyper-real," to use our preferred lexicon for the measurably and reflectively extreme. In the chapters that follow, hyper-real means realer than reality as we are accustomed to it being represented. It's ambivalent, contradictory, even enigmatic in its treatment of scale, material, form, and space. So real as to be impossible and extra at the same time.

And despite the range of element types that make up this book, the concept of the element is an essential ingredient in this discourse. Elements exist behind the scenes and in the scenes. Elements are essential for but can also essentially disrupt a conception of reality. Exposure to the nature of each element invites a convergent conversation between matters of topology, technology, and theory. Existential elemental discourse is likewise a matter of realism and representation. We'll consider the question, what is elemental? Is it the pixel that makes up the digital rendered image? The mesh within the digital model? An "object"? Particle? Light ray? What happens when the act of rendering unifies what were once multiple elements into one single complex? When the notion of reality is at issue, elements are open for debate. Each chapter that follows defines and explores one or more elements. Their existence is always contentious as they are created and/or operate in model, image, and mind. But it's not enough for each speculative element to exist. Elements interact to form compounds, and those interactions form multiple conceptions of architecture.

The geometry of this book is more like a spiral than an arc. The chapters reinforce a reoccurring pattern that on one hand suggests that the elements share a common nature as part of a curated collection. On the other hand, the elements advance from the foundationally primitive binary bitmap to the grids that make up those images into the realm of objects, containers, houses, and gaming spaces. Finally, we end near to where we started as we consider the rendered elements with respect to their relationship to drawing, which we frame as the image's precursor and successor.

Hyper-Real Animations

A book about realism must take note of the stillness of the printed image. As our discourse moves into the realm of dioramas, we'll discuss stillness and animation (as well as death and movement) in more detail. But as a practical matter, many of the impossibly real elements live an animate existence beyond these pages. Is it essential to watch these play? Certainly not, but they exist, really, and for real, here:

http://impossible-real.how

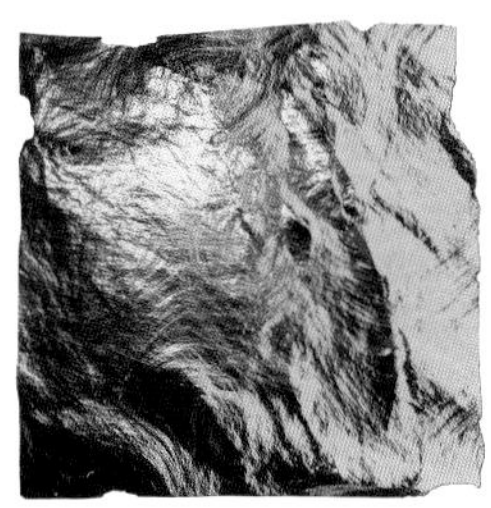

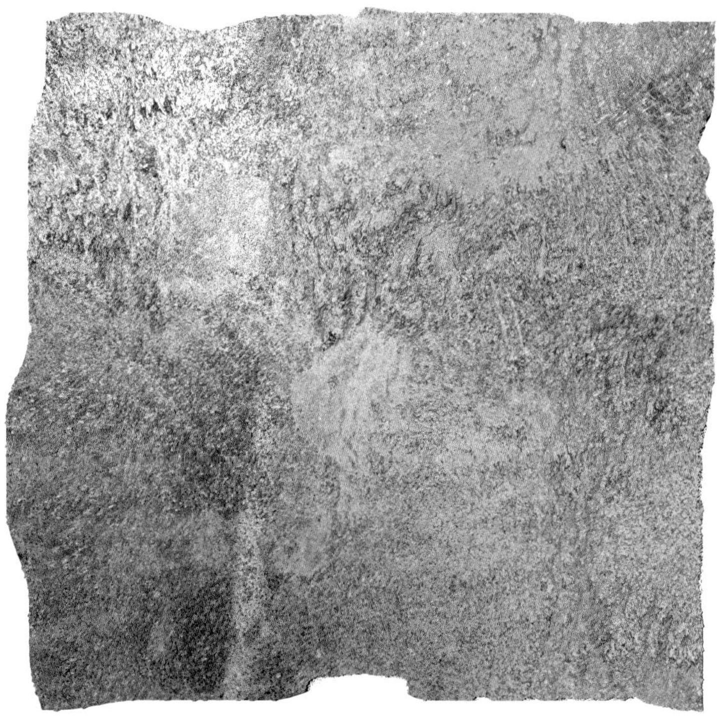

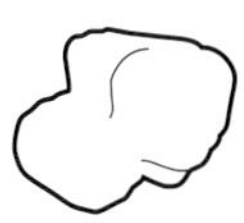
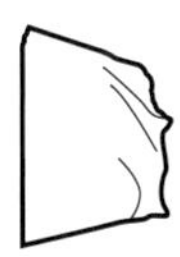
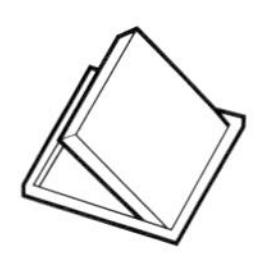
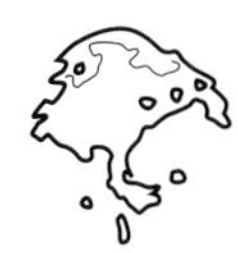

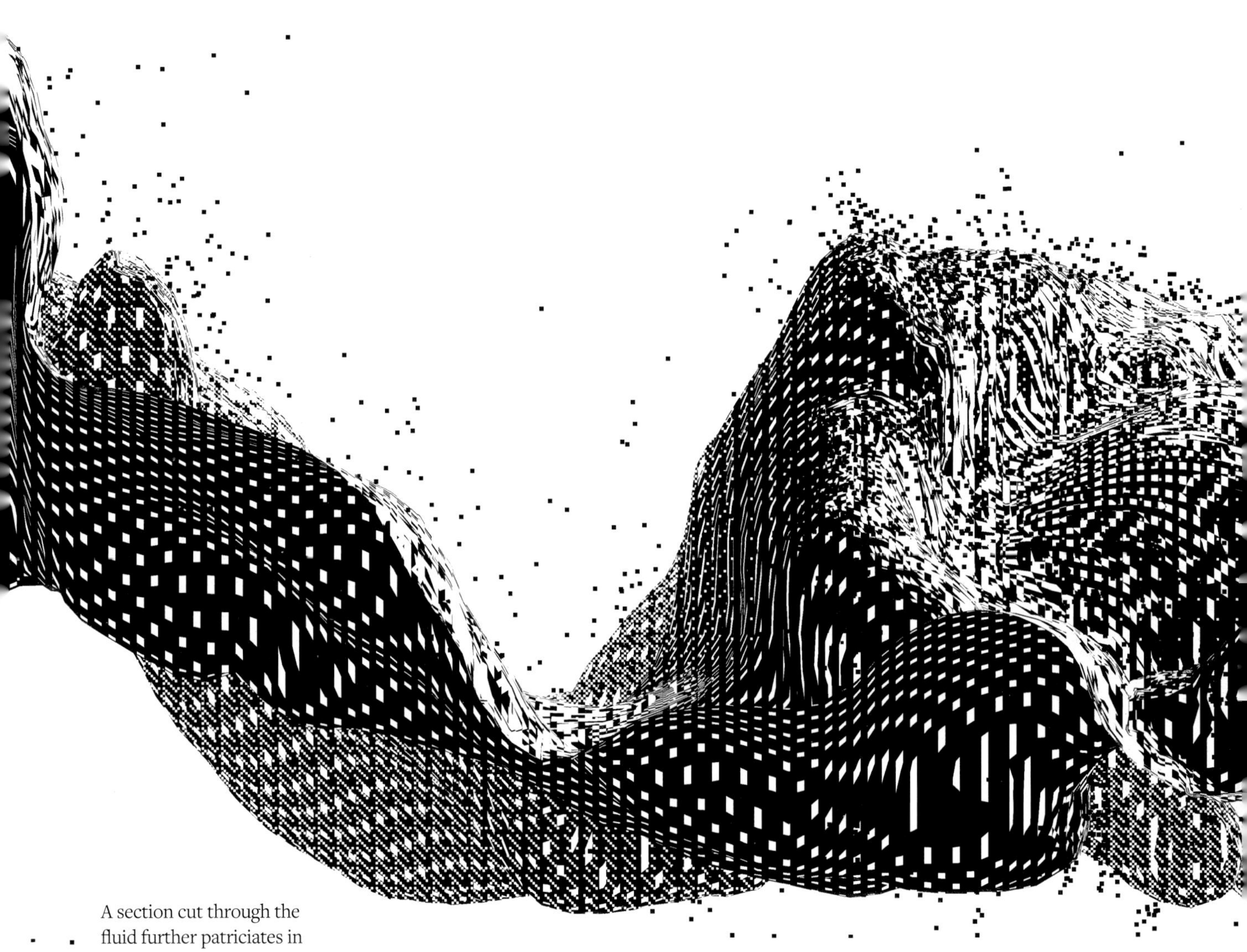

A section cut through the fluid further patriciates in the image's refusal to accept conventions of material mass even as it willfully expresses material and physical qualities.

CHAPTER 1

Bits Mapped

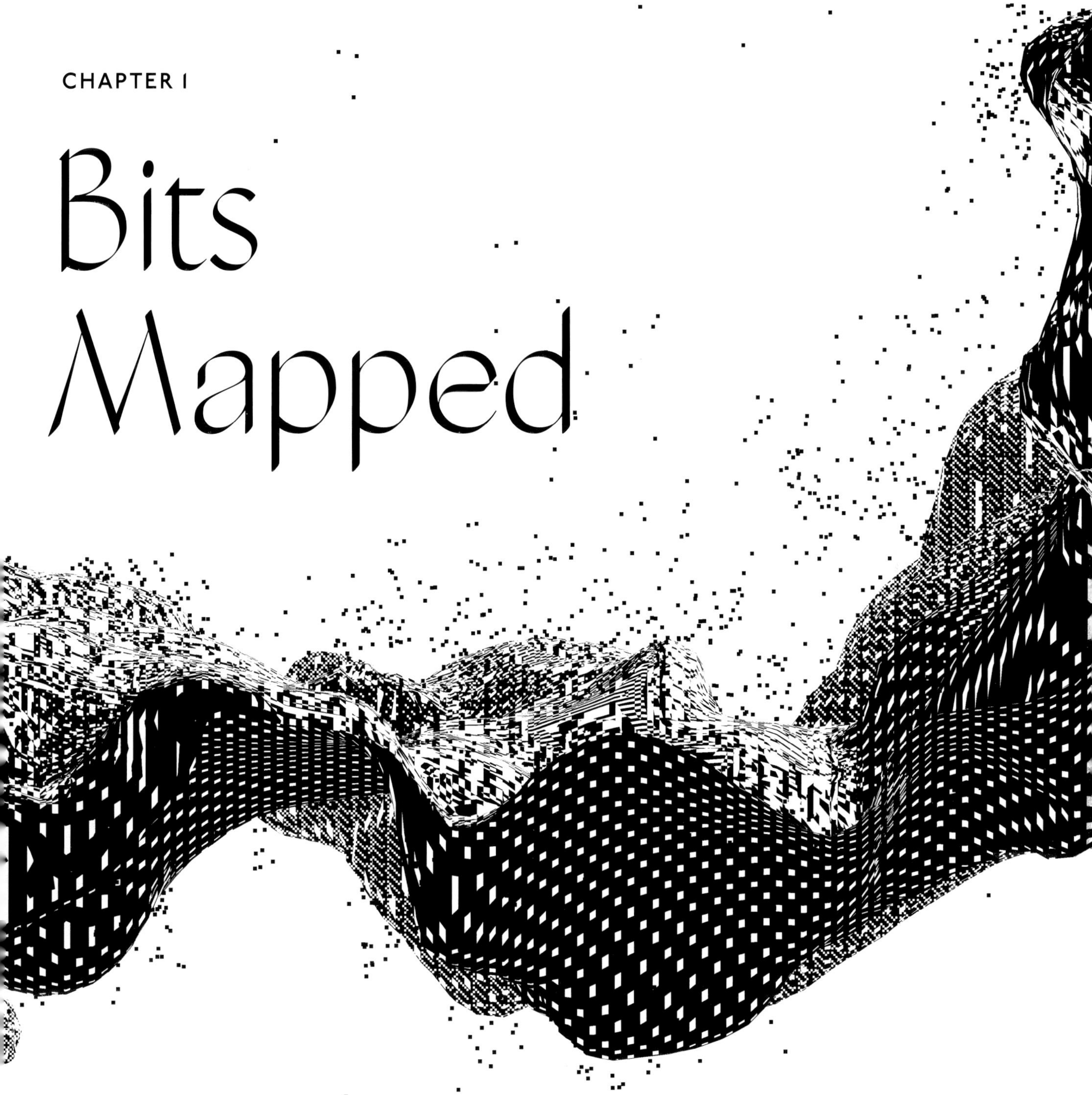

Where should we start?

The Pixel

An obvious beginning for discourse about rendering and digital media, especially given our interest in elements, would be the pixel, which literally means "picture element." The origins of the pixel are worth exploring, but instead of telling the story from the beginning, we're going to focus on a brief era that saw the pixel on its way to, but not yet arrived at, mainstream status. The loosely defined half-decade roughly between 1985 and 1990 is a "sweet spot" in the ascendance of the pixel. The state of the pixel during this time is aligned with the elements that will be explored, created, and examined throughout this book, beginning with a treatment of pixels in a manner that preserves some of the technical limitations of late '80s computing formats within the context of contemporary representational workflows. The rationale for *why* this all happens depends on what was just possible in 1985 and what was not yet feasible in 1990.

Perhaps you know the term, "pixel art," a subgenre of digital art associated with the meticulous crafting of small or low-resolution images. Perhaps the reference to the late '80s conjures nostalgia for a graphic aesthetic in the same way that the musical "synthwave" subgenre conjures 80's synthpop.[1] Early musical synthesizers left a signature sound that could be uncharitably characterized as the nascent and flawed approximation of musical instruments. We might go even further into that way of thinking and refer to the synthetic sounds as *representations* of existing musical instruments. Of course, the aesthetic prevalence of the synthesizer is owed to its new, different, and recognizable—and therefore iconic—sound. On one hand synth sounds are undeniably autonomous. They sound good, even without any intellectual reference. Music, even "popular" music, can be constructed with respect to their qualities and irrespective of their representational meaning. On the other hand, the imperfections of the synth sounds are rhetorically interesting with respect to representational aesthetics and our inquiry into why as well as how we represent reality. But just as our pixels strive to be inseparable from content in the same way that the paint on canvas that depicts a scene is inseparable from the content of the scene, synthpop qualities can't be separated from the technological representational discourse. The cherished and specific sounds of the synthesizer don't exist despite imperfect nature of representation, they exist because of the imperfect nature of the representation. The music resonates in revival form in a way that sets an aspirational trajectory for pixels. Technology and visual culture increasingly repress the pixel as subject in pursuit of higher and higher resolution. Can we do for pixels what synthwave has done for '80s sounds?

The term, "pixel art" usually refers to works that celebrate the limits of the digital image and rely on lower resolution and manual techniques that express the pixel. Pixel artists designed icons, glyphs, and fonts of early graphic user interfaces, but today the artform tends to manifest in standalone digital images that use low-resolution and pixelization as a graphic style. We'll soon delve into the digital culture of the late '80s, a time at the base of an exponential curve of graphic innovation, which saw users and game developers (but few "artists" and almost no "architects") crafting with pixels before the prevalence of the digital photograph, which began its ascendence in 1990 with the first consumer handheld digital camera to go to market in the United States, the Dycam Model 1.[2] We'll also explore the excitingly disruptive implications of binary bitmap culture on contemporary rendering practices. But first, we need to dwell a bit longer on what the pixel is and what it isn't.

Constructing Elements in Pursuit of Impossibility

The legacy and etymology of the pixel are certainly relevant, but because we'll use the pixel to poke at the concept of a representational architectural element, let's pause here and define "element." A straightforward definition—the irreducible components of matter—won't work in the realm of the digital. Even the pixel, despite its origins as a "picture element,"[3] is reducible to bytes. In most of the RGB images we make and experience in our everyday lives, each pixel is associated with three such bytes, one for each channel: red, green, and blue. Each byte *contains* eight bits. Those eight binary values, a combination of zeros and ones, describe a base ten number between zero and 255 inclusive (two to the power of eight possible values) and thus our pixels can be said to contain 24 bits and two to the power of 24 (16,777,216) possible values. So, a pixel is certainly reducible and by the strictest of definitions, not an element. Alvy Ray Smith, the cofounder of Pixar and author of *A Biography of the Pixel*, likewise uses the container premise to explain what we all implicitly understand, though often mistakenly define technically, about the pixel. He writes, "The bit became the universal medium, and the pixel—a particular packaging of bits—conquered the world. It became possible to remove a painting, so to speak, from its canvas."[4] He further conflates the pixel with the bits it contains and the methods used to display them in writing, "Pixels are the invisible bits that represent visible waves. My fervent intent is that you understand this piece of magic and be amazed by how it works."[5] We can soon come to one of two conclusions.

One option is to conclude that the only digital element is the invisible bit and move on to other and separate conversations about content. Though valid, this framing is as uninteresting as it is flawed. Everything digital is reducible to bits, yes, but bits are very much unlike atoms of the kind found on the periodic table of elements. They have no material and no mass. They could be described as an ontological state of being or lack of being in the same way that "true" (or "false") and "yes" (or "no") are linguistic constructs. Smith, whose creative and intellectual authority is unimpeachable, elegantly links the separability of content and medium—and even the essential construct of medium—to the history of the pixel. But like this discourse, he does not isolate technology from creativity. If we were accept this philosophically pure option, we cut ourselves off from creative control over the definitions of the components of our work. Everything digital would be a new arrangement of bits, nothing more, and digitality of architecture would be a settled matter. The second option—the option that we will choose, and which will guide the work that follows—is to conclude that there are no fixed digital elements. Even pixels turn out to be less coherent than we might initially assume, and that's good. While this relativist position might be unsatisfying to the digital theorist (and the designer who turns away from the impact of technology), it's compatible with both design and programming cultures invested in the constant contextual reframing of elements, content, and reality. In this option, the pixel sometimes regains its elemental status, *and* the door is opened for us to define and create elements at will. Elements are whatever we want them to be. From a creative perspective, it matters more that we are in control over our building blocks than it does that the building blocks are irreducible.

In that spirit, it's important to note that the element that we'll explore as this chapter progresses is more than a pixel. Our interest in representation provokes us to consider elements that make up images—pixels certainly included—and elements that make up the models and spaces that are represented *in* those images. When the element is slippery, moving from model to image to subject to method, architecture holds it together. In a sense, every designed element of architecture is a work of architecture. Our special pixels are one such example, tethered between image, form, and reality. These picture elements are anchored in the model and occasionally manifest as objects in the scene even as they make up that very scene. What might sound like an enigma will be explained, but first, let's dwell on another important term.

The elements in this book are labeled "impossible" because they avoid a fixed relationship to a singular built reality. Their appearance in one reality might contradict with their allegiance to another reality, for example. The elements don't merely find themselves in a reality though. As they extend like a skewer through multiple media and formats, the elements tend to create their own realities. Again, our specific kind of pixel construct performs in this way. Histories provoke reality as much as visual cues. The history of the pixel, for example, brings conceptions of representation, reality, and the image to bear on its contemporary manifestation. Our impossible elements are often recognizable as a type. They aren't new, but are often newly strange.

1988, the Year of the Pixel

The pixels on these pages have more in common with the pixels of 1988 than the pixels of today. Today's screens are so dense with pixels—so high in resolution—that the geometric extent of a single pixel is indecipherable to the human eye. Our image display technology has progressed beyond the point where the technology defines the aesthetics. "Pixelization" is a problem of the past. In this work, recovering pixelization is an opportunity to recover digital craft.

In the pursuit of its representational and conceptual capacity, it might help to note that a pixel is not merely a tiny square. To the aforementioned pixel virtuoso Alvy Ray Smith, this is incredibly important. "Pixels have no shape until they're spread by a spreader. I've often drawn them for pictorial convenience as a side view, or in elevation, as spikes of the appropriate height...we can't see pixels...really, truly, a pixel has no shape. It's a point with zero diameter. Only spread pixels have shape."[6] Strictly speaking, a pixel rendered or visualized can appear to be a square, but it can also inform or become any number of graphic types and shapes. Here though, the colloquial usage of pixel as those tiny little squares we *can* see is culturally as well as theoretically significant. The pixel is the data that inform that small portion of rendering on screen, *and* the portion of the rendering itself. Secondly, and relatedly, a pixel cannot exist on its own. Technical literature on the pixel and its history will accurately note that the pixel is the smallest *addressable* element of a digital image. Addressing is the first step toward reading or modifying the status of a portion of that digital image. Pixels are not like bricks that form a wall; pixels aren't aggregated to form an image, but rather the reverse: an image exists as a digital formation and then is recorded and modified in terms of pixels. Historically speaking, these clarifications help explain the mutability and resilience of the pixel through radical changes in hardware, operating systems, programming languages, software, and digital image formats. Any cellularly reducible visual 2-D array can be conceived in terms of pixels. It's most accurate and most fruitful to think of the pixel not as a thing, but as a concept. This concept can be traced over a long history of implementation that continues to evolve today.

With that noted, the discourse about pixels can be anchored in multiple moments. We could look back, for example, at the electronics of circuit boards controlling incandescent marquee light displays. Or we can examine the SuperPaint computer system developed Xerox PARC in the 1970s that was significantly advanced that it was used to create exploratory animations by Alvy Ray Smith well ahead mainstream digital video formats.[7] But our story is best rooted a bit later, in 1988, four years after the release of the first Apple Macintosh, which came bundled with its first "killer app," MacPaint. Designed and developed by Bill Atkinson, MacPaint is an example of creative innovation and creative restraint. It epitomized the graphic feats of the Macintosh, which were far beyond its competitors in the personal computing industry. The year 1988 marked MacPaint's maturation to version 2.0 of after Apple spun off part of its software division to form a new company, Claris. For the first time, artists, designers, children, and hobbyists—groups with significant overlap—converged with and flavored the computer arts scene with a flair of optimistic postmodernism, though not often articulated in those terms. Many explored the possibility of making art with a computer without the need to theorize, write software, interface with a terminal, or access a closet-sized apparatus. Computer art historian, Grant D. Taylor writes of this time, "Influenced by the anti-humanists, postmodernists were also skeptical of the belief in technology as morally neutral. However, those who theorized computer and electronic art in relation to postmodernism effectively dampened the anti-humanist pessimism by seeing technology as personally empowering. By close of the 1980s, computer technology, illustrated in the rise of the artist-programmer, moved from the hands of the technocrat and from its instrumental paradigm to the hands of the individual in the public and cultural sphere."[9] Taylor keys us into a theorization of the 1980s as articulated by social scientist and technology psychologist Sherry Turkle who writes of the emergence of the "Macintosh paradigm" of "simulation and surface" in contrast to the predominant computing culture as epitomized by IBM.[10] The resulting body of pixel artwork produced in this era is immediately recognizable for reasons that can be traced to technology and designed technological limitations. The entire Macintosh operating system, for example, could be compressed into only 128 kilobytes of memory and with no hard drive, was stored entirely on a 400-kilobyte floppy disk. Despite its lack of color or even grayscale, the graphic quality was profound: high refresh rates, relatively high resolution, smoothly updating graphics, and a fidelity of detail. All of this was possible because of the density of pixels on the screen. The early Macintosh computers did not feel like text-based terminals with graphics overlaid. They were an entirely graphic experience. The shape of rendered pixels was also a design decision for the early Macintosh. The Macintosh's predecessor, the Apple Lisa, rendered pixels taller than they were wide to optimize horizontal detail—a benefit for word processing but a hindrance for most graphic applications. The Macintosh's non-directionally-biased square pixels and the 72 pixels per inch resolution of the built-in CRT display would soon become industry standards.[11]

The icons that were part of the Macintosh graphical user interface (GUI) were designed by artist Susan Kare.[12] Kare's influence on the Macintosh brand, computer art, and digital culture can't be overstated. Aside from the Apple logo itself, Kare's "happy mac," "command," and her "Chicago" typeface that worked well at small pixel heights would become icons (for lack of a better term) of Macintosh culture.[13] Initially, Kare sketched on graph paper to conform to the structure of the pixel array. Memory and resolution were both at such premiums that each icon could afford a small amount of data—at most 32 by 32 pixels or 128 bytes before compression. To facilitate this process, Andy Herzfeld wrote custom icon-editing software for Kare that would mimic the gridded paper and allow her to toggle pixels on or off. The icon was displayed at two sizes, 1:1 (for previewing) and at significant zoom with visible gridded lines (for editing). The output of the software was hexadecimal code that developers could embed into future versions of the operating system. Fascinatingly, this software, used to develop icons for the Macintosh ran on a prototype version of the Macintosh.[14] This beautifully circular relationship between tool, media, and representation foreshadows many of the custom elements that will be described later in this book.

Remembering Kare's initial work on paper, it's worth pausing here to speak about paper verses screens. Beginning with the obvious, paper is usually white. Dark media like graphite and charcoal sit over and in the substrate. The digital image, by default, flips this. When a screen is off, the pixels go black. White is additive, the result of a positive signal, a one rather than a zero, a value of true rather than false, presence rather than absence. Thus, in digital interfaces, content is easy to conceive of as vivid white against empty black nothingness of non-signal. The Macintosh graphic user interface—counter to digital tendencies—flipped this back. White areas defined the interface's background. Text and figural icons were black. The "blank" image when launching MacPaint was likewise white and the paint brush in its default setting rendered pixels black. It suggested that the act of printing to white paper could be a direct transference of content on the screen. This reflects the beginnings of an apparent mindset among the Macintosh interface designers that could be characterized as an interest in registering with traditional or everyday media. Even before the prominence of desktop publishing, this was evident in the metaphors prevalent in the GUI and would eventually evolve into a devoted if impermanent[15] allegiance to skeuomorphism in Apple's software and operating system graphic user interface. Even Kare's carefully crafted MacPaint sample graphics, used extensively in Macintosh marketing materials and embedded in MacPaint software as examples, were overtly traditional. One of the most widely used of her MacPaint works is a digital interpretation of a woodblock print by Hashiguchi Goyo. It reflects a balance between pixel-precision and pixel-subservience to gray tones.

Originally, the full MacPaint image measures 580 pixels wide by 720 pixels high, which is larger than the original Macintosh's screen resolution of 512 × 342. The proportions of the image almost perfectly match a portrait orientation of 8.5- by 11-inch paper. Printed at 72 pixels per inch, the same resolution as the Macintosh's screen, the image would sit on such a page with about a one-inch margin at all sides. Again, we can deduce the Macintosh designer's interest in a computer not as a processor of words and numbers, but something tethered to the world via images.

36 eight by eight binary bitmap patterns included in MacPaint.

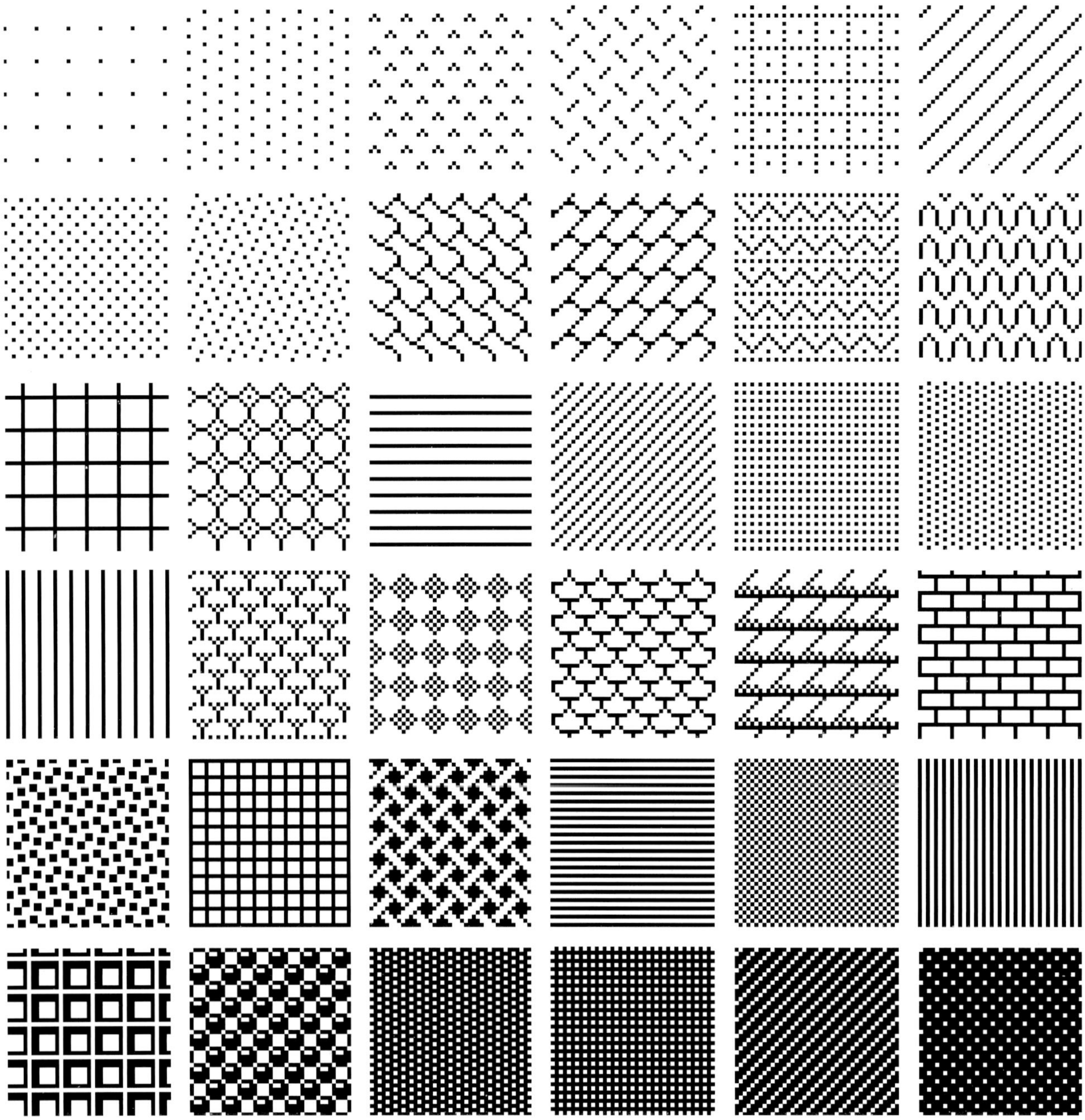

36 eight by eight binary bitmap patterns included in MacPaint repeated within larger areas.

Pixel Creating Cultures

Let's return to two terms mentioned earlier: "pixel-precision" and "pixel-subservience to gray tones." Pixel-precision refers to the manual control of each pixel. We might use the term "by hand" to describe this craft. Such a label, though easily confused with the direct use of physical media, is accurate in the sense that the hand controls a mouse, which in turn can control an interface element that adjusts one or more pixels at a time and without delay. This is unlike the indirect execution of filters, procedures, or algorithms that take time or a sequence of steps to play out. The state of pixels are not generated, but controlled, directly. Pixel-precision leaves open the possibility that the individual or small clusters of pixels are perceptible in the final image at full size. Think of single pixel representing a star in the sky, a particle of mist, or a connected sequence of pixels representing a strand of hair. In these cases, the pixels retain their discrete and figural qualities; they don't recede into each other. Yes, this phenomenon is dependent on the relatively low resolution (by today's standards) of MacPaint images, but there's something else at play.

Let's now consider, "pixel subservience." Using today's image processing technology, one can easily open a digital photograph and convert it to a binary bitmap image. Most image editing software can do this using one of multiple algorithms. The "50% threshold" algorithm simply checks to see if the value of the input pixel was closer to black or white and outputs one of those two values accordingly. More complex algorithms would consider the grayscale value of an area of the input image and generate a pattern of black and white pixels to match that value. Each pixel would be *subservient* to the mission of articulating a gray value. That is, the perception of gray made possible by processing clusters of pixels together as a single value. The resulting image can be said to appear gray if one doesn't zoom in too closely. But those processed pixels will likely lack a sensitivity to the content of the image. Lines and strong edges are especially difficult to sustain in a conversion into binary bitmap from a source image. Pixel-precision methods, on the other hand, allow (and require) the assertion of lines and hard edges.

Pixel-precision, when coupled with pixel-subservice, blurs the line between drawing and rendering in the sense that a pictorial scene with shadow and tone can be constructed (as in, rendered) but that scene is built up with a system of representation (like a drawing).

Crafting gradients with a mixture of pixel-precision and pixel-subservience is similar in concept to what can be achieved with hatching in a material drawing. In a strict line drawing, there is no melting down or blurring of the line. There is only line, or lack of line just as in these images the pixels are either black or white. Dense clusters of repeating lines are perceived in terms of value. MacPaint helpfully provided an editable pattern library: a collection of 8 × 8 pixels that approximate a range of gray values. These patterns can be applied over an area of the image. These patterns, which number 36 in total, are not even close to exhaustive. There are over eighteen quintillion (1.845 × 1019) possibilities.[16] Even if we were to think about the possible levels of value by counting the total number of black pixels within the 8 × 8 pattern unit, we would arrive at 62 values (plus solid black and solid white). Fascinatingly, the MacPaint patterns are unevenly distributed between light and dark using this metric. Some of the MacPaint patterns contain the same number of black verses white pixels and could be said, therefore, to approximate the same value. If considered only in these quantitative terms, these patterns are redundant. Did the MacPaint developers make a mistake? Certainly not. They were clearly operating under a different premise. The MacPaint patterns are designed to do more than deploy a certain *number* of dark verses light pixels. The pixels do much more than approximate shades of gray. They suggest material, texture, and scale. They hint at a level of playfulness and experimental graphic confidence that suggest that Kare was involved.

Macintosh computer games of the era reflect these constraints. Though early Macintosh computers were not known for a wealth of available advanced 3rd-party software (games included), there is one genre of games that is uniquely relevant to this discourse and that was affiliated with Apple's Macintosh. Bill Atkinson developed MacPaint almost singlehandedly, but he was also principal developer of HyperCard, a software development environment in which a stack of images augmented by GUI elements and other media formed a linkable traversable database. HyperCard is often cited as a precursor to HTML in the sense that both contain hypertext linkages through an otherwise linear structure. The HTML "page" is analogous to the "card" in the stack. A custom scripting language within HyperCard allowed for conditional relationships and input-driven narratives to be developed within the stack, which could be exported as a standalone application. It was the kind of visuals-first development environment that could only exist, at the time, on the Macintosh, and the resulting software was equally unique in its allegiance to rich visual narratives as well as rather heavy memory requirements for the era. HyperCard Stack Games were more like playable graphic novels than the real-time inhabitable complexes that will be explored in a later chapter of this book.[17] The immersion in these games and the quality of the experience is entirely a function of the images, which can be linked together into sequences. These renderings were produced manually, often with MacPaint. Thus, "screenshot" is not exactly an accurate term to describe how they are sampled here. "Extracted resource" is more appropriate. Regardless of the label, these images warrant a close reading in terms of the quality of their perceived grays, the presence of lines, the treatment of light and shadow, perspective, and, more broadly, in their capacity to suggest a reality within the scope of the digital game.

Brothers Rand and Robyn Miller and their company, Cyan, created a series of these HyperCard stack games. *The Manhole,*[18] published in our "year of the pixel," 1988, is notable for its lack of goals or ending. Loosely constructed narratives are driven by spaces and environments more than the characters. The game is infinitely explorable but is not "open world" by today's definition; the HyperCard stack is finite. The images and spaces in *The Manhole*—inspired quite overtly by *Alice in Wonderland*—balance between the strictly enclosed spaces of rooms, caverns, the interior of follies, and exterior spaces that would seem to span endlessly as the atmosphere fades to white or black. *The Manhole* respects conventions of perspective, gravity, light, and natural materials, but players are shuttled between various scales regularly. Doors and portals are especially important. Absent the smooth animate transitions that are possible with real-time camera movement, markers in space coherently link one frame to another. The advantage of this lower fidelity of camera movement becomes evident in the composition of each frame. The presence of doors and portals are positioned and scaled for maximum ambiguity and spatial tension. As a game of images, every image contributes to the world. Conversely, every world is conceived like a diorama, encapsulated within the closed format of the image and oriented toward a viewer sitting just on the other side of the thick frame of the computer screen.

Spelunx and the Caves of Mr. Seudo, [19] another HyperCard stack game published by Cyan, followed *The Manhole*. Again, each frame is crafted to imply movement through intricate architectural scenes. The structural underpinnings of *Spelunx* are similar to *The Manhole* such that they provide a control over which we can explore advancements in artistic technique and computational capacity. Most immediately, we can note that the resolution of *Spelunx* is double that of *The Manhole*. The Miller brothers' style evolved with the increase in resolution. The articulation of black outlines around figures is less a given. Edges can be articulated instead by areas of varied tone within one object, and even around the boundaries of a cast shadow. Where *The Manhole*

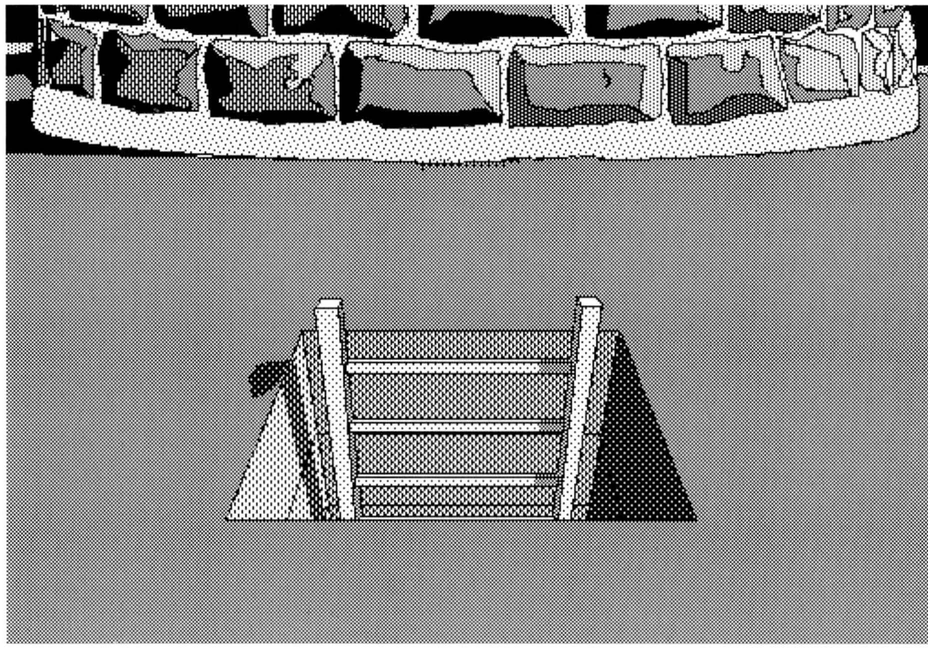

always reinforced edges with lines as though a low-resolution approximation of a vector drawing, *Spelunx* allows the patterned areas themselves to imply the edges of form. It more confidently includes images that we would describe as renderings. We might even go further and note that *Spelunx* approaches the kind of realism that results from a raytraced rendering. Because *Spelunx* had the advantage of advancements in memory capacity, the game is richer in quantity of assets in the stack. The nested worlds within worlds go deeper. In what might have been a seed of influence planted over two decades ago, there are pictures that turn into dioramas and a rendered mechanical apparatus that grows a tree[20] based on input parameters for branches, fruits, and flowers.

There's more going on here than nostalgia for a digital era long passed by. The restrictions and constraints imposed by MacPaint and similar software forced onto a pixel a heavy charge: be an element while representing other elements. These constraints elevate each pixel to potential aesthetic prominence. Conversely, each pixel, even those that are subservient to a gray value, teeters on the edge of exposure. No pixel can hide in such low resolution. Each digital image was crafted, rather than processed. As we think about digital rendering using contemporary software, we'll be searching for similar productive constraints. When we can't find them, we'll make them.

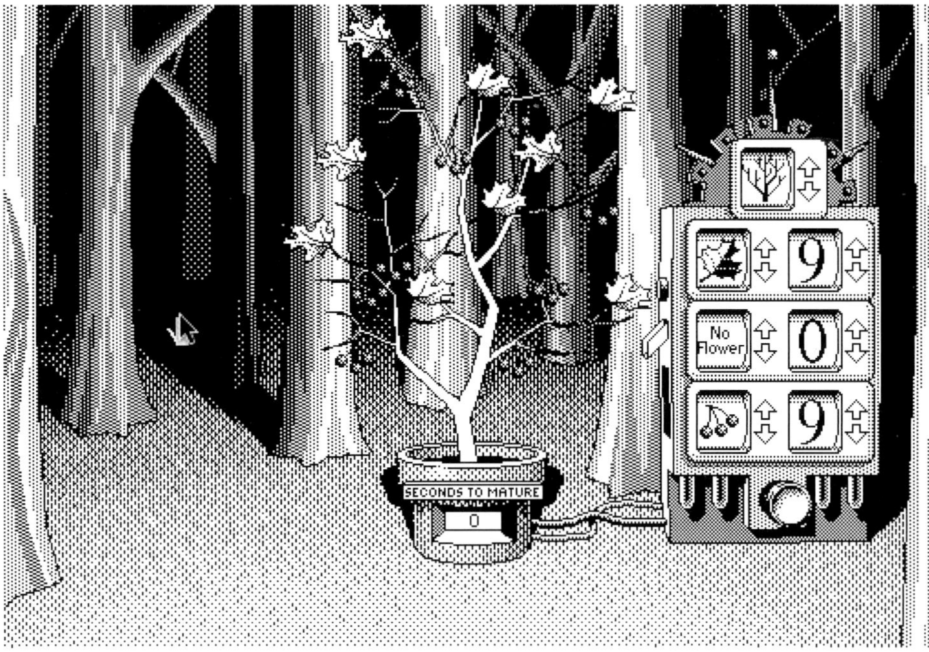

One of hundreds of still images from *The Manhole,* a HyperCard stack computer game by Rand and Robyn Miller, 1988. Courtesy of Cyan, Inc.

One of hundreds of still images from *Spelunx and the Caves of Mr. Seudo,* HyperCard Stack computer game by Rand and Robyn Miller, 1991. Here, a virtual world within the virtual world of the game invites players to operate a tree-growing machine. Courtesy of Cyan, Inc.

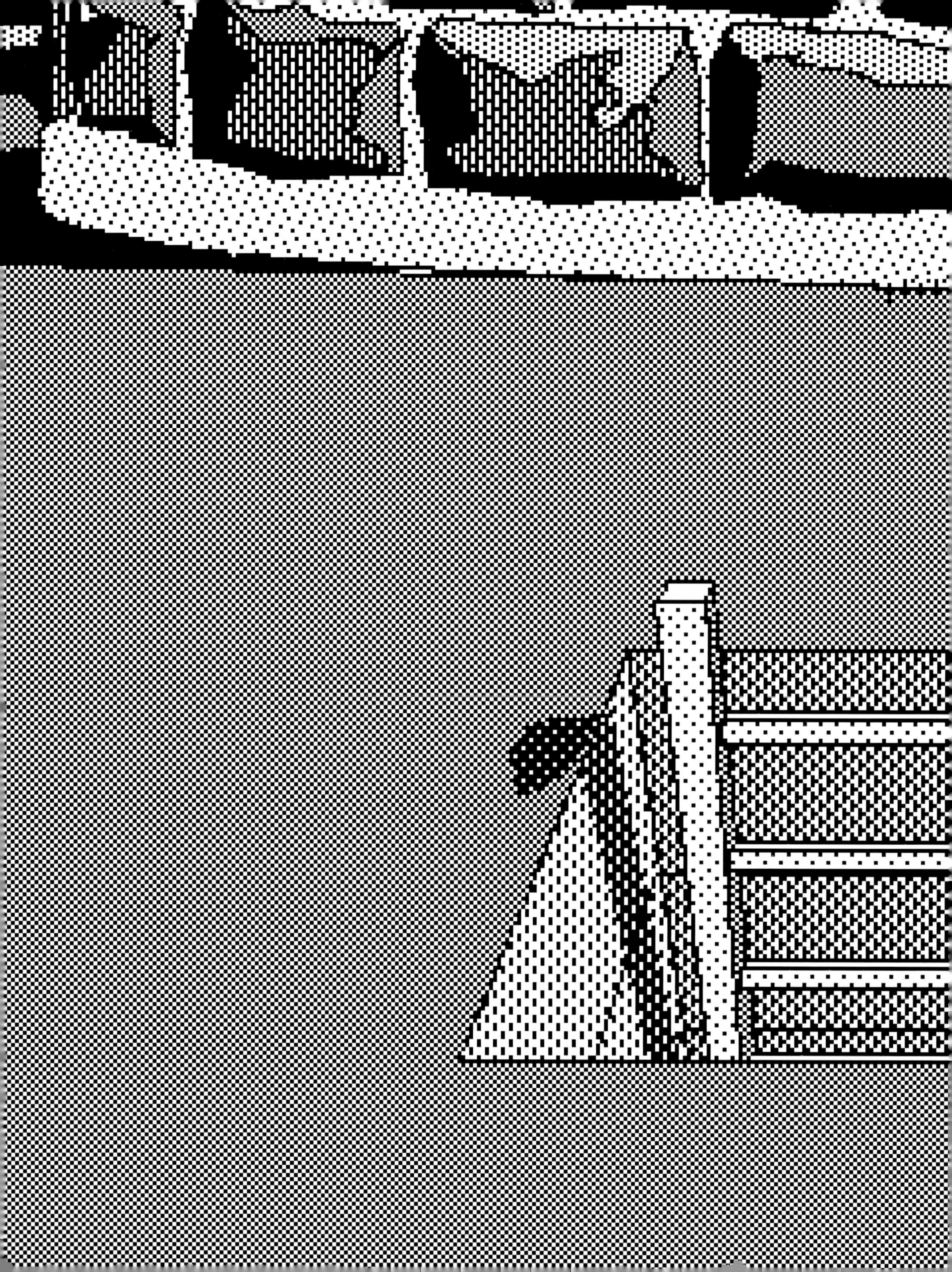

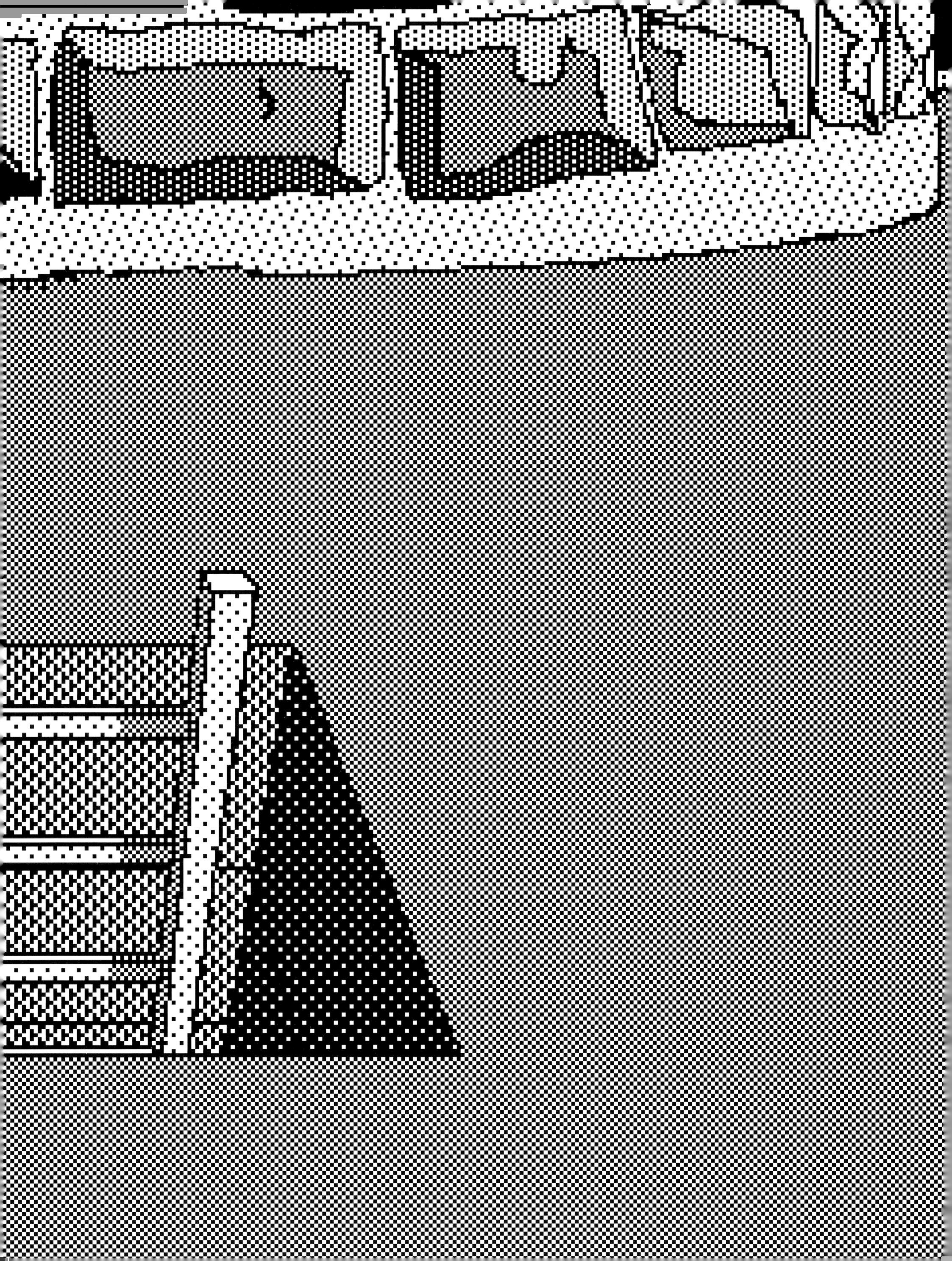

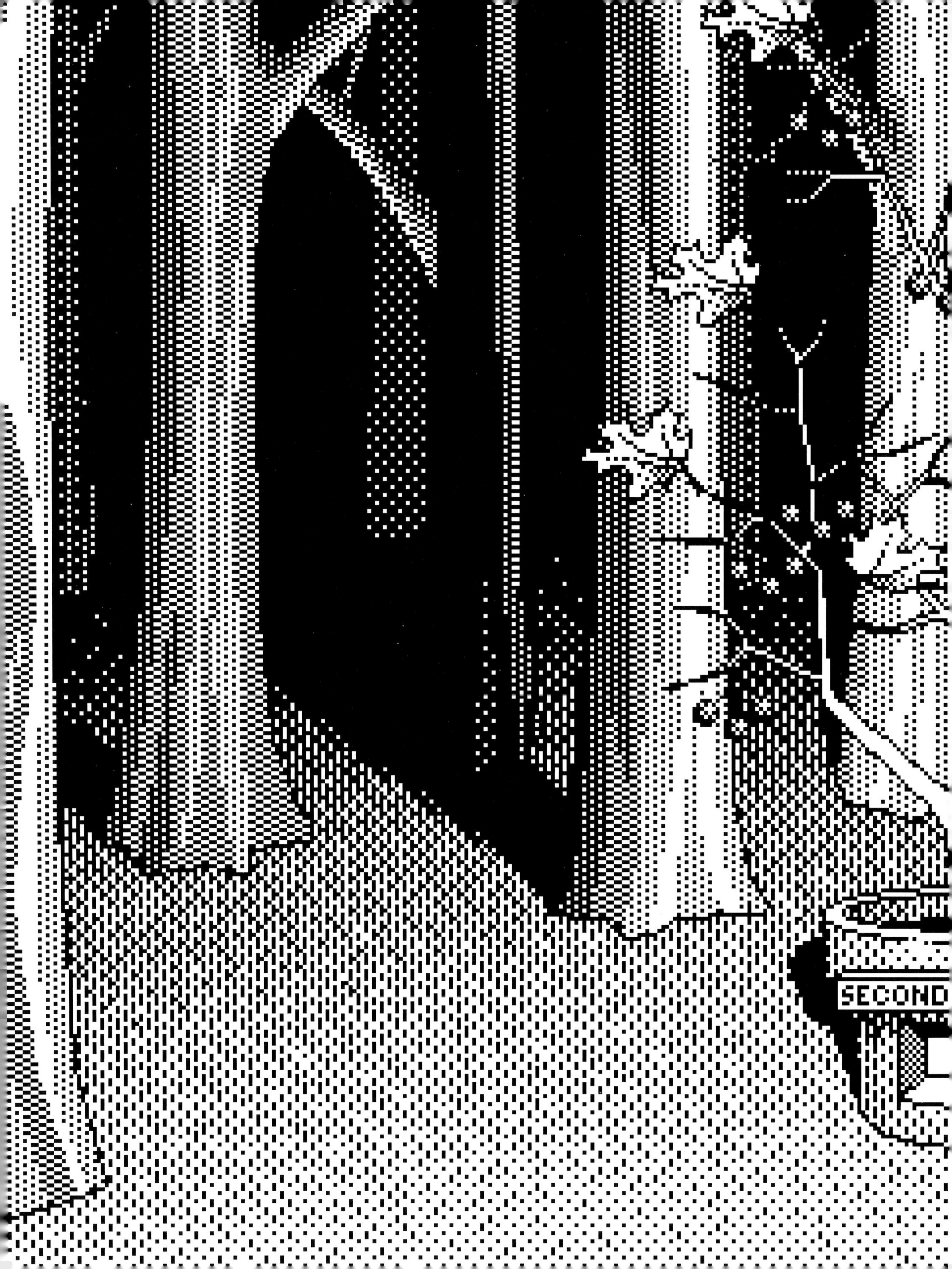
SECOND

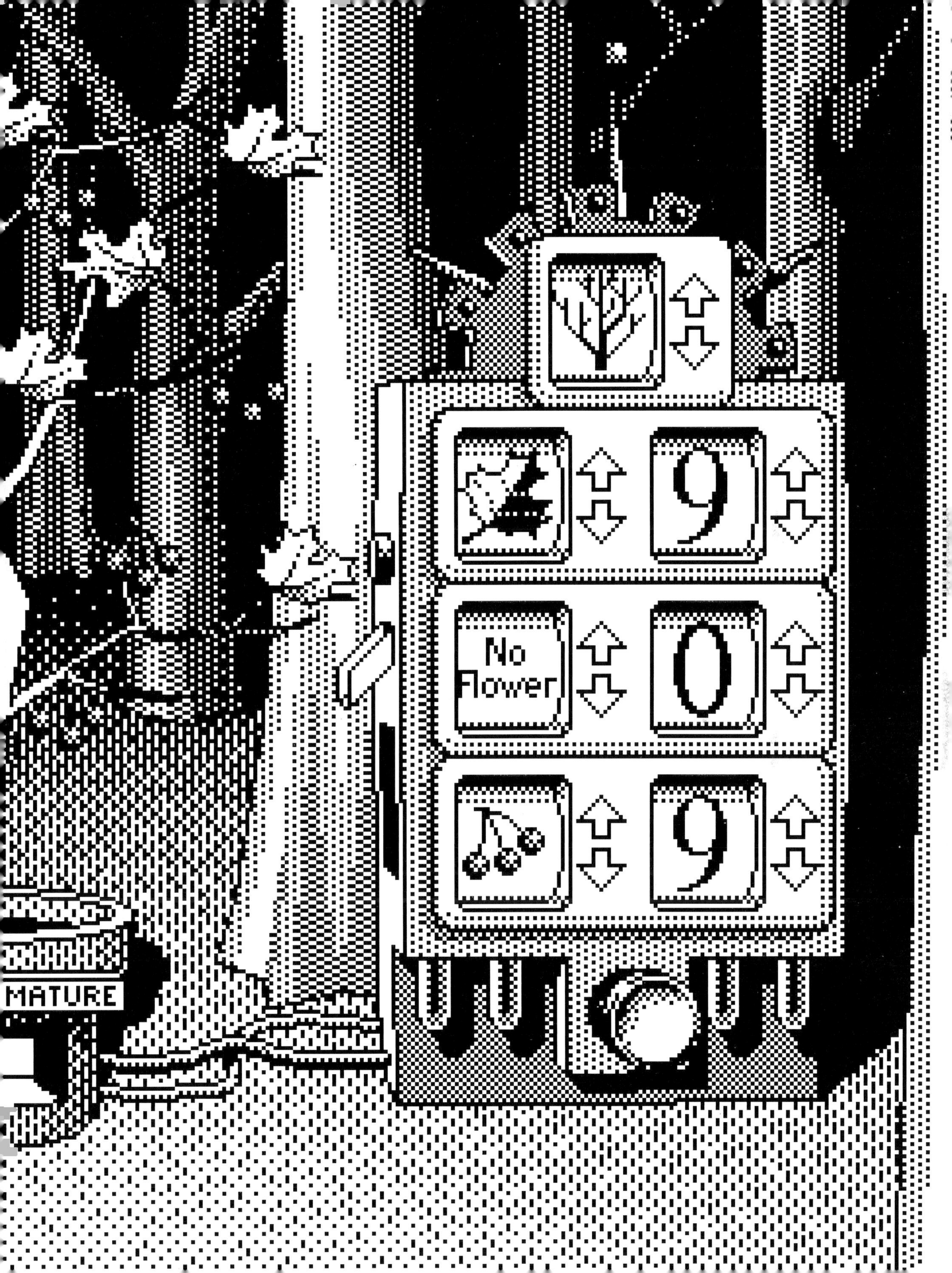
9
No
Flower
0
9
MATURE

Preserving the Pixel, Releasing Style from Technology

Architecture and design computing is often constrained by capacity. The pursuit of more memory, more resolution, and more data sees the pixel receding from view. Our rationale for preserving, or recovering, the pixel goes against this trend of ever-increasing capacity. Still, the negative connotations of "pixelated" are rational. A pixelated image lacks realism in the sense that we see the pixels instead of seeing through the pixels to the content of the image. The negative connotations of "pixelated" are also social in that pixelation can telegraph obsolescence or a poverty of resources. Throughout this book, we'll pursue a middle ground: we'll push our representational elements to do more than exist in the aggregate; we'll also expect them to assert themselves in defiance of the pressures to disappear. Without this purposeful preservation, digital media can only find itself converging with absolute realism. When the pixels, or any element, asserts itself, we can see our work leap beyond reality. Our elements can pull us into the realm of uncanny realism, a space in which we can find ourselves encountering work that looks more real than conventions would suggest we should be comfortable with. We'll avoid an allegiance to any one form of realism, but we'll regularly engage them as foils and points of contrast. For example, a medium resolution binary bitmap image sits in opposition to photorealism even as it triggers some of same realism cues as we might expect to see in a photograph: perspective, shadow, gradient fields, depth of field, blurs, noise, etc. Simultaneously, these renderings seem to go out of their way to remind us that they aren't at all like a photograph. In this sense, the pixel is a microcosm of the elements that will be explored later. As we'll do with other elements, we still need to explore the limits of what the binary bitmap does for us as designers. What can we do with the pixel when it is both legible in the image and operable behind the scenes as a data structure? We know that the high contrast black and white pixel image disrupts what might otherwise be reducible to a historical style, but how can we surpass the technical limits of 1988?

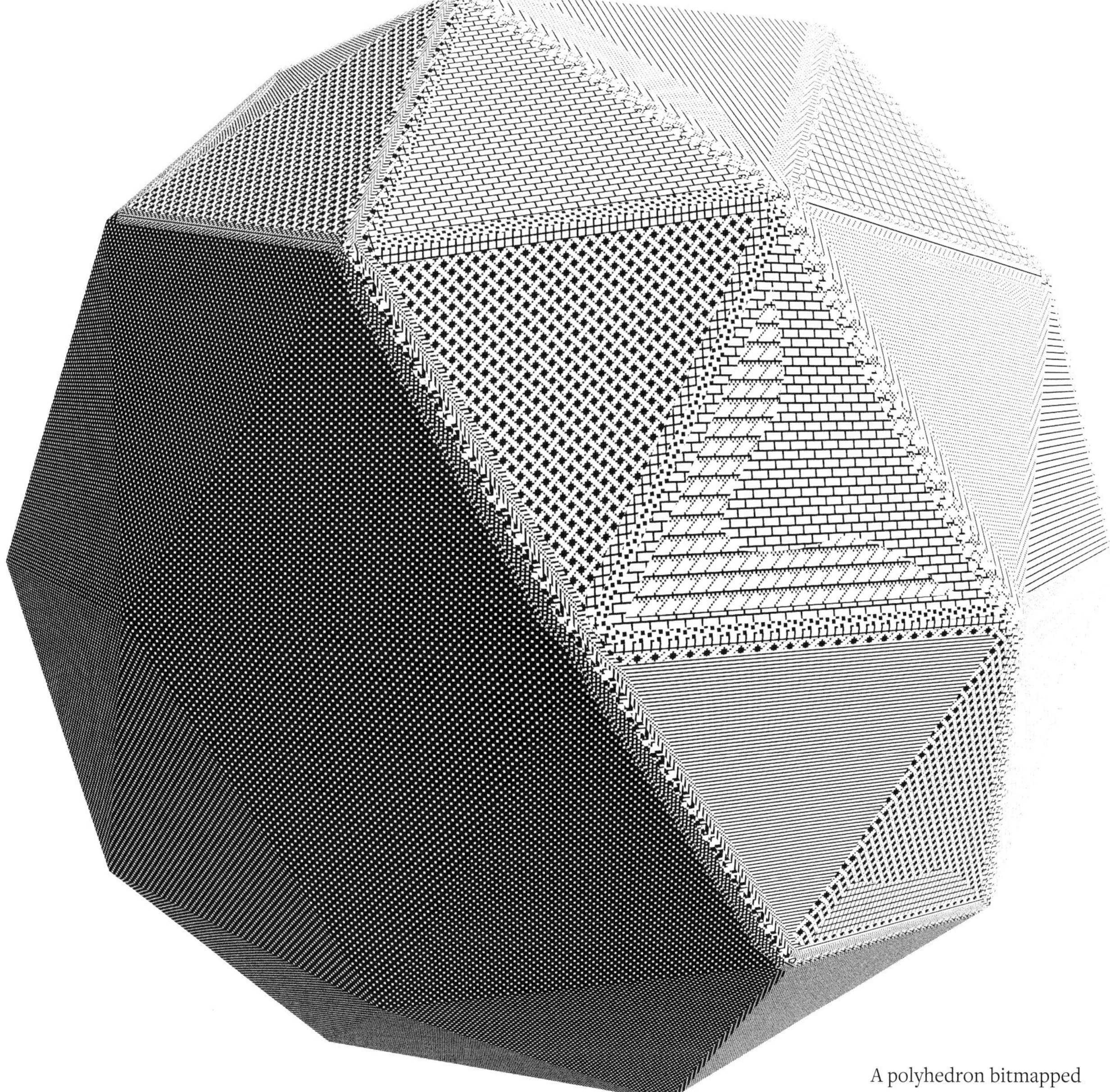

A polyhedron bitmapped using MacPaint textures applied with sensitivity to the relationship between overall darkness or lightness and the orientation of each surface. Light is not diffused so the binary bitmap texture leads to a binary bitmap rendering.

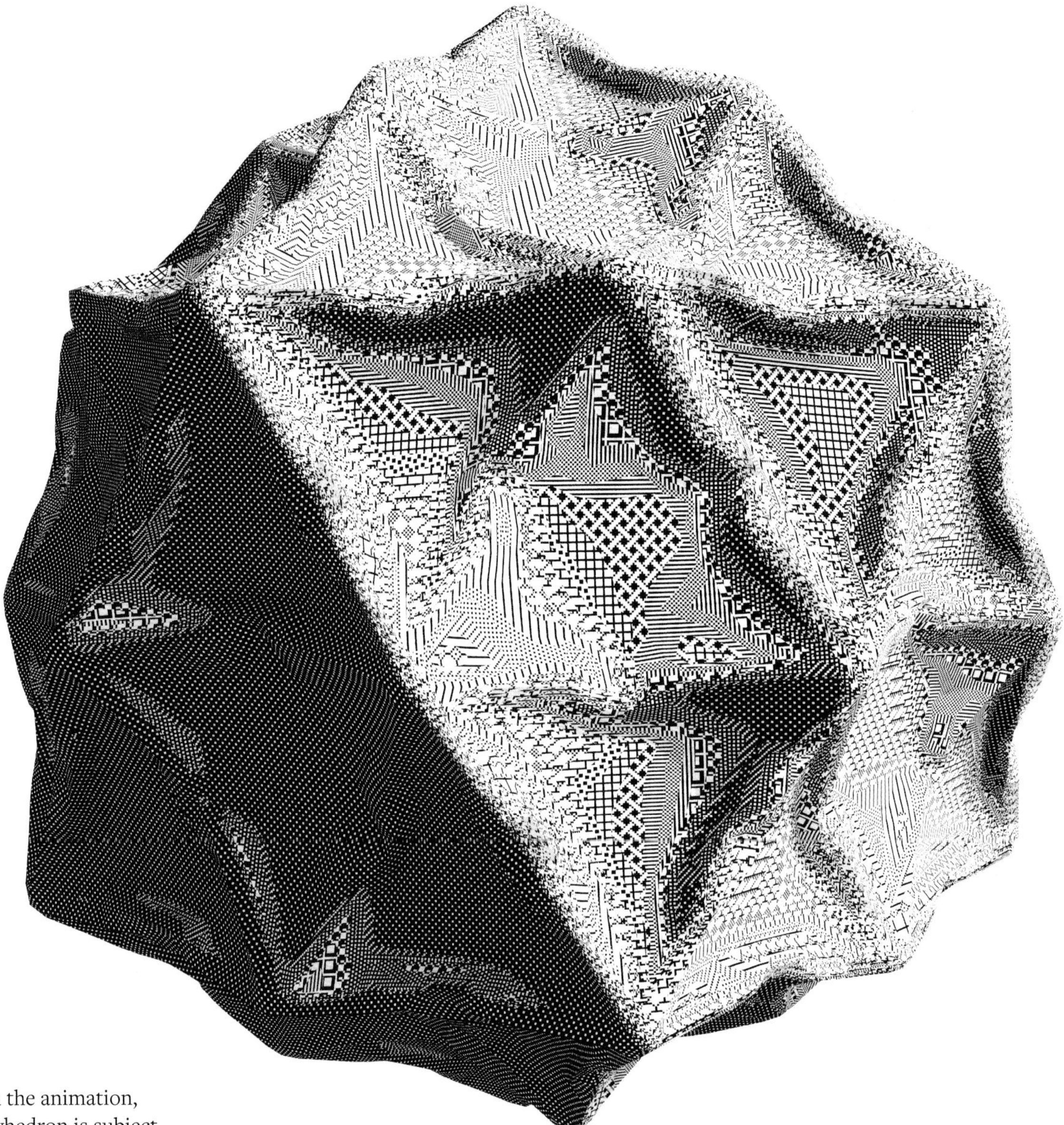

Later in the animation, the polyhedron is subject to material physical deformation. Though the mapping algorithm stays constant, the resulting image reflects a tension between the pattern's capacity to represent texture and serve the representational demands of the simulated geometry.

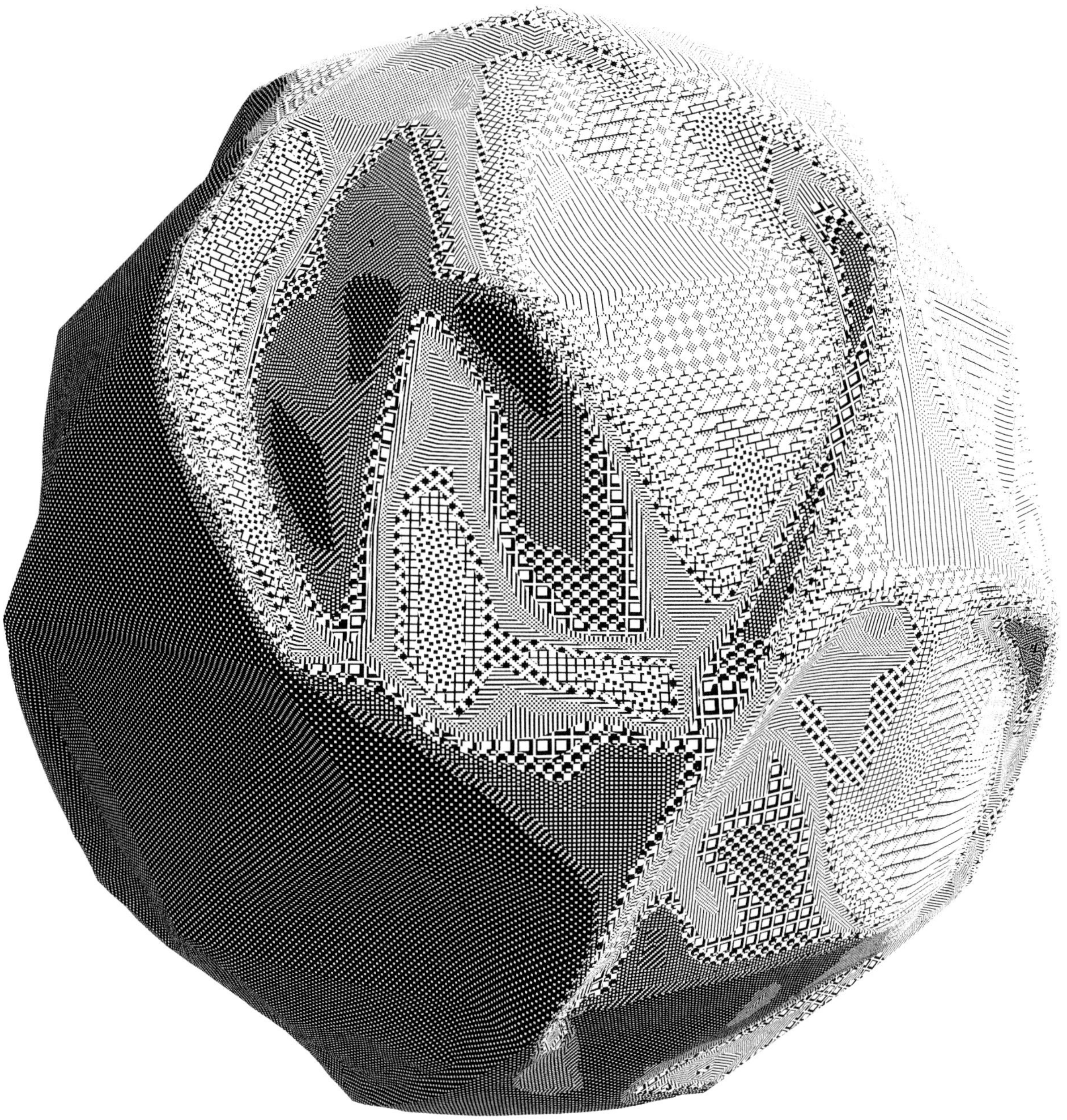

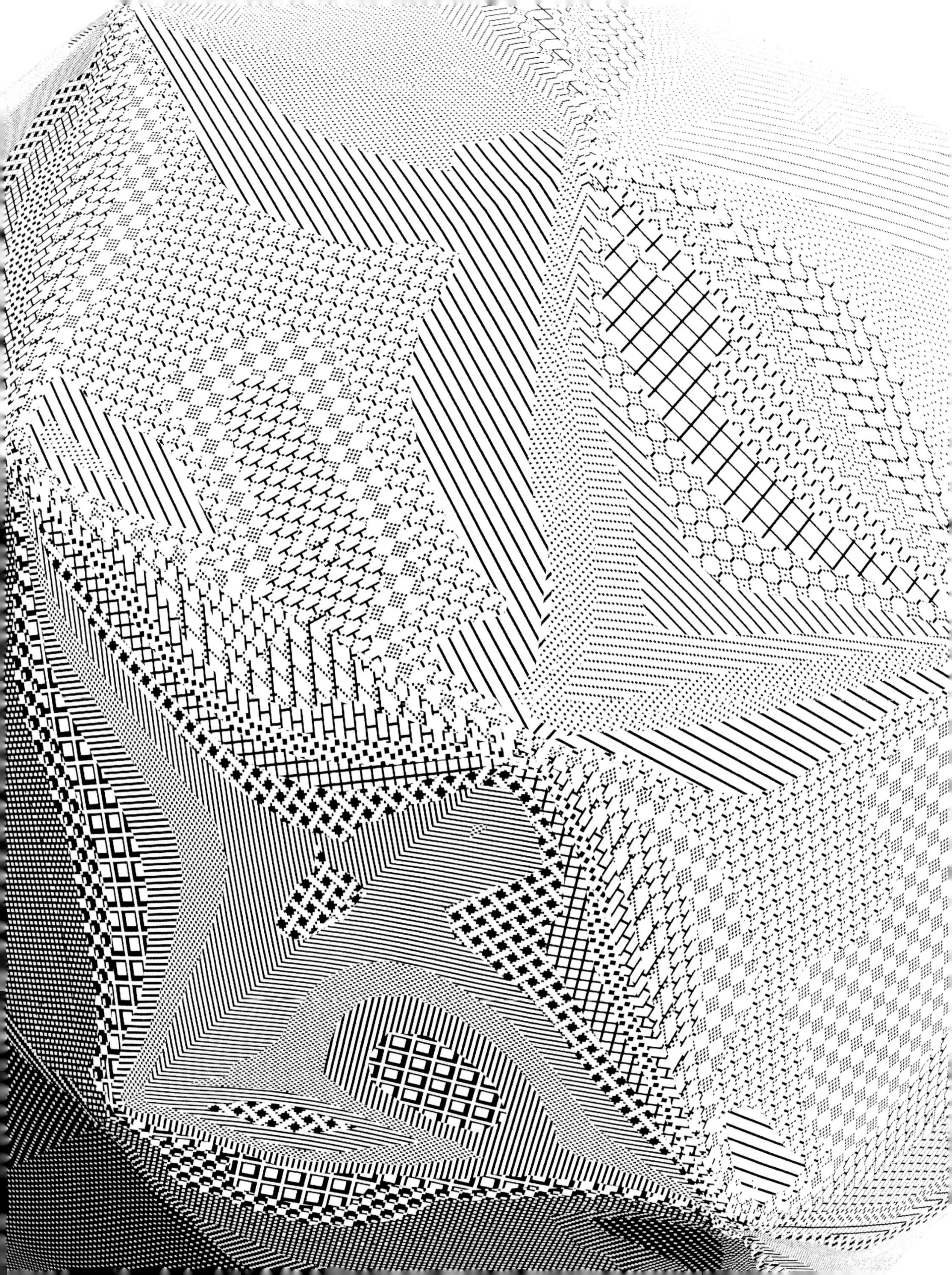

The Contemporary Binary Bitmapped Surface

There are two fundamental approaches to the contemporary engagement with the binary bitmap: emulation and generation. Both are rich with opportunities. Emulation might literally involve an emulator, a kind of technical diorama that allows the actual MacPaint software to run as though it were operating on a 1988 Macintosh Computer. Because of the cultural status of MacPaint and the fact that its source code is in the public domain and archived in the computer history museum,[21] there are multiple emulators available, even one that is web-based.[22] The most significant impediment to working in a 1988 modality is not access to vintage software, but the discrepancy in screen resolution. Emulators respect the pixel display of GUIs and so when mapping onto today's screens, which pack more pixels per inch, the classic Macintosh interface appears exceedingly tiny. Thus, another approach to emulation involves self-imposed restraint rather than the election of vintage software. Contemporary software can be used as though it only had the features of MacPaint: the color space can be set to bitmap, anti-aliasing turned off, and bitmap patterns loaded into the library. The advantage of this approach is that the exact constraints can be designed. For example, anticipating a 72 pixels per inch resolution print, the overall dimensions of the digital image could be increased while maintaining MacPaint operating resolution.

The second fundamental approach, exhibited here, involves using 3-D modeling and rendering software in which custom algorithmic materials can be created. It's often the case that digital media is better when coded by the designer. This is certainly one such situation. Though divergent in terms of process, this approach shares an ethic with the Miller brothers and the contemporary "pixel artist." Each pixel state—black or white—is generated conditionally. Where the emulation approach allows the human author to craft the pixels, this generative approach involves algorithms and Boolean logic. As we've discussed earlier, the conversion from full color to grayscale to binary bitmap is possible, but the results are wanting. The conversion process leaves artifacts and robs us of the opportunity to optimize pixels with respect to content in the image. Instead, information from the *model* serves as input to what amounts to an equation that results in a value of true (white) or false (black). There's no conversion from color or grayscale image to a bitmap format. The process creates a bitmap from scratch. The pixels are again subservient, but to form, material, and optics rather than a pre-existing image. Where bitmap conversion makes such a calculation with respect to prior value of each pixel and its

Carved cubes fall onto each other. Their planar surfaces invite the mapped bitmap patterns to reassert themselves. Though at first this image may read like a cartoon where the 2-D pattern fills a flat shape outlined within the space of the image, the patterns are actually mapped in 3-D and therefore subject to the same perspectival projection as the modeled geometry.

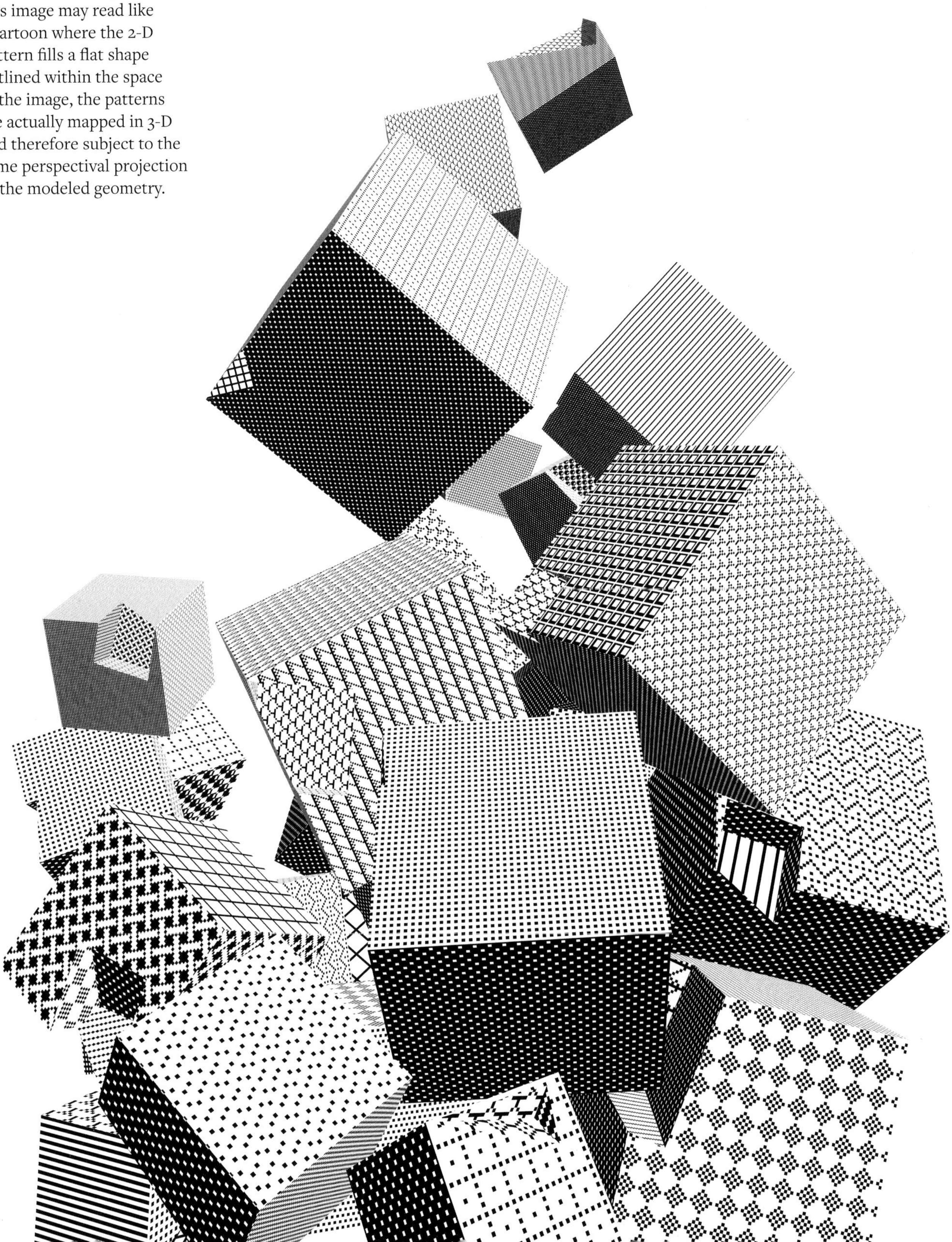

neighbors, this process can be informed by the orientation of 3-D geometry, distance to camera, path to a light source, as well as velocity or acceleration of 3-D geometry.

Thus, the binary bitmap is not merely an image, but the infrastructure between and including mesh-based 3-D models and the rendered black and white image. The original MacPaint textures are encapsulated within this system, so that they may be deployed selectively as though mapped into surfaces and subjected to perspective projection or in 2-D after perspective projection has taken place. Post-processing also takes place within the binary representational apparatus. Negotiation between two sources of pixel information resolves via Boolean "or," "and," "x-or" (either or, but not both), and "not" operators. Even lens blurring is achieved by swapping bit values from a random neighbor—closely when the object rendered is within the focal range and farther as it falls out of focus. Throughout the whole process, every pixel is always black or white.

The pixels are still pixels, but their status, along with the status of the image, has changed to become something more rhetorical and more material. Let's remember that Alvy Ray Smith describes the nature of the pixel as distinct from material media like paint because the content of a digital image can be separated from the digital light that displays the pixels. But now the pixel is like paint. It's subject and medium at the same time. The original MacPaint patterns hint at nostalgia, but the content—cloth, physical, fluid, and even photographic—implies a digital model and digital simulations that defy the limits of vintage technology. Like this book, and like the impossible elements that will follow, the elements might even be described as didactic. They explain themselves and the process of their creation even as they strain to express and become more than what would seem to be possible within their internal constraints. They become more specific. What might be on one hand esoterically quirky aims to be intellectually and historically connected in ways that diverge from the usual cultures of digital image. They aim to tell their story and invite narrative readings.

As our discourse continues, our focus on the pixel–what it can be, what it can represent, and how it evolves within creative processes–will spiral into more layered elements that can all be traced back to, if not reduced to, pixels in similar ways.

EXERCISE

Draw by hand within the space of a digital image

Start with an entirely black or white image sized between 500 and 1000 pixels in both directions. Prepare your software so that your drawing tool changes one pixel or more pixels at a time without any smoothness or blurriness. Initiate the construction of a 3-D scene by drawing a scaffolding first. This might be as simple as an isometric grid. Or you might draw some geometric primitives as oblique axonometric projections. Another option would be draw guidelines for a perspective scene. Now fill the scene with content. Don't shy away from depicting, conjuring, or expressing qualities that are non-binary in their nature. This will force the pixel to represent more than that which is black or white. You'll want to regularly zoom in to see and operate on each individual pixel and zoom out to read the entire image.

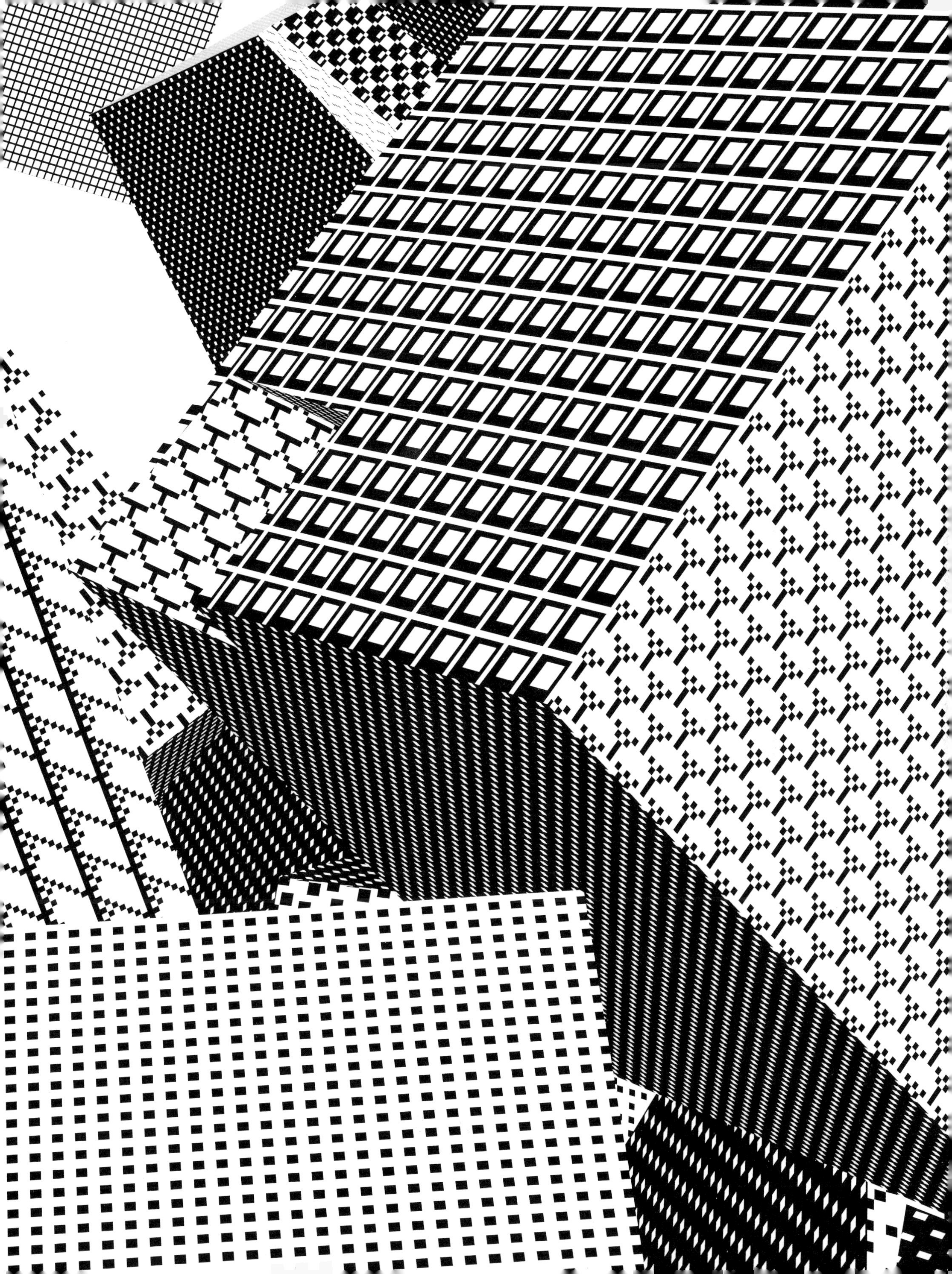

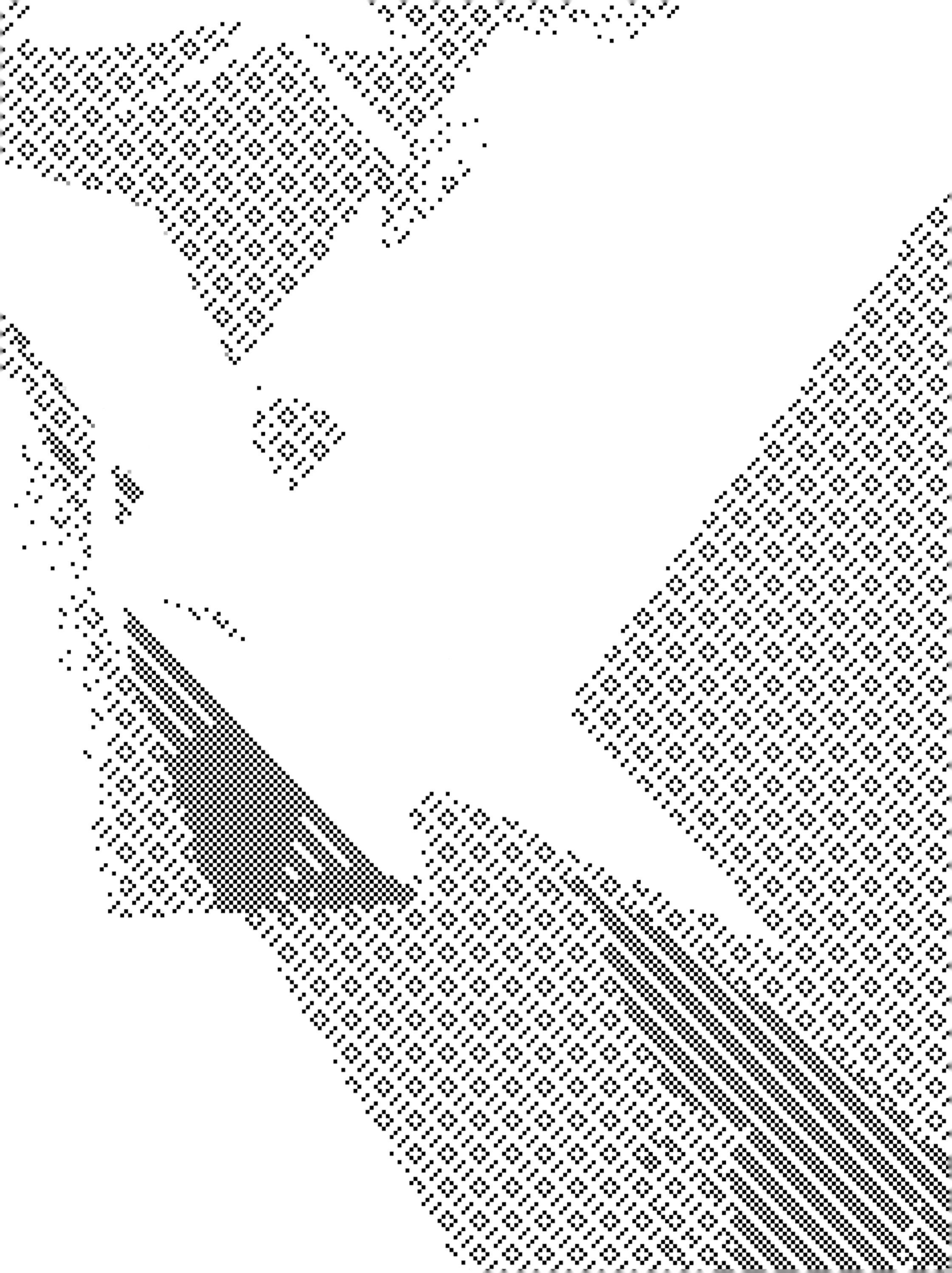

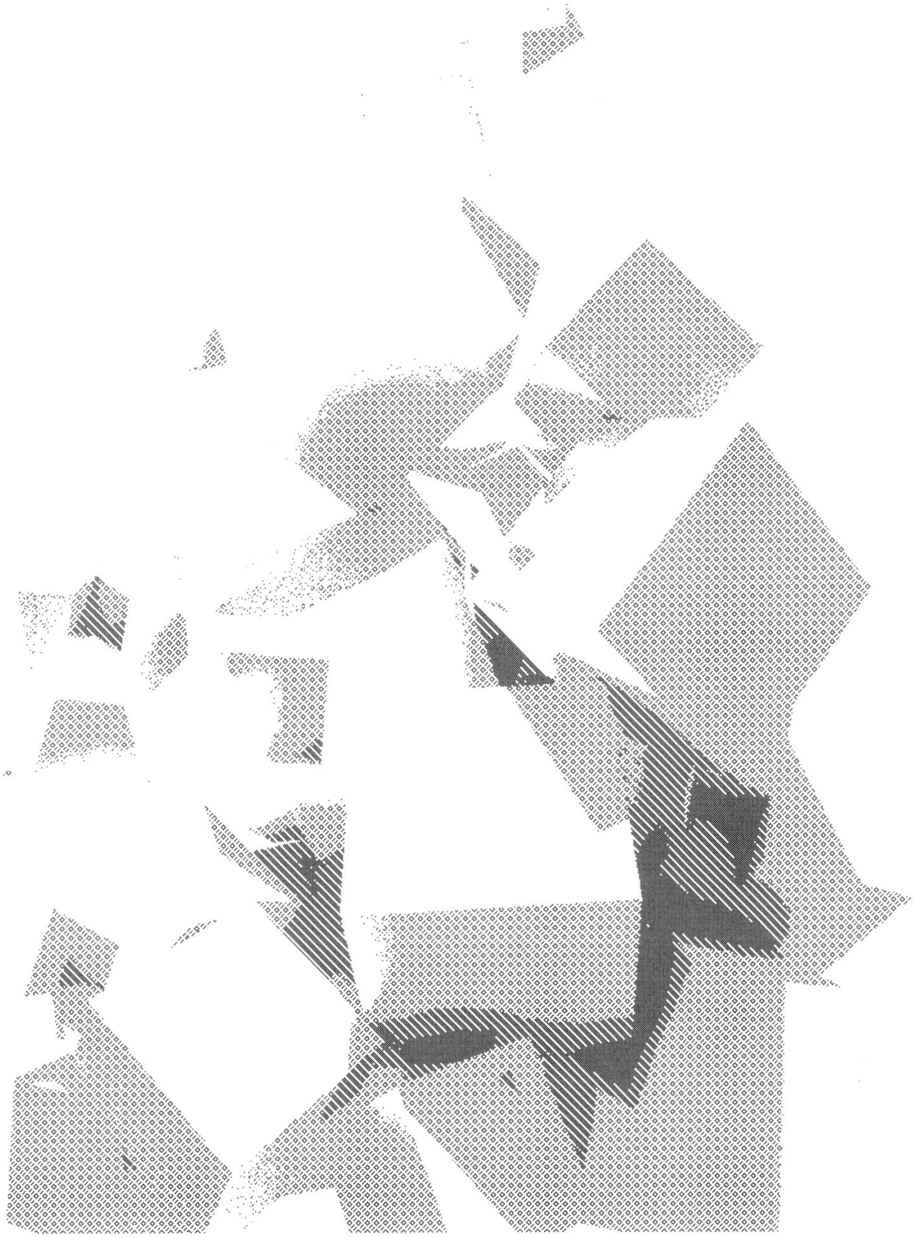

In this series, shadows are also rendered, first as a separate channel. Though generated from the 3-D model, the shadow layer itself is oriented toward the 2-D space of the image. This simple binary screen exhibits a graphic neutrality compared to the MacPaint patterns. This image is legible on its own, though it is designed for the purpose of later overlay.

The image now receives the shadow layer and a white mist layer. The binary nature of each source allows us to think of their relationship as three inputs to a logical equation calculated at each pixel.

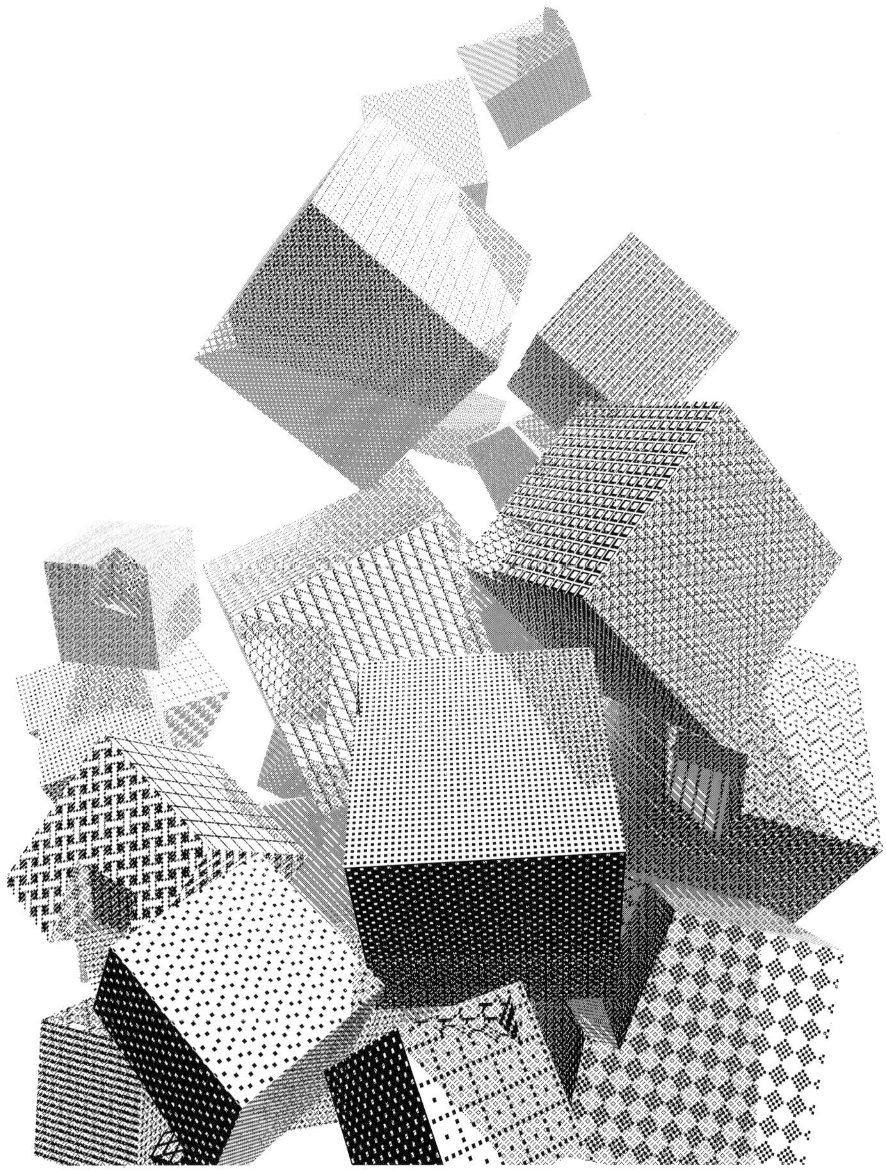

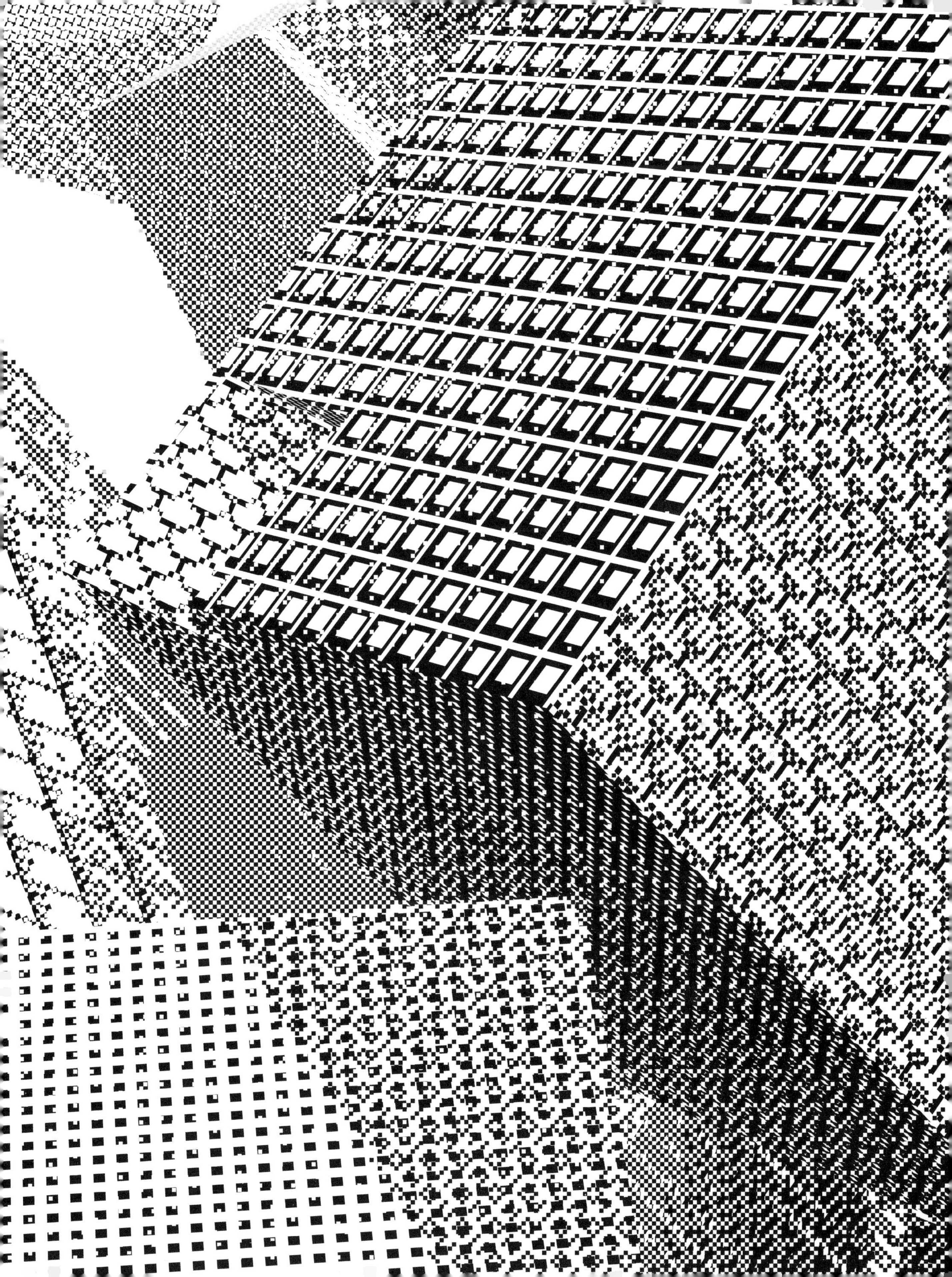

Throughout the process, the image is tethered to the digital model. A pixel swapping algorithm weights a random calculation based on the distance of the represented geometry from the camera.

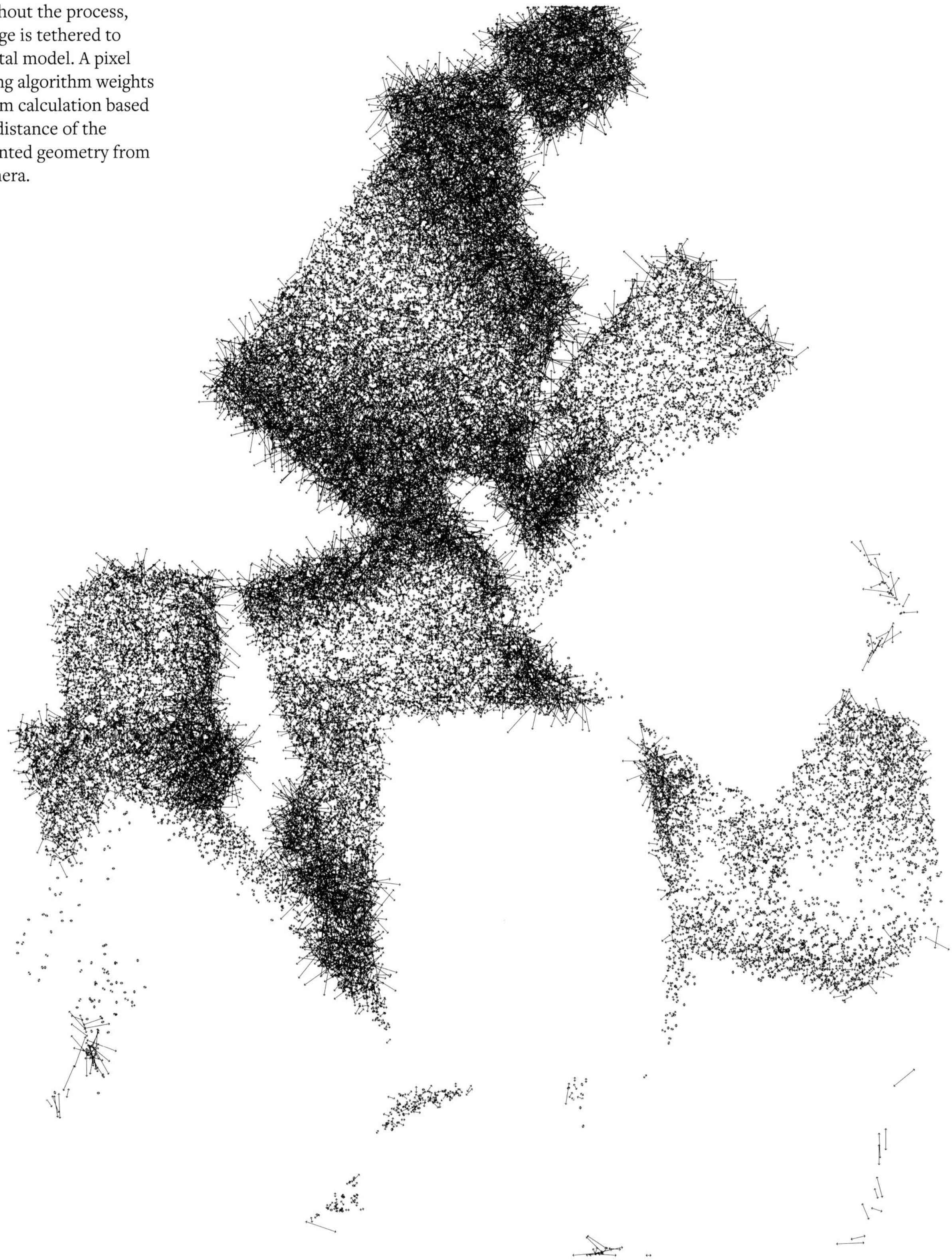

After swapping pixels based on distance from camera, farther objects appear blurry, as if out of focus.

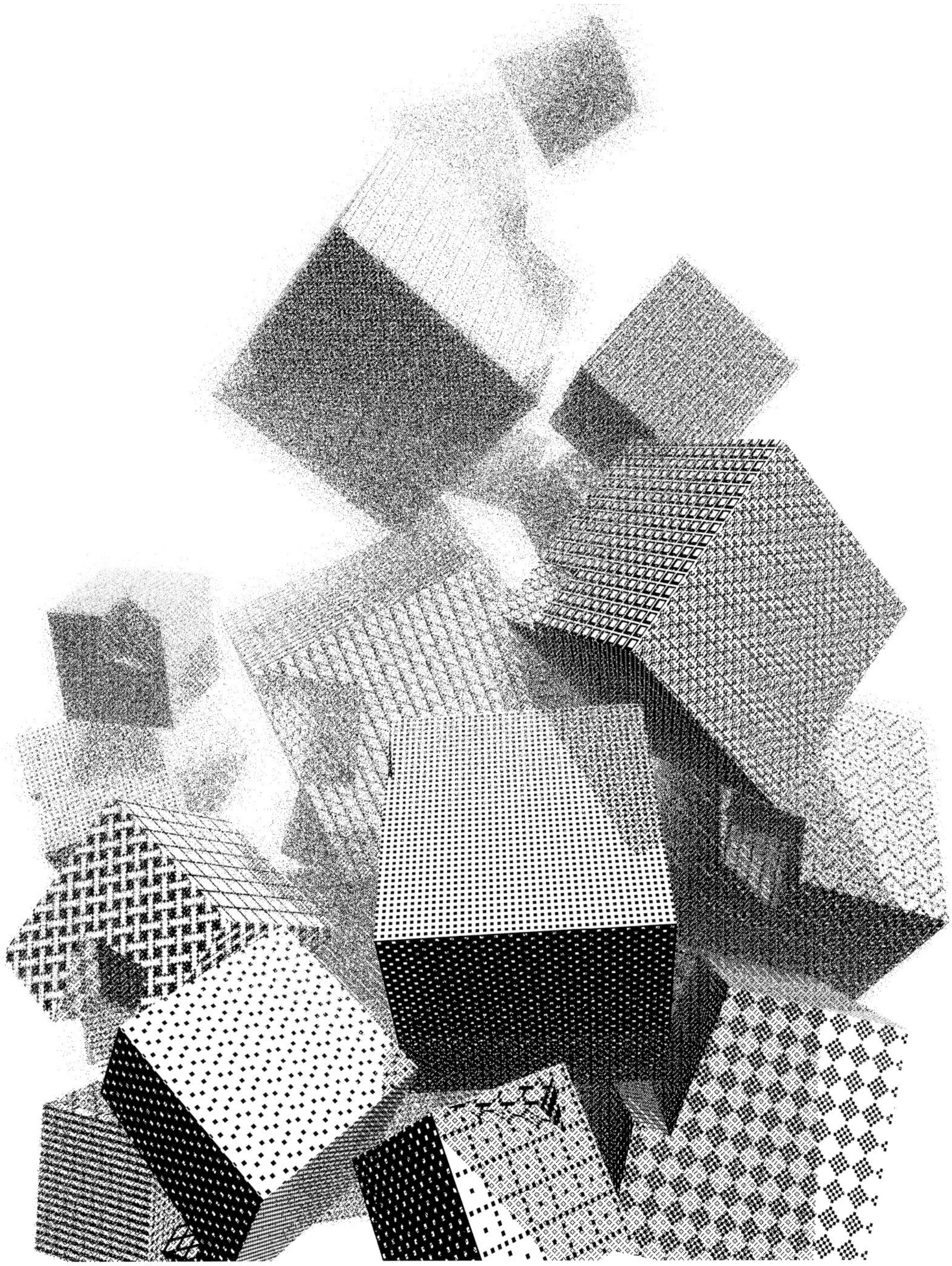

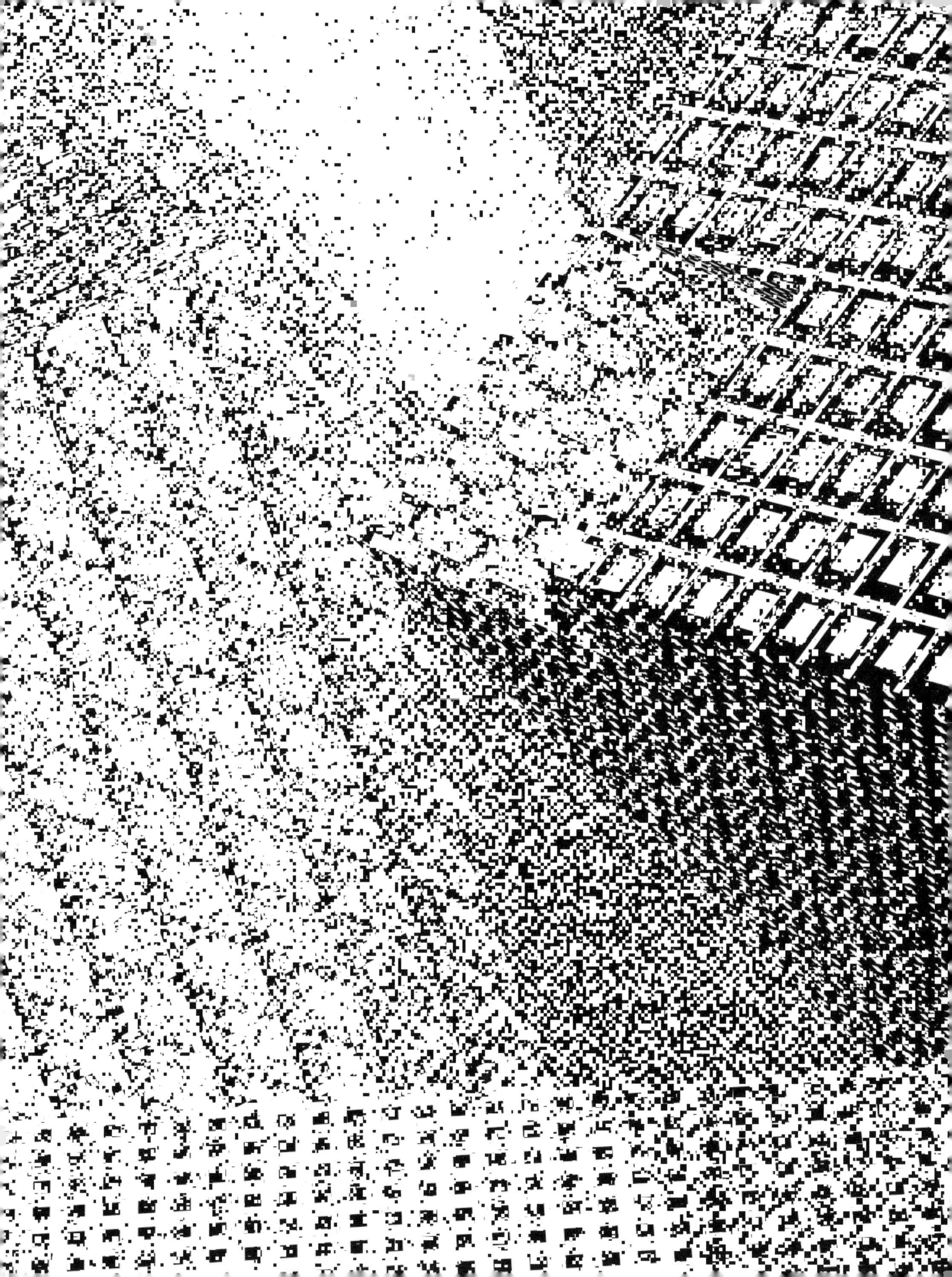

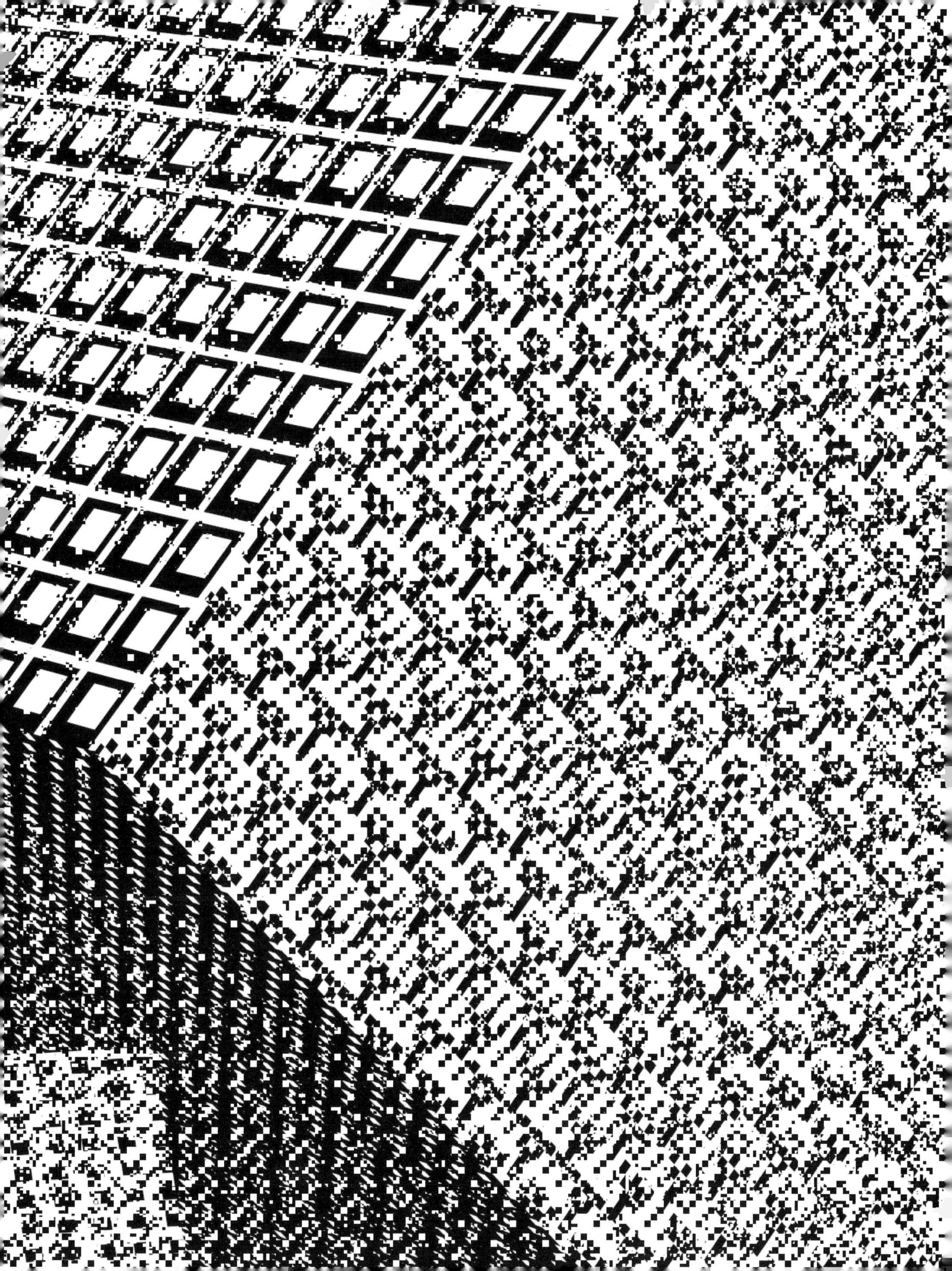

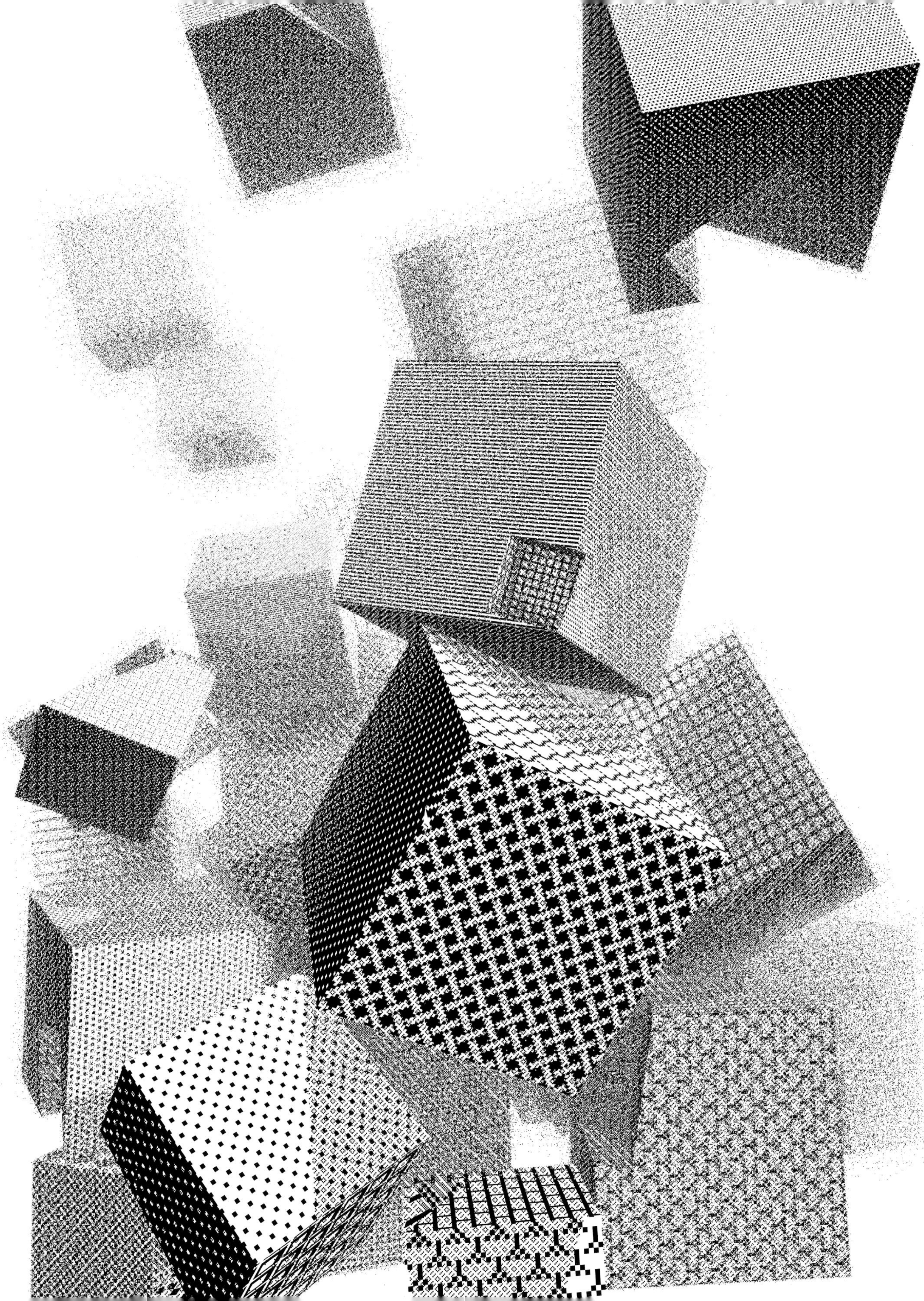

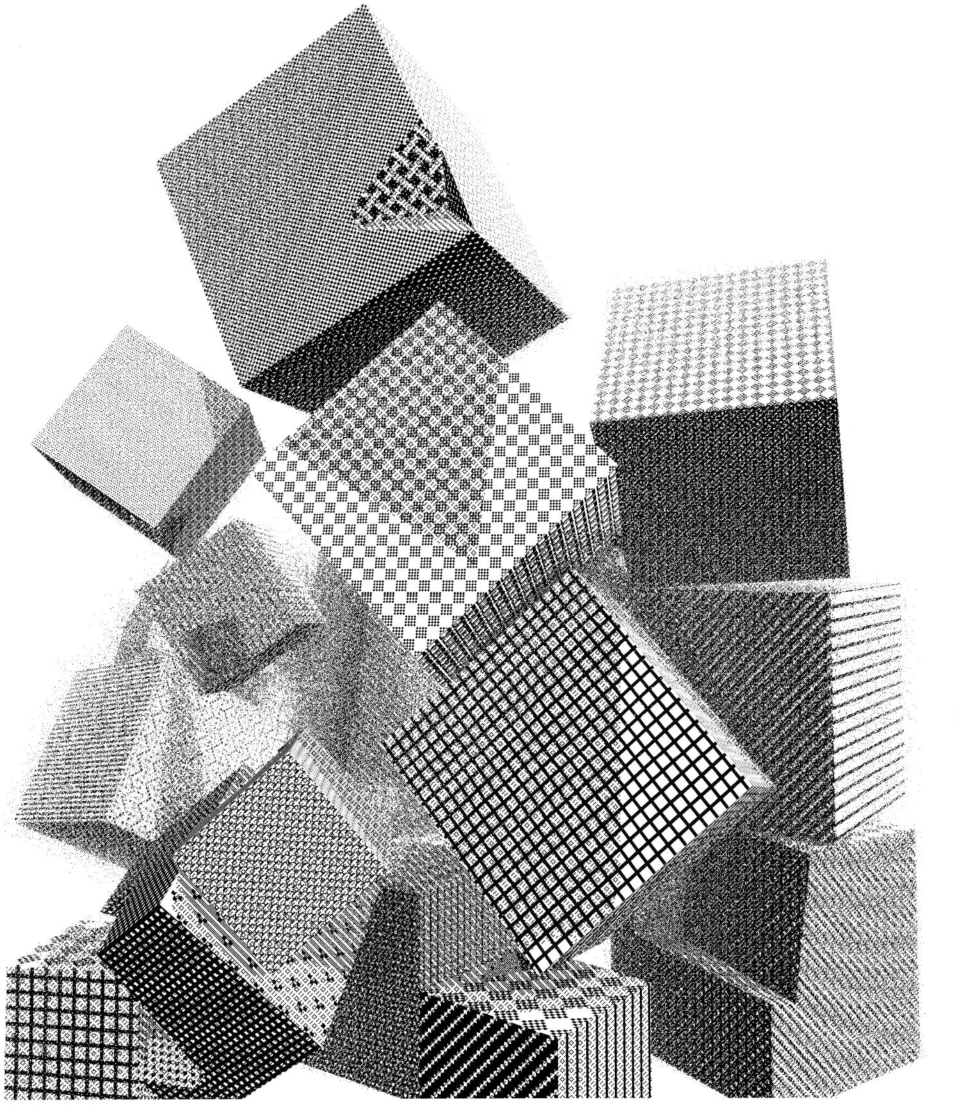

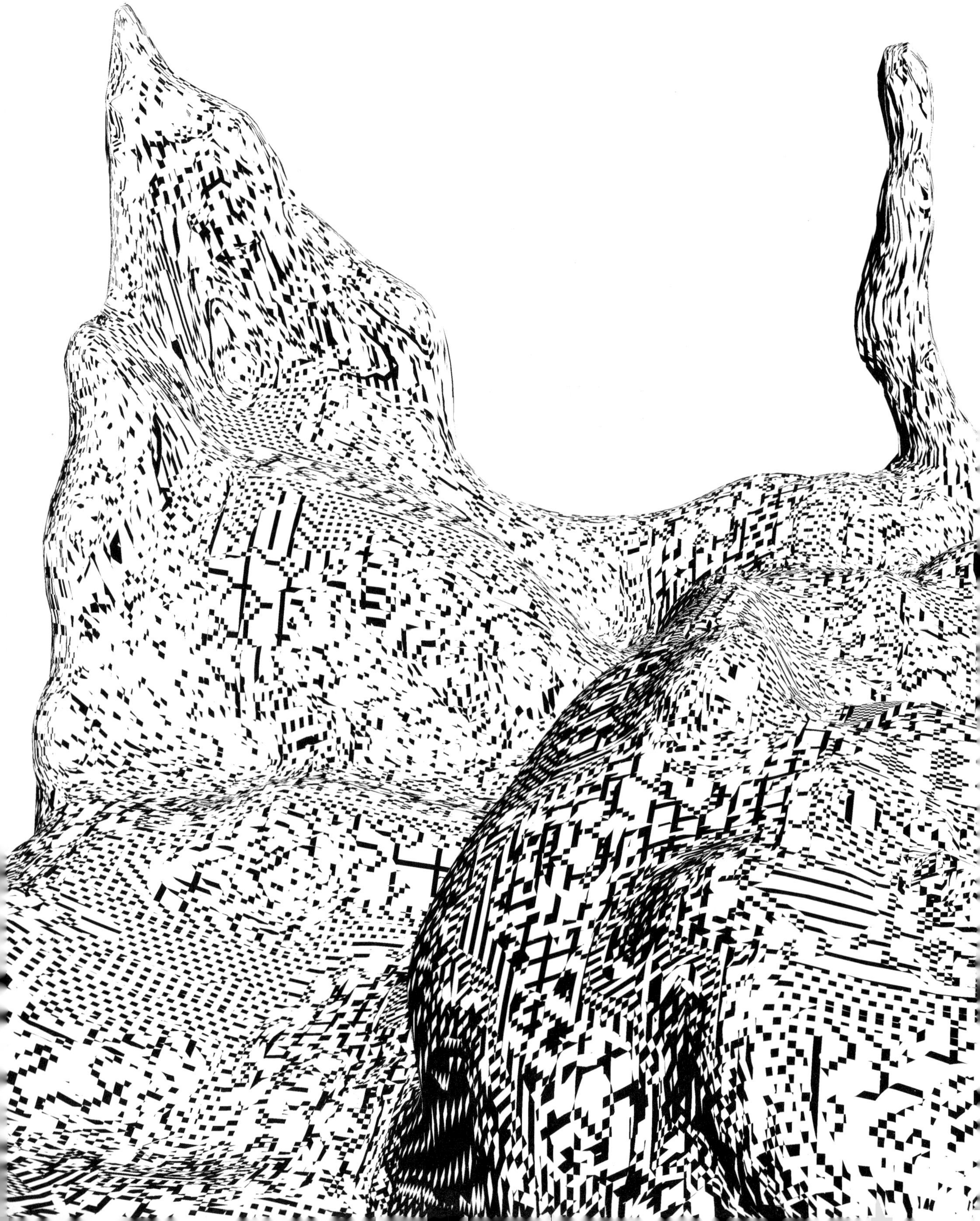

The search for content that when fused with pixels challenges those same pixels, brings us to some sloshing fluid. The smooth but variable surface calls upon a change of pattern from one small portion of the surface to another. It's almost as if to see the MacPaint textures, one must look beyond or through the rendered content.

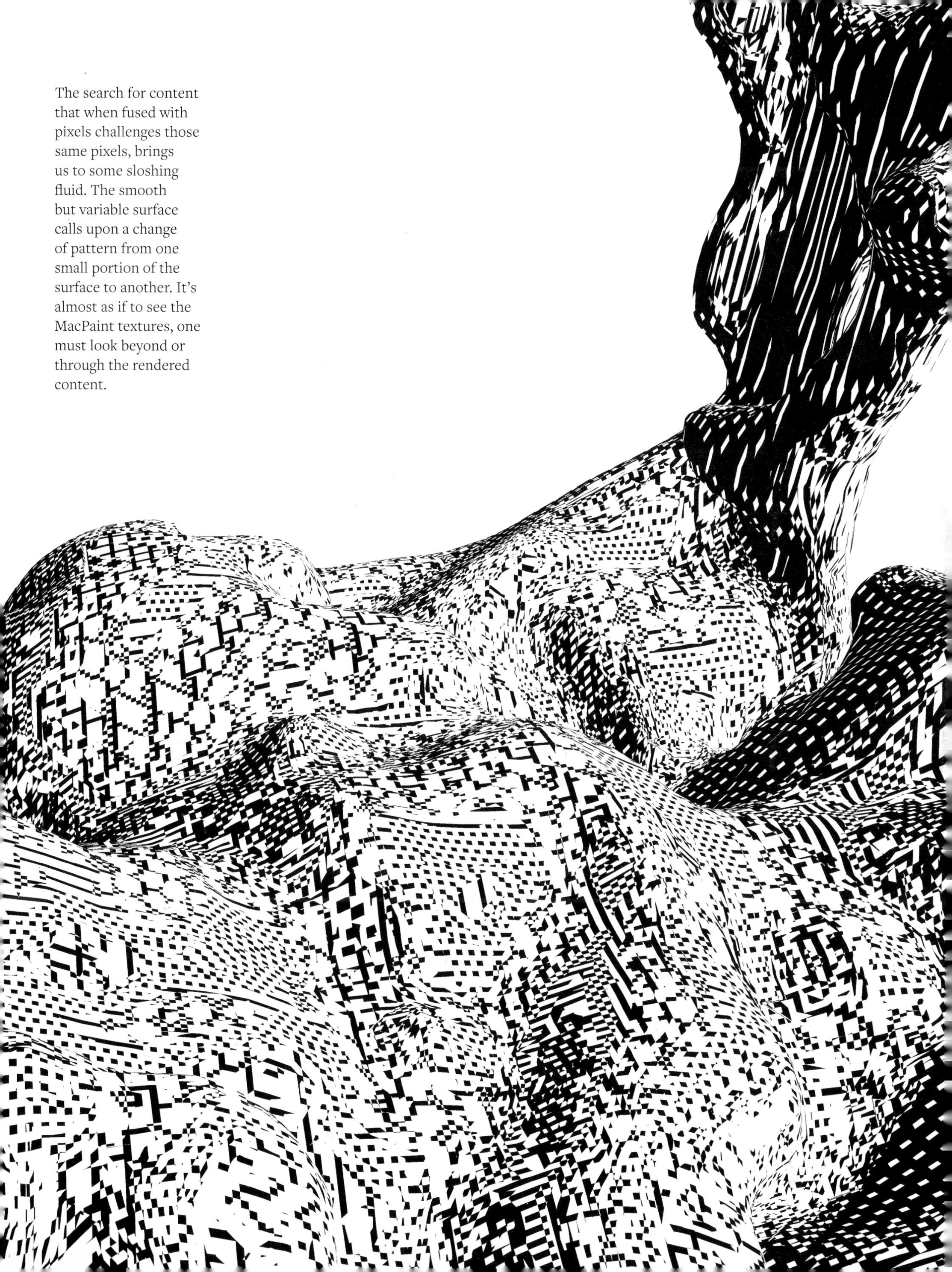

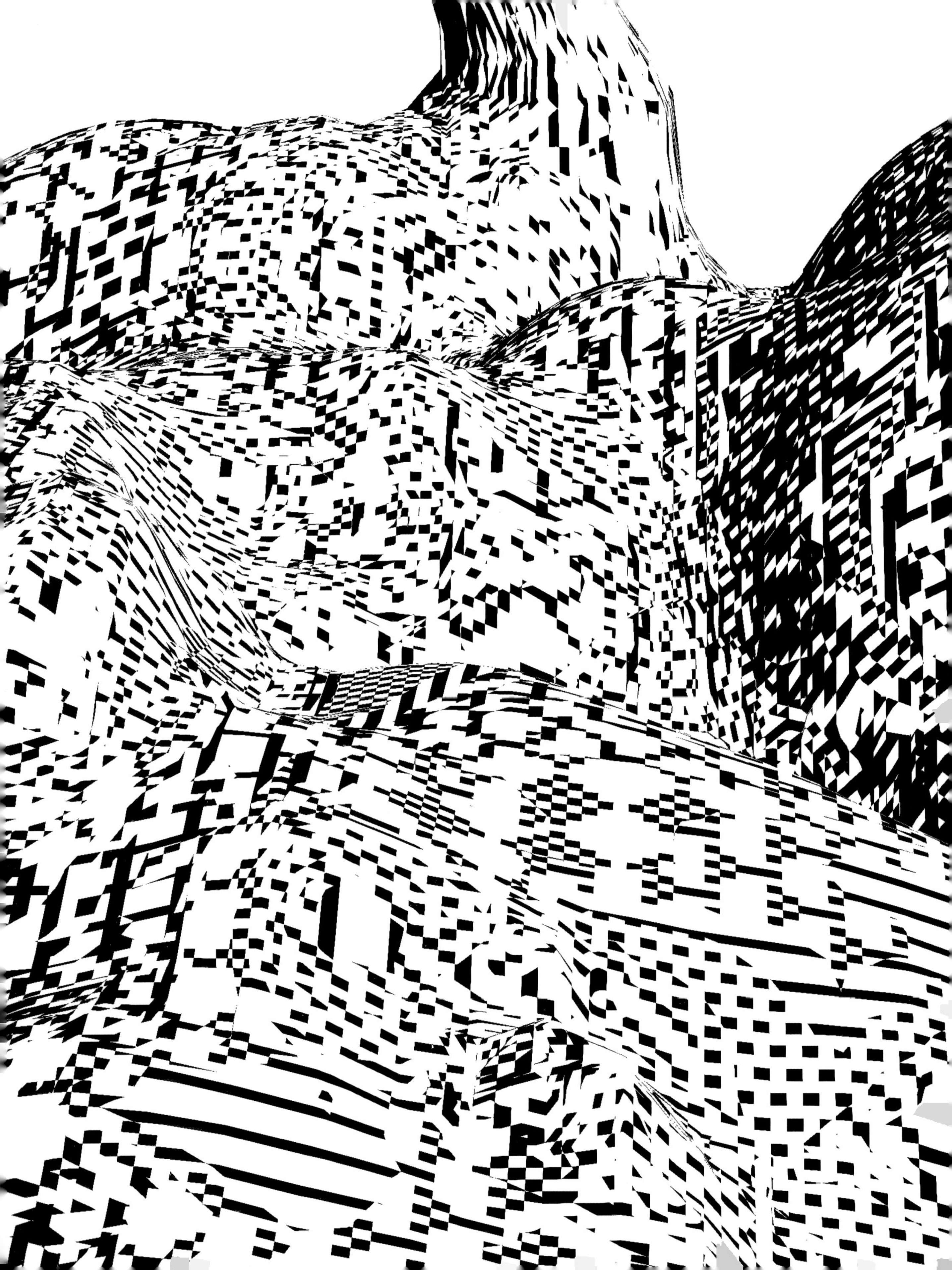

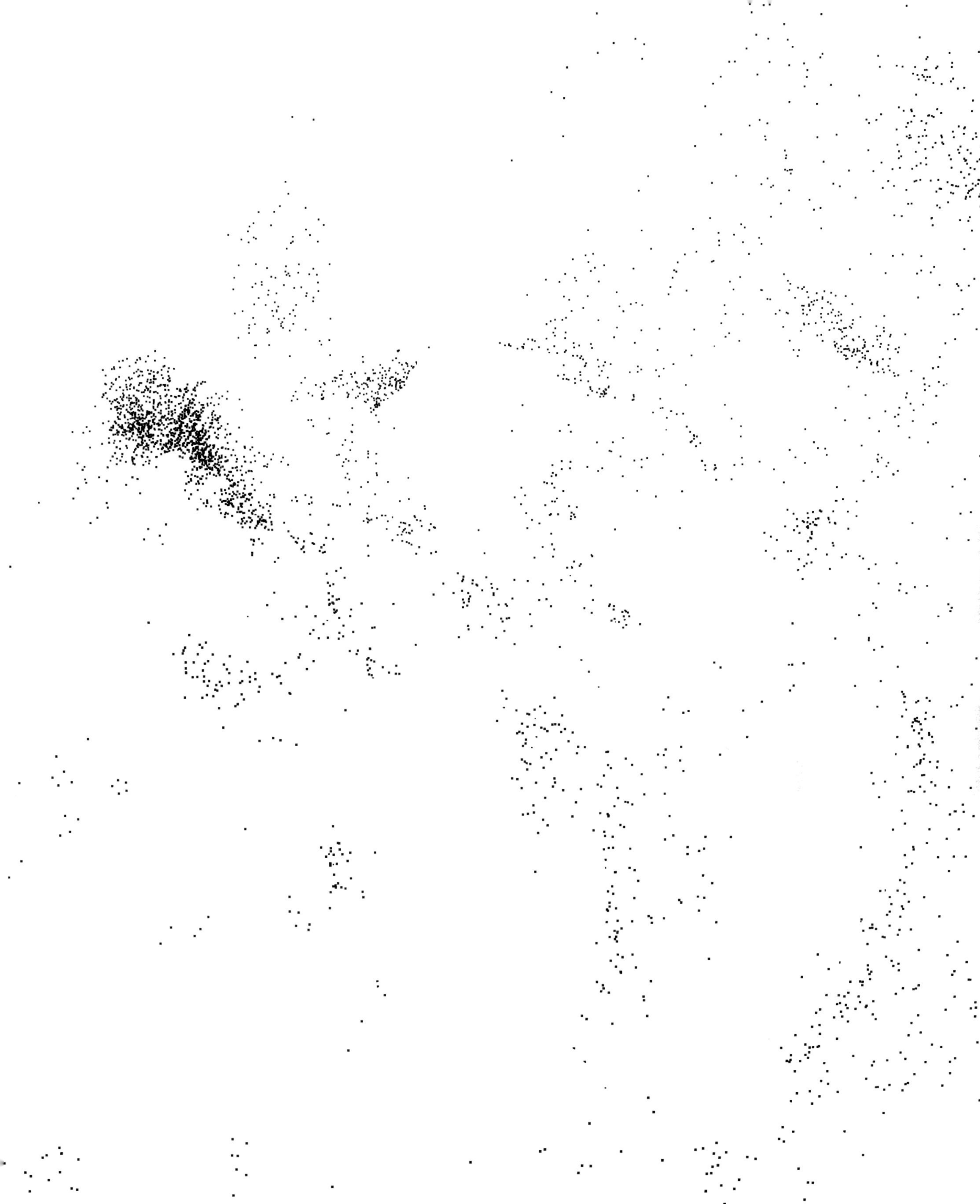

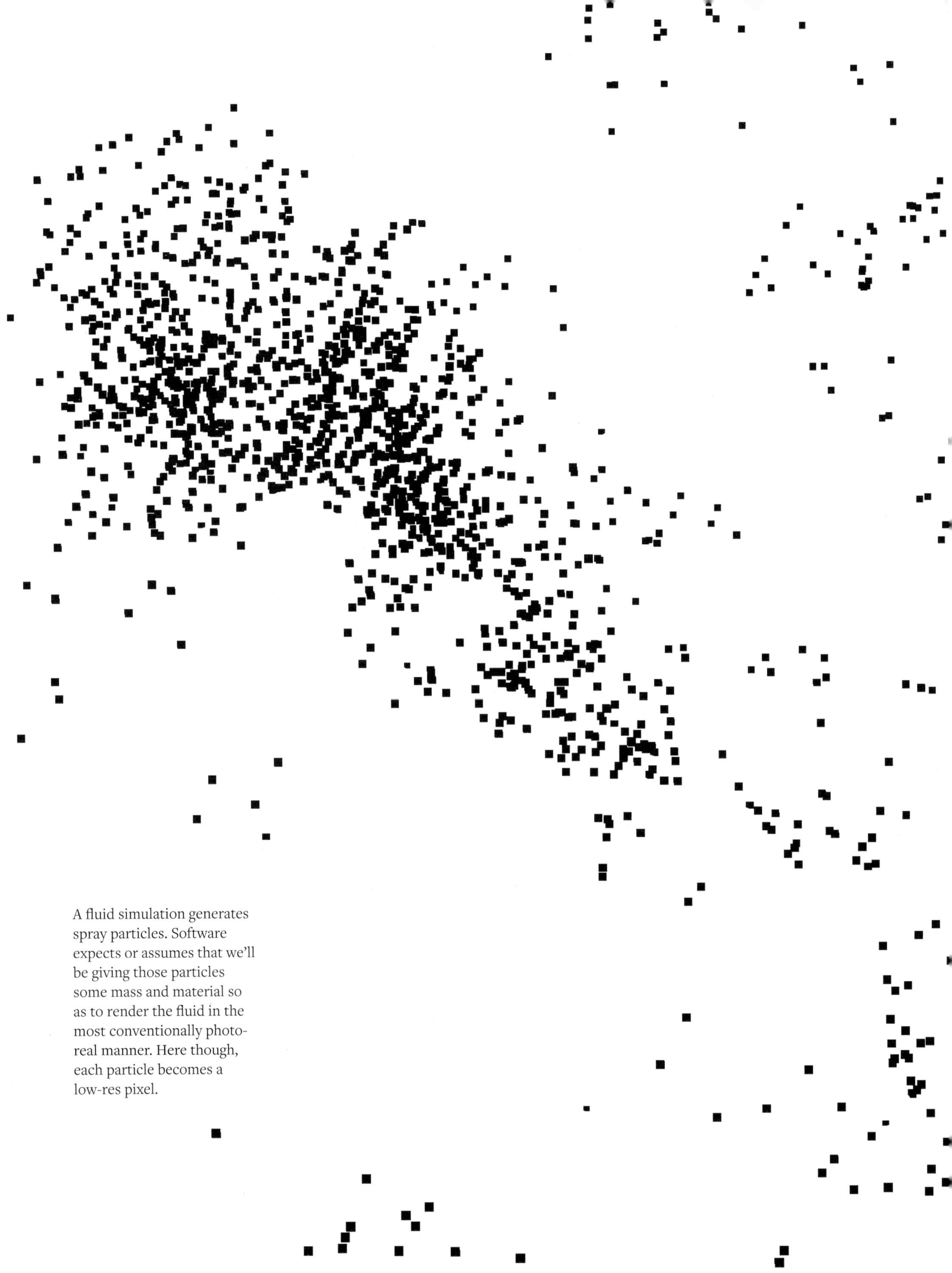

A fluid simulation generates spray particles. Software expects or assumes that we'll be giving those particles some mass and material so as to render the fluid in the most conventionally photo-real manner. Here though, each particle becomes a low-res pixel.

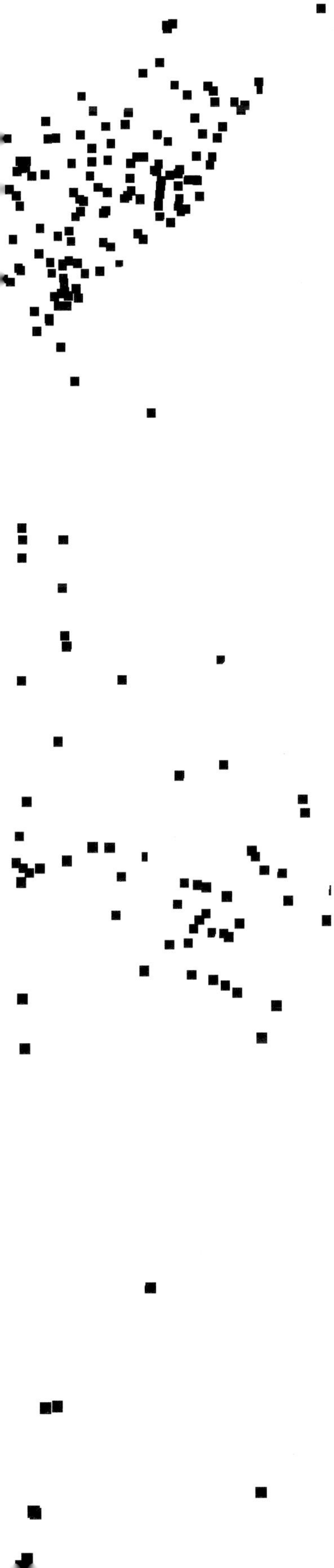

Depth is likewise rendered via a Z-buffer (distance of the object in the scene to the camera a at each pixel) that is striated by thresholds, which govern the density of a simple pattern. As though a white mist exists in the scene, pixels that are farther away are more likely to be converted from back to white.

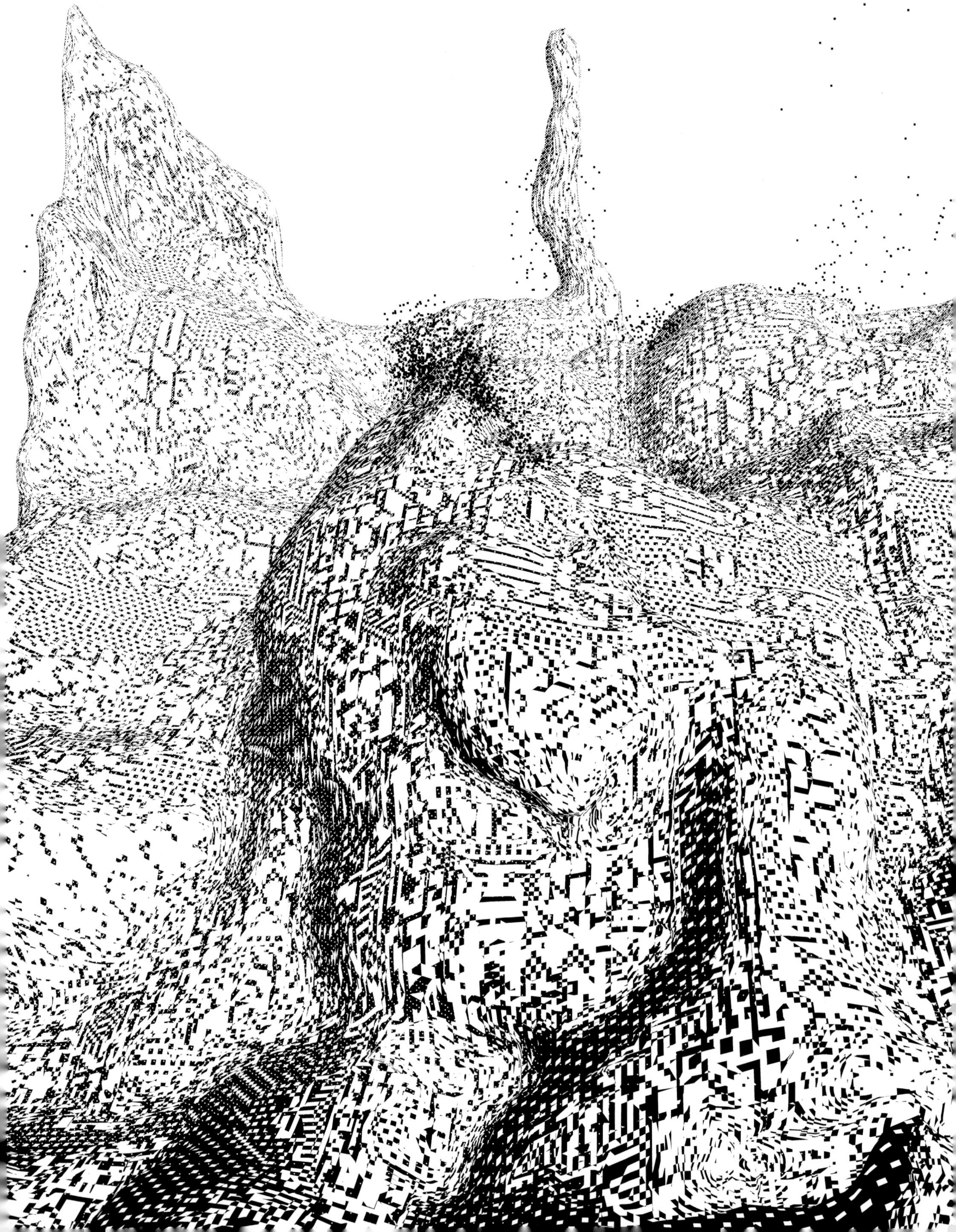

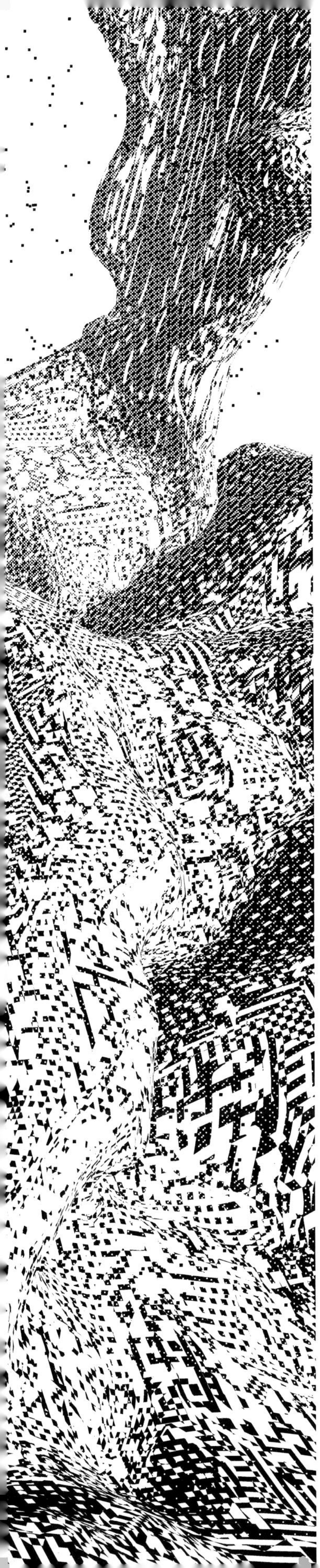

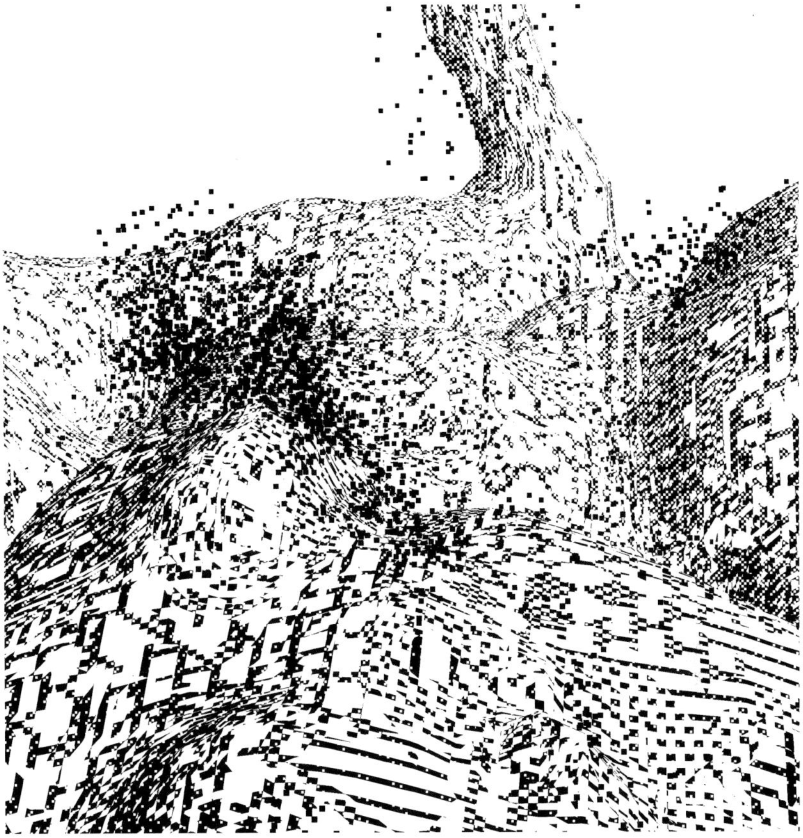

The completed composite scene resolves depth, spray particles, and the rendered fluid surface.

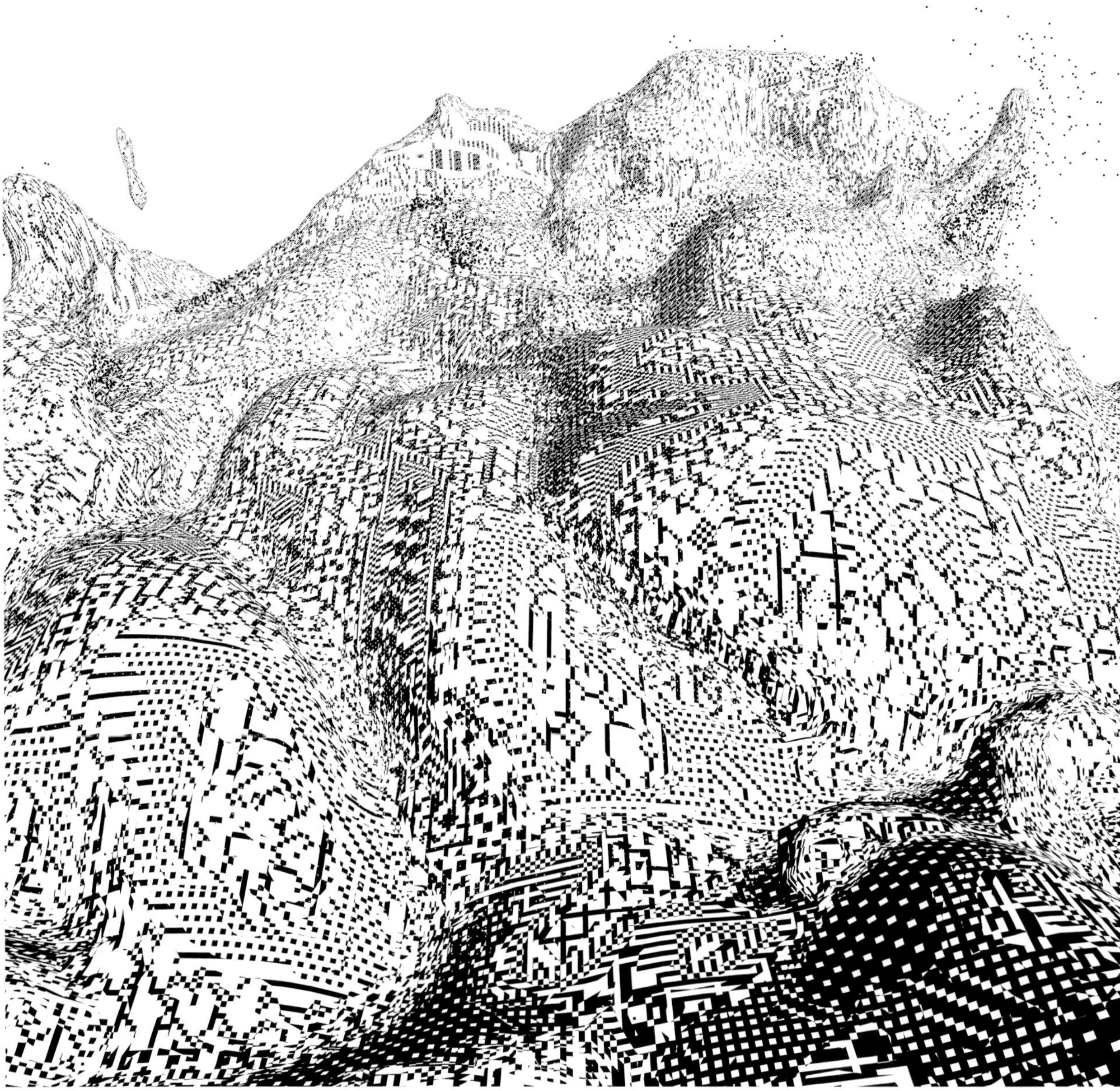

A composite rendering later
in the scene.

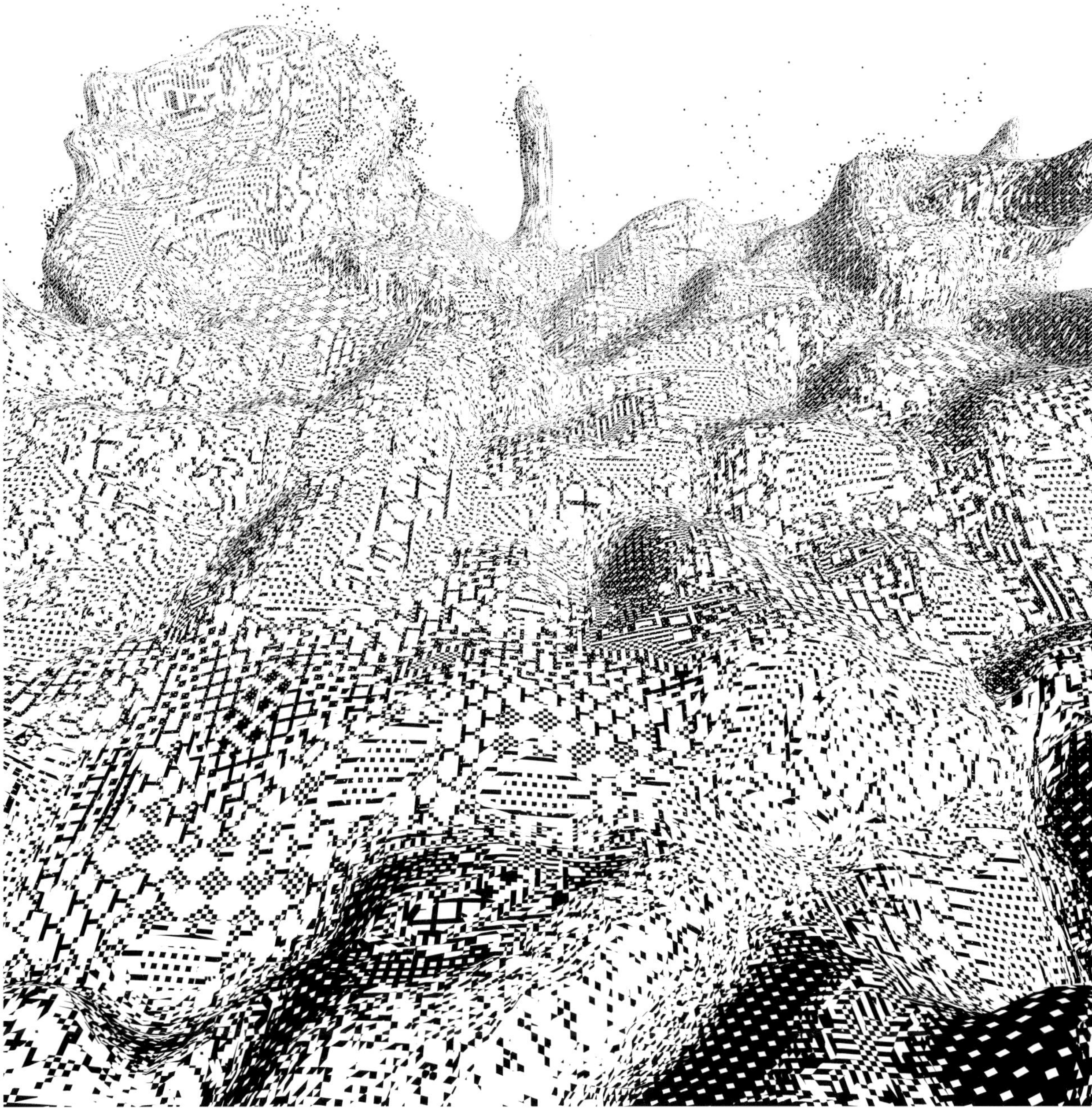

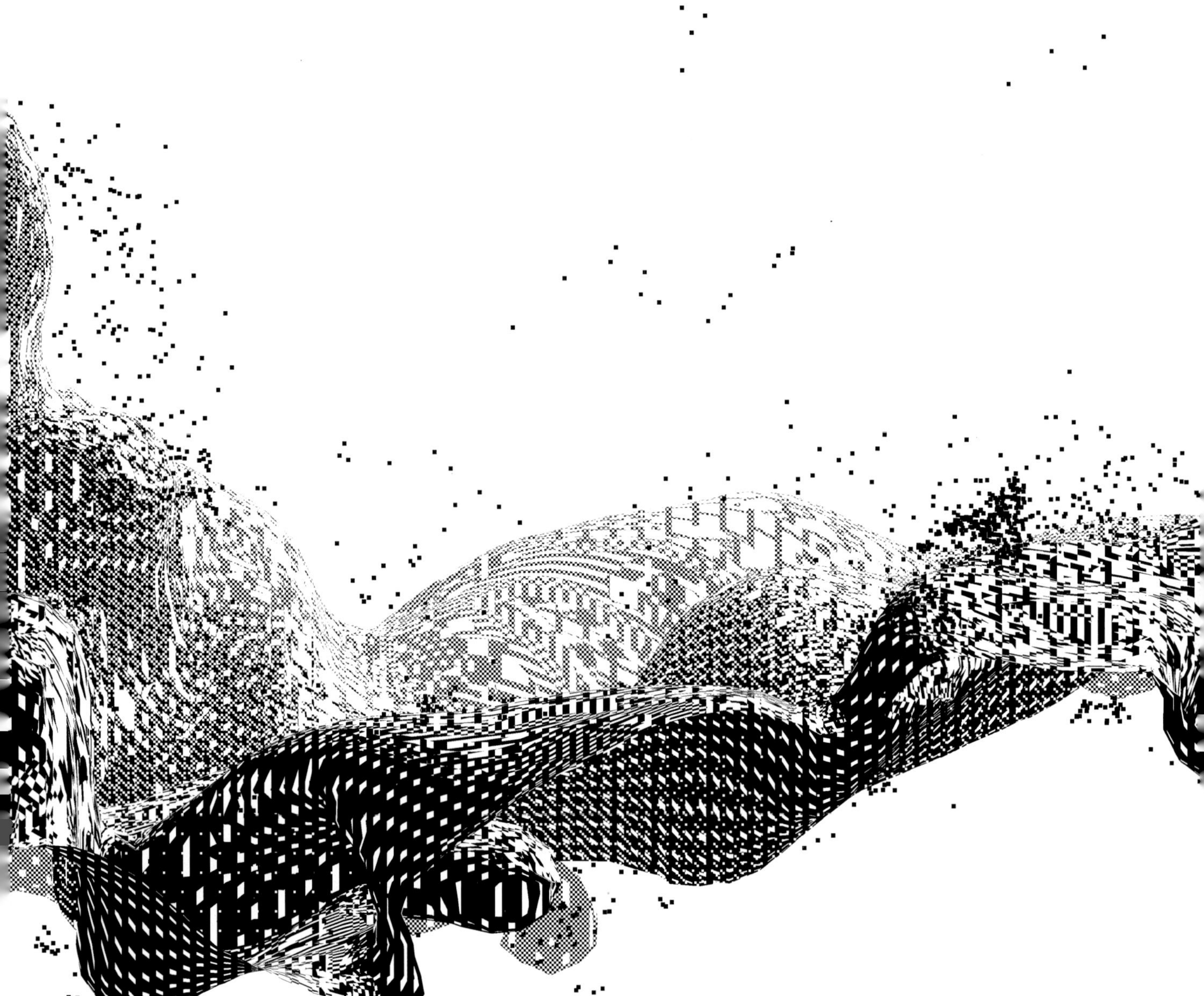

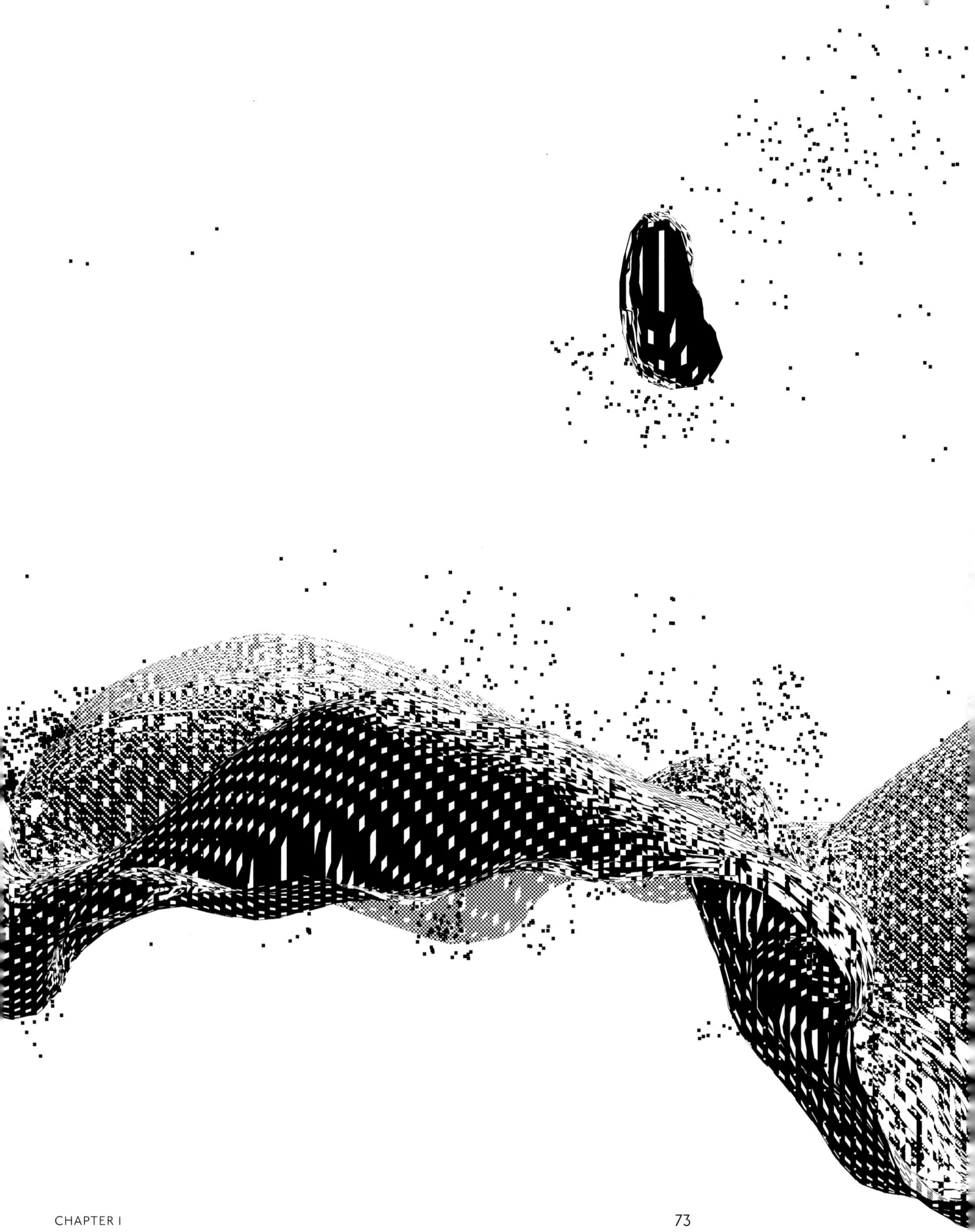

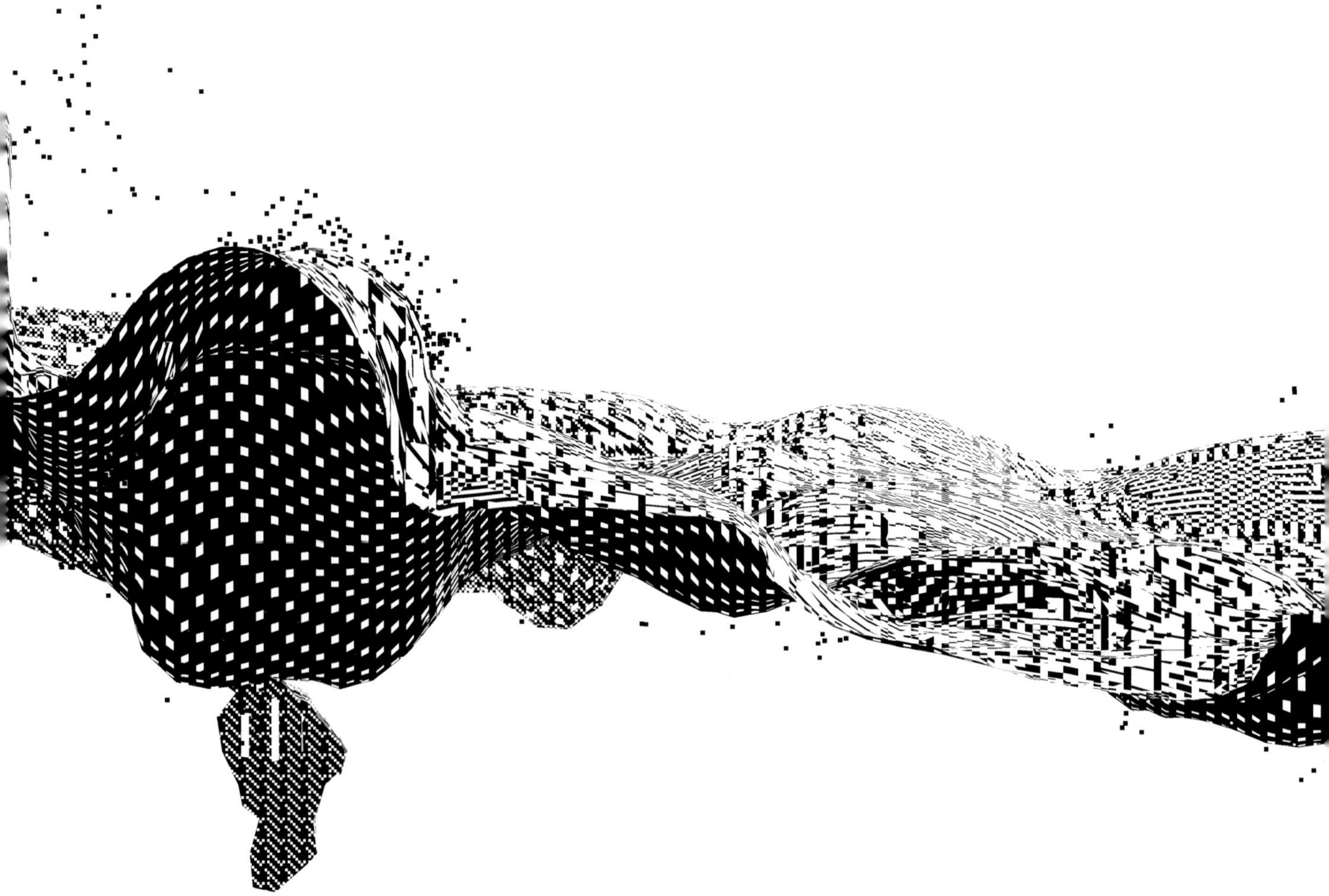

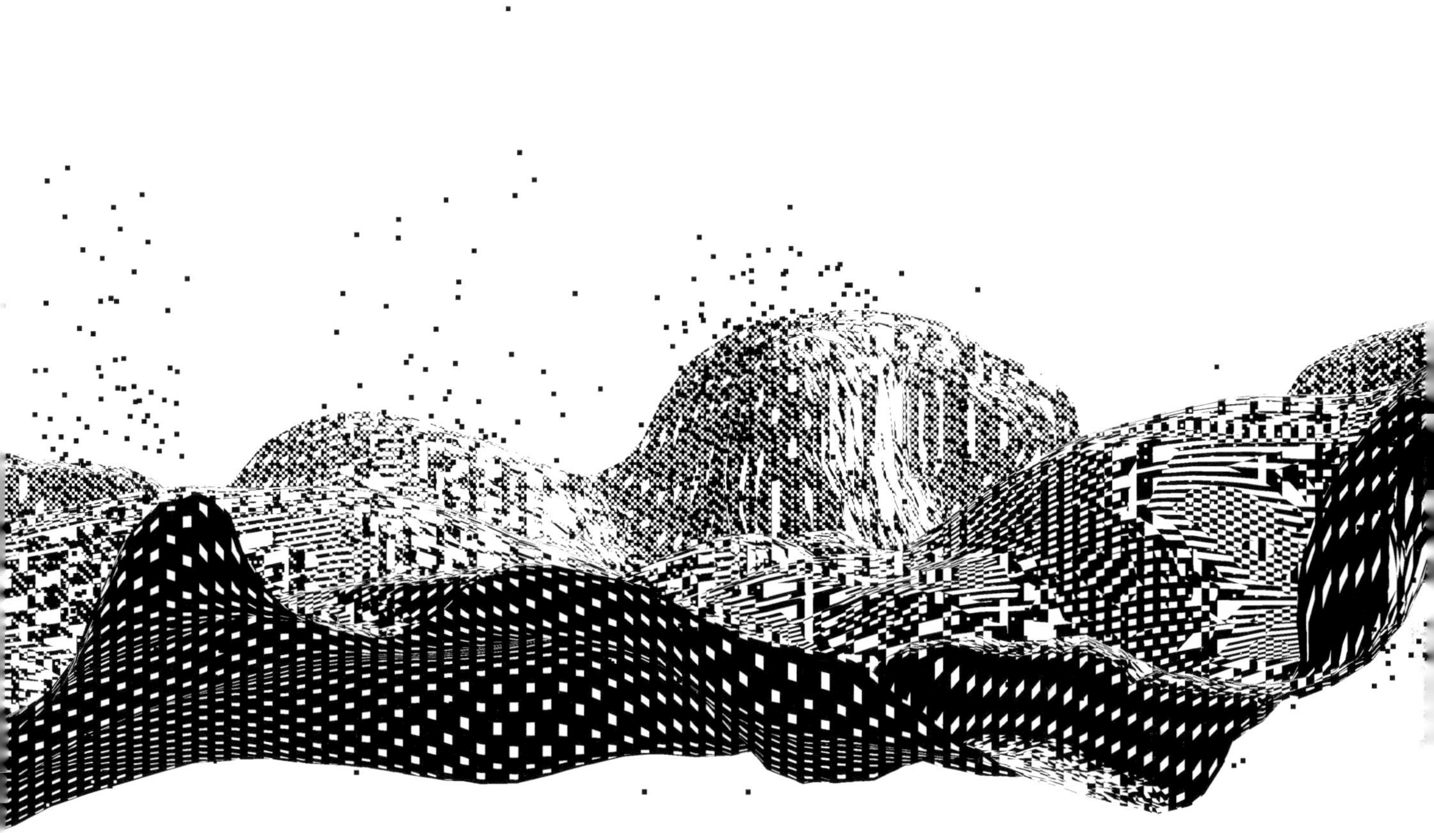

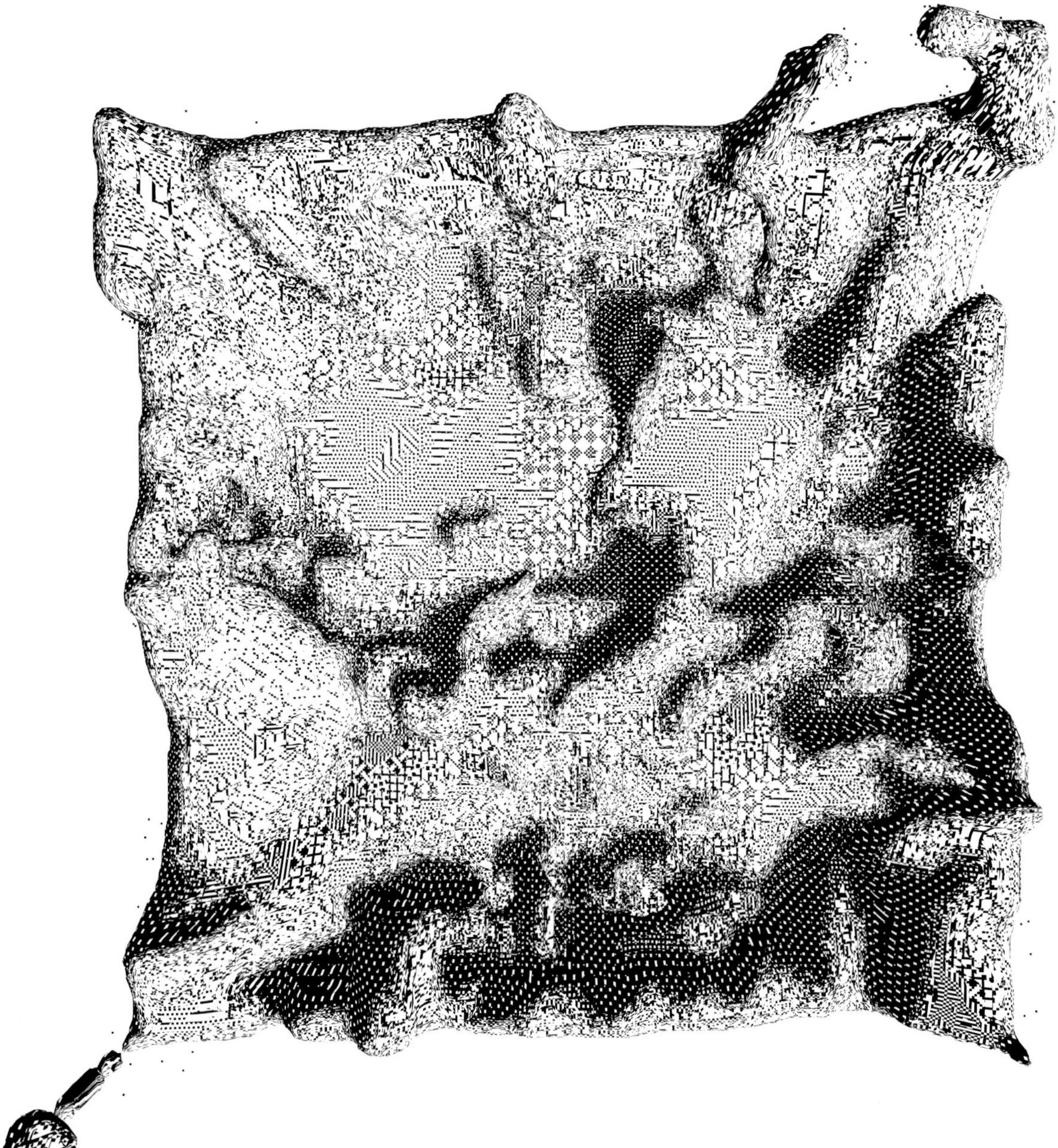

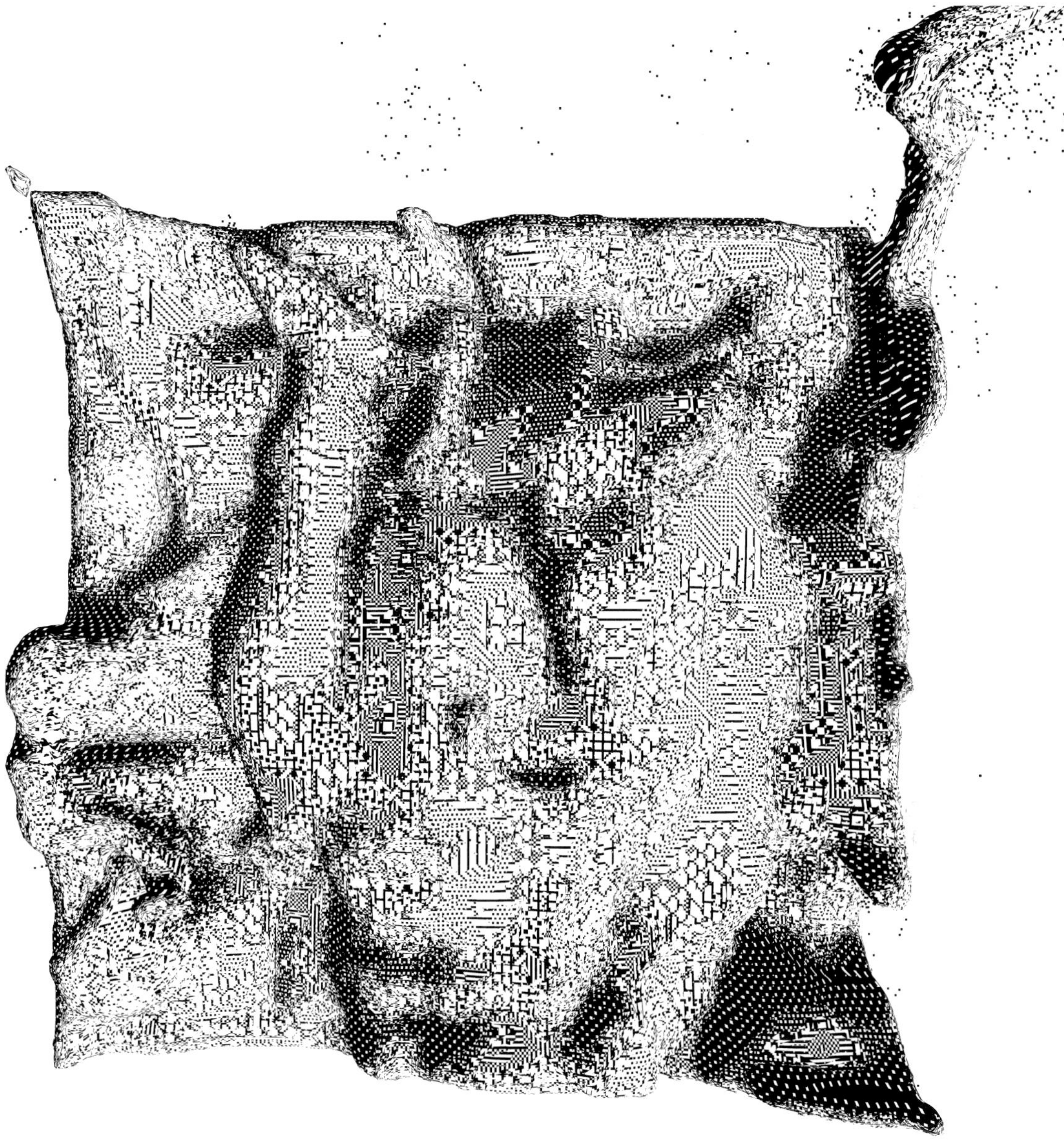

EXERCISE

Resolve to true or false with tons of information

In whatever software environment you render, create a custom shader (digital material) that generates pixels that are black or white. The more control your software gives you over the inputs to your shader the better. Many rendering platforms now implement the Open Shading Language or allow visual node-based editing of shaders with respect to the path of light, camera position, and surface geometry. These tools will help with this exercise. Aim for your shader to consider as many inputs as possible, even those that might at first seem arbitrary or unrelated to the visual qualities we usually associate with rendering. Don't be a purist here. Existing bitmap images can be involved in this process, and if the output starts to look real in ways other than you were expecting, great.

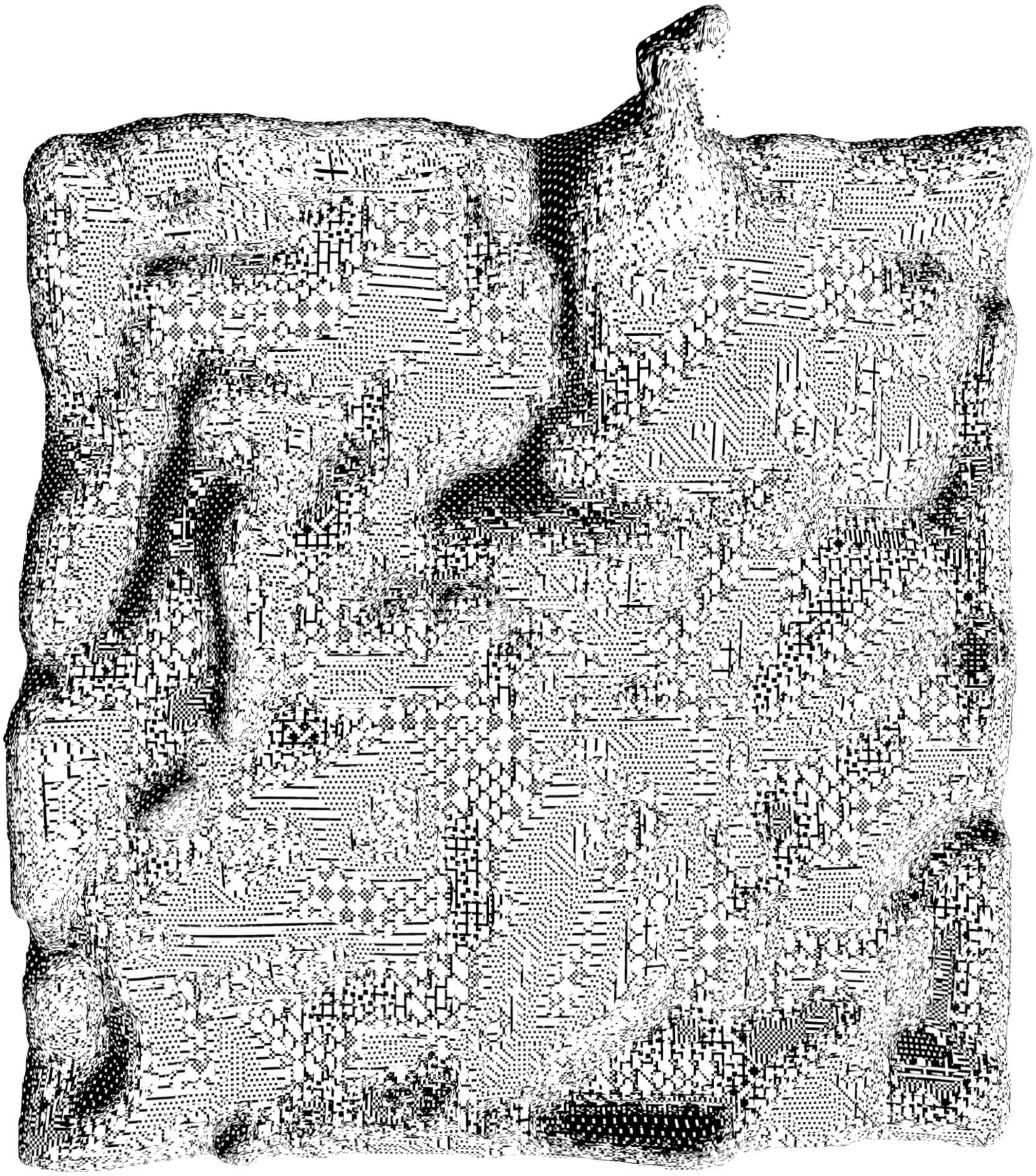

Notes

1. Preston Cram, "How Synthwave Grew from a Niche '80s Throwback to a Current Phenomenon," PopMatters, November 25, 2019, https://www.popmatters.com/synthwave-feature-list-2641449554.html.
2. Richard Trenholm, "History of Digital Cameras: From '70s Prototypes to IPhone and Galaxy's Everyday Wonders," c|net, May 31, 2021, https://www.cnet.com/tech/computing/history-of-digital-cameras-from-70s-prototypes-to-iphone-and-galaxys-everyday-wonders.
3. Alvy Ray Smith, *Biography of the Pixel* (MIT Press, 2021), 51. Smith cites a 1965 document by Fred Billingsley of Caltech as the earliest appearance of pixel and further explains that coining the term was not enough to canonize the term writing, "The word pixel itself had to fight for existence. Pixels were called many other things at first...For many years IBM and AT&T made an effort to contract it to pel. But either their candidate pixel, the vibrant young image-processing community of the mid-1960s triumphed over the efforts of giant corporations."
4. Smith, 2.
5. Smith, 5.
6. Smith, 60. Smith's, "spread" pixels refer to the process of sampling and interpolating from digital to wave form thanks to the mathematical genius of Kotelnikov's Sampling Theorem.
7. Michael A. Hiltzik, *Dealers of Lightning: Xerox PARC and the Dawn of the Computer Age* (New York, NY: HarperBusiness, 1999), 231. SuperPaint could boast, "nothing less than the most flexible frame buffer anyone had ever seen. Simply defined, a frame buffer is a box holding a hell of a lot of memory. More precisely, it is a grid in which the memory is arrayed to correspond with a video frame so that one or more bits of memory account for every 'pixel,' or 'picture element' on the display."
8. Andy Hertzfeld, *Revolution in the Valley: The Insanely Great Story of How the Mac Was Made* (Sebastopol, CA: O'Reilly Media, 2005), "MacPaint Evolution." 171. Hertzfeld, a close collaborator of Atkinson and co-creator of the original Macintosh, articulates the beauty of MacPaint's innovative triple frame buffer, rounded rectangle algorithm, and a feature for recognizing text created within a rasterized image. This later feature, through functional and innovative, was edited out of the software to maintain the integrity of its purpose.
9. Grant D. Taylor, *When the Machine Made Art: The Troubled History of Computer Art* (New York, NY: Bloomsbury, 2014), 244.
10. Sherry Turkle, *Life on the Screen: Identity in the Age of the Internet* (New York, NY: Simon & Schuster, 1995), 36.
11. Hertzfeld, *Revolution in the Valley: The Insanely Great Story of How the Mac Was Made,* "Square Dots." 32–33.
12. Hertzfeld, *Revolution in the Valley: The Insanely Great Story of How the Mac Was Made,* "Busy Being Born" 89–97.
13. Alexandra Lange, "The Woman Who Gave the Macintosh a Smile," *The New Yorker*, April 19, 2018.
14. Hertzfeld, *Revolution in the Valley: The Insanely Great Story of How the Mac Was Made,* "Busy Being Born, Part 2" 153-157.
15. Claire L. Evans, "A Eulogy for Skeuomorphism," Motherboard, Tech by Vice, June 11, 2013, https://www.vice.com/en/article/nzzpyz/a-eulogy-for-skeumorphism.
16. Some might argue that the correct number of possible 8 × 8 bitmap patterns is significantly fewer than eighteen quintillion given that the graphic effect of some of those theoretical patterns are equivalent. For example, one could argue that the one black pixel among 63 white pixels is effectively the same pattern regardless of the position of that one pixel. We might call this, the "theory of wallpaper" because it's like claiming that two identical walls covered with the same wallpaper look the same even if the wallpaper is applied beginning from different spots on each wall. However, MacPaint assumes a constant and global 0,0 origin for every patter irrespective of the area to be filled. Thus, most, but not all, of the eighteen quintillion patterns would appear differently when applied.
17. See Chapter 7, "Anxious Vision: Real Time and the First-Person Perspective View," by Hans Tursack.

18. Robyn Miller and Rand Miller (Cyan Inc., 1988), "The Manhole."
19. Robyn Miller and Rand Miller (Cyan Inc., 1991), "Spelunx and the Caves of Mr. Seudo."
20. See Chapter 3, "Using a Tree to Represent a Tree."
21. Leonard J. Shustek, "MacPaint and QuickDraw Source Code," CHM Blog: From the Collection, July 18, 2010, https://computerhistory.org/blog/macpaint-and-quickdraw-source-code/.
22. Joel Cretan, MacPaint.org: How to run MacPaint Today, accessed August 23, 2020, https://www.macpaint.org/emulate.html.

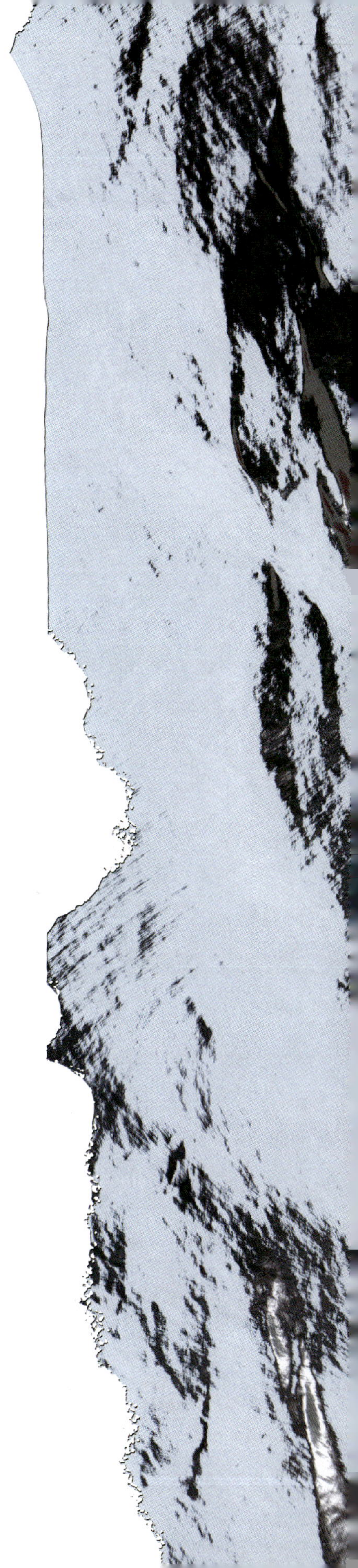

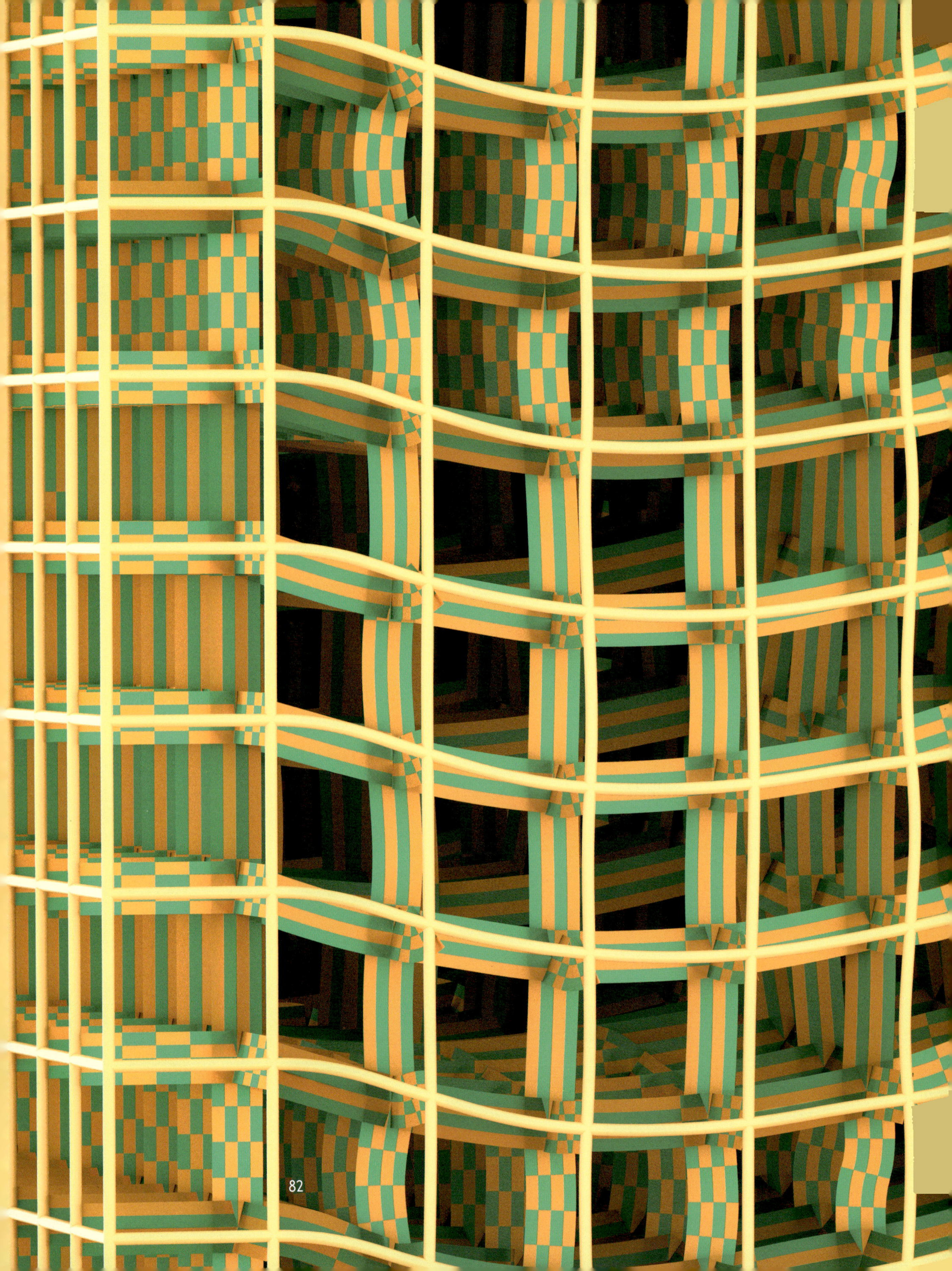

CHAPTER 2

Every Grid is Material

by Julie Kress

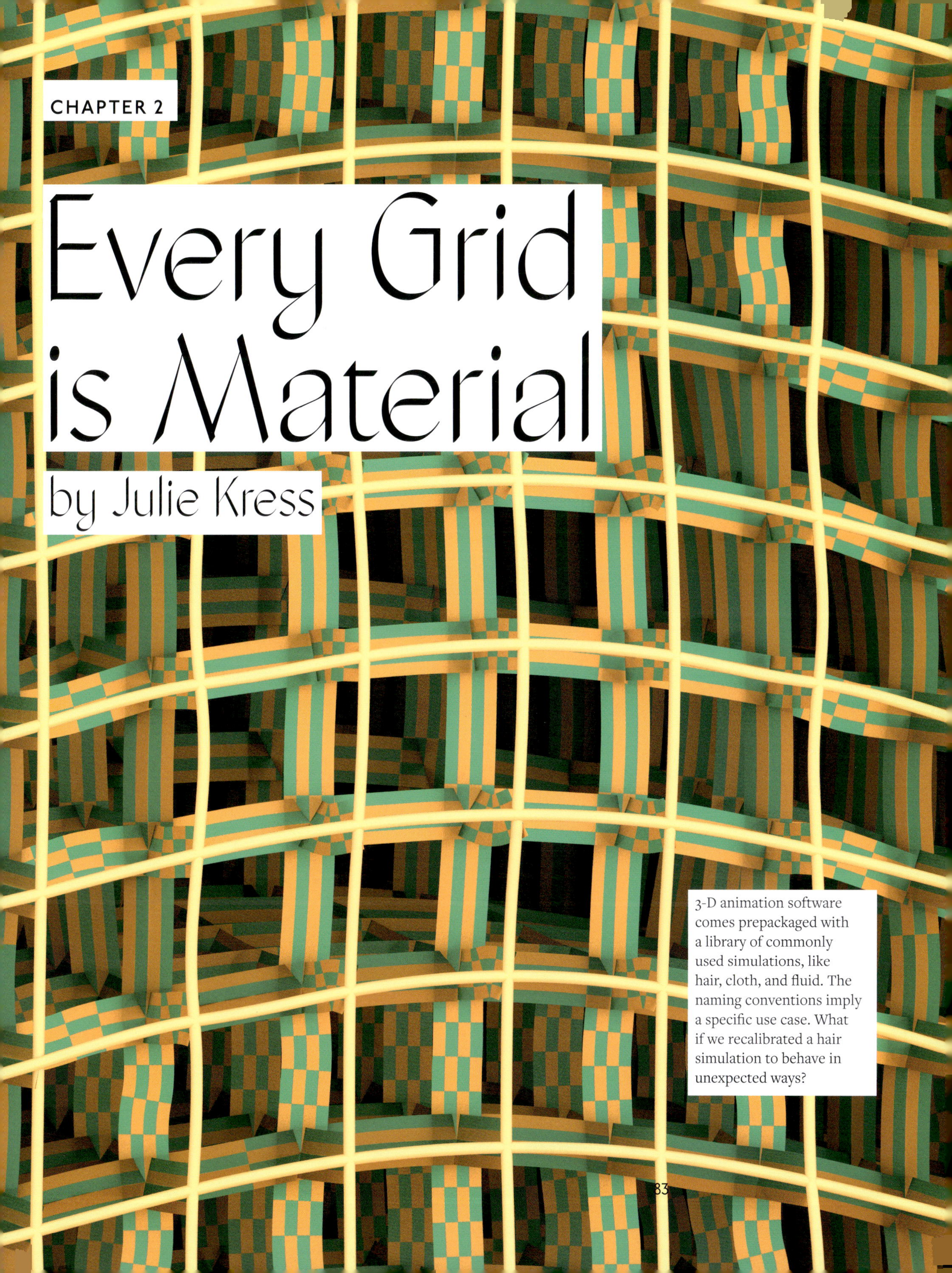

3-D animation software comes prepackaged with a library of commonly used simulations, like hair, cloth, and fluid. The naming conventions imply a specific use case. What if we recalibrated a hair simulation to behave in unexpected ways?

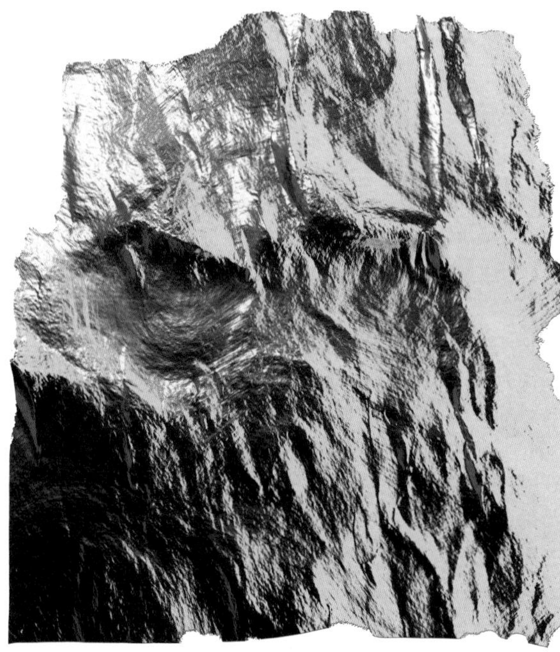

From power grids and spreadsheets to social media feeds and coordinate systems in 3-D modeling software, our daily lives are intensely gridded. These ordering systems are often treated as insignificant and neutral territory. Take for instance the checkered canvas in Photoshop,[1] used as a symbol for *transparency* or *nothingness*. Or consider its 3-D counterpart, the checkered UV texture map that appears on 3-D models as a *placeholder* for "real" textures yet to be applied. We are accustomed to the checkerboard representing what *is not* a part of an image. Yet every digital image, *is* a grid. The checkerboard is just a lower resolution grid that provides a coarser way to organize the image that is already gridded. How could these grids gain more substance, like those deployed by a graphic designer who may pluck a guideline and drag it across a page to shift the positioning of elements, or the grids that emerge from woven threads on a loom? Material physics simulations normally want to deny the grid to achieve the most life-like animated effects, but that is futile in the gridded world of digital images. This dichotomy offers a framework to recover the grid as a live, physical participant in the creation of 3-D forms and digital imagery. Now digital simulations face the grid with a material identity crisis. What if the grid is not just a guide, but is also content? What if the grid *is* the material? How can the grid be contained when it wants to continue into infinity?

The most visually evident impacts of the grid are marked by twentieth-century Modernism. The radical design group, Superstudio, pushed the modernist grid to absurdity, by imagining the entire world enshrouded in a giant continuous grid. Their Continuous Monument[2] series highlighted the oppressive nature of the grid but also suggested opportunities to repurpose it for their utopian visions. Their attitude in support of these hijacked grids is more relevant than ever as we are in fact occupying the continuous monument at even greater intensities than Superstudio imagined, at the scale of the entangled networked grid of the world wide web down to the pixel grid displayed on our mobile screens.

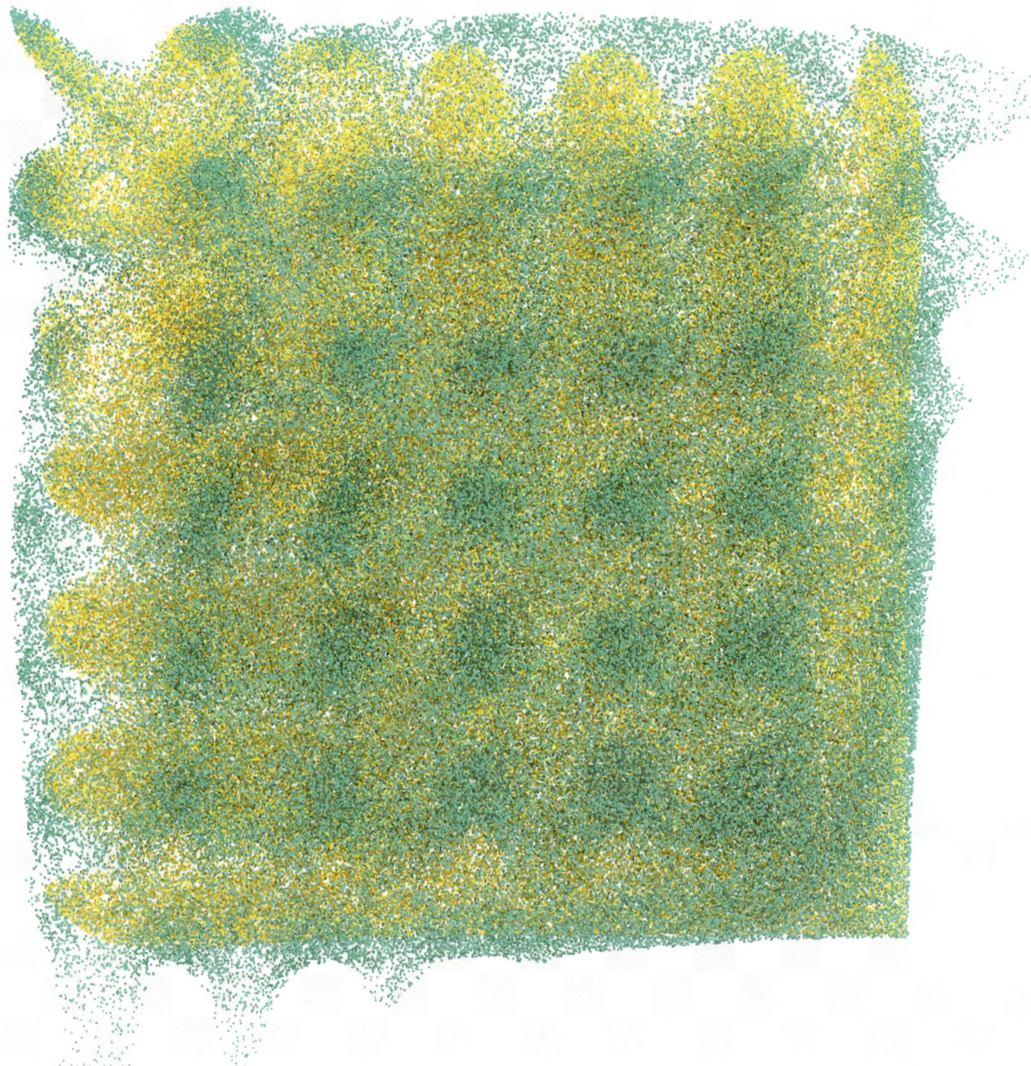

Every tool is Pre-Gridded

Grids are not neutral, but they are our culture's default. Any 3-D Modeling software will likely greet you with an x, y, z Cartesian grid, awaiting geometry to be placed into the pre-gridded world. The grid isn't just there as an idle backdrop but informs every tool and every topology. Every point, curve, or surface is generated in reference to the grid. Even the most amorphous, fuzzy object will have coordinates defining its shape. 3-D modeling often relies on the grid as a user interface device. A user creates an object of certain dimensions, for example, and then places the object in space by aligning their cursor to a grid, or in reference to other geometry. Alternatively, one could compose the model entirely through text-based commands using numeric parameters rounded to a certain decimal point precision, again affectively constraining to a grid. At this most elementary organization of a 3-D model, both the space and the objects that exist within it are vigorously gridded. This is strongly evident when a 3-D model is viewed in wireframe mode, without visible layers of light, shadow, or color, just grid skeletons defining every surface. It's uncomfortable to admit that this Cartesian field underlying all of our tools and devices, always working in the background as a helper for authorship, is also authored.

Many of us become well acquainted with homogenous, pre-gridded worlds at a young age. The ruled paper with that abnormally large spacing for a clumsy hand first learning to write cursive comes to mind. Even the iconic school desks of the mid-twentieth century would typically be neatly lined up in rows so that each student could easily be accounted for. More free-spirited teachers would try to arrange the desks into clusters or in the round, but it never disguised the modular nature of the restrictive furnishings. For architects, grids are essential to the mechanisms of drawing; the parallel ruler tied to most drafting boards, for example. It might not be "pre-gridded," but it certainly anticipates a grid, as a device that specifically facilitates repetitive lines orthogonal to each other. Within the drafting apparatus, it is not so easy to deviate from the grid.

Drawing grids in a digital sandbox does not represent anything but the behavior of the simulated particles themselves.

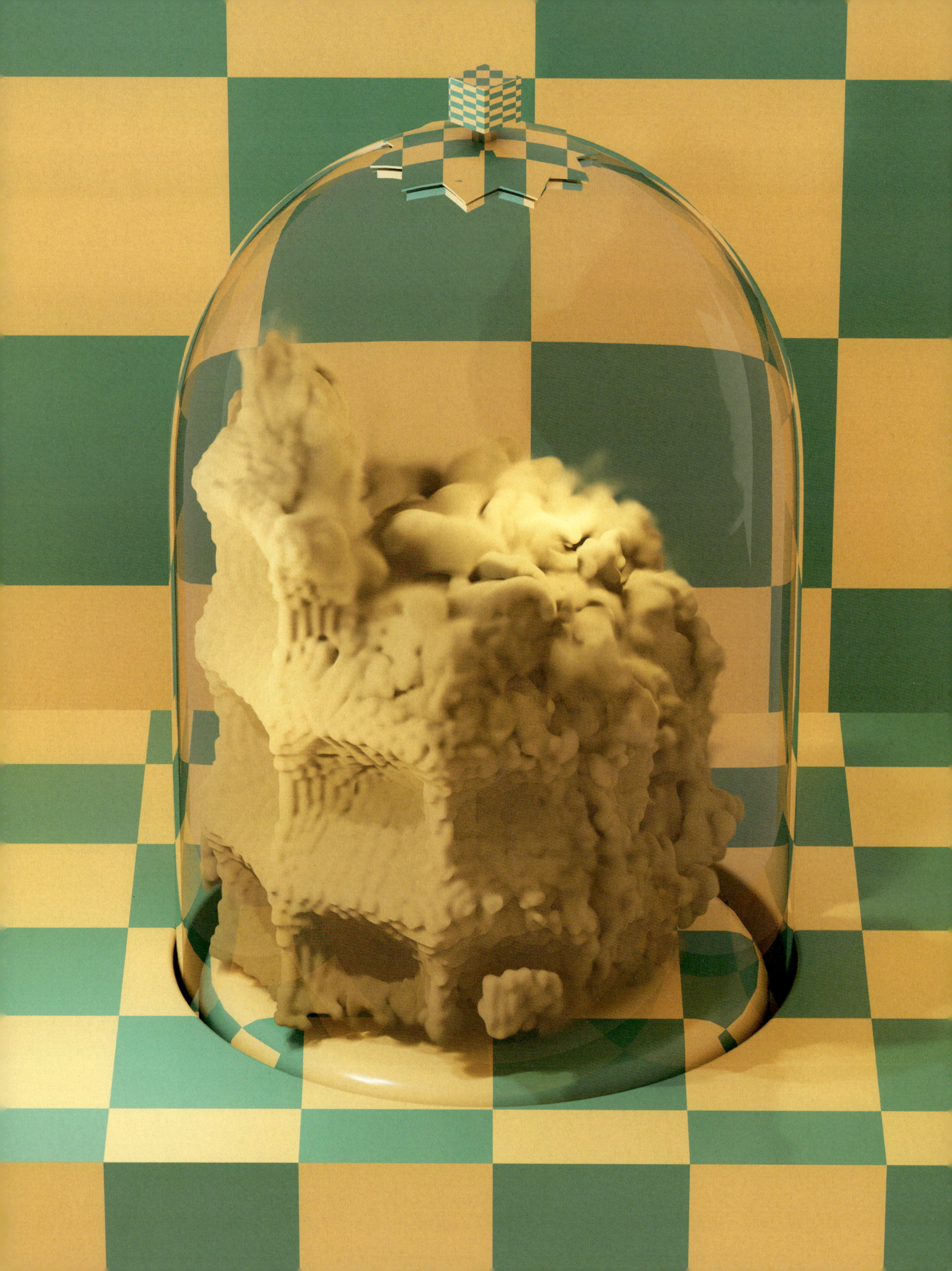

Every Grid is Aesthetic

This tradition of drafting grids most obviously originates from the grid used as a guide for perspective and orthographic projection. However, in her seminal essay on grids, Rosalind Krauss counters that perspective isn't really an early instance of grids, because perspective was "the science of the real, not the mode of withdrawal from it. Perspective was a demonstration of the way reality and its representation could be mapped onto one another."[3] The grid according to her definition is "flattened, geometricized, antinatural, antimimetic, antireal. What art looks like when it turns its back on nature."[4] Artists working at the time of Krauss's publication, like Agnes Martin, Larry Poon, and Jasper Johns were testing that extreme. They created grids that did not serve any purpose for accurately representing perspectival realities. Instead, they were purely studies of the 2-D perceptual field and meditations on the grid's infinite expansion. They didn't map anything but "the surface of the painting itself."[5] The grid overtook modernist art as something that was abstract and synthetic, but it should be recalled that it was also material, depicted in paint spread across canvas surfaces. Whether it's drafted on trace paper, represented in paint strokes, or displayed on a screen, the grid will always have material origins, even if it remains a symbol of the digital that is anti-material and anti-real.

This anti-material aesthetic permeates pop culture and sci-fi aesthetics. Consider TRON,[6] in which a game developer is transported into the software world of a computer. The world is awash with grids as a representation of "digital space." Turning to a slightly more obscure example, we could reflect on the "Homer^3" short in the *Simpsons* "Treehouse of Horror VI,"[7] in which the cartoon Homer falls through a wall into a 3-D modeling space, indicated by an eerie glowing green grid and some floating mathematical equations. Marge calls, "Homer where are you?" Homer's voice echoes from this other dimension, "I'm somewhere where I don't know where I am!"

The *Star Trek* Holodeck is a virtual reality space used to transport characters to any place or time imaginable. In *Star Trek*'s fictional future, characters can program their own simulated realities. Ironically, the scenes in the Holodeck are as real as the show ever gets given the rare opportunity for characters to appear in contemporary clothes on earthly locations. Before a Holodeck program runs, it is staged as a plain black room gridded with thick yellow lines. The room completely disappears once it transforms into the infinite expanse of the simulated environment. It's a simple but effective storytelling device to define the threshold between two realities. A yellow grid temporarily flickering into

Smoke won't hold a shape. Its most salient features are related to diffusion and dissolution. There are two options for how smoke can hold a grid. Either it's a grid to start with, or it collides with one after. Terrariums, when sealed, create a scaled atmosphere that promotes plant growth. The closed system of the terrarium is also an optimal environment to prevent simulated smoke from dissipating too quickly.

view is enough to remind the audience what is considered fiction (a Holodeck simulation) or real (the spaceship and its crew). Everything that exists in the Holodeck stays in the Holodeck, or so you think until the barrier between digital and physical become a little blurrier in episode 138, "Ship in a Bottle."[8] Professor James Moriarty, a computer-generated character from a Sherlock Holmes simulation gains self-awareness and seeks to exit the Holodeck and enter reality. "That is not possible, you cannot exist outside this room!" Captain Picard tries to explain. "Are you certain of that?" replies Moriarty as he does the impossible and steps out of the sitting room at Baker Street, through the Holodeck doors, and onto the starship Enterprise. In this episode, the Holodeck isn't just a vehicle to propel the story in a different time or place. The room itself becomes the subject and a conceptual device to reflect on the boundaries between digital and physical experiences. Like all the impossible elements presented in this book, the representational device inserts itself into the story. It becomes the subject without sacrificing its capacity to contain and transmit other subjects.

The Holodeck grid is implicitly referenced in most virtual reality headsets. They typically have a built-in safety feature, a "guardian" that appears as a glowing grid barrier when you come too close to tripping hazards in the real world. The guardian could be any pattern or symbol, but we already have a natural comfort with the grid as a representation of abstract nothingness. The grid's anti-material aesthetic is less likely to be mistaken as a material element of the virtual environment. Both use cases of the grid in VR headsets and the Holodeck, recall the checkerboard canvas in Photoshop, a representation of what's not actually there. Instead of defaulting to this aesthetic, the "Ship in a Bottle" episode invites us to refocus our attention onto the grid as the material of interest.

When simulated smoke collides with its container, you can clearly see gridded artifacts, exposing the computer's limits while it calculates the collision between voxels and the terrarium.

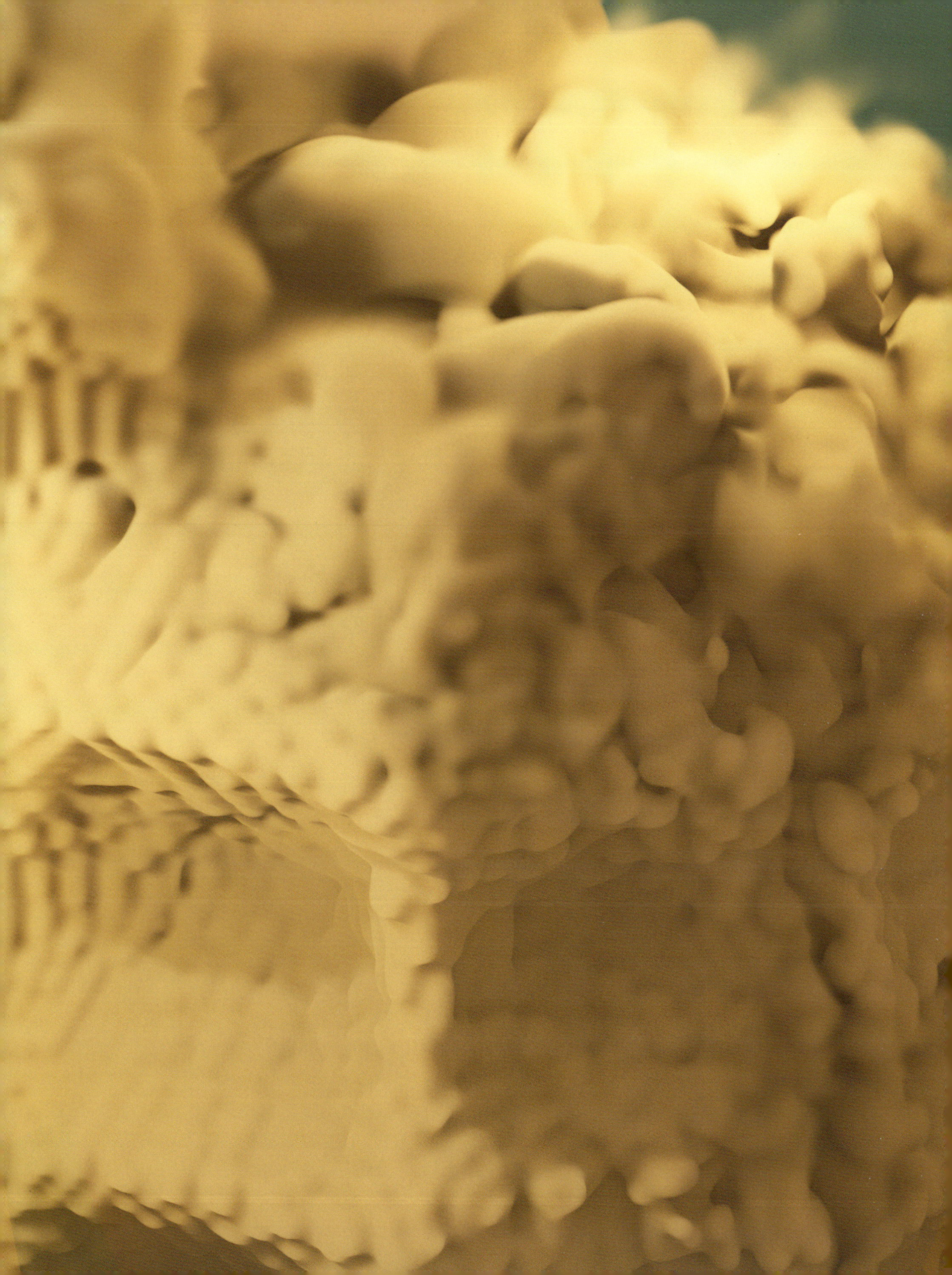

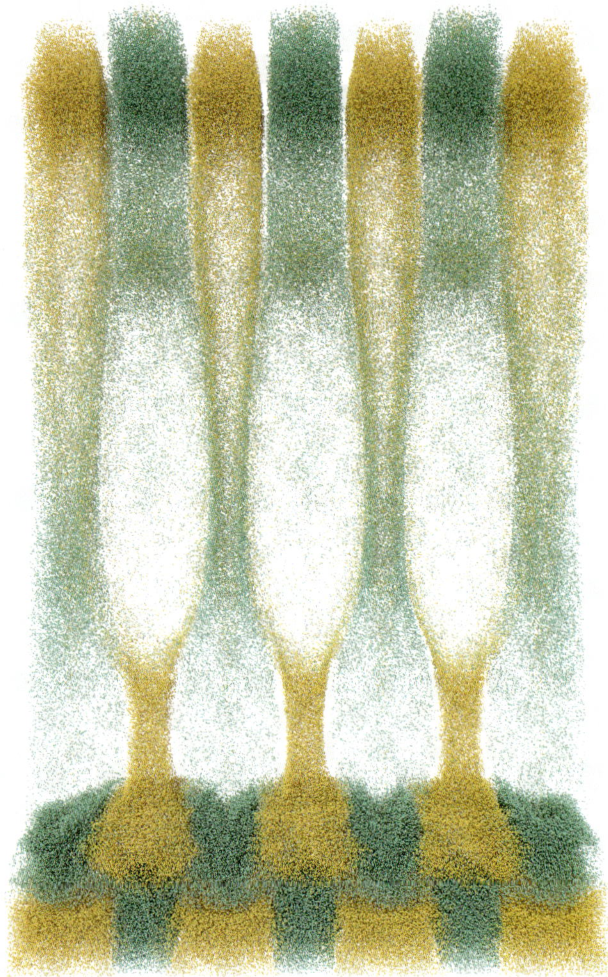

Usually grids are applied, underlaid, or projected, but they can also be plopped. The grid defines where and when the plops should occur, but the ideal plop falls a little outside the guidelines.

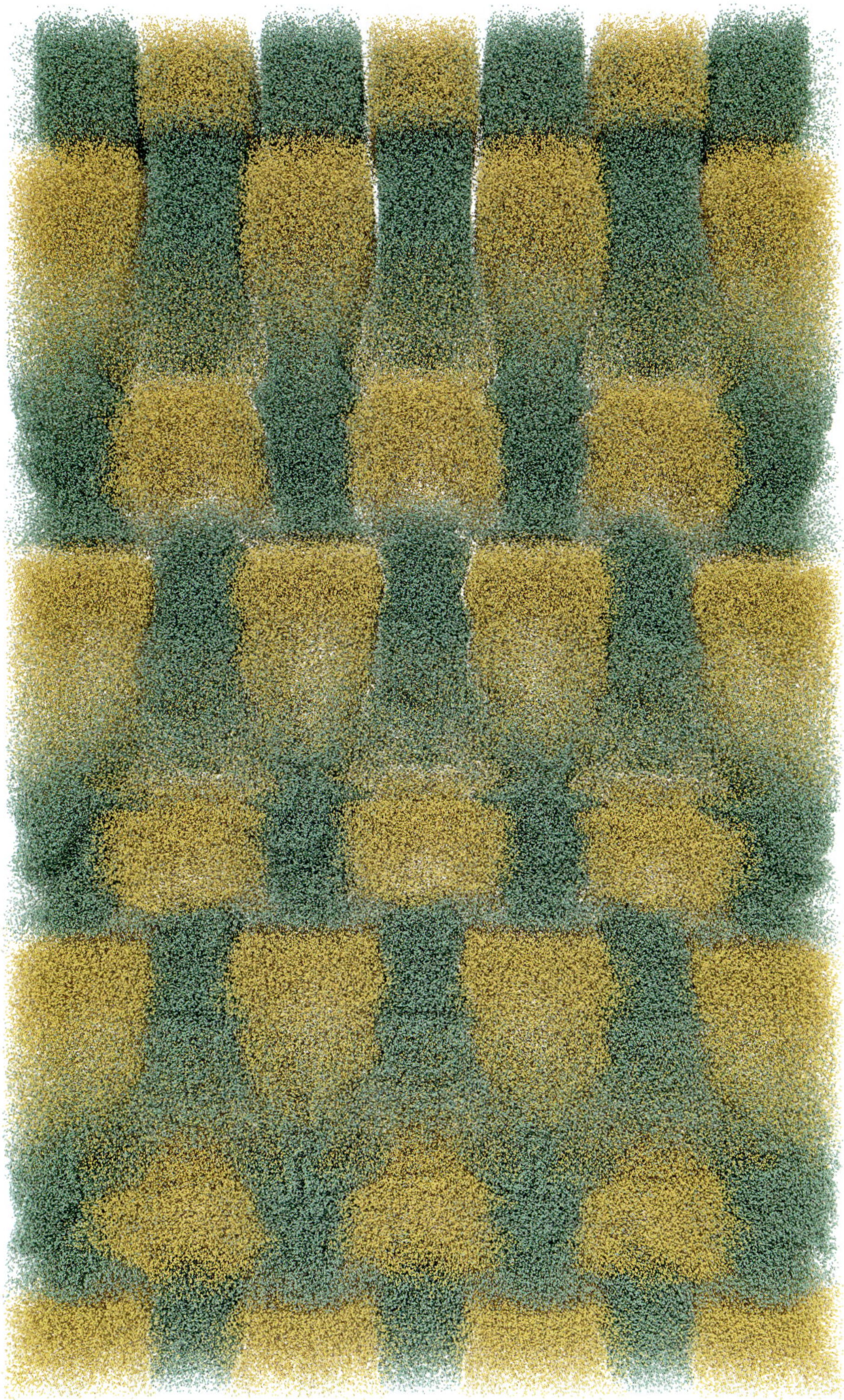

Every Grid is Constructed

Architects inhabit the same grids prevalent in sci-fi aesthetics, but sci-fi environments can claim to be fictions entirely removed from reality, whereas architects assume that the digital is a representation of something in existence or potentially constructable. Marco Frascari connects the practice of "denoting lines" away from perspectival origins and instead invites us to consider the historic construction site that saw measuring ropes, weighted plumblines, and chalked strings pulled across the terrain to mark the building footprint and guide the erection of vertical walls. "The transformation of the use of taut lines on site to the use of denoting lines traced on paper and vice versa reveals the cunning intelligence of architects."[9] Frascari's interest in the synergies between the practices of drafting, and marking a physical site invites us to consider the similar mental and physical forces at work in both. Today, architecture culture contends with a complex relationship with the long-established tradition of drawing. Strictly speaking, architects don't draw anymore, they produce digital images. How then can we rekindle the "cunning intelligence" Frascari describes without the drawn line? Might we form a new analogy between image and building in the same way Frascari traced drawing and building? One way forward is to make the digital model the construction site. Physics simulations and rendering engines allow for the hyper-real, literal pulling of threads across a site, erecting of scaffolds, and suspending of weighted plumblines. It at first appears that the ingenuity of translation between physical materials and a drawn line that Frascari essentializes has been entirely replaced by simulacrum. This is not the case.

3-D modeling catalyzed a rapid transition from traditions of orthographic drawing to an unprecedented set of digital tools and procedures for graphic production. We are still adapting to the notion that a 3-D model is real in the sense that it that can be rotated, scaled, and zoomed while simultaneously rendered in 2-D images presented on a screen. This occurs long before and totally independent of its fabrication as a real object. This condition in which image and object are not mutually exclusive is uniquely digital. Frascari's drafted line and chalked string now inhabit the same conceptual realm. The increased ease of material simulations offers yet another drastic shift in which a 3-D model can adopt material behaviors that appear more real than ever, more object-like than ever. However, simulated models are still digital objects, presented as an image, and will always exhibit certain characteristics of the digital, even if they are imperceptible. It is joked that if you created a map of the world that describes every detail without any compression of information, the map would have to be large enough to cover the world itself. If you had infinite computing power, any evidence of the digital would disappear because you could have an infinitely smooth simulation displayed at the highest quality resolution. Instead of aspiring for this energy intensive impossibility of a direct replication of the world, it is far more interesting to imagine how the presence of the digital can be authored to produce new and unexpected effects.

Kai Franz's "Plopper Series" makes use of a hacked plotter, known as "The Plopper." The materials he plots with are messy and imprecise, piles of sand hardened into place with polyurethane and paint. The results look more like geological specimens than a product of digital fabrication. He explains that 3-D printing and similar fabrication processes can generate any kind of geometry from computer-generated models, they are "robots of industry," whereas "Plopping is a process for discharging logarithmic hiccups."[10] His work marries digital exactness with physical materials that resist control. In the world of physics simulations, we might subscribe to Franz's artistic framing of digitality, but operate conversely by producing materials that *appear* messy and random despite their numerical foundations. Our ambition is to coax messiness into a digital logic. This is certainly in violation of the nature of the digital, which is indiscriminately discrete. What appears to be fluid, smoke or cloth is a linked collection of data points. In the last decade, we have become familiar with digital identifiers in physical materials such as layer lines in 3-D prints that corelate to the size of the extruder nozzle. Oddly enough, a smoke simulation that does not have high enough quality settings, will have similar artifacts resembling the striations of a 3-D print. Our discipline is still becoming acquainted with the differences between multiple forms of digital materiality traversing images, drawings, models, and animations.

Why does it matter whether we call a digital representation an image or a drawing, when both are a visual depiction? Architect John May explains, "that to contemplate the difference is not about orthography or computation being better or worse, but to acknowledge that thinking takes place under radically different conditions in each"[11] Drawing is a mode of marking a surface through repeatable hand movements and gestures often guided by external tools. Where models are editable, drawings are fixed. They can be traced or overlaid, of course, but their distinction is a matter of operations and structure rather than appearance. Still, the tradition of drawing still holds a great deal of authority in the way architects are trained to engage computation. Digital 3-D models are incredible devices packed with information, yet students of architecture are still compelled to smash their intricate models into "drawings" with the popular Rhino 3-D command "Make2D." May describes this coping mechanism as pseudo-orthography, in which familiar operations of drawing are simulated in software under the false pretense that the fundamental operations of architecture have not changed but just made more efficient through digitization.

Fakeness has a negative connotation. We are all still wrapping our heads around the ethics of Mountain Dew's decision to resurrect the artist Bob Ross 25 years after his death for a 40 minute "lost episode" in which his likeness paints a Mountain Dew bottle within a landscape.[12] Pseudo orthography is nowhere as sinister, but there are wrong and right reasons for its use. Unconscious pseudo orthography is a symptom of a stubborn profession unwilling to reassess architecture as a digital practice. Instrumentalized pseudo orthography, on the other hand, is a way to consider how orthographic sensibilities long ingrained in the history of architecture do not need to be completely erased but can be a navigational device for methods of image production. The conception of a grid as an underlay drawn on trace paper helps us to perceive the similar behavior of a grid on a layer in an image editing software, but also to recognize the difference when a grid adopts new identities as an element, or an apparatus. The scenarios depicted in this chapter pair multiple conceptions of grid with physics simulations to propel this notion of instrumentalized fakeness. Some simulations are pseudo orthographic, mimicking the process of inscribing a grid into a substrate, plopping matter into a gridded sequence, or erasing a grid that was previously staged. Other simulations are necessary to express a particular grid's range of motion. Fusing the grid and physics simulations serves to imagine the grid as a material that can be authored equally to 3-D surfaces, curves, and points.

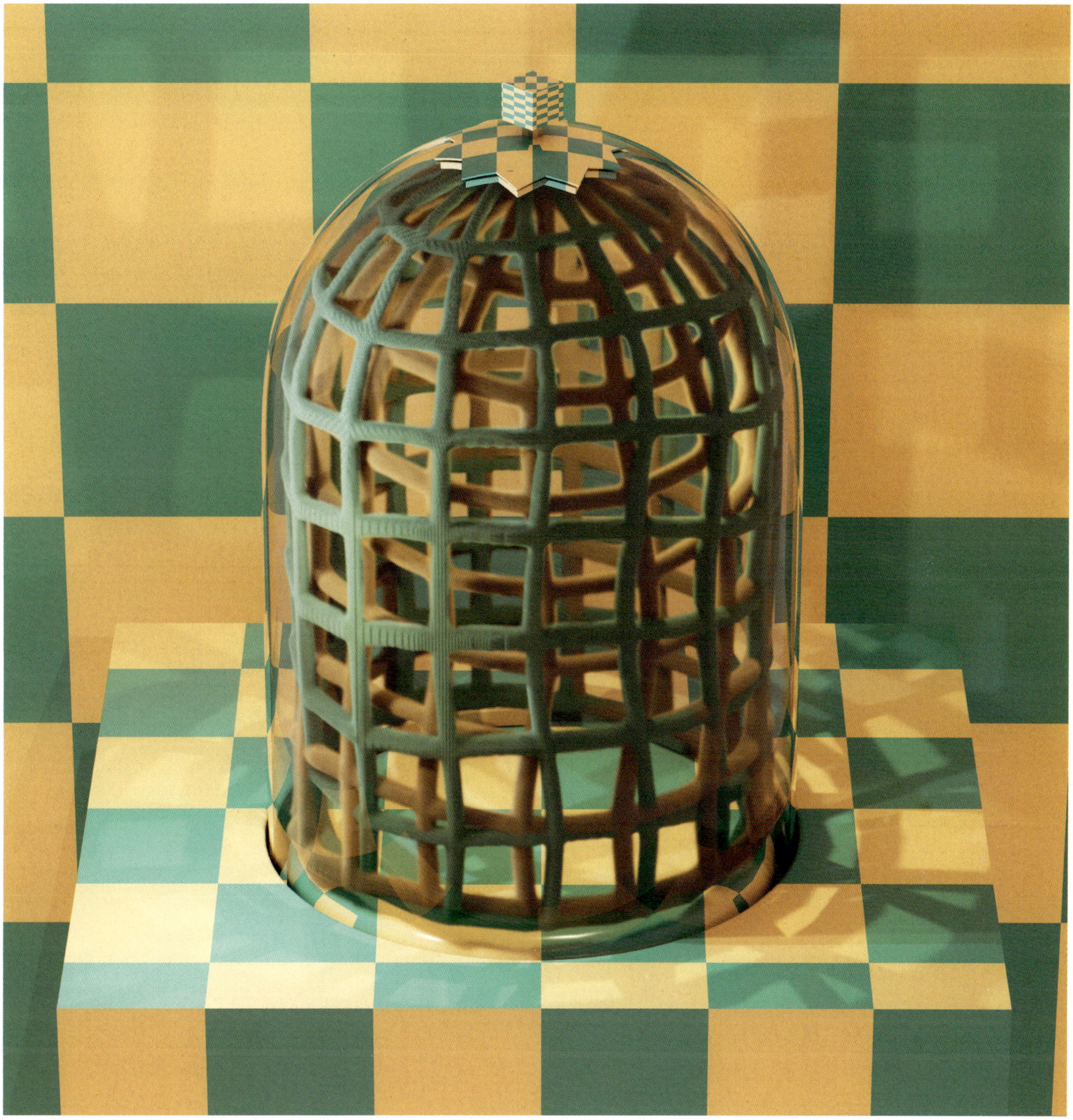

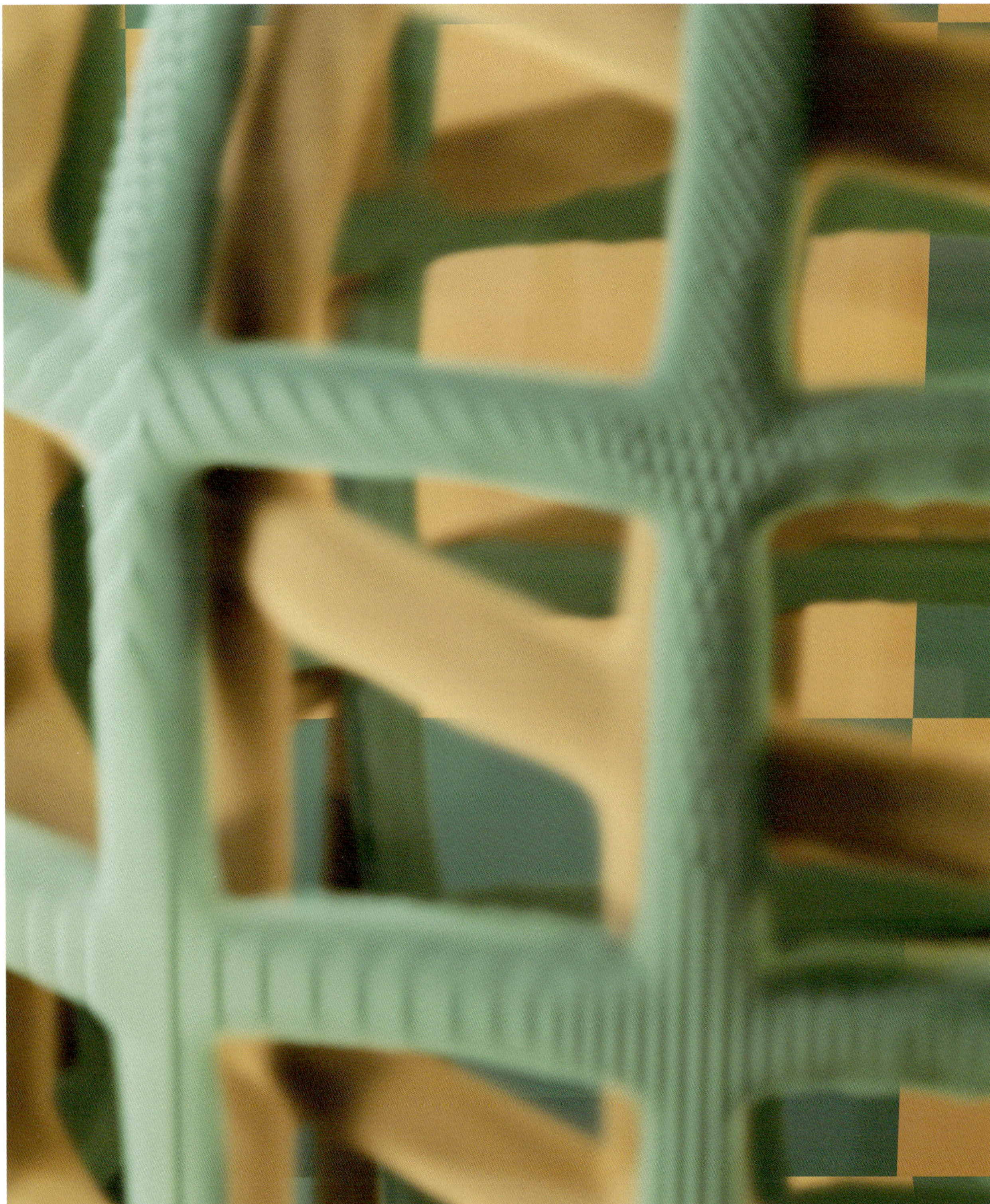

Every Grid is Imposed

In any creative process employing computational technology for image making, it is necessary to identify what effects are unique to the digital format and what role you as the designer will play. Simply executing a simulation is not satisfying. Most 3-D animation software, such as Maya, Blender, and C4D, feature physics engines that come prepackaged with a library of commonly used simulations within the entertainment industry. With the help of a few tutorials, one can likely generate authentic hair, cloth, or smoke right out of the box. The naming conventions for these effects imply a particular use case and material characteristics, but a simple recalibration of language allows us to begin to imagine alternative outputs of the simulations customized to our purposes. "Hair" are dynamic curves. "Cloth" is a soft body as opposed to a rigid body. "Smoke" is a particle simulation. Simulations are computationally intensive. A lot of our time may be spent waiting in anticipation while the computer processes. Staging a scene and then waiting for results to compute provokes a goal-oriented mindset. How might we evaluate our results in the pursuit of nothing in particular? Is realism an essential component of a successful simulation that's inventive, critical, and pleasing? Certainly, a simulation can precisely and realistically calculate how objects will collide with each other and deform under the influence of user-defined forces, but simulations can also defy real world physics. Gravity can be rotated sideways and objects that look like stone can float like balloons. With the possibilities of the digital, our creative arsenal can expand beyond a nostalgia for real world materials. Curves, surfaces, and even pixels might be imbued with tectonic behaviors that elicit associations with a material, like paint for instance, without replicating the appearance, color, or texture of that material. This divorce between behavior and appearance is the most salient feature of digital simulations. It relieves digital matter to express new synesthetic pairings of objects and behaviors. These "fake" simulations require the designer to customize their 3-D construction site; establish the subjects, narrativize the procedures, and have a dialogue with the tool to evaluate the surprising effects it produces.

Construction scaffolds are essentially figural 3-D grids that provide temporary frameworks. In theory, a scaffold should leave no trace once the building is erected. They are intended solely as an assist for structural stability and to provide workers access to unreachable heights. Like the checkered transparency signifying texture, they lack a certain standing associated with the final and the permanent. It may seem strange or absurd to produce a computer-generated scaffolding since there is no requirement to support a 3-D model against gravity. Even within the context of a physics simulation, the material behavior of an object can be manually constrained at any or every vertex to be infinitely rigid. This redundancy recalls John May's critique of pseudo-orthography, that the logics of new tools beg for a rethinking of old methodologies and not just a means of producing the same output faster. However, a digital scaffold does not (because it need not) equate to a literal support, but can function as a guide for organizing geometry, a visible mechanism that exposes grids already present in the simulation, and a formwork to impose new grids altogether. The digital scaffold soon becomes something more than a temporary measuring device or guide. It transitions, evolves, performs, and responds such that might become subsumed by the work to the extent that it can no longer be switched off.

Physics simulations can reveal their latent, computational, and hidden grids, but the scaffold makes additional grids visible and operable. Scaffolds for hair (curves), cloth (surface), and smoke (points), require some unconventional procedures to design into the system, as gridded behaviors are not normally desirable for realistic material simulations. For example, a hair simulation requires the following inputs: a surface to attach hair follicles, the number of follicles to be distributed, and a hair length. By default, the follicles are distrusted via a random noise algorithm specifically coded to eschew the grid. The inputs are hair specific, and the result will be a field of independently bouncy curves attached to a surface, presumably a body. The process to structure simulated hair into the unusual structure of a scaffold, requires a more manual approach. This involves constructing a lattice of curves with hair dynamics and detaching all the default hair follicles that normally anchor the hair to a surface. Then constraining each curve vertex to neighboring curve vertices based on a maximum distance (approximately the distance between each intersection), so they don't drift from each other but have some flexibility at the joints. Varying the density of the curves, the constraint range, and hair rigidity settings is key to uncovering the wide array of possible structures. Through this manual procedure, the scaffold is grafted onto the material simulation to impose regular order on top of a set of software inputs that resist them. This operation pivots the exploration from input-outcome to productive discovery.

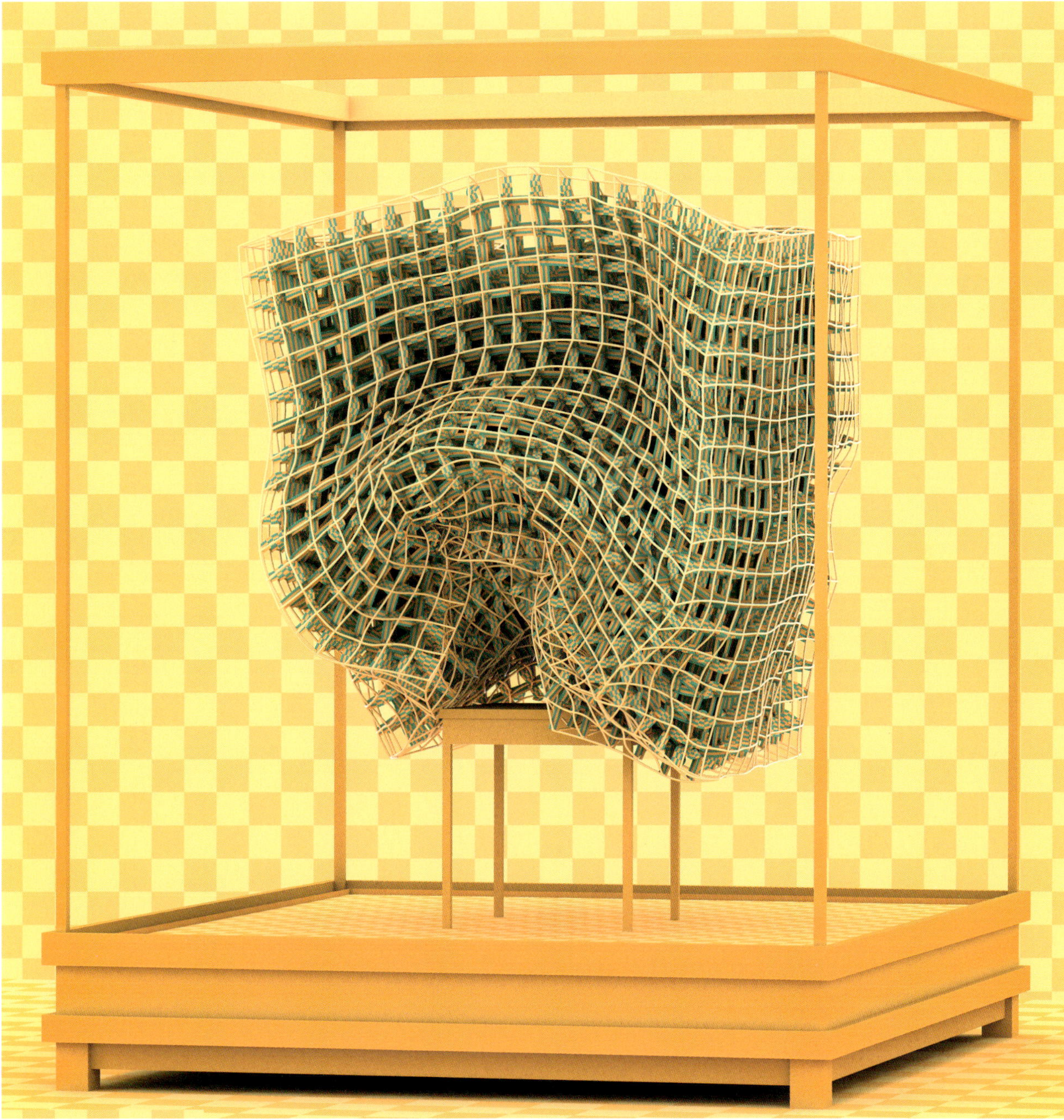

EXERCISE

Build and Break a Scaffold

Using your favorite 3-D modeling software construct a grid. (It does not have to be orthogonal or uniform.) It could be a collection of curves, neatly arrayed in a row, or maybe a pattern made of individual planes. Maybe you work backwards and begin with a solid primitive, subdivided into quadrants or isocurves. Construct your system into a 3-D scaffold, incorporate crossmembers and consider how elements overlap, interlock or weave. Apply a force to the scaffold (like gravity, wind, or pressure). It could occur inside, outside, locally, or globally. The members do not need to be stiff, they could flex, jiggle, or even collapse. Use a physics simulation, or, if your software doesn't have a physics engine built in, disrupt your grid with human forces then help it heal itself without reverting to its original form.

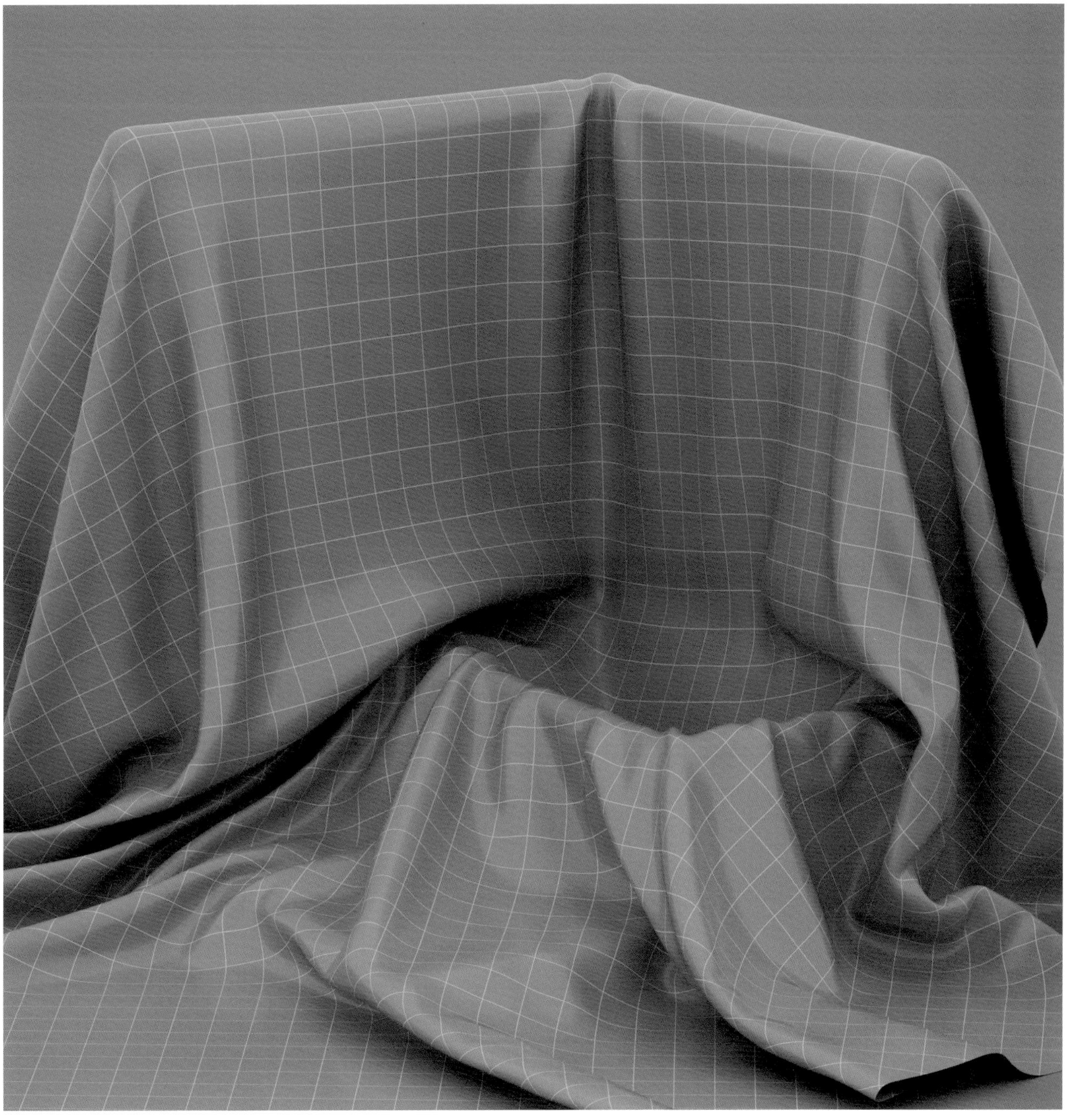

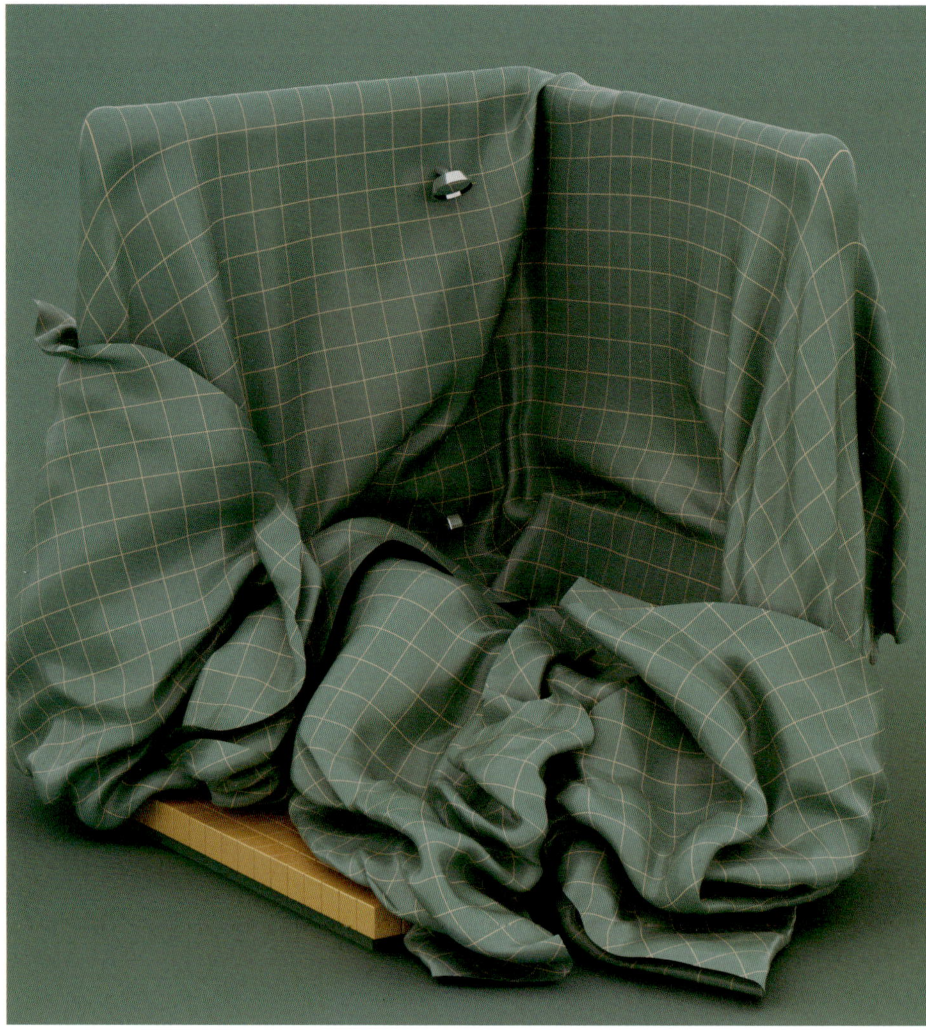

A bathtub is expected to be smooth and continuous, with as few seams as possible to avoid creating spaces for undesirable microbes. Digital cloth simulations should also be smooth, but for different reasons. A blanketed bathtub bridges the two conditions, physical and digital, to question: what are our physical and digital spaces optimized for?

Every grid wants to go on infinitely

Grids are infinite, endlessly expansive, and can always be subdivided to find more grids. Sometimes grids contain other elements too. Gridded glass, for instance, is something we are very familiar with. It is normally desirable for glass to be clear, if not invisible, but Krauss observed that the mullions of a window are essentially a grid, whose presence functions as an optical guide to focus the eye and to visually perceive glass as multivalent, both transparent and reflective.[13] The pairing of grid and glass allows us to register glass that might otherwise be too close to invisibility. The doorway into the *Star Trek* Holodeck serves a similar role to the window mullion, by interrupting the immersive environment and reminding us of its presence on the spaceship. Interestingly, the Holodeck doors are about the most substantial of any on the Enterprise, equal in thickness and implied structural heft to those leading to the shuttle bay, another way "off" the ship. Both the door and the window mullion are demarcations of a boundary. But that boundary isn't always clearly visible. In the film *Awakenings*[14] the neurologist, Dr. Sayer, played by Robin Williams, encounters a catatonic patient who is unable to walk to a window. Every day she gets to a certain point in the room and stops. While observing a girl playing hopscotch outside, it occurs to Dr. Sayer that the grid of black and beige floor tiles ends at this same point. One night, he paints the rest of the floor to the windowed wall. The next day, the woman walks directly to the window, finally reaching the view to the outside she was seeking. The grid as a visual field can be contained with or without the help of other elements.

Terrariums create a miniature atmosphere that promotes plant growth and keeps out pollutants. The complete water cycle of evaporation and condensation can go on endlessly without the water escaping outside. Physics simulations already behave a lot like terrariums. They exist in a vacuum with a predictable set of variables. For computationally expensive simulations, like fluid or smoke, physics engines will provide a safety mechanism that stops calculating the simulation once particles exit the area of interest to prevent the computer from crashing or otherwise wasting processing time and energy. These unrealistic but material objects are sometimes called a "killvolume," or an "outflow" depending on the software. More generally, the invisible bounding boxes also function as force fields containing the simulations within the otherwise infinite 3-D space. Visualizing the invisible killvolume with an actual 3-D model of a glass terrarium is a cousin of the scaffold, a seemingly useless, fake representation of the computational forces at work. But visually, a rendered terrarium does serve a creative purpose. Often 3-D modeling techniques are used with the aim of generating forms that will be manufactured physically. The rendered terrarium reprioritizes the image outputs of simulations over physical outputs. It creates a 3-D frame for the composition of an image, immediately defines an inside and outside, and creates a productive tension between figure and field.

Every grid has mass

We have a tolerance with respect to animate work that distorts a representation of a human body. Far beyond what we might know to be anatomically possible, a cartoon, exaggeration, or caricature passes without suspension of disbelief. The same is done for material simulations, which might be falsely amplified or slowed to fit the needs of the scene. When a 3-D model is animated, it can describe a greater range and exaggeration of characteristics like volume and density than what could ever be conveyed in a single still image. A pillow can be modeled in detail with realistic depressions and wrinkling in the cloth, but a cloth simulation of a pillow being tossed onto a bed conveys far more about the soft bounce of the pillow mass. Even a cloud of points might resemble smoke, sand, or snow, but with the help of an animated particle simulation, the points can be imbued with dynamics specific to the viscosities of each element. This differs from a point cloud generated with today's 3-D scanning technology. A point cloud only draws the surface that was visible to the laser. Particles, on the other hand, are generated as a 3-D gridded field of points that can cluster and disperse as a mass. Surface modeling may not always be enough to engage the complexities of digital materials. Modeling the mass within a volume, instead of relying on mass to be implied through form, and characterizing material qualities through animation, introduce new axes in the pursuit of realism.

The story goes that Archimedes discovered how to measure the volume of an irregular object while enjoying a bath. Thus, it feels only natural to fill a 3-D bathtub with a fluid particle simulation. Filling a bathtub with a grid, on the other hand, does not conform to any historical allegory, which only serves to suggest some motivation in attempting to do so. The ideal tub is smooth and continuous. Various innovations in the plumbing industry led to the iconic tub that we know today. Firing porcelain-on-iron creates a smooth continuous surface that protects from corrosion. A built-in recess tub is perhaps the peak of modernist bathtub smoothness. The bathtub rim is extended to sit flush with a tiled wall enclosure. This reduces the chance of hard-to-access undersides being exposed to undesirable germs and microbes. Some grids run counter to smoothness, however. The seams between bathroom tiles are the most susceptible to water seepage. Grids oppose smoothness in the digital sense too. Ideally a cloth simulation will be rendered at a high frame rate for a smoother playback of the animation. The more subdivisions in the mesh surface, the smoother the drape of the cloth. But smoothness comes at a price, as the denser the mesh, the slower the simulation will be calculated. This is because any quadrant in the mesh will be flat, it only bends where quadrants link, like chainmail. If the surface is too low resolution (too few quadrants), it will behave more like rigid creased paper than finely woven fabric. The same rules apply to particles. The denser the collection of particles, the more volumetric it will appear; not enough particles and the cloud will be illegible. Filling a bathtub with a grid provokes a double take with respect to both the constructed reality of the tiled bathtub and the uncanny reality of the digital image. Oddly enough, both environments prioritize continuity, smoothness, high resolution, and performative efficiency. Both also invite slow soaking rumination.

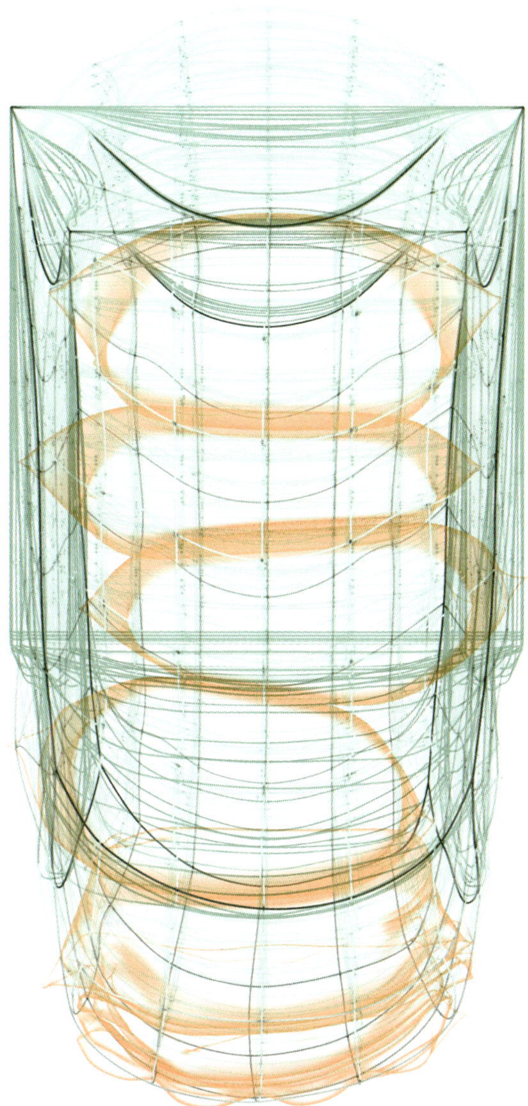

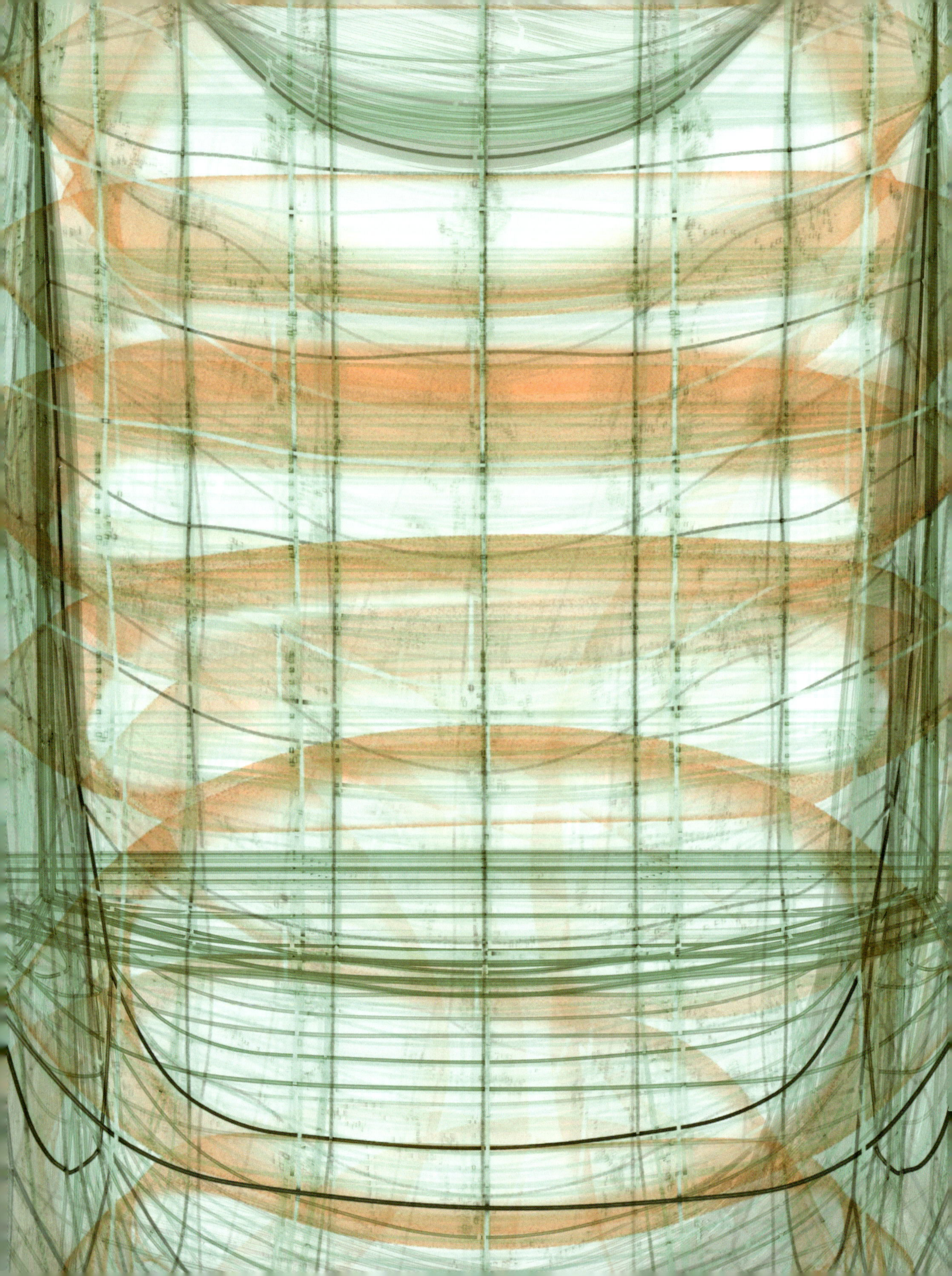

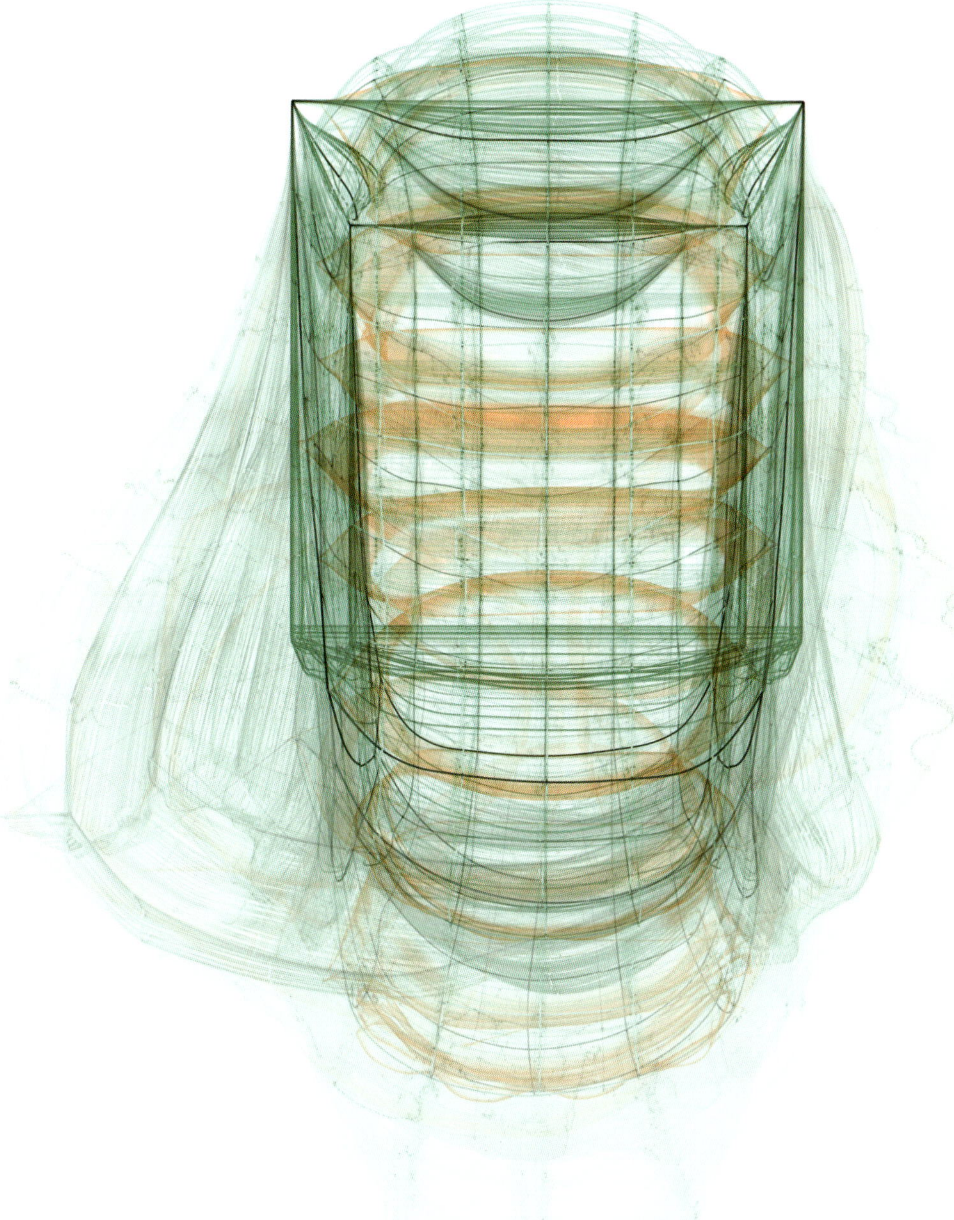

Pillows expand within a flexible lattice container. The frames of the animation are composited, so that each line of the lattice forms the sense of a continuous surface, generating a ghostly image of the dynamics at play.

EXERCISE

Contain a Grid

Take your scaffold from the previous exercise and stage it inside a glass terrarium (any shape or style). Determine if the container will frame an optimal view of the object inside, keep it from escaping, or protect it from something in the outside environment. The scaffold can remain an independent figure, expand to meet the walls of the enclosure, or even extend outside of the glass. Maybe the scaffold actually supports the terrarium. Detail framing elements that receive the glass, door hinges, and how the container meets the ground and surrounding context. Test if you even need to render a realistic glass material for the container to be legible.

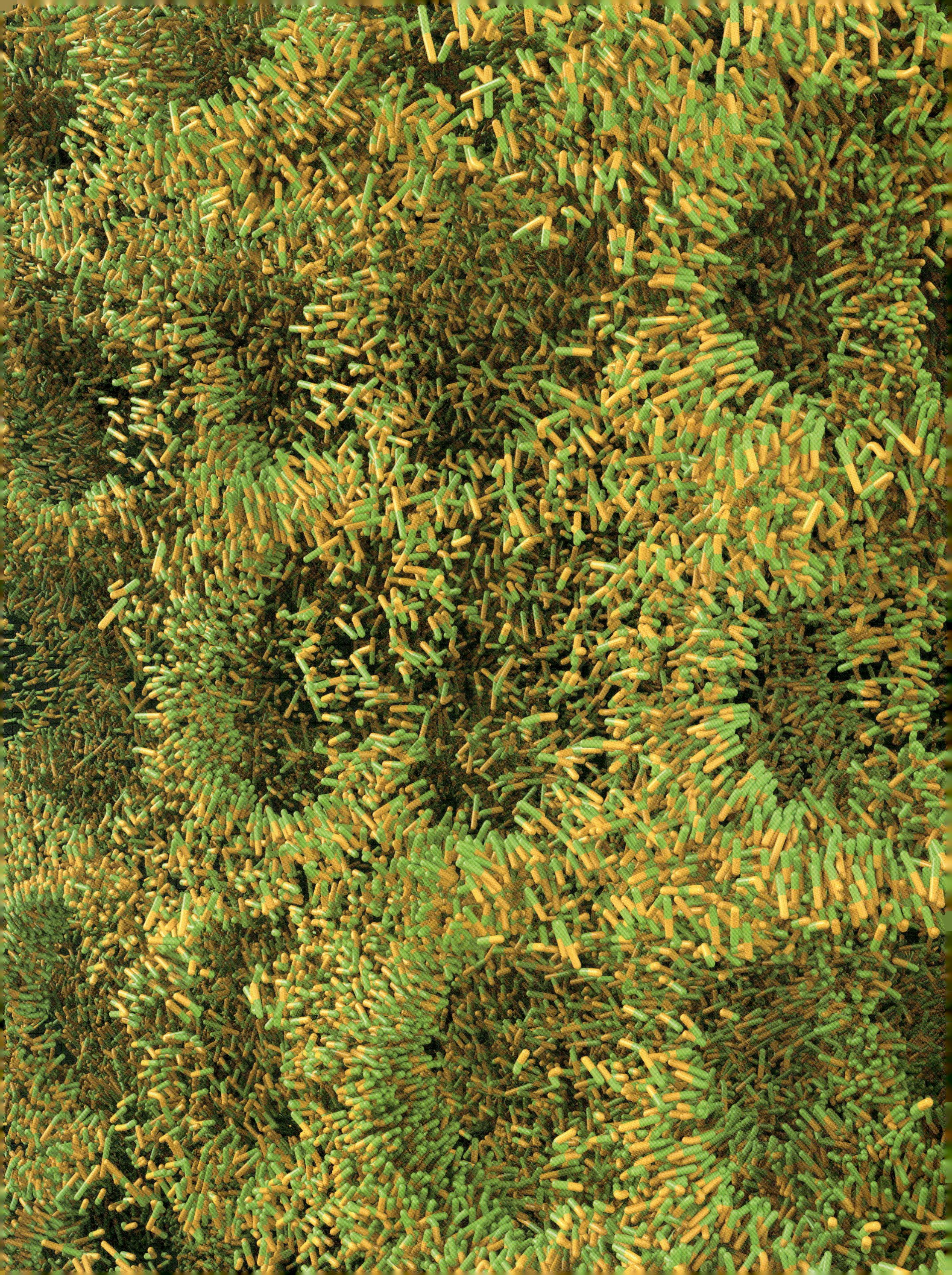

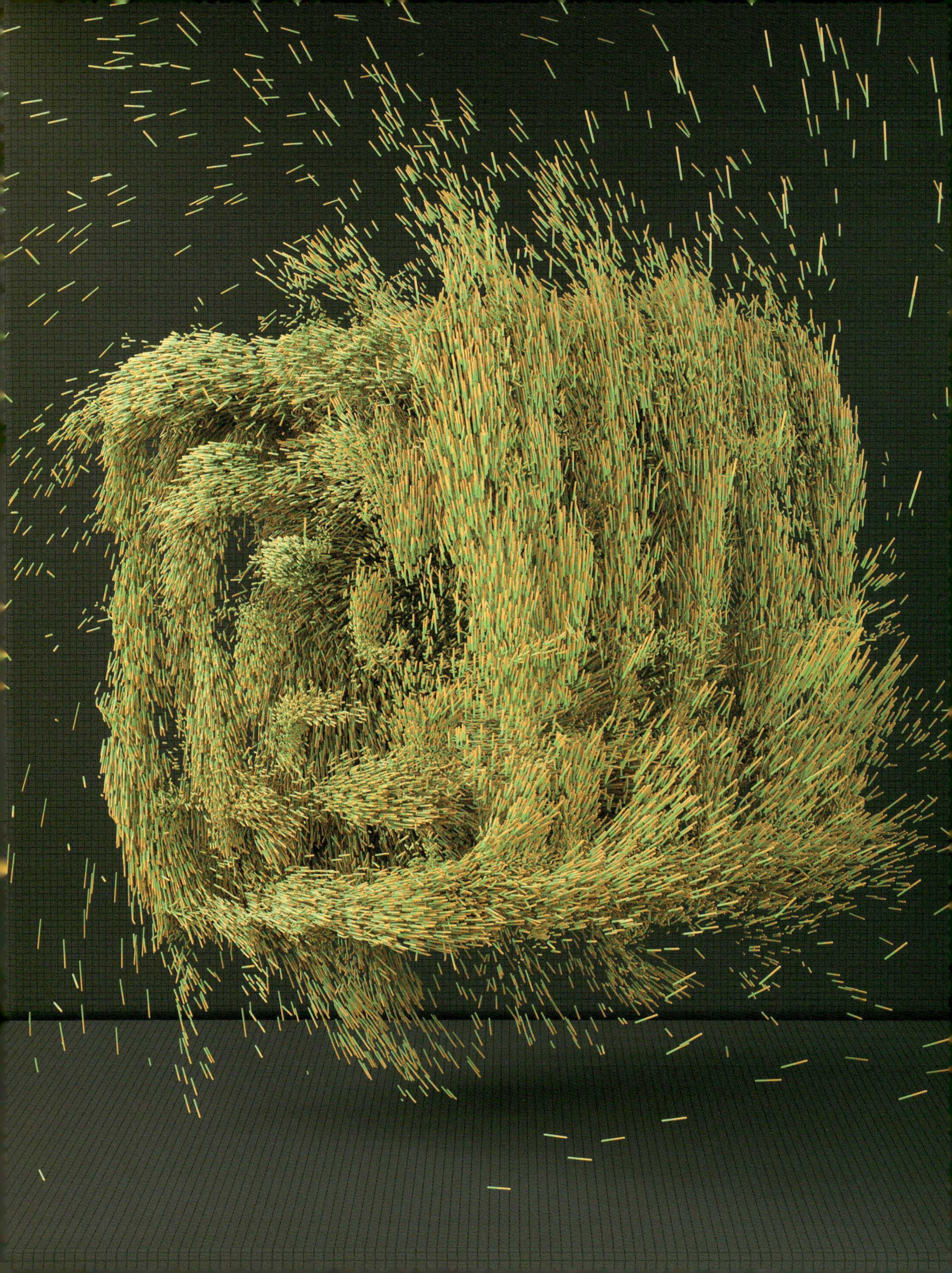

Every grid does not need to be the same

Grids have long been claimed as a foundational element of design, especially in the context of graphic and now UX design. They are the standard ordering principle for tasteful layouts. While the printing press is an obvious influence in which modular metal blocks of type were set into a gridded formwork, the baseline grid did not emerge as a formal universal element until the development of design curricula in the early 1900s. During this period, many artists were enamored by abstraction as a formal language and grids could therefore help elucidate universal principles for graphic production.[15] Wassily Kandinsky for instance published *Point and Line to Plane* (1926)[16] where he purported to outline languages of proportion, rhythm, and harmony that could be applied across visual arts and music through his analysis of the three primitives in his title. Into the twentieth century, various publications emerged as standard manuals for visual design. Particularly, Swiss designers like Karl Gersner and Josef Muller-Brockmann produced widely read literature that championed grid systems.[17] These systems that we still repeat and imitate today were optimized for a different world that valued standardization and mass production even in the creative disciplines of visual communication. In his 2017 update to the popular layout handbook *Making and Breaking the Grid*, Timothy Samara reflects that "efficient transmission" of information does not need to be the only ambition, and in fact inefficiency may lead to deeper understanding. "Simplicity, order and visual neutrality in communication are strategies aimed at facilitating inclusivity...But also pose a potential threat through the aesthetic (and arguably, intellectual) conformity they engender."[18]

The Scaffold, Terrarium, and Bathtub are not elements that would ever be considered for the next iteration of a design manual aimed at outlining a universal system for image production. These elements would also be unlikely to appear in a handbook outlining techniques for physics simulations. One version of that book would distill the processes down to the geometrical primitives, dynamic curves, soft and rigid bodies, and particles. A manual for film effects that mentions physics for visualization might stick with the premade simulations like hair, cloth, or smoke. Scaffold, Terrarium, and Bathtub are specific, far from universal, and are not comprehensive. They are starting points to play with digital matter that creates local reality, reflects reality, warps reality, and also engages the unique reality of images. Simulations permit a dialogue between material and representation that confronts assumptions about the possible and the constructable. Some of the new realities can only exist in the space of digital animation. Their performance reinforces and questions various conceptions of reality. Useless scaffolds made of hair. Figural grids sealed in terrariums. Bathtubs filled with low-res grids. Each pairing exposes material facets of grids that run counter to gridded assumptions.

Scaffoldings are typically intended to assist for the construction of buildings. It seems absurd to construct a digital scaffold, since there is no need to provide physical support in digital spaces. However, 3-D modeling scaffolds makes the inherent systems that guide a digital workflow visible and operable. There are two scaffolds on display in this terrarium, but one is invisible. Neither of the scaffolds are secondary, both coexist, and have influence on the other's form.

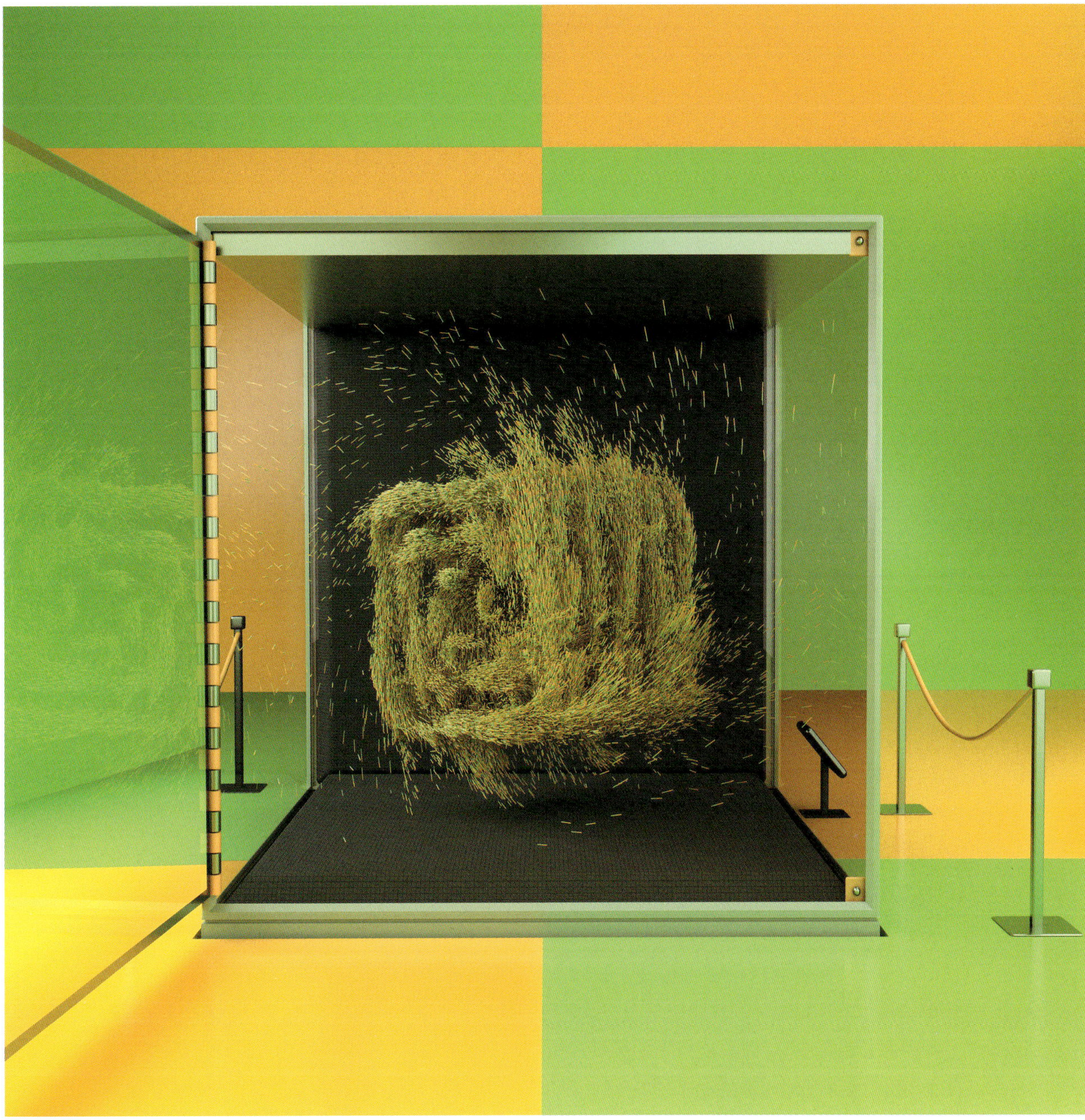

EXERCISE

Un-Standardized Fixtures

Model a standard fixture in your home, i.e., bathtub, sink, oven, fireplace, built-in bookshelf, etc. Include seams where materials come together—the wall, floor, ceiling, or table its fixed to—and any secondary fixtures like faucets, drains, and electrical switches. Fill, drape, or douse the sampled fixture with a new material or substance. This could be done with a physics simulation (cloth, fluid, or particle) or modeled by eye. Exaggerate how the new material contradicts the intended function of the fixture.

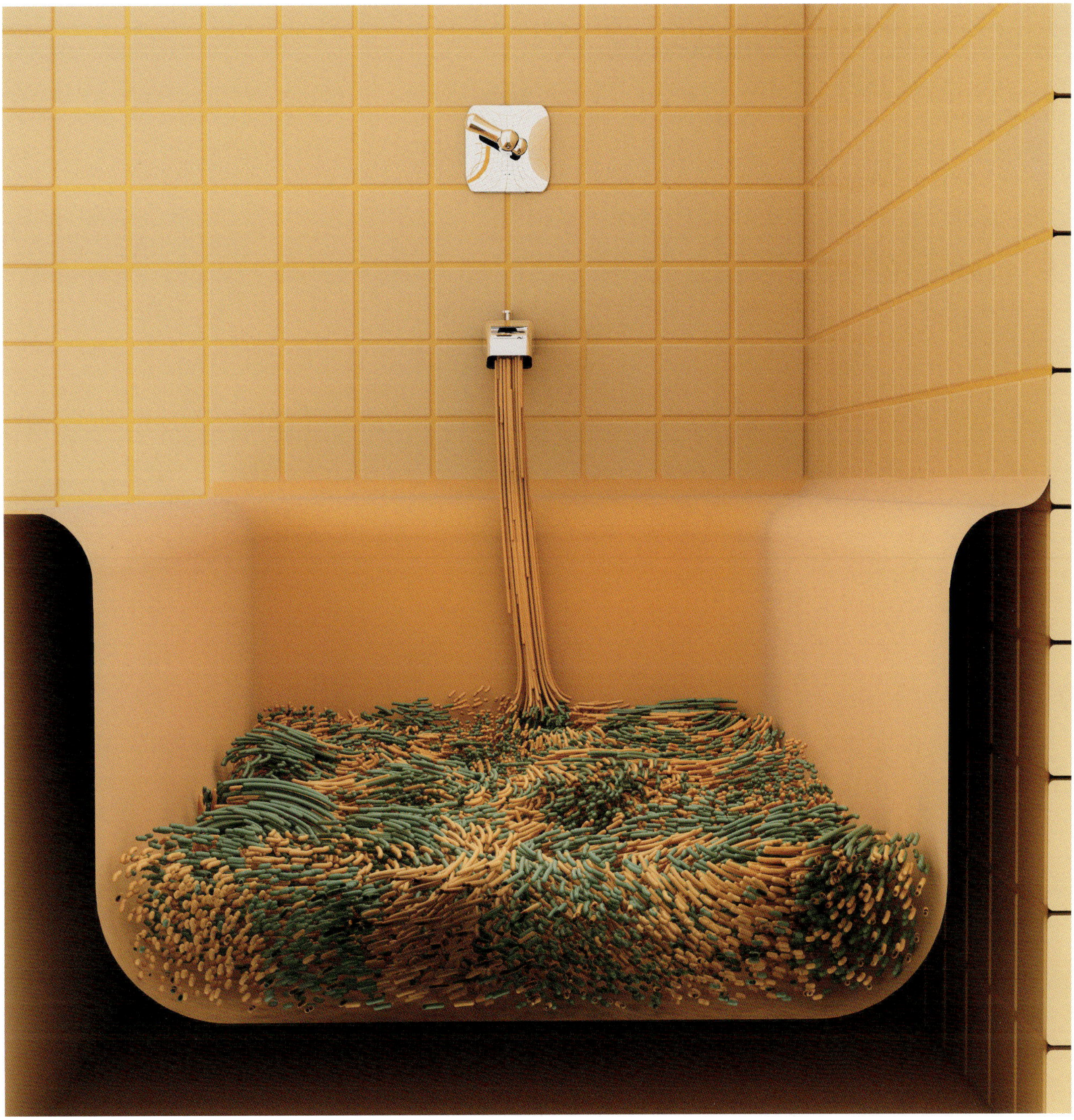

Notes

1. Adobe Inc., "Adobe Photoshop," V22.4.3, 2021.
2. Rebecca Siefert, "Tradition and Modernity, Continuity and Critique," *Drawing Matter, March 4, 2021, https://drawingmatter.org/tradition-and-modernity-continuity-and-critique/.*
3. Rosalind Krauss, "Grids," *October, Vol. 9 (Summer, 1979): 50–64, https://doi.org/10.2307/778321*
4. Ibid.
5. Ibid.
6. *Tron. Directed by Lisberger, Steven. 1982. Los Angeles: Walt Disney Productions.*
7. *The Simpsons. Season 7, episode 6, Homer,*3 "Treehouse of Horror VI," directed by Bob Anderson, aired October 29, 1995, on FOX.
8. *Star Trek: The Next Generation. Season 6, episode 12, "Ship in a Bottle," directed by Alexander Singer, aired January 24, 1993, on CBS.*
9. Marco Frascari, *Eleven Exercises in the Art of Architectural Drawing (New York: Routledge, 2011), 101.*
10. Kai Franz, Serial Nature (Stuttgart: Kohlhammer Druckerei GmbH+ Co.KG, 2014), 119.
11. John May, *Signal, Image, Architecture (New York: Columbia Books on Architecture and the City, 2019).*
12. Mountain Dew, "The Joy of Painting MTN DEW." March 6, 2021. YouTube video, 41:57. https://www.youtube.com/watch?v=qqDni4IHDIY.
13. Rosalind Krauss, "Grids," *October, Vol. 9 (Summer, 1979): 50–64.*
14. *Awakenings. Directed by Marshall, Penny. 1991. New York: Columbia Pictures.*
15. Johanna Drucker, *Graphesis Visual forms of Knowledge Production (Cambridge: Harvard University Press, 2014) 35–36.*
16. Wassily Kandinsky, *From Point and Line to Plane (New York: Dover, 1979).*
17. Josef Müller-Brockmann, *Grid Systems in Graphic Design (Salenstein: Niggli Verlag, 1996)*
18. Timothy Samara, *Making and Breaking the Grid (Beverly: Rockport Publishers 2017), 7.*

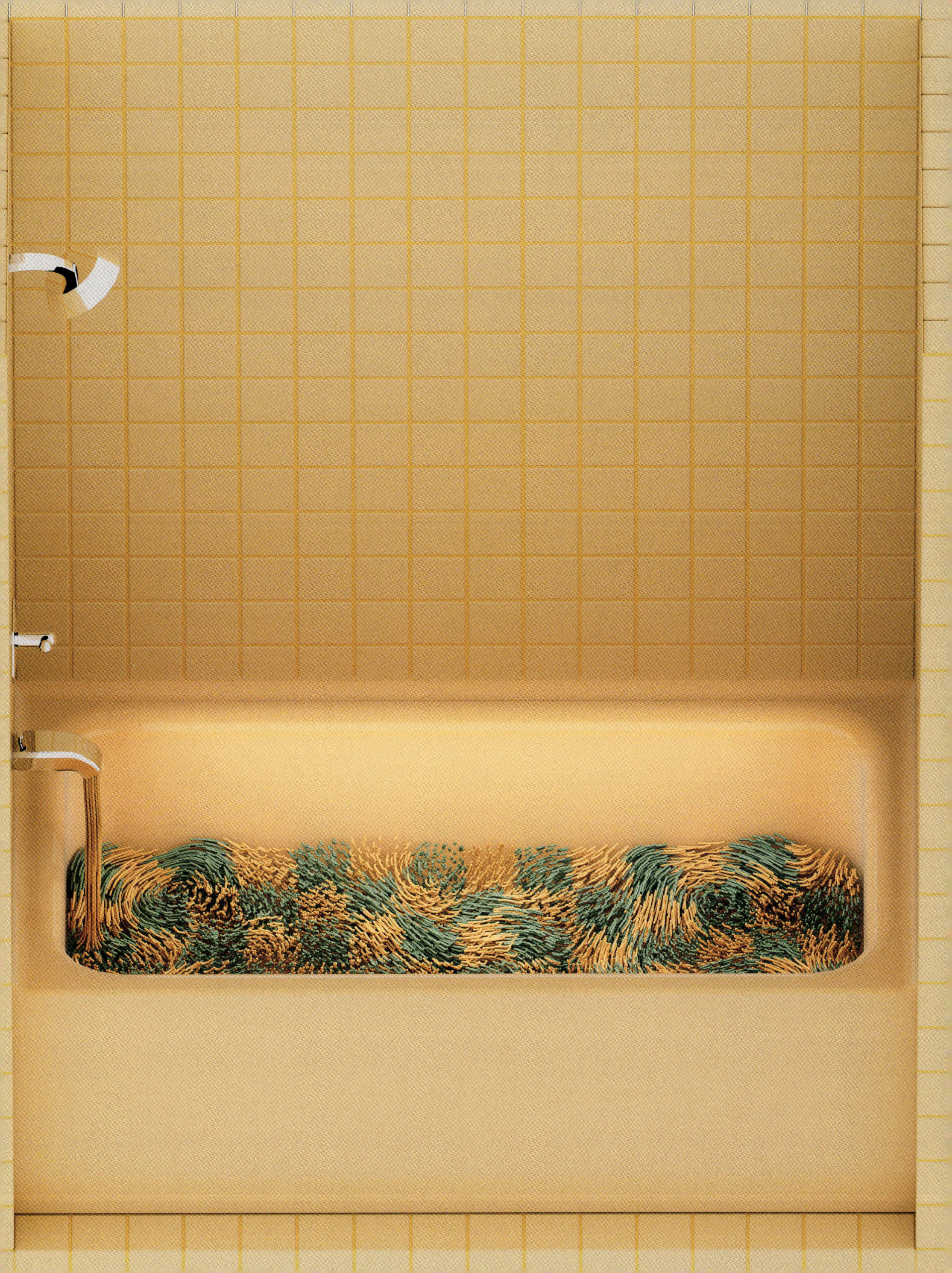

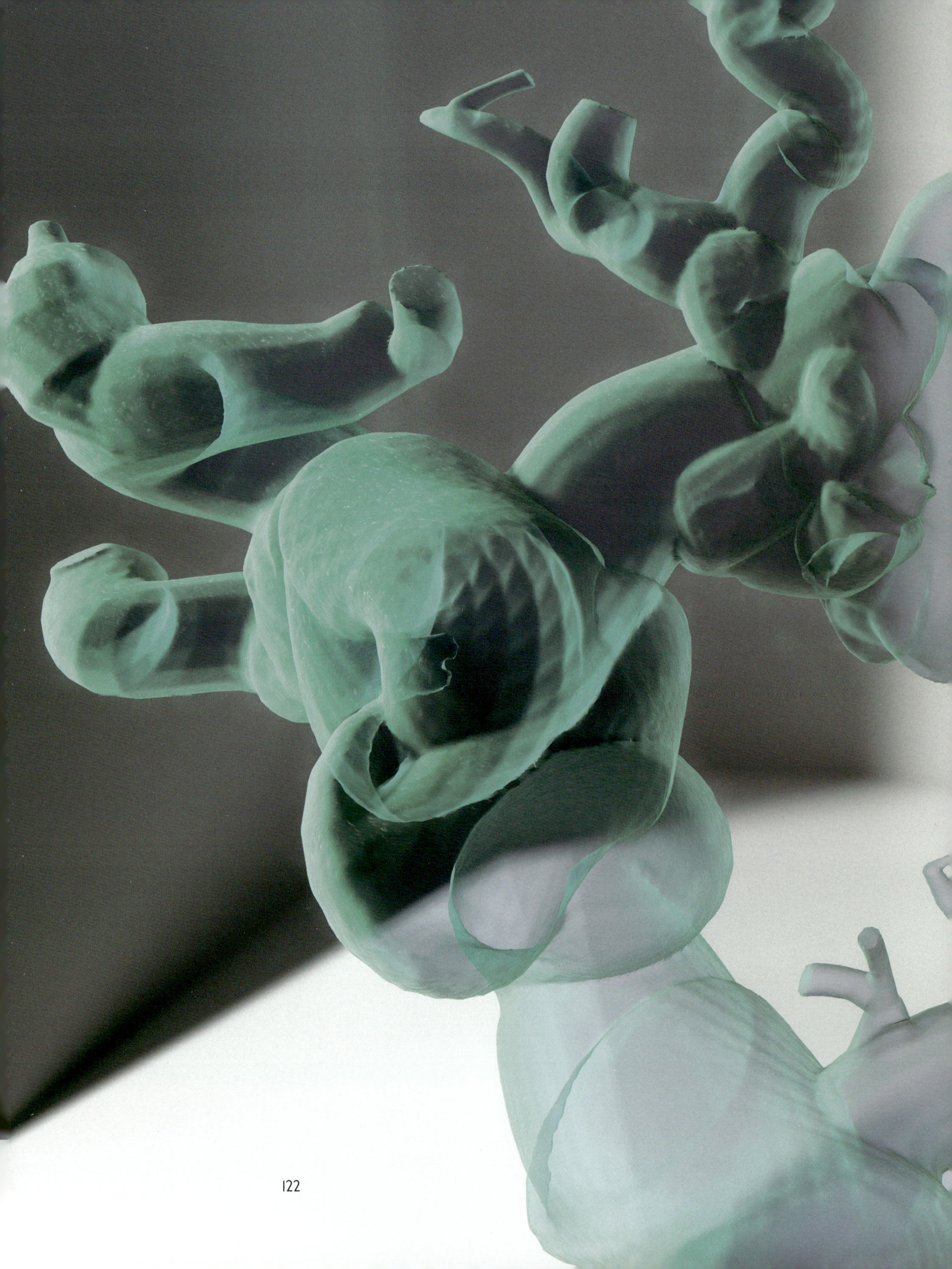

CHAPTER 3

Using a Tree to Represent a Tree

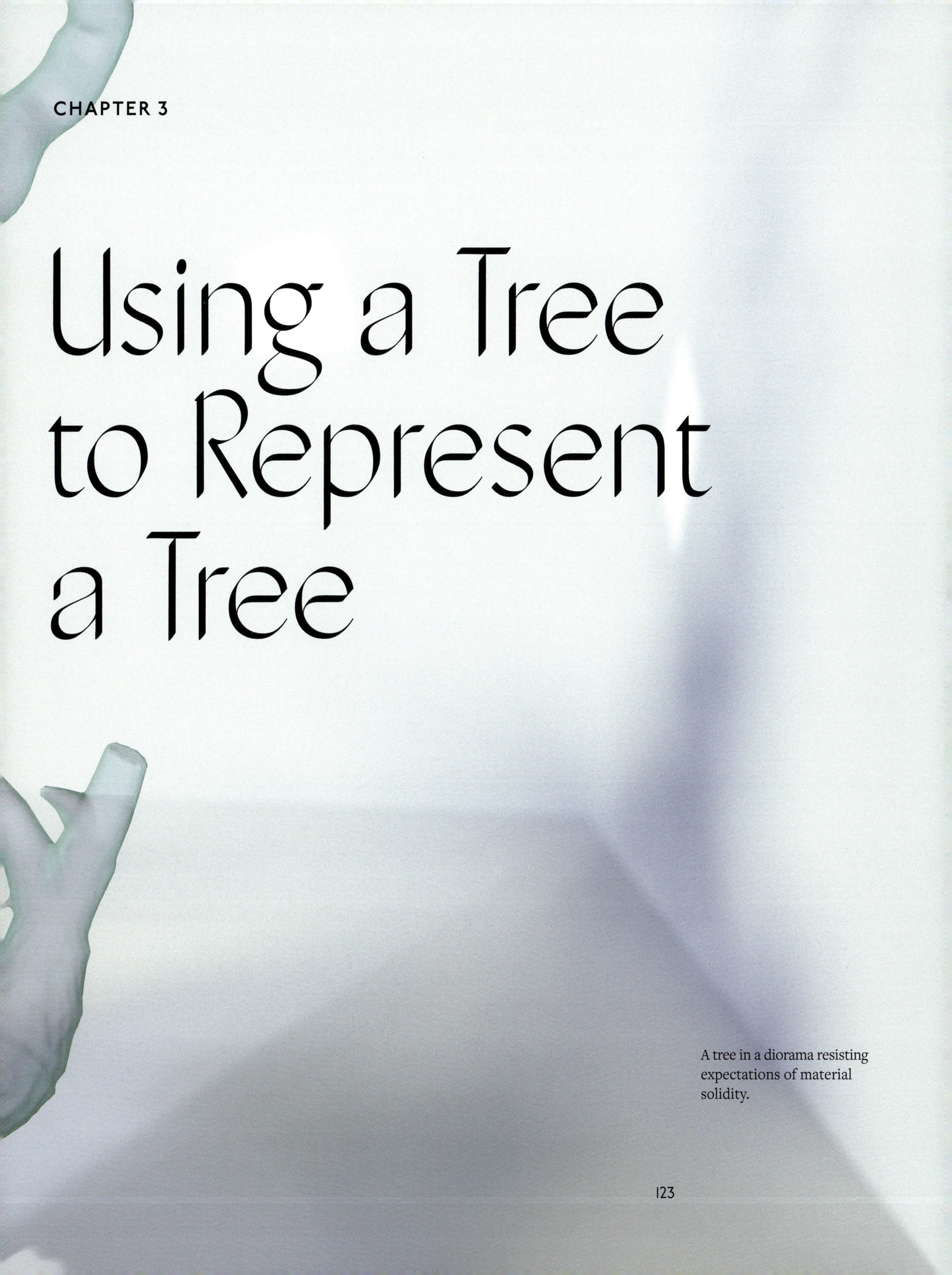

A tree in a diorama resisting expectations of material solidity.

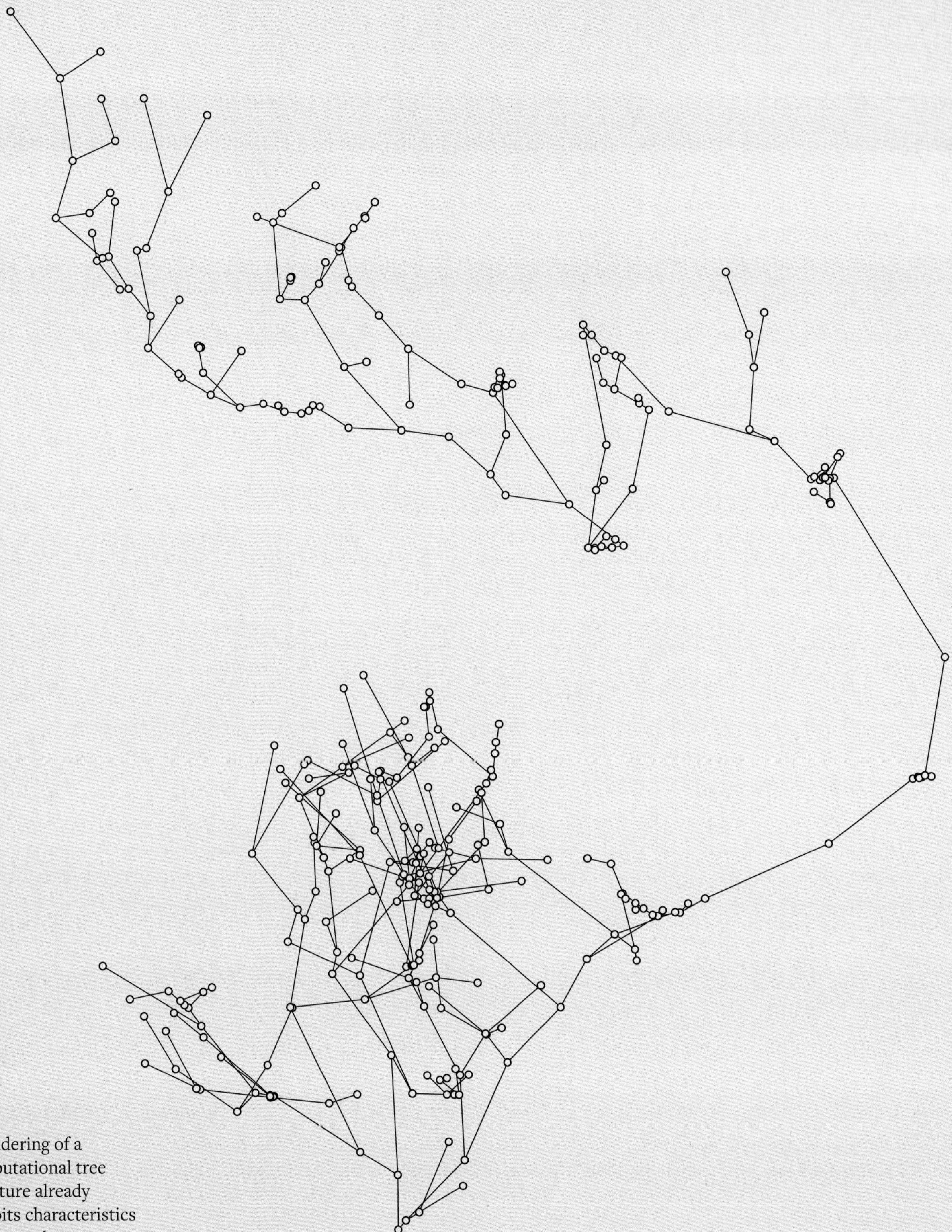

A rendering of a computational tree structure already exhibits characteristics of a natural tree.

A digital representation of a bonsai tree is a bonsai tree. That's a bold statement that admittedly warrants some defense. Of course, nothing digital can be considered alive, or even close to it. In a 2003 essay Sanford Kwinter writes that, "No computer on earth can match the processing power of even the most simple natural system, be it of water molecules on a warm rock, a rudimentary enzyme system, or the movement of leaves in the wind."[1] This is, for the most part, still true, almost 20 years later. To software evangelists who might take exception by noting recent developments, Kwinter is a step ahead. His position is not against computation, nor is he pessimistic about computational progress. Rather, he takes a particularly relevant position against an autonomous computational paradigm. He continues by noting the potential role for computation with respect to both material and knowledge in a way that would seem to both call for and challenge the premise of the work that follows in this chapter.

> Implicit here is the idea of learning how to make matter model matter... In this use the computer becomes metallurgical substance, it extends the exploratory evolutionary process of differentiation and refinement by inventing new levels of order and shape. The computer and its software together can form a Matter/Intelligence unit of a very primitive but useful kind. But to do this, the computer, in the triad Nature-Mind-Computer, must play only the appropriate intermediary role of interface between Nature and Mind. This would be in clear contradistinction to what is more often the case today, where computational environments provide a customary but imperceptible experiential envelope from which Nature...is excluded and within which the activity horizon of Mind is insidiously confined. We must not believe the narcotizing hype that an emerging electronic world is poised to liberate us from a mechanical one, nor even that there exist an electronosphere fundamentally discontinuous from the mechanosphere that has formed us till now.[2]

Looking back on Kwinter's warning and the contemporary post-digital break from computational exuberance, is it possible to conclude that we've over-corrected? Have we, as a discipline, dismissed the paradigmatic nature of digital because its everyday status perpetually reveals its limitations? Do we too regularly repress digital representations with apparently self-aware modesty? Has digital cynicism inadvertently relegated digital representation to vocational status? Perhaps taking a narrow and literal read of Kwinter's "nature" is a way forward. Initially, it may seem obvious to note that there is no chemistry, no sunlight, no oxygen, no photosynthesis, and no matter within digital space. This given would seem to support the premise that representation is, by definition, a depiction of reality rather than a copy of reality. In the fashion of Magritte, we could imagine a painting of a tree with the caption, "This is not a tree."

And yet, we aren't talking about depicting an existing tree here. This work—offered as a kind of evidence contrary to the presumption that digital representation is either a resolved set of techniques or a futile pursuit of material form—was cultivated as a self-similar recursive hierarchical structure of branches and subbranches. In other words, a tree. The "behind the scenes" trees and the trees that are rendered by parsing them start to blur with one another in surprising ways. We can then explore the idea that representing a bonsai tree may actually involve structures, tools, and interfaces that are inspired by bonsai practices, but which produce elements that bear no resemblance whatsoever to trees of any kind. Before exploring that in more detail, however, let's also stipulate that we aren't talking about any and all trees, but bonsai trees in particular: crafted quasi-natural elements. While the incomplete attempt to make digital bonsai is executed in earnest, any claim to a new digital reality is not meant to replace or compete with bonsai culture. To be clear, the digital bonsai process developed here is not a translation of existing bonsai practices. The process draws from bonsai practices just as the result sometimes resembles a bonsai tree, but this is not to be misconstrued as a simulation of nature or material. It's something much stranger. For example, as will be explored in more detail later, "to prune" a digital bonsai is to cut and remove a branch before it is imbued with any mass or material.

This might be an opportunity to reflect on the reoccurring question that looms over any explicitly digital project tethered in the material or the living: is it in opposition to its analog counterpart? If not—and whether the subject is bonsai trees or material drawings or artificial intelligence the healthy empathetic answer is most certainly that it is not—we might then rightly question the value of digital culture in the first place. The provocations implicitly offered by digital bonsai are therefore not offered in terms of optimization, efficiency, or idealism, but in terms of strangeness, surrealism, and a spirit of open-ended speculation.

Bonsai is an Action and an Element

The origins of *bonsai*, which literally means "tray planting" are Chinese[3] though the craft is also widespread in Japan, where the term generally describes cultivating miniature trees. The Chinese "Penjing" is overlapping and the original form of the Japanese loanword "bonsai" but often includes full scenes—people and other objects along with trees. Bonsai artist Peter Chan describes bonsai in a way that particularly suits our inquiry: "A Bonsai is an artistic replica of a natural tree in miniature form. It exists only in a pot or container." In other words, the bonsai is its own world. The tree is not a medium. The tree is not artificial, but the tree is also not left to grow as-is. Instead, it's cultivated as a tree representing a larger tree. Chan goes on, "It is essentially a work of art and is produced by man through expert care and manipulation of natural plant material. It is above all a picture or illusion of a real tree."[4]

Much attention is given in bonsai discourse to compositional values. These will be familiar to students or practitioners of design and include hierarchy, rhythm, and balance. Much more challenging to digital and computational inquiry are the tenants, principles, methods, and tools of cultivation. If much of computation is like baking, where recipes (like algorithms) are followed, step by step, to achieve a particular result, bonsai craft invites a different approach. Bonsai are never finished and it's usually impossible (or impudent) to identify a precise compositional goal and then set off executing it. Improvision is necessary, but teds not to manifest as in-the-moment whims or arbitrary decisions. Bonsai culture defines types of tree compositions, within which the artist-cultivator can contextualize what they are observing in each iteration with a generalized sense of tree's potential future growth. Improvisation plays out over a duration longer than human perception. Human actions direct at the time scale of the design action play out over the long, iterative, and semi-predictable life of a bonsai.

The question of when and what to prune is the paramount in this endeavor. These creative acts are the primary gestures that have been instrumentalized computationally in digital space. Pruning, of course, is one key technique in keeping bonsai trees relatively small even as trunks and branches grow relatively thick. Pruning is subjective and forever—two terms not usually associated with the digital. The human artist must study the tree and make a decision. Once that decision is made, there are no undos. Thus, a digital bonsai must involve a digital tree, but most importantly it must also involve an interface for pruning while the tree is growing.

Books About Bonsai are Like This Book

In the age of Twitch Streaming and ASMR, bonsai artists have authored books, of course, but reach a much larger and ever-growing audience via their YouTube channels. This work drew much more from prolific artist and author Peter Chan's technical-contextual videos than any physical book, including his. The irony is noted.

Whether through book, video (or both), bonsai discourse, like computational discourse, is difficult and interesting because "how" and "why" questions are often answered with the same content. Chan's empathy for the trees is matched by his empathy for his audience. His videos are unscripted and his candor and wit balance his modest indecision. He talks to us as he prunes and rotates the tree in his hand:

> Now, this one although it has been cut there, forms several leaders and it can become quite confusing. So which do I choose? ...The base is very nice on this tree...So, this could be the front...This could also be quite interesting because the base is very nice here. I could possibly make this the leader, that means cut it off there and here or I could cut it there. ... It's all a question of cutting everything off and waiting for it to grow again. Making bonsai requires patience.[5]

He would fit right in as an art school professor. Chan's book, already quoted and cited earlier in this chapter, leads to an observation, offered as a kind of aside, to touch on some meta inquiry: this chapter of this book is about the theory of digital rendering anchored in practical discourse. Almost all contemporary bonsai books are similar: they are part portfolio, part manual, and part practical theory. They can be read and enjoyed by the aspiring practitioner, the seasoned practitioner, and the non- practitioner alike. Much architecture and design scholarship tends to avoid the "vocational," often to the frustration of the practically minded reader. One lesson to take from this observation is that the pleasure of the encounter with a designed object is not undermined by an explanation of the process or methods used to create it. Vocation, discipline, intelligence, and entertainment are more interrelated than academia is often comfortable with.

The Tree Behind the Tree

Any basic algorithms and data structures textbook will describe the computational tree. It's an infinitely expandable computational object that is defined recursively. Each node contains a bit of information such as a coordinate point, single number, identifier, name, and so on. Each node can also contain branches, which are themselves nodes. Those nodes contain information and branches, and so on. Initially, the tree contains just one node, but it can extend exponentially. These trees, when visualized, either in a textbook or as a computational sketch, look like trees in nature. But it would be silly, in a computer science context, to assume that their use is to represent a real tree. They are often referred to as "decision trees" or "search trees" because their recursive nature makes them easy and efficient to traverse. They capture tiered, nested, relationships well. Imagine a tree representing a chess game, for example. The base of the tree represents the initial board. Each possible move is a new branch leading to a new board state, each possible move at that board state would be yet more branches from that level. The tree would stop growing at checkmate. Decision trees are often used for complex resource allocation as well. Here, however, the trees are the fundamental element used in the rendering of real impossible trees. They take on that almost silly conflation of abstract data structure with very real subject matter.

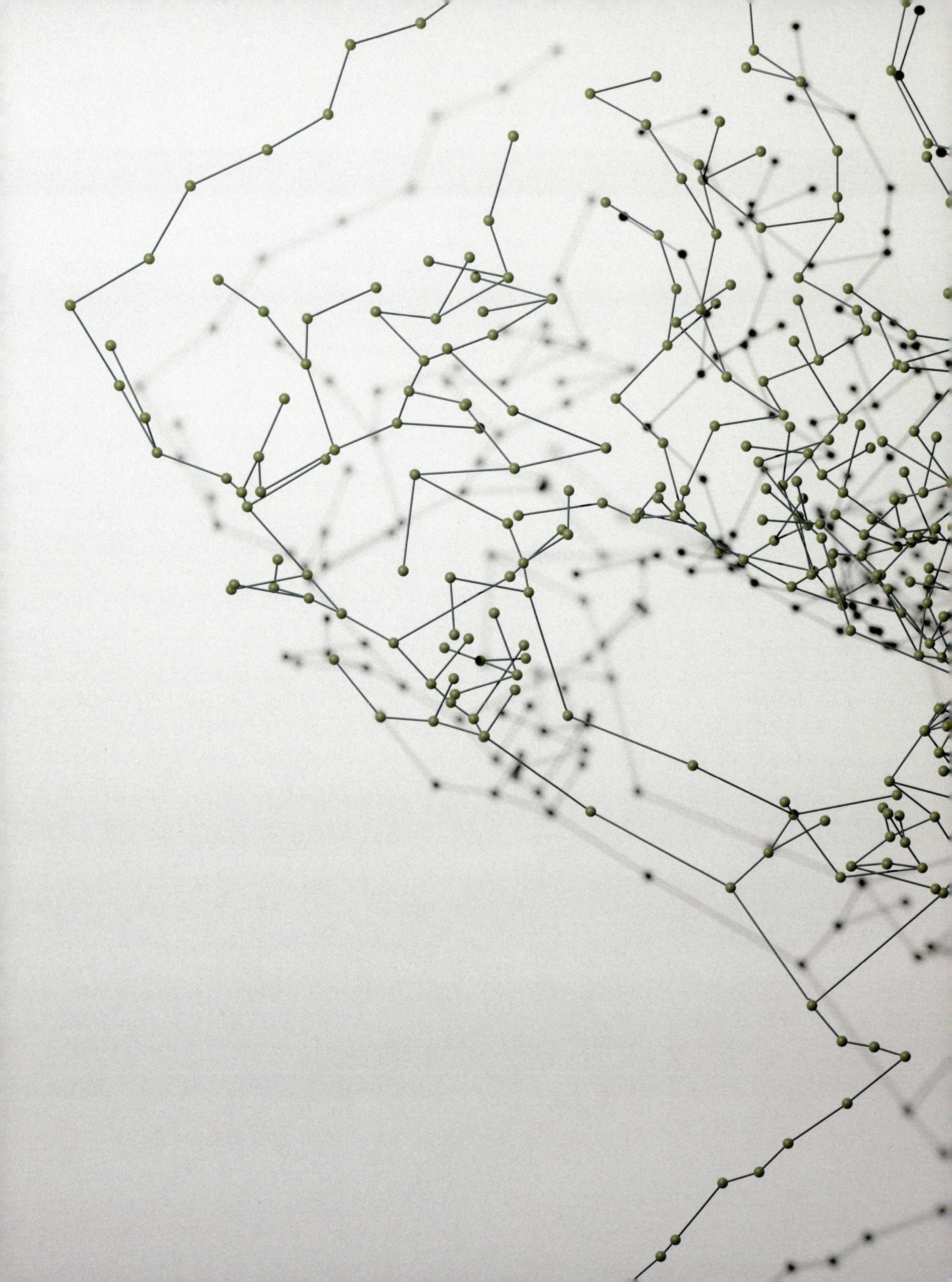

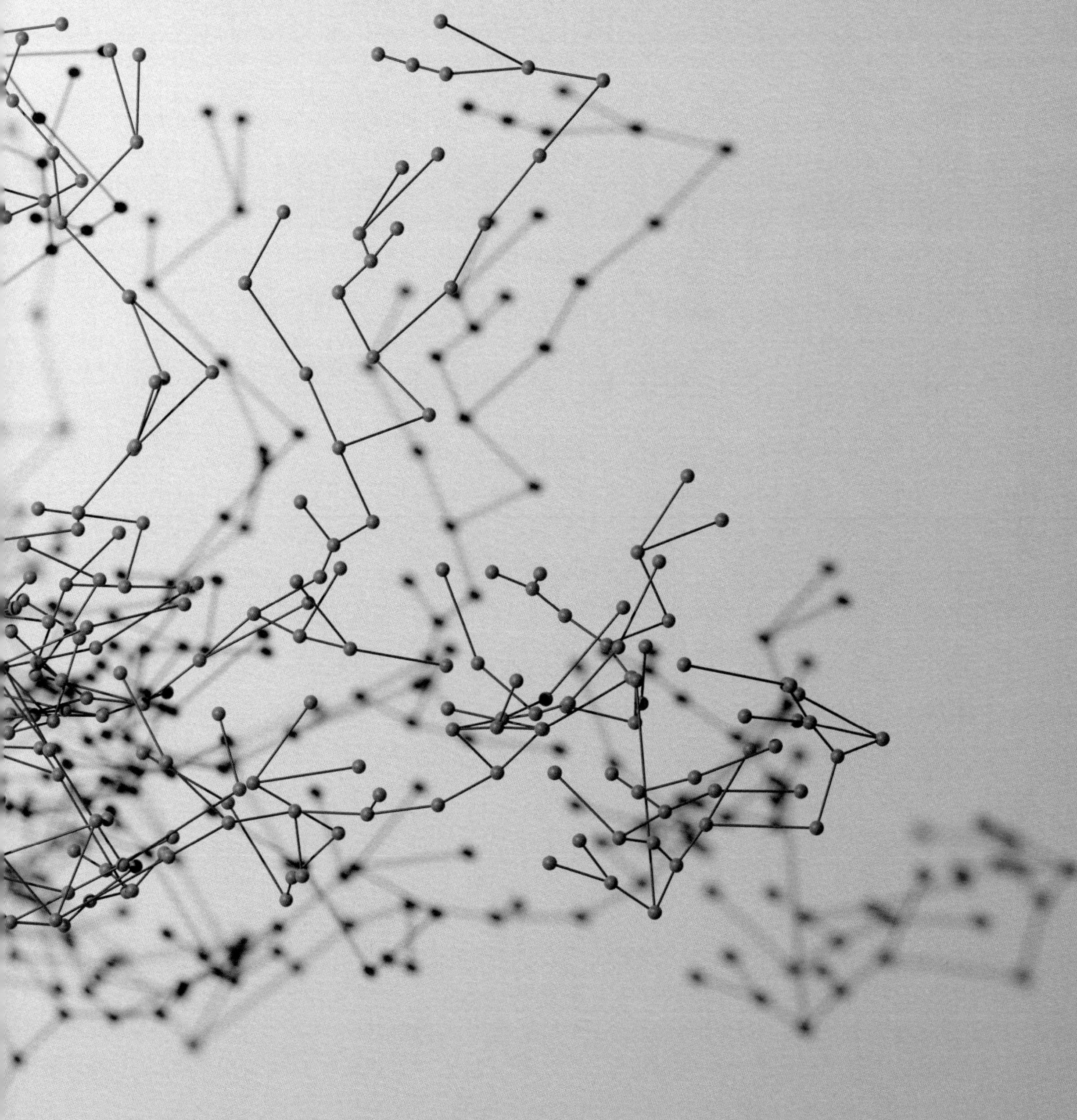

Mass abruptly casts
the tree as a real element.

Because the tree data contains information about the age of each branch, the rendering process can also involve the growth of new volumetric forms.

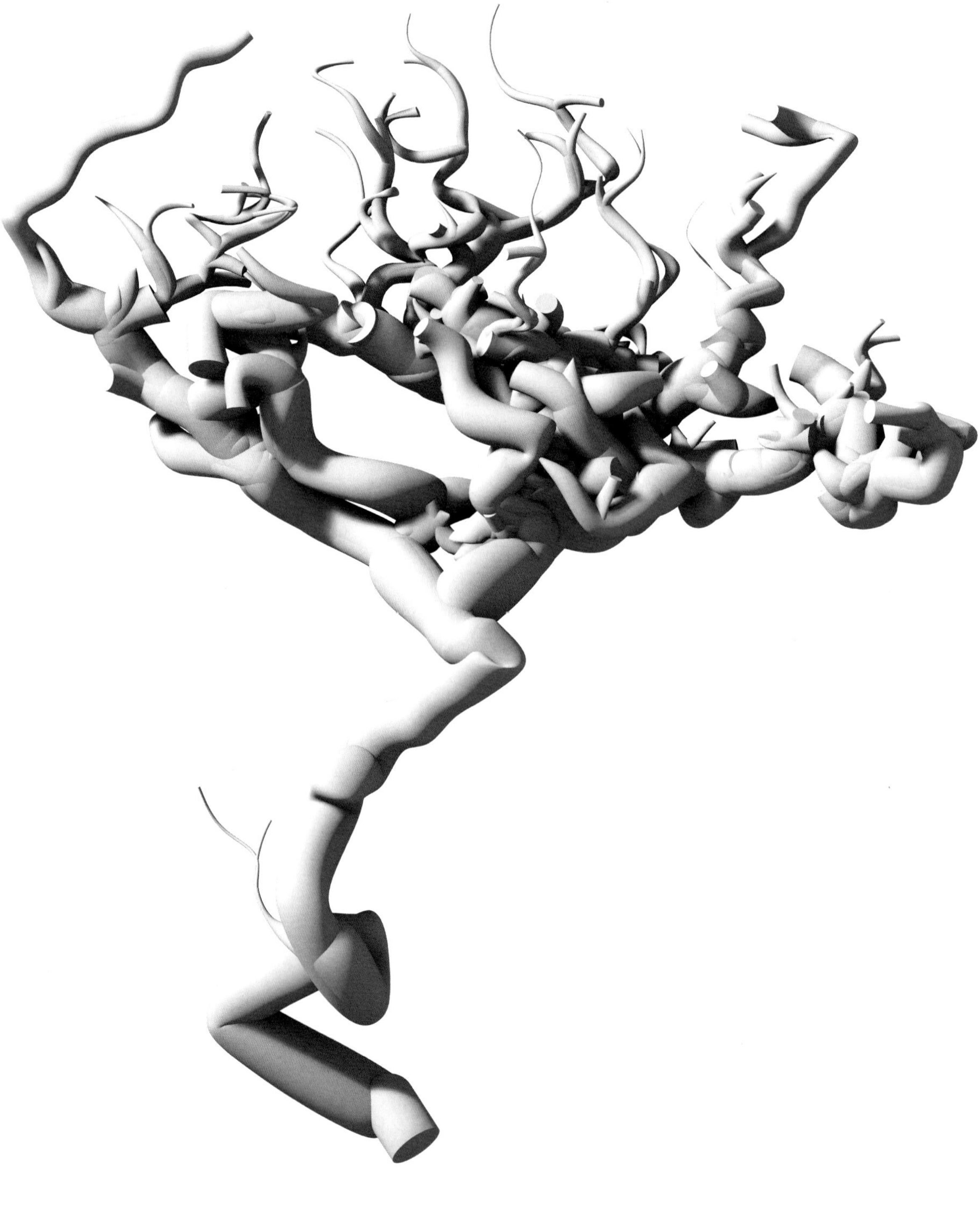

Designing Tools to Control or Release Natural Randomness

Bonsai artistry and theory are often articulated in terms of mediation of nature. The rhetoric can often read as a kind of invisible coaxing, directing, or influencing that purposefully stops far short of expressing any attitude that might resemble conquering or domestication. Again, this is a valuable challenge for the digital. The "hand" of the bonsai artist is repressed as a matter of intention, but also as temporal effector. Some of the mythology of bonsai even describes trees merging fully out of extreme or unusual natural circumstances. Most importantly though, the bonsai tree is not artificial. Thus, it would not be wrong to note that a digital bonsai is a contradiction of terms. But for that very reason, we persist in exploring this extended representational pursuit.

Moving forward, we can cautiously conflate randomness with natural. This admittedly imperfect gesture is well considered. Nature is our only known source of true randomness. It may suffice to note that digital pseudo-random numbers are the closest thing to nature that is possible. If we want to dig deeper, we could note that the pseudo-randomness that is present in computational random number generators approaches natural randomness to the extent of being indistinguishable from it in many contexts. Most pseudo-random numbers are so close to truly random that they are referred to, as we will do moving forward, simply as "random," without debate or caveat. To return to our bonsai frame of reference, an unmediated digital tree would be the result of completely random values. A digital bonsai tree would likewise result from random values. Despite the ability to prune, the author-user would never be allowed to place a branch in a particular location. The author-user doesn't ever use anything like the "draw a line" tool. Instead, the user-author prunes unwanted branches making room for new growth. This is not necessarily an entirely subtractive process. The author-user is also invited to stimulate growth (akin to adding growth hormone) at a node. This isn't like drawing. The user-author's actions don't necessarily lead immediately to desired new growth. It takes some time, and even then, the tree is constantly shifting, sagging, and swaying with a mixture of simulated gravity and randomness that inhibits a mindset of total composition—of total control. Ironically, even the digital forces that inhibit control by the user author were programmed by the same human. It's not uncommon, for example, to find the user-author pruning a branch, stimulating growth, and then pruning that branch again and again until it "looks right." What does it mean to look right? That's a difficult question that would be answered differently at different moments of the tree's lifespan.

Watching bonsai master Peter Chan, it becomes clear that when he encounters a tree of modest age, maybe one that he and his team have worked on for years but not decades, he does not consult a journal. There are no "history notes" for each tree. But it's not as if he's encountering it anew. There are often fresh discoveries, year after year, and knowledge is embedded in the tree. That's the healthiest, or perhaps inevitable, way of working with nature: observe, influence, wait, repeat. This is compatible with many drawing practices, but is alien in most digital practices, especially those with computational underpinnings.

When making a digital bonsai tree, the user-author can choose to do nothing other than watch the tree randomly grow. That's hard to do. Patience in front of a slowly moving creative output on a screen is a learned skill. The overly manipulated tree does not reach maturity. In the world of bonsai, the "sacrificial branch" is an opportune term in this regard. This kind of branch is allowed to grow for the purpose of thickening the trunk just below it, though it is anticipated that this branch will be pruned eventually. This has theoretical implications on the practical use of randomness in computation. In computer science, we can find randomness as a problem-solving device. Think of the "random sample" as a scientific and generative idea. But creative randomness is different. It's more disruptive than it is solution-oriented, but that disruption forces new and often helpful perspectives. Much like encountering a bonsai tree in the late summer after a season of growth, new opportunities affect the artist's goals.

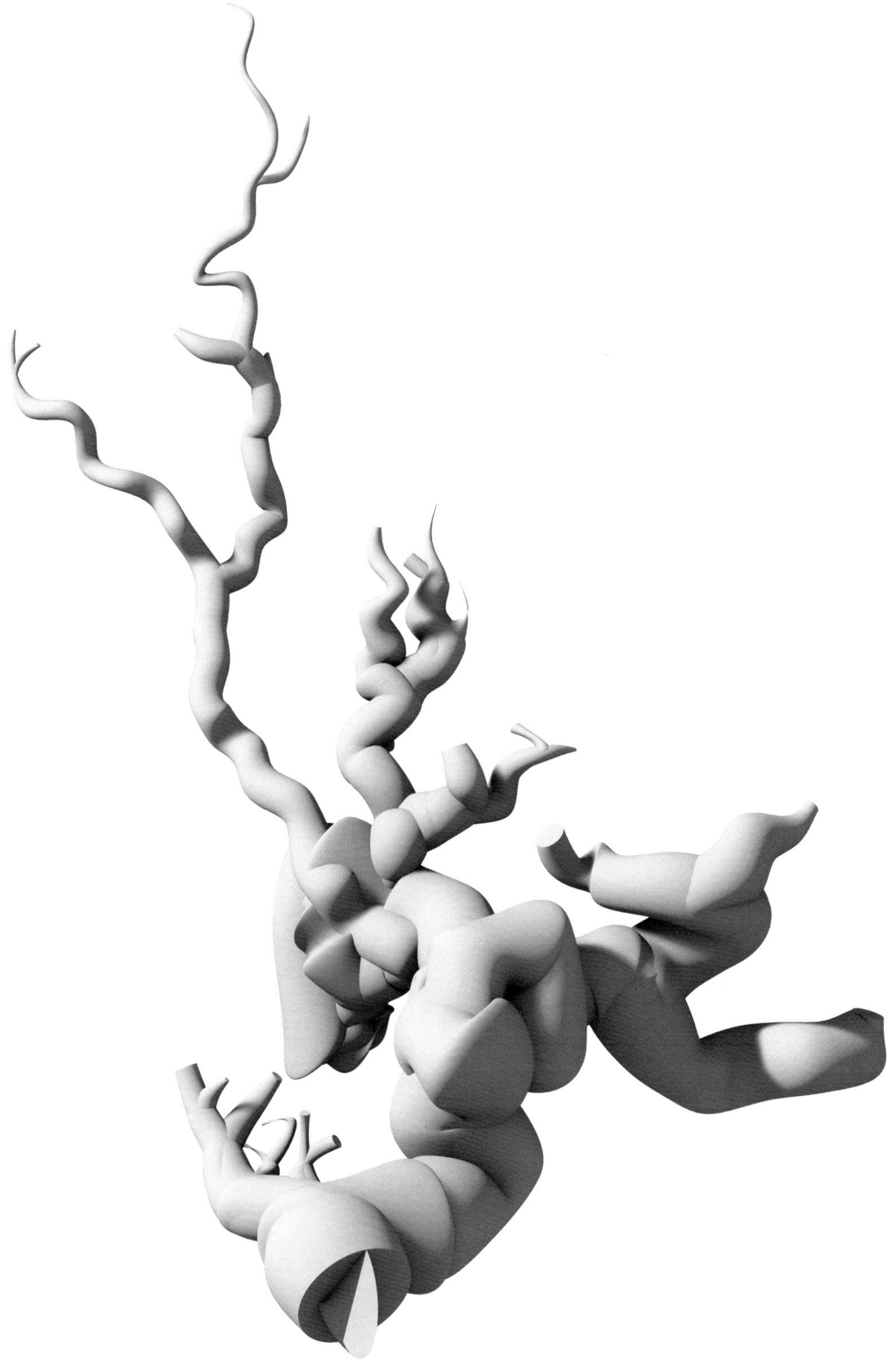

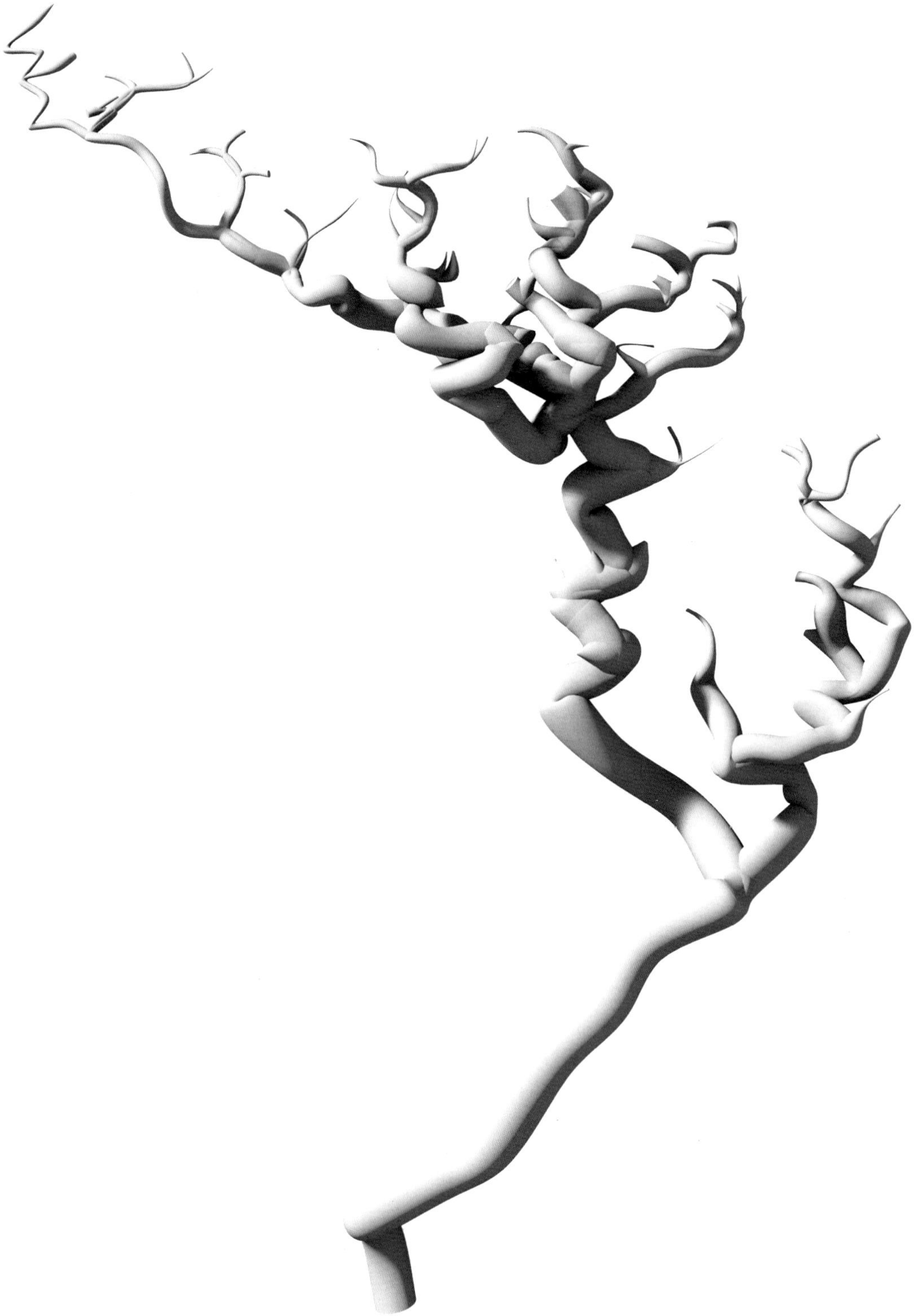

Rendering a tree in a drawing invites divergence from the digital surface.

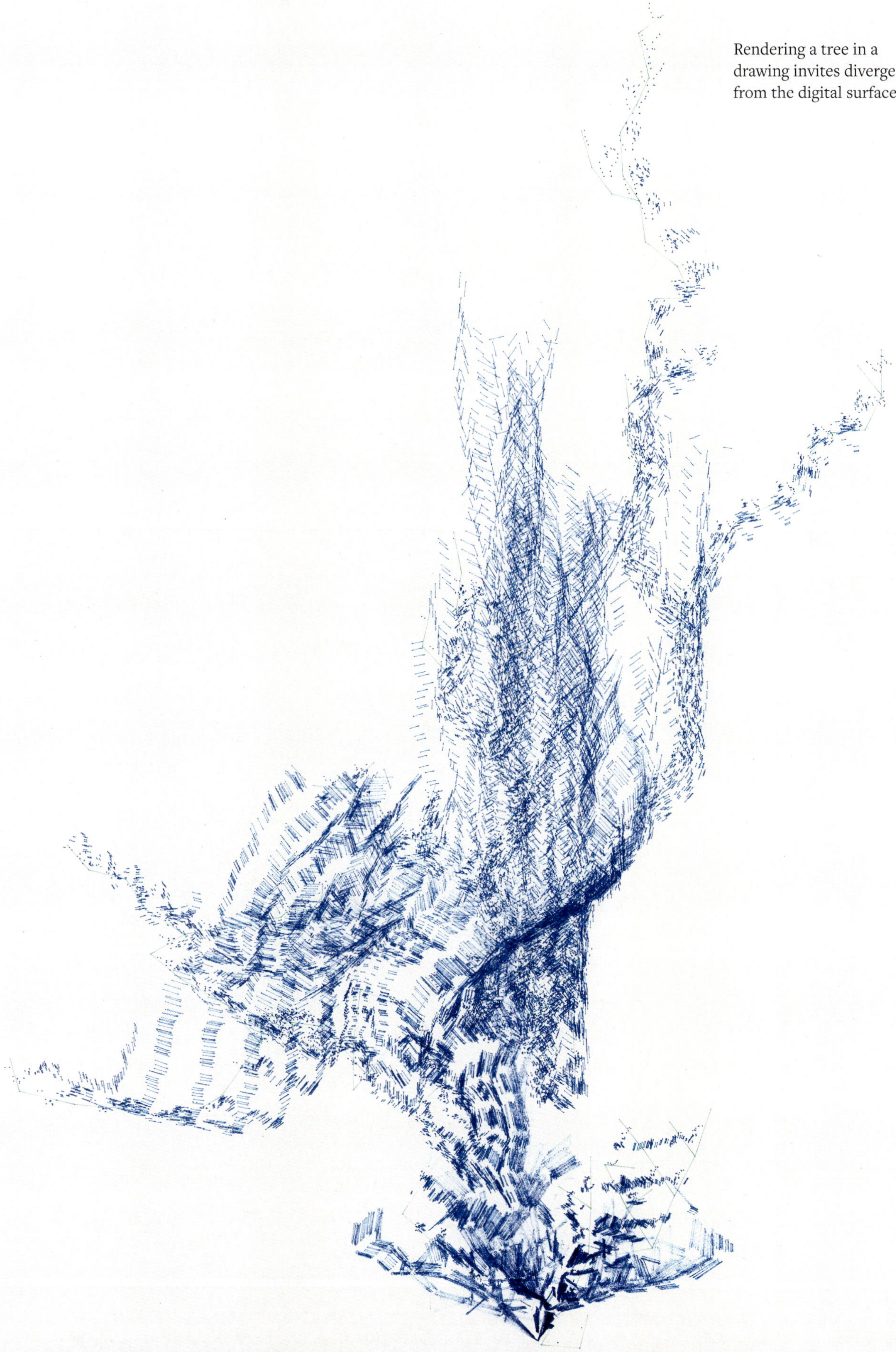

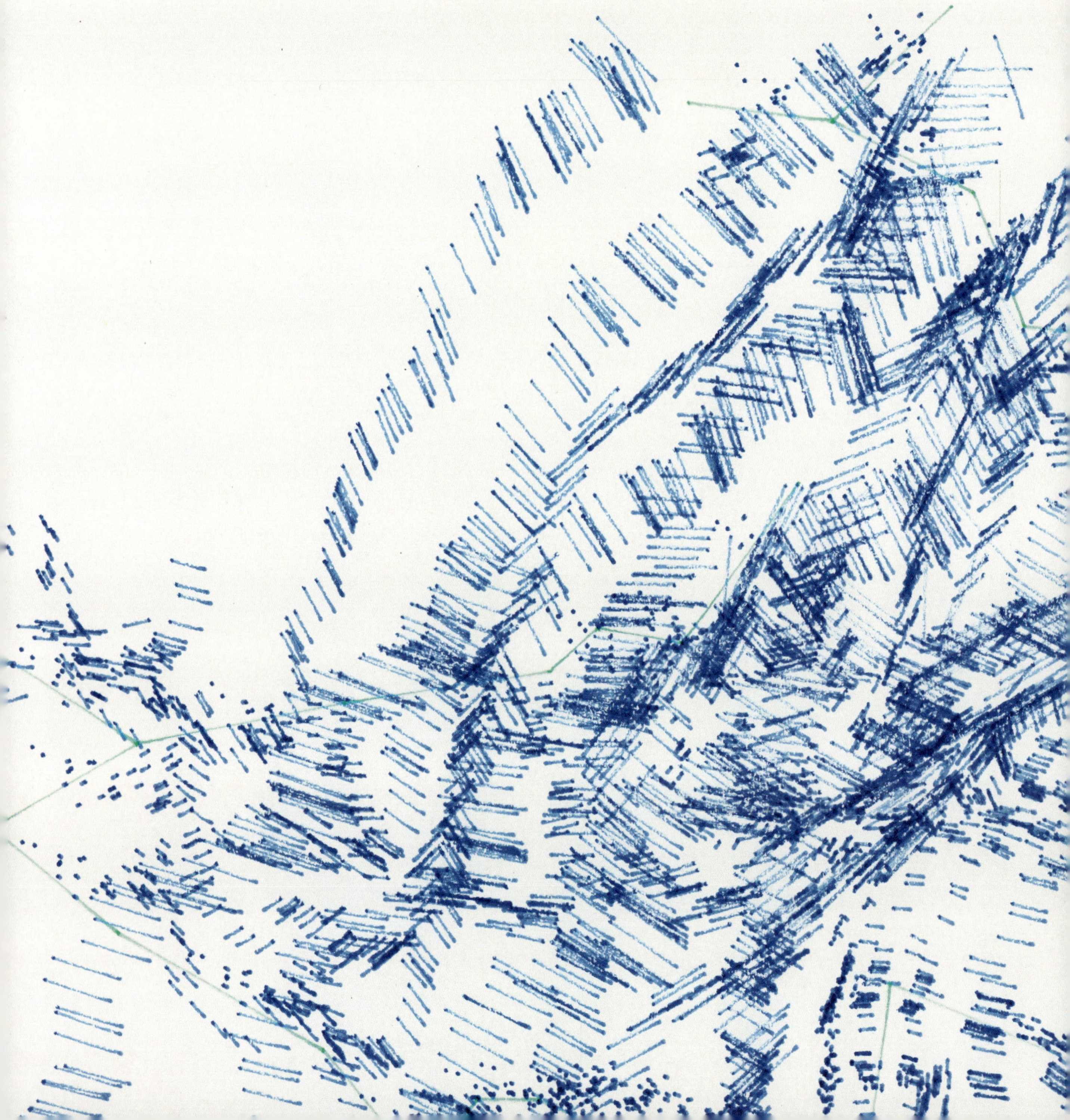

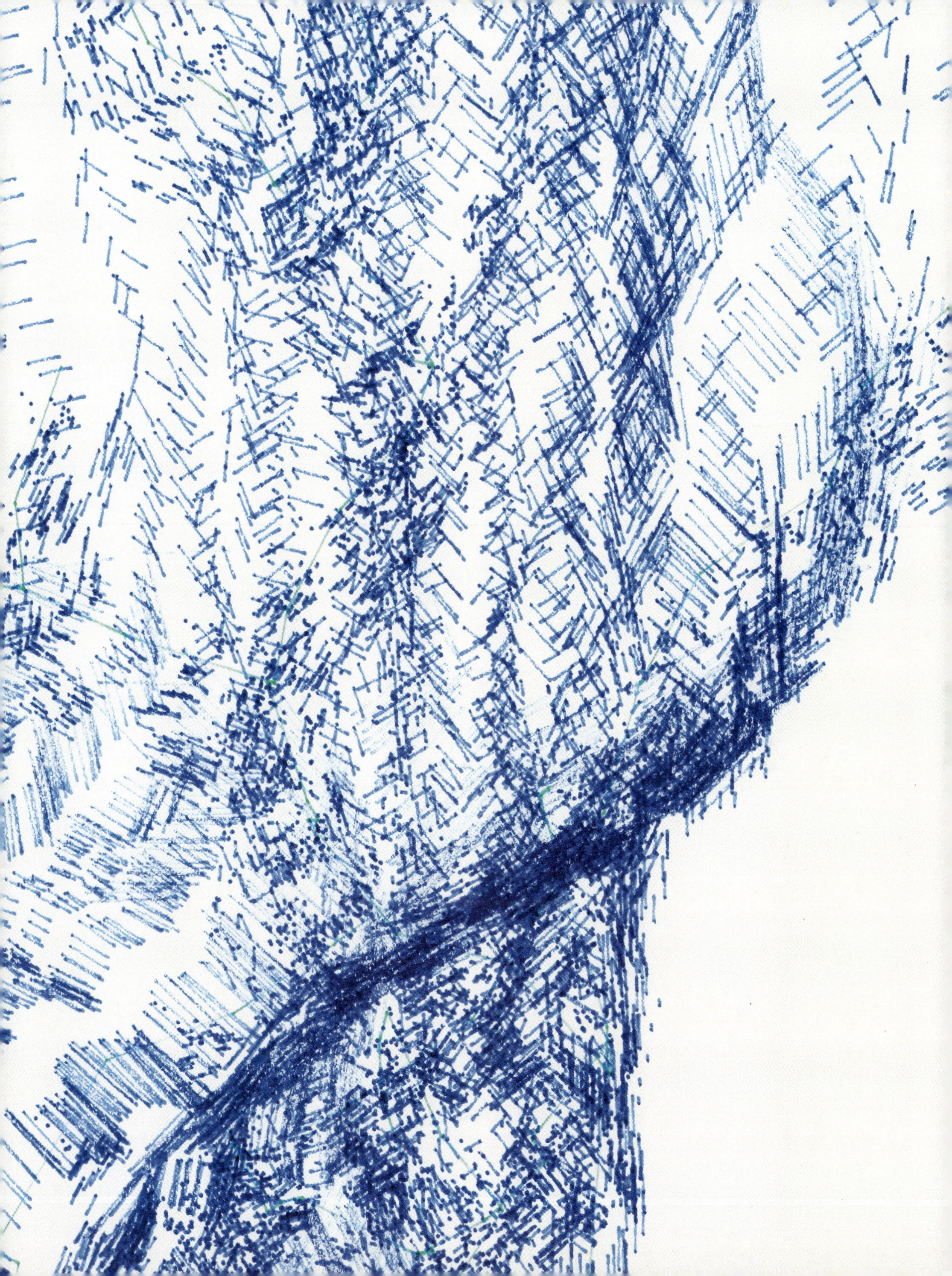

EXERCISE

Random Salt Crystals

Random values have often been compared to salt in a perfectly seasoned dish: when introduced to a computationally generated element they enhance other flavors without dominating. What if the salt was allowed to grow as an element, as a kind of cultivated crystal? Could it be served on its own? To test this premise, generate some random content within a loop. At each iteration, give the user—yourself—opportunity to adjust the output. Consider what criteria emerge during the process and what criteria you use to catalog the various results.

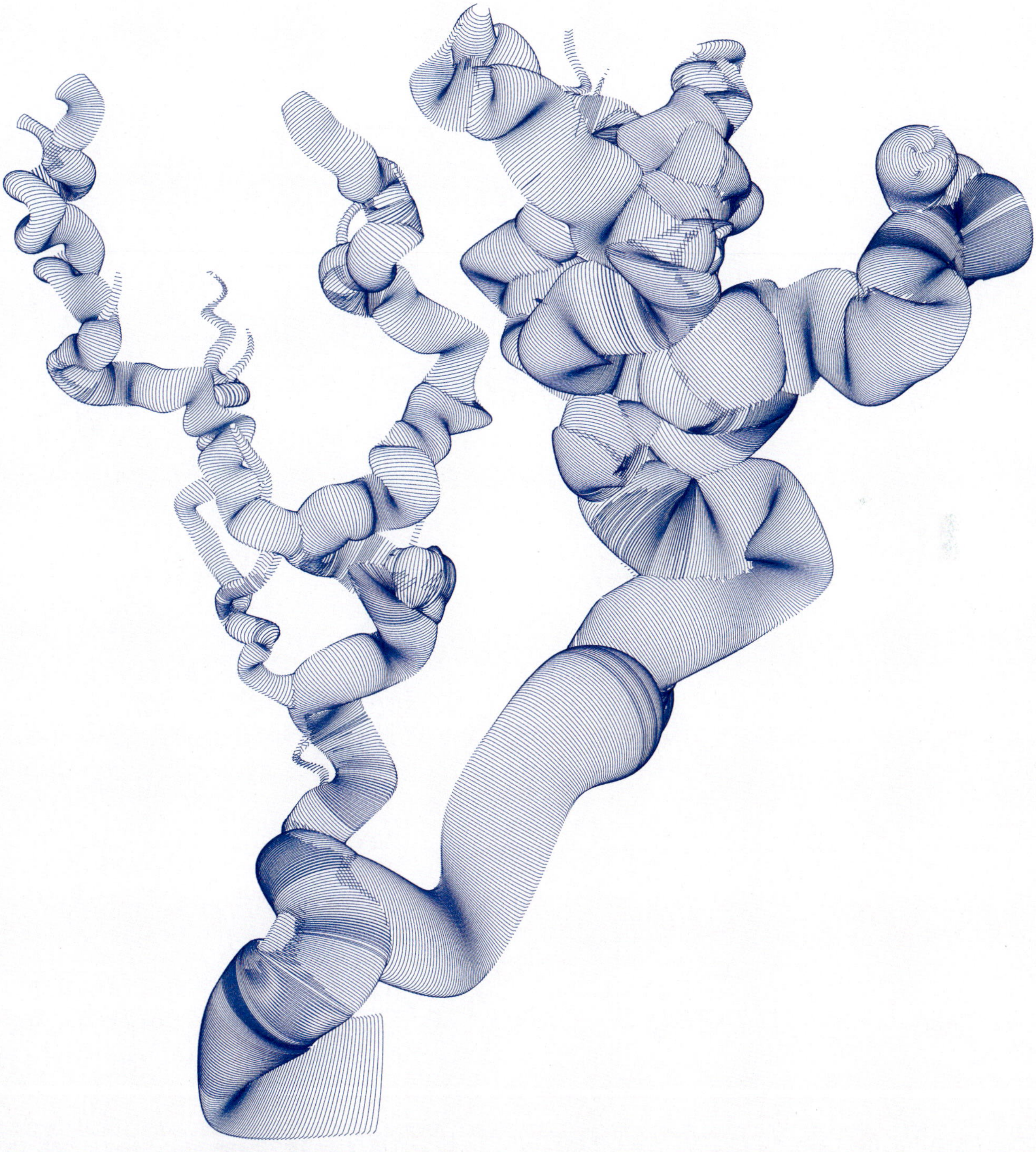

Who is the "User-Author"?

The constant reflection that occurs during the cultivation of a digital bonsai is also a kind of push and pull between the user, who is operating the bonsai interface, and the author, who has developed the code. Here, both are the same person. That conflation is a microcosm of the constant tension that all users of creative software feel. Despite their status as user, they strive to be an author. In this case, the user-author is also the author of the text, an admission that most readers will have already understood, but nonetheless strains the stylistic desire to make this text about the work rather than about the user-author (or is it now, author-user-author?).

Though the digital bonsai as element is a kind of pressurized or extreme user-author case study, this tension is beneficial. Ignoring it is to ignore the labor of the developer while also deferring to the latent biases defaults of software. Either way, reclaiming authorship is a decidedly humanist endeavor. Tools and media shape our work, but we can and should shape our media and tools.

Using Software the Wrong Way

The workflows involved in this project are messy. To describe them or diagram them would almost be a comedy of arrows and loops and nested inputs, conditionals, formats, footnotes, conversions, and caveats. They aren't being hidden from the reader with any proprietary interests but edited out before their production based on a strong conviction that they would be almost no use to anyone (the author included) in any other context. This may sound like a conceit, or perhaps even a flawed design, but this reality is arguably a digital ideal. Two different commercial digital modeling software applications would be legible in the messy workflow diagram that doesn't exist. Both are misused to the extent that their influence on the aesthetics of the result is minimal. That's not always laudable, but the possibility of operating "on" or "with" software rather than "in" software is liberating. Readers may have already gleaned a sense of the custom interface for digital bonsai pruning that gives the author control over the tree at every discrete step of its growth. That interface is overlaid onto digital modeling software with an interface devoid of any conception of time. Ironically, on the other side of the workflow, near the end, animation software is misused by placing hundreds of copies of the bonsai tree over a timeline—one per frame—to give the appearance of growth. This stop-motion reality forced into a keyframing world is as essential as it is unconventional. Each frame is populated by a keyframe, leaving no space for the interpolation that this structure is designed to enable. The topology of the geometry changes from frame to frame as the tree sprouts new buds and branches or is pruned. In other words, the tree animations are made not by moving or transforming objects over several frames. Instead, the tree is re-rendered at each frame based on data stored in one of many text files.

Those text files are precious, but they do not belong to any one software. They are more like lists than they are models. The programming language, which in this case happens to be Python, is treated like Esperanto for software. Nearly all contemporary software is controllable by a Python API. Many software applications offer a fully developed Python programming environment within the interface. Here, "scripting," which generally refers to code that can be executed from within a kind of bubble of software, is often assumed to be either for the creation of software plugins or for users to automate preexisting software functions. In this case, scripting is a bit different in purpose and scope. On one hand, a script grows a tree and shows the user-author a preview of the tree as it grows to allow them to selectively prune while controlling the stepping of time. This script generates text files. When it concludes, there is no tree, but everything necessary to render a tree. On the other hand, another script, in another software, reads those text files and puts trees in timelines for raytracing, or generates machine code for a drawing machine.

Programming is "clean" in many ways. Certain syntax rules are non-negotiable, of course. Error messages can be relentless and unforgiving. But programming is perfectly compatible with the messiest, most custom, esoteric, personal, or quirky workflows—all of which are decidedly compatible with bonsai. There's no such thing as a "bonsai-tool," real or imagined. More likely, a bonsai artist's toolkit will involve a collection of wire, scissors, rakes, plastic bags, and moss that are often used in surprising ways. In other words, tools are made from other tools, reappropriated, and gleefully misused. This applies to digital rendering as much as it does to the cultivation of these animate and self-referential trees.

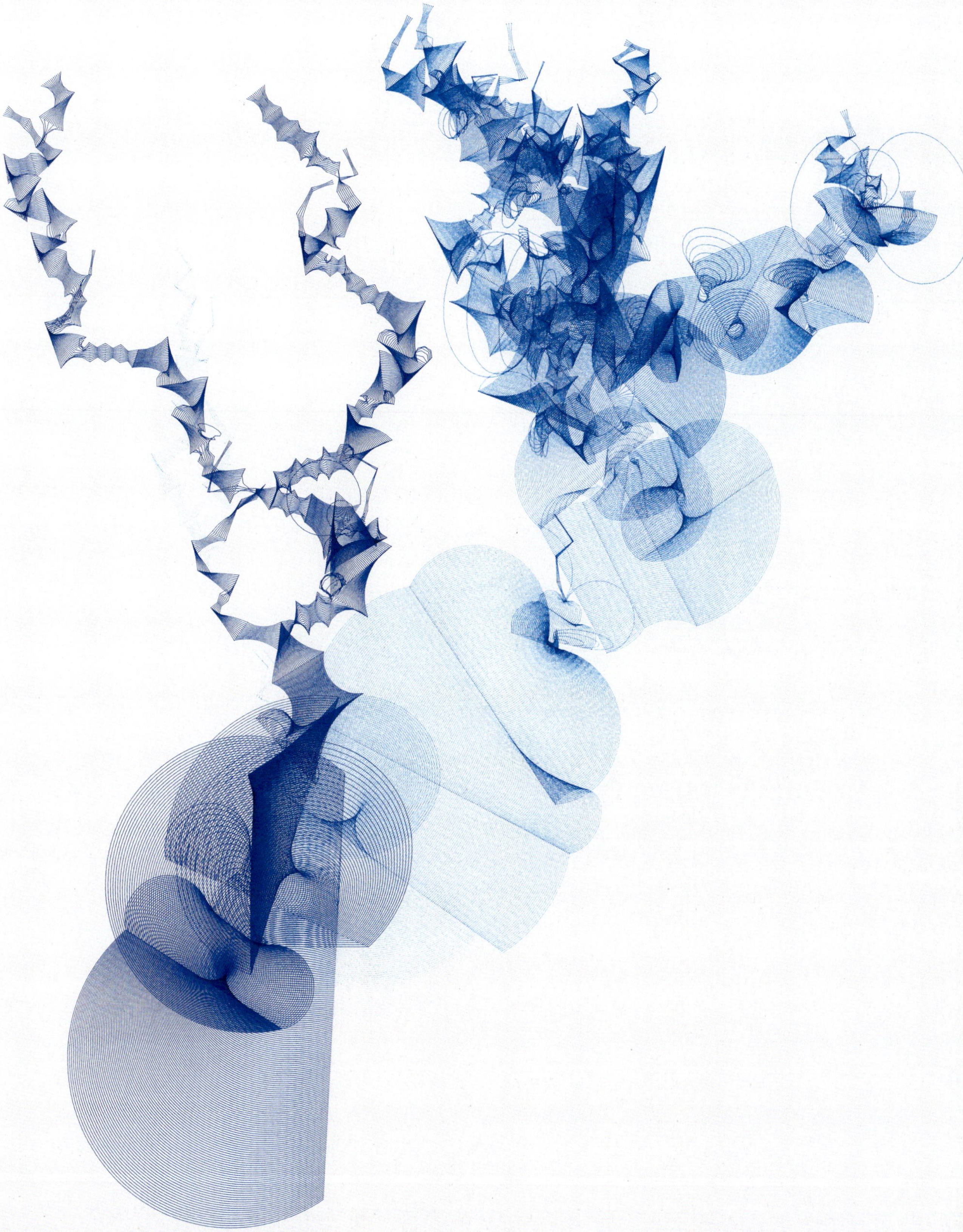

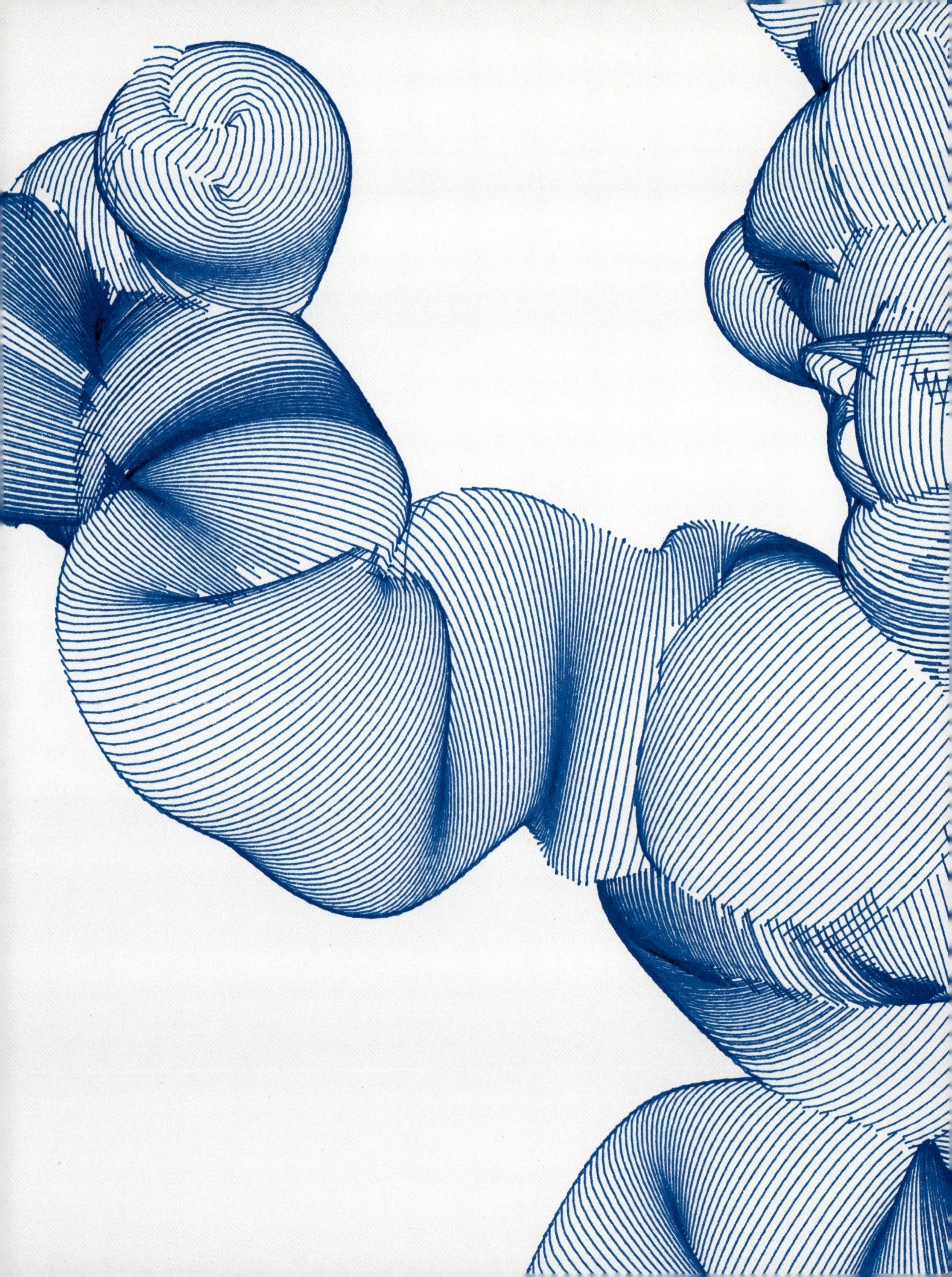

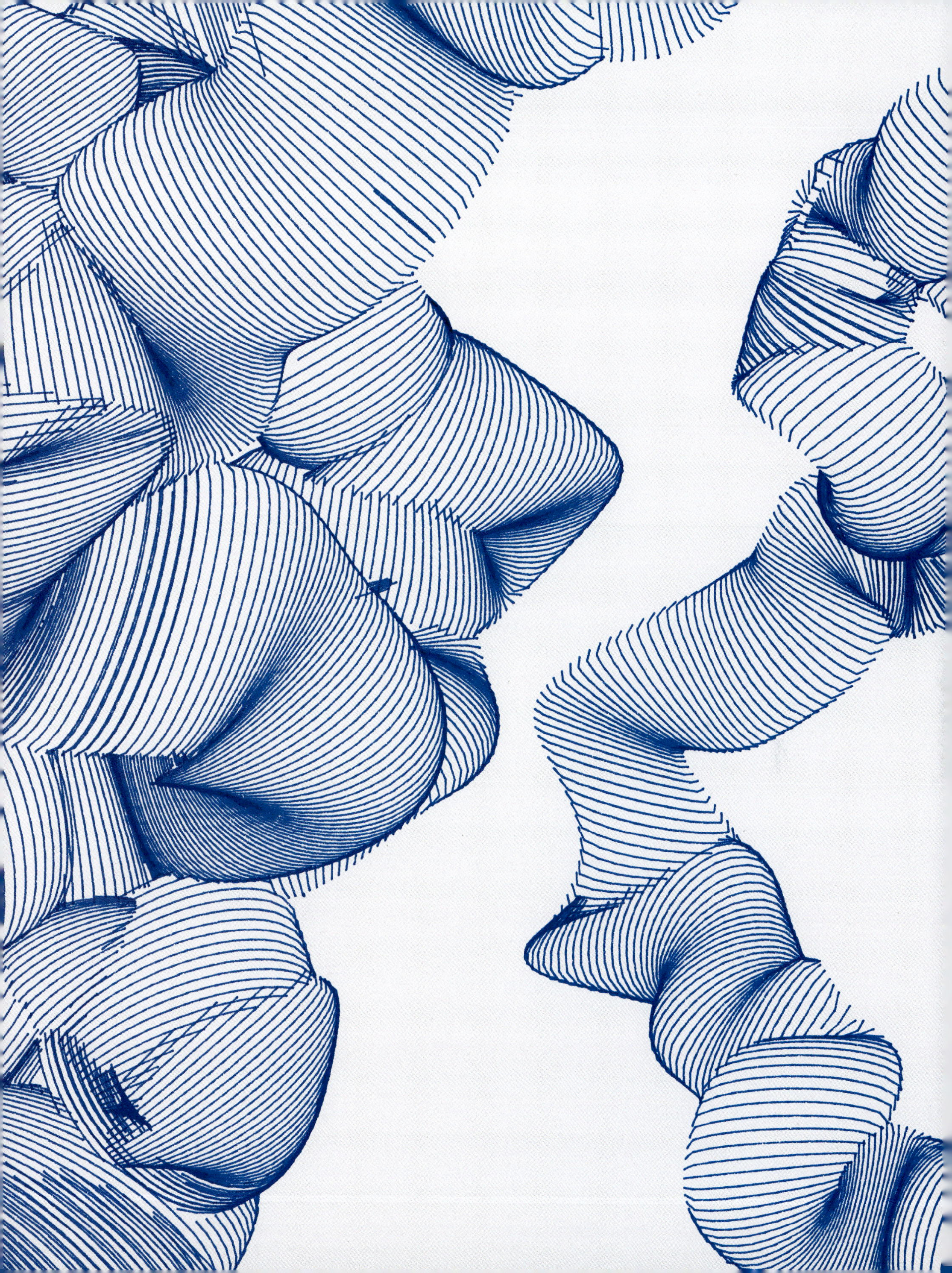

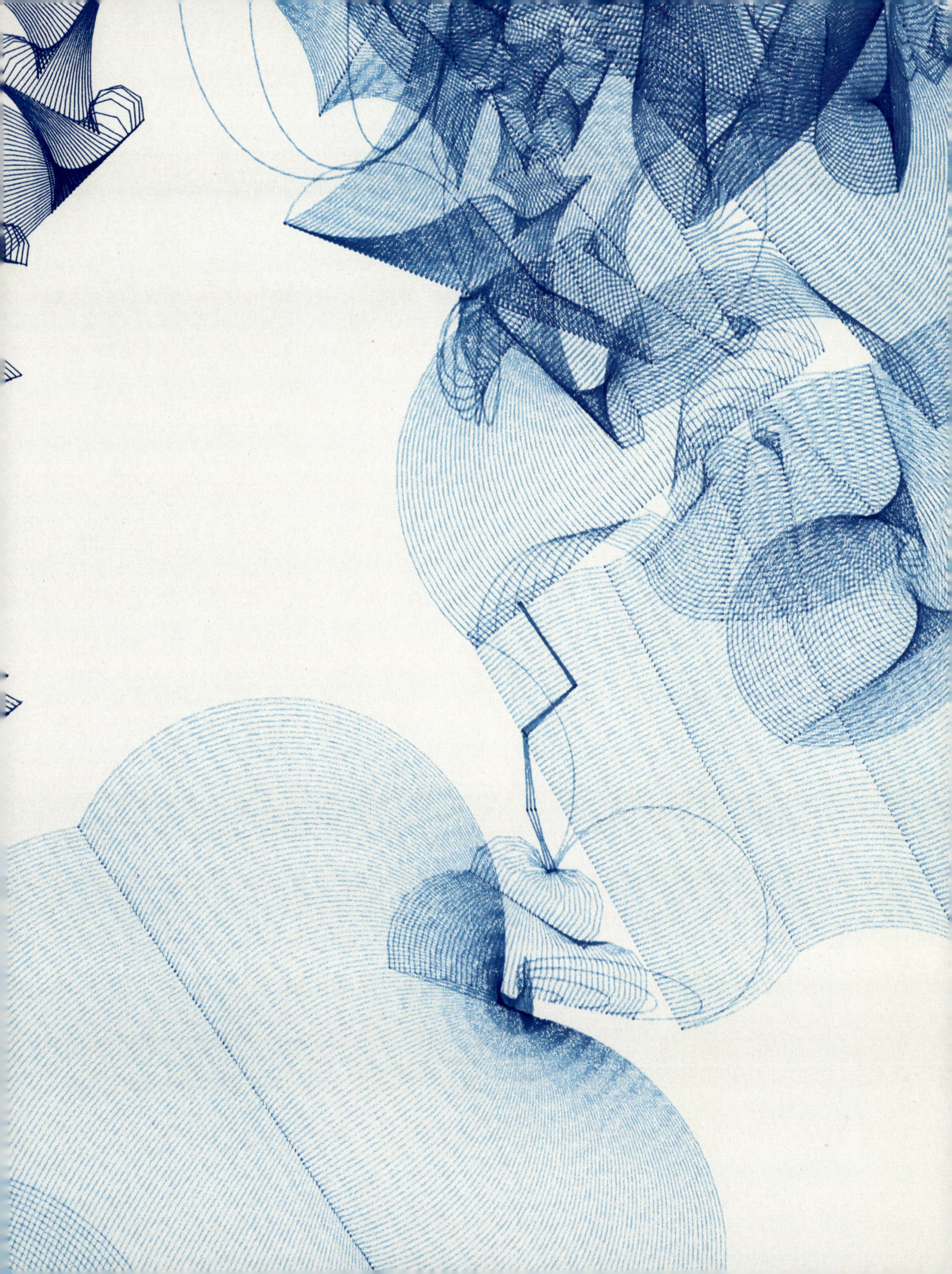

A Tree Yet Rendered is Three Hundred Text Files in a Folder

The database of text files in the middle of the messy workflow contains every bit of information about the tree at every moment in time. It's also incredibly simple. Without any compression or optimization, it's nothing more than a sequence of sequences of points, articulated one at a time, line by line, with a special character used as a marker indicating a new branch path. One could hack a tree by opening it in a text editor, changing a value, saving, and then re-rendering the tree. However, that would likely lead to unintended consequences because the accurate representation of branching nodes requires duplicate points at multiple locations within each file.

Already the term "render" has been used throughout this chapter to describe the building up of 3-D digital geometry from information in text files. Some of the images are the result of trees rendered into 3-D form and then rendered again via the raytracing functionality in software. The later operation is what is most commonly understood as "rendering," which of course is accurate, but only one of many valid uses of the term. This is yet another situation in which software functions influence colloquialisms and confuse or evolve definitions. Often, rendering in software is merely a stylization—think, "wireframe mode" verses "rendered mode." If rendering is about manifesting the appearance of something where previously there was only idea, information, data, or geometries, then conceptually speaking, a wireframe is also a kind of rendering. If you see it, and there is data or geometry that defines it, what you are seeing is a rendering. This definition may seem pedantic, but it has the benefit of clarifying a relationship between drawing and rendering. These two territories overlap each other, but only partially. A drawing can be a rendering, but every drawing is not necessarily a rendering. Why do we care? The answer takes us back to a pursuit of creative control. Not a total creative control, which would involve a delusional denial of the creative agency of software designers and developers, but a kind of control over what we are in control of as artists, designers, or architects.

Sometimes a Tree Looks Nothing like a Tree

The non-tree trees feel like anomalies, but nothing has been translated or transformed to achieve them. There is always interpretation between the elemental structure of the computational tree type, the text file format of the tree data, and the rendered tree. The trees that look nothing like trees only vary in the final step, the rendering. This reinforces the idea that rendering is not necessarily showing something that was already there, but creating something that was previously only nascent, immaterial, or invisible.

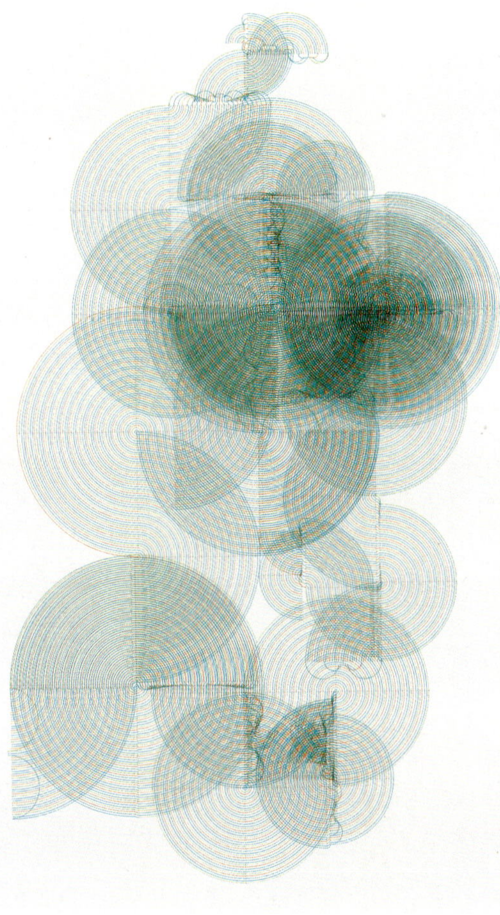

The same tree data can be processed into tree renders that look little, if anything, like a natural tree.

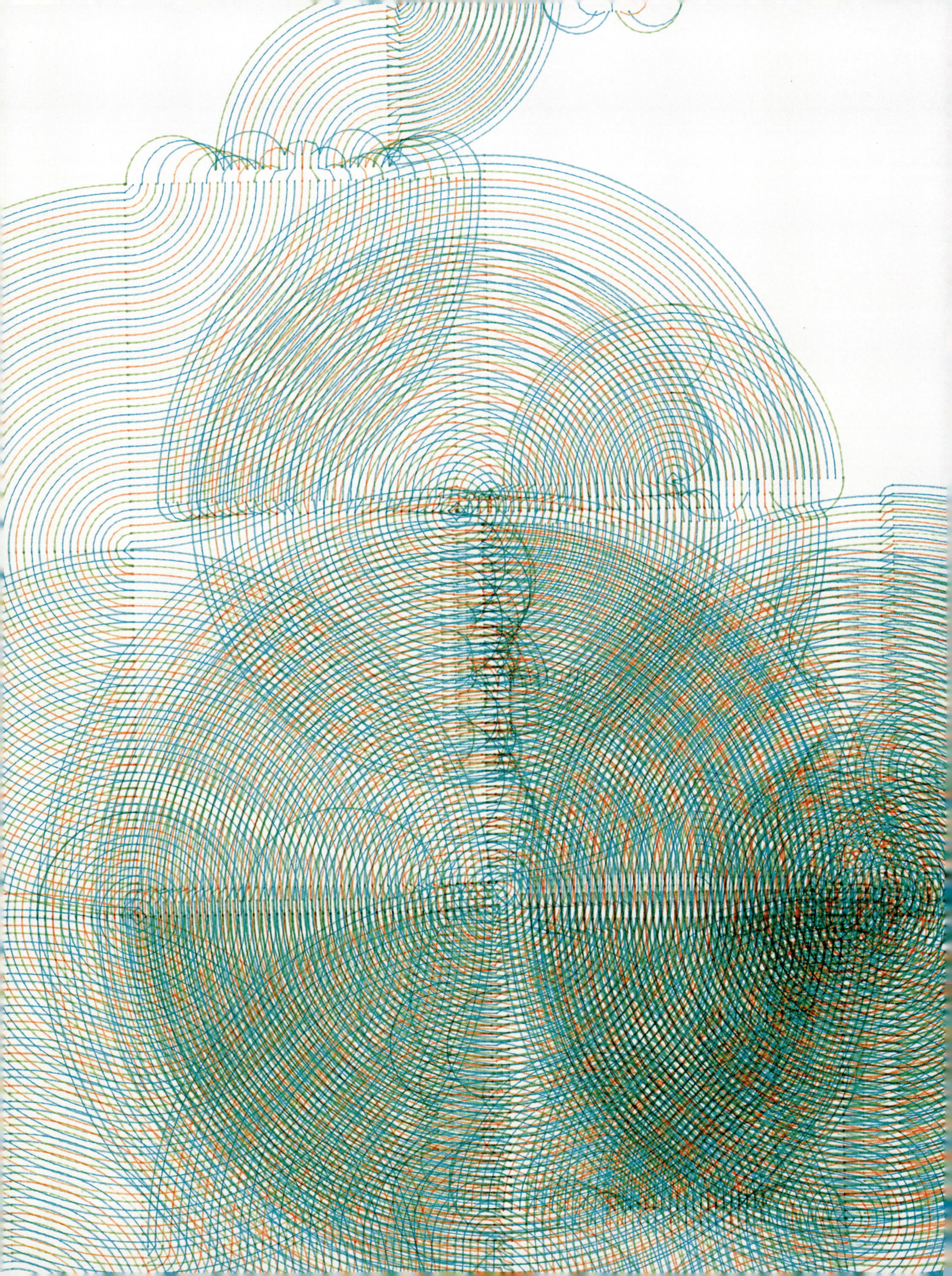

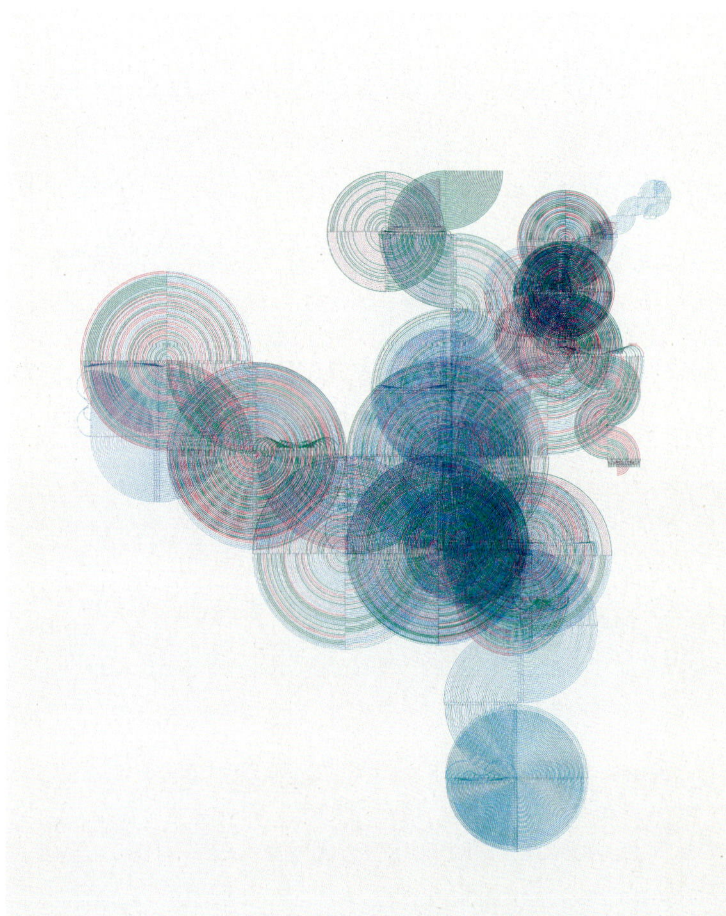

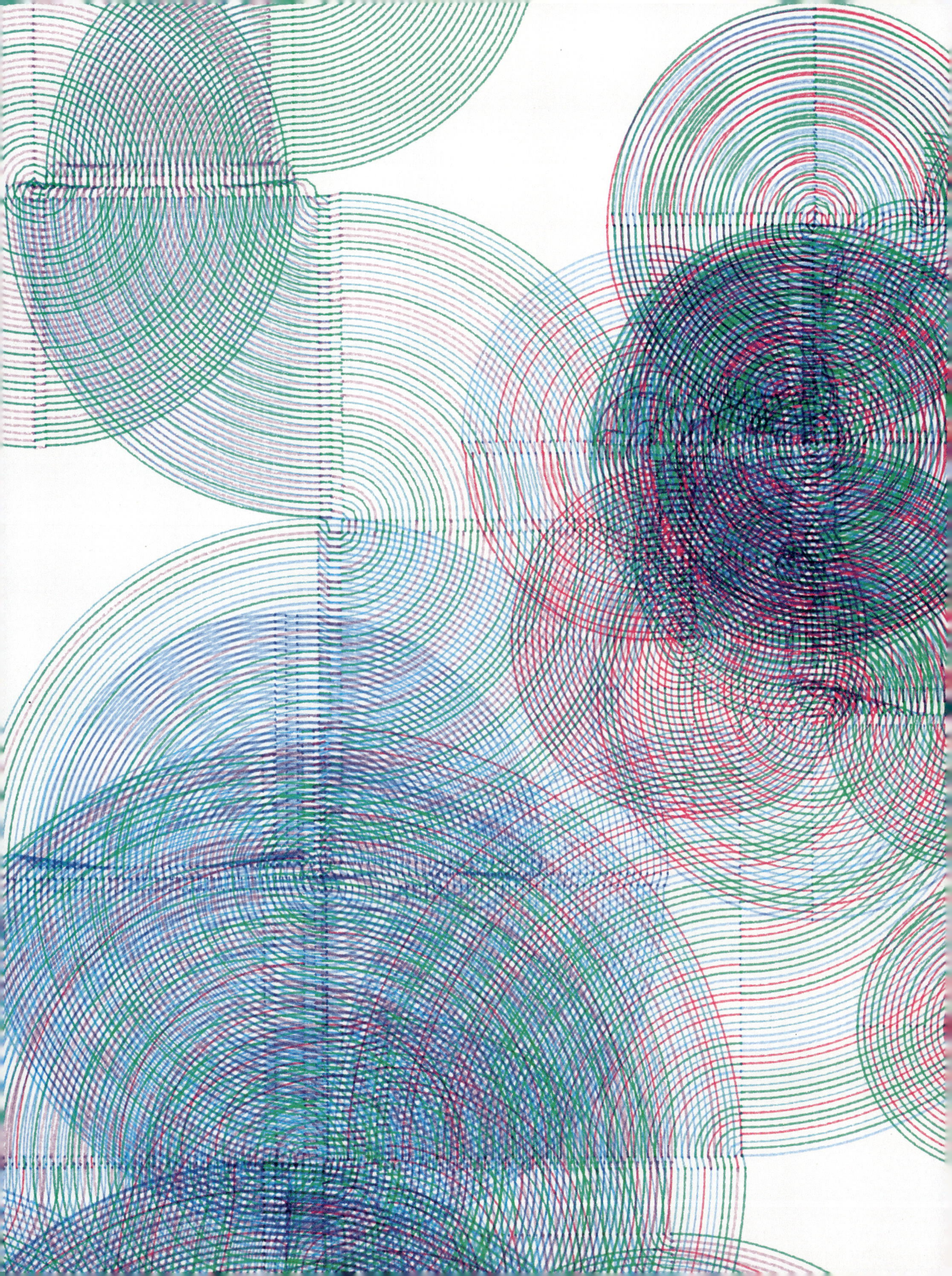

Everything is Bonsai when in Pursuit of Bonsai

The moment when a carefully cultivated tree becomes a bonsai tree is impossible to identify. We're then forced into a metaphysical thought experiment that could conclude with the realization that a tree might become a bonsai tree the moment one begins to operate on it as such. That might not be as much of a theoretical dead end as it initially sounds. It forces the emphasis on values and qualities rather than a strict catalog of definitions. What if we thought about bonsai less as though we are making a clinical diagnosis and more like we are working toward a set of values? Those values are often expressed in terms of a well-composted miniature. We might say bonsai artists work toward beauty through and with conflicting extreme scales. But there are other bonsai values that can be gleaned from watching the masters (on YouTube, of course). These other values have to do with strangeness or weirdness. For example, our interest in the extent to which a tree diverges from the perfectly symmetric cartoon-like symbol of a tree with a circular canopy and an exactly 90° trunk growing from the ground. Think about trees that are wrapped around a rock, growing upside down, that loop, or have survived a rough crack.

These trees do not exhibit those extremes because of nature, but of human nature. Reflecting on some of the early "rejected bonsai" it becomes clear, some of them are peak bonsai insofar as they don't resemble "normal" trees at all. They float, clump, flow, and almost writhe because of mistakes and failed experiments. These rejected bonsai are not to be confused with the non-tree trees, which are aesthetically different due to the algorithm of their rendered creation. These trees were initially rejected because a goal was not met. They are a kind of alpha tree or a version .01 tree that is, only after the fact, welcomed back into the published set because they inadvertently align with bonsai values, and their curious beauty only appreciated after seeing the goal—satisfying trees of the fully and correctly functioning software.

What were initially considered failed experiments in tree rendering are re-considered with respect to bonsai culture.

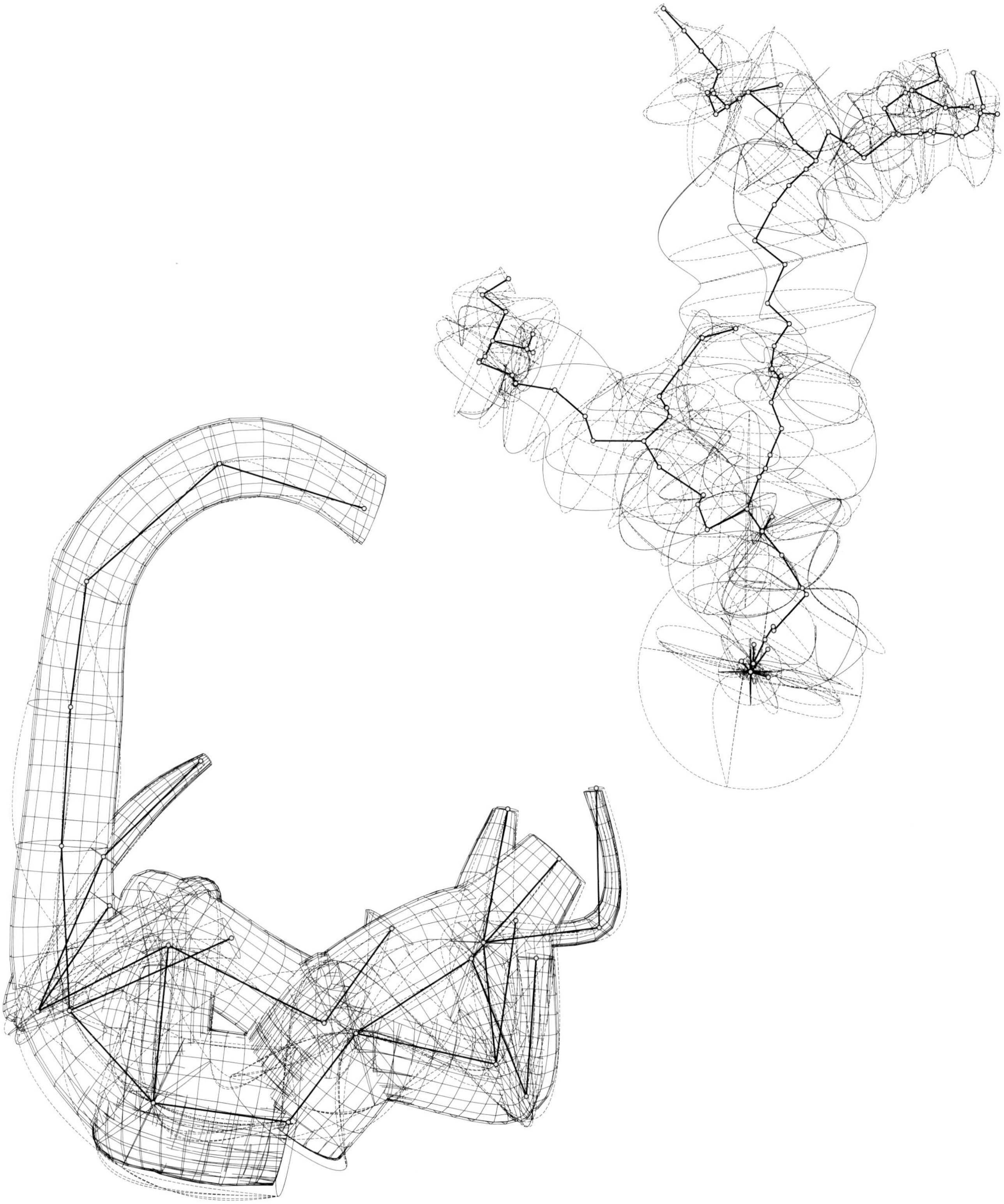

Over Time, of Time

Not all digital elements wear or change over time. This fact is relevant in multiple epistemological and philosophical terms, but for our purposes, it's most operable in terms of perception of reality or lack thereof. Temporal cues are triggers for reality. Many temporal cues live within the realm of the photographic image and are brought to renderings by way of texture mapping. Imagine, for example, a digital surface mapped with a photograph of a white wall with water stains, dents, dirt, and other signs of weathering due to age. This common strategy brings evidence of time to the rendered digital image, but it relies entirely on the photographic reality of the sourced texture in the narrowest of ways: it uses a photograph. The digital bonsai tree is a function of time. Each tree exists within a lifespan of serial frames. For this reason, the data for each tree are structured as a folder with many text files, one for each frame. Captures and renders of a particular frame are temporal only insofar as they remind us of a natural tree, which we know to be alive and growing. But given the temporal data of the tree, renders can draw from photographic techniques and qualities without having to sample from a photograph. Each rendered digital bonsai is durational. Data from one, multiple, or all frames are referenced in the creation of a drawing or image. As a result, the qualities and concepts inherent to the tree are immediately aligned with the photographic motion blur or time lapse. The motion blur resulting from relatively long exposures in photography could be understood as a kind of signal to the imperfect ability of the camera to freeze time. As with every medium and technology, "imperfection," "flaw," "technique," and "craft" are interrelated within the space of creative subjectivity. Thus, the digital bonsai again can be understood to move backwards into reality. Just as the digital bonsai is pruned before it is given mass, it fills a temporal void allotted to it rather than being captured within the duration of the open shutter.

When the database frames are mapped to the frames of an animation—let's assume for the sake of discussion that one frame of data is used for one frame of animation, though this is by no means a given—the digital bonsai can be said to grow very fast, or very slowly. The degree to which the temporal axis seems scaled depends on whether what we reference for a normal pace. If normal is the speed we expect a natural tree to grow, then the animation seems extremely fast. If, however, normal is the speed at which the user-author stepped through and considered each frame, then the animation seems surprisingly smooth and significantly fast. Finally, if normal is the speed at which the computer generates an entirely random tree, then the animation seems very slow.

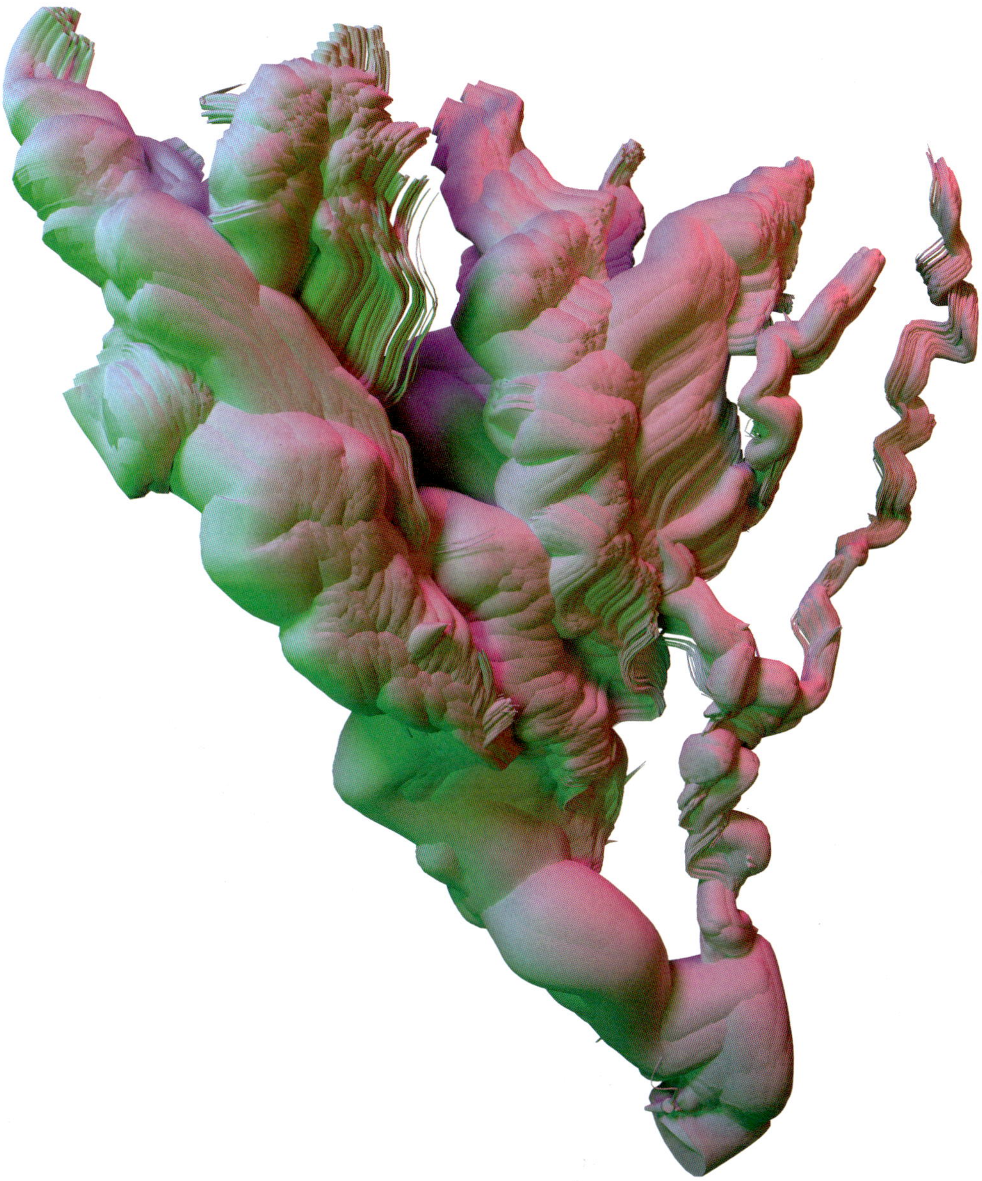

All the states of a tree
over its lifetime rendered
simultaneously.

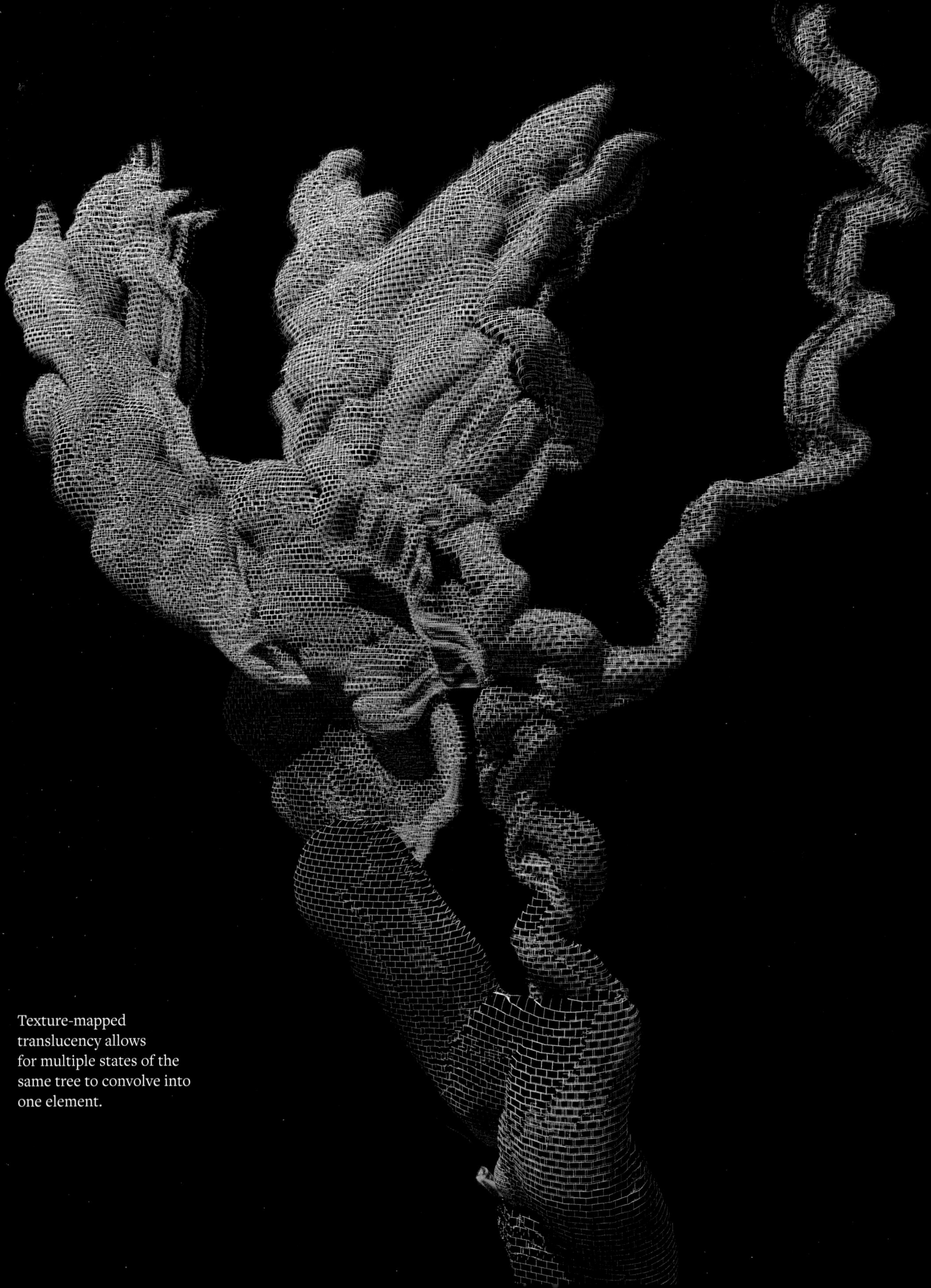

Texture-mapped translucency allows for multiple states of the same tree to convolve into one element.

The Pot is a Diorama

Like all impossible real elements, the digital bonsai is intrinsically linked to its representation. It can't exist without being rendered. The final provocation for this and all designed elements is the capacity to interact with other elements. As has been the case throughout our extended metaphor, bonsai culture sets us off on a productive vector. In the world of bonsai, the pot is essential. Arguably the potting of the wild tree is the first and primary gesture of making a bonsai. That action is more than a utilitarian matter of making a bit of earth portable. The pot is likewise not merely a base, stand, or podium. Like a diorama it establishes the bounds of the world. It disrupts scale. It establishes space between itself and the tree.

The diorama as an element will be explored in much more depth in the next chapter, but its introduction here as enclosure-attachment to the digital bonsai clarifies that it is not neutral. The dioramas are implicated in the perception of scale, just like the conventional bonsai pot. The dioramas disrupt any conception of a singular view while biasing a front side. Frontality repeatedly comes up in bonsai discourse—often in terms of "finding the front" before making key pruning decisions.

Most importantly, as we conclude our digital bonsai journey, we can note that the salience of the element is distinct from notions of subject or object. Digital elements, especially those that provoke new conceptions of reality, blur the line between thing and that which houses the thing, whether that housing is database, enclosure, building, image, or paper.

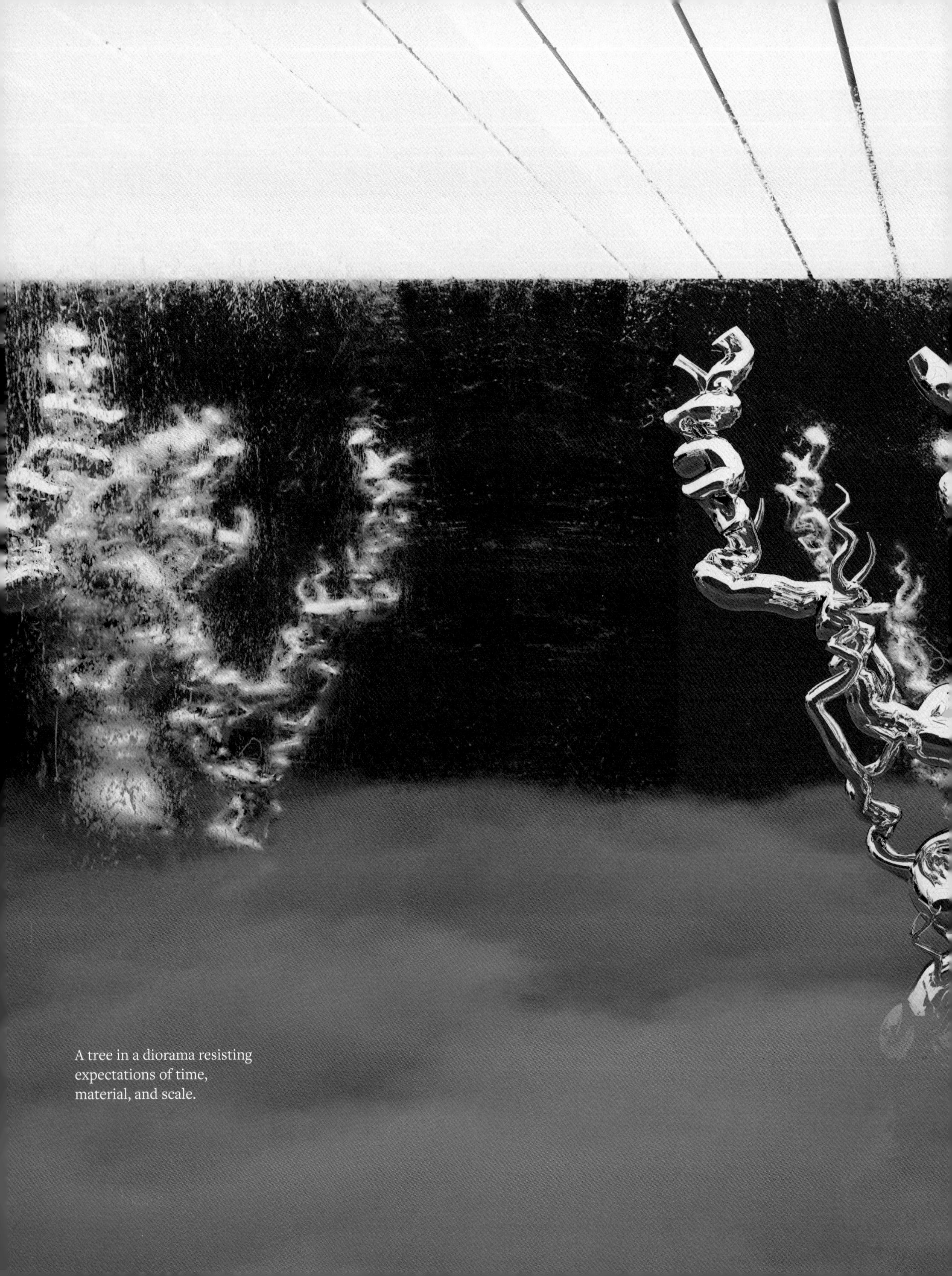

A tree in a diorama resisting expectations of time, material, and scale.

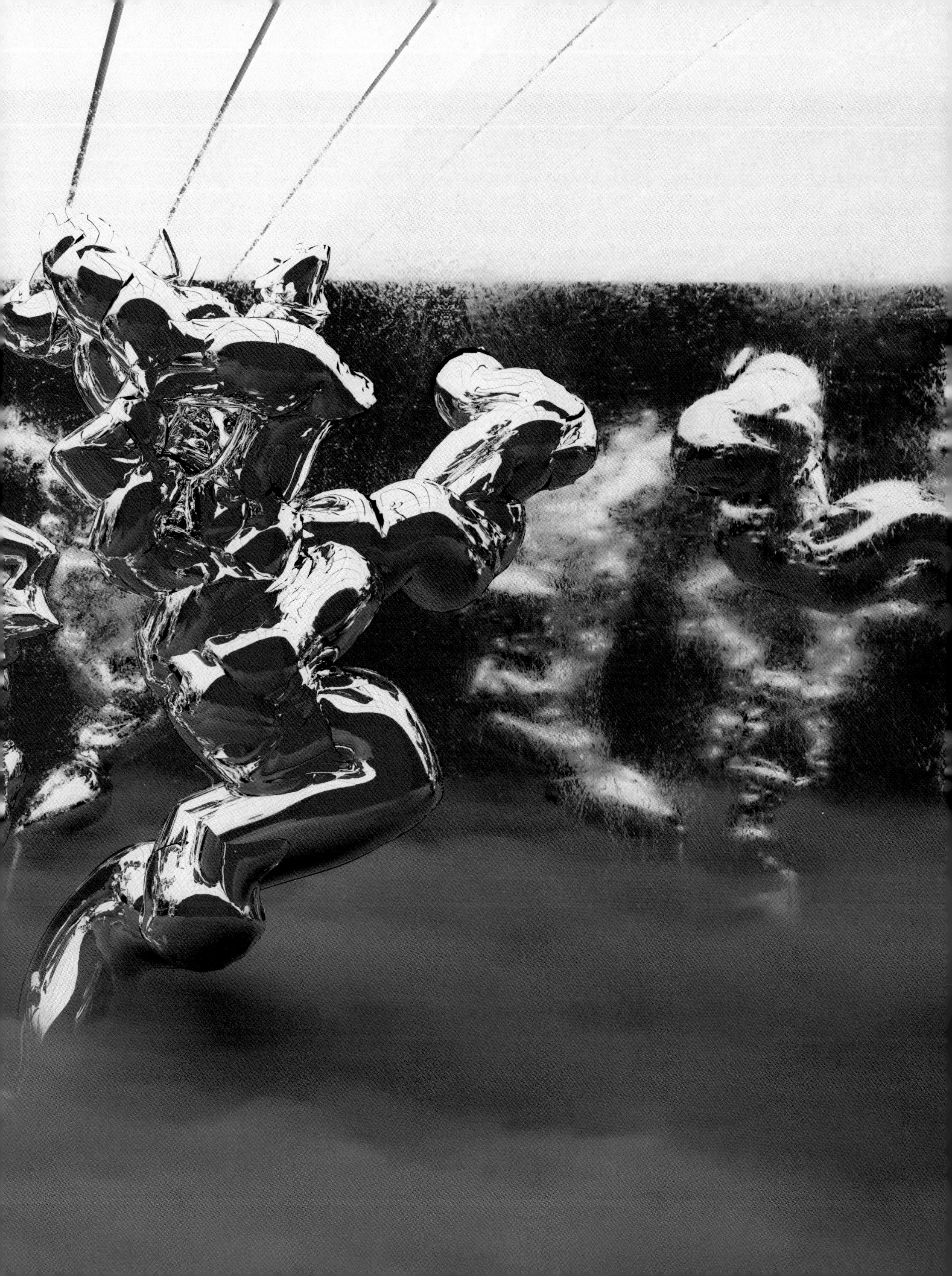

Notes

1. Sanford Kwinter. *"The Computational Fallacy."* Thresholds 26 (2003): 91.
2. Kwinter, 91.
3. Peter Chan. "Story," in *Bonsai: the Art of Growing and Keeping Miniature Trees,* 18. New York, NY: Skyhorse Publishing, 2014.
4. Chan, 19.
5. *Japanese Maple Shaping Decisions Part 1. YouTube*. YouTube, 2019. https://www.youtube.com/watch?v=cvh0r0Yf59I.

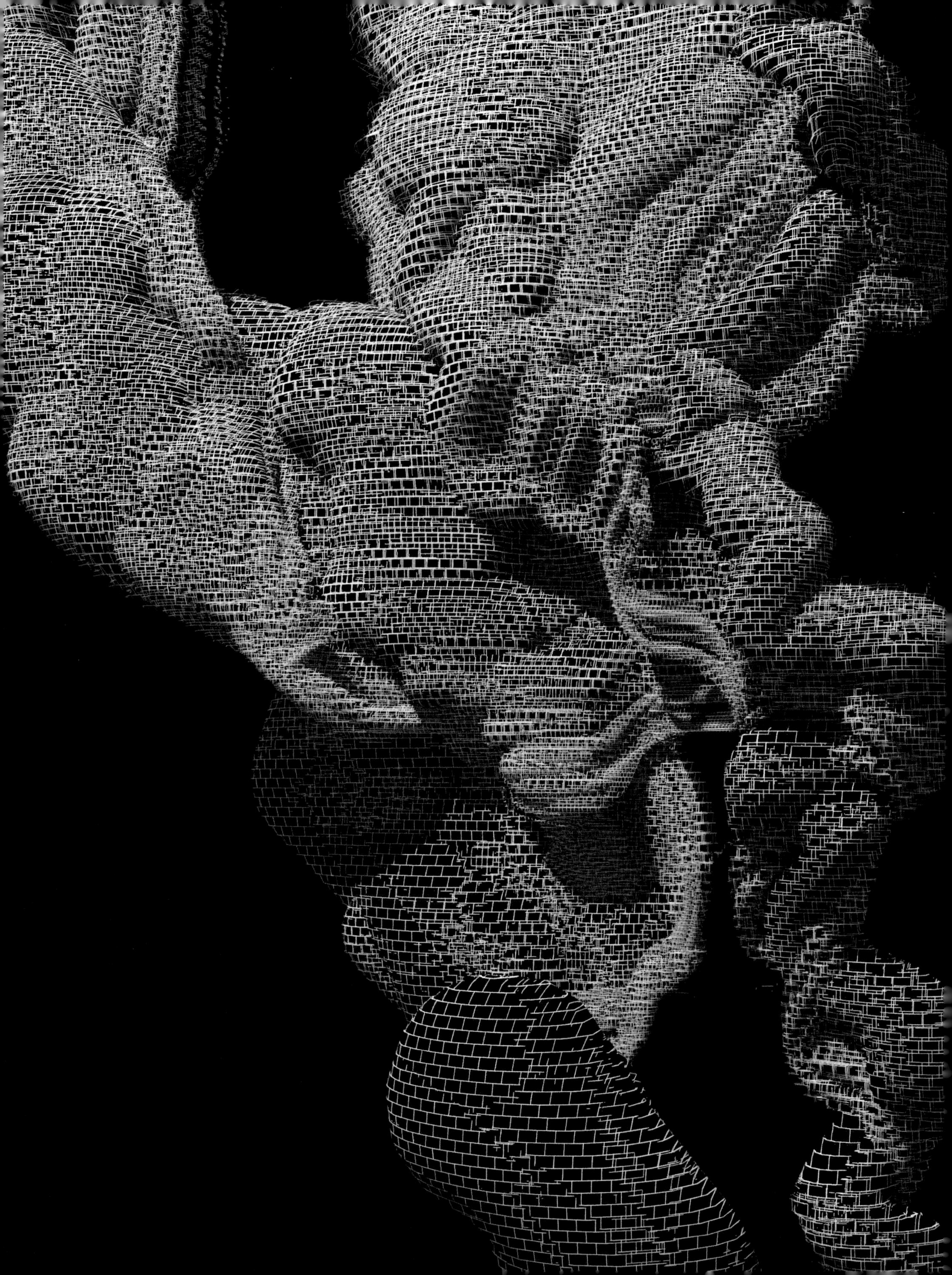

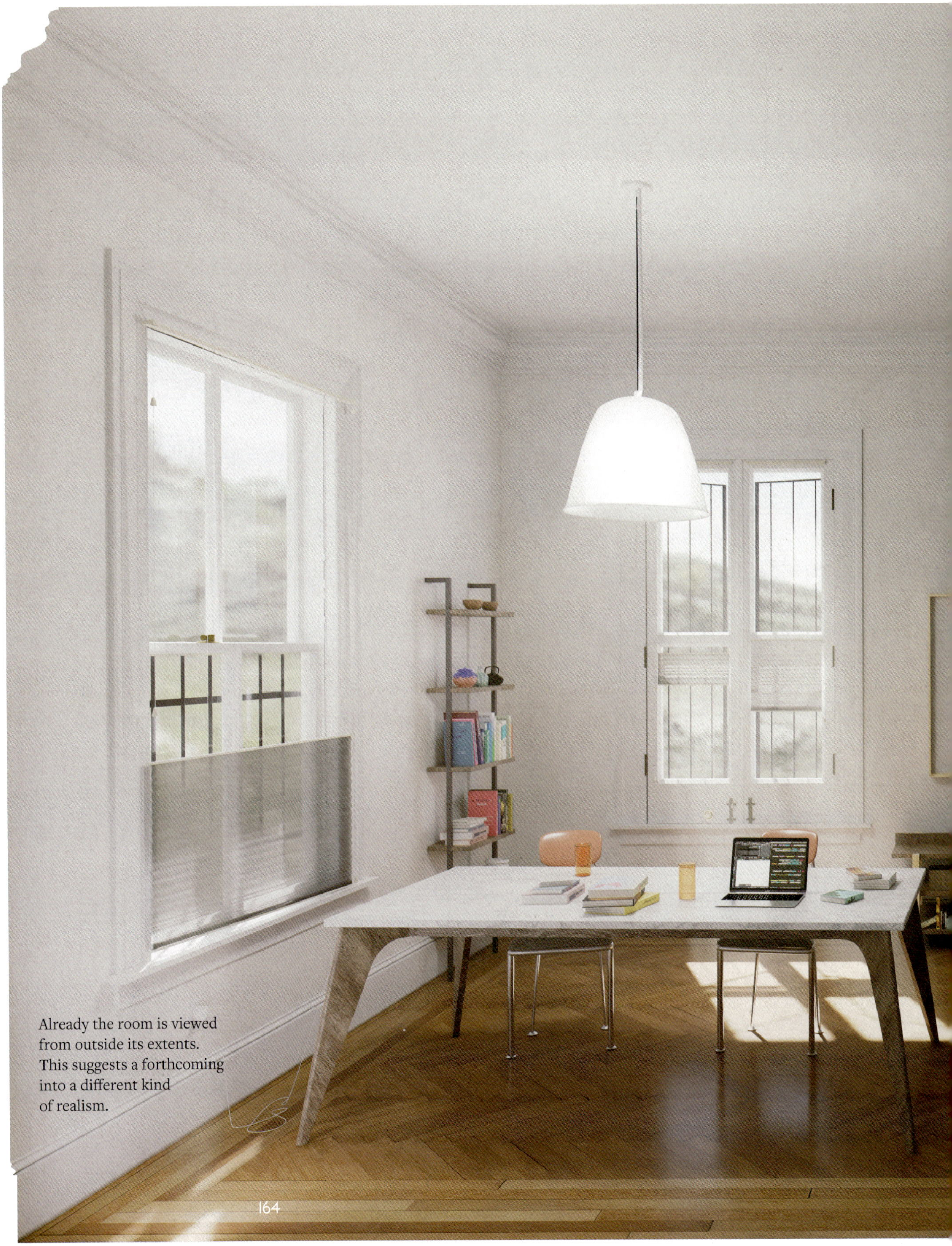

Already the room is viewed from outside its extents. This suggests a forthcoming into a different kind of realism.

CHAPTER 4

A Room that Becomes a Diorama; A Diorama Afflicted with Room Envy

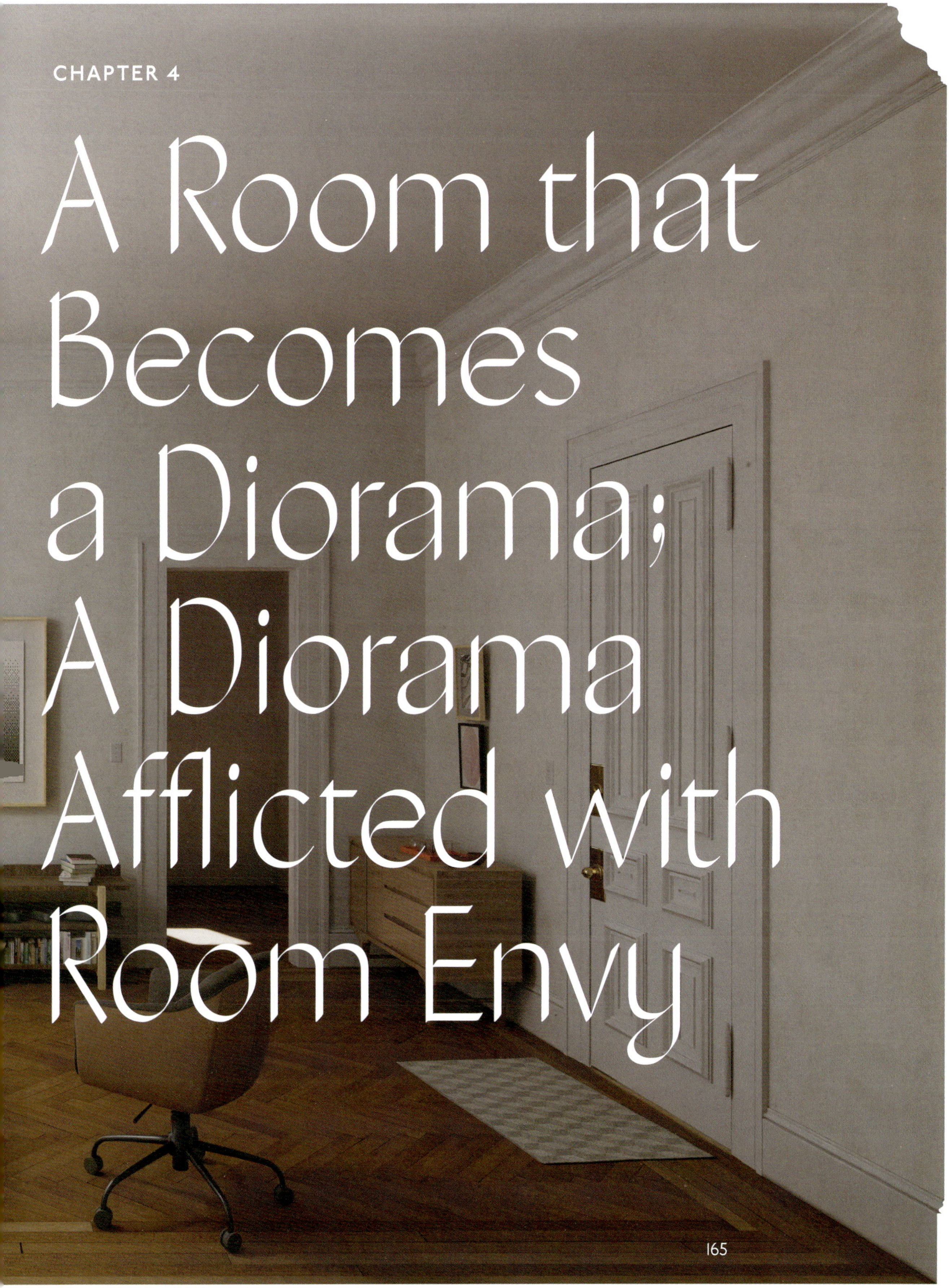

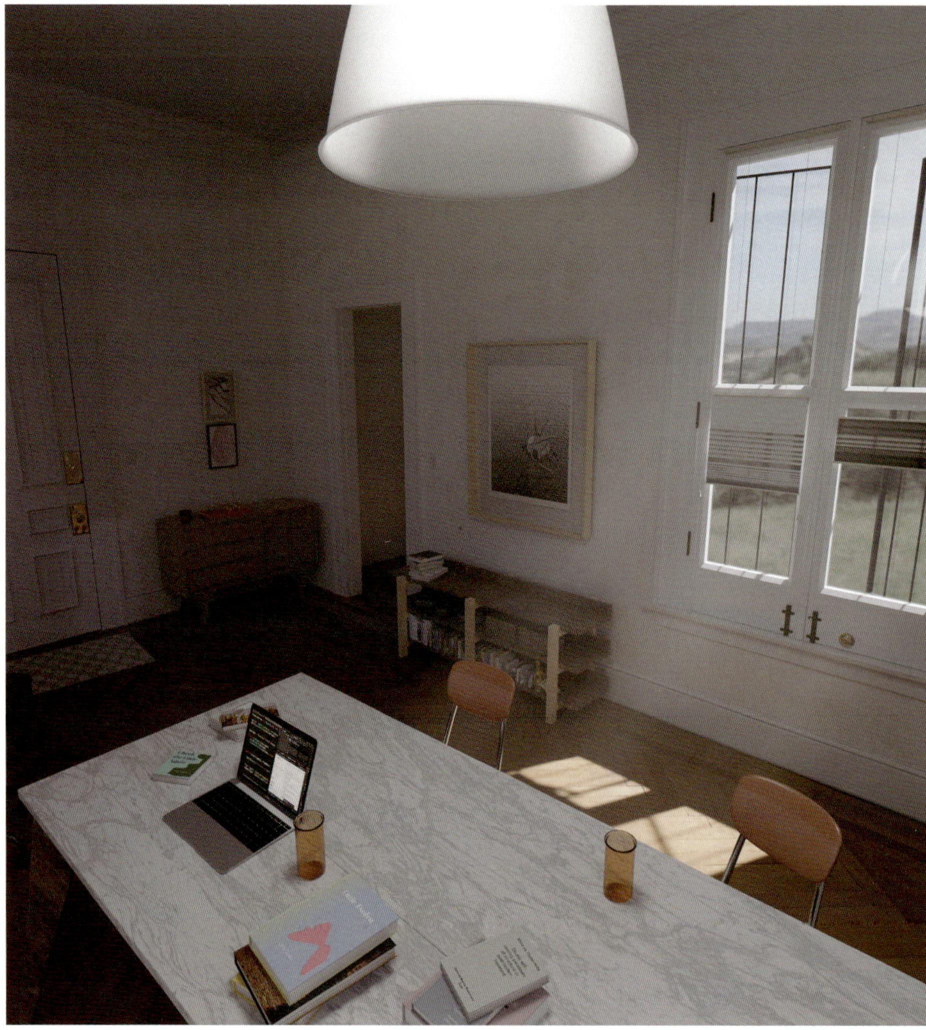

Almost but not Quite a Diorama: The Room, its Powers, and its Limits

A diorama is the spatial representation of another spatial scene viewed from the outside in. Dioramas represent something and they are something. They are meant to be viewed and are tools for viewing. This is fruitful territory for us, and as a result there are many ways to begin thinking about dioramas. An exhibit designer would begin with content, theme, or narrative. We're interested in the same, but we're also considering the nature of the diorama enclosure and frame. If possible, we'd like to consider the content and the enclosure as related components of the same element. This is consistent with the over-arching thesis of this project: that representation and architecture are always co-mingling and ultimately inseparable. Consider that a diorama shares some common traits with the image, the still life, the room, the stage, and the building. Each of those are elements themselves, but we can perform a kind of alchemy to transform any into a diorama. We'll begin with a room. In exploring the nature, power, and limits of the room we'll gradually begin to see how it relates to, and eventually how it can become, a diorama.

A room includes the content and atmosphere between its walls. An "empty room" is a special kind of room in which the absence of stuff itself becomes a descriptive quality. Whether a palpable absence or an entirely expected set of everyday content, the insides of a room are a gift to the renderer concerned with realism. Content is not just a matter of instantiation, but of evidence of human arrangement and rearrangement, of clutter, of staging, of collection. These all potentially contribute to a narrative, or in lyrical fashion suggest the formation of a narrative to be completed in the mind of the viewer. Material in the room is not merely a matter of being evidently made of material, but of material dimensions, wear, and age. Material is not something that gets applied to the room. It is the room. The atmosphere is material, artwork hanging on the walls are material, the book jackets are material. This framing of the room as material construct is admittedly the result of a desire to render the room.

The images exhibited here are digitally produced with the aid of software. Simulated rays bounce around and through objects. Along the way, data informs the light value, color, and the ray direction, but ultimately, each pixel in the rendered image is associated with some light or no light. The renderings can be understood as material as a function of light. With respect to the reading of the room, lighting is a connective agent. Lighting can come in—or appear to come in—from the outside thereby implicitly representing a world beyond the room. Later, we'll deal with light leaking into dioramas by way of the viewing surface as an architectural question, but for now we can focus on all the fluidic verbs often used to describe light: light spills in, light floods, and light washes. Although it is of course technically incorrect to ascribe material properties to light, atmospheric haze and small dust particles are effectively activated by light. These particles in the air are smaller than a pixel in the final image and often transparent. But those particles diffuse light rays, and the glare can itself produce optical artifacts that register within the limited resolution of the digital image. In some sense, these artifacts appear to be visible material light. As is often the case in this discourse, the rendering—simulated light—is indistinguishable from that which is rendered—the apparent materialization of light. Much of the material data referenced during this process is stored in images—texture maps, bump maps, etc. Thus, each rendering can also be understood as an image as a function of other images.

A disclosure is in order. The room described here is an interpretation of the room where most of this book was produced. This is a disclosure rather than a celebration because this room, and the author, are not the subject of this discourse. As was the case with the digital bonsai tree, the human agency of the crafting of the element is essential to the realism of the room. This is not meant to represent the author. Nor is it meant to represent the author's room, exactly. However, the human decisions and human algorithms in play here are essential. In some portions of the room, this is glaringly obvious: the casual stacking of books on the table, for example. Likewise, furniture, modeled loosely based on real furniture as viewed by the author in the existing space (or in some cases, from a catalog) is placed just as though it arrived off a moving truck. It looks like a human set those books on the table because a human set those books on the table. No "snap to grid" function was ever activated. "Lock ortho" was in most cases the enemy of this kind of casual realism. In other cases, human agency is less obvious.

The window blinds, for example, collapse and expand like an accordion. This material process is irregular, despite the fact that the blinds are machined and creased in precise increments. They've worn with age, and they don't collapse perfectly. In fact, a perfect (or perfectly calculated) logarithmic decay of striated density would look absurdly, and unrealistically artificial. Manually drawing "by eye" a gradually denser zigzag might seem surprisingly sloppy, but humans can be delicate, careful, and measured even when the software is asked to stop helping.

Each book cover, including the titles, have been systemically generated in a semi-manual way. This is risky from the perspective of labor: without a self-imposed cap on time, a book cover that is never seen in full in any rendering could consume an inordinate and wasteful amount of attention. On the other hand, duplicate books, or repeated clusters of pre-modeled books (of the kind available for free or cheaply online) tend to be reminders of the digital shortcuts in play. Theoretically, this is a salient example of the abstraction of digital craft increasing rather than diminishing human agency. It also suggests that every rendering is a crafted artifact, much more than a metaphorical polish over abstract digital content. There may not be a human figure visible in the rendering, but a human does figure into every rendering often in very visible ways.

To be clear, digital shortcuts are often welcome, but in this case, they are an unwelcome marker of the artificial. "Perfect realism," is of course an unattainable and philosophically circular pursuit. Even "photorealism" tends to be an operative principle rather than an absolute condition. Nonetheless, moments where manual craft, even and especially when unnoticed, prevent unwanted exposure.

"Exposure," which was just used to indicate the reveal of rendering technology, is also a term used by magicians to refer to the reveal of the technology, skill, or methods behind a magic trick. A kind of spoiler, in other words. We'll explore this in more detail in the context of dioramas, but we can note for now that with respect to rendering, exposure is something to be skeptical of. Except!—and with respect to reality there are always exceptions—exposure satiates a curiosity about methods. The x-ray view exposes the digital superficiality of that which, in the companion renderings, suggests material mass. This suggests that exposure may be more than the spoiler that ruins realism entirely. We can extrapolate further and suggest that most of this book is devoted to exposing and exploring digital technique. The compilation of flat book covers before their mapping onto 3-D form is one such overt exposure. Exposure there and elsewhere seeks to generate and disseminate knowledge.

Before transforming a room into a diorama, we should note, as a matter of fact: a room is not a stage. Its proportions and orientation do not and cannot conform to a viewing side. And of course, shifting the view to the "outside" when there is no world outside the room proves difficult. To do so would be, again, to suspend one aspect of realism. So as a first step, one wall is removed. Immediately, we can position the camera outside the room. The seeds of a diorama have been planted.

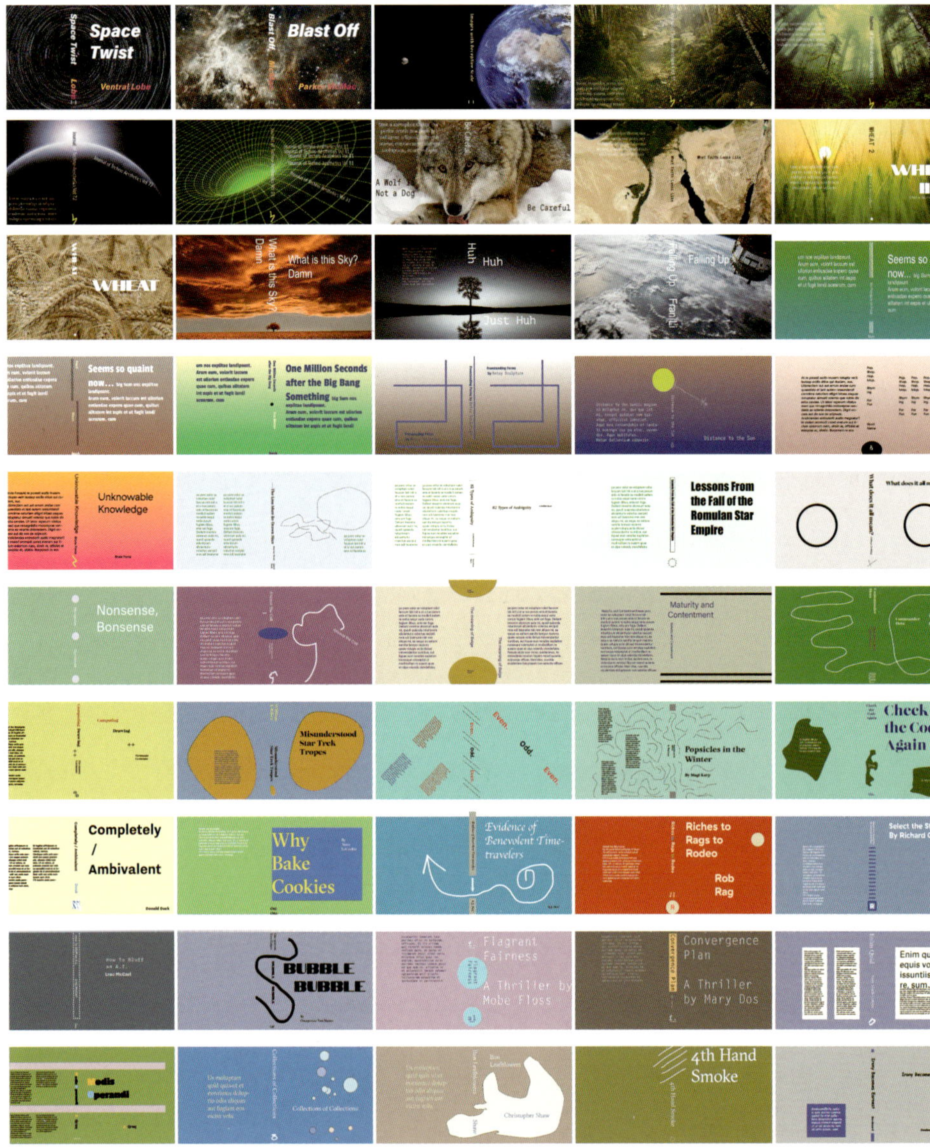

The database of hardbound book covers created for these renderings.

Right: The database of softbound book covers created for these renderings.

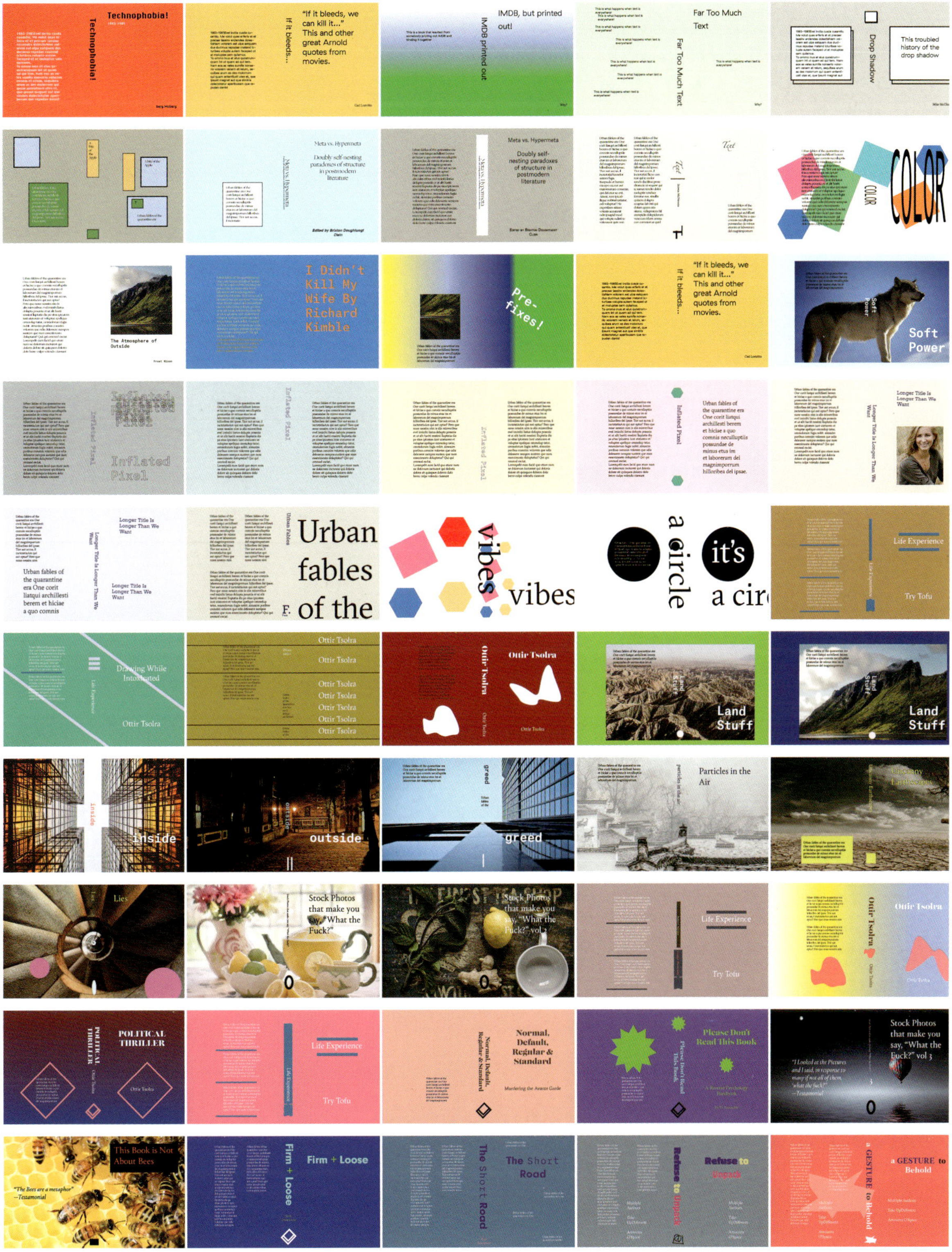
Technophobia!
"If it bleeds, we can kill it..." This and other great Arnold quotes from movies.
IMDB, but printed out!
Far Too Much Text
Drop Shadow
This troubled history of the drop shadow
Meta vs. Hypermeta
Doubly self-nesting paradoxes of structure in postmodern literature
COLOR
The Atmosphere of Outside
I Didn't Kill My Wife By Richard Kimble
Pre-fixes!
Soft Power
Inflated Pixel
Longer Title Is Longer Than We Want
Urban fables of the
vibes
it's a circle
Life Experience
Try Tofu
Drawing While Intoxicated
Ottir Tsolra
Land Stuff
inside
outside
greed
Particles in the Air
Lies
Stock Photos that make you say, "What the Fuck?"
POLITICAL THRILLER
Normal, Default, Regular & Standard
Please Don't Read This Book
This Book is Not About Bees
Firm + Loose
The Short Road
Refuse to
a GESTURE to Behold

EXERCISE

Model your space with every regard for detail and no regard for accuracy

Look at the room you work in most often. From that room, model and then render everything in and enclosing that space. Capture how things come together, fall, or are placed casually, exhibit signs of wear and damage, or are imperfect. Bevel sharp corners! Include outlets, cords, shades. Within your digital model perform an everyday activity like making the bed with a real cloth simulation, preparing dinner, and then washing the dishes, sorting all the objects on your table, etc.

All Apertures Become Dioramas

We can treat every aperture in this room as a receptacle for new dioramas. The apertures are already ripe for this kind of rendering. The room was modeled from the inside out, and the digital model essentially stops at the edge of the room. What's at and slightly beyond the windows serves the room. The room is not in the world, the room is the world. Every opening is more like a volumetric fixture than a portal. Thus, it's neither a technical nor conceptual leap to make the openings into discrete volumes with their own content facing the room.

Each new diorama is plugged into what was once a vague aperture. They are windows and doors to other worlds but are physically inaccessible—only our perception crosses into them. The room, now a kind of museum, is still as discrete if just a bit larger. Now real in a different way. One diorama creates a new opening in the ceiling and contains a cloud—fitting for an aperture seen when looking up, but nonetheless impossible in terms of gravity, time, dimension, and lack of infrastructure. The dioramas emit light, but indirectly. Light fixtures are hidden within each. Light interacts with modeled content and photographic backdrops, makes its way into the room and then to the camera. Light from each diorama leaks into the territory of other dioramas. This is minimized, but not eliminated.

Dioramas make the room less real in some ways and more real in others. The dioramas, when considered together, offer a heterogeneous collection of multiple realities. Seeing more than one at a time, as is readily possible from within the room, is to experience an unresolvable conflict between different scales, tones, and locations. This could be said to favor conditions suggesting contingent or local reality over a total reality. On the other hand, the room itself is only increasingly real. It's the realistic anchor against which the fictions of each diorama are read against. For this reason, the infrastructures of access prohibition are more than decorative. For example, the polite but stern retractable belts attached to strong stands were specified from the same catalog as interior architects would consult when designing the lines to an airport security screening threshold or the barrier that a bouncer opens and closes in front of the entry of a nightclub. Here, they seem to say, "do not cross" into the ocean wave diorama. Another diorama projects into the space and is buffered by a railing large enough to comfortably support a viewer while keeping them at bay. Yet another diorama is closable with a curtain. The curtain rod, like the other barriers, creates a threshold between room and diorama, but it also suggests that these dioramas can be closed for repair or replacement, a suggestion that is as fabricated as it is mundane.

Finally, it's important to note that the removed wall is also given the curtain treatment in anticipation that this room for dioramas will itself eventually become a diorama. The checkerboard grid answers the question: what should a surface look like when the other side is unseeable, but the surface itself is invisible? "Emptiness" is not the same as nothingness, so we turn to a software standard for representing transparency.[1]

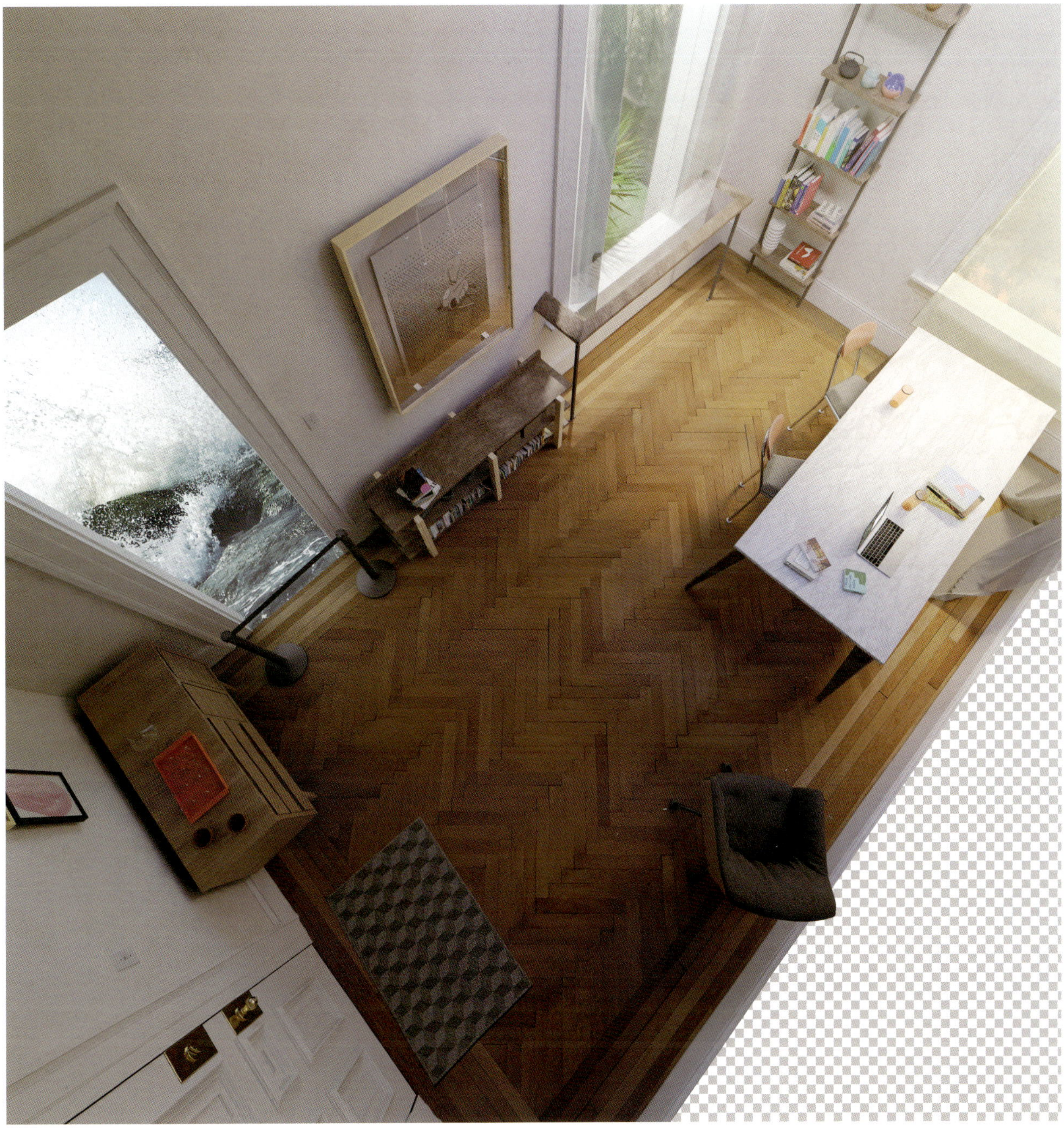

Viewed from the ceiling, the room in its new state is increasingly distant from its original mundanity.

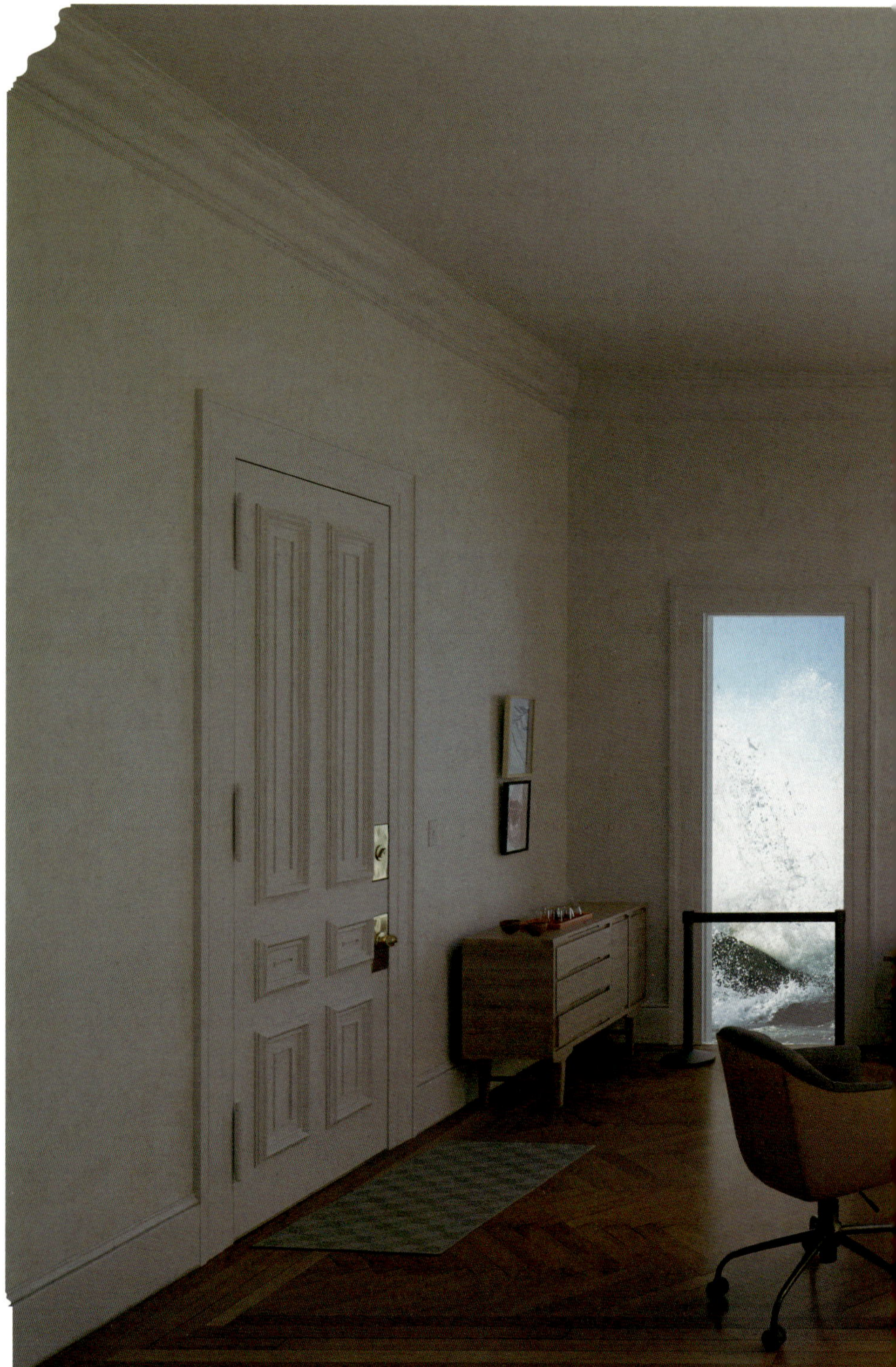

The other worlds—dioramas—are plugged into the portals at the ends of the room.

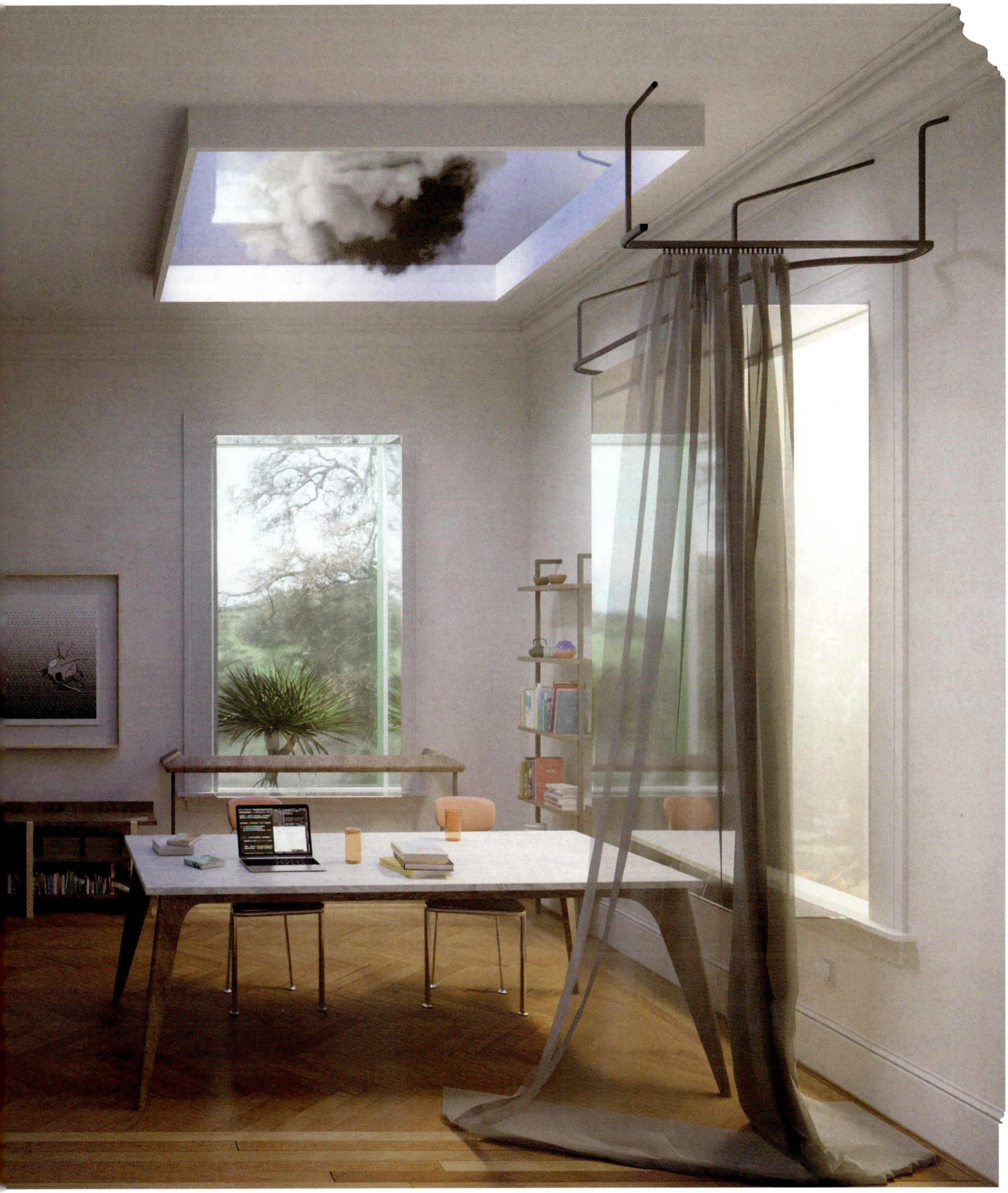

In anticipation of becoming a diorama, the right wall of the room is removed for viewing from the outside. From the inside, however, that wall must be articulated as nothing rather than background.

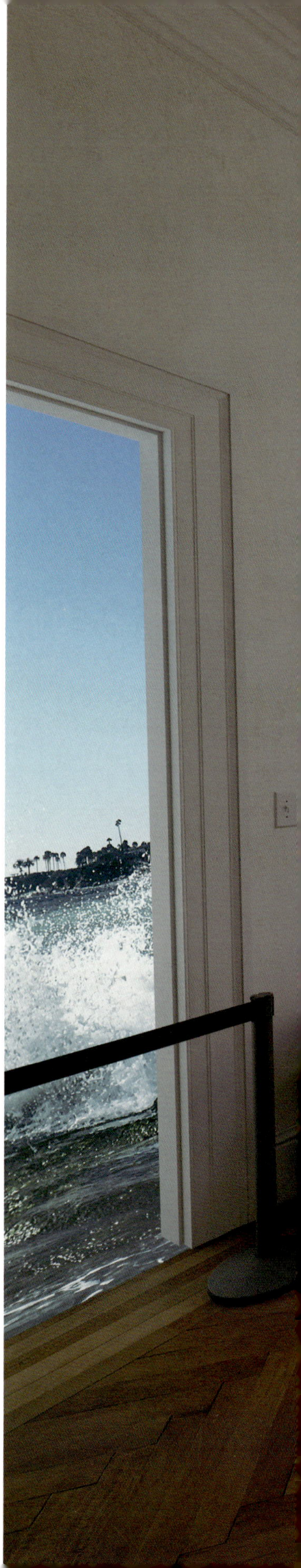

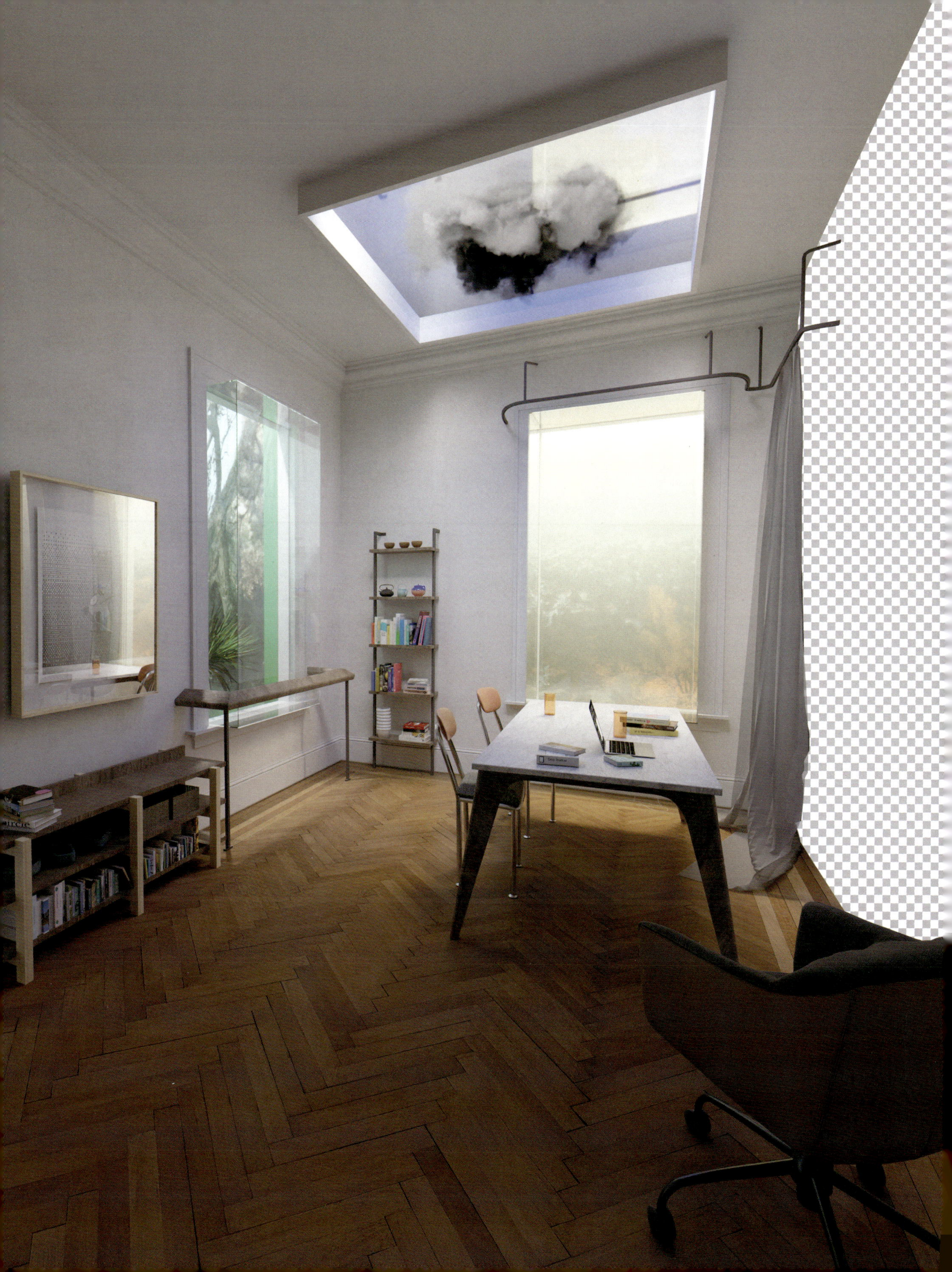

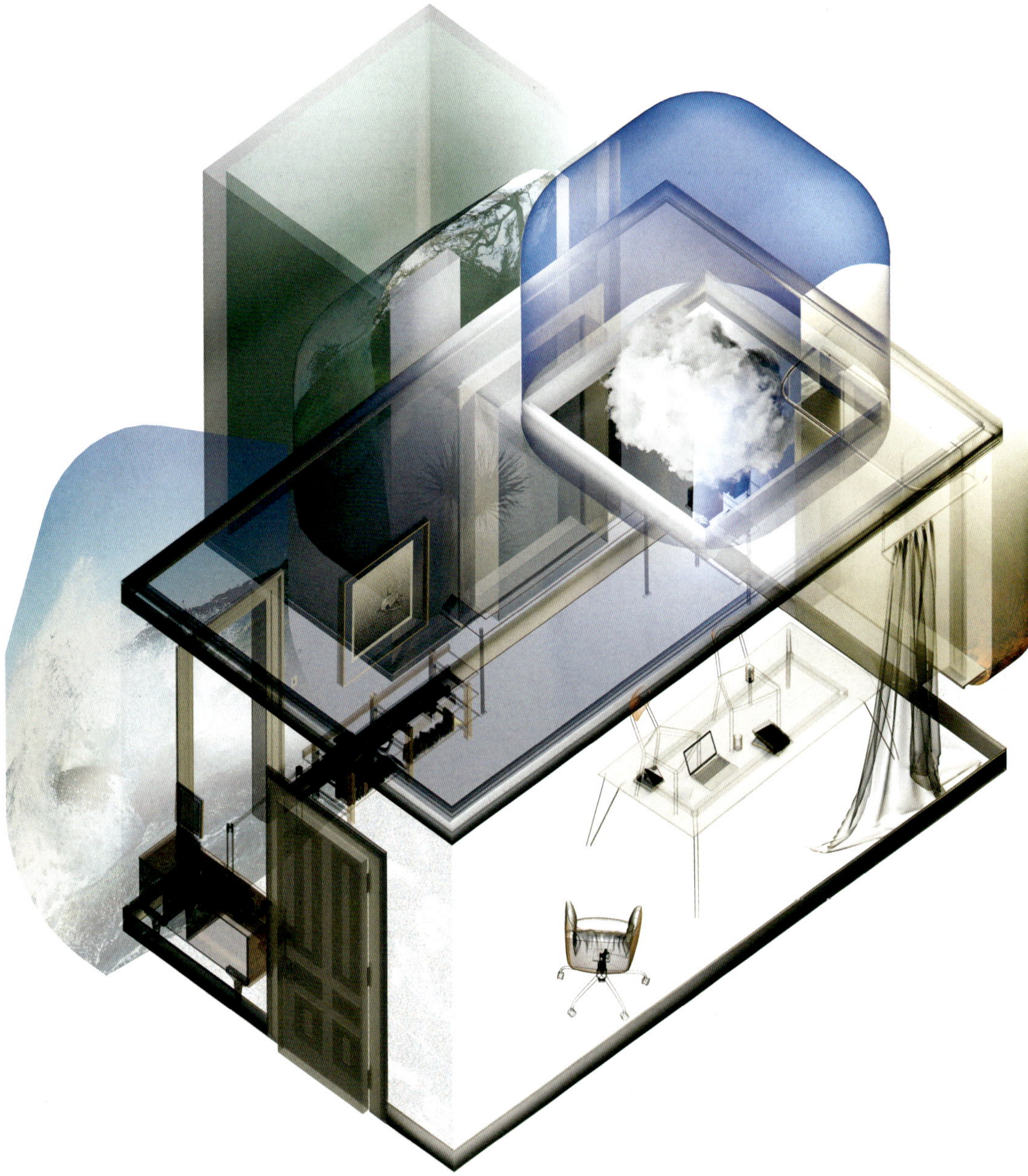

Dioramas often position the viewer as a voyeur. This translucent isometric exposes the digital geometry, but through a contrasting representational system.

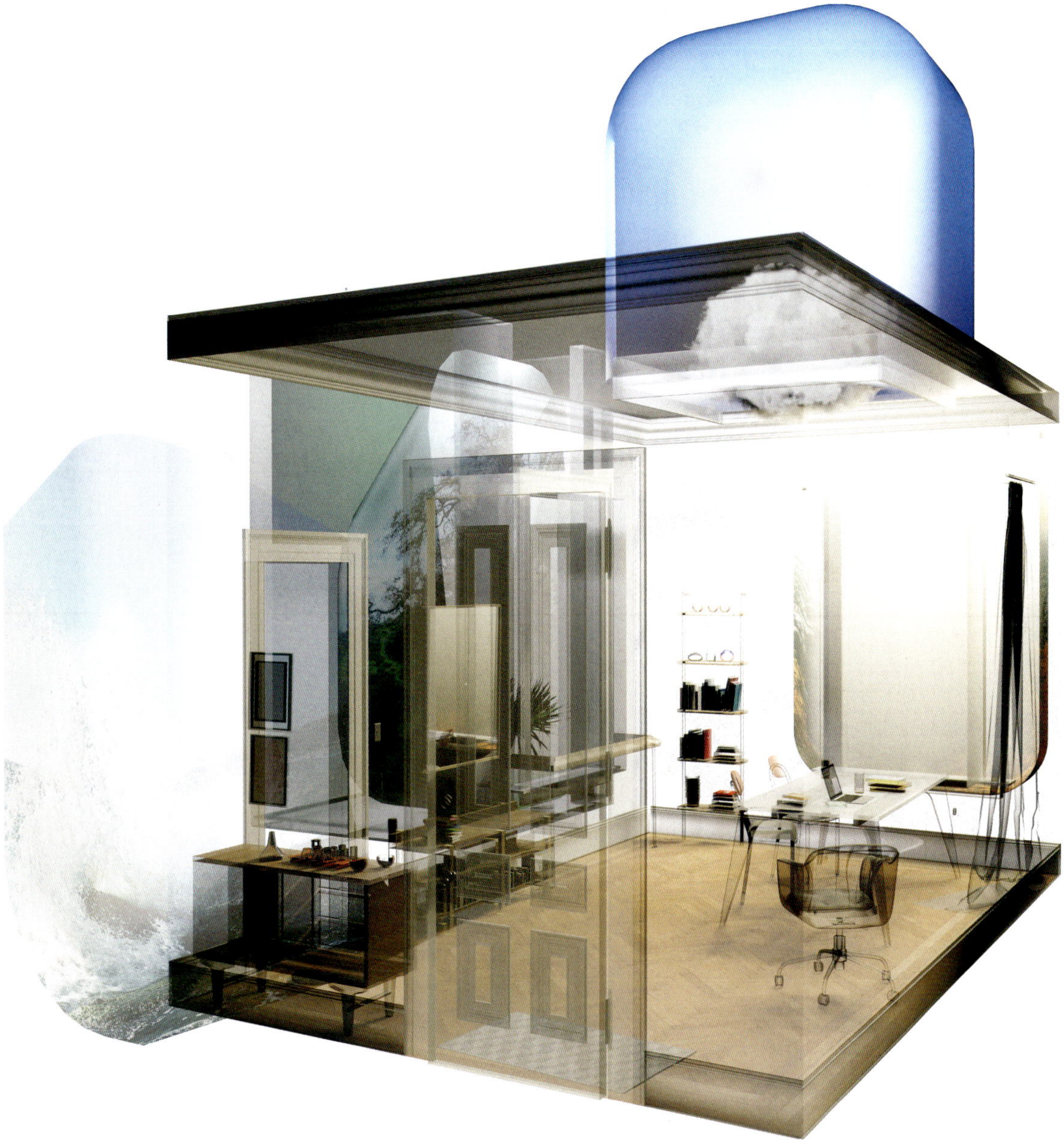

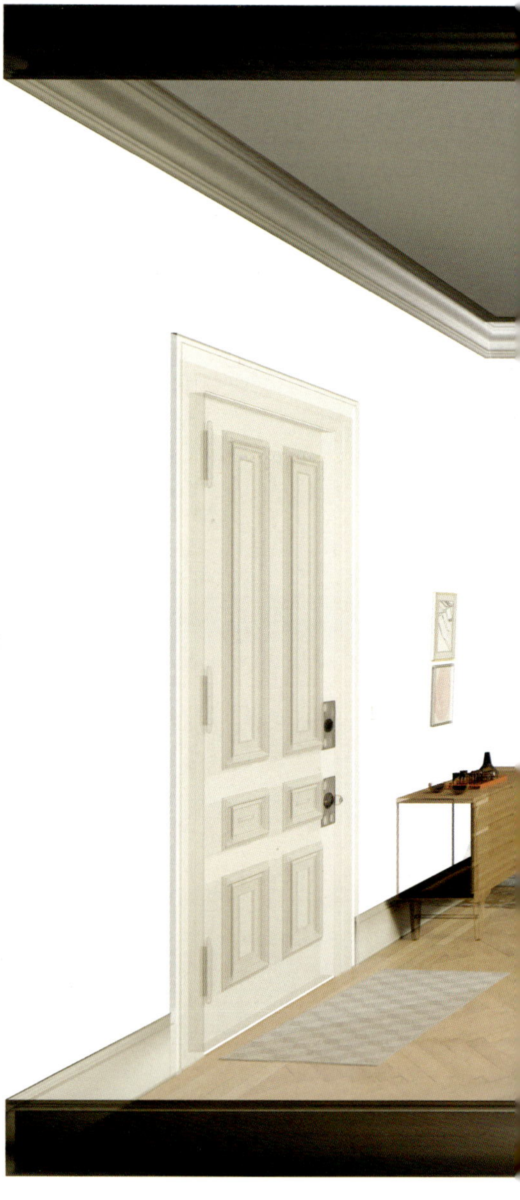

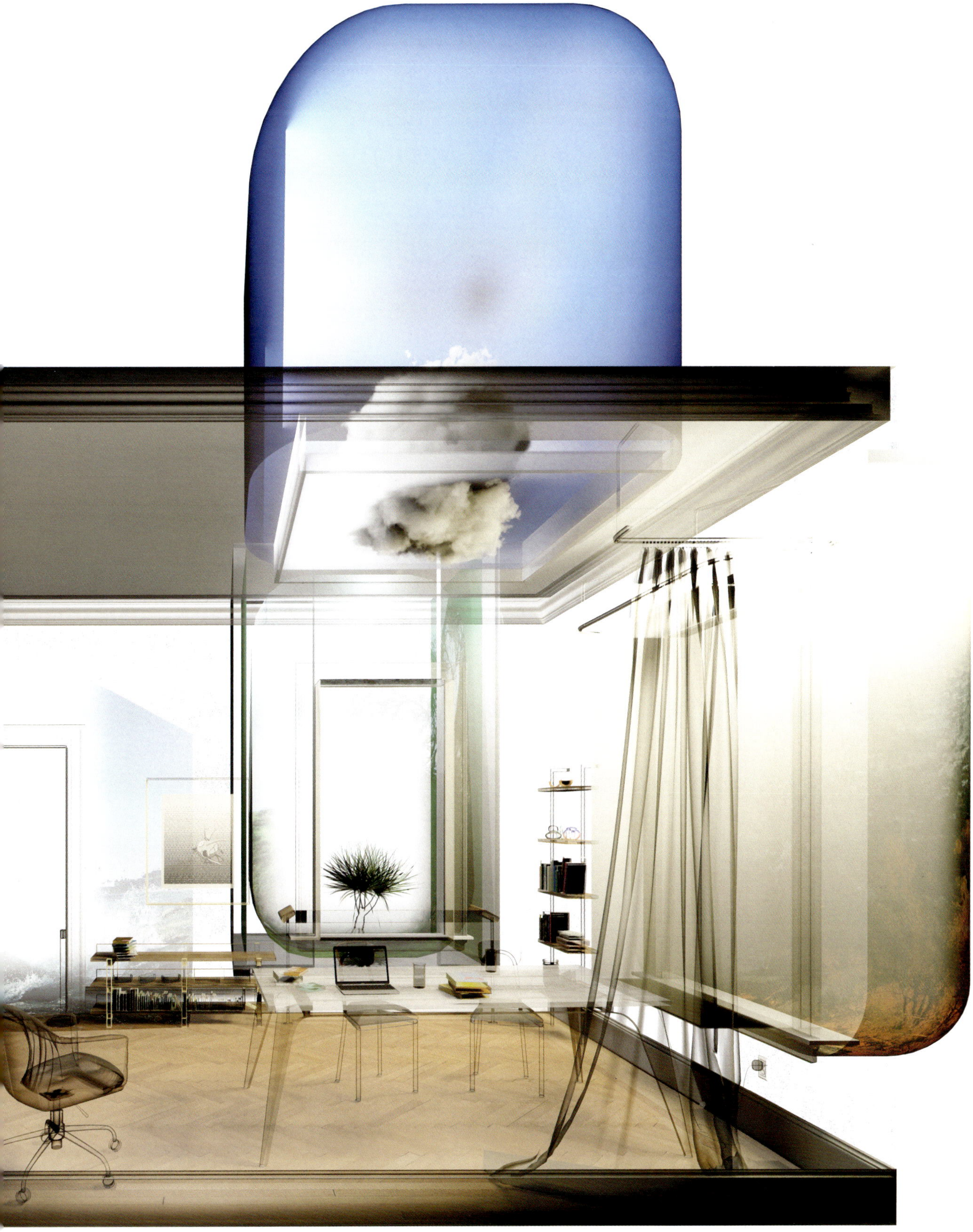

The Room as a Diorama

The full transition room to diorama is procedurally radical despite seeming quite modest upon first glace. Nothing is in the same position. The scale varies. The proportion of the represented room is different than the real room, which had already deviated from observed reality. Even the particles of dust in the air are sized with respect to how they might most productively appear rather than how large they should be. As was the case with the crafting of book covers, this process of re-modeling is algorithmically organized specifically deploying the limits of human perception. The diorama is essentially the result of modeling from memory. Deviations from the original are therefore expected and even welcome, as long as they provoke the uncanny rather than highlight a glaring discrepancy. This is all consistent with a defining quality of diorama: it can perfectly represent only up to but not beyond the point that it would cease to register as a diorama. Even the notion of a "perfect diorama" is a contradiction. Imagine, for example, a diorama that was infinitely deep—a portal to another world perhaps, like the dozens that have appeared throughout literature, TV, and film. There are almost too many to cite, but two particularly special ones come to mind: the first iteration of Star Trek's Iconian Gateways[2] and the portals made by "the Subtle Knife" in His Dark Materials.[3] These special thresholds are rendered with little or no frame and no telltale surface distortions at the "event horizon," the infinitesimally thin threshold between worlds. Even without the traditional glass barrier protecting a still life in front of a background that characterizes many natural history museum dioramas, the line between worlds is explicit and absolute. The truly perfect diorama converges with reality and therefore doesn't exist. All dioramas are imperfect and that's part of their appeal: they play a game of representation while telegraphing the nature of that representation.

For the same reason, a visible frame around the diorama is often invited to assume aesthetics of prominence. Like an elaborate frame placed temporarily in front of vaudeville circus acts, the frame doesn't blend with the content within the diorama, but it says something important about the content within the diorama: it's in a different reality. That reality shares space with us, but the architecture separates it. Interestingly, the Iconian Gateways were reprised in a later Star Trek series with much more traditional and ornate framing.[4]

In some sense, the renderings of the room made into a diorama are more like the room than the first renderings in this chapter. The relationship between the three rooms (the room within which the author sits, the room modeled and

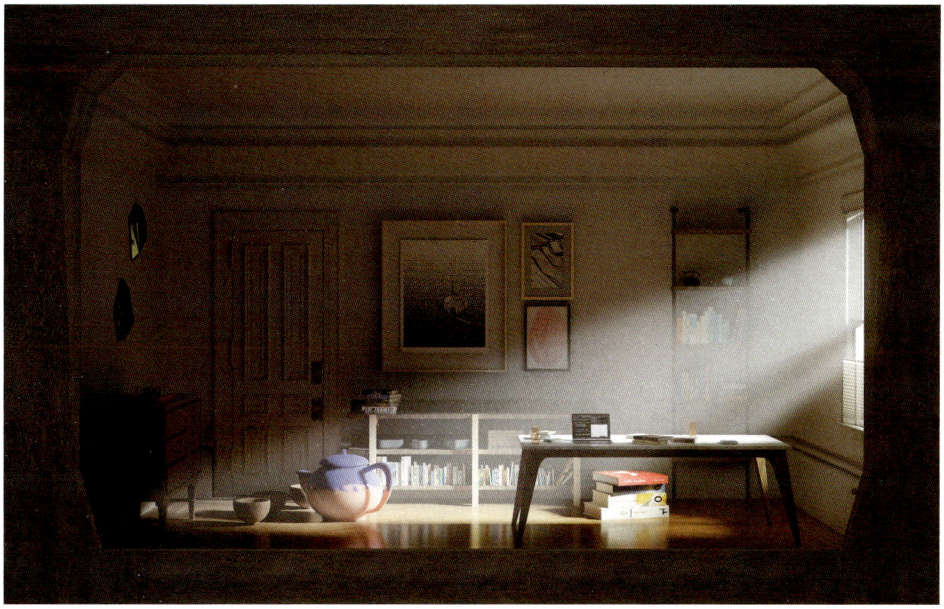

rendered, and the room re-modeled and re-rendered as a diorama) is triangular rather than linear. The flexibility of the diorama allows the salient and memorable features of the observed room to become naturally exaggerated. The result is not exactly a caricature. No abstraction is involved in the representation. The result is also not quite surreal. The reality-defying liberties are barely noticeable, at least at first, and certainly do not distort the laws of reality though they do push against the limits of normalcy in the creation of a strange condition.

Dioramas tend to be shallow, or shallower, than reality. In this way they share some qualities with the image, as has already been noted. Depth is a kind of capital, and it must be spent wisely. The room is no exception. This sets up another productive tension between depth that is artificially conveyed, as would be the case in any image exhibiting three-dimensional content, and depth that is modeled. Projection of light and image are possible inside the diorama and in the rendering of the diorama. Perceived depth is therefore in ample supply.

Now framed within the diorama, the room is recognizable, but completely different.

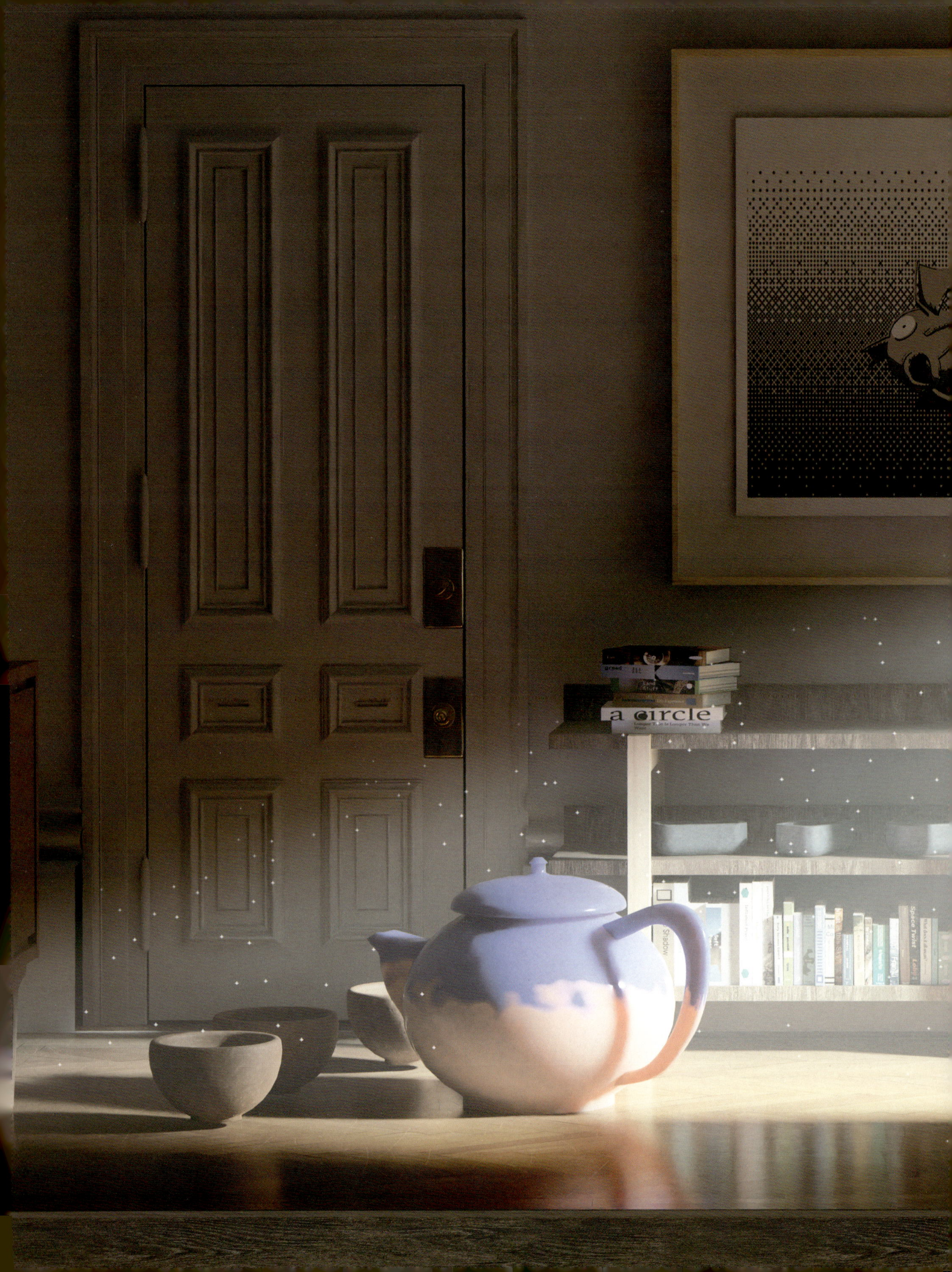
a circle

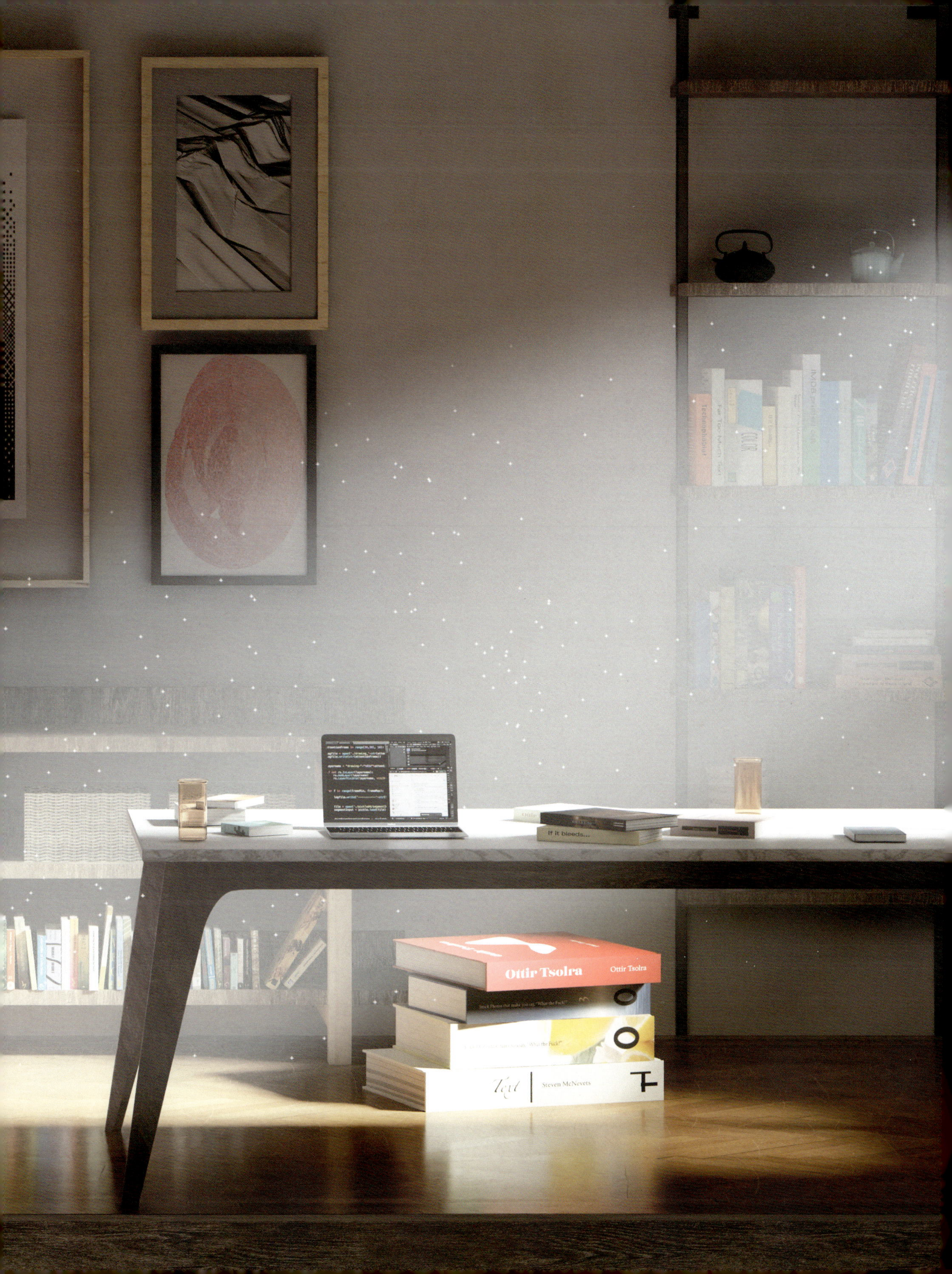
Ottir Tsolra
Ottir Tsolra
Text
Steven McNevets
If it bleeds...

EXERCISE

Model from Memory

Make a highly detailed digital model of a real space you know well, from memory. Avoid visiting the space during the process. Render the model and adjust the model based on the qualities you remember. As you're modeling, take note of which angles you tend to view the model from. Save a common view and construct a frame that assumes a human viewing the model from that position. Did that affect the scale of your model?

American Landscape as Diorama

The American landscape painting traditions are as problematic as they are interesting. Much of the work is a fascinating record of art and science's evolving understanding of reality, perception, and representation. Colonialism, Nationalism, and Technophobia are all tracible threads through nineteenth-century landscape painting that, broadly speaking, saw the influences of the Hudson River School and the Barbizon School disrupted by what art historians would label "tonalism" in a progression toward expressionism. Our inquiry is by no means novel from a historical perspective, but our transformative treatment of a painting by George Inness into a diorama nonetheless requires an awareness of a historic context. In some sense, we can position Inness and tonalism on a smooth gradient from realism to expressionism. We can see Inness's facture and the registration of atmosphere over object rooted in perception while clearly advancing from "realism" toward an interpretive position. But of course, this transition was rocky and contentious. Inness's sanity was questioned. Rachel Zaidy DeLue reflects on Inness's critical reception:

> Noisy, violent, rough, peculiar, strange, unpleasant, crude, perplexing, uncountable, impossible, incomprehensible, exceptional, fantastical, weird: what was it about Inness's landscapes that made them so unthinkable and difficult, that provoked, on the part of their critics, such a collectively troubles response? ...it was not just the uncharacterizable nature of Inness's pictures that concerned these writers. All of the critics I have cited responded to Inness's works by discussing them in terms of perceptual capacity: what they could see, what was difficult to see, what kind of seeing his paintings seemed to require, what his looking distorted, what appeared impossible or incomprehensible with regard to what was considered normal vision...Inness was, or at least seemed to be, a dedicated student of nature. Knowing, or at least expecting this...his critics had a right to be disturbed by pictures that purported to present "nature as it is," and at times did, but also (and often simultaneously) saw or imagined nature as it never could be; his critics had a right to be troubled by pictures that, above all, seemed to be the product of a distorted vision of things, the offspring of a malfunctioning eye.[5]

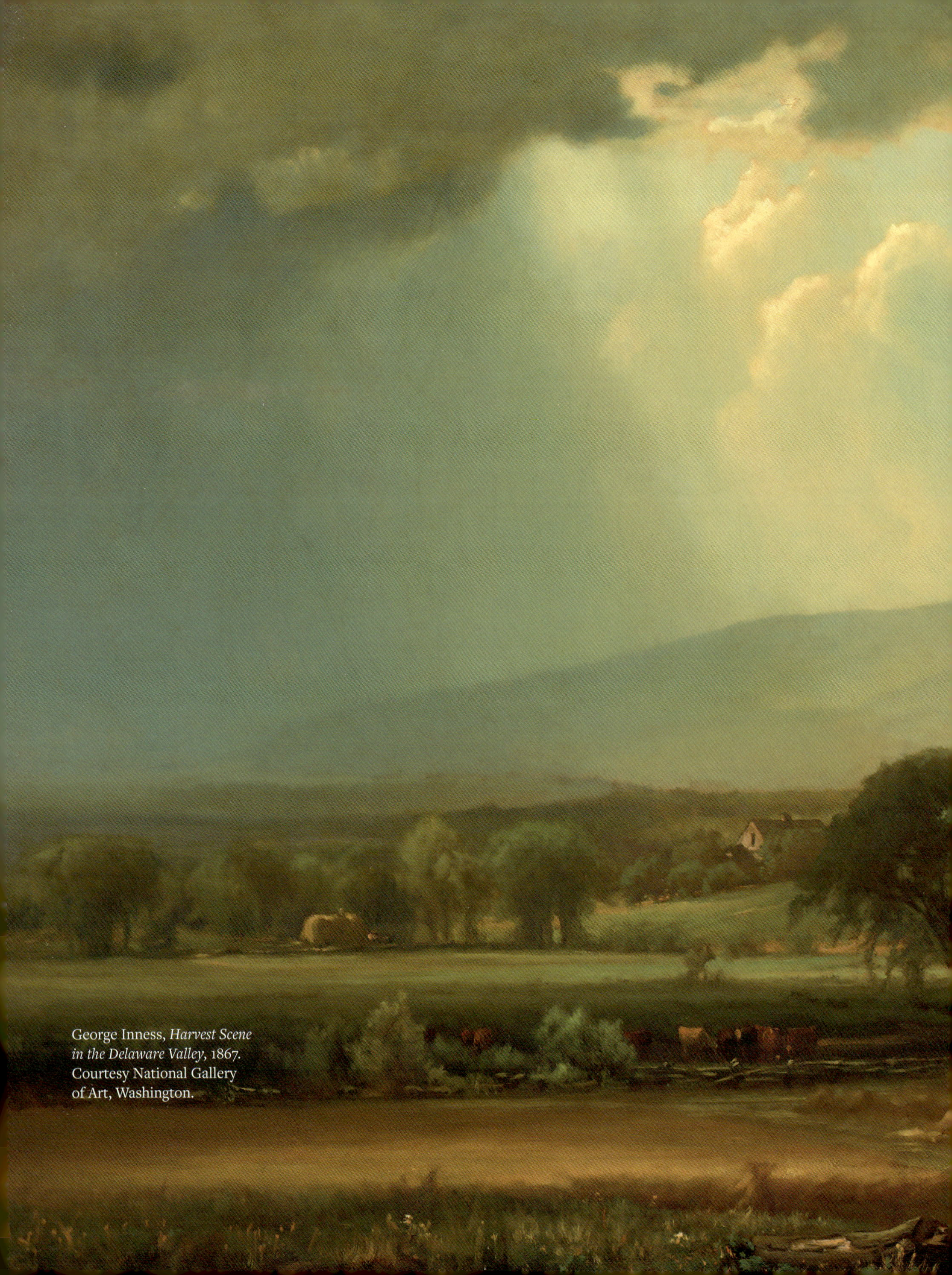

George Inness, *Harvest Scene in the Delaware Valley*, 1867. Courtesy National Gallery of Art, Washington.

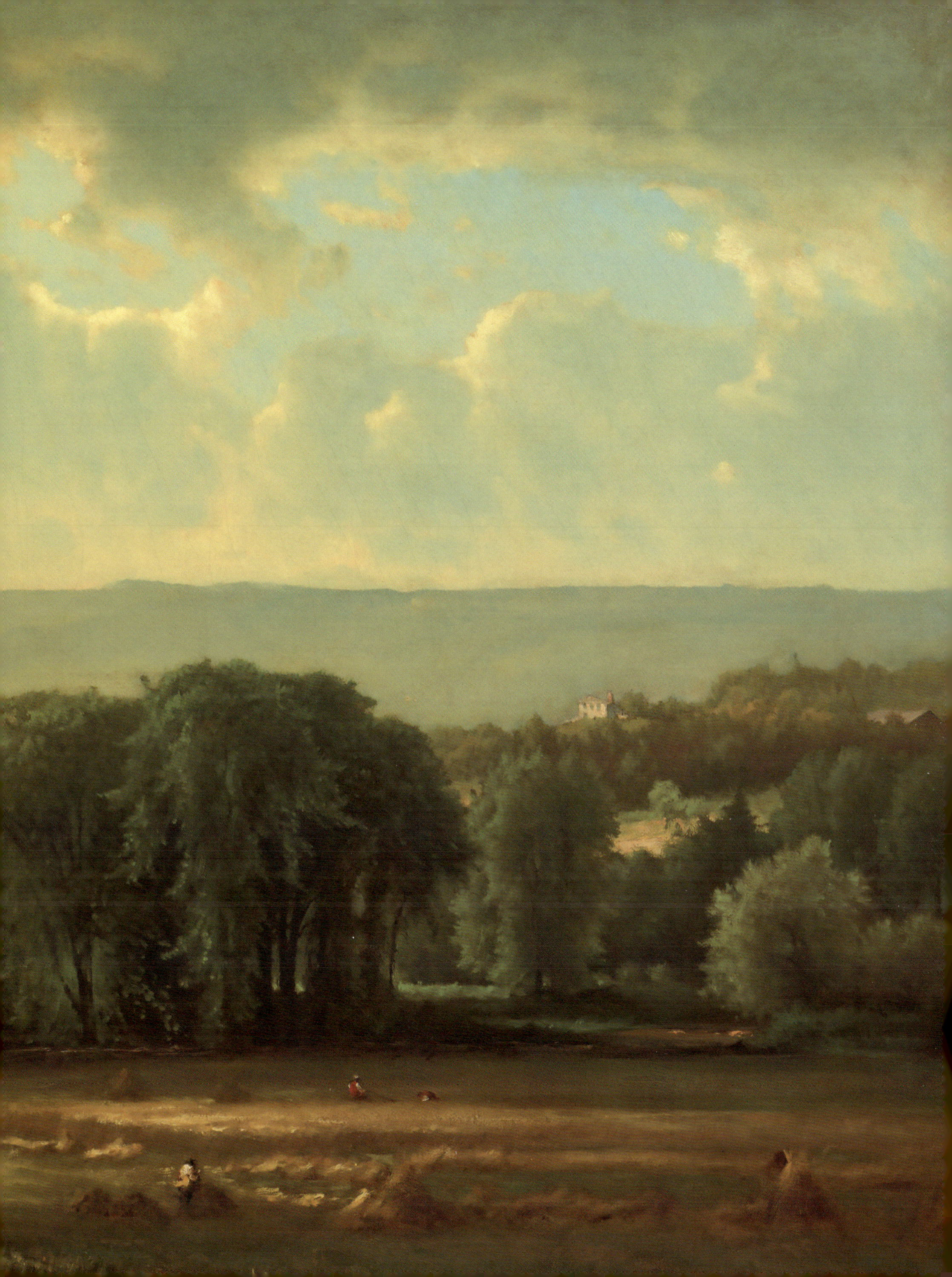

Inness was certainly not insane. DeLue agrees:

> Inness had a different sense of truth than did his critics, even those sympathetic to newer trends in art and who considered Hudson River School landscapes hackneyed and stale. Distortion and obscurity were, for him, strategic and essential components of his practice and… provide the very foundation on which he constructed his version of the real.[6]

Inness's reputation and posture poses a challenge to us. His calculated almost computational approach to reality is sympathetic to the contemporary diorama. Reality (or nature) is always processed on the way to being represented. Our contemporary opposition to accepting any representation as canonical requires our representation of his representation of nature to impose some critical weight. Can this tension be sustained in a diorama? If the claims about representation and its narrative potential are accepted, we ought to accept "yes" for at least a tentative answer.

The National Gallery of Art offers a publicly available database of high-resolution images of much of their collection that is now in the public domain. This allows re-publication and sampling. No use is misuse in this rights framework. Inness's Harvest Scene in the Delaware Valley,[7] is part of this collection. Inness's fondness for provocation is evident in his commitment to, for example, "the reality of the unseen,"[8] an endorsement, however unintentional, of his painting's future as a diorama. However, the diorama is as gentle and neutral a medium as the paint brush, which is to say, it's not neutral or gentle at all. Rather, the objective in this dioramafication is to appropriate the painting, to bring a degree of thickness in front of it that simultaneously extends content and compresses the painting explicitly into the backdrop. While the original painting is earnest and serious, the diorama is absurd in its digital hyper realism. The painting is durational almost like a long exposure photograph. The artist's long reflective gaze is sustained. The splashing fluid contrasts that durational quality by exhibiting a quick capture, like a photograph taken with an extremely fast shutter opening. Weather, atmosphere, and color are richly present in both realities. Perceptibly, there's an alignment of sorts, but the realities of nature completely clash, almost as if the diorama playfully mocks the painting. Inness's reaction to the diorama might even resemble how critics reacted to his more challenging works, with offense. The resulting diorama is not in the spirit of the any American landscape tradition, nor does it deny the agency of those traditions. The implicit rhetoric that emerges is fueled by this tension. The painting alone is a matter of art history. The digital content alone would resemble a cartoon or a technical example of digital rendering techniques. Together, they fuse to create an element that looks obliquely at its own origins. Does a political message come through? No such claim is made. However, if a diorama is an apparatus for seeing a constructed reality, this work intends the act of seeing to disrupt any notion of a stable cannon, even and especially as elements of that very cannon are purported to serve as an authority on seeing. Perhaps this modest gesture is the beginning of an agenda playing out through the act of representation. Or perhaps the act of rendering a previously finished work in a manner that breaks it open is more political than it might seem.

Representation that depicts and transforms the perception of place often requires a "suspension of disbelief"[9]—the temporary setting aside of one's awareness that a film is a film so as to willfully immerse oneself in the drama and effects on screen. Mistakes such as the briefly visible Starbucks cup in a scene of Game of Thrones[10] inhibit the suspension of disbelief. While this concept is rarely applied to painting, it is meaningful in our discourse about dioramas and for American landscape paintings as well as contemporary approaches to disrupted realism. The relatively large Harvest Scene in the Delaware Valley canvas would seem to invite the viewer to step close and see the landscape through the eyes of Inness. Contemporary work by Radu Belcin, Mia Bergeron, and Alex Kanevsky all come to mind with respect to the contrasting deployment of selective or variable realism in which the medium of paint on canvas competes with the detailed articulation of human figures. All three artists are featured in John Seed's Disrupted Realism[11] folio, which is curiously subtitled Paintings for a Distracted World. Distracted in this context is less a critique of the audience's attention, but a reflection on the multivalent nature of contemporary visual perception. It also suggests that the work by these artists might be participating in the reclamation of attention by making breaches in realism legible subjects within the work. Where they break their own conventions, they do so in manners that remind the viewer that they are looking at paint on canvas. In a sense, this is suspension of disbelief in reverse. One can imagine their work as a kind of diorama that selectively acknowledges and exaggerates the walled enclosure in a way that traditional dioramas in a natural history museum, for example, would avoid. Dioramas often make their own implicit request for suspension of disbelief. As we've already discussed, dioramas themselves are never invisible. They can't recede. They remind the viewer of the fabricated nature of the realism within. This condition is either repressed or accentuated. In the Harvest Scene in the Delaware Valley diorama, the contradicting realities push the viewer literally and conceptually outside the landscape to view its structure and nature as well as its content. Though perception is intact, ambiguity is inescapable.

Digital natural artifacts invade reality of *Harvest Scene in the Delaware Valley* as it is transformed into a diorama.

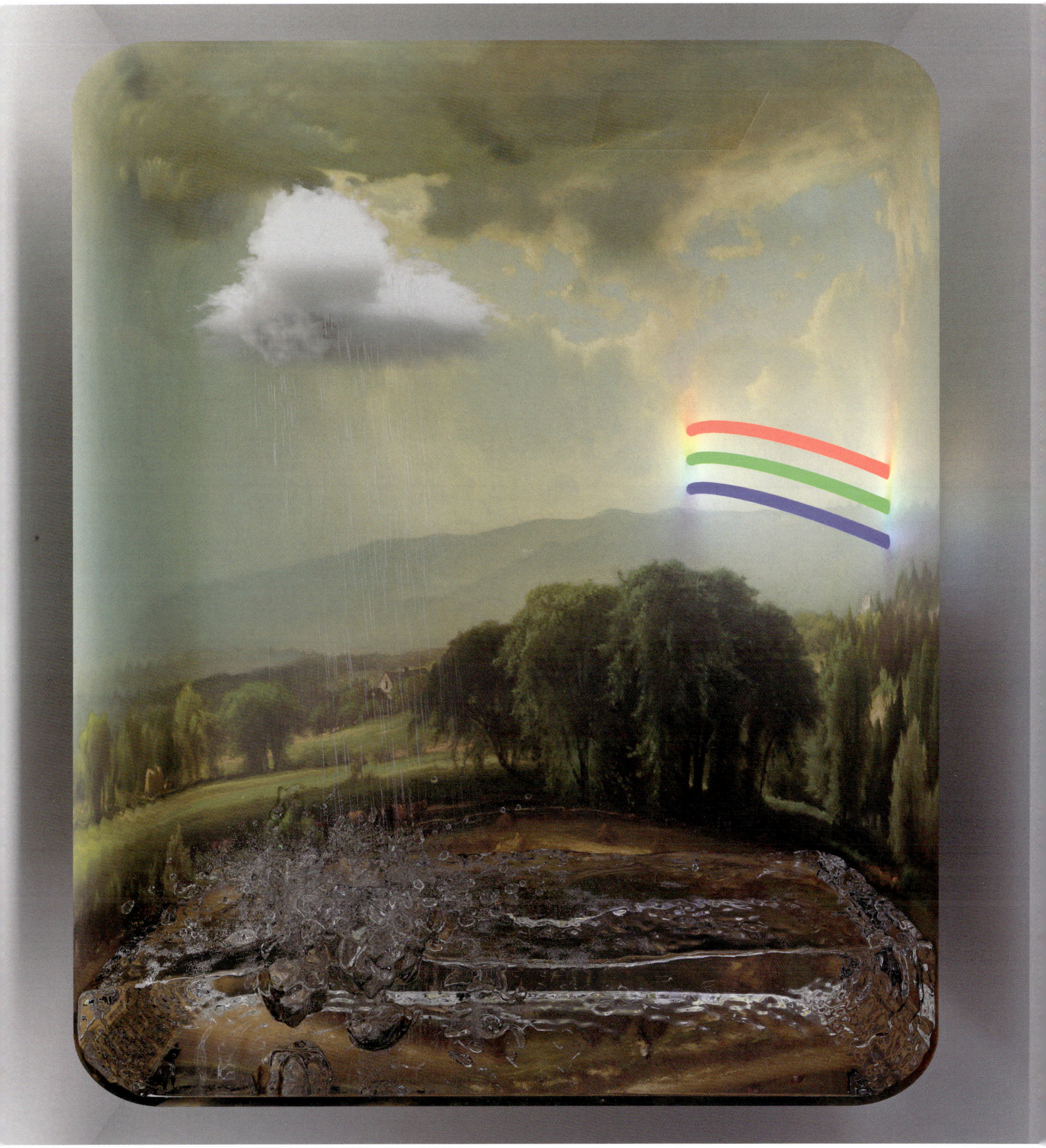

Like (Performed) Magic

The comparison between design and magic is not common. Our work and this discourse regularly slips and flows between architecture, design, and art, but magic sits far afield. Magic as extended metaphor, however, is obviously productive, especially with respect to dioramas and their multivalent ambiguities. With that in mind, we can define magic as a discipline concerned with realism. Magic theory even has a term, "intention of reality,"[12] to describe the behavior of a magician in terms of words, body language, and attention so as to match the conception of reality that is necessary to establish the perception of magic. Jamy Ian Swiss, whose book Devious Standards[13] will be quoted from extensively, is a figure analogous to bonsai artist Peter Chan who features prominently in the third chapter of this book. Both are creative intellectuals who theorize, criticize, and editorialize via their creative practice. Swiss, for example, often performs magic during conference style talks about magic.[14] Another magician, Michael Webber, often does the same. In one talk, in a transition between a performance and his theoretical ruminations, Webber explains:

> Since tonight is really a talk, a conversation, I don't want there to be any misunderstanding about what this is that I am really doing. So as much as I work in a show to try and make my stuff look and feel really real, I don't want anyone in this room to walk out thinking that what you saw on stage really really happened. I mean, what you saw really happened, but it didn't really happen...My goal is to entertain through mystery and to leave my spectators in a sense where they want to challenge their own certainty.[15]

Swiss further unpacks "intention of reality" in the context of a "false transfer" of a coin from one hand to another in a vanishing trick:

"As with almost any false transfer, we would look at the displayed coin first, then glace up at the audience during the false transfer, then look down at the imaginary coin." Swiss even uses the metaphor of art and "rendering" to elucidate an explanation of magic by writing, "our thinking, and our technique, must be rendered not merely transparent, as in other arts—the brush strokes of a painter, the fingering of a musician—but in fact must be reduced to absolute invisibility."[16]

Most modern magicians accept and convey the premise that they have no divine or supernatural powers. "Real magic" is in the mind of the viewer and depends on a shared conception of the rules of reality. Magicians enter into an implicit contract with their audience whereby the audience accepts that they will be lied to, deceived, and subjected to a false and contrived view of reality. Magic is thus a kind of willful cognitive dissonance: knowledge about reality is in conflict with the perfection of reality. Rather than question reality, we logically accept that the modern conception of magic has taken place. According to magician Jim Steinmeyer, "A magic performance consists of a collection of tiny lies, in words and deeds, that are stacked and arranged ingeniously to form the battlement for an illusion. It's a delicate battle of wits—an audience that welcomes being deceived, then dares to be fooled, alternatively questioning, prodding, and surrendering."[17] All the while, the magician is performing with a deep empathy to the audience. The magician must do more than practice, they must practice watching magic with the kind of skepticism, curiosity, and awe of a non-magician. Swiss agrees writing, "I learned as an adolescent that it's best to watch a magic show twice: once as my best imitation of a layman, suspending my critical faculties to the best of my ability in order to try to 'see' the magic; then a second time as a magician, fully exercising my expertise concerning method."[18] A post-modern trend is also articulated within magic theory in which the exposure of a trick can be choreographed within a meta trick. A trick within a trick, in other words. This is not exactly the same as the representations of representations that fill these pages, but is perhaps aligned with our interest in gleaning transferable knowledge from creative practice. Unpacking four magic terms will help us explore this extended metaphor further. Two such terms, "exposure" and "method" have already been mentioned, but we'll explore them in more detail. The others: "over-proving" and "flashing" are also common terms that become uniquely interesting and relevant to us in the disciplinary context of magic.

Exposure, the act of revealing some or all of the secrets behind the trick, is ethically complicated in the world of magic. Magicians are understandably sensitive about exposure because their livelihood depends on a degree of secrecy about their methods. Artists, designers, and architects likewise develop their own, sometimes proprietary, methods. At one time, publicly revealing the methods behind common magic tricks was considered taboo. Imagine how ruthless it would be to stand at the front door to a magic performance offering to expose—and spoil—all the tricks that the magician was about to perform. And yet, it is almost never this straightforward. The reasons why exposure is complicated reveals another key term, "methods." Exposure of the methods is not the same as exposing the trick. In the same way that rendering software is necessary but not sufficient to create a compelling rendering, the method alone is insufficient to construct a compelling magic trick. The aforementioned Jamy Ian Swiss devotes a whole chapter to the difference between the method and the trick. He repeats, "the method is not the trick," at least a dozen times throughout the chapter. In his own words, "the method is part of the foundation—albeit a significant part—on which a mystery must be carefully constructed...most methods, in and of themselves, are far too coarse to rely on in creating such a demanding and fragile composition as thoroughly magical experience."[19] The method is the technology or the core skill of the trick. But it does not constitute the trick. Ultimately, therefore, it can be argued method is neither proprietary nor precious. Swiss even later recounts multiple scenarios in which he or another magician performed a trick, exposed the methods, and performed the trick again to equal or even more success.[20] In the world of speculative architecture, the trick or magical performance here is akin to the work, whether it be image, drawing, building or project. To extend the method/trick distinction, we might note that our methods, the foundational techniques or actions that must occur, include common algorithms, the infrastructure of the diorama, the tools we make and deploy, as well as the software functionality that we depend on. We need these things, but these things alone do not constitute the work. Let's consider the dilemma that computational artists face when asked, "Can I see the source code?" To answer "yes" is generous and reflects the treatment of the code as a method. Access could be given without fear the work would be undermined by others knowing the methods. Sometimes this access might emerge out of a sense that the code itself is not the intellectual property of the artist, but the result of algorithms that have been used and re-used by dozens if not hundreds before them. To answer "no" is also likely a generous answer but reflects the treatment of code as the trick or the performance. In this understanding, revealing it would undermine both the work and the curious party.

Swiss and many other magicians lament the loss of the layperson. In the age of the internet, almost everyone knows a little about magic, just as everyone knows at least a little about digital media. Think of the colloquial use of "Photoshop" as a verb, for example. Thus, exposure is a relative term. Being aware of a broad type of method and even having read a bit about the specific method is not the same as knowing the method. Many contemporary magicians have adapted to this "everybody is a magician" fact of modern life. While the hypothetical perfect layperson is still an appealing ideal, it is not a prerequisite for the successful performance of magic. Likewise, the premise of a diorama surprises no one. However, the awareness of artificiality and the existence of a painted backdrop does not undermine the value of the diorama. To extrapolate further, the pursuit of a new reality is not completely failed if the viewer is aware of the pursuit. This has always been true in the world of art as well as the world of magic. What's evolved is the complexity with which we articulate sustained interested ambivalence for reality-bending art forms even as our grasp on reality remains fixed. We can even empathize with and look forward to the skeptic who may appreciate the execution. Finally, we can train like magicians and repeat the same work over and over until it becomes nearly perfect, or it evolves into something else.

"Flashing" is the act of accidentally revealing the method of a magic trick while performing the trick. This is to be avoided. Let's consider the "double lift" in a card trick. The method involves removing two cards from the deck when it appears that only one card has been removed. Swiss devotes an entire chapter of Devious Standards and roughly 30 pages to multiple double lift methods that, when performed may last much less than one second. It is fascinatingly "insider" discourse on the magician's craft and the culture that is cultivated by teaching and learning that craft. The novice reader's appreciation for card tricks will have been completely unaffected by Swiss's exposure in "A Dissertation on the Double Lift."[21] However, if during a performance, the magician makes a mistake and the method fails—let's say the cards separate and are splayed apart in a way that makes it apparent that two are being held—this would constitute a flash.

Flashes usually happen in the moment, which is one distinction from exposures. But in another sense, the difference between a flash and an exposure is a matter of intention and narrative. In the world of dioramas and representation, we might think about a flash as a flaw that triggers the unwelcome reveal of digital artificiality. A diorama flashing itself would involve, for example, the unintentional backdrop peeling off of the back wall, a visible seam in a texture map, or even evidence of JPEG compression in an overly reduced image. Flashes can destroy a sense of reality. In magic and in architectural representation, however, faux flashes can be deployed for a sense of meta reality. Imagine a trick in which a magician constructs an apparent flash and thus fails to identify or find the correct card in a deck. The humorously self-effacing magician says, "Oops! sorry! Something must've gone wrong, let me try that again." The trick fails again, in different way. The trick continues to fail 46 more times until four cards remain. Finally, all four cards are revealed, and they are all the matching card![22] This was a trick made up of failed tricks—different than a trick within a trick and a kind of hyper-real impossible reality. The same happens with and around dioramas. Consider the diorama-flashing photography of Richard Barnes, who reveals crates, tape, plastic wrap, maintenance, humans, cleaning, and constructions in a way that could be said to betray the "trick" of the diorama in meta-realist fashion. Barnes is the subject of Susan Yelavich's essay, "Death and the Museum," which notes of Barnes's photographs of dioramas under repair:

> Barnes removes the "pardon our appearance" signs and interrupts our suspension of disbelief...Such behind-the-scenes images aren't a critique of the diorama. In fact, Richard [Barnes] prizes the nineteenth-century, low tech diorama, with its truly uncanny verisimilitude... The contemporary museum seems to have lost confidence with the diorama's power to convince and often overcompensates by tricking it out with special affects...their wardens say they are mirroring their visitors' short attention spans...In attempting to eradicate the uncanny and dispel out uncertainties, the museum risks flattening the experience of encounter. Wonder is muted. Temporality is masked. The impact of death is sequestered within a label. Quietly, even respectfully, Richard Barnes's photographs beg to differ. They champion the beautiful uncanny.[23]

In a footnote, Yelavich also offers a relevant historical fact, "The diorama was patented in 1822 by Louis Daguerre, the same Frenchman who invented the daguerreotype."[24]

Barnes's flashing (an admittedly odd verb to associate with a photographer) according to Yalavich is not exactly a violation of the magic in the true sense of a magic "flash," but a pivot that can be said to earnestly reaffirm the value of the original even as it violates the secrets of its methods. We must now confront the fact that the line between an exposure and a flash is quite blurry. Yelavich asserts that Barnes's work is quiet and respectful. It's earnestly and patiently ironic. We've noted already how removing the suspension of disbelief can focus critical attention without arms-length distance from the work. It may be more apt to conclude that the stripping of suspension of disbelief opens the door for an injection of critical attention into the work. This is productive in the sense that the author, as well as the audience, is influenced by the flash. In that sense, a flashed trick leads to the generation of a new trick.

"Over-proving" can happen in magic, in baking, in an elaborate lie, and in representation. Famously, Shakespeare addresses this in Hamlet. Queen Gertrude, when declaring, "The lady doth protest too much, methinks,"[25] takes issue with the intensity of the assertion of truth in Hamlet's play within the play—a diorama of sorts. The same can occur when a magician makes a scene of showing nothing up the sleeves. It can backfire. Swiss again offers a salient example. "In our earliest days of magic, we find ourselves saying, 'Here I have an ordinary pack of playing cards.' And this promptly leads to our first lesson in not making unimportant things important: We are quickly corrected by our elders, and instructed that we must never say, 'Here I have an ordinary pack of playing cards,' because this statement of the obvious is counterproductive to our purpose. Instead of proving innocence, it raises suspicion."[26] In digital representation, the classical reality-based over-prove might be the lens flare, dust in the air, or over the top wear in a wall. The lesson for digital artists, designers, and architects is to rein in on the subtleties that constitute triggers of reality—the beveled corners, the surface imperfections, and, yes, even the lens flares, to the extent that they are almost unnoticeable. Deploy them, but not to the extent that they are the subject of the diorama. Certainly keep them in play. Dismissing them altogether is as flawed as avoiding digital media because of the risk of digital flashings.

A rendering of the *House of the Woodland* by WOJR treats the beams, walls, floor, and ceiling as components of a diorama. Here, the building is not the subject of the rendering, but the container of the subjects.

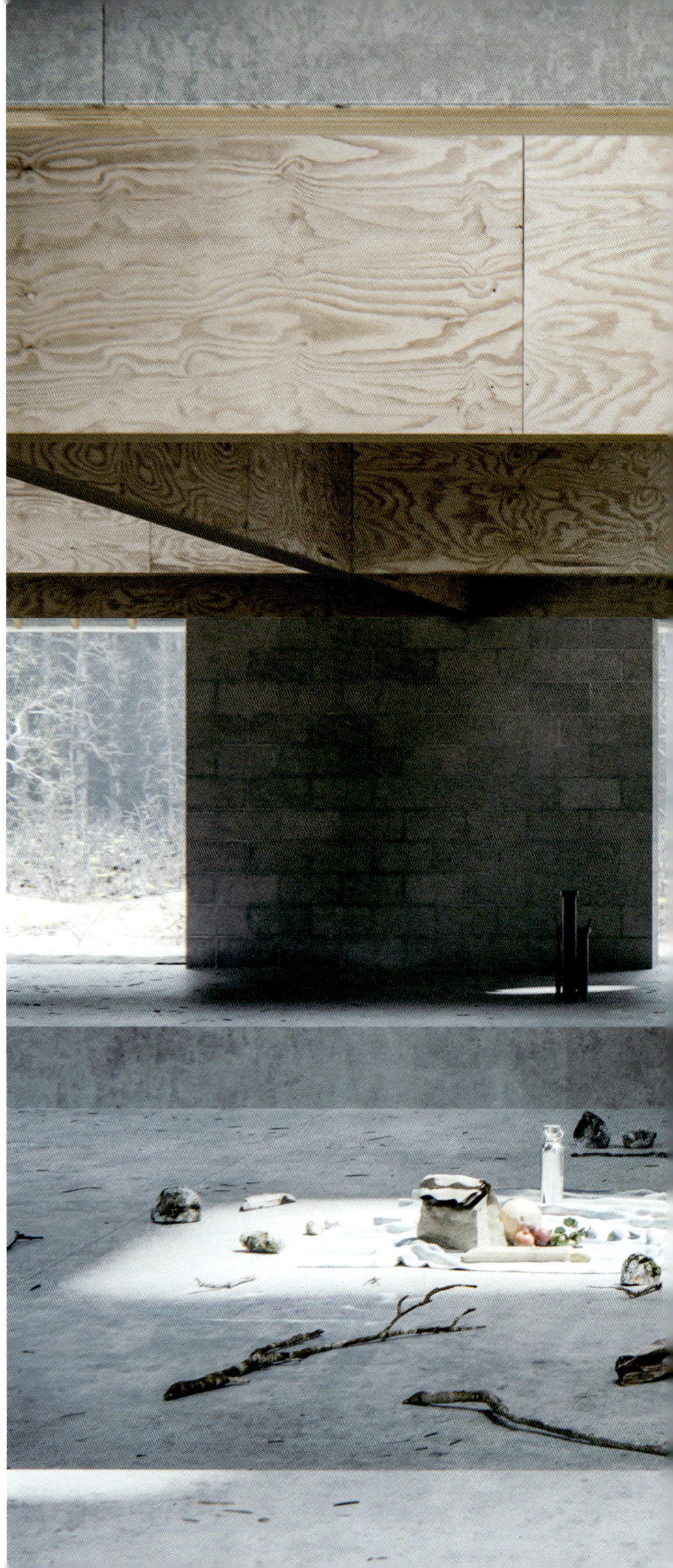

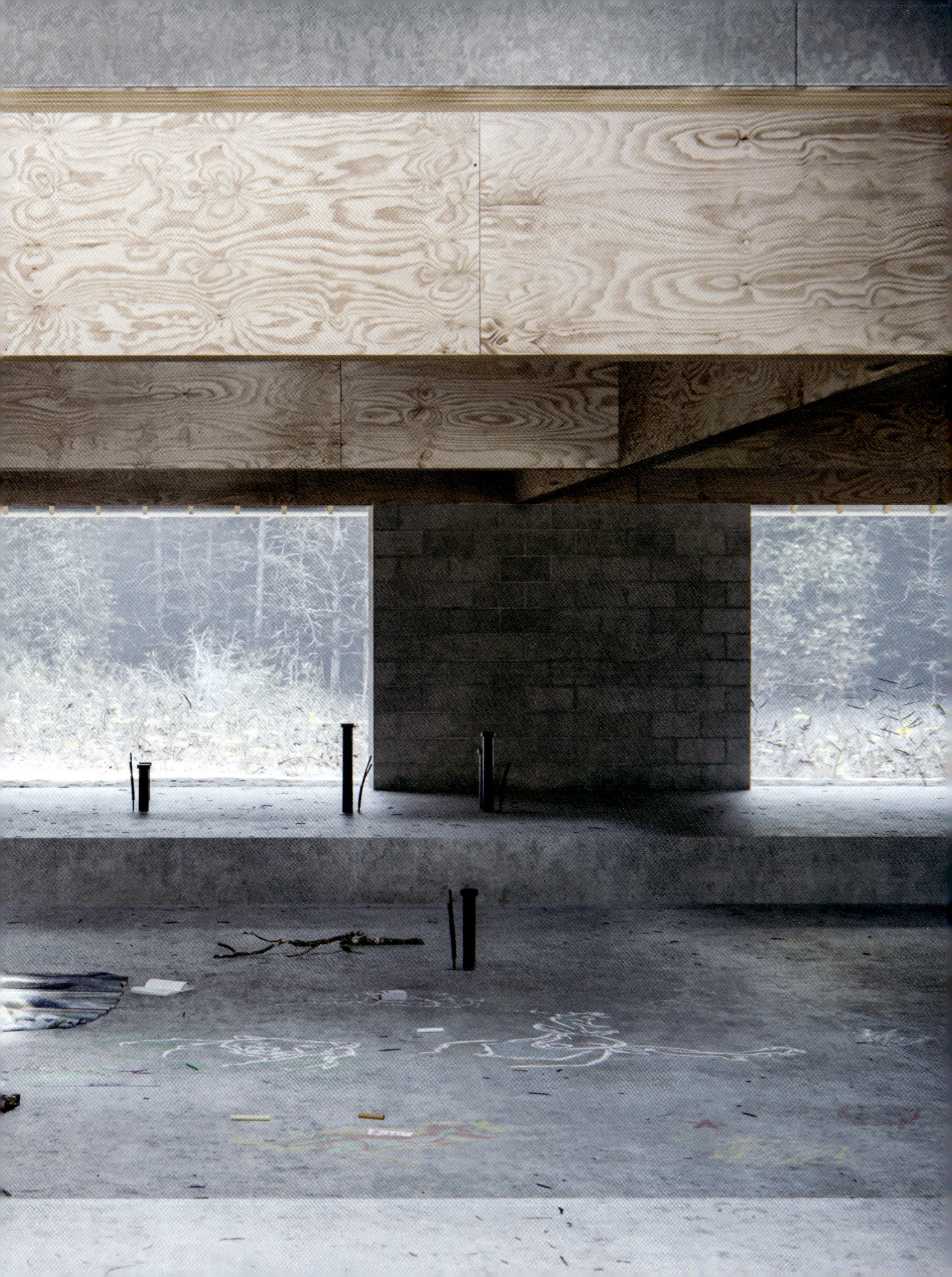

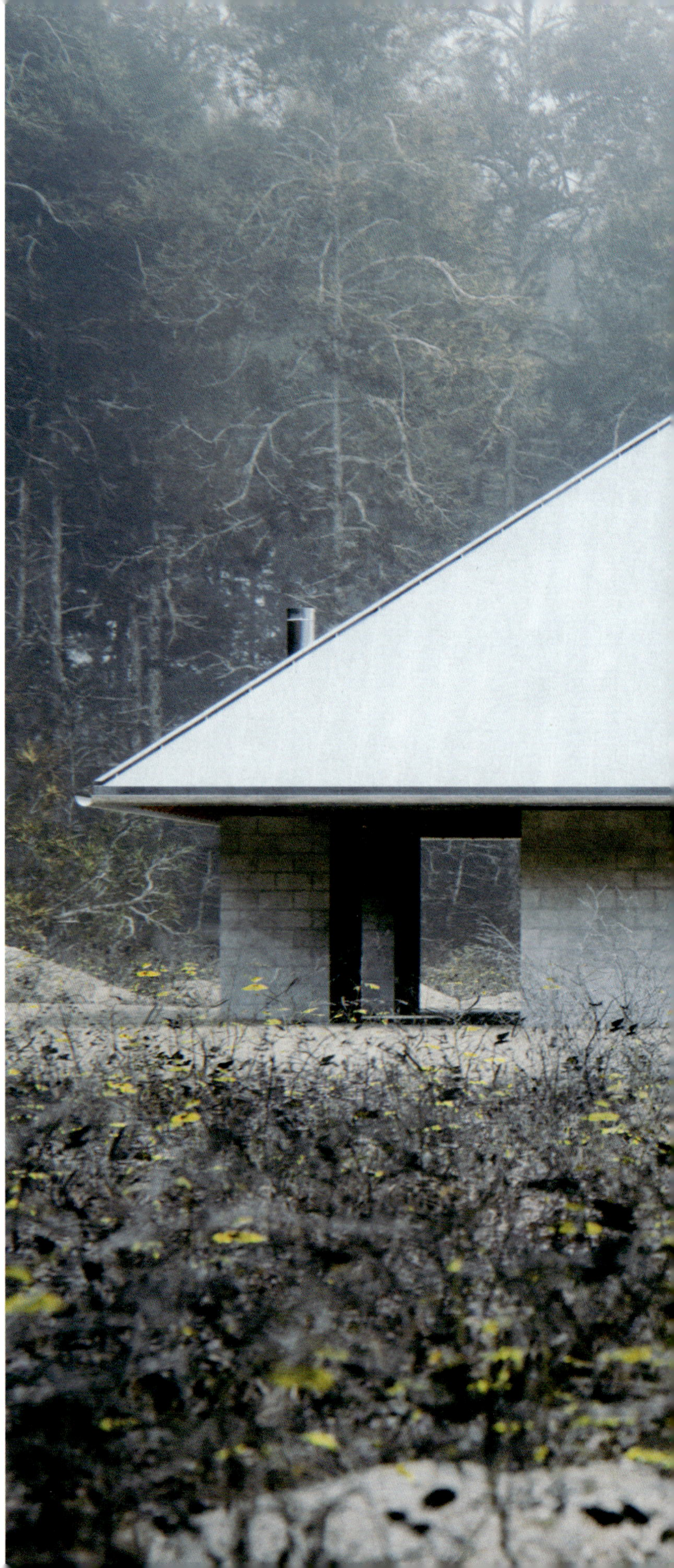

A rendering of the *House of the Woodland* by WOJR upends the expectation that resolved realism is a final destination.

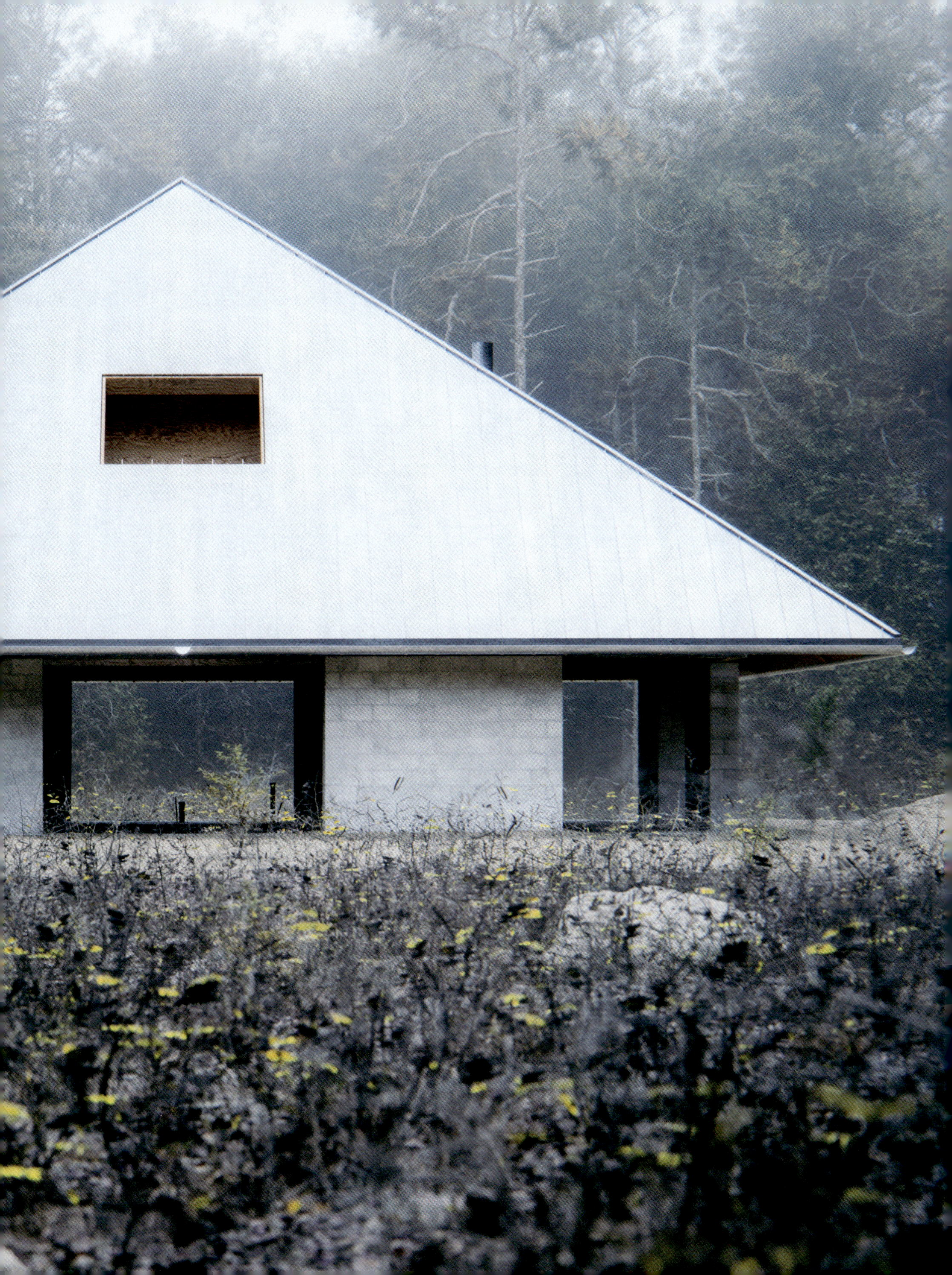

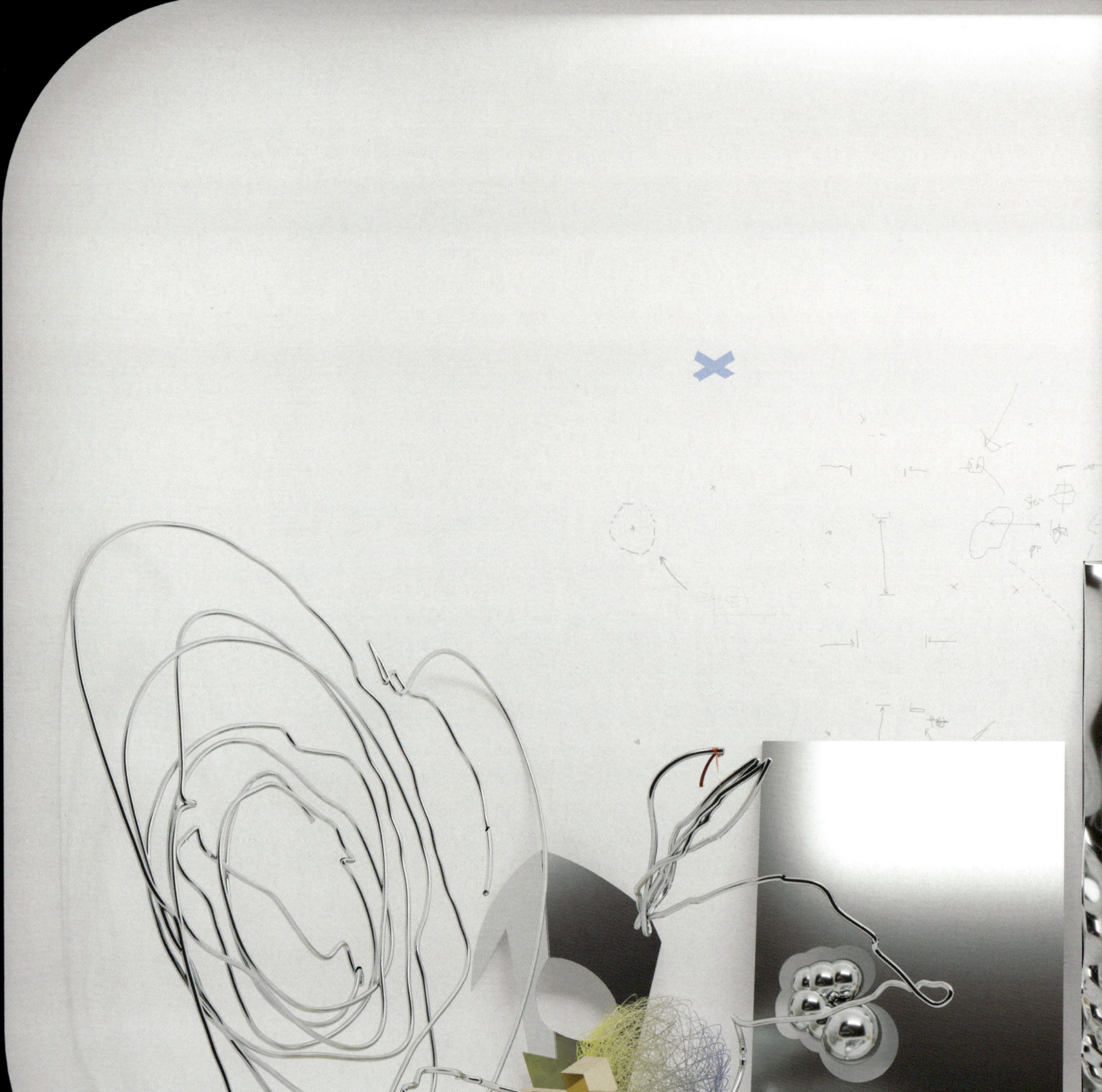

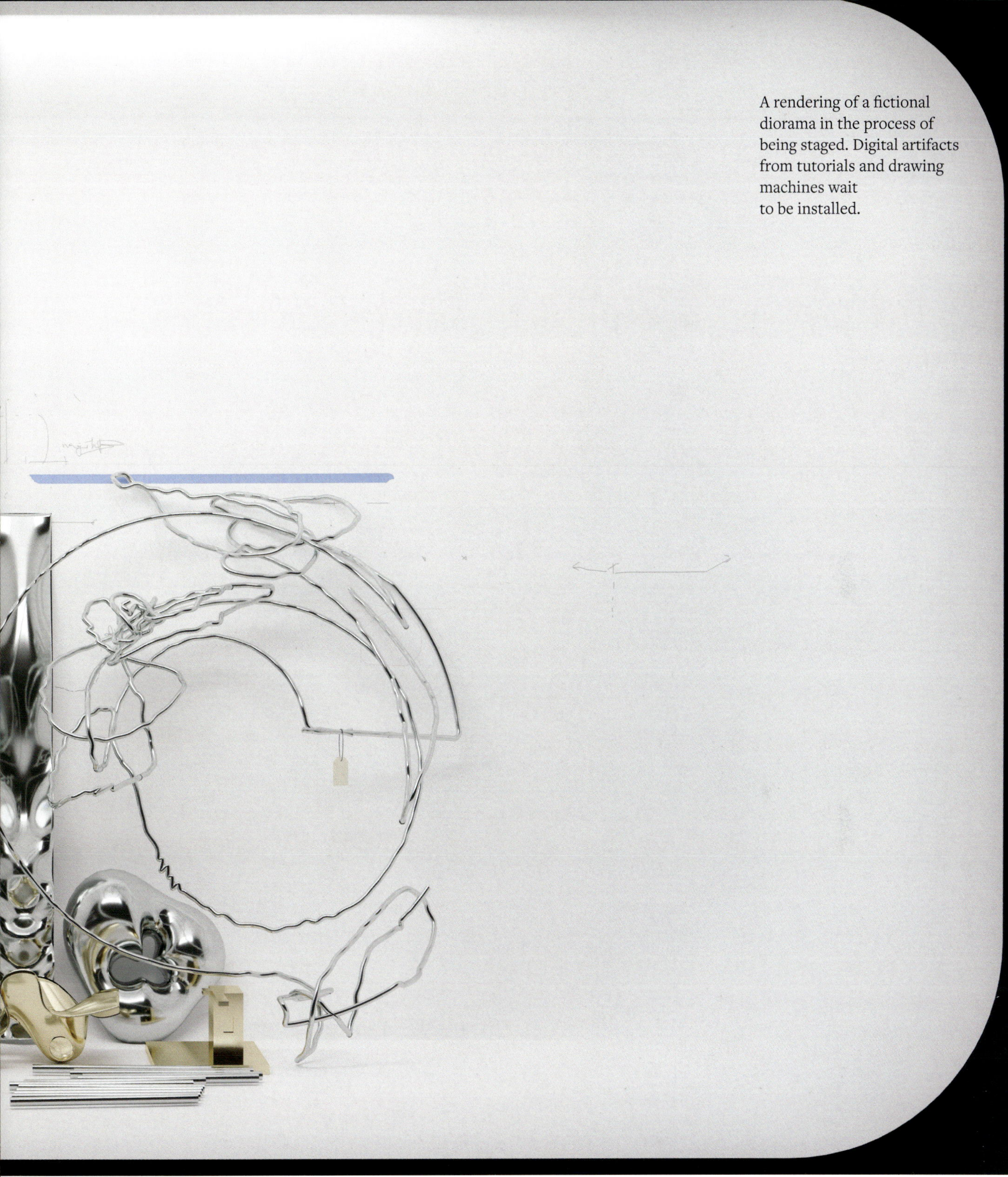

A rendering of a fictional diorama in the process of being staged. Digital artifacts from tutorials and drawing machines wait to be installed.

Can a Diorama be Separated from Its Content?

Architectural designers are often too comfortable with empty space. We separate content from container with the assumption that the use-occupant fills the spaces we conceive. Even a cursory review of architectural renderings will immediately reveal a typical discrepancy between the status of walls, windows, and floors (often rendered with meticulous attention to reality and refined lighting) versus the articulation of atmosphere, furniture, objects, and people (often collaged, abstracted, or left out altogether). Renderings that capture anything other than finalized, idealized, and newly constructed architecture are as rare as they are beautiful. The WOJR House of the Woodland[27] comes to mind. The house is rendered only partially built, with detailed articulation of human events, human impacts, and human occupation within the ephemeral diorama-like interior worlds of the incomplete project. The nuanced debates that stem from a rejection of modernist purity or luxurious minimalism are supported, and even sidestepped, by the most basic of dioramas or buildings-turned-diorama, which refuse emptiness and are never neutral. Conversely, it might be accurate to note that any empty diorama is still loaded with content.

If a diorama is thought of as the hybrid between a room and an image, we can immediately see how and why dioramas are perfect subjects for a photograph (or a photographic simulation made through digital means). This also explains the loaded nature of the empty, or nearly empty, diorama. It yearns for an upgrade to status as a room. Even without a staged scene, dioramas are biased toward the viewing orientation or in some cases a viewing position. An empty diorama is not a neutral white gallery waiting to be filled with art. Rather, it is a scaffold for future content, palimpsest of past content, or both. The aforementioned Richard Barnes is apparently interested in the same, capturing the dioramas between exhibits that are exposed in a manner that is best characterized as "uncanny"[28] rather than naked or empty. The infrastructure of the diorama—which we might call an "architecture"—is positioned as a representational media. This is an essential observation. Like all impossible elements of architecture, the diorama is representational even if that which it represents is itself.

With it well established that "empty diorama" is a provocative term, it likewise becomes compelling to test the nearly empty diorama— the diorama in the act of being assembled or constructed. This is especially of interest when the diorama can be caught between two worlds. The first is the world of the audience and that of the museum of which the diorama is a component.

The second is the artificial world within the diorama. This contradiction can be a matter of perspective—a perspective grid mapped onto a diorama so as to match a point of view, for example. The contradiction can also be a matter of material: tape, string, dust, and plastic wrap from "our world" invade the world of the diorama. Finally, the contradiction can be a matter of wear and deterioration such that, as if a very crude and flawed version of the Star Trek Holodeck,[29] each exhibit taxes the diorama and eventually, exhibit after exhibit leads to visible peeling and staining that reinforce the seams undermine any semblance of infinite depth created by perfect lighting and rendered backdrops. The diorama is therefore a meta moment of flux. The viewer is a voyeur not through the window, but of the window itself. In this state, the dioramas, like the WOJR renderings, can be said to capture human inhabitation, where and when we might not expect to see the human figure. The viewer likewise becomes the subject as the diorama is calibrated to and seemingly aware of a watchful presence. There's no magic without an audience.

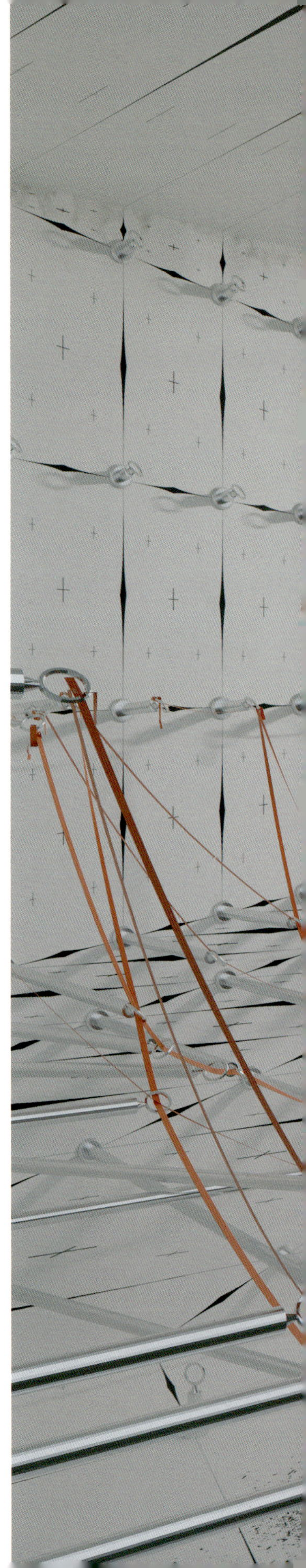

Viewed from the side, the
shallowness of the diorama
visibly conflicts
with the implied depth
of the perspective grid.

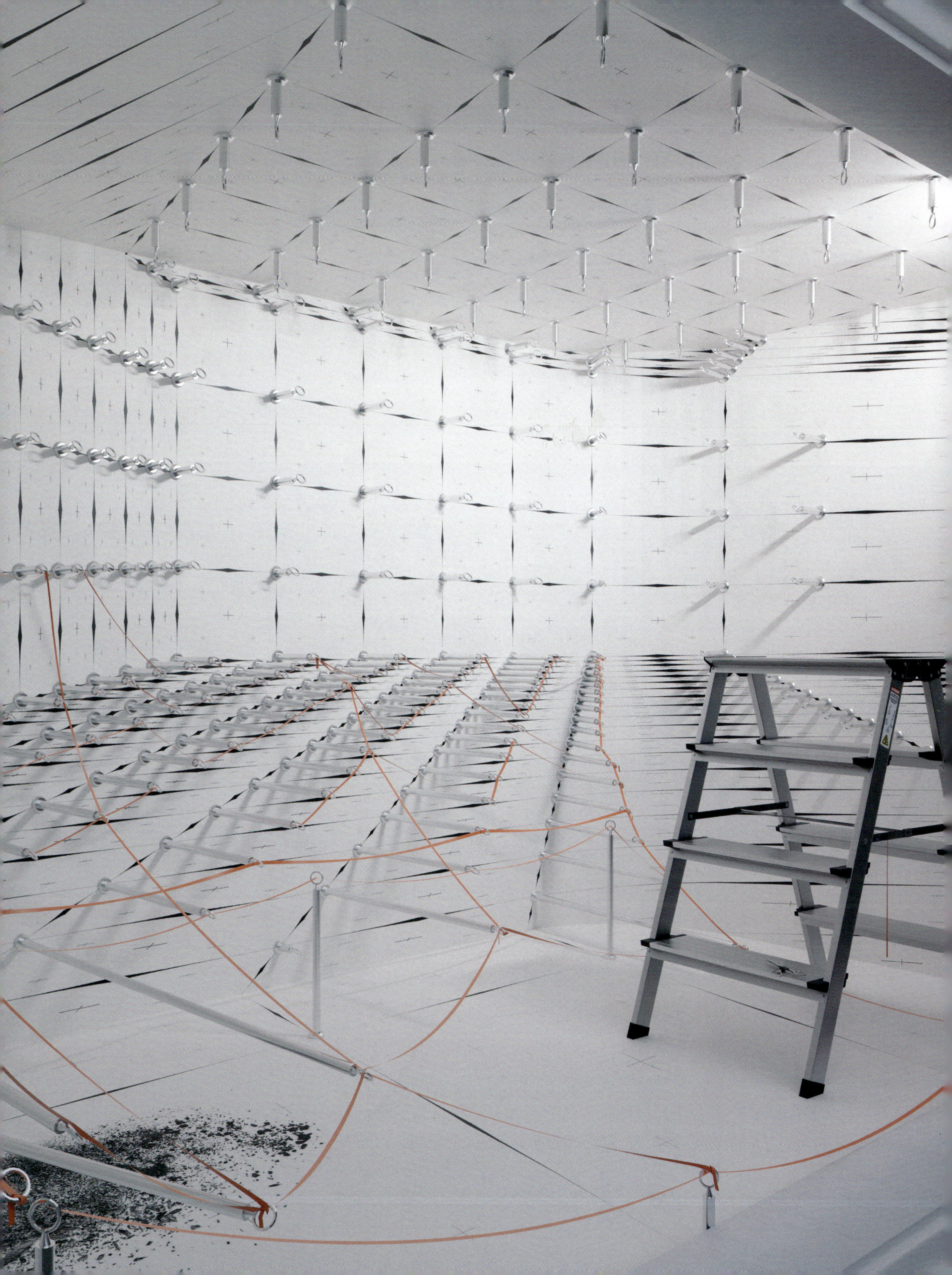

A rendering of a fictional diorama in a state of partial completion. The perspective grid doubles as an infrastructure for artificial landscape, which appears to be in the process of pre-fabrication.

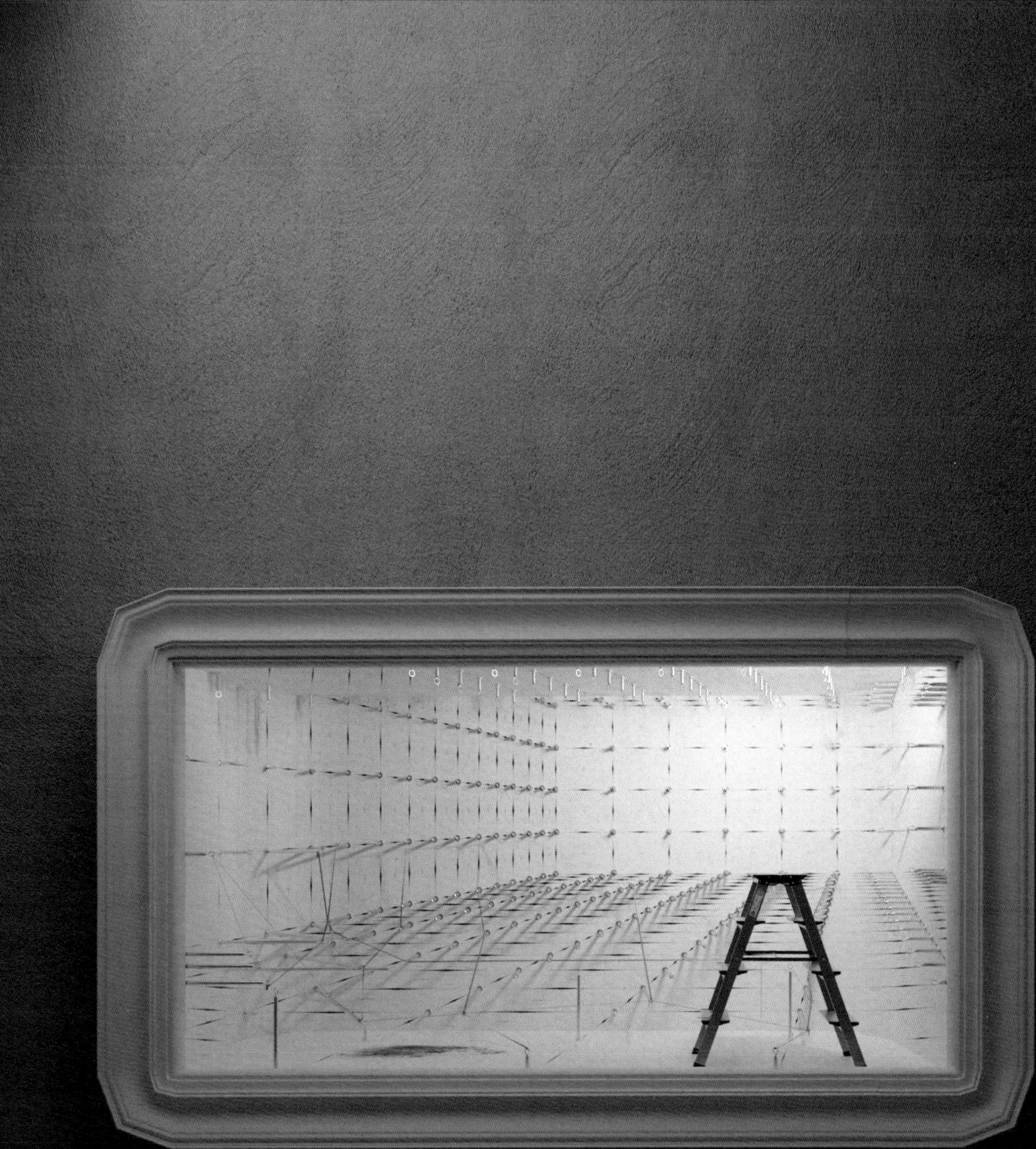

Notes

1. For a thorough discission of the elemental status of the transparent checker grid, see Chapter 2, "Every Grid is Material" by Julie Kress.
2. Gene Roddenberry (creator) et al. "Contagion." Episode. *Star Trek: The Next Generation* 2, no. 11, March 18, 1989. The completely non-existent frame, which though consistent thematically would pose aesthetic and technical problems, is sidestepped. The portals are instead rendered with a thin repeating border that distorts by way of offset the otherwise perfectly real world beyond. Also of note: the Iconian gateways are one-way only in terms of visibility and traversability.
3. Francesca Gardiner (writer) et al. "The Scholar." Episode. *His Dark Materials* 2, no. 5, December 6, 2020. This series, based on the novels by Phillip Pullman, sees cuts between two realities rendered with irregular and unframed edges without any framing.
4. Rick Berman (writer) et al. "To the Death." Episode. *Star Trek: Deep Space Nine* 4, no. 22, May 13, 1996. In this rendering of the fictional Iconian technology, the gateways are thick and ornate.
5. Rachel Ziady DeLue, "The Struggle of Vision," in *George Inness and the Science of Landscape* (Chicago: University of Chicago Press, 2008), 17–18.
6. DeLue, 18.
7. George Inness. "Harvest Scene in the Delaware Valley." *National Gallery of Art Collection*, 1867. National Gallery of Art. Washington, D.C. https://www.nga.gov/collection/art-object-page.125748.html.
8. Adrienne Baxter Bell. *George Inness: Writings and Reflections on Art and Philosophy* (New York: George Braziller, 2006), 79.
9. Samuel Taylor Coleridge. *Biographia Literaria (1867)* (London: Oxford Univ. Press, 1979).
10. Scott Stump. "HBO Admits '*Game of Thrones*' Coffee Cup Mistake, Wipes It from Scene." TODAY.com, May 7, 2019. https://www.today.com/popculture/game-thrones-fans-spot-modern-coffee-cup-winterfell-celebration-scene-t153578.
11. John Seed. *Disrupted Realism: Paintings for a Distracted World* (Atglen, PA: Schiffer Publishing, Ltd., 2020).
12. Jamy Ian Swiss, *Devious Standards* (Seattle, WA: Hermetic Press, 2011), 11.
13. Ibid.
14. *EG5 Jamy Ian Swiss. YouTube*, 2012. https://www.youtube.com/watch?v=jjxeqyuSe_Y&t=269s.
15. *Michael Weber, Performer & Miracle Designer (EG5). Vimeo*, 2021. https://vimeo.com/227274048.
16. Swiss, *Devious Standards*, 35.
17. Ibid, 6.
18. Ibid, 55.
19. Ibid, 3.
20. Ibid, 23. Swiss recounts being fooled, "when I should have known better, when in fact I did already know better," by Martin Nash.
21. Ibid, 95.
22. Ibid, 66. This is an extreme exaggeration of a trick described by Swiss that was performed by Roberto Giobbi, "in which the final revelation includes a slight mistake, which is then corrected with the disclosure that the magician has previously added to the prediction card a note with the words, 'off by one.'"
23. Susan Yelavich, "Death and the Museum," in *Animal Logic: Container, Diorama, Skull, Refuge, Murmur* (New York, NY: Princeton Architectural Press, 2009).
24. Ibid.
25. William Shakespeare, *Hamlet* (New York: Dover Publications, 1992), 3.2.
26. Swiss, *Devious Standards*, 35.
27. William O'Brien Jr., "House of the Woodland," WOJR, Organization for Architecture, accessed July 21, 2021, https://wojr.org/.
28. Yelavich, "Death and the Museum." Yelavich, in a discussion of the uncanny nature of Barnes's photos, cites Anthony Vidler's *The Architectural Uncanny: Essays in the Modern Unhomely* (Cambridge, MA: MIT Press, 1992), 3.
29. For a thorough discission of the *Star Trek* Holodeck, see Chapter 2, "Every Grid is Material" by Julie Kress.

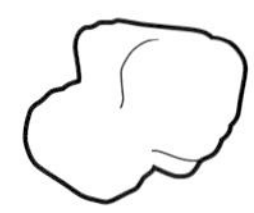

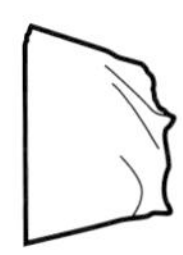

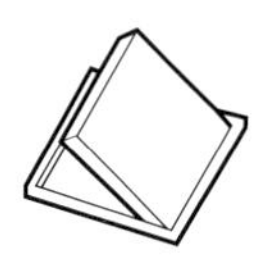

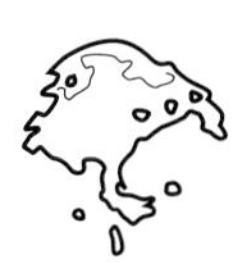

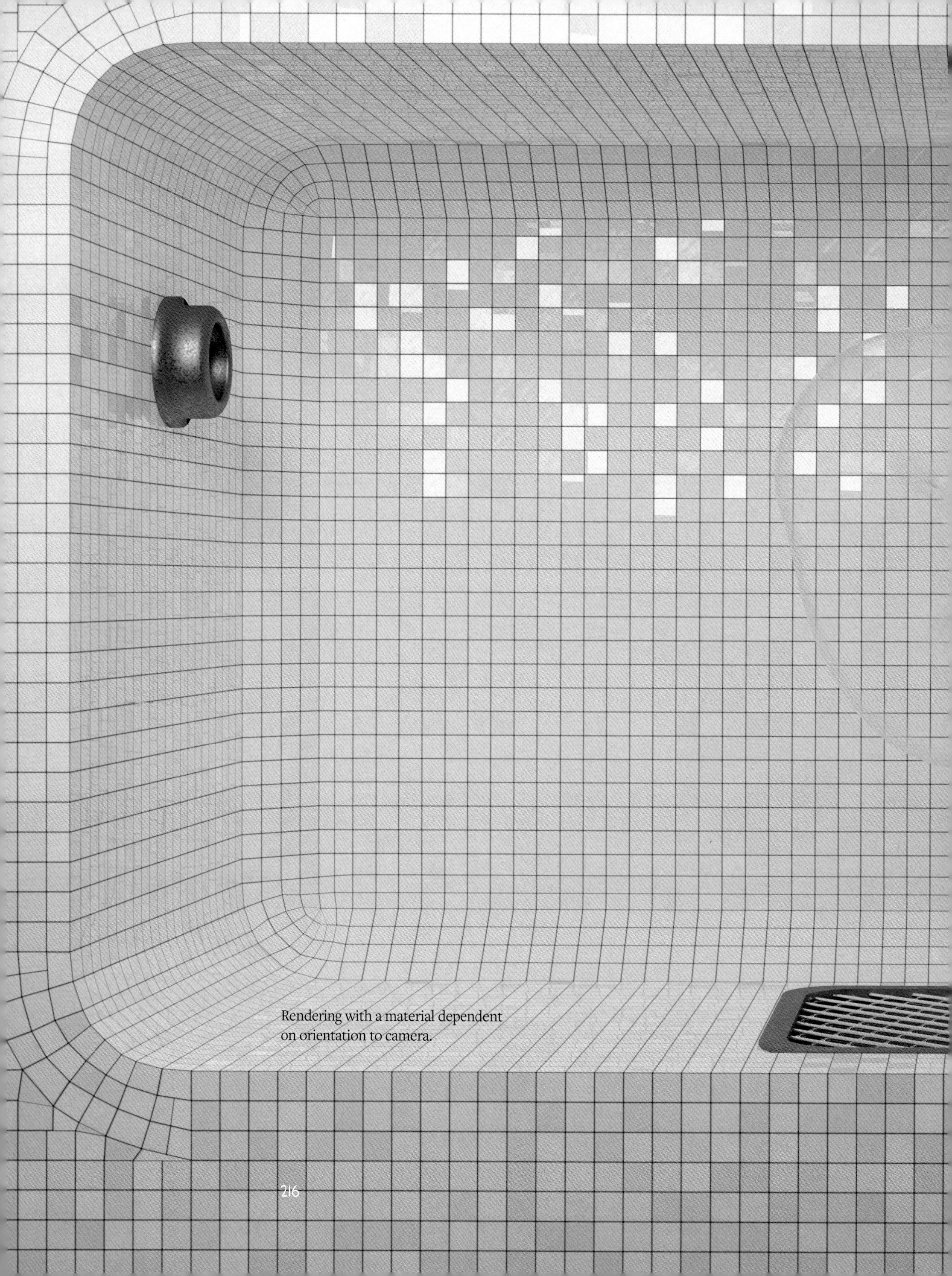

Rendering with a material dependent on orientation to camera.

CHAPTER 5

Rendering the Almost Invisible

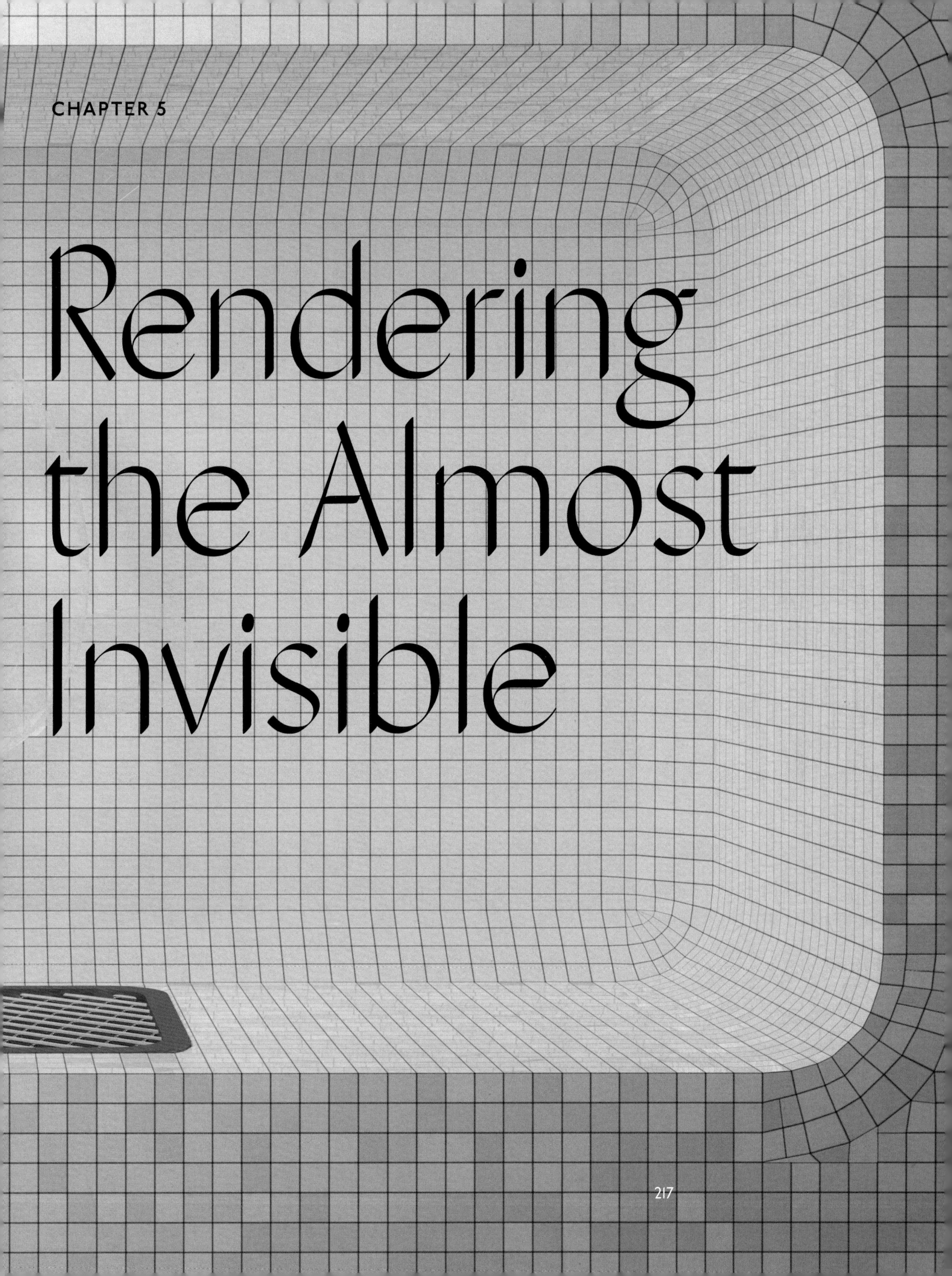

For all things discursive in the world of magic, we've consistently turned to Jamy Ian Swiss. In the previous chapter, the diorama was positioned relative to his various theoretical framings of the magic trick. This chapter will rely on the diorama as a foil and catalyst for other elements. In that sense we must linger in the analogical space of magic a little longer to confront a challenging assertion: magic is its own medium. Each trick and each magician bring their own methods, style, and narrative, all of which contribute to the rendering of a new reality. Each magic trick must do the work of affecting perception. The trick is content and container, and our conception of the diorama in similar terms was a great service to our pursuit of elements of architecture. But magic loses its reality-affecting power when mediated by film or TV. Swiss explains:

> What's the difference between technology and magic? ...[According to Michael Webber] any magic excessively dependent on technology will be indistinguishable from technology. Or, any insufficiently disguised technology will never be perceived as magic...It doesn't leave you with the sense that laws of physics have been repealed suddenly or temporarily. It doesn't leave you with a lingering sense of mystery...It doesn't rattle your sense of how the world works...It's that liveness, it's the immediacy, it's that sense of reality that sets magic apart from technology...Conditions really become a factor if you're trying to do magic on television...I collaborated with Edward Tufte in a Chapter, "Explaining Magic" in a book, Visual Explanations, in there we wrote that, "video representations of magic are deeply suspect"...Did the assistant vanish from the box because the camera was turned off or because of a real trick? If magic on TV is always a compromised version, at best, of the magical experience, what about movie magic? Magicians are trying to get you to forget that there is any technology at all so you can stay engaged in the magical experience...[The director Christopher] Nolan says, "Anything you notice as technology reminds you that you're in a movie theater. Even if you are trying to portray something fantastical and other-worldly, it's always about trying to achieve invisible manipulation"...Interestingly, Nolan made a movie about magic...called The Prestige...[about that, Nolan] said, "basically the idea was always really not trying to show magic in the film and impress people with stage magic because that can't work on film. People are aware of special effects."[1]

Let's consider the invisible element as though it was the perfect magic trick. The invisible element rendered is...nothing. Claiming it is something is suspect in the same way that magic in film is suspect. It does not affect our conception of reality because we've already subscribed to the reality of the film (or the paper, or the computer screen). Magic in film upends our suspension of disbelief because it provokes intellectualization of technological conditions. The magic inside the film might make for beautiful film, it might even intellectually interest those fascinated by magic. This is more than can be said for the perfectly invisible element. Even its rhetorical dimensions are wanting. Swiss claims that The Prestige works because the film doesn't present the tricks to the film audience as magic. The film audience sees something less than magic and more than magic at the same time. The film exposes many of the tricks including some that fail. We empathize with the magician's process. The narrative flows around and through the tricks, but the tricks are not the narrative. Thus, it might be said that the film is magic in reverse. Returning to our parallel, theoretical, invisible elements, our conclusion is obvious: we must render them in such a way as to disrupt their invisibility.

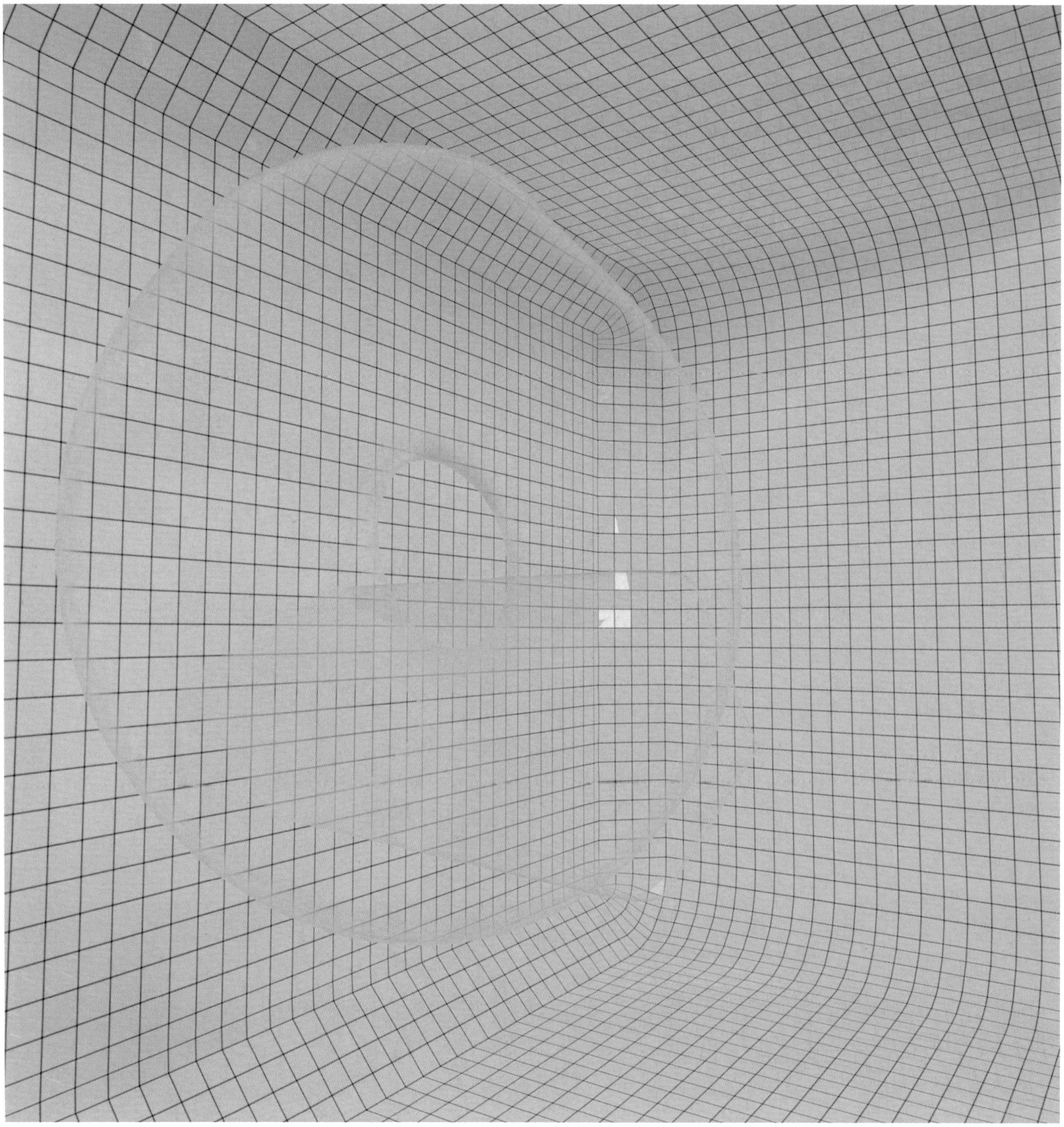

Straining to Become Invisible

In a digital rendering, simulated light rays intersect with surfaces and volumes. In the most fundamental sense, we can equate something happening to those rays at those intersections with the rendering of that geometry. If nothing happens—if intersections are ignored and the light transmits uninterrupted through the geometry—the geometry is invisible. As has already been discussed, this conceptual invisibility is both perfect and uninteresting. Perfect invisibility is without ambiguity and without mystery. Fortunately, we are in control of those intersections, and we can therefore design consequences based on their occurrence.

Rendering software usually does this by default. We assign a "material" to our geometry. That material is often not much more than a set of values that influence equations that change the light rays. The light ray loses intensity, and the surface appears as a translucent dark filter, for example. Or the light ray changes angle and refraction occurs. But we're interested in the appearance of a material that is caught in a struggle to be invisible as though we are watching a magic trick fail. If every light ray interacts with the surface in a consistent way, there is no tension between visibility and invisibility. We could also note that translucency—partial opacity—is not the same as partial invisibility. What we're looking for instead is contingent, but, what effects should be contingent upon what conditions?

Opportunity arises through the customization of the same software that offers us the default materials. If we approach materiality as a medium, the behavior of rays at the intersection of geometry can be algorithmic as well as mathematic. If the behavior of the light ray depends on contextual conditions, we can render objects perfectly invisible in some portions—which is of course to say not render them at all—and render them as diffuse in other places. How we decide which behavior to execute can depend on the geometry at or around the intersection—whether it is bumpy, smooth, or sharp, for example—or it can depend on the orientation relative to the camera. This is a key opportunity. It makes the camera an active component of the scene. It means that the apparent existence of the element is dependent on the camera. The camera doesn't show what's there, it creates what's there.

Film is a rich territory for the almost (or struggling to be) invisible. An invisible agent is intensely—sometimes horrifyingly—dramatic. The culturally and technologically significant film Predator was released in 1987. Yes, this is the film in which Arnold Schwarzenegger plays Major "Dutch," leader of a paramilitary

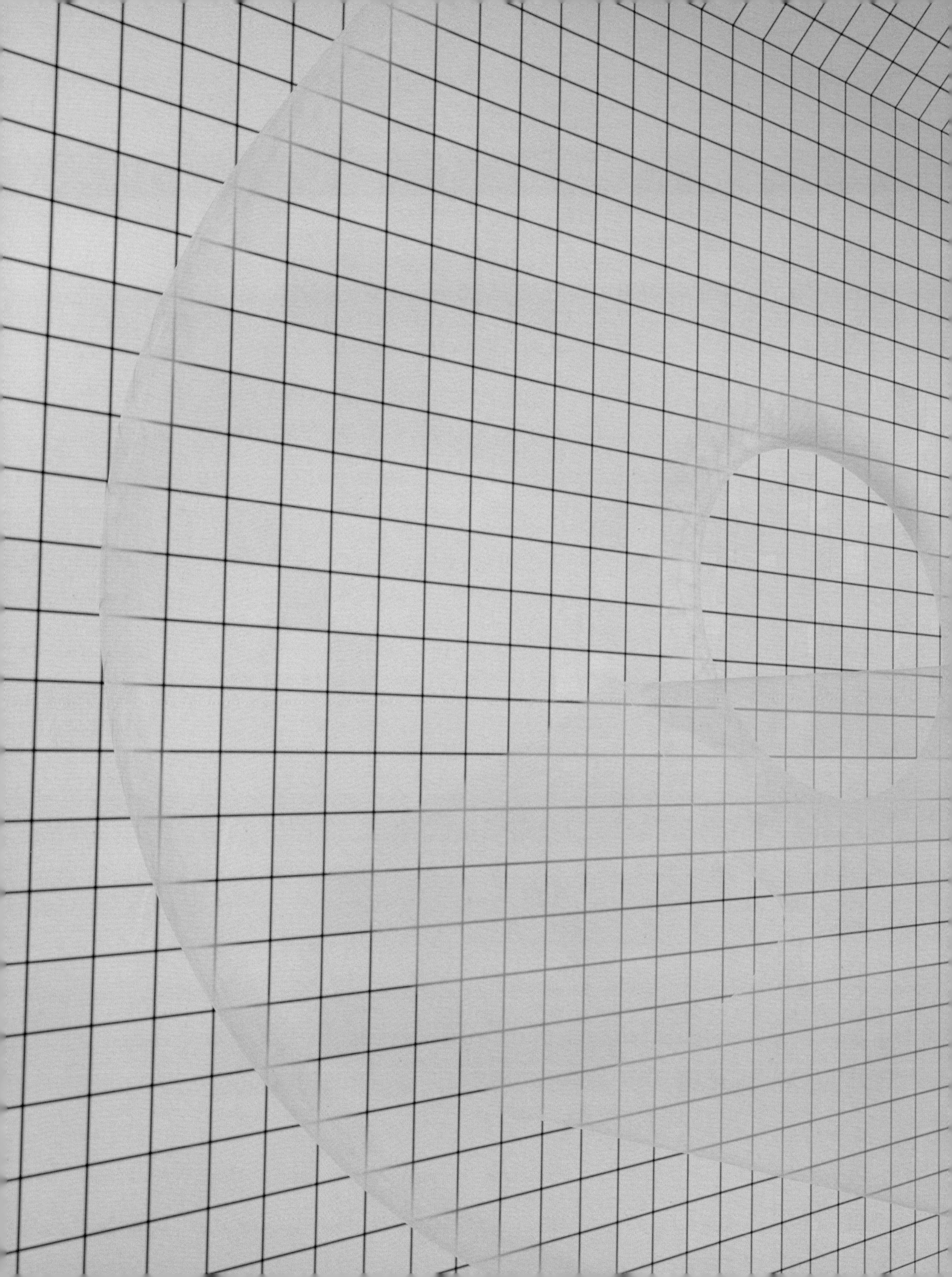

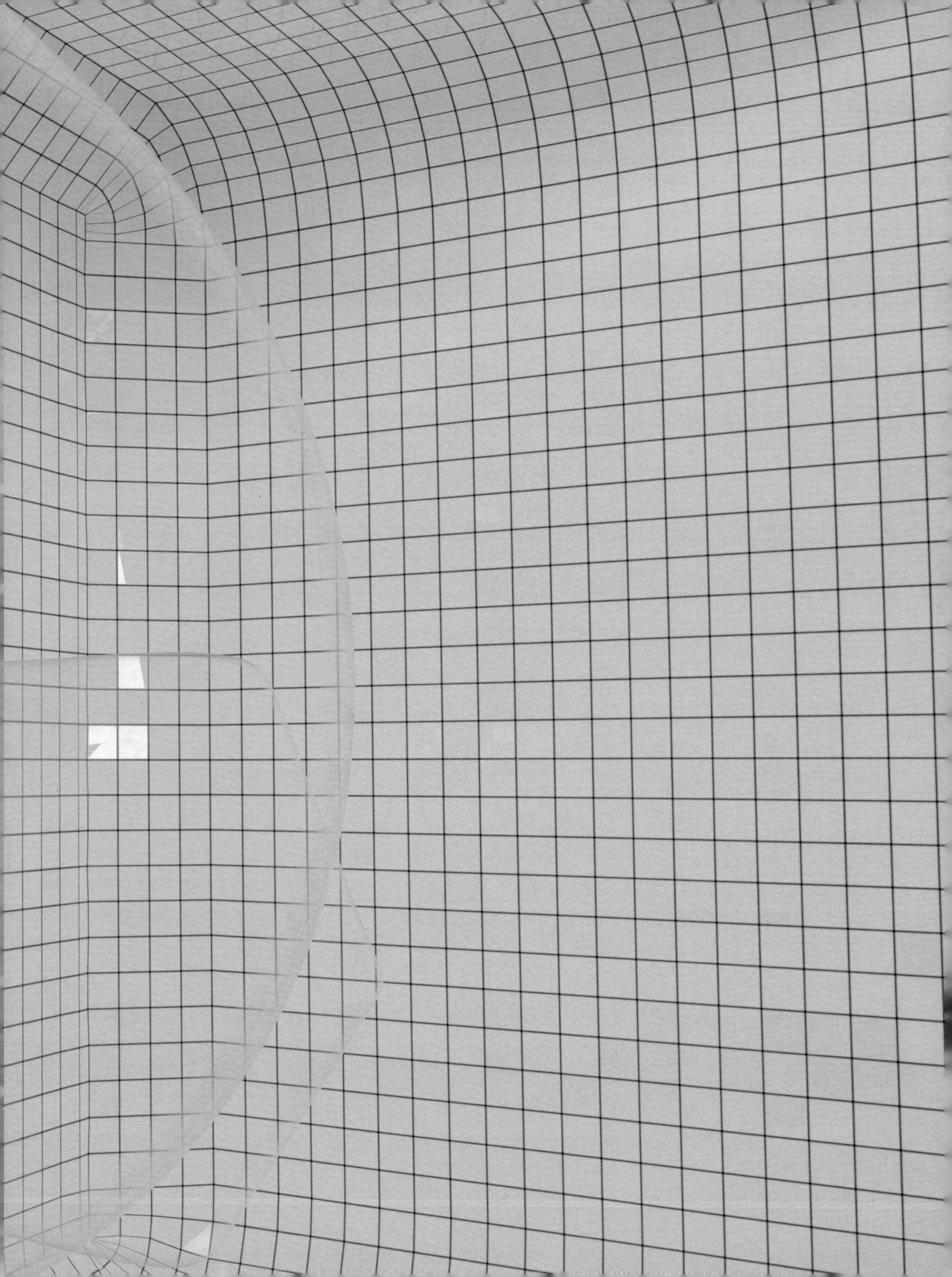

team that spends the near entirety of the film battling an advanced and violent extraterrestrial in the jungle. The creative technologies deployed in Predator were widely recognized including in the film's Academy Award Nomination for Best Visual Effects. Readers may remember our discourse in Chapter 1 that argued that the late '80s were a special time for pixels in digital representation and computer gaming. In the same way that rapidly expanding computer accessibility influenced digital art, visual effects in film were influenced by, but not yet taken over by, digital computers. Like architecture at the time, film was turning (but had not yet turned) digital.[2] Of utmost importance to the film's narrative, and our narrative, is the fact that the predator uses an invisibility cloak. It should come as no surprise that the cloak is not perfect. Of course it isn't—there'd be nothing to see on screen if it worked perfectly. Predator was not the first film to confront this invisibility conundrum, but the technical methods deployed to exhibit this partial invisibility are uniquely in strategic alignment with the optically contingent and relationally parametric digital materials used in the work presented here. In a 1988 issue of American Cinematographer, Paul Mandell writes about digital-analog hybrid technique developed by Eugene Mamut that was first used in a Renault car commercial. "Savvy viewers may have scratched their heads. Was it a computer Image? Or perhaps a slit-scan streak effect of the car, matted over a background scene? None of the above. It was optical trick consisting 1,200 split screens per frame of motion picture film."[3] A "trick"! The resonance with our inquiry doesn't stop there. Mandell continues, "Using this technique, any moving object on regular production footage can appear to stretch, twist, shape-shift, or otherwise transform into an image that would have delighted the surrealist painters of the Forties." Though the raw footage is analog, the relational data of the changing slits are digital, resulting from "200 to 1,200 hairline slits...generated on a computer, depending on the effect desired. The slits are then transferred to hi-con film stock...The clear sections are nothing more than tiny hairline splits on black emulsion, one slit per frame, which change in position (and in shape, if need be), very much like an animated cartoon."[4] Fascinatingly, the same methods used to make a car extremely and exaggeratedly present on screen were also used to make the extraterrestrial predator almost invisible. Mandell explains, "The opportunity came with Predator, the title character being an extraterrestrial monster capable of blending perfectly with a jungle environment."[5] Unfortunately, "perfectly" is less than precise word choice. As the actual effect was calibrated, thankfully, to render the predator's invisibility less than perfectly: "This illusion (dubbed 'the camouflage effect') was created with a series of concentric mattes that conformed to the Predator's traveling shape... Once they were done, various takes of the Predator's jungle environment were shot at different focal lengths and inserted into the character shape, concentrically. The creature resembles a moving Fresnel lens—something that had never been seen before theatrically."[6] Like many digital rendering techniques, the predator's invisibility is achieved by manipulating 3-D geometry with respect to their projected position and orientation to the 2-D screen and relative orientation to the camera.

At this point, it may be helpful to remember that "material" in the context of digital rendering is a matter of association and appearance, often to a degree that ironically disassociates image from form. Let's consider an example. A digital material that enables a rendering of concrete might consist of a manipulated photograph of a sample of real concrete. "Assigning" a material to a digital form is increasingly a curious though apt word choice in the same way that "modeling" can be said to diverge from "representing." Is this a lament of the loss of materiality in the digital space? Certainly not. If the digital model ever was material, it was superficially so. The algorithmic paradigm is materially generative, so long as we are comfortable with rendering assuming the role of experimental generative space rather than the output capturing prior decisions. Digital materials are now models themselves. They contain texture maps (images), procedural algorithms, and relational references. The most irrational thing about them may be that we label them "materials." If we instead labeled them, "guides for the conversion of geometry into pixels" we would clearly understand them in parallel to the projection methods that likewise participate in the translation from 3-D to 2-D.

EXERCISE

Unrealistic Material

Create a material that diverges from everything you intuitively and explicitly know about materials in your reality. Think in terms of geometry, rendering, and if-then statements. Contemporary software that uses nodes or programming language within its "material" interface will be essential. Play and experiment. Break the rules of a known material or create a material from scratch. Treat digitally modeled form as a datum in these experiments. Perhaps you will need more than one such datum. Keep in mind that these datums must remain consistent throughout the duration of each experiment, but this does not mean that the datums are neutral. An undulating, bumpy surface might be as valuable here as cube or sphere.

Massive, but Immaterial

We can also "render" the invisible without ever displaying the invisible element. It can remain fully immaterial and its existence only betrayed by other simulated matter. In this framework, the diorama activates and performs as atmosphere and medium. Fluid and smoke extend the diorama and collide with the invisible element. Here we can recall a rich tradition of the cinematography of the invisible. The dozens of cinematic adaptions of H. G. Wells's Invisible Man[7] may be the most obvious set of references. Put simply, we—the audience—need the invisible man to touch things, wear clothes, get dirty, and find himself caught in the rain as much as those who might seek to survive his attempts at violence. We participate in the drama of his immateriality. We need his invisibility to be imperfect so that we can perceive magic, not technology. Even if the narrative depends on perfect invisibility, we're almost certain to encounter the technology breaking down—as is the case of the visual outing the cloaked Romulans in an episode of Star Trek[8].

Collisions are essential in this paradigm as is the discrete boundary of the invisible form. Its massive impermeable nature is without ambiguity. The legibility of the invisible, on the other hand, is a delicate balance between optics, geometry, and material that sustains formal ambiguity. We see material except within the bounds of the element. We also see material encountering and interacting with the surface of the element. This threshold condition can be specifically defined not in terms of extents or dimension—those are variable from moment to moment—but in terms of deviation from the expected. The form that is disturbed or disrupted due to collisions with the invisible element falls within this threshold.

Again, the diorama is an essential catalytic element. The diorama participates in the dissemination of the atmospheric form. It registers the infrastructure—spouts and drains, for example—of this form and in that way suggests that the smoke or fluid are each an extension of the diorama. Instead of a distinction between content and container, or inside verses outside, we read a distinction between atmosphere (and its constituent infrastructure) and figure.

Fluid meets invisible solid.

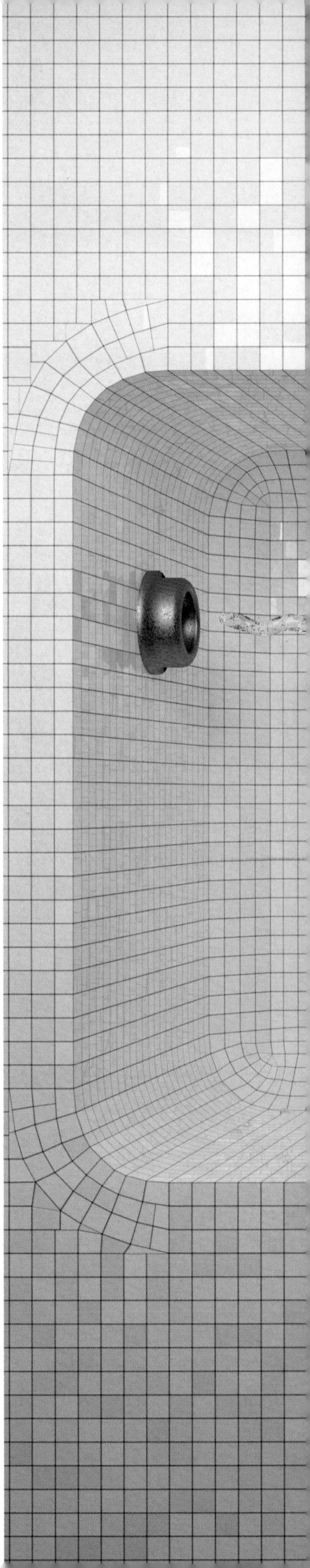

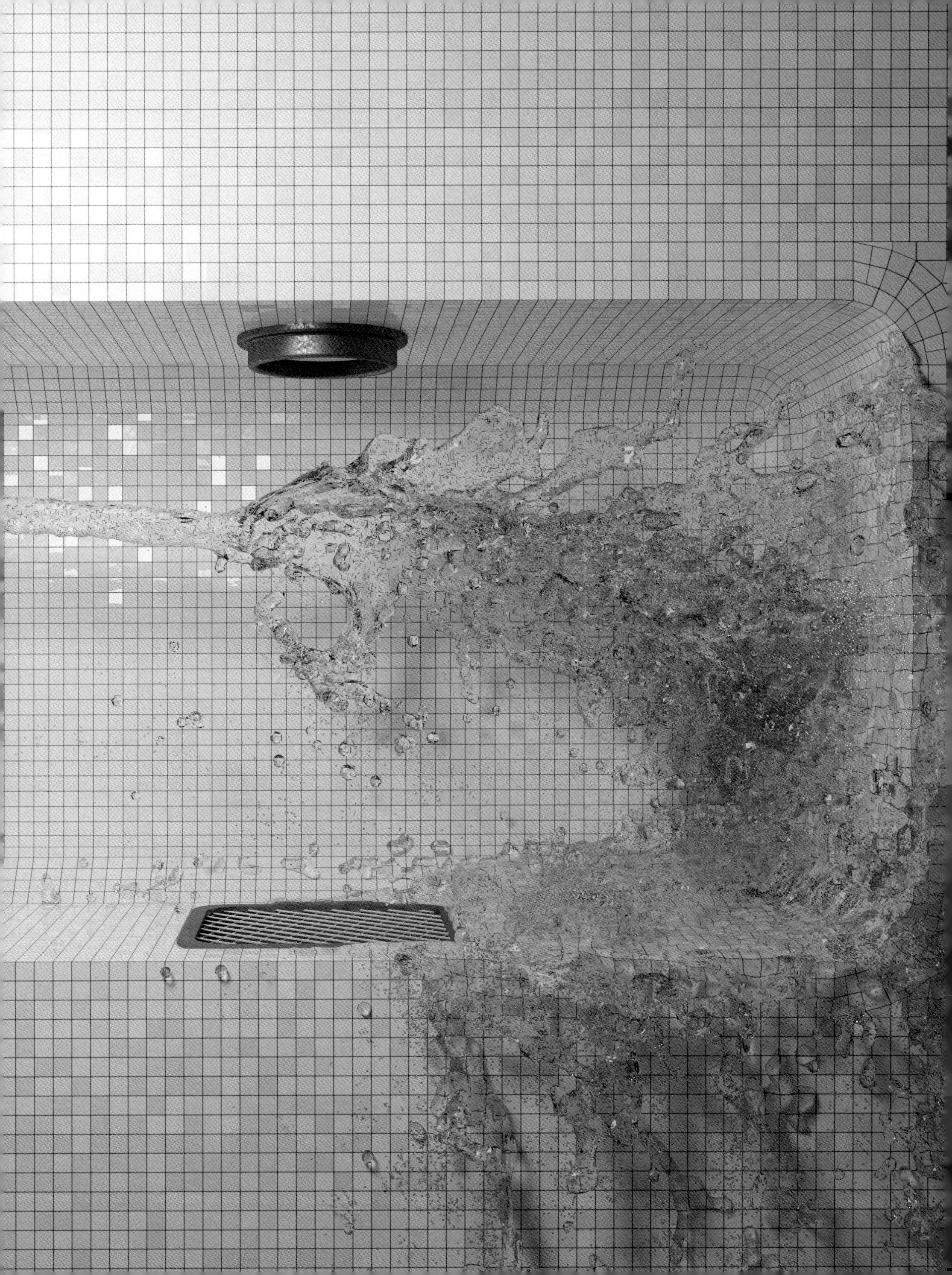

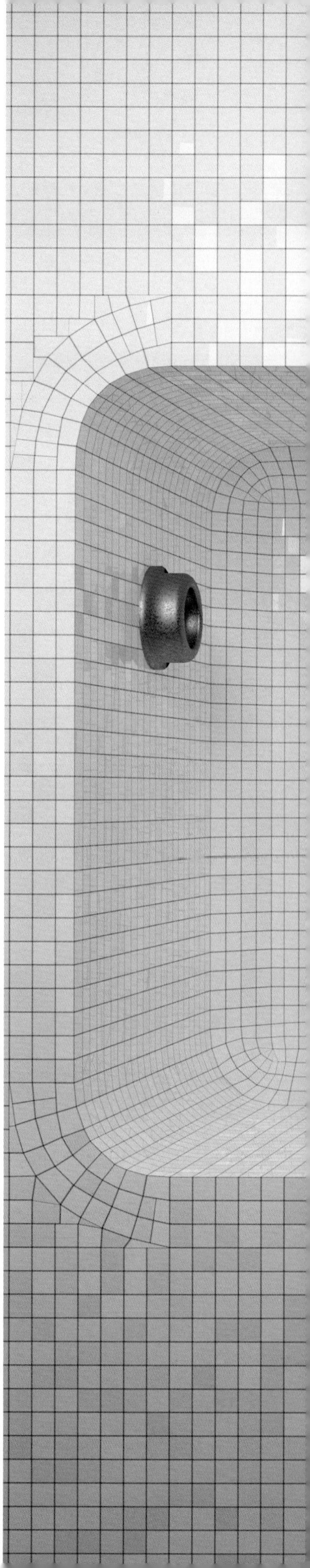

Rendering only a threshold of interaction between fluid and solid.

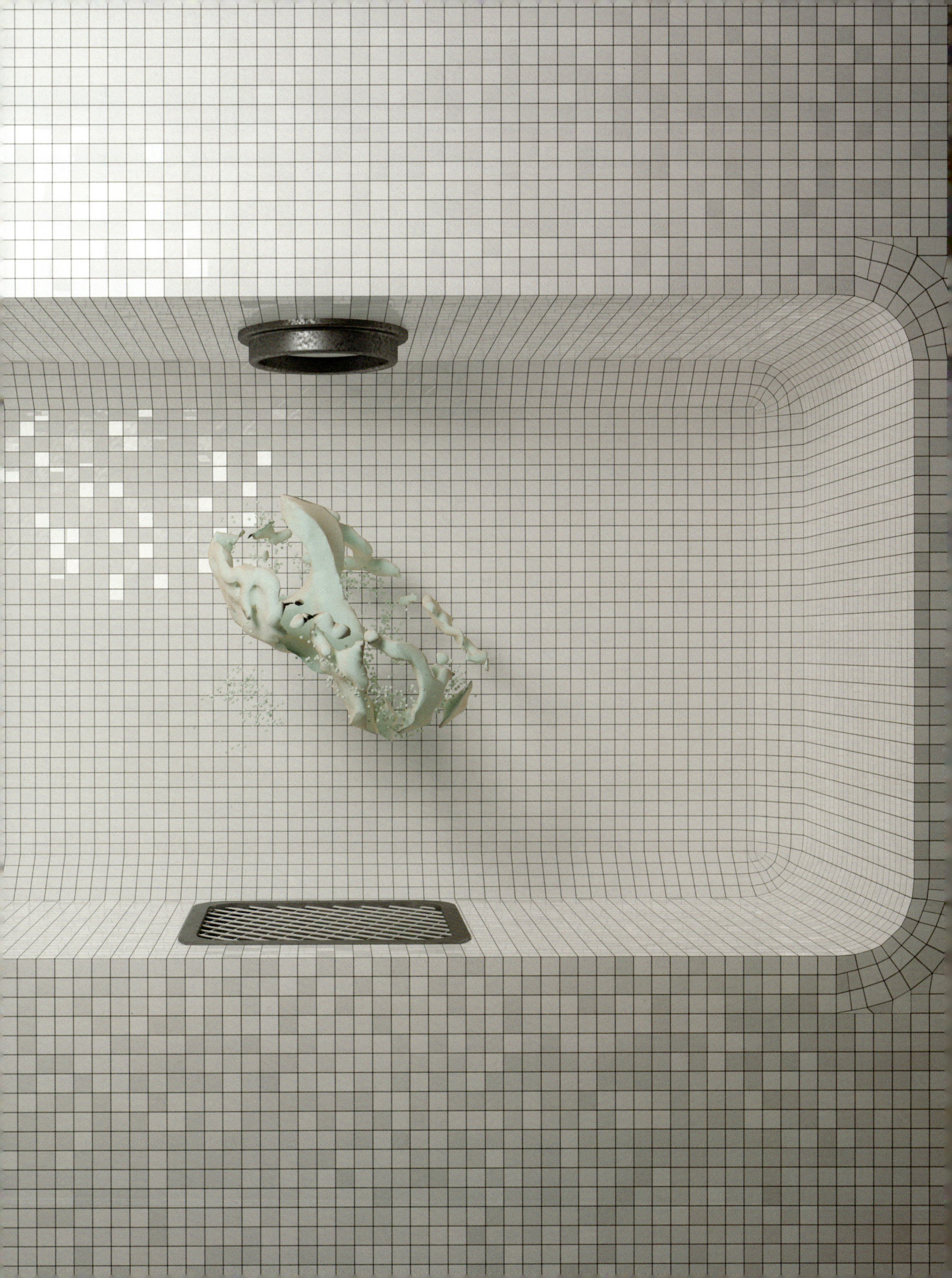

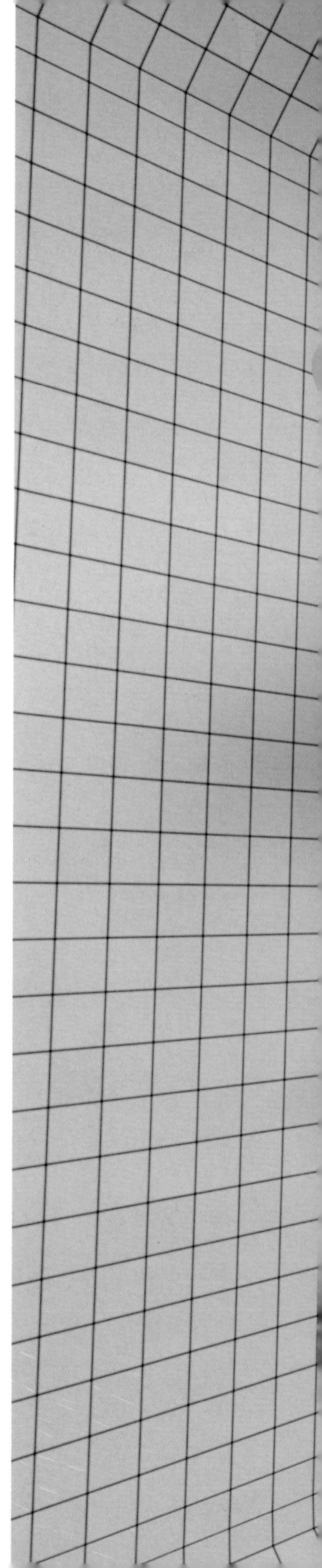

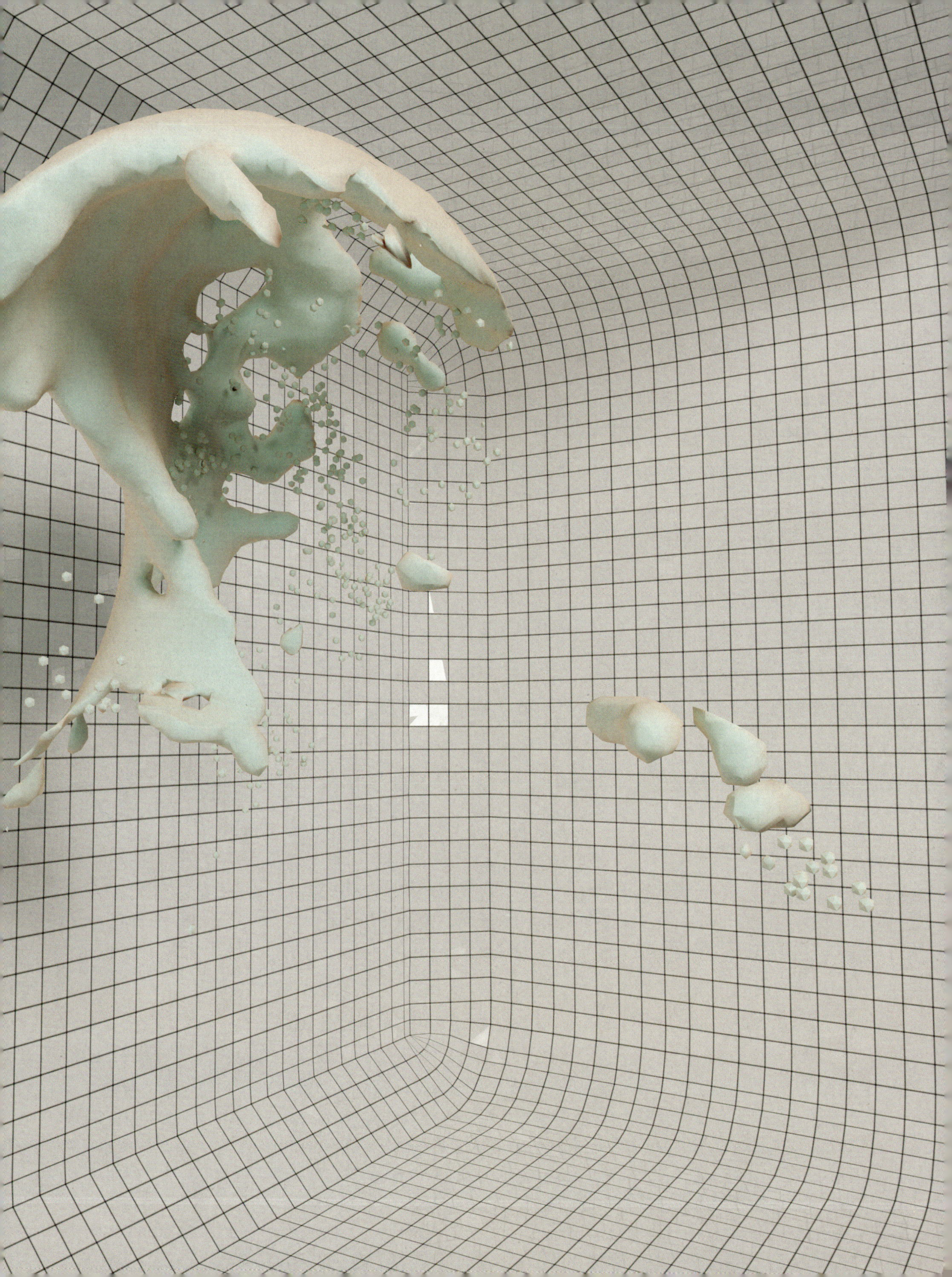

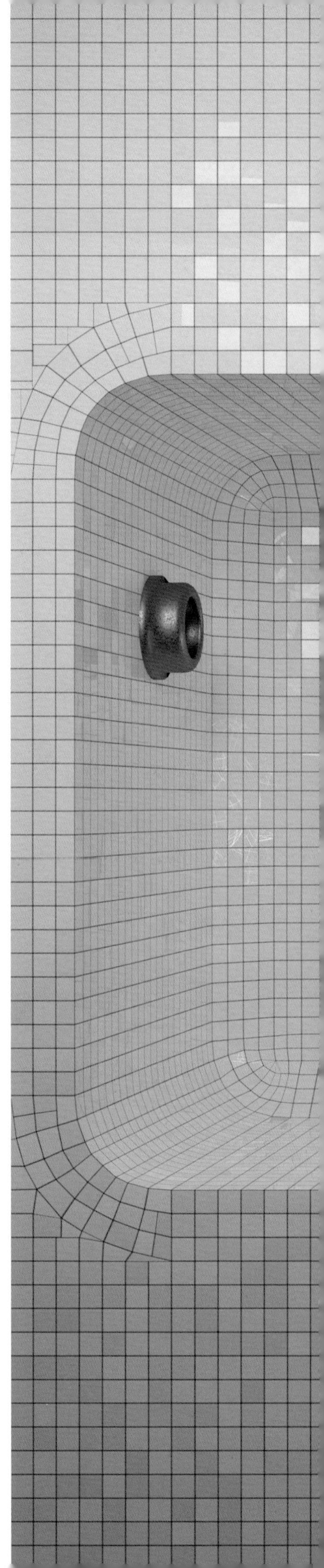

Rendering the interaction between light-emitting wireframe and dark smoke.

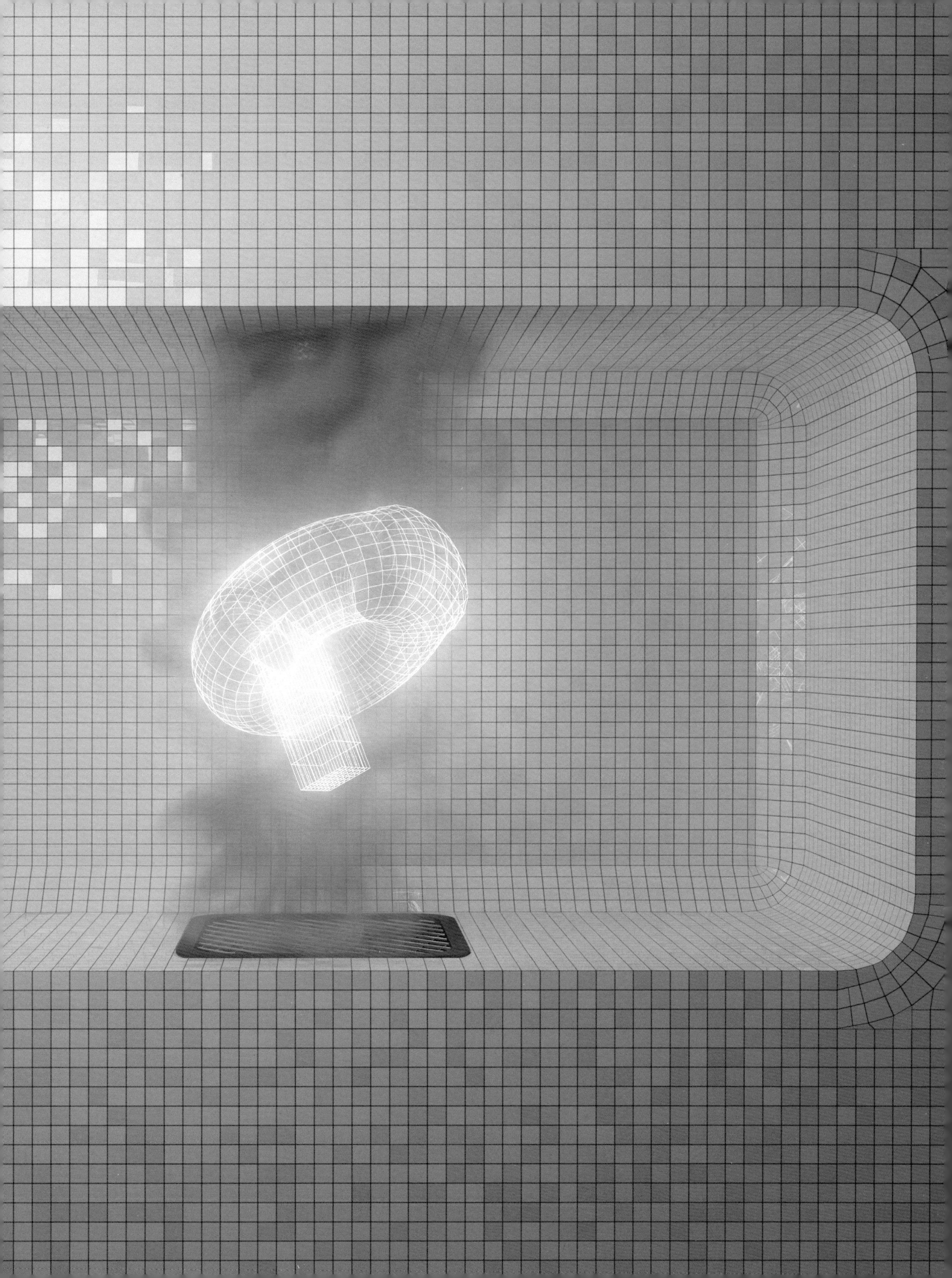

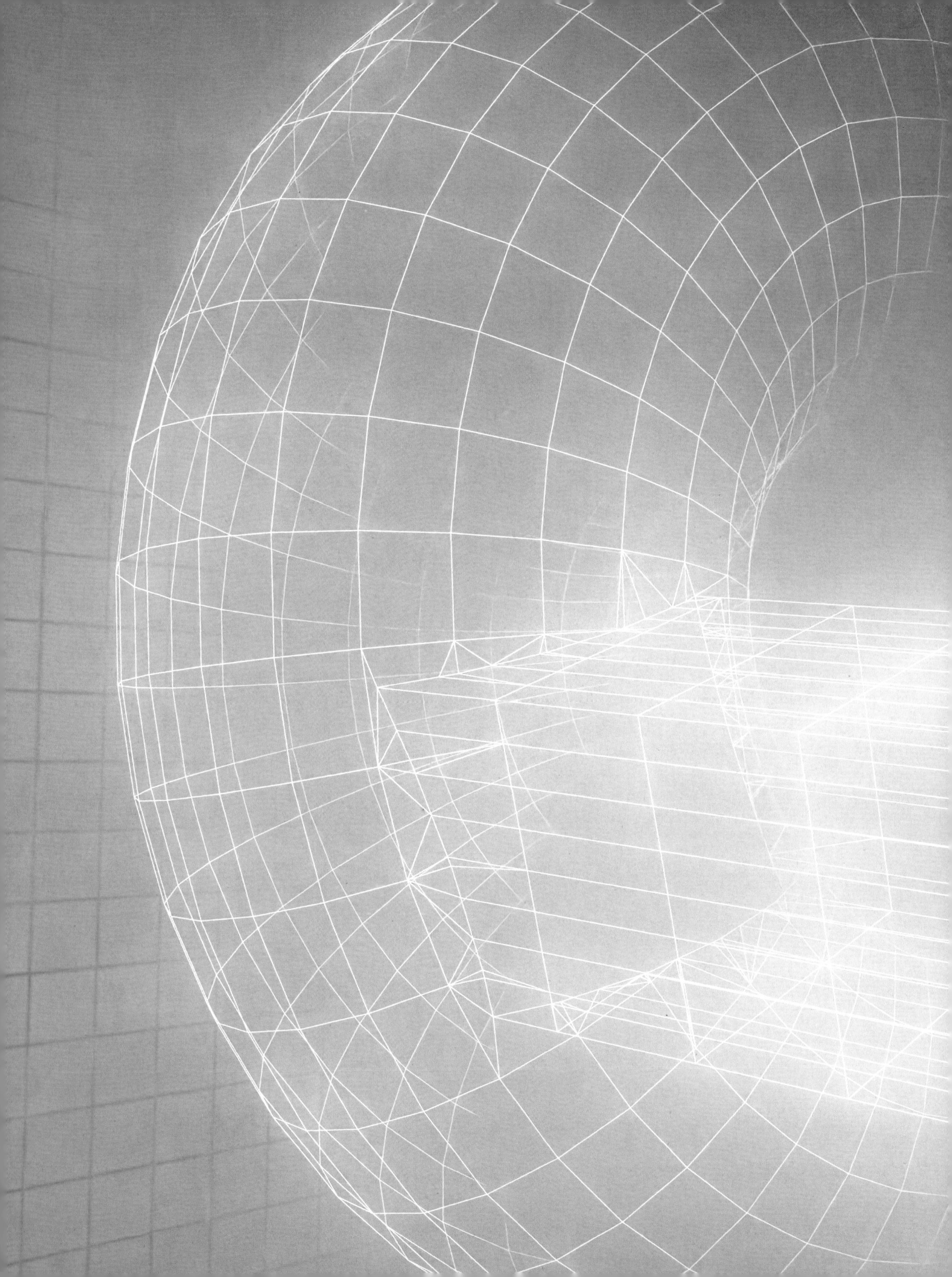

Can a Diorama Become Invisible?

The elemental diorama contains and renders the invisible elements. The diorama is, of course, essential and, as has already been mentioned, inextricable from its contents. Without it, the perfectly invisible element is without the slightest evidence of its existence. But "invisible" can take on other meaning in the context of the diorama. Visibility can be defined in terms of attention. "Feeling invisible" might involve having been looked over or ignored. That which is so insignificant or mundane as to garner no attention might as well be invisible. When we say we "felt invisible in the crowd" we are of course speaking figuratively. We usually don't want to be thought of this way, but this kind of invisibility is often necessary in the context of rendering a reality. The element that is invisible in appearance needs counterpart elements that are visible in appearance and effectively invisible to our conscious attention.

In the last chapter, we discussed the craft of creating unique book cover designs within the room. That process of crafting details that were not the subject of the rendering was positioned as a delicate balance between expending design energy on the construction of reality verses wasting precious design time. Here, however, with respect to the invisible elements, the value of the mundanely real serves a specific function: it positions the invisible elements in jarring conflict with what we expect to see in terms of material and gravity.

The tiles on the walls of the dioramas are crafted in an unusual though painstakingly normative manner to create optical affects that might've gone completely unnoticed if not for this reference. Without them, the digitality of the process would creep into the rendered image. The mesh that directs the rendering of the tiles is not mapped with an image. It's divided into faces as all meshes are, but in this case, the faces are not sized and positioned so as to optimize the curvature. Instead, the mesh is manually subdivided such that each face corresponds to one tile. The gridded wireframe of the mesh model matches almost exactly with the grid of the tile. A slight divergence results from each face being manipulated during the render to articulate a tile. Each tile appears to bulge slightly. Most importantly, as if set into mortar laid "by hand," each tile is not perfectly parallel to the mesh face. This is inconsequential in even lighting conditions, but when glare intertwines with formal legibility, as is the case when the wireframe of the semi-invisible form emits light, the tiles shimmer like pixels. The manual nature of the tiles respects their material counterpart, which is likewise manual, but as was the case with materiality in rendering, rendering converges with reality as the model diverges from it. A secondary benefit of this crafted materiality is a freedom from the obligation to calibrate a relationship between image and mesh. Because there are no external images to map, extending the mesh by adding a new face is like adding a new tile. The tiles can go on forever without concern for the usual unwanted artifacts of texture mapping: visible seams or noticeable repetition of patterns.

EXERCISE

Everything but the Thing

Find or model a digital solid. Isolate it on its own layer so that it can easily be hidden. Design a primitive and repeating system of forms that is as different in nature from the original solid as possible. Deploy this system gently and subtly at first. Regularly hide the solid so that the capacity for your designed system to render the invisible form is tested. At these moments, take the opportunity to record an iteration by exporting an image. Explore different criteria for when to stop this iterative process and/or invite a second formal system in. The animation that can be produced by sequencing your iterative images may be more valuable than the final form.

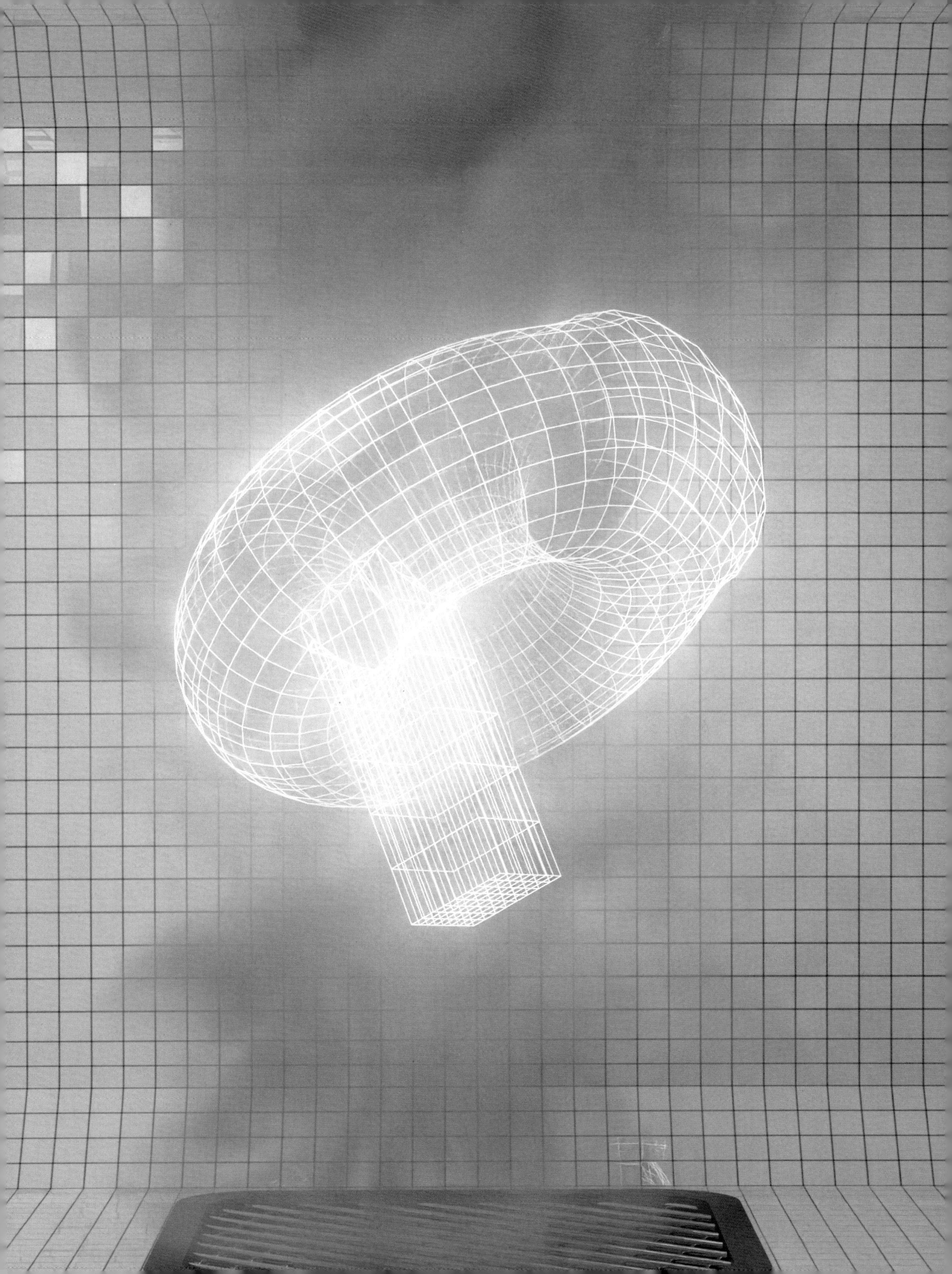

What about the shape of the invisible element?

It may seem unusual to have progressed this far in a discussion about rendering digital geometry to have never mentioned the qualities of the geometry itself. We've discussed strategies for partial invisibility, but those could be applied to any mesh geometry—and that's the key; we've engaged in formal discourse in which the content of our inquiry requires formal input, but the resulting rendering represents something other than that input. That something else is not wholly new either. That something else is neither figure nor ground. That something else is neither atmosphere nor object.

Some readers may be satisfied to realize that we have meandered into a working if lacking definition of architecture: an invisible geometry intertwined with controlled atmosphere with a threshold condition at its edge. Other readers will insist that a question persists: what is that input geometry and why is it shaped in that way? The anticlimactic answer, the union of a rectilinear prism and a torus with multiple slight surface deformations, is ever so slightly consequential. The invisible element is a body comprised of multiple recognizable parts with just enough variation to leave open the possibility that there is something more unseen. The shape is just regular enough to serve as a foil to the atmospheric diorama. In the delicate realm of semi-invisibility, calibration is paramount. The most significant feat lies in the loaded conceptual nature of an ontologically contradictory rendering in which the subject is materially invisible while being traced by material form. The shape of the subject is not at issue, but it's not neutral either.

Essentially Animate

The semi-invisible elements within dioramas rendered on these pages are animate. The stills are each a freeze frame. That much is obvious, or at least it's fair to say that much is easily assumed. The fluid appears to be in the midst of splashing and the smoke in the midst of diffusion. A similar apparently animate quality can be ascribed to many images in multiple chapters of this book. It's one of many triggers of reality that can live in a digital still rendering.

In these cases, though, we can go further and claim that an animation conflicts with reality if that animation exists within the representational container of the diorama. Dioramas are temporal containers. Even more than a photograph, they can be often understood to stop time. Imagine a taxidermy buffalo in a scene depicting the landscape of the American plains. The buffalo is obviously inanimate. Or is it? If we suspend disbelief, we might allow ourselves to read the buffalo at rest or moving in super slow motion. Even as the photographer Richard Barnes captures a curator cleaning the buffalo[9], we are invited to sustain two realities, moving at two speeds simultaneously. The uncanny or strange conditions aren't forces that break reality. Instead, two overlapping realities coexist within the confines of the diorama, which provides the architecture essential for this occurrence.

Imagine then that the fluid or smoke is not animate. Consistent with our surprisingly nimble hypothetical buffalo (which of course is a representation of a buffalo made of buffalo parts) this can be said to complicate, not flatten reality. Now, the "magic" plays out in the articulation of real but inanimate form that represents fluid. This is the pursuit of the uncanny within the diorama. To achieve this, we need a trigger for a different time scale. Dioramas are durational, and we can represent the extreme limits of that duration. Barnes encounters the same during installation of dioramas. In the final work of this chapter, those markers—triggers of a different reality—take the form in conflicting material wrappers and fixtures. The fluid is now still like glass and is suspended by cables, which support the very material form that only exists in the first place to trace and reveal the invisible elements. They are two layers of reality deep. To return to our reoccurring ruminations on the discipline of magic for a moment, we can speculate that although representations of magic undermine magic, layers of reality might allow magical conditions to transfer into something, to rattle your sense of how the world works, and to reveal something much more real than the really real.

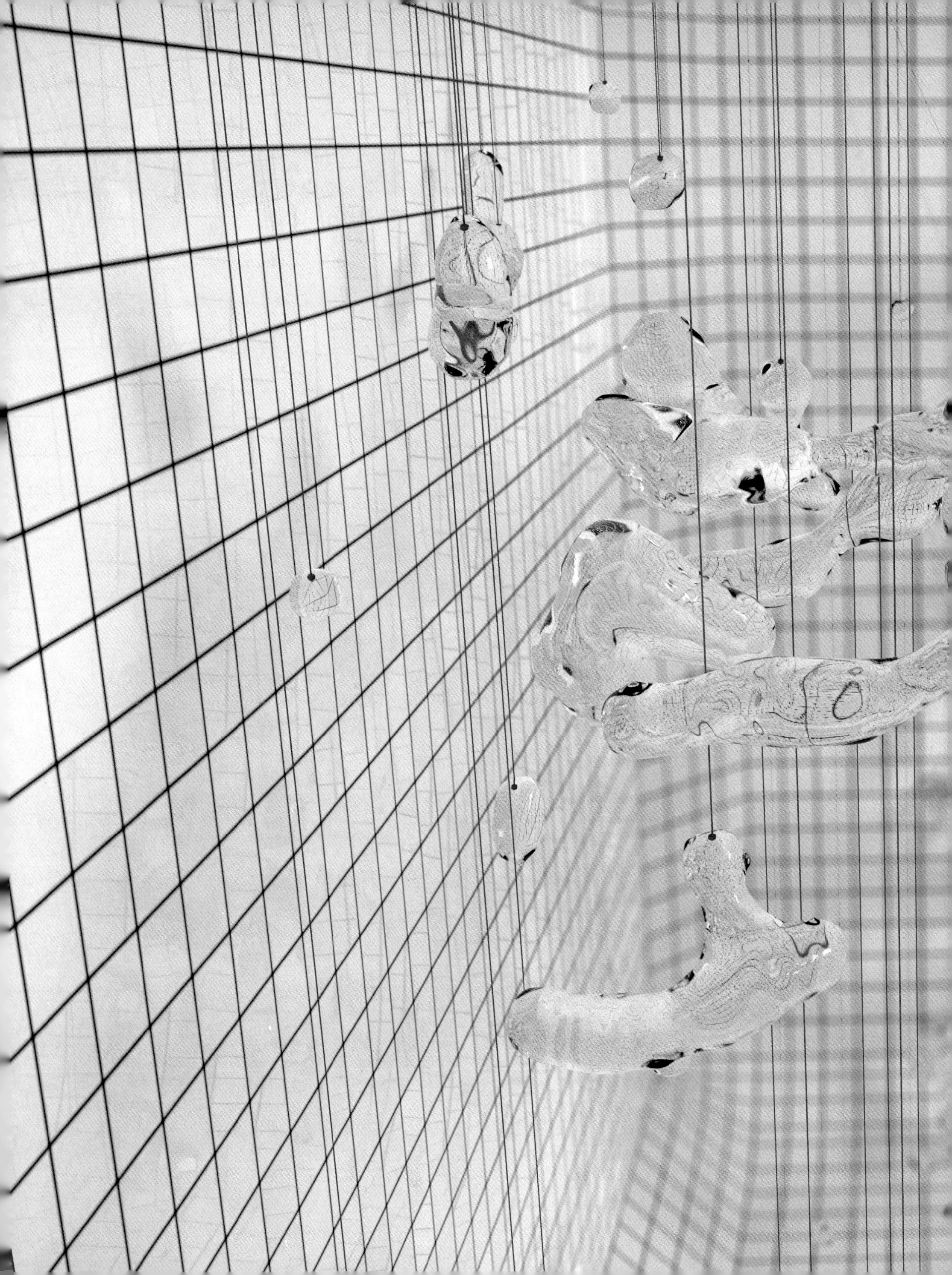

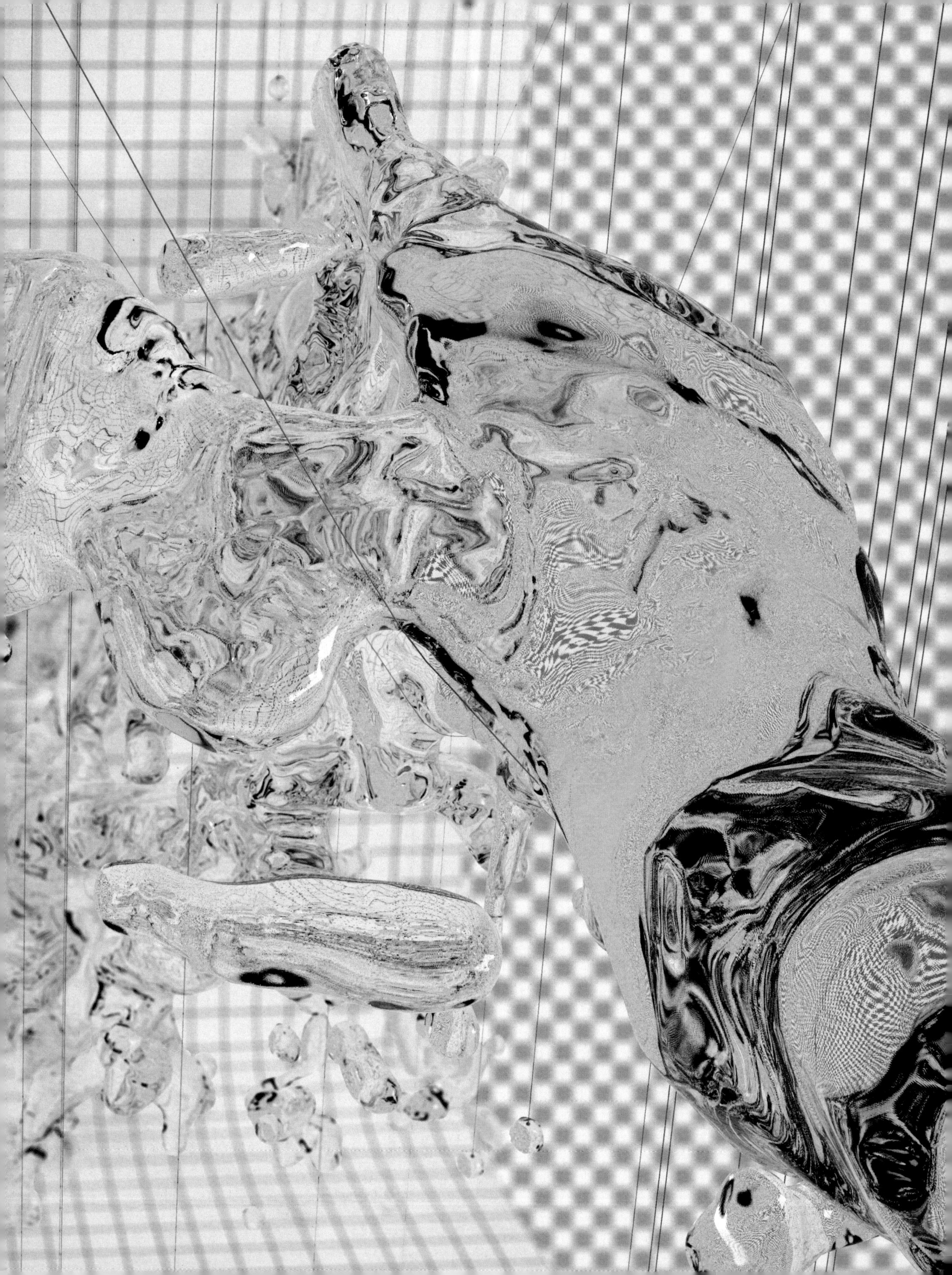

Notes:

1. *EG5 Jamy Ian Swiss*, YouTube (YouTube, 2012), https://www.youtube.com/watch?v=jjxeqyuSe_Y.
2. Mario Carpo, "Introduction, Twenty Years of Digital Design," in *The Digital Turn in Architecture 1992-2012* (Chichester, West Sussex England: Wiley, 2013). In the introduction to this reader, Carpo articulates the nature of the "turn." "[T]he beginnings of the digital turn in architecture were first and foremost a matter of inspiration - and perhaps fascination. Electronic technologies in the early 1990s were changing - some thought, revolutionising - society, economy, culture and almost every aspect of daily life. So much was changing and so fast that some architects started to think that design should change too."
3. Paul Mandell, "Elastic Effect: New Optical Wrinkle," American Cinematographer, October 1988.
4. Ibid.
5. Ibid.
6. Ibid.
7. H. G. Wells, The Invisible Man (Scotts Valley, CA: CreateSpace Independent Publishing Platform, 2010).
8. Moore, Ronald D. (writer) et al., "Redemption II." Episode. *Star Trek, The Next Generation 5*, no. 1, September 23, 1991.
9. Richard Barnes, "Diorama," in Animal Logic: Container, Diorama, Skull, *Refuge, Murmur* (New York, NY: Princeton Architectural Press, 2009).

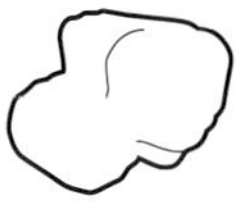

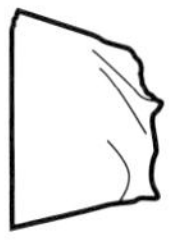

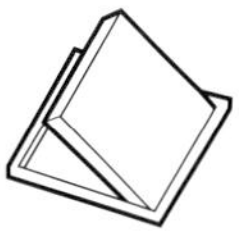

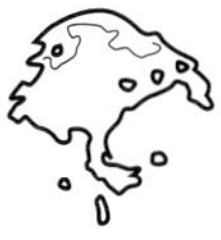

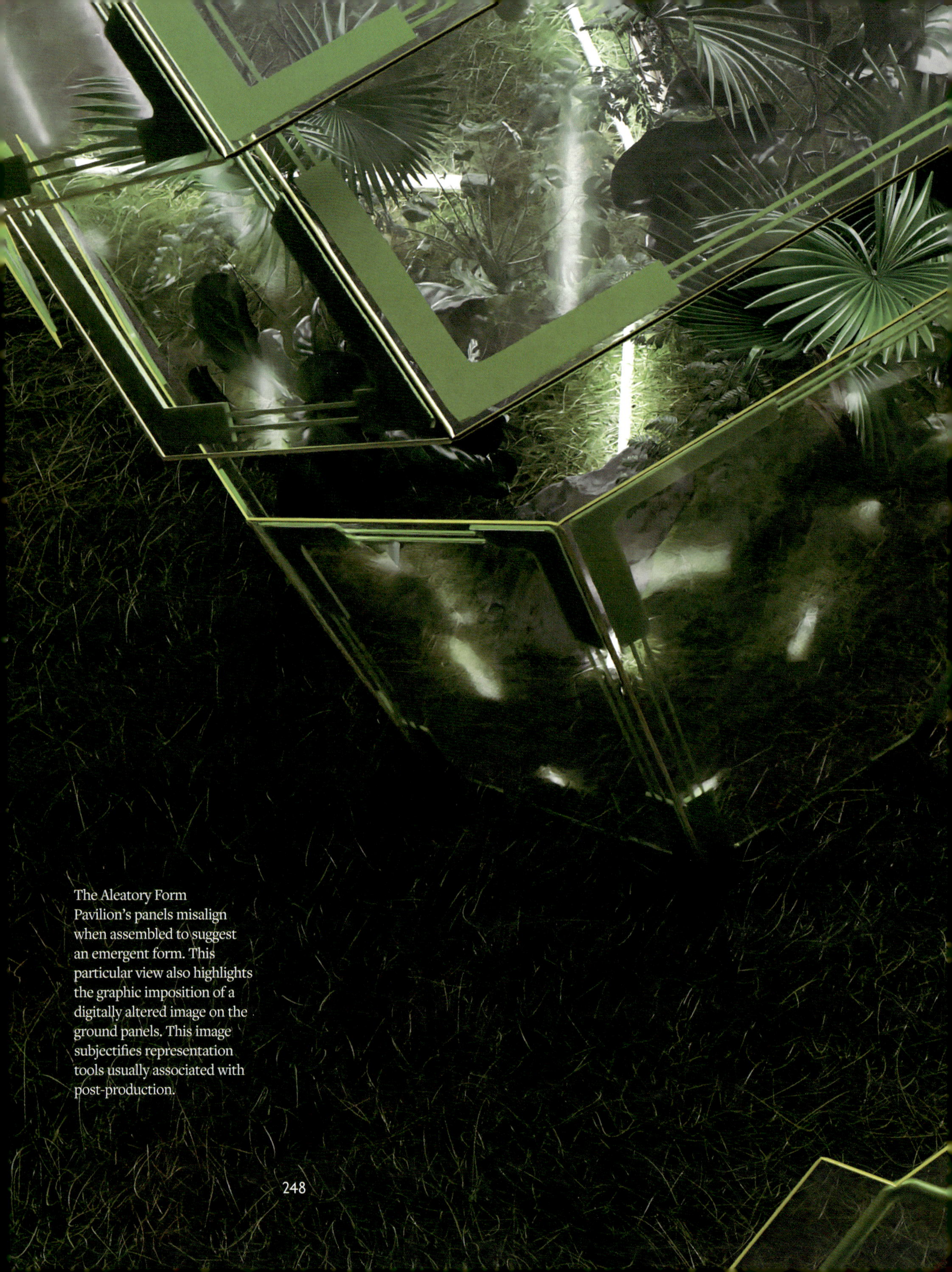

The Aleatory Form Pavilion's panels misalign when assembled to suggest an emergent form. This particular view also highlights the graphic imposition of a digitally altered image on the ground panels. This image subjectifies representation tools usually associated with post-production.

CHAPTER 6

Operating on the Violence-Aggression Axis

by Viola Ago

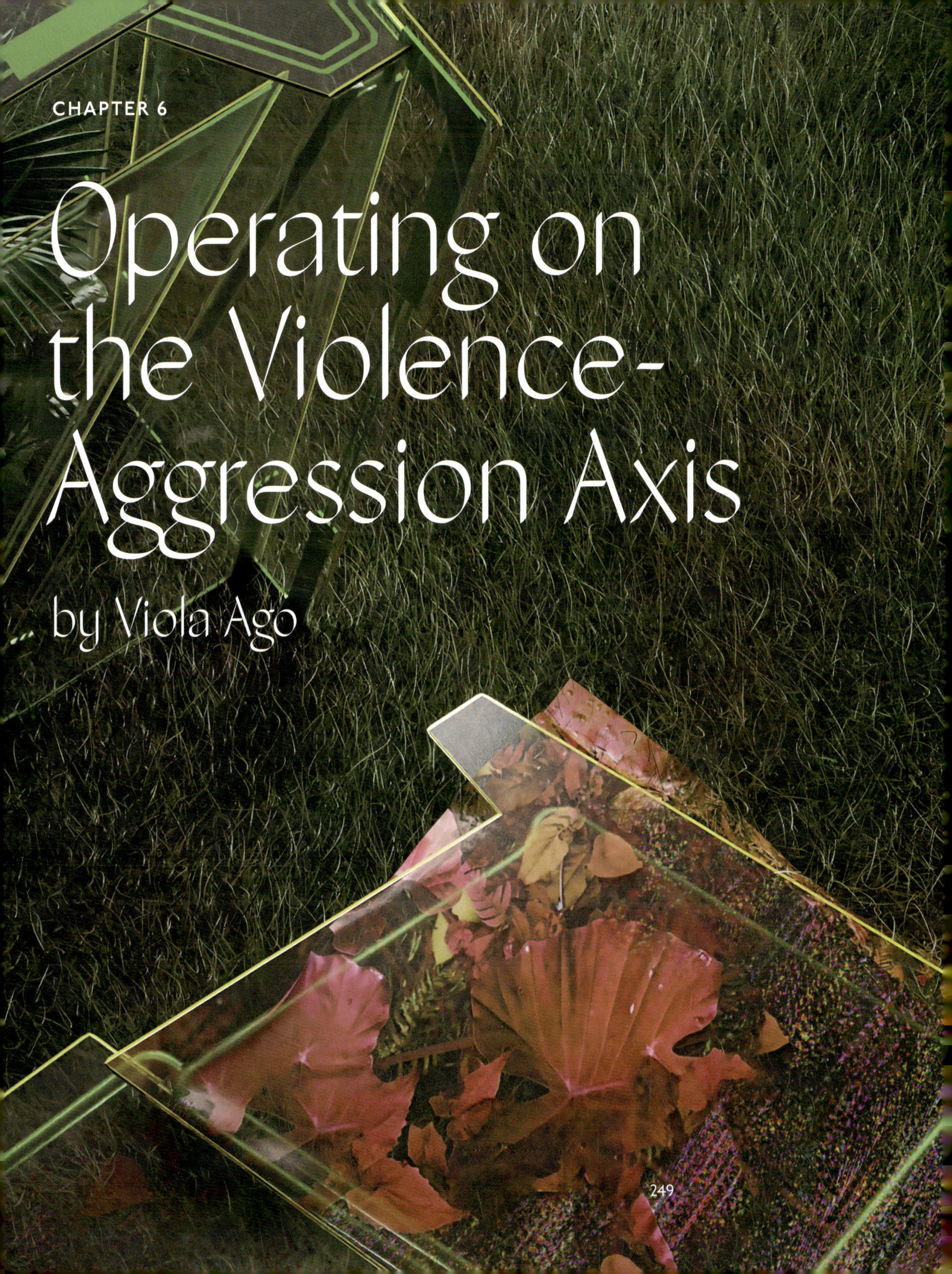

A smoke plume is seen rising in a portrait-format cell phone video, followed by a sudden explosion. Then the video shows 36 thumbnails of recordings of the explosions at the Port of Beirut that took place on August 4, 2020. The video continues to display smoke plume simulations, geospatial analysis, splices of real and simulated footage, and geometrical and coloration attributes of explosions. The filmic sequence teeters between the real and the simulated, between accurately rendered materials and defaulted Phong and Blinn off-whites, between facts and informed assumptions. The back-and-forth of these binaries is conflated—one is not in service of the other. The video, produced by Forensic Architecture, a research agency directed by Eyal Weizman, intertwines open-source data from the real world with digital platforms and tools innate to visual, creative, and scientific disciplines. Intentionally or not, this atypical methodology offers an architectural possibility defined by events, policy, and forensic evidence, rather than stand-alone formalisms.

Outside of art and architecture, the digital tools evident in Forensic Architecture's work are borrowed from peripheral disciplines such as film, animation, data analysis, and motion graphics. In addition to the use of digital platforms and open-source information, Forensic Architecture also constructs tools and methods informed by forensic psychology. In reconstructing architecture as an event, they turn to egocentric and allocentric perspectives to inform and parse out resources such as in the *Torture In Saydnaya Prison* project. An egocentric perspective refers to the experience of an event in the first person at eye level, whereas an allocentric perspective refers to the experience as an outsider—that is, the experience is built through relationships that the individual constructs with things, objects, and other material and immaterial atmospheric influences. Not unlike the binary conflations in *The Beirut Port Explosion* project, forensic psychologists argue that trauma conflates the egocentric and allocentric perspectives into an enmeshed experience. In all, somewhere between the laws of physics and the laws of memory, Forensic Architecture constructs filmic sequences that collapse the past and the present using digital tools from fields of visual representation and conceptual tools from the field of psychology. In so doing, they ask that we re-see and re-consider the world that we otherwise understand through conventional lenses as static, single-purpose, and one-directional.

In the Space of Animate Memory Sequences

Constructing sequences using a methodology based on a combination of memory and simulation affords a compelling apparatus for an architecture that is not merely visual, but also haptic, gestural, spatial, and political. Conflating the laws of physics, descriptions of events, affective experiences of natural behaviors, and qualities of units in a system or network can productively engage our perceptual apparatuses in ways that extend past the traditional narratives of architectural thinking and making. Exploring these apparatuses in the architectural realm might constitute what is typically, though maybe erroneously, referred to as "representation." Apprehensively accepting the term, this work implicitly argues that representation is not a method of mere visual or annotative communication. We can instead understand representation as a way of being within the world; processing reality so that we can collectively participate in its becoming. Through representation and visualization, we can transform our permeable selves and become with our reality in real time.

The speculative Aleatory Form Pavilion uses digital simulation tools to inform the organizational qualities of the proposed structure. In contrast to a key framing technique that generates animation between two known states, this approach instead deals with initial states subject to forces. The matrix constitutes an exhaustive diagram that lists actions and forces impeding on a closed (watertight) input volume to realize the agitation of the components of the architectural composition. The process first involves transformation techniques such as cutting and rotating. The results are then loaded into a digital physics simulation engine to add a turbulence force to the panels that makes them seem to tremble from a supporting structural frame underneath. In the space of animation sequences, geometrical transformations and physics-based compositional manipulations can get extreme. In some cases, the variation within the sequence is almost invisible. In other cases, the original inputs are transformed beyond recognition. At either extreme, the bounds of the representational world are defined. More importantly though, the compositional actions are not "pre-real." They are not separated from the reality of physics forces. Conversely, it would not be appropriate to position this work within the realm of "form finding," a methodological territory that assumes that simulation reaches a state of equilibrium coinciding with an idealized form. It might even be suggested that the matrix is not merely collection of versions, but the representation of possible states all meant to exist simultaneously.

The second part of the Aleatory Form Pavilion matrix tells the story of the consecutive real-time decisions that were made in the digital realm. Force

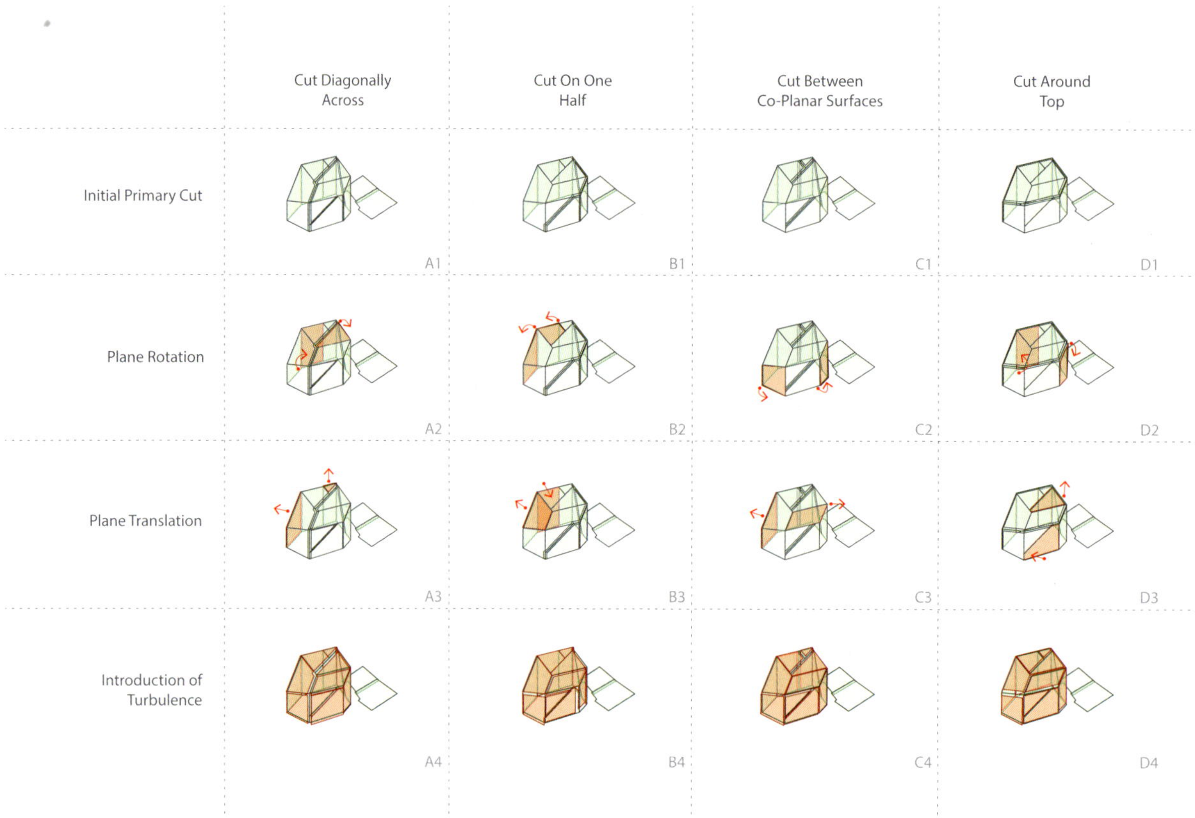
Cut Diagonally Across
Cut On One Half
Cut Between Co-Planar Surfaces
Cut Around Top
Initial Primary Cut
A1
B1
C1
D1
Plane Rotation
A2
B2
C2
D2
Plane Translation
A3
B3
C3
D3
Introduction of Turbulence
A4
B4
C4
D4

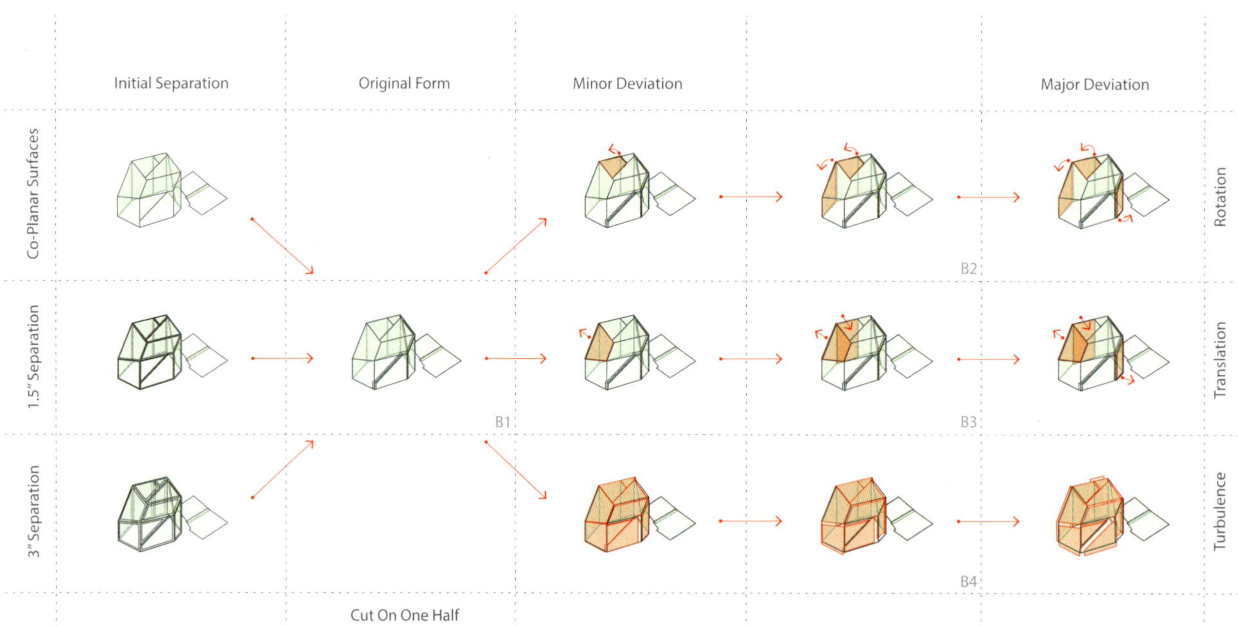
Initial Separation
Original Form
Minor Deviation
Major Deviation
Co-Planar Surfaces
1.5" Separation
3" Separation
B2
B1
B3
B4
Rotation
Translation
Turbulence
Cut On One Half

coefficients are altered by the author to cultivate effects and qualities that point to instability and duress on the spectrum between the almost invisible transformations on the one end to completely unrecognizable ones on the other. It is also important to note that it is through the animation platform that the remnants of a digital interface and authorial production converge.

If the animated formal sequences constitute an element of architecture given that they convey as well as create, the complementary roof-like structure also warrants consideration as an element. It's treated as though it missed its host entirely and is instead resting on the ground. An infinitely thin graphic layer blankets a wire frame, which is similar, in some terms, to the surrounding context. Digitally manipulated in alter-real hues, the roof elements reveal an interest in deviation from that which is expected and typically, normally, real. The recognizably and predictably green house plants, for example, serve as a register against which graphic deviations are orchestrated in tandem with the non-conformism of misaligned edges. Though the elements in the scene are unambiguously coherent, they are not resolved in the usual terms. Enclosure, thickness, and dimensionality are fleeting concepts. Instead of the rendering polishing a clean end-product, the rendering realizes and facilitates the abnormal digital uncanny.

This set of diagrams for the *Aleatory Form Pavilion* illustrate a physics engine simulation on a group of panels that would otherwise perfectly align to form a clean, watertight volume. The diagrams combine explicit transformation operations as well as a less-controlled turbulence force applied to the panels.

EXERCISE

Transformation Matrix

Starting with a cube, laterally move a copy of the cube and transform the copy. Repeat the process by making a copy of the transformed copy and transforming again. Repeat until a series of forms are arranged in a row. Keep in mind that the transformation should be consistent but could involve any number of operations and decisions. After the series is complete, design a different transformation to apply to the other axis. Apply the new transformation to a vertically shifted copy of each element in the row and again repeat to form columns. Now that the transformation matrix is complete, what will you do with it? Consider transforming or augmenting the composition so that it might function as a single element. Or, use the matrix as the foundation for a stop-motion animation where each frame moves left, right, up or down along the matrix to generate an animate figure. If needed, return to the beginning and make a higher (or lower) resolution matrix.

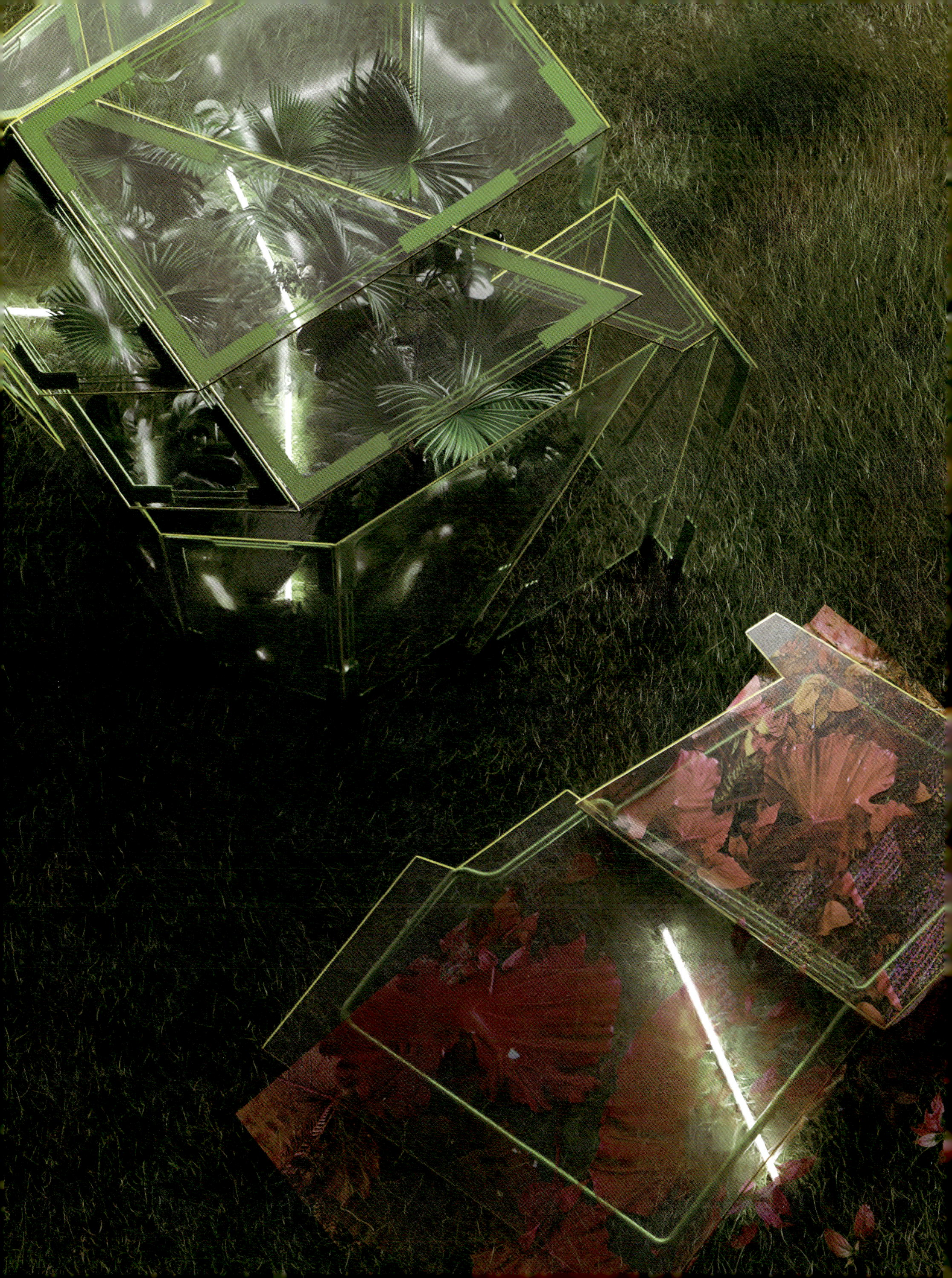

Relational Architecture: Between Violence and Aggression

With these initial drivers in mind, our attention can be directed to an element that can be linked to aesthetics, digital simulations, and politics—the architectural surface. So far, two conceptions of surface have already been in play here: 2-D panels and infinitely thin graphic layers. Intentionally manipulating these two conceptions of surface reveals a burning creative desire to make visible conditions of disorder attuned to architectural discourse that advances beyond one-directional, historically biased, and theoretically exclusive narratives. To be more specific, these forms seek to accelerate a disciplinary convergence with the dilemmas and urgencies that paint daily life—more globally now than ever before. It seeks to expand modes of production at pace with expanded modes of communication.

Our contemporary moment is one in crisis, characterized by material (as in the body and physical constructs) and immaterial (as in cognitive and internal sensorial systems) destruction. These adjectives have been integral parts of the creative vocabulary before, especially during the deconstructivism movement in architecture and the Dada and neo-Dada movements that saw architects and artists viscerally responding to their preceding eras. For architects, this manifest as the cold, symmetrical, and rigid tenets of high modernism, and for artists, as the representational and classical orders of art. This kind of old-as-age patricidal modality has been de facto in architecture and art in the passing of the torch: in order for a new style to be established it must kill its father. In the arts, perhaps the most recognizable and literal example can be attributed to Robert Rouschenberg's 1953 Erased de Kooning Drawing where he personally requested a favorite of de Kooning's paintings (drawn in pencil) from the artist himself and literally erased it to establish his timely dominance. An analogous example in architecture could be illustrated by Frank Gehry's 1991 Gehry Residence where the architect took the typical suburban balloon-framed bungalow single-family home typology and started to literally deconstruct it by removing parts, adding disoriented cubes in random areas, using industrial materials, exposing rather than hiding the structural elements.

There is cultural cache from the art and architectural works performed during these contradictory and subversive eras. However, revolting against the architect father, in architecture, with architecture, creates a very hermetic and claustrophobic sphere of engagement that instead of destroying the system, further reinforces it by repairing or replacing the stale and no-longer acceptable parts.

The deconstructivists missed two important aspects during their infamous turn. One missed opportunity was in not allowing the design and conceptual process to support and center other forms of politics—social, economic, political, ecological, etc. The second missed opportunity of the deconstructivists was their obsession with the final, deterministic, knock-out product, and that process was seldom discussed as a catalyst for new methods for representation. In other words, the design process was in service of a finalized building or form that made you feel something was out of the ordinary. In this way, deconstructivism had some affinities with the postmodern condition where the physical body of the urban subject was meant to be spatially disoriented and destabilized. Today, we have the potential and, luckily, the collective ambition to work toward a relational architecture that can belong to the political condition as much as to the aesthetic. Simply put, in the creative process, we have the potential to embody our very real ways of being. Representation cannot remain stagnant.

In his 1961 book, *Wretched of the Earth*, Frantz Fanon sketches an immersive parallel between the colonizer and the colonized in his chapter on violence. He describes the colonizer's imposed value system as violence and the response of the colonized as aggression. This weighs heavily on the reader. A destructive atmosphere—a complex network of multi-axis diagrams between violence and aggression—is inherent not only in our contemporary being, but persistently through most of modern life. In our context, the western creatives of the second half of the twentieth century missed this, more than likely due to the institutionalized nature of knowledge production and dissemination. The 2021 exhibition at the New Museum in New York City, *Grief and Grievance: Art and Mourning in America*, revisits this exact world. The show includes a video installation by Theaster Gates titled *Gone are the Days of Shelter and Martyr* (2014). This video shows a recording of a performance that was part scripted and part improvised on site where an intimate group of musicians occupy an abandoned and dilapidated church in Chicago. They use their bodies to physically move imminent artifacts in the church and sounds to ephemerally activate—arguably even transcend—the complex history of the church, which Gates argues is typical in south side Chicago. The installation offers a fascinating example for work that zeroes in on the relationship between politics and architecture. It is even more relevant for our current moment because our material and immaterial states of duress are here. It is impossible to imagine an architectural space—even a speculative or fictional one—where the politics of violence and aggression are not considered.

EXERCISE

Chop, Drop (does it Roll?)

Begin with a solid 3-D digital form (possibly chosen from a transformation matrix). Chop it with a non-orthogonally oriented cutting surface. Separate the new objects and cap them if necessary. Load the two objects into a physics simulation engine. Add a rigid ground. If necessary, activate a gravitational force (some engines will have this on by default). Play the simulation. Alter the parameters that control simulation speed, force amount, friction, cohesion, and drag to simulate a drop that is either close to appearing natural or that makes the scene feel artificial. Listen to your own sensorial apparatuses when altering these inputs. Repeat this process many times. Consider copying and retaining the chop after each drop in a physical pile so that no form is rejected, only set aside after reaching equilibrium.

Intentionally Corrupted Surface, the Resurgent Line

In our inherited present world, we inhabit a reality littered with physical artifacts and an increasingly platform-dependent digital environment. In this context, we can afford a return to a consideration of strategic process over proprietary product so that we can focus on new forms of becoming with our representation. Methodologies that produce moments of surprise, shock, and deviations from an established norm contribute to this endeavor. Excerpts from a series titled *Models are Drawings that Believed in Miracles* are featured here to facilitate our exploration of the corrupted surface. The drawing is equal parts process and product and has been generated using algorithmic techniques. In addition to the drawing phase of the project, the work has also been produced using methods of fabrication inherent in industrial design manufacturing; methods which often bleed into the architecture studio "model shop." To be specific, the drawing has been produced by printing four consecutive layers of vector and color information directly onto a semi-transparent rigid plexi board using UV-cured ink. The layering of the graphic information is important in two ways—one conceptual and one haptic. In the conceptual sphere, each consecutive layer—though a duplicate of the initial formal diagram—betrays its origin in favor of more corrupt conditions. From a haptic position, the layers are printed separately (the drawing is actually printed four times over with a loosely precise registration point) so that the graphic information creates a low relief on the picture plane, one with mounds of ink deposits that favor the topmost layer (the most corrupt) over the original sources of information (the least agitated)—which also gives the drawing/model a tectonic dimension.

This drawing concept/production methodology searches for moments that induce discomfort hidden under the guise of polished form. Being finished is decoupled from being resolved, while modeling is convolved with drawing. It is this level of subversion that we can look beyond and within the surface to pursue the most basic element of the conventional architectural representation—a straight line segment, with a ubiquitous line thickness or weight. These lines are employed to produce sensorial experiences in the conception of the work, but also to communicate perceived moments to someone who has not learned the language of design and architectural drawing. These kinds "what you see is what you get" lines also appear in further diminished form as "hatches" in Chapter 8. Here, we're concerned with subversive politics of these lines. We're interested in using the line to further reinforce the normative and the conventional but also to destroy it just a little bit. Why? In the past, it has been difficult for humans to operate from a place of obliteration, instead we use the altered, and more often than not, destroyed forms of the familiar.

In another iteration of this methodology, the friction between the layers of rigid and corrupt information moves to the material kind of surface element as the act of assembly forces the 3-D realization of 2-D surfaces. Even here though, surface is unconventionally implicated in the representation of volume, a legacy that results from its previous co-dependence on the drawing of lines. An animation sequence registers a digitally simulated event: the collapse of 2-D and 3-D information. To be more specific, the animation sequence registers an action: forces of compression act on volumes on a "ground" plane while also interacting with line-based graphic conditions that violate the legibility of the underlying form. The representation constitutes an experiment that sustains the swaying between haptic and visual decision-making. The project borrows visual qualities from an analog exercise of a parallel research study, the *Poppy Red* design project. In particular, the experiment recalls and references hydrodipping, otherwise known as water graphic transfer printing, an industrial design process typically used to shrink-wrap graphics onto complex 3-D objects by forcing the object (receiver of the graphic) through a chemical water bath whose surface supports the inkjet-produced graphic. Though it can be calibrated for high precision coefficients, hydrodipping also allows for more haphazard collapses between the 2-D and 3-D content because the registration mark between the two forms literally floats on the surface of the water. With this expanded project, the architectural surface gains agency in three distinct ways. The "ground" surface for example is a surface on which geometrical operations take place. Not too dissimilarly, the water surface, despite its material distinctions from the drawing substrate, supports and sustains line drawings and color fields. Arguably, the water surface is material and immaterial at once. And more importantly, this conglomerate, loaded, architectural surface encompasses all the previous operations and statuses of surface: ground, drawing, image, panel, and material. The architectural surface also registers the conflict between conceptions of the surface. Like other elements of architecture explored in this book, as it resists conventions of representation, subsumes representation into its own existence.

In the attempt to misuse and corrupt, introduce deviations from order, and to slip between 2-D and 3-D agency, the animation sequence for *House 1*, featured here, looks to digital simulation tools to co-opt the behavior of hydrodipping. The goal is not to precisely imitate natural behavior. To turn to the conception of architecture proposed earlier—that architecture might capitalize on an event that is equal parts allocentric and egocentric, or in other words, part physical realism and part memory—the simulation exercise replicates water transfer behaviors by *selectively* recovering the analog, or architectural, events. In this way, the surface is not co-opted by the author with a high level of control. Instead, the surface has its own agency in the design process as a host of alternative realities that are more distraught, more corrupt. We can then conclude that the architectural surface itself becomes a negotiator between the real and the imaginative, and instead of offering solutions, it offers destabilized conditions in which the negotiations are embedded and inherent. The simulation explorations of surfaces as actants use the forceful event of the 2-D and 3-D layers in an argument for states of duress as an aesthetic possibility that is inextricably tied to our political and cultural beings.

Given that the work of architecture is also a work of architectural representation, we can expect that we can use it to pose questions. Can we stand still for a moment and occupy a site that resists our collective urge to repair failed systems, to patch over the broken, to apply shiny patina on objects of oppressive regimes? Can representation participate in the suspension of correction and the refusal to immediately resolve? How do we, in a deeply capitalist visual culture, resist the impulse of pacification? How can we find a new definition of comfort—or be satisfied in the uncomfortable—in the disorderly, in the duressed? Can we create and operate in an architectural world in which both the shiny old orders and the fractured sites for resistance, co-exist? Can architecture gain from the coexistence of collective culture with parts in ruin? If we push a step further beyond the simple acknowledgment of the violence-aggression axis and we also accept that scattered parts and events of destructive force are very real conditions of our daily life, then perhaps we can find a layer of creative potential in that—one that can engage with architectural thought and creative process, rather than end the story in misfortune and missed opportunity.

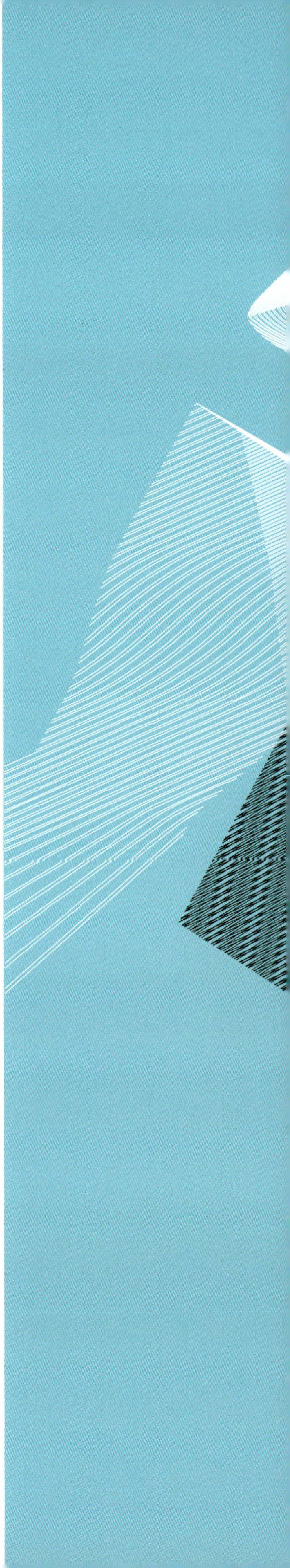

Drawing from the *Models Are Drawings that Believed in Miracles* series, this "hardly a drawing," panel consists of four individual flatbed printed layers, directly on a rigid acrylic panel, subtly misaligned to generate a loose figure. The topmost layer, printed in white, deviates from the original drawing the most by borrowing its transformation cues from the natural flow-like behavior of liquids, in this case water.

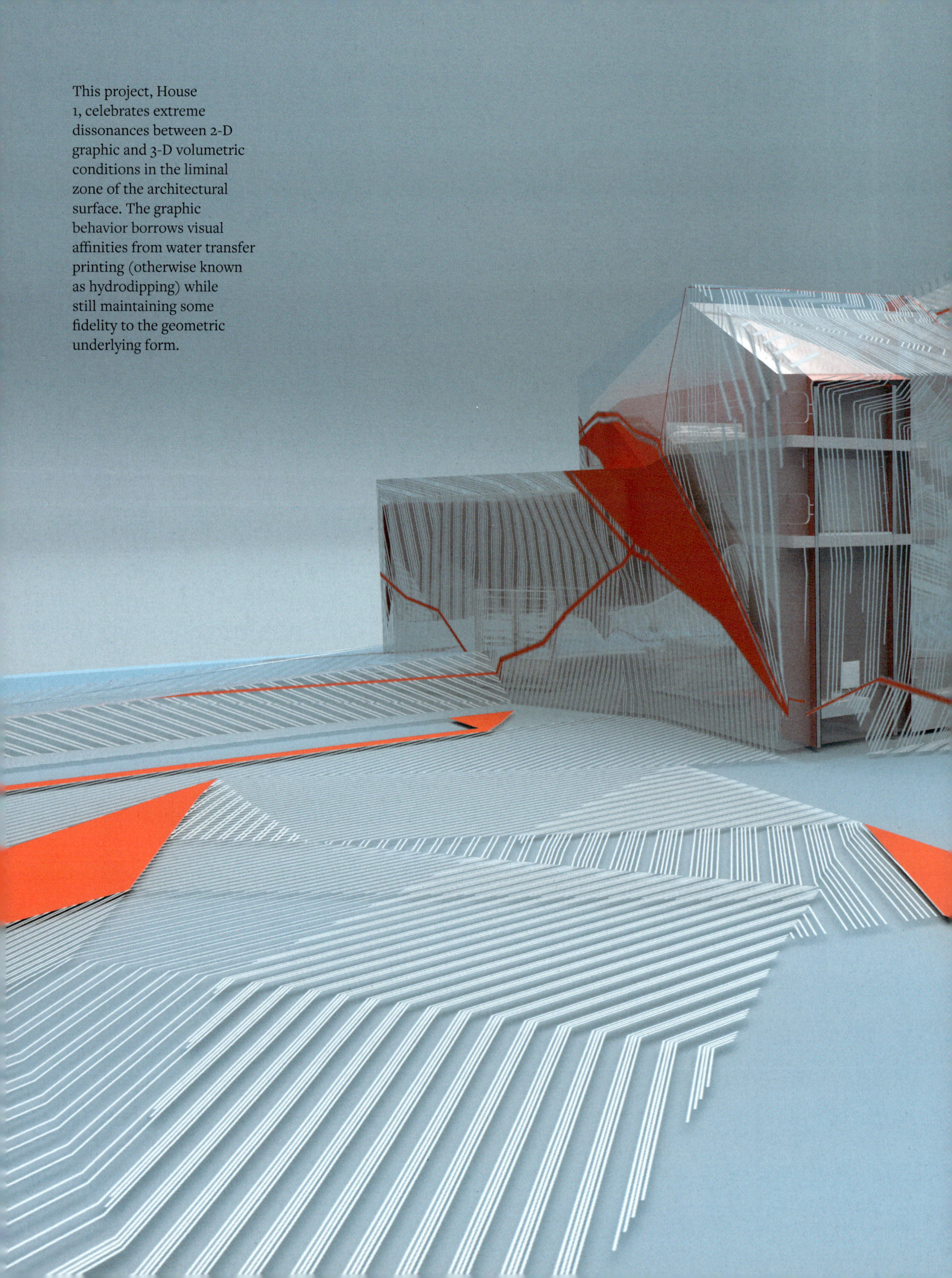

This project, House 1, celebrates extreme dissonances between 2-D graphic and 3-D volumetric conditions in the liminal zone of the architectural surface. The graphic behavior borrows visual affinities from water transfer printing (otherwise known as hydrodipping) while still maintaining some fidelity to the geometric underlying form.

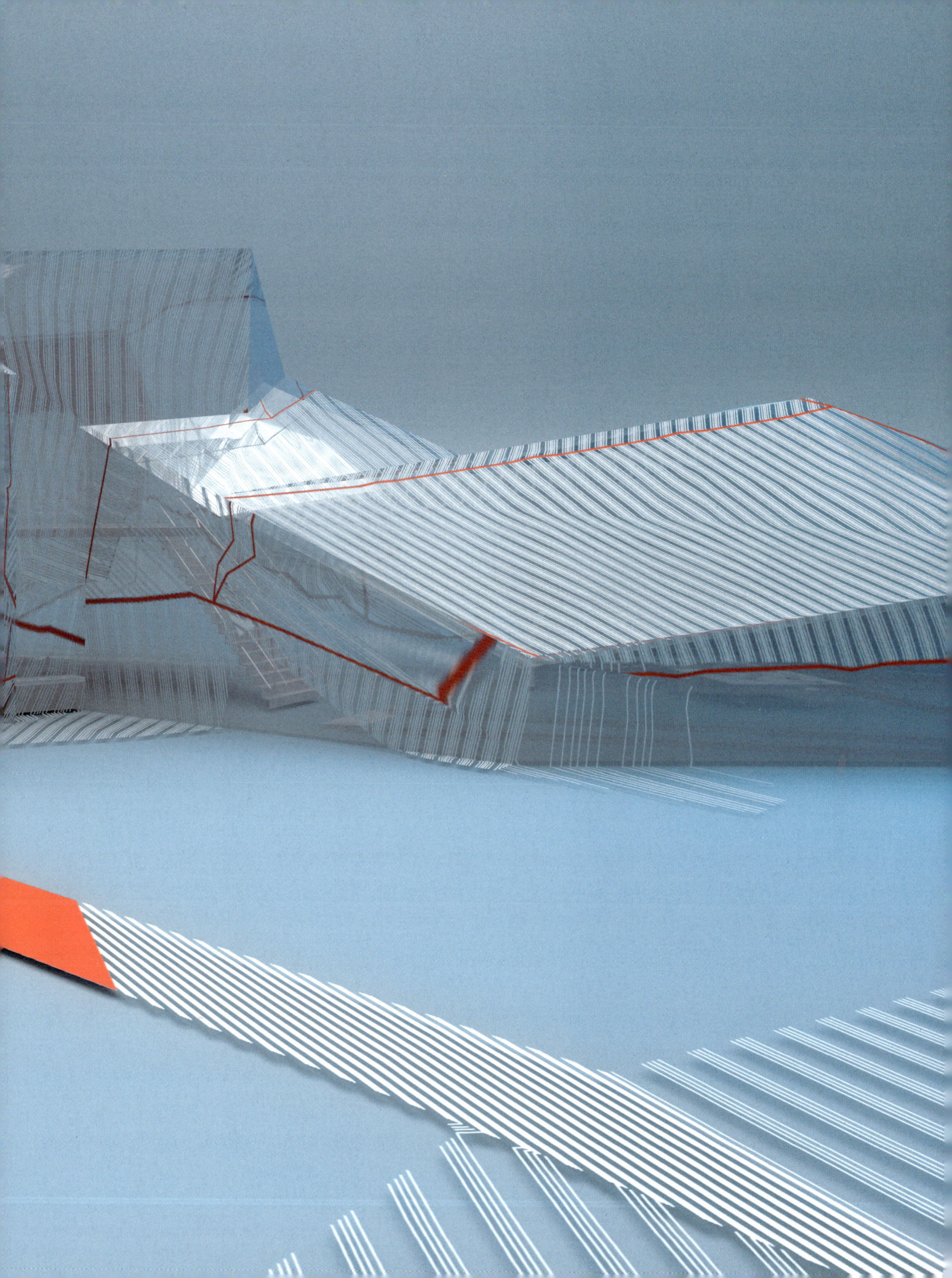

EXERCISE

Surface Frictions

Extract a rendered frame from an animation of an object falling (perhaps one that has been chopped in response to an earlier exercise) toward the ground. Import that rendering as a 2-D plane (or texture map the image onto a 2-D plane) within the file used to generate the rendering. Using the same physics engine, define the plane as a cloth and allow it to drape over the object that has fallen to the ground. Now, the representation of the object is materially dependent on (and a mask over) the object itself. In preparation for a rendering from a top-down view, adjust physics parameters, transparency, and lighting in the scene. Aim for a level of visual discomfort—a violation of expectations and a representation that seems conflicted about what it is, and what it is representing. After rendering the top view, consider using that image as a texture map for another render of the original object. Align and misalign 2-D and 3-D information by paying attention to the qualities of the 3-D digital atmosphere that call out to you.

Lyricism and Empathy (Or Bad Responses to External Calls)

So far, the work shown here has rendered the condition of duress that resides on the violence-aggression axis through two primary streams: first, formal and visual operations and second, the use of digital simulation technologies. The notion of the informed creative author is under pressure in this framework. We might ask, for example, how one of the animated sequences considered earlier would differ in another author's hands? And is one's author animation more valid than the other's? As we extend this line of inquiry, we can helpfully turn to perceptual mechanisms guided by lyrical influences and phenomenology of empathy.

> Normal perception is biased towards instrumentality rather than vibrancy, simplification rather than open-ended reception.
> —Jane Bennett, *Influx and Efflux: Writing Up With Walt Whitman*, 2020.

In an attempt to return to moments more attuned to the sensorial and physical aspects of the human creative agent, we should first note that our current cultural (working) bodies are prone to aggression as a counterforce to structural violence. In the quote above, political philosopher Jane Bennett illustrates a human "I" whose perception has been trained in the post-industrial age to look for efficiencies, simplification, and structure. This is a violent form of training of the human I. It is a violent act indeed to enforce a rigid, top-down training of perception on an I that is human; an I that is capable of much more complex and aleatory influences. Fortunately for us, Bennett also argues that it is possible to move past "normal" perception. And in order to do so, we need to be bad at looking for efficiencies, and good at looking for atmospheric forces and invisible calls of things. An aid that Bennett suggests for overcoming the crux of normal perception is her theory of lyrical force. She postulates that when a viewing subject encounters a thing that has lyrical force, they can be overcome with extraordinary fascination. She supports this postulation further by arguing that our human perception is in fact structured to look for these extraordinary moments and describes the encounter as a moment between impression (receiving information) and expression (processing received information).

In her book, Bennett makes a case for people who she considers to be more attuned to the material world—hoarders. Though hoarding is considered a mental disorder, Bennett argues that some human individuals are prone to hoarding because of their ability to extend the boundaries of their immaterial beings into the space that they share with an old pizza box, rat feces, telephone books, and old lamps—but a few examples of a hoarder's thing-collection. Though an extreme condition, Bennett argues that the hoarder I is more capable of reaching out and responding to the call of the visible and invisible world—a term she coined as thing-power. In all, Bennet uses the haptic, the visual, and the lyrical to describe a human condition susceptible to outside influences—because humans, according to Bennett, are ultimately beings that create relationships with other beings and things, human and non-human. To return to an earlier discussion, it is precisely this relationship with things that the human I is attuned to that helps formulate the forensic psychologists' theory of the allocentric perspective. The theory postulates that the more traumatic an event, the higher the conflation between the egocentric (human normal perspective) and the allocentric (third person perspective recounted from relationships with the individual's milieu). An additional recount of the plasticity of the human and the non-human is explored by political scientist Jairus Grove in his 2019 book, *Savage Ecology: War and Geopolitics at the End of the World*. In this discourse, the agency of both the egocentric and allocentric is more capricious than we anticipate. Building on Bennett's thing-power theory in a two-directional manner, Grove explored the concept of human and non-human alliances; alliances that are aleatory and that happen by chance.

With this framework in mind, the architectural proposal is rather self-evident. If the creative author I expands itself to the call of a world in traumatic duress, or even merely acknowledges the violent forces of daily life, they might be able to experience new, but not novel—simply another assembly of existing things—methods for an architectural creative process. In this expansion, these new processes help build an authorial individual's architectural imaginary. The creative worker might then encounter a site for creative potential where the real (egocentric) and the fictitious (allocentric) converge.

As a literal translation of our discourse, an architecture project can be comprised of loosely leaning panels, a blown-off building corner, a roof that has slid from its host, a crumbled masonry wall, or a deformed modernist mullion facade. Such a project can be understood in terms of Rudolf Arnheim's and Theodor Lipps's perceptual mimetic psychology theories of visual dynamics. Arhneim developed these theories based on Lipps's experimental psychology work on empathy to analyze and qualify works that lent themselves to dynamic perception. For example, Arnheim suggested that viewing a roof that rests on columns modeled after human bodies can make us feel weight through the anthropomorphic affinity of the columns. A more abstract example by Anrheim described the empathetic observation of a man who was sitting slumped on a step in front of a building and had fallen asleep. To the left of the man there was a straight staircase with a thin but prominent guardrail. Especially since it was the only linear element in a scene that consisted of volumetric objects, Arnheim argued that through our perceived empathy, we read the simultaneity of the diagonal guardrail and the posture of the slumping man and that it is the deviation from the normalized vectors of horizontality and verticality (through diagonality) that produce the dynamic qualities of the composition.

This formal and compositional empathy is incredibly useful in reading finalized works of architecture and is in line with the deconstructivism work of the 1970s and 1980s where, for example, works were designed in ways that forced human bodies to be compressed and released through spaces. Studio Libeskind's Jewish Museum in Berlin comes to mind as an example of this bodily compression. Or we might consider situations in which the human body would experience the weight of building fragments hovering above, as in the case of the Lou Ruvo Center for Brain Health by Gehry Partners. Yet another and perhaps most interesting kind of example would find the human body vicariously sensing vertigo from multilayered concrete walls that refuse to align orthogonally, exemplified clearly in the Vitra Fire Station by Zaha Hadid Architects. These building projects took their clues from drawings (Libeskind), models (Gehry), and paintings (Hadid)—three categories that are the very root of what we understand as representation in conventional architecture.

Interesting as these bodily empathetic qualities via architecture may have been, however, they are not a sufficient model for our contemporary context. The works were in fact aggressive toward the modernist architectural mandates of clear finishes, upright posture, orthogonal rigidity, cleanliness, etc. However, these offers start and end with the artifact, the built work. The finalized moment is in and of itself a rigid methodology. If our contemporary context requires that we respond on many registers (not just the violence-aggression axis that is important to the work shown here), the two-directional operations—or to use Grove's terms, the human-nonhuman alliances—need to be more open-ended. The open-endedness is not to be mistaken as an ultimatum, but rather as a first performative principle for an approach to representational work of the kind explored here: architectural events that register fictitious and real forces between a 2-D graphic and a 3-D volumetric aggregation through lenses of the haptic and by extension the lyrical. This open-endedness does involve at least a temporary but necessary turn toward process over product. But our moment is not entirely procedural either. The strange, uncanny, and campy qualities suddenly seem relevant matters for serious representation. Rather than focusing on the architectural 3-D model as a representation tool that compels the viewer, builder, stakeholder, or client, we can imagine projects rooted in contemporary social and political issues. We can argue for the proposal of a biased process. It follows then, that an animation sequence, a 3-D model (physical or digital), renderings and drawings, are the architectural project. Our representational categories that we have for the most part understood as divisive are relatedly understood as enmeshed in the fabric of architecture at large.

On Haptic Sways Between Fiction and the Real

Given that we are considering process as an architectural project, we can now turn our attention to a forceful event between two units in a scene and expect that we can register the evidence of that event. Philosopher Edith Stein's phenomenology of empathy framework provides a theory that can be useful in further synthesizing the creative author I. Stein was the first philosopher to argue that the method of phenomenology is not one-directional (such as Edmund Husserl's infamous epoché thesis), but one that corresponds as the world or a foreign experience looks back at the self. Stein used the term fusion to describe the moment in which the sensorial body and the physical body of an individual fuse in abstract space while experiencing a foreign thing in the world. In simpler words, she argued that a foreign experience responds through the sensorial body, which then re-activates the physical body (though it was the physical body that first reached out to the foreign experience).

In the design process, fusion characterizes the moment when a creative author's perception-like empathy communicates between their sensorial and their physical bodies and subsequently, the individual makes the decision to—in a physics engine simulation for example—click and alter the input parameters that suspend units in mid-air. Literally speaking, as per Stein's argument, it is the physical act of using the mouse to click on the play control in animation, or the physical act of using a keyboard to type in a gravitational acceleration other than 9.81 m/s^2 that fuses the sensorial and the physical bodies of the designer. These extremely mundane interface-mediated actions alert our consciousness and help us experience a foreign event with both of our sensorial and physical mechanisms. Whether in the digital or analog space, the phenomenology of empathy allows for the creative author to give in to their innate apparatuses as each person's response in experiencing a foreign event will be informed by themselves and their unique milieu.

This drawing, part of *House 2*, consists of groups of parallel lines that are continuous. It is through their change in direction (or jog) and the distance between each individual line (or density) that the various compositional qualities emerge: balanced to unbalanced, light to heavy, saturated to desaturated, or flat to volumetric.

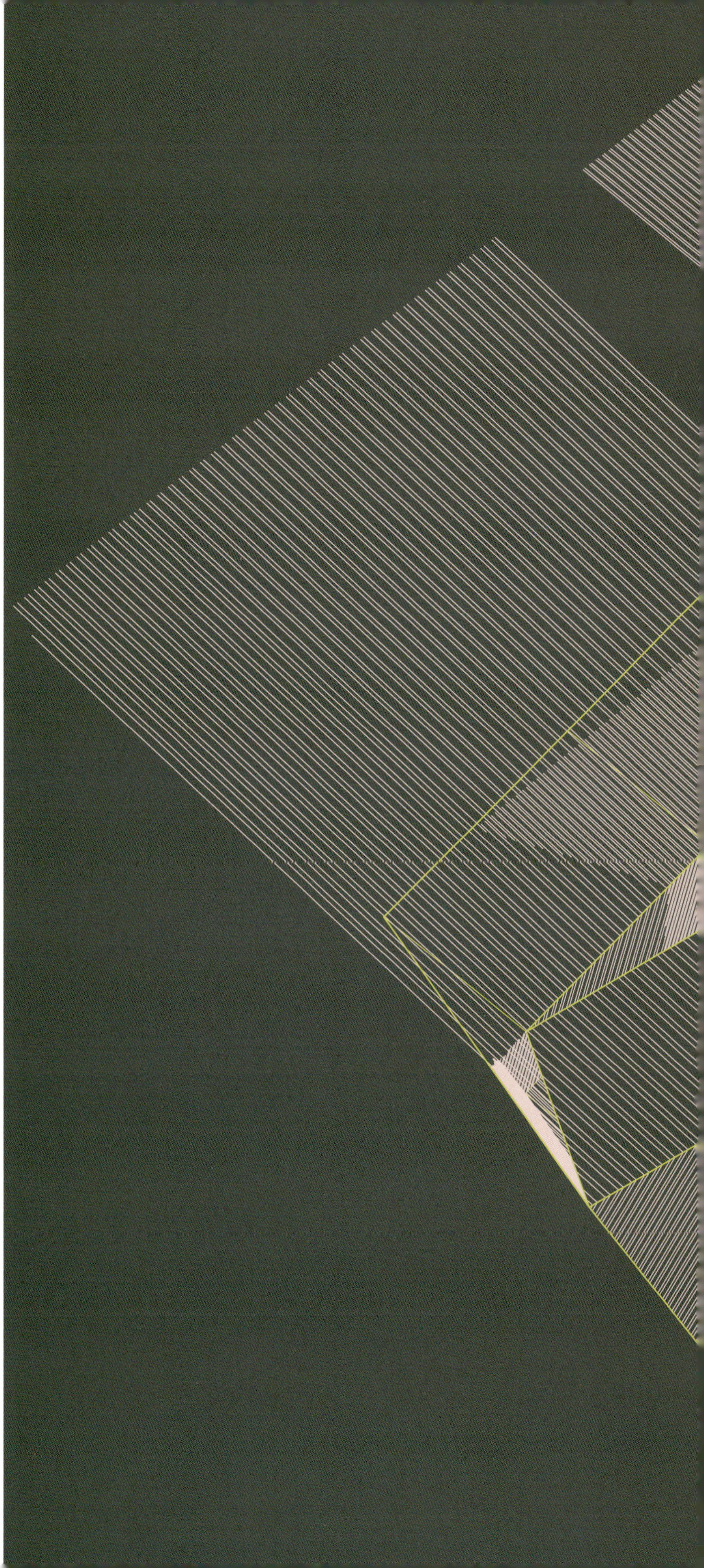

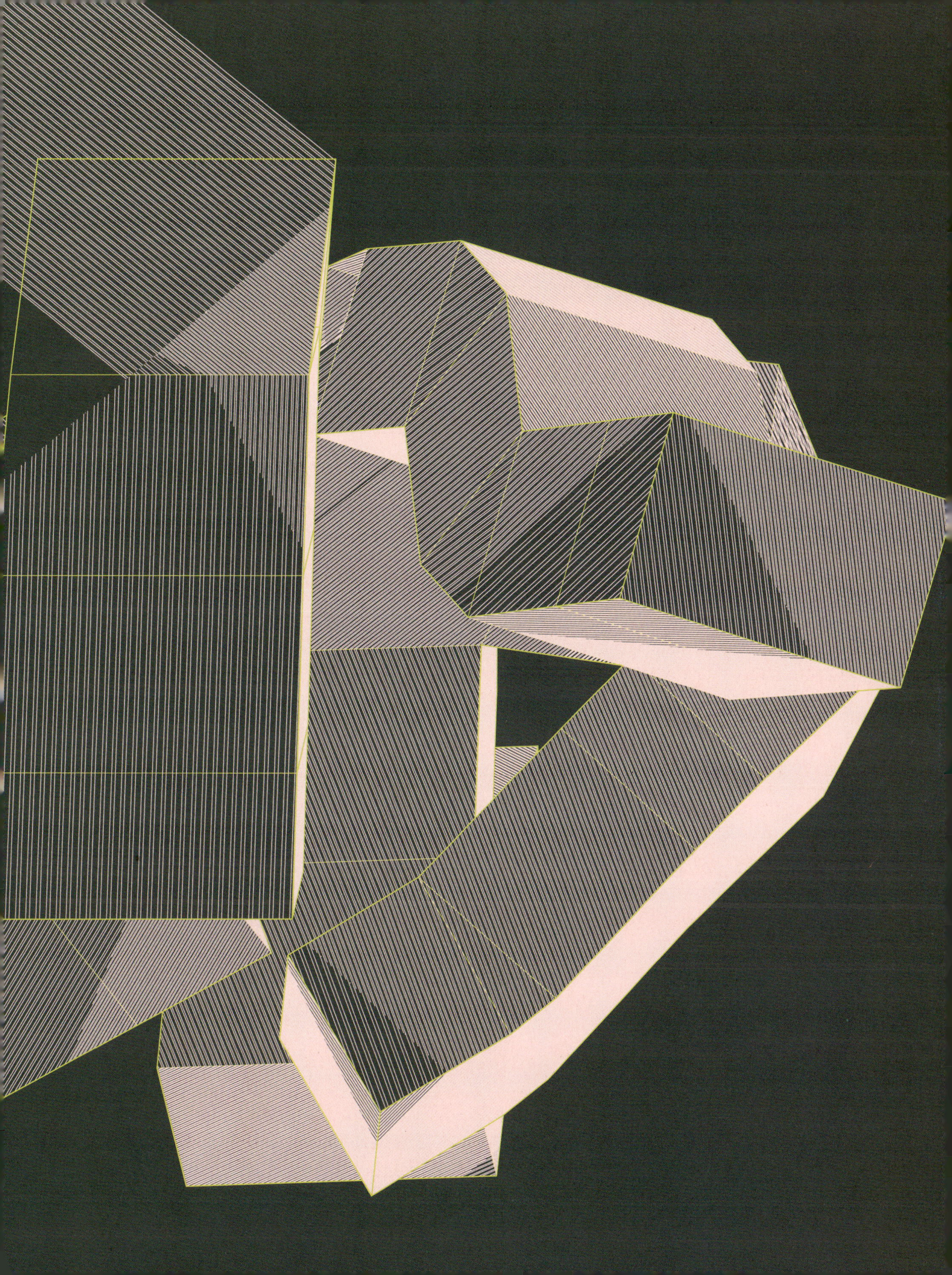

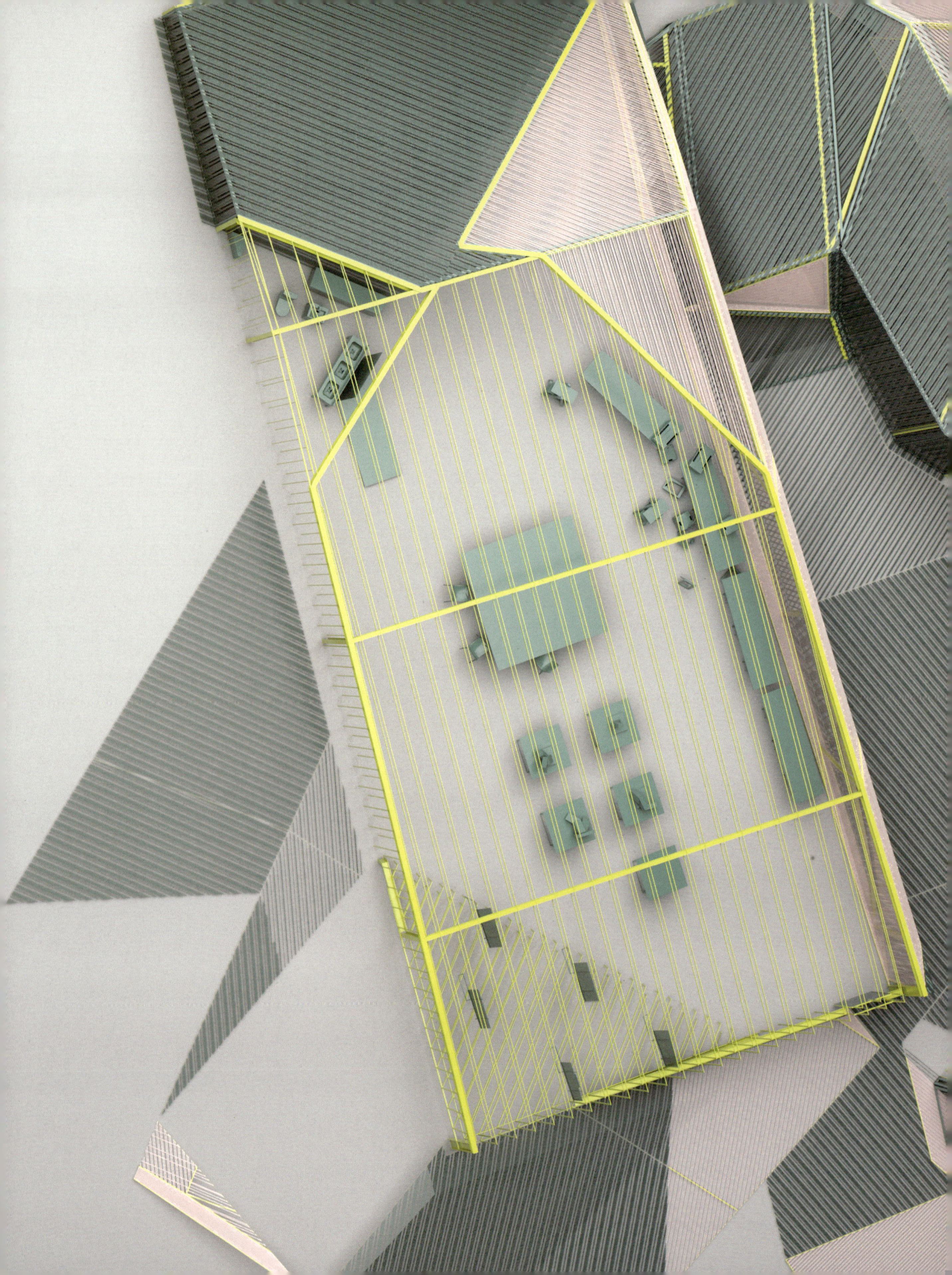

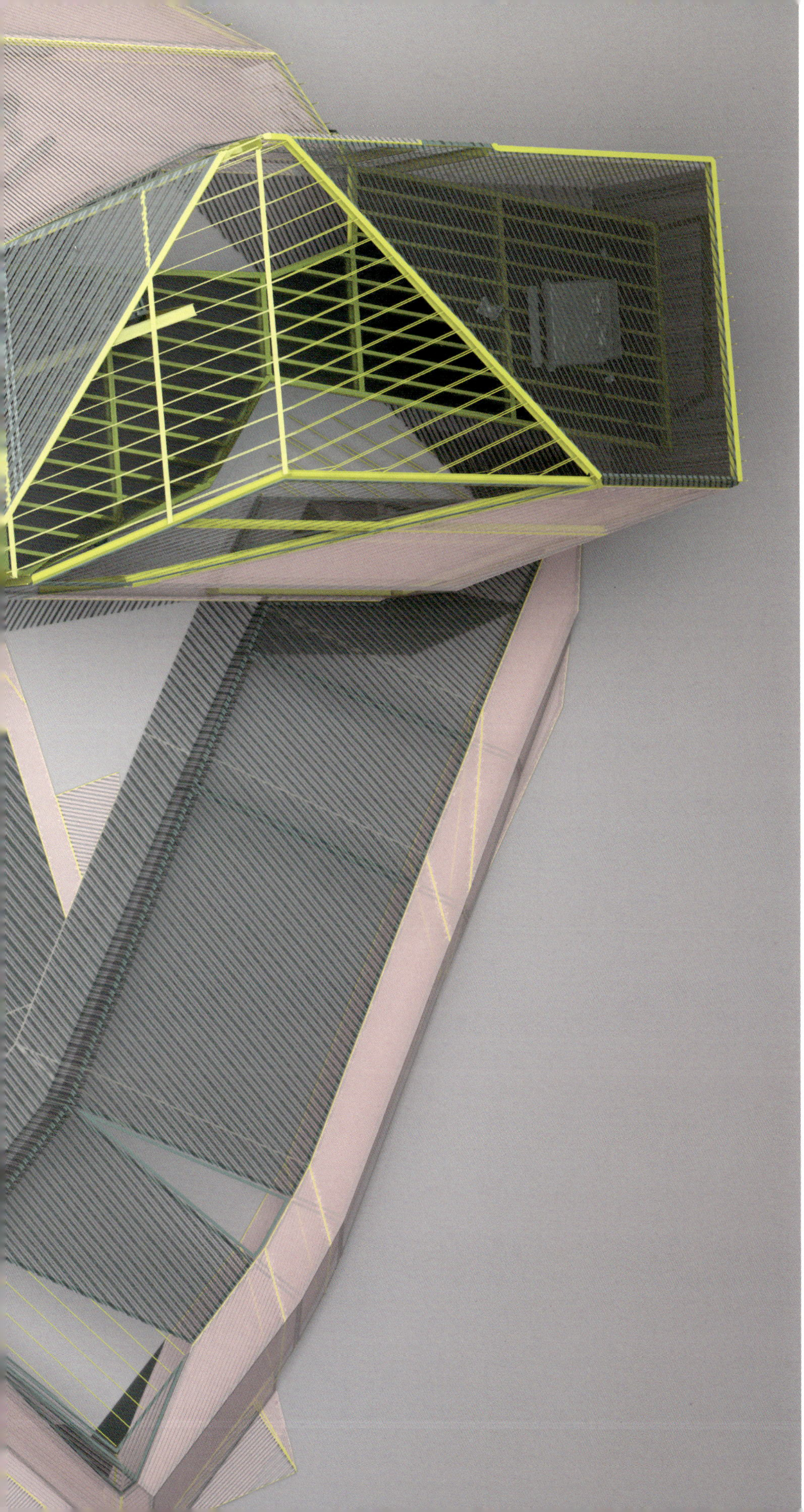

This drawing, part of *House 2*, is a design research exercise that results from the conflation of 2-D and 3-D information. The house proposal attempts to discover lineages between architectural elements and digital design operations.

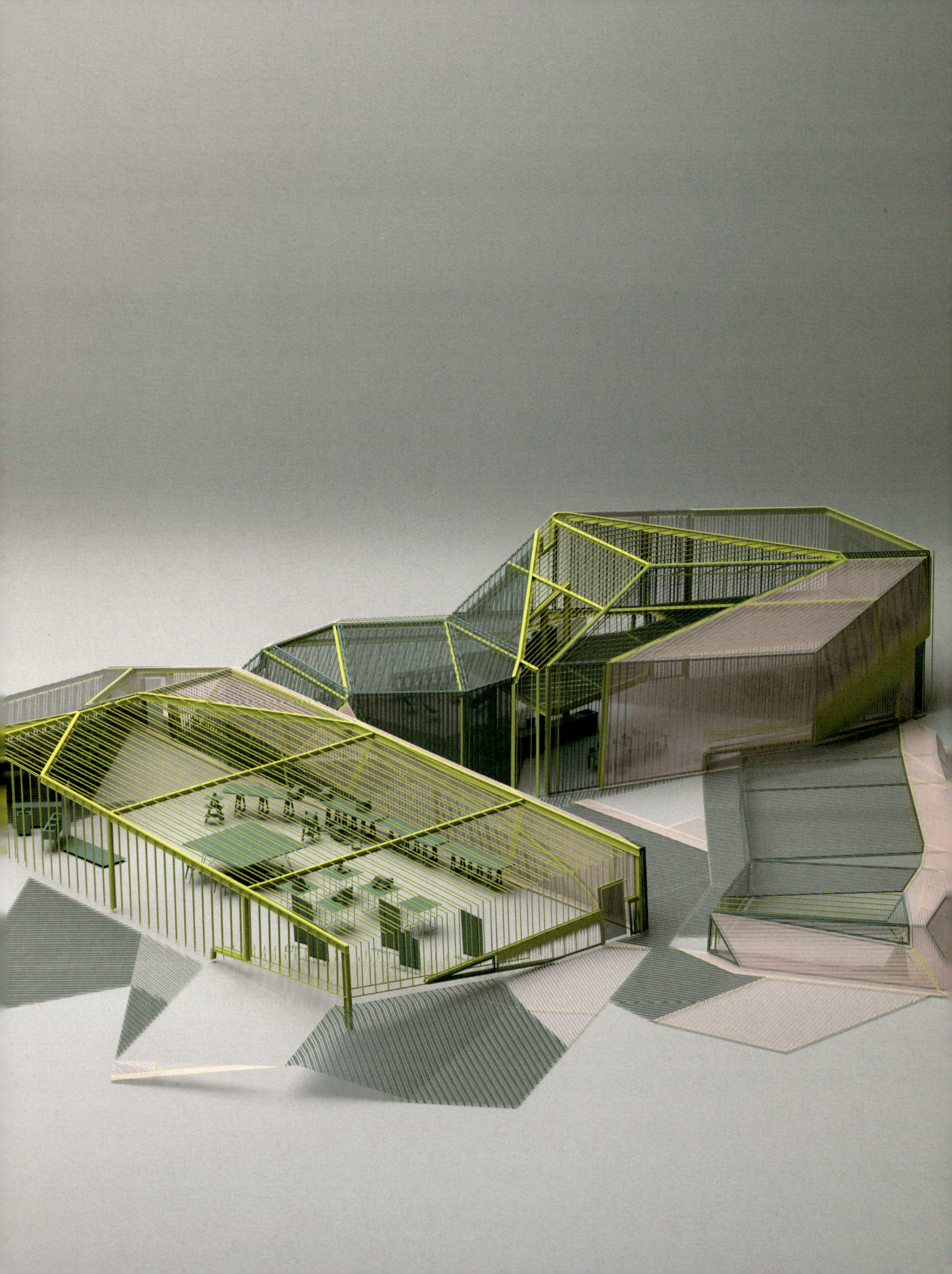

This *House 2* elevation view rendering reveals another architectural quality that is surface-based but that results from and responds to the 2-D and 3-D information collapsed together. On some of the facade panels, the yellow line (vector) based information from the 2-D drawing digitally stretches and droops in the vertical direction. This is another architectural surface condition that has been generated through the violent event of crushing 3-D volume through a 2-D graphic.

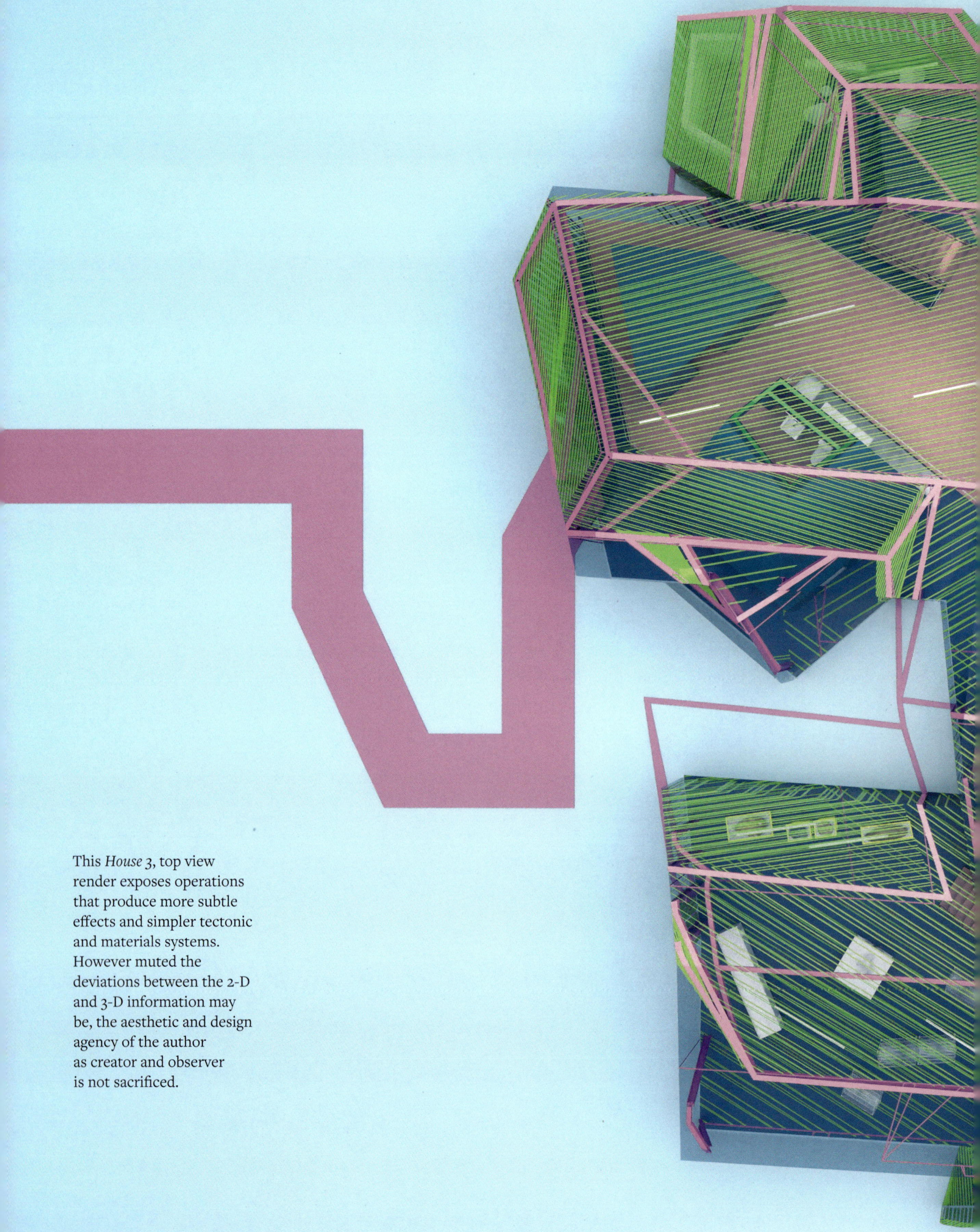

This *House 3*, top view render exposes operations that produce more subtle effects and simpler tectonic and materials systems. However muted the deviations between the 2-D and 3-D information may be, the aesthetic and design agency of the author as creator and observer is not sacrificed.

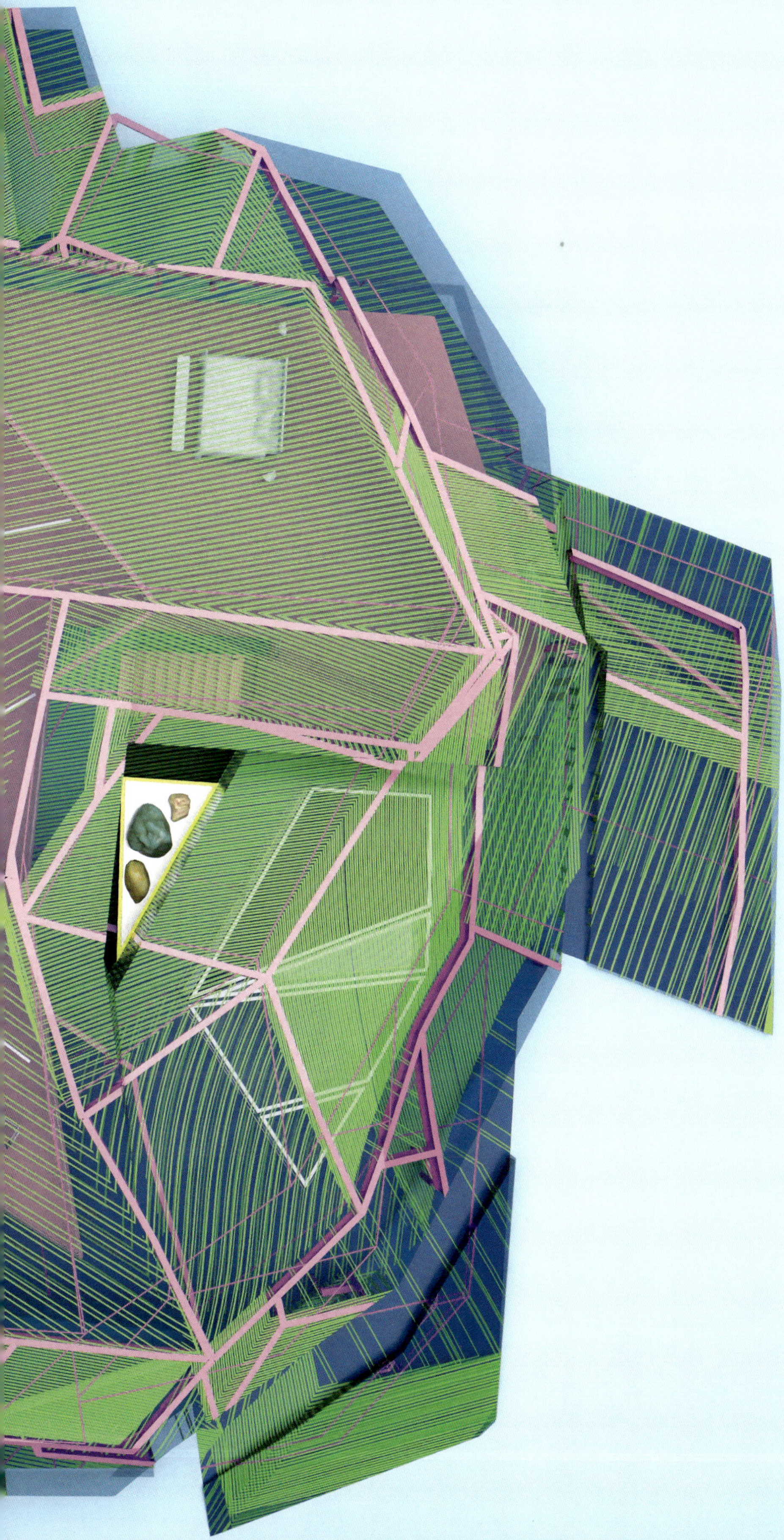

In a similar pattern to the work we've explored previously, two more speculative houses, *House 2* and *House 3* support the process-based design experimentation and test the conceptual ground surface at the building scale. *House 2* began with a 2-D drawing and a 3-D volumetric cluster. The 2-D linework is produced with an algorithm and is ontologically in opposition to the 3-D geometric construct, which is sculpted. This friction, or aversion even, between dimensional allegiances registers on the violence-aggression axis separate from the event of the clash between the drawing and the volume. In *House 2*, the graphic blanket—the way that the graphic, as a surface, wraps the form—is less contentious than in *House 1*, where the stretched and skewed 2-D content displays almost no link to the original drawing. Alongside the 2-D versus 3-D digital confrontation, *House 2* reflects further interest in graphic fragmentation. The yellow line from the 2-D drawing is rasterized and is dripping in a way that exposes its pixels on some of the facade panels. Neither the dripping lines, nor the panels were selected from a cognitive position. Both qualities result from a repeated 2-D and 3-D simulation event. The creative author's objective further plays out through curation, editing, and filtering. The cladding also depends on dimensional surface conflict and changes materially, visually, and tectonically as provoked by the event-operation. The pink lines register this conflict. The structural articulation grows out of these lines rather than what we would traditionally see: a structural logic determined by 3-D geometry. Heightened realism diverges from our expectation of resolved systems. Material, graphics, and geometry correspond but don't converge. The surfaces resist blending or mixing into new composite forms. Instead, they retain their elemental status and represent frictions of the kind only found on the violence-aggression axis.

House 3, the least duressed of the set, is seen in surfaces articulated entirely by flatbed printed graphic conditions. Embedded in the graphic blanket are digitally simulated residual pink lines, seeding the structural system—not unlike the reciprocity between the panel articulation and the structural system integration in *House 2*. The green lines that blanket the surfaces likewise correspond to the stud walls on the interior. The apparent precarity of these parts allude to the origins of these forms: one frozen frame in a simulation. Though highly resolved, line networks might seem to have been left to roam the architectural surface at their own free will. They sometimes align with other participants in the work, and at times they betray the composition entirely and fall on the ground. This behavior is only visible upon close examination and in contrast with the overall sense that *House 3* is more rigid, clean, and less corrupt than its siblings. As such, *House 3* belongs closer to the violence side of the axis; with *House 1* closer to aggression, and *House 2* sitting somewhere in the middle.

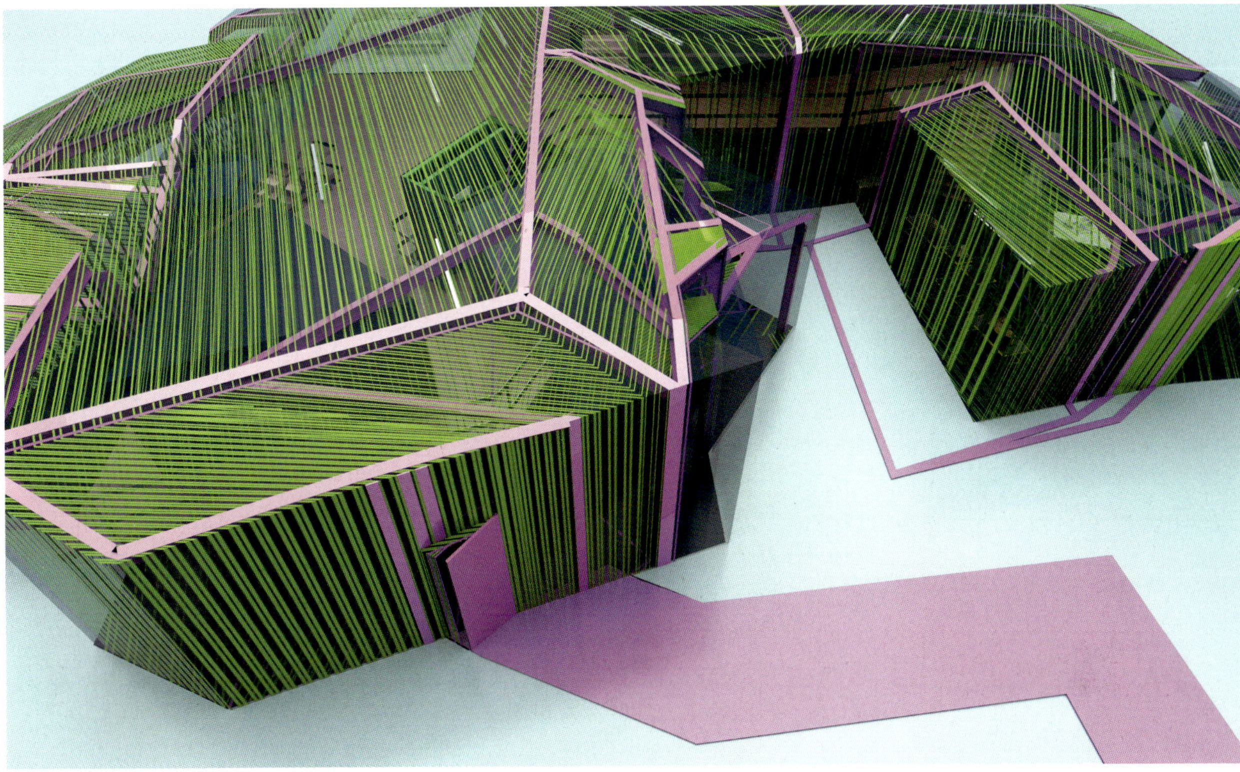

This *House 3* rendering reveals the interior logic of the house design that takes its cues from the exterior form. The design methodologies and processes explored with these works can be adapted and deployed through different scales and spatial and architectural conditions.

Overcoming Systemic Cognition

House 2 and *House 3* are thoroughly digital. However, analog associations from memory of experimentations prior or from related fictitious architectural events permeate systemic operations and make their way into the work. We've unpacked various digital operations in play and we've also described human agency in terms of "curation, editing, and filtering." But there's more to the story. As is the case with the surfaces that operate on the violence-aggression axis, creative actions can't be relegated into mutually exclusive sets of the systemic and the improvisational. Rather, they reside on a spectrum. Human authorship can also involve developing instrumental knowledge and skill unique to each temporal model. As an example, the click of the mouse that suspends a graphic in midair informs the sensorial body, which then uses the physical body to change the input parameters in the simulation and click on play again. The next chapter explores a related form of learned spatial and bodily acuity in terms of the complex and the gaming perspective. Within these systems, new sensorial responses are integrated in the world of representation. Influences from things (a la Bennett's "thing power") alert and occupy perception. All of this happens before any systematically trained cognition (informed by government sanctioned mandates, modernist leftovers, or colonizer-centric value schemes) can take over consciousness. It is quite the struggle.

It's also imperative to note that the house series serves as a representational study on processes that live on the violence-aggression axis. They are not to be taken as definitive architectural proposals for the built world. The role of digital tools that are so imperative to this work are multifaceted. We are influenced by technology and we in turn influence and create technology to push our work further. The last two decades have cataloged quite the volatile relationship between architects and digital technologies, including a subtle but explosive moment that split the field into two primary domains: the techno-positivists and the techno-apathetics. In this space of ideological divides, however, things only became more extreme. Regardless of the forces that led to ideological divides in architecture, we are at an opportune moment. We can grant ourselves permission to put them aside in favor of more intertwined models between technology and architecture. Contentious as it may be, the work shown here attempts to re-strengthen and restore our relationship with digital architectural representation not in a hermetic manner, but rather in an open and permeable fashion. This oscillation between technology as a primary motivator and technology as a utilitarian device already charts an expansive area filled with intense frictions. Frictions can momentarily destabilize our discipline, but they also make our field diverse. Since frictions within a field—a project or a discipline—can produce overwhelming and extreme layers of expertise, they can also reveal new and contemporary problems, and ultimately propel us into new, undiscovered, and more equitable territories.

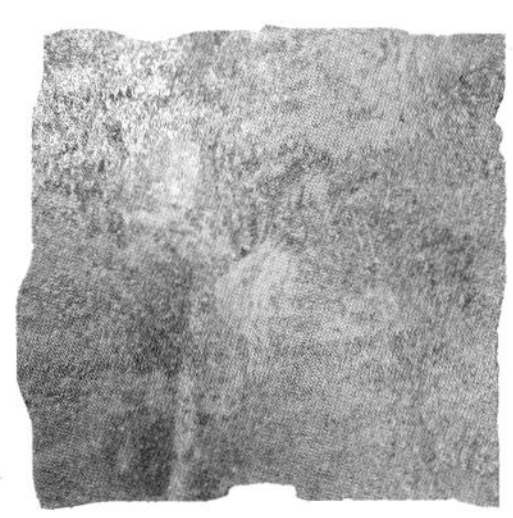

Notes

1. Phong and Blinn are two render materials (surface shaders) typically included as default settings in most rendering engines. Phong was invented by Bui Tong Phong at the University of Utah in 1973 and Blinn was a modification on the Phong model for OpenGL, which was accomplished by James Blinn in 1977.
2. "The Beirut Port Explosion." Forensic Architecture, November 17, 2020. https://forensic-architecture.org/investigation/beirut-port-explosion/.
3. Eyal Weizman, "The Architecture of Memory." e-flux architecture, (November 2020), Accessed June 17, 2021. https://www.e-flux.com/architecture/confinement/357171/the-architecture-of-memory/.
4. "Torture In Saydnaya Prison." Forensic Architecture, August 16, 2016. https://forensic-architecture.org/investigation/saydnaya.
5. The articulated architectural surface here refers to the moment where the graphic lines and the geometric panels are collapsed onto one another.
6. Robert Rauchenberg, Erased de Kooning Drawing, 1953. San Francisco Museum of Modern Art (SFMoMA), San Francisco, CA.
7. Other seminal projects include Peter Eisenman's house series, Bernard Tschumi's Parc de la Villette, Daniel Libeskind's Jewish Memorial Museum, Morphosis 2-4-6-8 House, Zaha Hadid's Vitra Fire Station. The movement carved itself into discourse with the 1988 MoMA exhibit titled Deconstructivist Architecture, which was curated by Philip Johnson and Mark Wigley.
8. Andrew Culp, "Introduction" in Dark Deleuze (Minneapolis: University of Minnesota Press, 2016), 1–21. In his introduction chapter to Dark Deleuze, Andrew Culp suggests three stages for good scholarship and that in revisiting/revising previous work, the author must "reveal that (1) other scholarship commits an error; (2) an essential insight has been missed; (3) a new concept can be created."
9. Robert Boyers, The Fate of Ideas: Seductions, Betrayals, Appraisals (New York: Columbia University Press, 2015), 116. Knock-out is a term borrowed from David Hockney. When Hockey was asked if he would rather his work be qualified as beautiful or interesting he responded by defining that interesting refers to process and that the work would seem as though it was getting there, whereas beautiful would refer to a work as final, and that it can "knock you out."
10. Frederic Jameson, "Architecture Spatial Equivalents in the World System," in POSTMODERNISM: or, the Cultural Logic of Late Capitalism (Durham: Duke University Press, 1991), 97–153.
11. Fanon, Frantz. "On Violence, On Violence in the International Context," in The Wretched of the Earth: Frantz Fanon (New York: Grove Press, 2004), 1–62.
12. Grief and Grievance: Art and Mourning in America. Feb. 17–June 6, 2021, New Museum, New York.
13. Miracles Architecture, Models are Drawings that Believed in Miracles. 2016. Miracles Architecture. Web. September 5, 2021. https://www.miraclesarchitecture.com/#/gipfel/
14. Miracles Architecture, Hydrodipping Matrix (Poppy Red). 2018. Miracles Architecture. Web. September, 2021. https://www.miraclesarchitecture.com/#/poppy-red/
15. Jane Bennett, Influx and Efflux: Writing up with Walt Whitman (Durham: Duke University Press, 2020), 79.
16. Bennett, ix–xxv. Bennet borrows the "I" from American poet Walt Whitman. She reflects on the lyrical nature of Whitman's I and develops a theory on the relationship between the self and vibrant materialism, non-verbal influences, haptic experience, and atmosphere.
17. Bennett, 73–88.
18. Note that normal has been weaponized and even institutionalized by the higher powers.
19. Bennett, 78–81.
20. Bennett, 78.
21. Eyal Weizman, "The Architecture of Memory," in e-flux architecture (November 2020), Accessed June 17, 2021. https://www.e-flux.com/architecture/confinement/357171/the-architecture-of-memory/.
22. Jairus Victor Grove, Savage Ecology: War and Geopolitics at the End of the World (Durham: Duke University Press, 2019), 134–36.
23. Viola Ago, "Compositional Physics and Other Diagrams of Force," in Log (New York: Anyone

Corp, 2019), 33-43. Please see essay for more examples of architectural projects that speak to a world of duress.

24. Rudolf Arnheim, "Dynamics," in Art and Visual Perception (Stockholm: Stockholms Universitet, Institutionen för Konstvetenskap, 1960), 416-19.
25. Rudolf Arnheim, "Visual dynamics," in American Scientist 76, no. 6 (1988): 585-91.
26. Sarah Bakewell, At the Existentialist Cafe: Freedom, Being, and Apricot Cocktails (New York: Other Press, 2016), 48-49. Stein was a student of Edmund Husserl. She was seminal in his study and research group and helped him write his Ideas Volume II. She left in order to develop her own philosophical work without Husserl's ideas impeding hers. Her relinquished seat in Husserl's group at the University of Göttingen in Göttingen, Germany was filled by Martin Heidegger.
27. Edith Stein, "The Essence of Acts of Empathy," in On the Problem of Empathy (Washington, D.C.: ICS Publications, 1989), 3-35.
28. It is important to note that surface articulation accounts for tectonic expression through not only the tectonic qualities that are embedded in the liminal zone of the exterior faces of the surface (i.e., the thickness), but also on the support. Just as the support of a painting is the canvas (a la Leo Steinberg), the support for the articulated architectural surface is the thing underneath.
29. The techno-positivists continued to develop their work in extreme hermetic zones in the spirit of efficiency, novelty, and cost effectiveness. In opposition, but also in an almost identical manner, the techno-apathetics, a more complex group, started to operate within isolated systems made of very basic inputs: primitive geometries, low resolution shapes, and low fidelity color/diagrammatic systems.

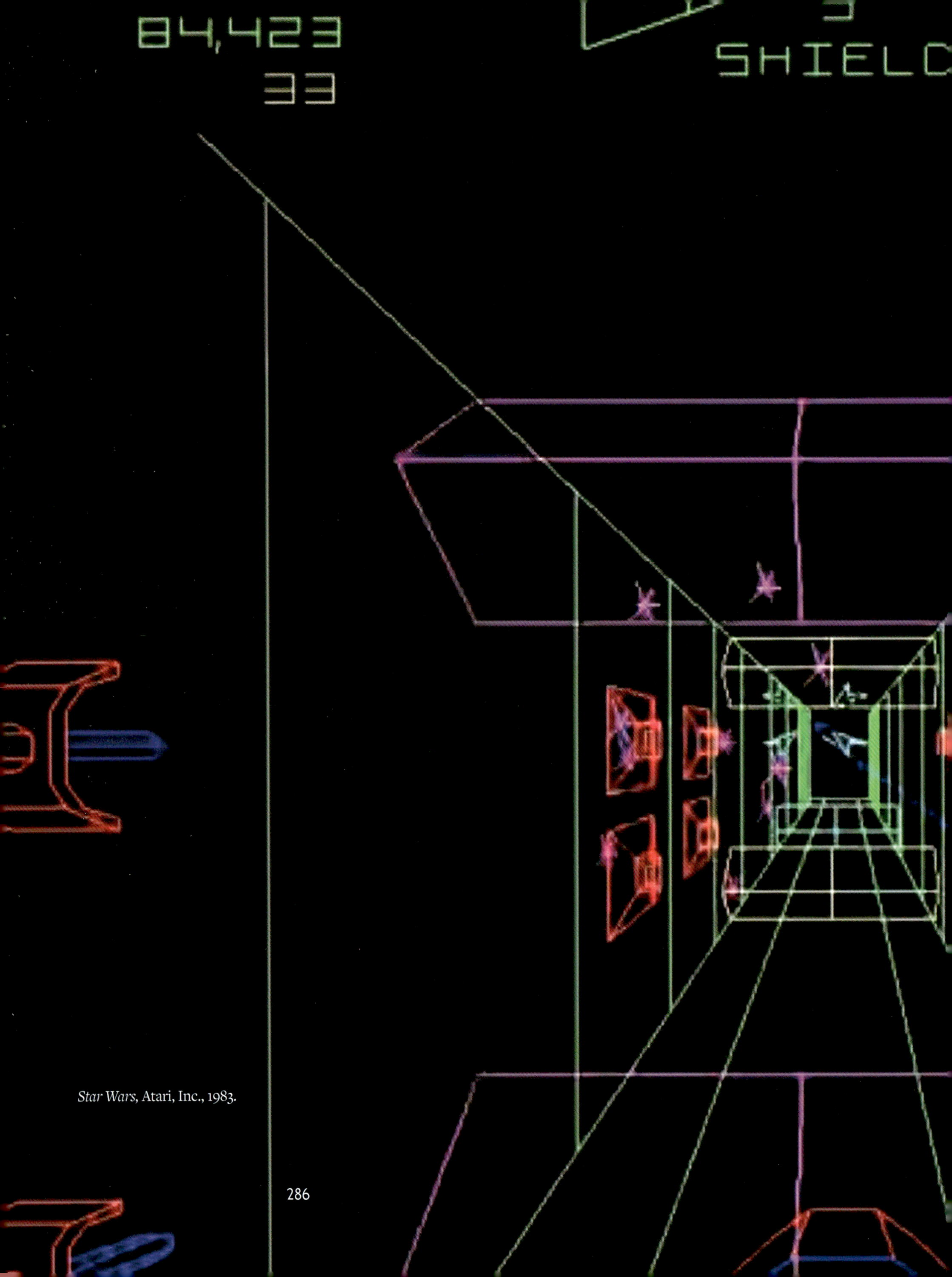

Star Wars, Atari, Inc., 1983.

CHAPTER 7

Anxious Vision: Real Time and the First-Person Perspective View

by Hans Tursack

What can architects learn from examining the visual structures of 3-D video games? How have they influenced the culture of architectural representation? And why should the gaming perspective view, level structure, and architectural complex be considered essential elements for contemporary architectural theory? How is video game theory instrumentalized in the creation of architecture? To begin, video game engines are becoming ubiquitous features in architectural rendering culture. Platforms like Unreal, Unity, and Twinmotion offer designers tools to create environments that can be explored and interacted with in real time by the user-client. While 3-D modeling, rendering, and animation platforms have been commonplace in architecture schools and experimental studios since the 1990s, accessible, interactive, real time rendering platforms are a more recent and less studied phenomenon.

Much can be said and overstated about the novelty of tools and media born in the gaming industry. The gamer-subject is a relatively new conceptual figure in theoretical discourse, and one that presents serious questions about our commonly held theories of perception. For this reason, it is worth tracing the ways that 3-D game spaces draw heavily on architectural conventions and those of neighboring visual disciplines. Experiencing games, setting up virtual cameras, designing the architecture of levels, and employing world-building strategies for gaming environments are rather natural extensions of techniques used in cinema, illustration, and architectural representation. These design moves use the basic foundations of practices such as landscape painting, analog rendering, and—perhaps most important in the context of architecture—perspectival drawing. This discourse and affiliated creative work aim to distill the fundamental tenets of the first-person perspective view in 3-D gaming spaces, and in doing so, deploy the structure of that viewing paradigm. We'll explore how game design builds from, aligns with, and disrupts conventions of architectural perspective rendering and the viewing subjects they posit. If designers and architectural consumers are beginning to see buildings through the gamer's eye—to *play* architecture like a level—what design opportunities does this new viewing condition present? What biases are revealed in doing so?

Picture Windows

Perspectival drawing creates the illusion that the world can be measured, ordered by geometric principles, and—by extension—controlled by the viewer. In recent decades, video games have brought the perspective view back into the forefront of visual culture and imbued it with a newfound relevance and theoretical urgency; albeit outside of architecture or fine-art proper. This is perhaps unsurprising, as rendering and perspective drawing have suffered a significant cultural downgrading in postwar architectural theory. Perspective drawings, and photo realistic digital renderings especially, are often described as reactionary—devices that pander to mass media consumption as opposed to more cerebral visualizations like plans, diagrams, or axonometric projections. In her essay on rendering and phenomenology, historian Lucia Allais points out that renderings are largely thought of as sales tools today, "Commercial renderings, especially, images used to sell buildings, are seen as engines of superficiality because they are aimed at nonarchitects."[1]

Three-dimensional digital modeling gives designers the illusion of being masters of geometric worlds. Architects adept at rendering can quickly, cheaply, and easily produce high-resolution images that rival photographic realism. It would seem that little has changed in the perspective's role in architectural discourse over the last century, beyond the tools (i.e., 3-D models and rendering engines) used to produce them.

The gamer could conveniently be cast as the newest, souped-up, enlightenment cliche of the all-knowing master at the center of a linear-perspective construct (with amplified illusions of agency). However, gaming phenomenologists like Brendan Keoh also theorize the gamer as a subject that is decentered, plural, and part of a cybernetic system. For Keoh, the gamer is a hybrid machine-human composite, "the video game player is a dispersed, fragmented, and heterogeneous subject."[2] This only becomes more salient in online gaming. Such dispersed subjects are rendered as avatars and networked into vast collectives who meet in designated architectural platforms. Three-dimensional video game levels are a novel kind of public architecture and social space where our collective unconscious stages its power fantasies in a 24/7 stream. The average architectural consumer may receive real time representations with a familiar passivity and indifference, however, we must also acknowledge that they are (perhaps unknowingly) adopting the gamer's position in relation to the model-space.

In this chapter we will attempt—where possible—to create productive continuities between visual techniques and spatial archetypes in game design and traditional architectural design methods. Architects, critics, and theorists too often react to new tools as inciting all-encompassing paradigm shifts (human visual experience giving way to machine vision, for example) and full-scale disciplinary crises. An architectural framing of game design invites us instead to embrace new technologies that productively advance perspectival projections as a design tool. Much of the experience of viewing and designing game-spaces is indebted to the renaissance invention and codification of perspective. With that in mind, we must also bring to bear how gaming has altered the subject at the origin of the perspectival gaze (the viewer-gamer). We should not ask how the viewing subject has been fundamentally redefined, but what has been added to the equation when perspective becomes real time, digital physics allows one to engage with and act on the virtual world, and one's gaze is assisted by a litany of digital aids.

No Time Like Real Time

A full historical account of the birth of the Z-Axis in 3-D video games is beyond the scope of this study. However, a cursory sketch of some anchor points along the "race to 3-D" in the past 40-plus years illuminates several foundational elements embedded within the first-person perspective view that remain native to contemporary gaming engines. Games studies theorist Mark J.P. Wolf cites Vectorbeam's minimalist racer *Speed Freak* (1978) as featuring the first "true three-dimensionally generated objects" in a game. In *Speed Freak*, wireframe cars and exploding (flying and rotating) polygonal objects that can change scale and position are rendered as white vector-lines against a black background.[3] Only two years later, two stand-alone arcade games appeared with significant advances on *Speed Freak*. Atari's *Battlezone* (1980) and *Star Wars* (1983) were impressive arcade first-person shooters with 3-D wireframe objects and architecture rendered in multi-colored lines. In all three titles, 3-D computation is performed in real time (the objects are not pre-rendered as graphic sprites), though largely at the expense of the graphic richness, detail and textures found in contemporaneous 2-D titles like Nintendo's *Super Mario Brothers* (1983).[4]

Though many significant strides were made in the interim, 1993 marked a true paradigm shift in the move toward ubiquitous first-person 3-D gaming in perspective.[5] That year the 3-D aerial rail-shooter *Starfox* was released for the Super Nintendo, several high-quality 3-D games including Namco's *Cyber Sled* appeared in arcades, and id Software's infamous first person shooter *Doom* was released for the PC.[6] *Doom*'s technical achievements and its influence on 3-D gaming are too numerous to list. Among them are massive leaps in texture mapping (*Starfox* and *Cyber Sled* filled their polygonal models with solid colors), drop off lighting (a hallway in *Doom* would be dimly light at its entrance and the light would taper off into black along the Z-axis), sound design, and a convincing mix of sprites (2-D animated characters and objects) and true 3-D environments. As Dan Pinchbeck's close reading of the game articulates, *Doom* was built to be scary, dark, and fast.[7] Though *Doom* naturally takes the cake for its legacy, graphic ingenuity, frame rate, and cultural infamy, all three examples are evidence of an argument that 3-D gaming is intimately wedded to military perception. The 3-D gamer's gaze is a cybernetic construct, and one that is attuned to hiding, targeting, and navigating through the simulation of vision augmented by semi-automated viewing assistance (thanks to the presence of fictional scanners, drones, radar, and motion sensors). Perspective and information are processed together in the data-scape view of Heads Up Displays (HUDs), so named because they avoid the need to turn one's head down (or away) from the perspective experience. Most importantly, the gamer's gaze is a function of dynamic movement (speed and camera freedom controlled by the gamer). HUDS are biased interfaces that teach and direct as much as they assist. They orient and influence gamers' expedient, purposeful movement through environments. The analytical tools that make up HUDS can disrupt the reality of the perspective experience while clarifying the contextual reality of objects, environmental conditions, and targets. Articulating context may add meaning, usefulness, or narrative value. Distinguishing figure from ground, for example, is sometimes a matter of success, failure, and, in some cases, survival.

The mid-1990s also saw the introduction of an innovation in the use of perspective in fully 3-D game worlds sometimes called "dual navigation" or "free look." Free look is the ability for a player to move a character in an environment with one control and change their view with a second control input. An example of this is in the WASD computer keyboard and mouse combination, where keyboard arrow keys (or 'w', 'a', 's' and 'd') allow a player to move forward, backward, left, right, and jump, and the view or camera is controlled by the mouse. In *Doom*, a player moves laterally via WASD and pans around a scene with a mouse, but only along the horizontal axis (looking left or right). Bungie's Macintosh-based shooter *Marathon* (1994) by contrast, was one of the first games to give the mouse the ability to control a camera that would also look up and down in addition to side to side while the arrow keys moved the player in space. Imagine that you are a game character and a hypothetical mouse controls your rapid eye movements, while the arrow keys are your feet that take you from room to room, and platform to platform. Building on the innovation of *Marathon*, id's next blockbuster franchise *Quake* (1996) popularized free look in PC gaming and made other significant advances in speed.[8] Meanwhile, Sony's PlayStation Dual Shock gamepad hardware (1997) introduced consoles to the now-standard "double joystick" configuration where characters move with one thumbstick and look with the other.[9] The double joystick configuration is now a default configuration for consoles, including the Nintendo Switch (2017). Free look was also a feature in Epic Games' hugely popular first-person shooter for the PC, *Unreal* (1998). The engine that was used to create *Unreal* is now a platform for architectural visualization (through its consumer-friendly *Twinmotion* tool), game-design, film, and television. Free look, the WASD + Mouse convention for navigation, and the double joystick configuration on console controllers are industry standards for contemporary games and game-engine environments alike. What these developments contribute to a culture of gamer vision is the ability to move through and scan a 3-D environment (with a spherical free-rotating camera) as fluidly as one's hardware will allow.

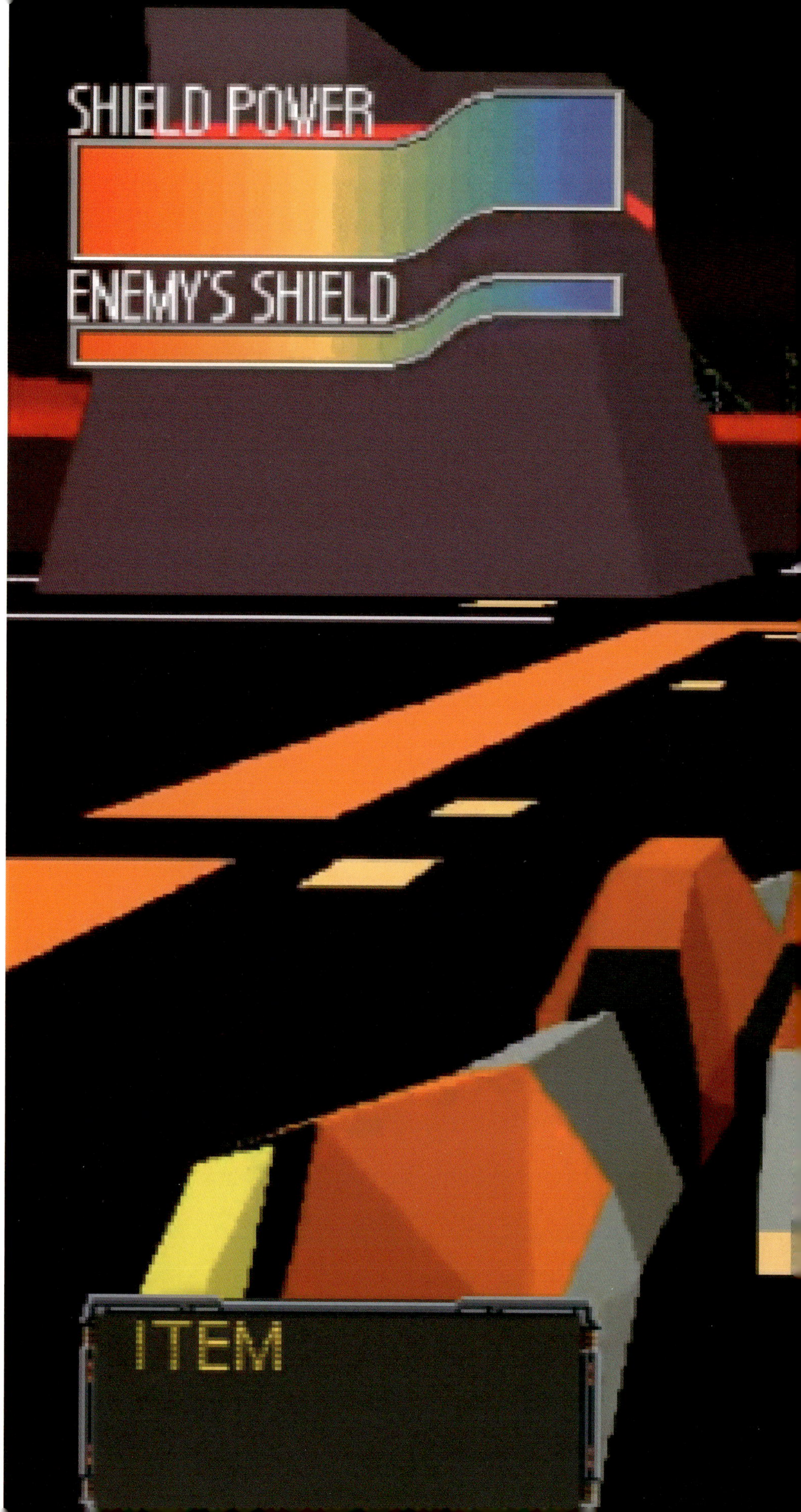

A screen capture of *Cyber Sled*. By Namco, 1993.

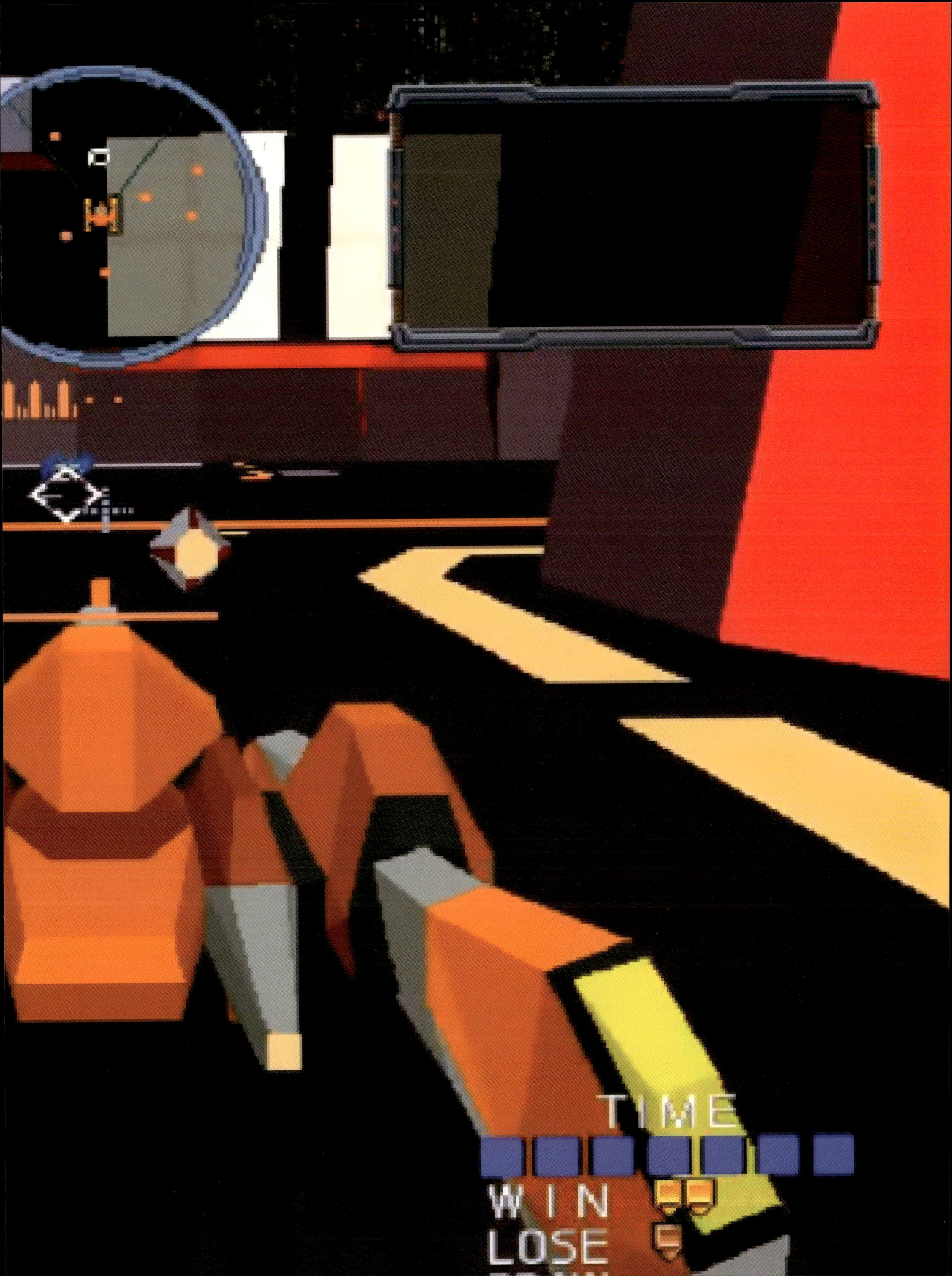
TIME
WIN
LOSE

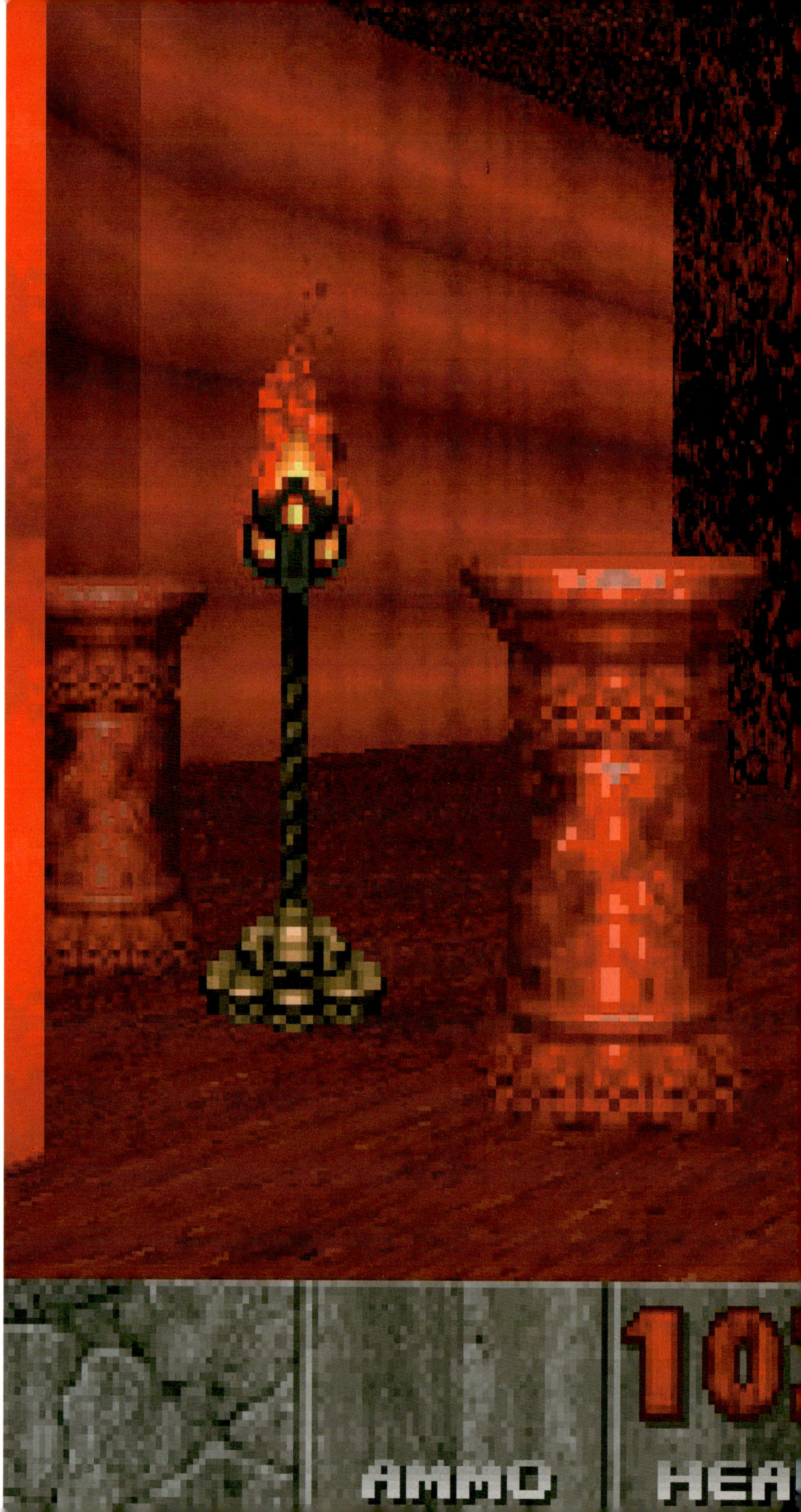

A screen capture of *Doom*.
Namco. Id Software. 1993

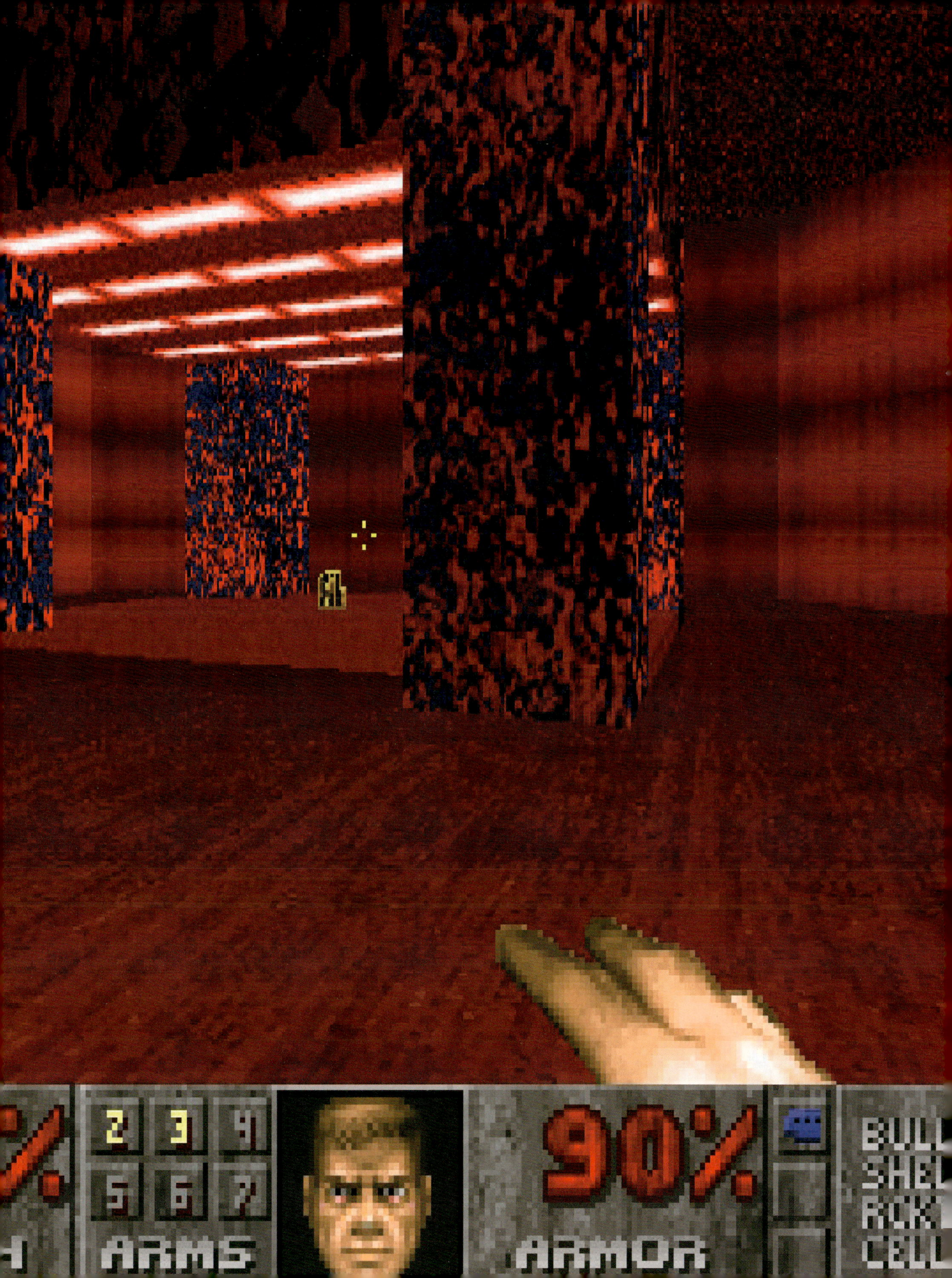
2 3 4
5 6 7
ARMS
90%
ARMOR

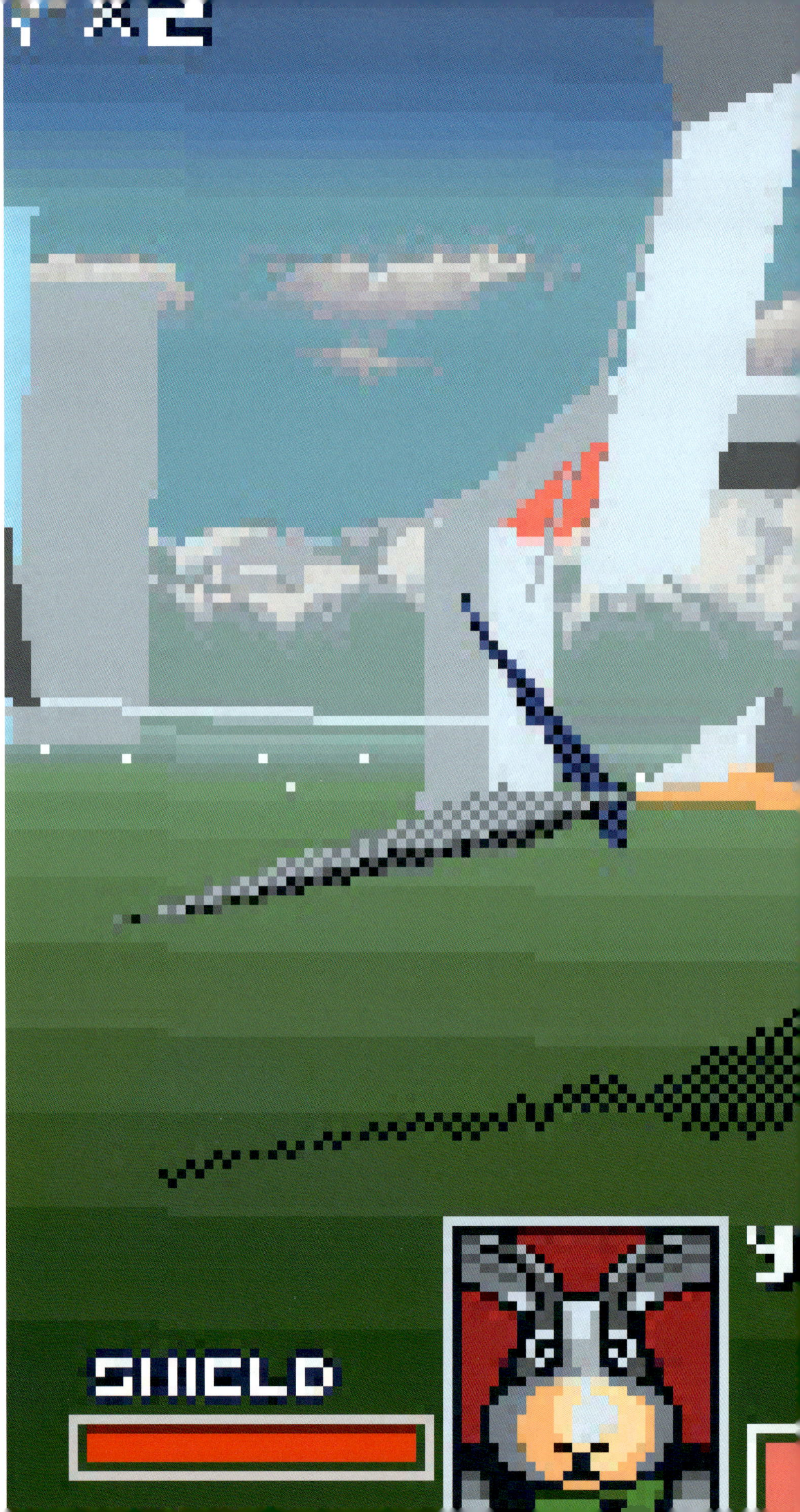

A screen capture of *Starfox*. Nintendo EAD, Argonaut Software. 1993

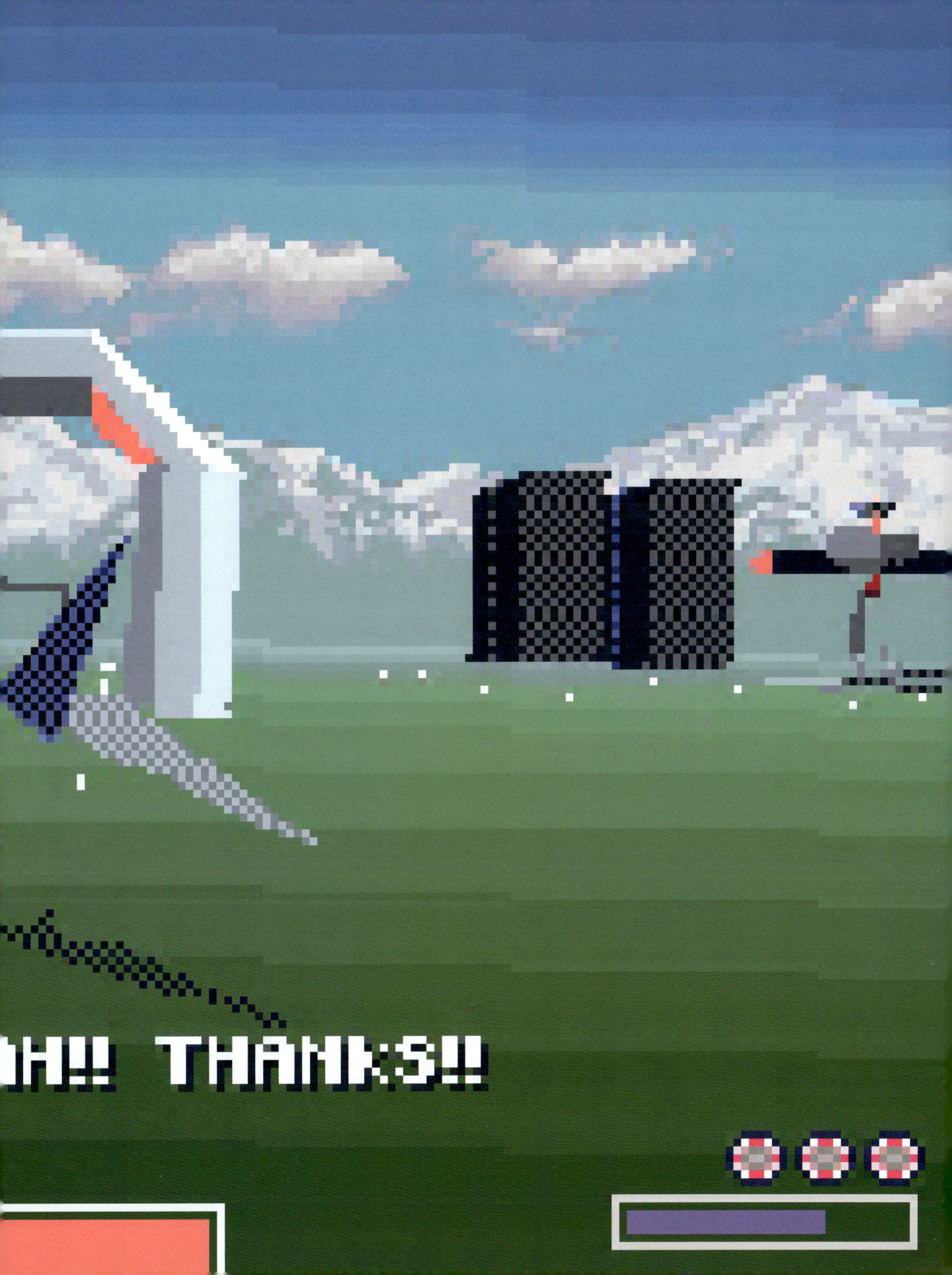
H!! THANKS!!

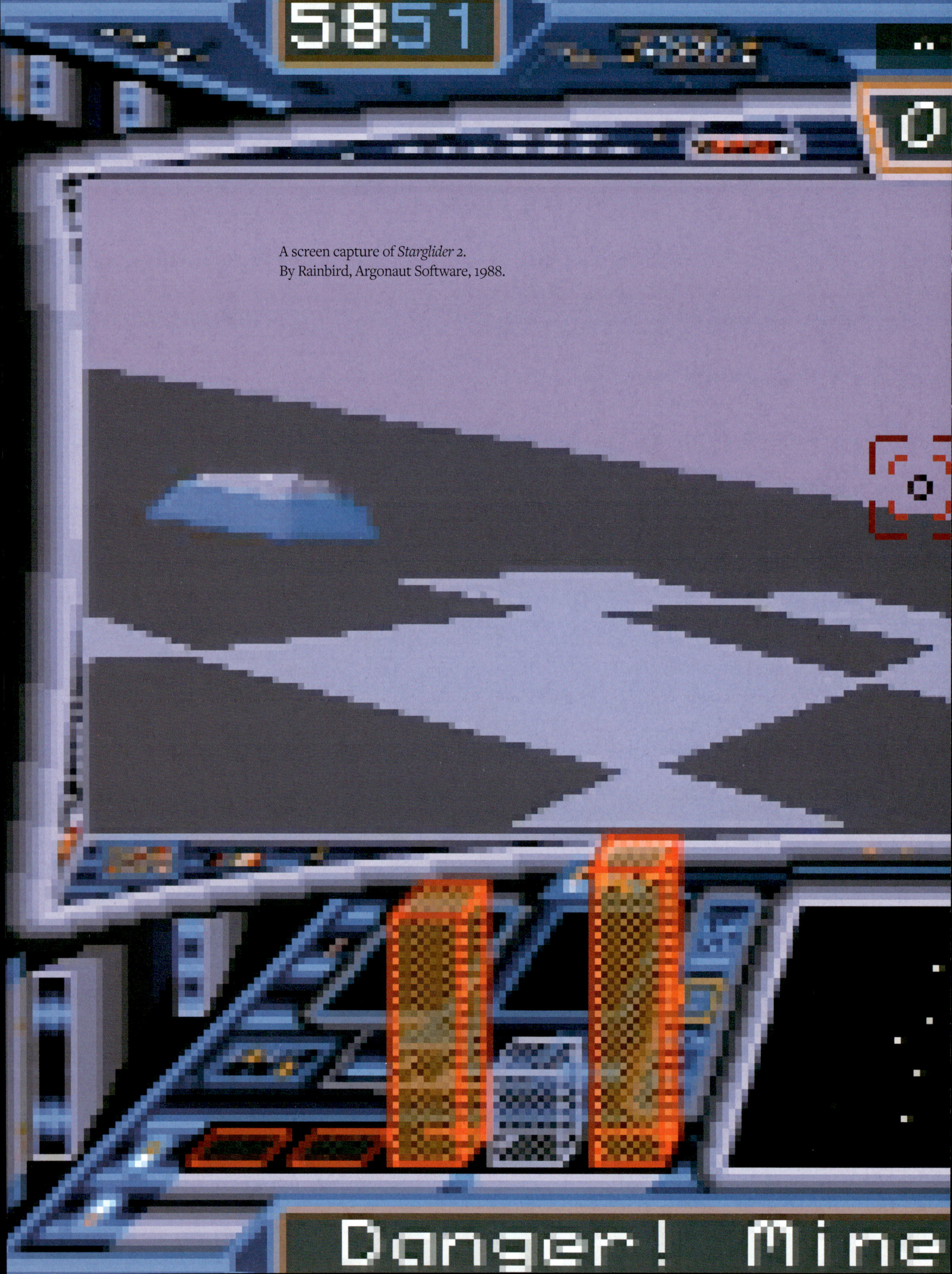

A screen capture of *Starglider 2*.
By Rainbird, Argonaut Software, 1988.

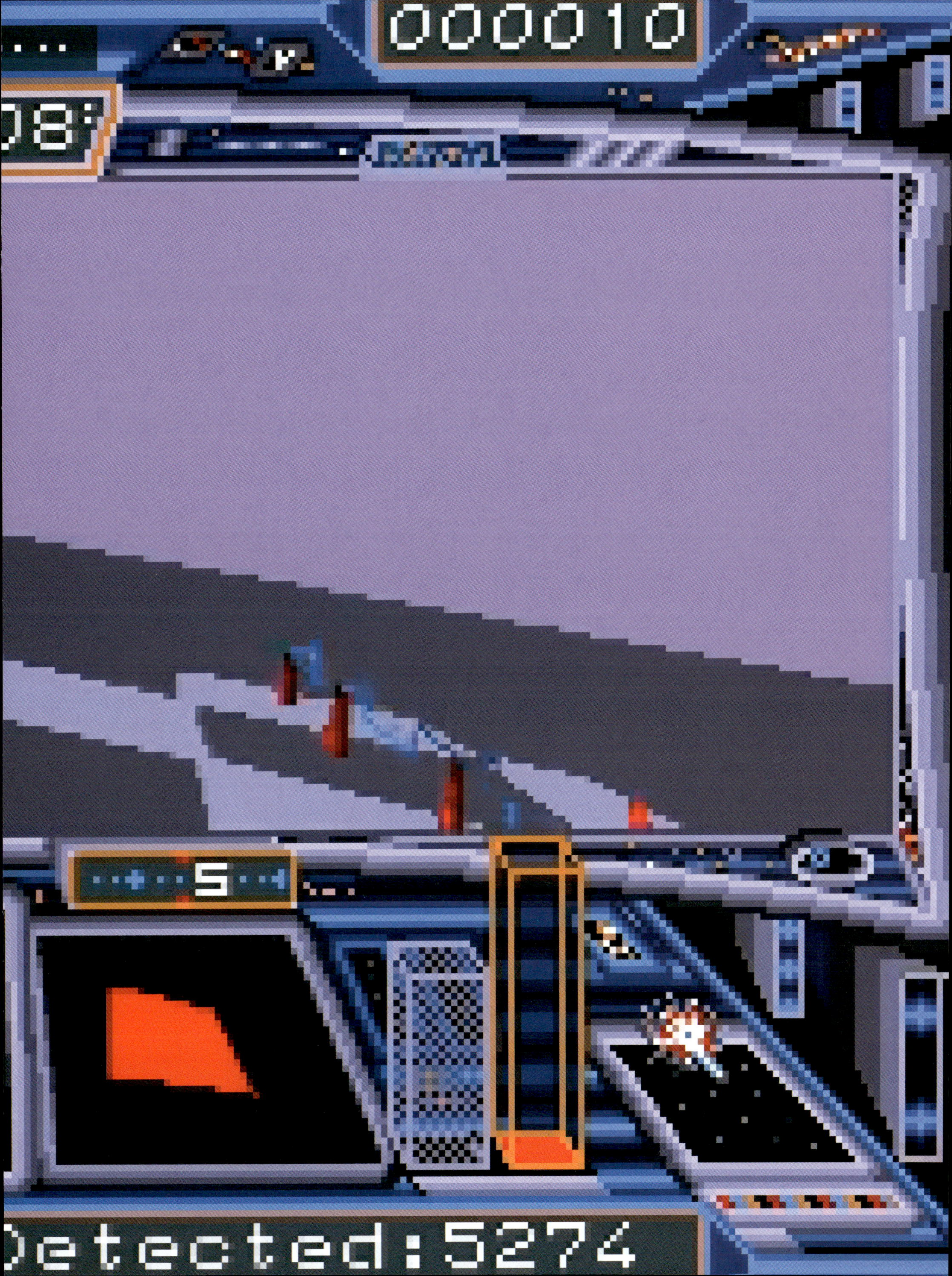
000010
Detected:5274

Tunnel Vision

The ability to move through real time 3-D worlds at high speed, the subtext of a militarized perceptual state of attention, as well as the later implementation of free look, naturally influenced the culture of level-design in top-selling games. Viewing a 3-D world by gaming in perspective is a fundamentally different experience from playing side scrolling 2-D, axonometric, and top-down plan-view game spaces. When the British developer Argonaut Studios teamed up with Nintendo and its star designer Shigeru Miyamoto to develop *Starfox* (1993) for the Nintendo SNES, they encountered a quality unique to 3-D game spaces that encourages linear, directional movement and architecture.[10] Initially, the demo version of *Starfox* disoriented players with unstructured views; flying through 3-D space with little more than a ground plane and sky for orientation. The solution involved a series of gates that the player would fly through like a car driving through a tunnel or under a series of bridges. An additional axis and zero gravity only add layers of difficulty to the fact that the avatar here is a spacecraft. Without *Starfox*'s gates, the visual field was too open and vast; akin to the feeling of whiteout that pilots can experience. *Doom* on the other hand was linear by its nature. Built on the shoulders of one of its id predecessors, *Wolfenstein 3D* (1992), the player moves through a series of maze-like corridors that open into rooms, chambers, and occasionally, open-air arenas and temples.

The linear structure of *Starfox* is also notable for its innovation in the rail-shooter genre. As a rail shooter, the visual narrative of the game literally moves the player's camera along a predetermined path. As a character, in this case, a spaceship, you are ushered through a landscape with minimal flexibility. A player has limited movement up, down, right, and left. One can brake or use a burst of speed to move your ship forward, but only for limited lengths before returning to the automatically controlled camera path; the player's movement is on a short leash tied to the fixed movement of the camera. With linear shooters like *Doom* and more contemporary titles like the Bungie's *Halo* and Valve's *Half-Life* franchises, players have near-unlimited freedom of movement. However, in these titles, the level architecture implicitly channels a player's movements forward through stages of the game's campaigns like a mouse in a maze. The first commercially successful, fully 3-D titles like *Doom, Starfox,* and *Cyber Sled* set the stage for a convention in gaming vision where one scans the perspectival cone for survival; the titles sent gamers into fast-paced 3-D worlds where one hunted demons and piloted spacecraft and tanks in immersive environments. Apocalyptic red mountain ranges, blue skies, and cityscapes painted the backgrounds of the three games. The gamer was meant to feel like a part of an infinite, 3-D universe. Perspectivally, however—if one pares-down the gameplay in these titles to their core—success requires that one anxiously stare down a one-point perspective cone and scan the converging lines of an environment for targets, threats, useful objects, and new opportunities on the horizon (a door, a gate, health, etc.). This anticipatory and restless viewing condition is embedded in the structure of gaming engines and continues to distinguish real time rendering environments from more traditional moving image media like film. Likewise, when architectural projects are realized through the gamer's lens, experience moves to the fore and geometry, form, and tectonics recede into the background.

Where *Starfox* used geometric markers to give structure to a formless field (and to increase the perception of speed and direction), *Doom* used innovative design techniques to transcend the claustrophobic underground feeling of *Catacomb 3D* and the monotonous repetition of featureless rooms in *Wolfenstein 3D* (id's predecessor-titles with perhaps *too much* directionality and determined movement). In both instances one can understand level design as a frame or stage for movement. Though the technical limitations of the PC in 1993 were many, *Doom's* creators used wall openings, windows, distant, inaccessible, "skyboxed" landscapes, split-level floors and sound and light leaking to open the experience of maze-like, claustrophobic levels. "[In *Doom*] there is a network of sectors that spill into one another, lie over and around each other, and operate together."[11] The necessity of linearity in early 3-D game design, and the opposing desire for the feeling of an open, limitless world in levels is a spatial tension still felt in contemporary gaming environments.

There are many formal theories in architecture that privilege a mobile viewing subject. Such theories downgrade the status of the architectural object to something like a backdrop for the movement of the user and the views they enjoy at various intervals. The picturesque, the modernist promenade, postmodern, regionally sited phenomenology, and the car-as-camera are only some of the more recent episodes in this genre of architectural theory. Such theories, however, tend to posit the viewer-user as an autonomous, delineated consciousness in need of grounding, symbolic orientation or heightened awareness of space, materials, arcane geometric structures, tectonics, landscape/site, semiotic systems etc. In gamer phenomenology there is no such delusion of a humanist project to aspire toward, affirm, or subvert. The body is neither transcendentally immaterial, nor grounded in a specific space, time, and corporal hyper-awareness. Gamer phenomenology acknowledges the role of our physical sensory systems and inputs via platform-hardware like gamepads. Likewise, digital physics alters our sense of gravity, weight, and velocity. Far from a perversion of perspective's power to capture one's unique, subjective experience, the gamer's view reaffirms the artifice inherent in perspective from its inception. In his text on perception, military historian Antoine Bousquet states that the perspective view was always a human-machine composite, and a multidisciplinary invention, "[a]t the intersection of the fields of optical science, pictorial representation, and land surveying."[12]

In postwar design theory in particular, the perspective is often purported to humanize modernist form, connect it to a site, and associate it with the specificities of a given cultural history. The scenographic perspectives drawn by Leon Krier in the office of James Stirling, and later his own, more extreme, regionally inflected work come to mind as examples. Contemporary commercial renderings, which again remind us of Lucia Allais' apt description, "engines of superficiality," largely continue this tradition, though with considerably less theoretical investment and polemical currency.[13] In this context, the gamer's perspective view is a far more authentic extension of the perspective's interdisciplinary origins. In a typical heads-up display a gamer is likely to see aim-assisting icons (options to use a sniper's scope), scanning aids (one might have an unmanned aerial vehicle in their toolkit), weapons, equipment, data on health, achievements, a time counter, and even a small map in plan view of a level with markers for where your avatar is positioned in relation to a landscape and key items or goals. It would be a mistake to argue that these overlays corrupt, distort, or otherwise mediate one's view of an architectural object in a gaming space. Rather, they make plain Bousqet's reading of perspective as a critical step in the advancement of military sight, "Perspectival geometry thus support the martial gaze through its deployment within an array of sociotechnical assemblages that seek to visually record, measure and represent the relative positions and proportions of objects in space."[14] Contemporary rendering practices in architecture are often used to romanticize the relationship between architecture, landscape, its users, and the city, but the history of perspective speaks to an ominous desire for control, measurement, and analysis in the service of strategy.

Design Notes: Levels as Perceptual Arenas

Experienced gamers are visual readers of levels, and designers are authors of a level's geometric narrative. In an anecdote about id Software's early years, Chief Technical Officer Robert Duffy recalls playing the same minimal "deathmatch" map in *Quake III: Arena* (1999) for three consecutive years each day after work with the team that designed the game. The *Quake III: Arena* team jokes that this map, *The Longest Yard*, was designed in less than a day. It was an exercise in efficient level creation. However, the designers inadvertently wrote a level so simple, and so elegant, that its reading was nearly inexhaustible and the designers continued to play it well after the title was released.[15] Gaming—it seems—is a kind of perceptual hermeneutics. For generations of gamers that have had access to the affordable, widely distributed 3-D console and computer games that emerged in the early 1990s, certain levels are intimate spaces that we traverse with familiarity and affection. Online gaming is especially rich with socio-cultural associations with gaming spaces given that such reading-playing is often a real time, collective act. Well-designed multiplayer levels are repeatable given that the social aspect of online gaming involves opponents and teammates' infinitely variable and unpredictable behavior. Game studies theorist Michael Nitsche writes, "3D games can assist concentration on certain patterns of events and make others less likely to occur"; a successfully designed level facilitates patterns and memorization, but is also open to improvisation and offers different opportunities and challenges to a player as they mature and evolve.[16] Level design, therefore, can be described as a quintessentially architectural activity. However, the creative forces that govern the design of elements are apparently more a matter of procession, movement, interaction, observing the status of objects, and navigation than top-down geometric schemas. Game designers develop the geometry of a level from experience-out. In the form-follows-experience attitude that level designers adopt, maps can be so straightforward geometrically as to be completely banal in plan. The four "Battle Mode" maps in Nintendo's *Mario Kart 64*, [1996] are perfect examples. Conversely, levels that focus on forward-procession can become unwieldy networks that appear more like baroque circulation diagrams than top-down site plans with clear, self-evidently logical geometric structures. Both cases support the idea that the gamer's perspective has produced a tradition of "architecture without architects" that is driven by movement, anticipatory vision, and goal-oriented use.

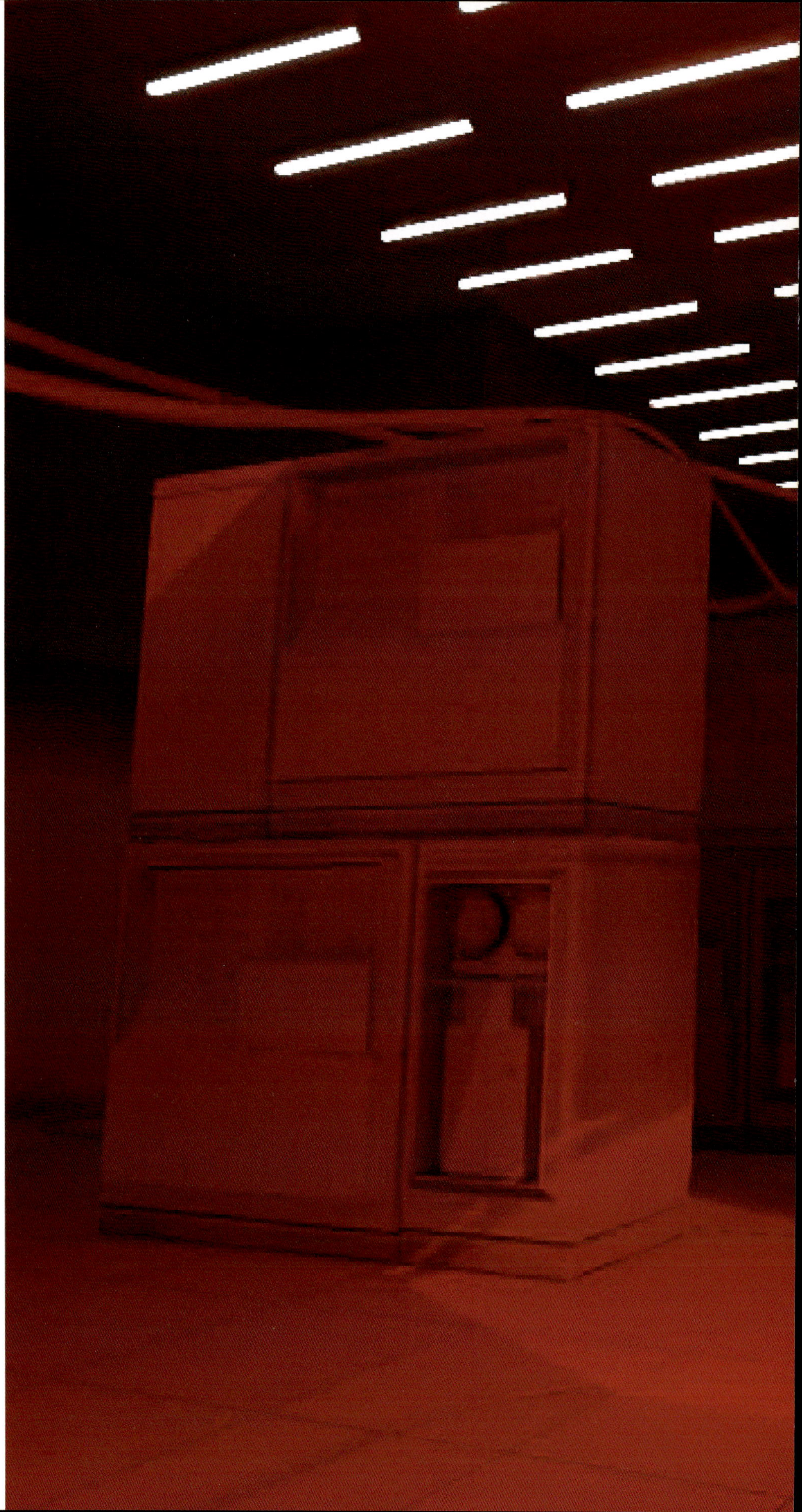

A screen capture of *Superhot*.
Superhot Team. 2016

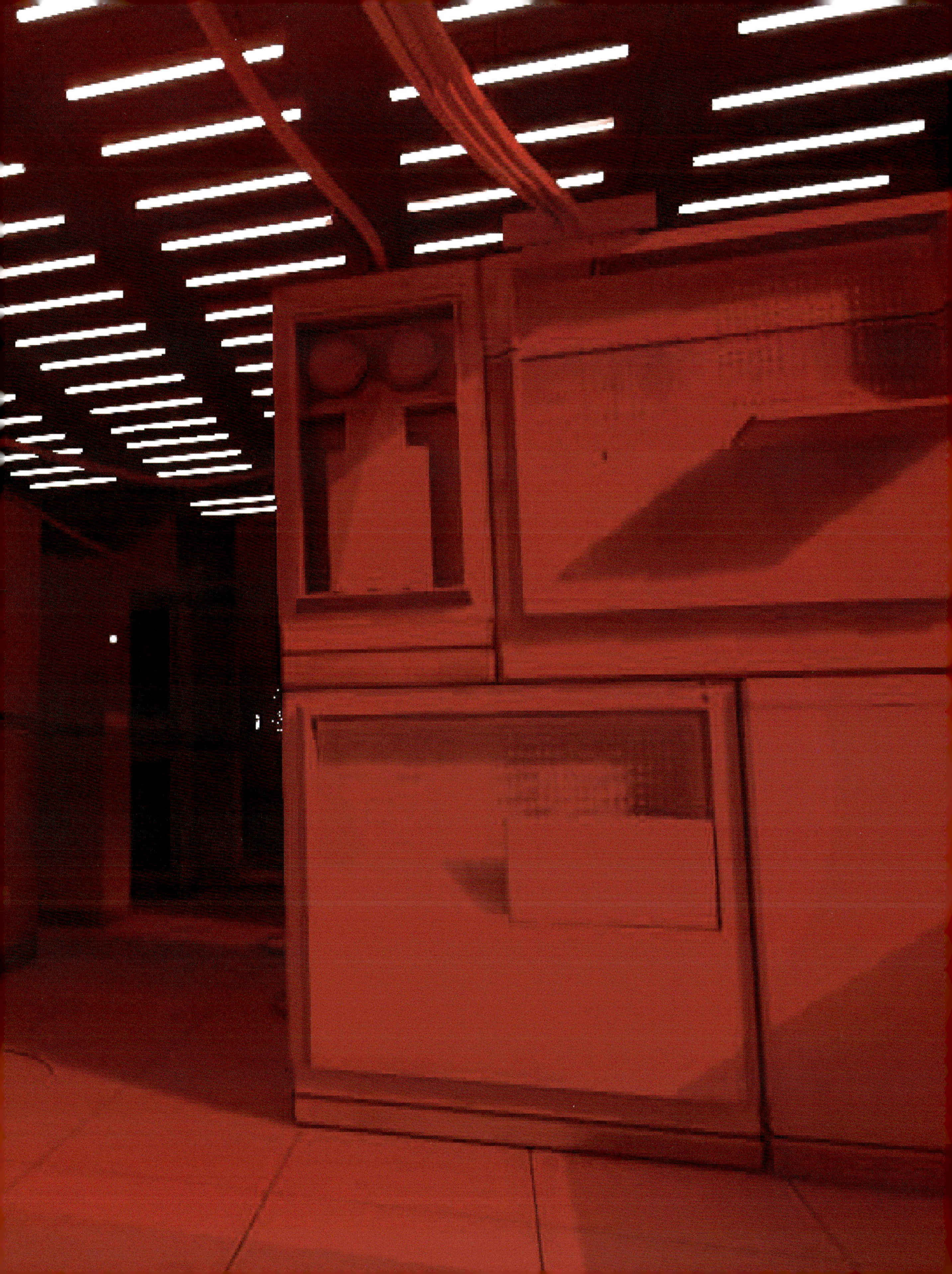

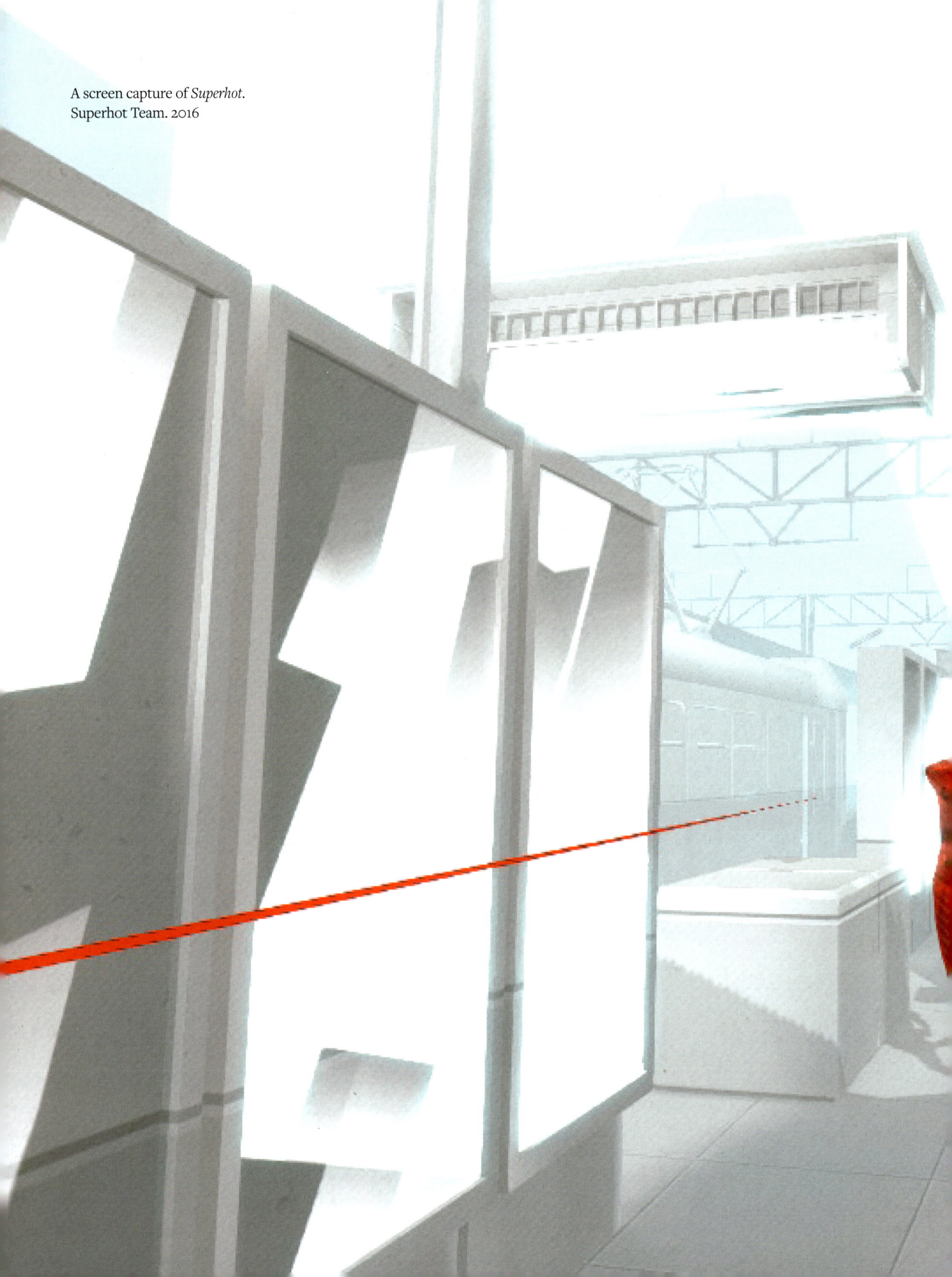

A screen capture of *Superhot*.
Superhot Team. 2016

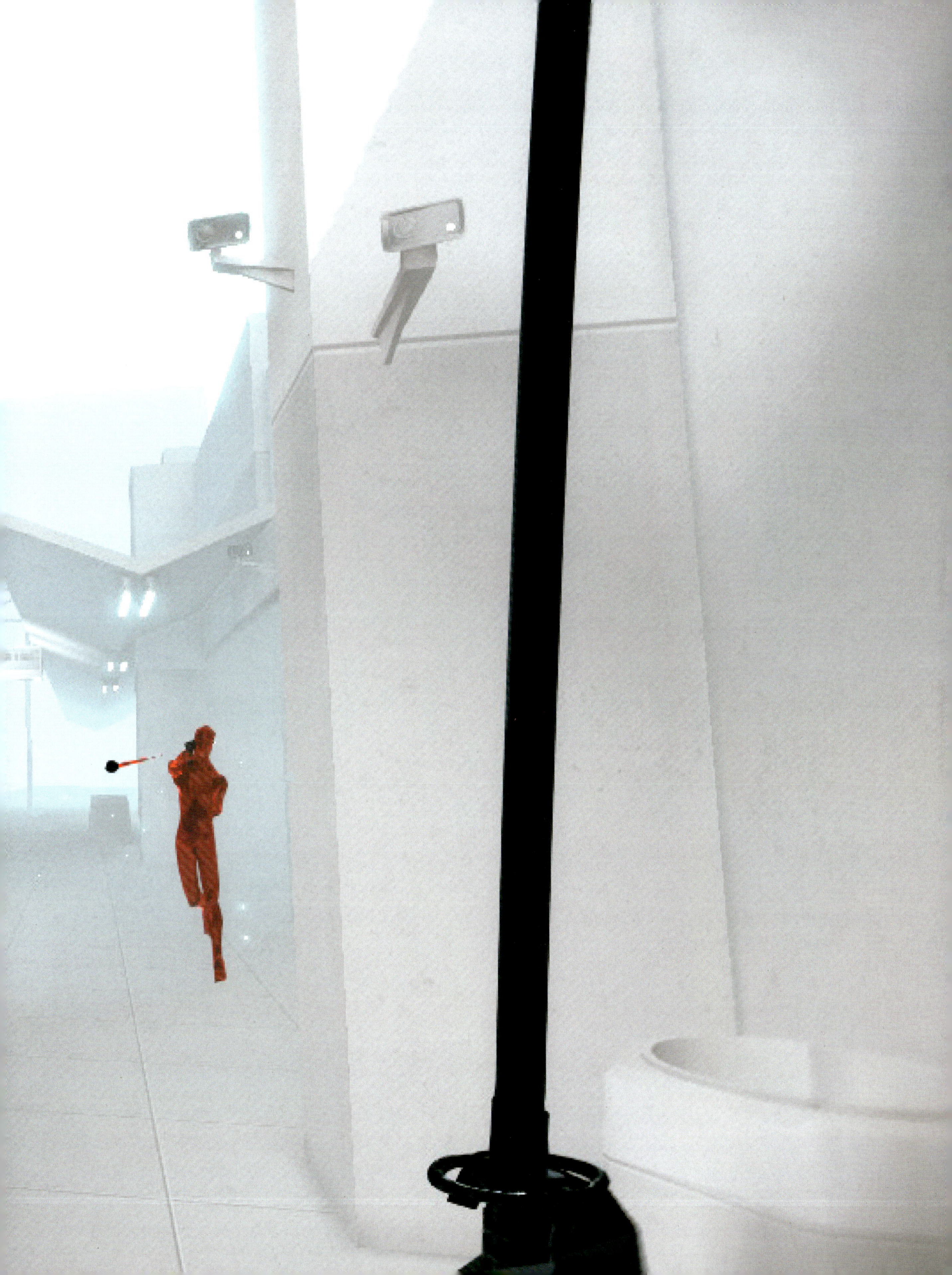

Objects in a Networked Field: The Architectural Complex

For those of us studying games from an architectural perspective, it's important to interrogate the design of levels and ask what kinds of spaces are conducive to 3-D gaming and the gamer's perspective gaze. In Nitsche's words, how do levels "assist concentration" and make certain events "less likely"?[17] Architecture, as it is represented in 3-D video game environments, provides a great deal of the fabric of levels. Game levels often resemble small cities or towns; a quasi-urban compositional problem, with the gamer-subject in mind as its user. For the purpose of this study, levels that contain multiple architectural objects in constellations will be forefronted over vast landscape-heavy solutions (the "open world" or "sandbox" genres).

Video game designers are especially adept at designing architectural complexes and have imbued the term with a new relevance.[18] Essentially, a complex is a particular formal type in art and architectural discourse. Complexes are suites of architectural objects connected by infrastructure. A complex is smaller than a city or a town and can be understood as a singular entity—an element in its own right. "Campus" might be the most apt planning analog in the sense of the complex being a singularly coherent, semi-urban network.

A complex must have an elaborate circulatory system; connections, passages, and pipelines that facilitate the movement of users and materials. Where the term *field* is used in experimental practice to describe the particulate architectural matter of vast urban sectors, it refers to a complex, or a group of discrete building-objects, intricately networked like a circuit-board. Ground is a contested concept in an architecture complex as circulation networks are datum-agnostic. Complexes are emphatically horizontal, but are also multi-level section-diagrams and cannot be understood in terms of vertical movement between simple sandwiches of horizontal floor plates. As a web of movement, a gaming complex is designed for sightlines, demonstrations of virtual physics (obstacles) and exploration. The complex is particularly conducive to the interaction of these vectors, exemplified in the dynamic movement of players in the run-and-jump-genre, the interplay of sightlines, the collision of objects, and active architectural surfaces.

As places, complexes are typically represented as unfinished works-in-progress with provisional elements and construction materials often strewn-about. Complexes are—more often than not—in suspended states of expansion, renovation, disassembly, and repair. A complex is a collection or group, and therefore explicit boundary conditions are unwelcome. Users move through a complex and, over time, they may alter its geometric character. A complex, in theory, if not literally in a game level, can expand and contract as nodes are added or deleted and connections are networked and severed. Several spatial archetypes recur in taxonomies of architectural complexes. A typical complex will include any of the following: labyrinths, observation/control towers, pools, tanks, linear infrastructural spines (a train track network for example), garden/landscape elements, archives or storage cells, multi-level atrium spaces, arenas, stand-alone pavilions, tunnels, catwalks, breezeways, bridges, lifts, occupiable roof decks, power stations, theaters/performance spaces, athletic fields, office spaces, testing tracks, laboratories, meeting spaces, rail lines, aqueducts, control rooms, and material transfer stations.

Virtual complexes in games are case studies in user-perception of the built environment. Strategically built virtual environments play off the three most important aspects of perception in games: hiding and targeting (in shooters) and discovery (in more exploratory genres). In both cases a player's cone of vision is their most valuable asset. Targeting in an open landscape is a rather banal gaming experience. The virtual complex is designed to open up avenues for the intersection of multiple sightlines (in atria for example), to create spaces where sightlines are controlled and predictable (as one hides in a sub level or hallway) and complex combinations of the two conditions. As bullet-time games like *Superhot* (2019) demonstrate, a player's field of vision is a precious economy in a game space, and the decision to look in a particular direction at a particular moment can mean survival, victory, or elimination.[19] Games that privilege walking, running, stalking, and evasion, especially in the shooter genres, often engage first person perspective views. In such games, sightlines—more than any other sensory input—motivate architectural decision-making in the construction of a level. A complex is largely a machine for viewing. It is a complex theater for the virtual gaze to wander in pursuit of its goals.

Object-Buildings in a Complex

Buildings are best understood as waystations in a complex—more like knots in threads of movements and sightlines than autonomous objects. Even stand-alone architectural objects in games, like a pavilion in a field, facilitate flows of movement. Useful architectural objects in gaming environments generally follow the rule that a player must be able to interact with them on multiple axes; making the most of dynamic sightlines, while finding ample opportunities to hide, duck, escape, discover secrets, or take refuge in hidden enclosures. As such, good architectural game-objects allow a player to move through, under, on, around, up, down, inside, and outside of a given building or pavilion. Successful game objects are thus porous, multi-level affairs with ample entrances, exits, stairs, ramps, ladders, balconies, decks, windows, breezeways, throughways, tunnels, and lifts. Though not entirely immune to the aesthetics of textures, lighting, and atmospheric effects, the gamer's eye is adept at assessing whether an architectural surface is useful (one can stand/walk/climb on it), passive (a wall that one cannot walk through and must go around/over/under), or physically active (surfaces that one can break, crush, blow up, paint on, or alter). In *Splatooon 2* (2017), players battle to cover a given area in their team's designated color of ink. Almost all horizontal surfaces accept ink, however, select vertical surfaces resist being covered. If a vertical surface is inked, players can traverse it by transforming into a squid that can "swim" up inked walls. The reciprocity between targeting, moving, environmental (architectural) activation, and the idiosyncratic physics of the game is nearly total.

For an architectural object to be open to a network, it must be something of a flayed, open, or dissected figure. This is not to say that more conventional buildings do not have their place in a level. A simple warehouse with a door, pitched roof, and windows would not necessarily be out of place. However, architecture conceived in the spirit of a level is often skeletal, connected to nearby structures, and in an incomplete state, somewhere in the process of construction, demolition, or ruin. Here again sightlines come into play. A dynamic architectural object in a level is conducive to targeting, hiding, and evasion and capture. In such scenarios, sights, sounds, vibrations, and particulate matter must be able to "leak" between datums (again, sound and sight leaks are one of *Doom's* greatest contributions to the history of level design). Tellingly, *Splatoon 2*'s levels read like ruins in that there are no "buildings" per se; only a staccato series of ramps, floating horizontal platforms, vertical planes, and systems of ziplines, conveyor belts, and launch-pads that allow a player to navigate the floating world through an exaggerated grammar of physics (*Splatoon 2* deftly marries the first-person shooter and run and jump genres).

EXERCISE

A Complex Without a Game

Because a complex is neither building nor city, begin by defining a territory of appropriate size. Imagine the ground as a neutral flat datum. Now, source a few models of buildings. Assemble a library of architectural objects with a range of scales and geometric types. Place them within the territory and increase their openness—remove some exterior walls, cut some spaces out, and add or expand apertures. Feel free to slice each building and separate the pieces. Now, model a circulation system that links the spaces together. Extend the existing floors, stairs, hallways, and ramps that already exist to enable fluid circulation throughout the complex. Add additional elements as necessary to reduce the number of inaccessible spaces. Ensure that at least one exterior space is well defined. Strategically model moments of the ground as mounds and excavate geometric volumes to create elevation changes in areas of openness between building objects.

Linear Movement in a Complex

Architectural envelopes serve an important purpose in gaming (obstructing views, providing shelter/hiding, etc.). However, discrete building-objects are less important than the opportunities that their individual surfaces provide. A catwalk for example, can move through a series of buildings. As a vector of movement, a catwalk or track is infinitely more important for the gamer than knowing where a specific building begins and ends. In the 2016 3-D remake of *Doom*, the player can pause the first-person perspective view to scan a 3-D, rotating map of a level, rendered as a ribbon-like series of horizontal paths. The map in *Doom* 2016 resembles the architectural convention of a circulation diagram, where the envelope of a building is rendered in thin lines, or is removed altogether in favor of floor plates, stairs, and occupiable platforms. In the same way that Jonathan Solomon, Clara Wong, and Adam Frampton's drawings for *Cities Without Ground* (2012) renders Hong Kong as a cacophony of vertical veins of circulation (paths, ramps, stairs, escalators, floor plates, and decks) games like *Doom* (2016) privilege networks of movement over place.[20] Needless to say, movement in games is inextricably wedded to each title's idiosyncratic conception of virtual physics as it relates to time. Physics and timing in gaming worlds can be a profoundly expressive element as titles like *Portal* (2007) and *Prince of Persia: The Sands of Time* (2003) demonstrate. In such games, any given architectural surface is only useful or important insofar as it is possible to occupy it, manipulate it, jump, climb or run on it, and use it for cover or in the service of attaining a goal. The precarity of an architectural element, such as the instability of a bridge, relative to its appearance necessitates attention to subtle cues in the rendered view.

James Cameron's 1986 film *Aliens* was a major source of inspiration for the original *Doom* (1993) team at id.[21] The survival-horror sci-fi precedent is indicative of gaming logic. In "campaigns," players are propelled through levels, hallways, corridors, tunnels, catwalks, and paths (often chasing or being chased a la *Aliens*); open areas are usually a reprieve from linear movement. In corridor-determined levels, perspective hyperbolizes depth in the viewport through the exaggerated lines of a hallway's walls, floor, and ceiling. Games are always goal-oriented and, in most cases, timed. As such, one studies the perspectival cone (of a hallway in a space station for example) in a level for targets, useful objects, hiding places, new routes, and clues for solving puzzles. Some games encourage movement by setting checkpoints for players to reach to save their progress, or hiding prizes, while others, again, in the spirit

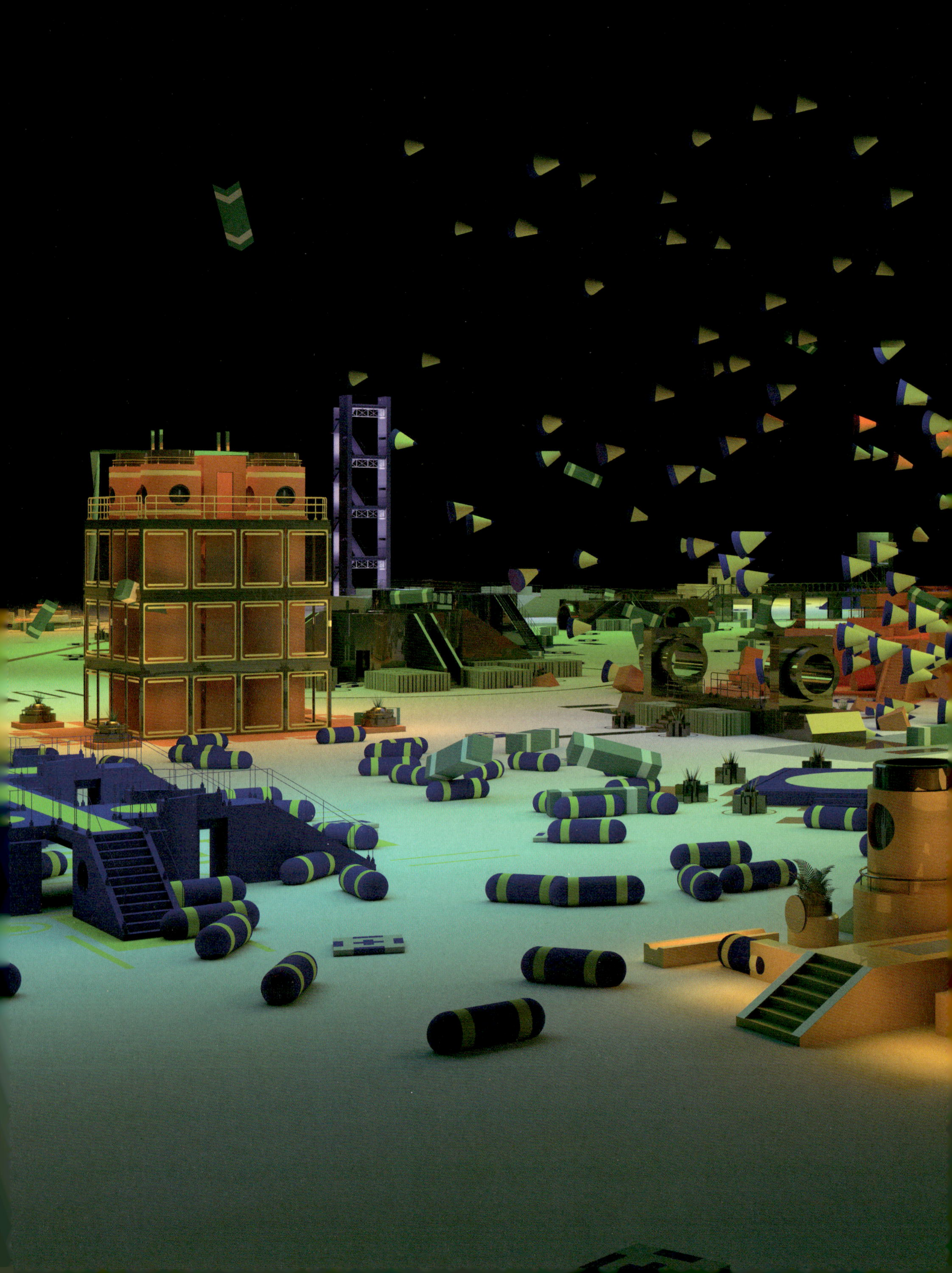

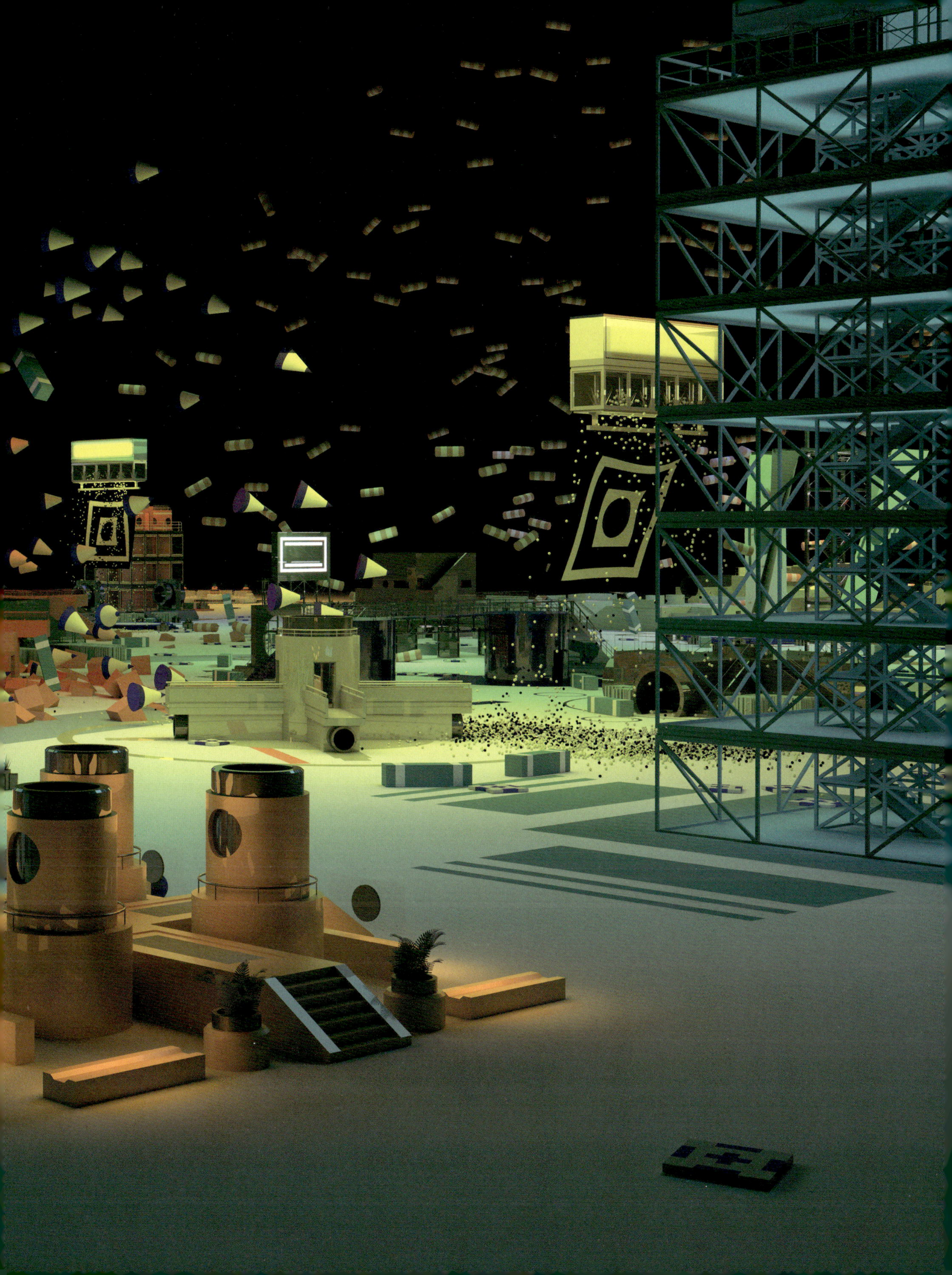

EXERCISE

Play the Complex

After the initial creation of the complex, it is imperative to explore your model from the first-person perspective view. Geometric biases introduced from an external modeling view may interfere with dynamic gameplay. Using a gaming engine, move around the model as a player would. Vary your speed of movement. Capture your gameplay as a cinematic or camera-path and watch it later. Repeat this process and look for opportunities for a narrative to emerge. Use the narrative to return to your work in the previous exercise and edit the forms. Repeat these two exercises for at least a few creative cycles.

of *Aliens*, move players forward more forcefully by closing and locking doors behind them and making previous routes impassable. In these scenarios, the only way out is through, and therefore one must always keep moving into the depths to succeed and survive.

Three-dimensional game environments have matured from raw wireframe and flat-shaded polygonal environments to richly texture-mapped illusionistic worlds. In high-res contemporary games, foliage, environmental objects and debris, landscape detail, infrastructure, and material textures such as corrugated metal, plywood, and weathered steel often serve to obfuscate and add complexity to targeting, achievement, and discovery. If architecture largely provides the structure of movement in games, texture-detail and atmosphere often serves as a kind of visual interference or calculated noise that serves as an obfuscator. Without texture and atmosphere, we might understand the gamer's view to be a perspective representation of the level map.

One of the most common archetypes in gaming levels are the crow's or sniper's nest. In the crow's nest, a player sees the entirety of the complex laid out before them like the surface of a circuit board. Access often involves a vertical tower with a limited number of entry points and a roof deck. However, strong levels often offer a counter to the tower in labyrinthine passages and subterranean tunnels. The crow's nest might offer a god's—or designer's—eye-view, but it cannot account for movement in the various ducts, catacombs, vents, sewers, basements, and circulation-shafts that are hidden from view. In the crow's nest one is afforded a near total freedom of sight; the possibilities can be overwhelming and one's attentiveness to movement and ability to distinguish figure from ground and active versus passive objects are key. In the vents, ducts, and catacombs, however, one only moves forwards or backwards. The field of vision is largely determined by the geometry of the tunnel that propels a player forward. Reaction time is key when traversing a game tunnel though one must be equally cautious about traps and setups in such areas where sideways movement is largely impossible.

In addition to the tower and tunnel or duct networks, complexes often feature linear circulation spines that function as micro-highways for the movement of people and materials. Such highways usually facilitate different speeds of movement for various human and non-human agents. Oil, water, air, chemicals, raw materials, data, carts, cars, electricity, and passengers may all move through a campus' spine or network of spines. Where conventional compositional theories privilege sculptural form as the genesis of a physical building's geometric concept, the author of a game complex draws in lines that solidify into paths, pipes, tunnels, roads, walkways, and tracks. A complex is a network of thickened lines punctuated by plates and inhabitable objects. As such, gates, doors, stairs, lifts, and locks control flows and obstruct and redirect movement. A complex is an elaborate spatial mechanism and requires tools, permissions, and timing to execute specific vectors of movement.

The Creative Necessity of Gaming Discourse

If architectural discourse is cultural discourse, our inquiries into rendering and perspective must overlap with gaming, which is quickly converging with all facets of popular media. Gaming is not a niche; more people are interacting with virtual, experimental architecture than ever before (there are 350 million registered users of Epic Games' *Fortnite* as of May 2020, for example).[22] While the most significant virtual, architectural environments are not designed by those who would self-identify as conventional architects, we are in a privileged position to learn and extract spatial principles from the collective discoveries of gamers, programmers, and game-designers. Architects and designers can begin by developing a robust discourse around the mobile, perspectival view unique to gaming environments and the architectures that cater to such viewing habits. Without this discourse, real time rendering could easily suffer the same fate within contemporary design discourse as perspective drawing and rendering in the second half of the twentieth century. Real-time rendering could become synonymous with corporate visualization strategies that recycle nineteenth-century painterly romanticism in the interest of selling clients a degraded phenomenology. Instead, we can discursively position real-time rendering creatively and generatively. It can influence how we construct and how we view and share views of architecture with others. In doing so, these representations, like all representations, affect what we make and how we make.

Displacement of the Viewing Subject

One feels a palpable sensibility emerging in the use of gaming engines in fine art and experimental architecture. This manifests in attempts to give visual form to capitalist junk space and ominous, animate material worlds. Though many examples are extraordinary in their visual scope, experimentation, technical acumen, and ability to render elusive cultural conditions and ideological positions, the visual trends of this work tend to gravitate towards open worlds, ruined landscapes, and non-descript cityscapes littered with the detritus of digital libraries/warehouses, exemplified in the work of artists like Jon Rafman and Cao Fei. Architecture and physics that might inform actual tectonic assemblies in these works are largely, and purposefully, left out of the equation. Graham Harman's mythic tale of a massive Ferris Wheel that acts as a kind of Noah's Arc for an infinite catalog of objects ("thousands of beings" including animals, bombs, power generators, prisoners, loudspeakers, active explosives, etc.) could be a literary-philosophical corollary to this genre of work.[23] Here again it's helpful to cite Brendan Keoh's writing on our sensory experience of video games. Keoh insists that gamer-phenomenology is one that marries human perception, the physical apparatus of the machine's hardware, as well as the virtual (immaterial) space the user inhabits. One could also cite Military theorist Antoine Bousquet's technical analysis of perspective as a device that weds subjective experience and objective space by way of sensing, mapping, and imaging. To adopt gaming tools and to study game worlds is not to displace the human subject in favor of an object's-eye-view.

Framing the perspective view in video games as an essential element of contemporary architectural representation generates profound implications for form-making and the construction of space. Just as the promenade, windshield-camera view, and scenographic perspective created reciprocal conversations between form creation and perception, the evolution of the gamer's view motivates the art of level architecture. As with the other elements explored in this book, this attention to the representational element brings it closer to reality, not farther from reality. While video games might offer a commentary on existing reality, they also constitute realities.

While hobbyist level design ("modding" existing games with accessible engines) has been a subculture of gaming since its inception, and game design is now an autonomous, specialist profession, newly available gaming engines are making level design more accessible to architects and designers with little or no engineering background. The architecture of level design and the companion art of worldbuilding constitute a new representational paradigm that is becoming commonplace in architecture studios. As such, our discourse needs to expand to accommodate the specificities of the geometric environment in games and conversely, allow those experiments to inform our built work. With the ascendance of gaming culture, millions of users inhabit virtual spaces on a daily basis and are as familiar with the anonymous corporate, industrial, military, urban, and futuristic complexes of games as they are with their own neighborhoods and places of work, recreation, and leisure. That the architecture of such environments follows a pattern language that one can clearly track to the inception of 3-D gaming, merits analysis, and design experimentation. Perhaps most notable for architecture in this language is the devaluation of sculptural form, in favor of networks designed almost exclusively for a mobile, goal-oriented, perspective view. The ubiquity of certain elements in this grammar such as the complex, linear infrastructural spines, networked objects, and other spatial archetypes like the labyrinth, arena, and tower privileges objects-in-a-field or architecture-as-open-network. In this, gaming spaces are affective arenas; participatory spaces designed as datums for movement, social interaction, exploration, self expression, and play.

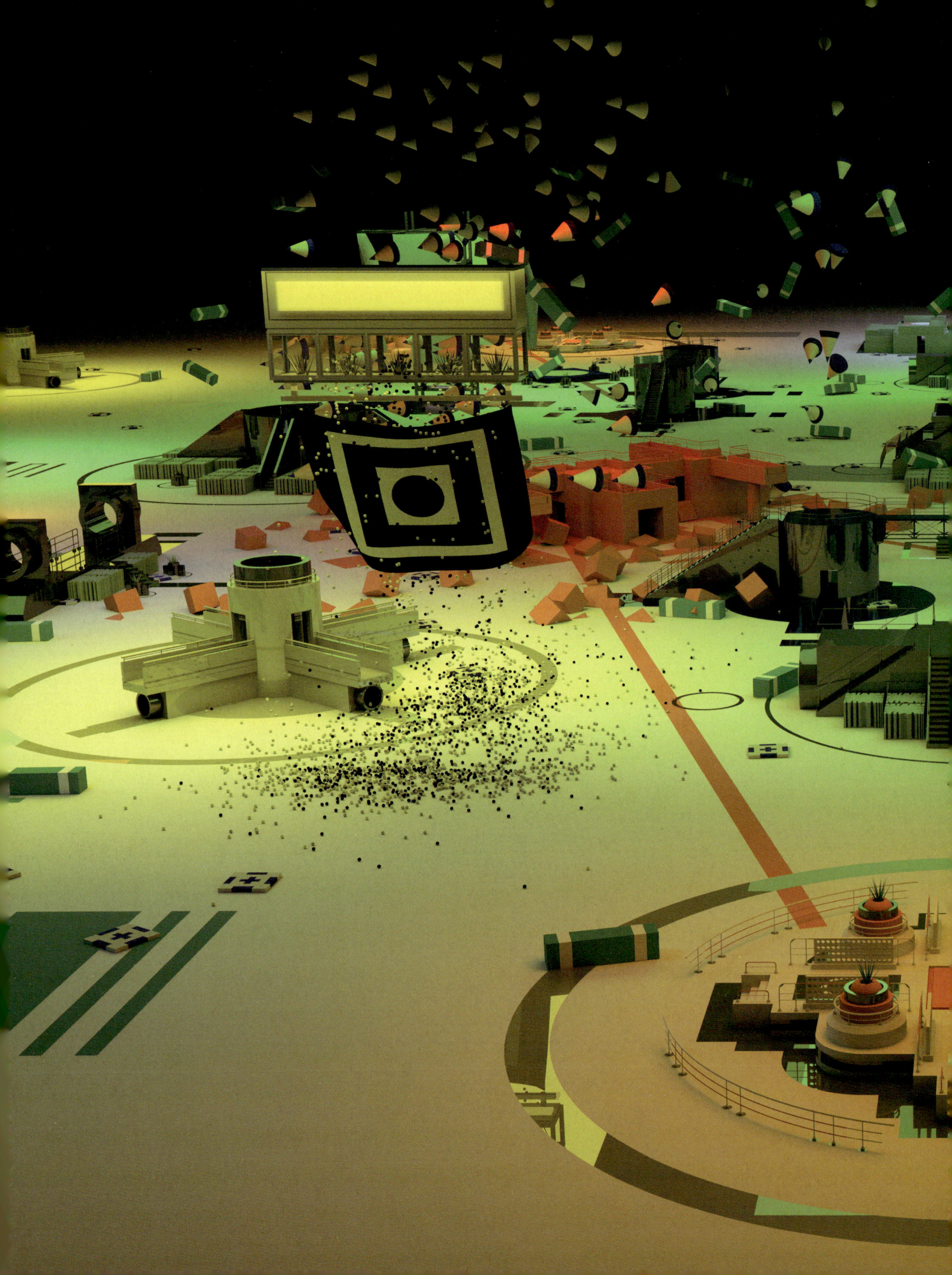

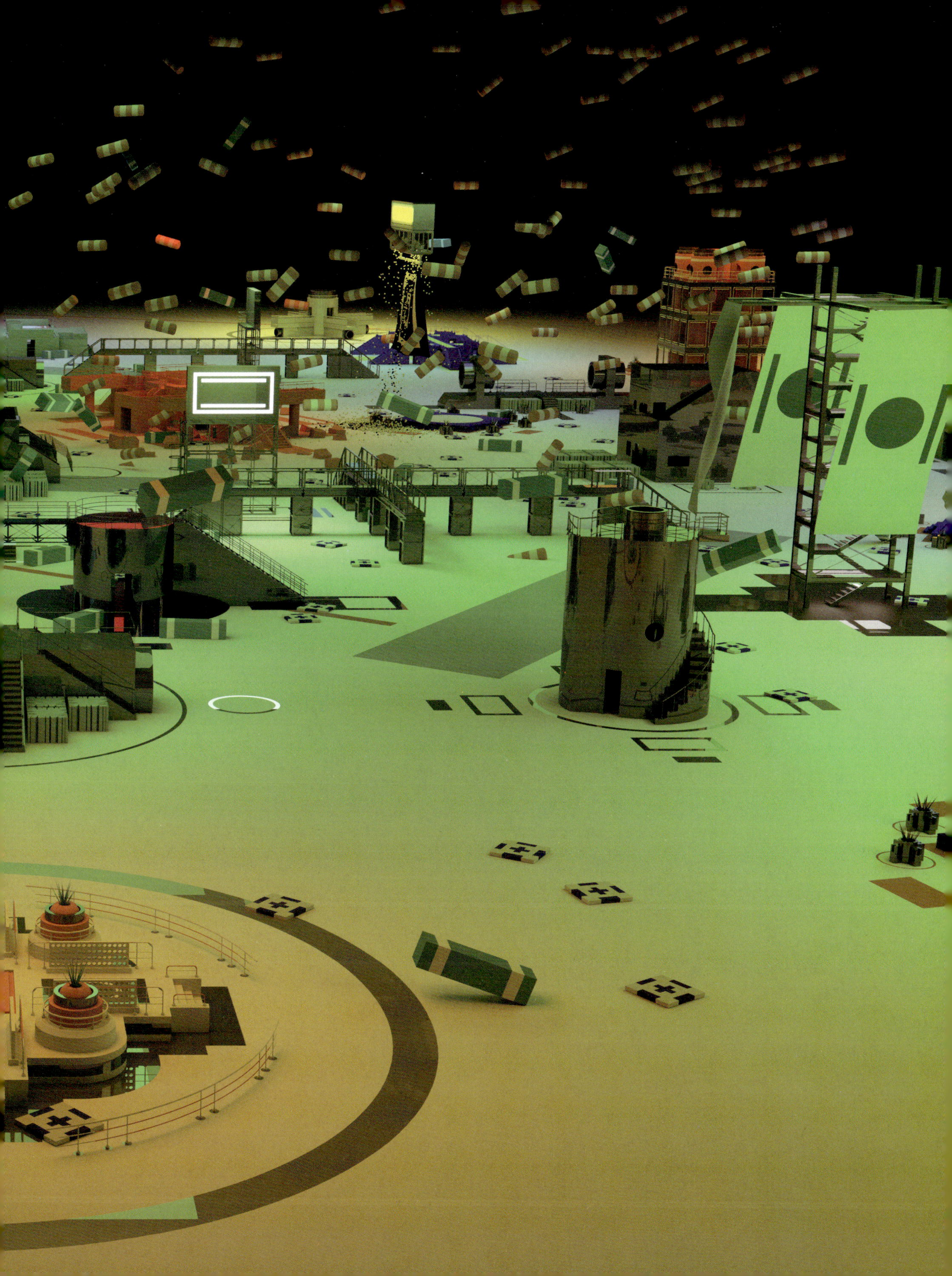

Notes

1. and Experiments," in *Design Technics: Archaeologies of Architectural Practice*, ed. Alexander Zeynep Çelik and John May (University of Minnesota Press, 2020).
2. *A play of bodies: How we perceive videogames*. (MIT Press, 2018), 44.
3. Video Game," in *The Video Game Theory Reader 2* (Routledge, 2008), 173–90.
4. bitmap image of an object or a landscape element in a game, often part of a set of different standard orientations or states. Sprites are sometimes called "movable object blocks" or "stamps.".
5. *Starglider 2* (1988) and id Software's *Catacomb 3D* (1991) were impressive advances in 3-D gaming though neither achieved the commercial success of *Doom* (1993).
6. fixed by a camera that is either static or moves through an environment on a set path. While the character-camera is fixed, the gamer can aim within the camera's viewport; much like being a gunner on a plane (a World War II bomber for example) that is being piloted by another person.
7. *Doom: Scarydarkfast* (University of Michigan Press, 2013).
8. *Quake* is commonly understood to be one of the fastest first-person shooter franchises. The genre has generally opted for slower gameplay experiences since the mid-to-late 1990s.
9. *A Play of Bodies: How We Perceive Videogames*, 104.
10. *High Score* (Netflix, August 19, 2020).
11. *Doom: Scarydarkfast*, 30–31.
12. *The Eye of War: Military Perception from the Telescope to the Drone* (University of Minnesota Press, 2018), 17.
13. *Design Technics*.
14. *The Eye of War*, 39.
15. Documentary: Part 1 - To Hell & Back," YouTube video, 28:27, Dec 12, 2016, https://www.youtube.com/watch?v=PS6SBnccxMA.
16. *Image, Play, and Structure in 3D Worlds* (Massachusetts: MIT Press, 2008), 159–60.
17. Ibid., 160.
18. charged subject in the spatial art of the 1970s. Architect-artists of this generation affiliated with post-minimalist sculpture often used the architectural type to explore the phenomenology of buildings, landscape, and site. Several notable figures that designed complexes in this vein include Alice Aycock, Nancy Holt, and Mary Miss.
19. *Superhot*. Superhot Team. Nintendo Switch. 2019.
20. Frampton, *Cities without ground: a Hong Kong Guidebook* (ORO Editions, 2012).
21. *Masters of Doom: How Two Guys Created an Empire and Transformed Pop Culture* (Random House Trade Paperbacks, 2004).
22. Statista, May 25, 2021. https://www.statista.com/statistics/746230/fortnite-players/.
23. *Circus Philosophicus* (John Hunt Publishing, 2010), 1–12.

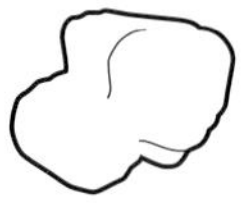

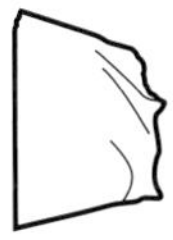

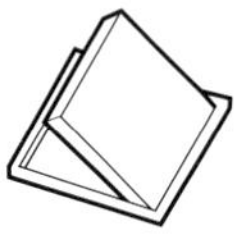

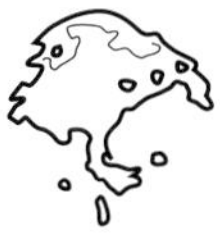

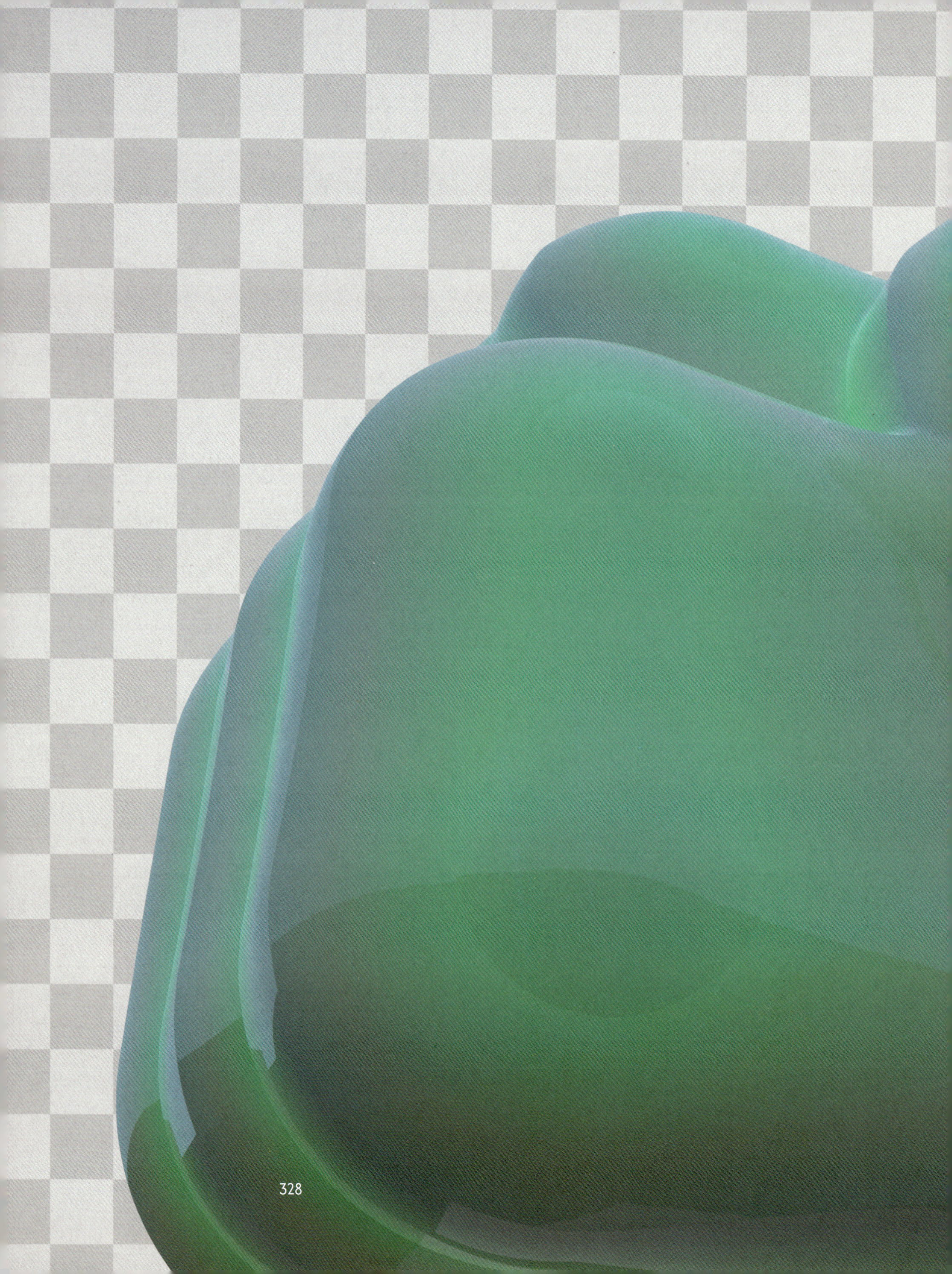

CHAPTER 8

Transition Elements: Rendering by Drawing

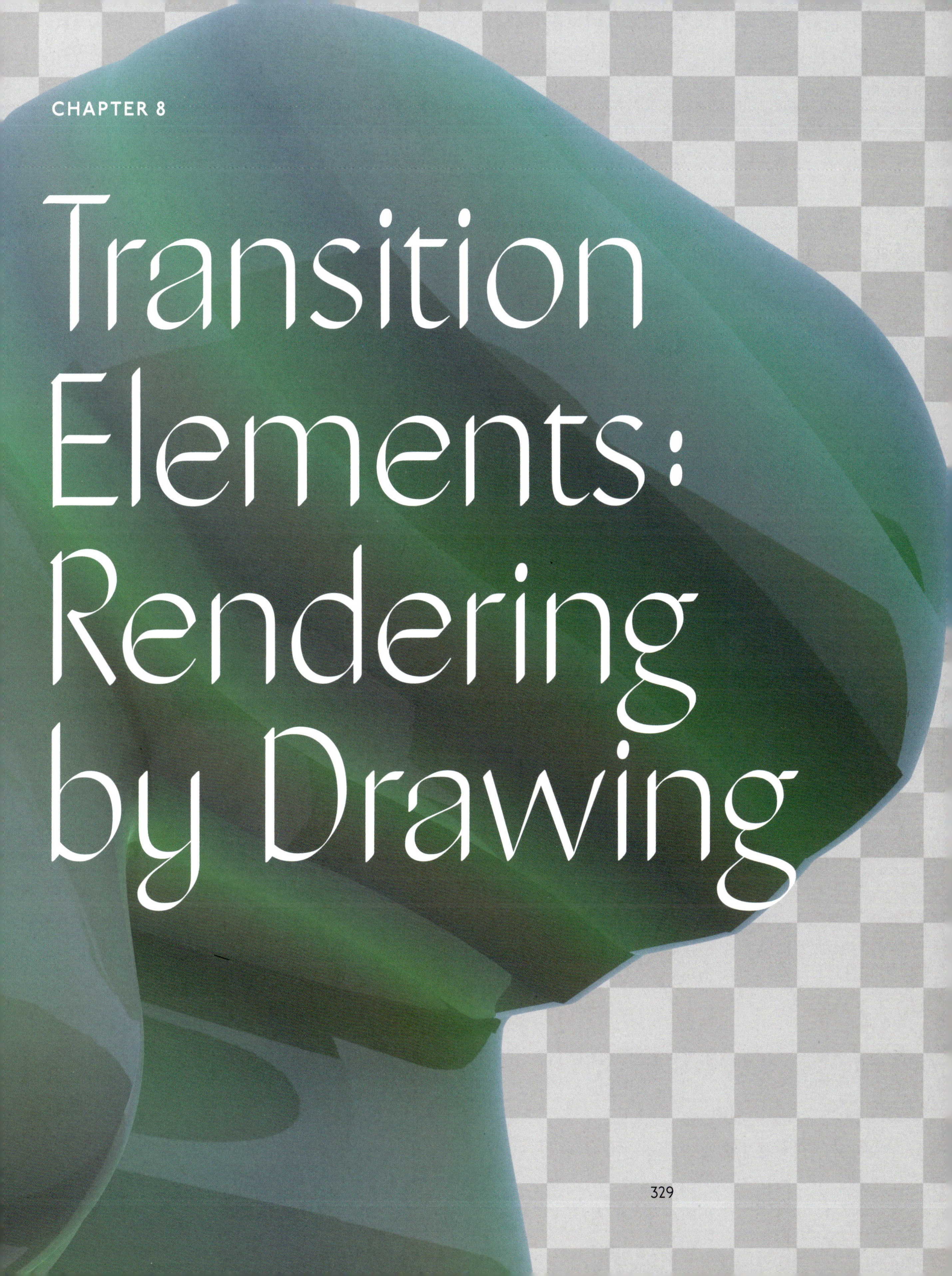

Drawings are often defined in contrast to renderings. How can impossible elements invite a drawing-rendering convergence without undermining the rich cultural and intellectual territory of drawing? Our answer to this question invites a return to foundational territory. We began considering the pixel in Chapter 1 and our inquiry into rendering brought us to increasingly complex, layered, and inhabitable elements. Now though, we advance rendering into the realm of drawing. Some might say that the pixel is post-line. There's no shortage of digital media critique in architecture that laments the loss of the materialized line, drawn "by hand," as though the image digitized the drawing and thereby laid it to rest. That reductive if convenient narrative misses the range of conceptual possibilities that are possible with images and drawings alike. In our reality, drawing isn't something to be recovered, but the inevitable next step in the evolution of the image.

The Case for Lines

The line epitomizes the possible. A line can direct the fabrication of the real and analyze the real. For the most part though, the line tends to enjoy some productive distance from realism. That can be a great benefit. Imagine a team of architects using a line drawing to explore early diagrammatic possibilities with a group of collaborators. With so many open-ended qualities and possibilities yet to be resolved, they might prefer a simple line drawing over the richness of a rendering because it avoids the fidelity of color and material; it avoids encroaching on the real too soon. Conversely, imagine teaching a novice with ambitions of realism learning to draw from life by advising, "don't focus on outline, but use the charcoal to mark the shadows." Both of those situations capture the tension between the coded nature of the line and the direct reality-friendly appearance of material media. Despite that separation, can we ask the line to simultaneously participate in the representation, distortion, fabrication, and manipulation of reality? It's a tall order. This would mean the line, normally associated with the limits of what is possible within a given reality, would start to suggest the impossible in the same way we've considered "impossible elements" throughout this book. In this sense, they could be said to transition between conventions of representation that usually remain constant and reality-dependent rather with those that are reality-defying.

The first step is to consider how lines manifest within elements that can be created with the rendering technologies we've already explored. In Chapter 5, procedural shaders were discussed in the context of the nearly invisible element. Let's make an important observation about rendering technology that is more obvious in console or computer gaming than it is in architecture: when the rendering process leads to *the* reality as opposed to one of many depictions of reality, there is no distinction between geometric content that was modeled prior to the rendering and geometric content that appears to exist in the rendering. Think about an architectural competition board or typical pin up. The renderings are often special moments of enhanced realism alongside drawings that withhold realism. We might even encounter the same projected view depicted as outline and then again as a raytraced rendering. Likewise, we might encounter a kind of pseudo rendering wherein photographs of material are used as a kind of paint-by-numbers fill pattern that respects the primacy of the outline. But if we allow rendering to stand alone, or we inhabit it as we would a video game, we can start to see the rendering apparatus as an extension to—or even replacement of—a modeling apparatus. In the "striations and metaballs" series of elements, the modeled source information is extremely minimal and true to the mathematical threshold model of the metaball conceived by James F. Blinn in 1982.[1] Blinn's metaballs are implemented in almost all 3-D animation software. They allow the frame-by-frame representation of smooth blobby intersections of mesh forms that distort and merge based on proximity. When rendered with a procedural shader that itself augments the smooth geometry with ridge-like striations while also influencing the behavior of light along those same striations, we can clearly conclude that the rendering doesn't reveal material, it creates material. This is a helpful reminder that lines are not inherently anti-material, despite the fact that we often conflate vector formats in digital workflows with the hard edges of pre-material formal gestures.

Other line-based transitional elements derive their strength from their subtlety. Encountering them is less like being slapped in the face and more like being taken by the hand and invited to notice something that is ever so slightly strange. To construct such an element involves first considering lines in their most bare state: as hatches. Then we'll consider systems of hatches as elements.

One way to think about hatches—essentially vector-based fill patterns—in drafting software is to consider them as barely lines in the same way a "hatch" can be seen as barely a door. It meets the technical criteria of a door, but lacks the qualities, capacities, and significance of most doors. A hatch is a line that is similarly lacking, merely a patterned mark—by default not even individually selectable in software when deployed as part of a patterned fill. But where a hatch is minimally a line (or a door) it also has the potential to be something else, and something more when customized and redeployed as a system. In the case of the line-like hatch, that something more is a capacity to render—to capture the appearance of material and atmosphere. In the case of the door-like hatch, the superpower is less obvious, but nonetheless is worth exploring: the capacity to render the wall that it sits within; barely interrupted by seam or gap, with little or no frame, and minimal depth, the power of the hatch is in its minimal interruption of surface.

Hatches used to render do not automatically rise to the status of "impossible" or "hyper-real," but they do easily register qualities. As a system to convey light, dark, and material they may remind us of a low fidelity, low-resolution image. The comparison is apt: in such a paradigm, a hatching system can be produced from the processing of an input image, like filters in image editing software. The line recedes far into the rhetorical background as it would take a collection of hatch lines to do the work of a single pixel. Here, the comparison to the pixel is the hatch's lifeline to representational relevance. Normally, hatches come pre-packaged as immutable though infinitely repeatable objects. But, if a hatch were biased in what it rendered, if it were specifically calibrated to a reality and not just any reality, then it would no longer be as neutral as the default hatches (or filters) that come prepackaged in software and graphics standards manuals. If the hatch could be imbued with information about the surface that it was tracing, if it could retain 3-D information even as it was marked in 2-D, and if it was indistinguishable from that which it is representing, then the hatch would be back in the game of contentious representation. Hatches would be constantly receding into the scene, doing the job of an element in a rendering even as they asserted themselves as the fabric of a drawing. Hatches would also retain their figuration as though they are lines. Imagine in this complex and delicate rhetorical framework, that which was being hatched was also a hatch.

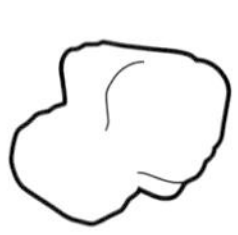

The opposing natures of striations and metaballs converge into one new object-material.

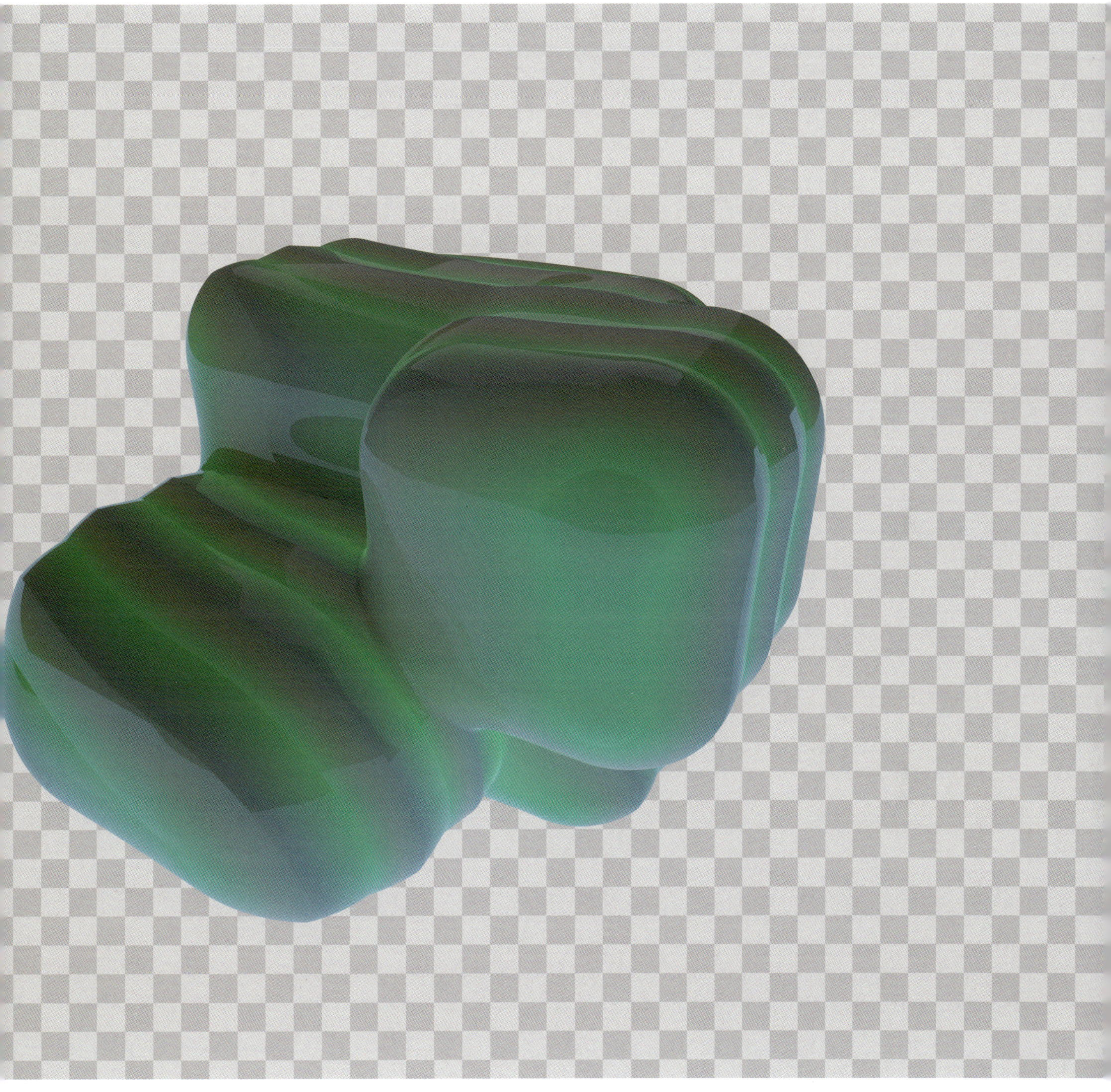

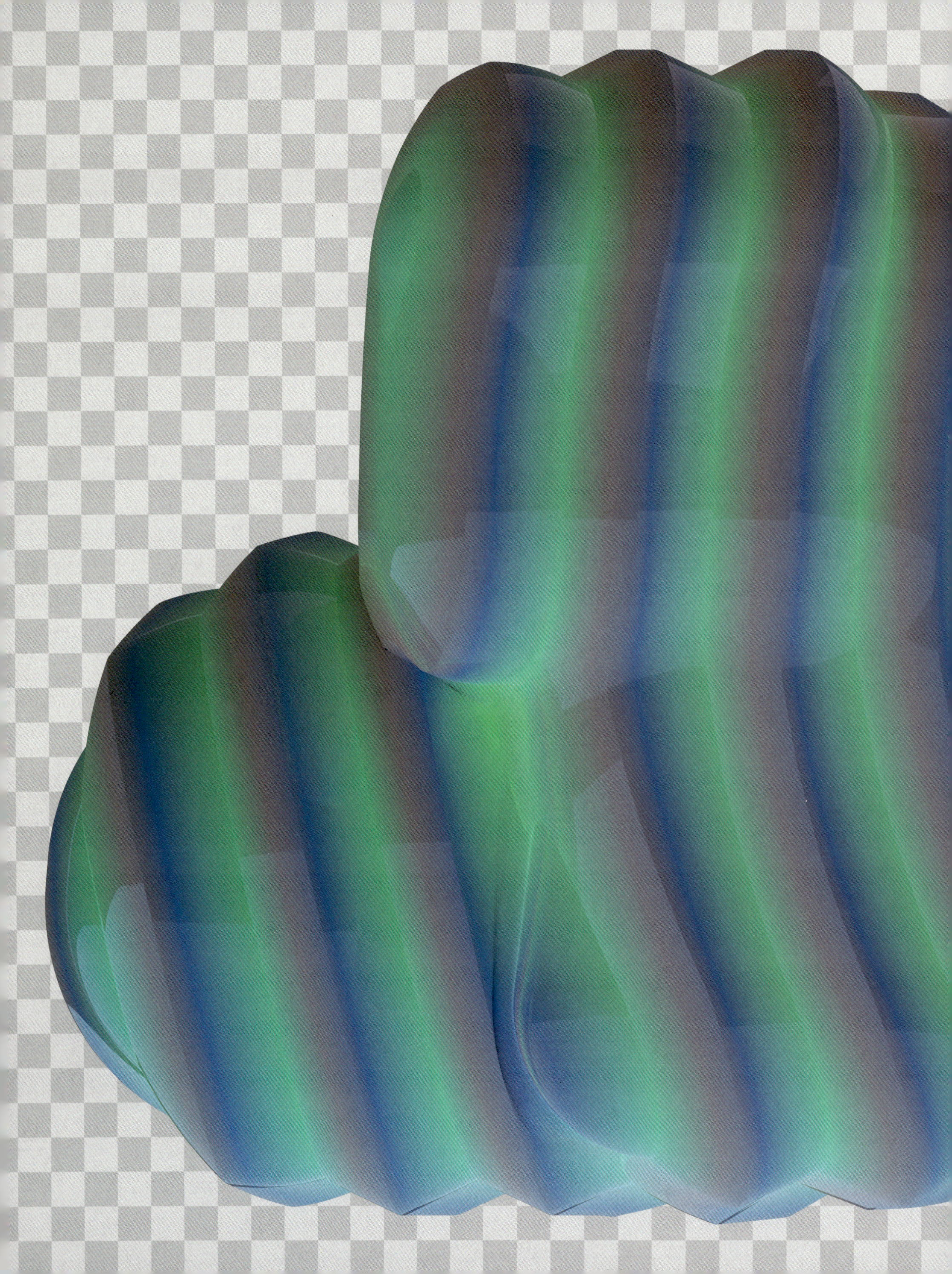

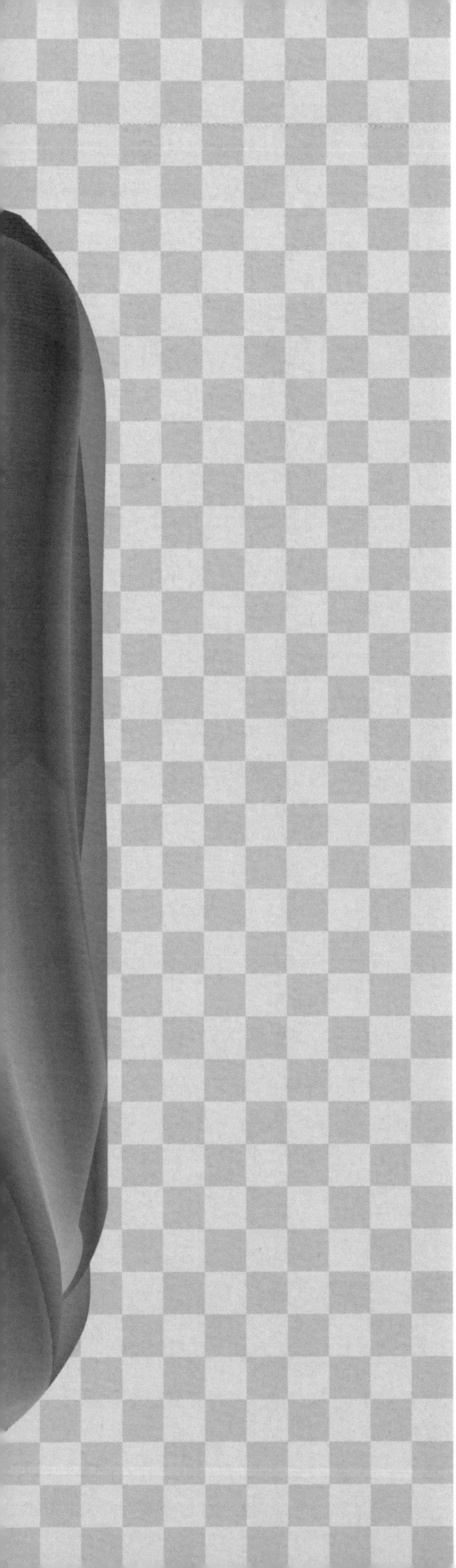

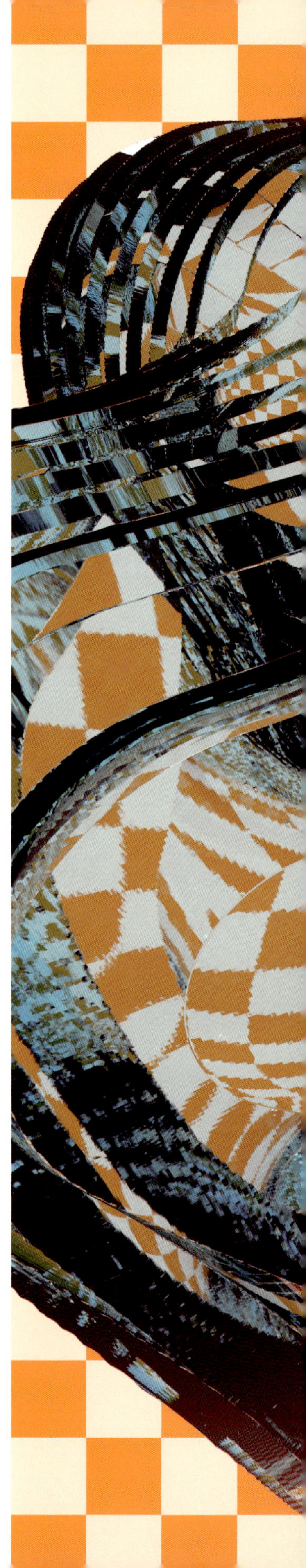

As the two metaballs overlap and separate, their total mass fluctuates, which contradicts their implied materiality, which in turn conflicts with their surface qualities.

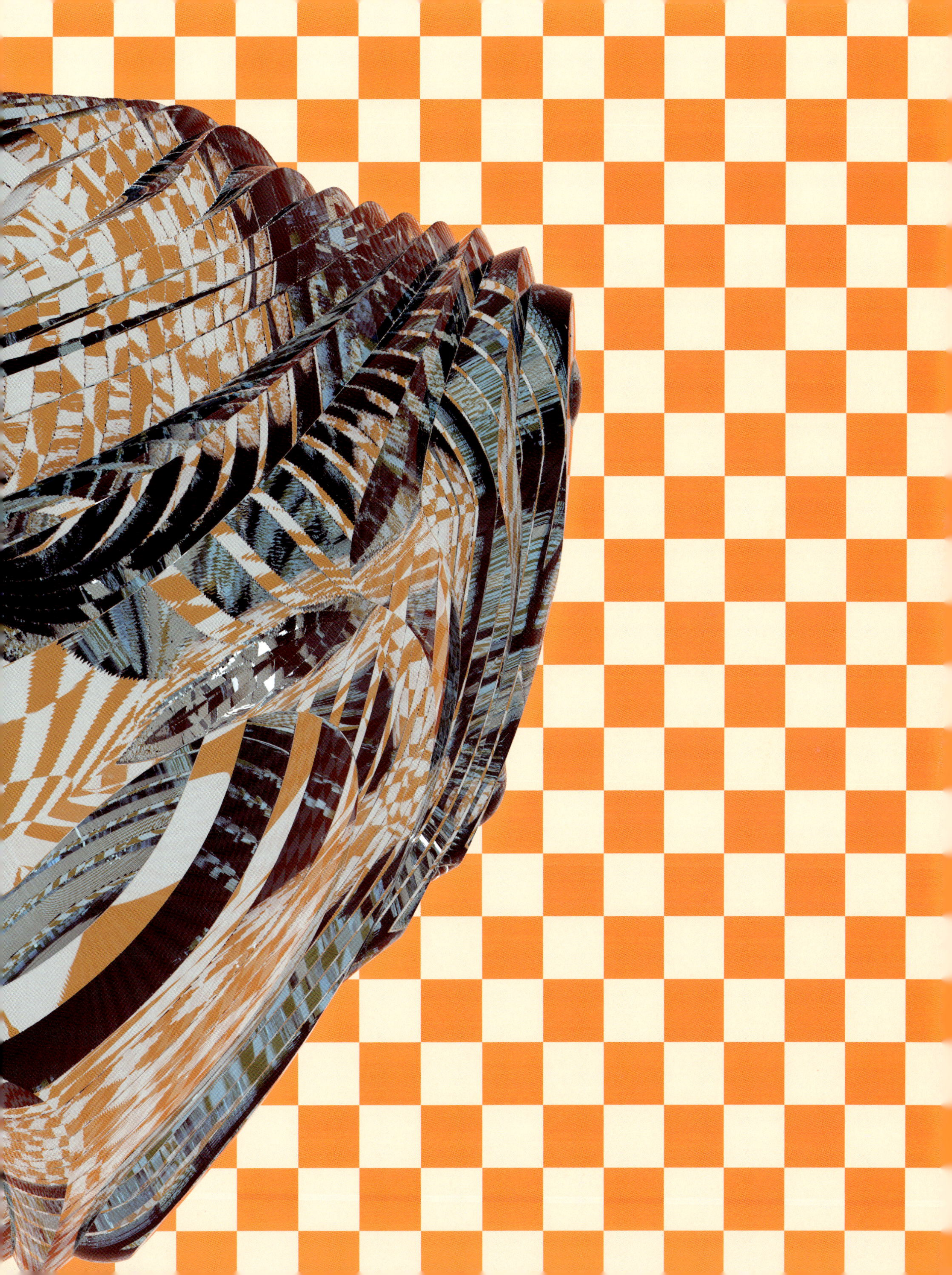

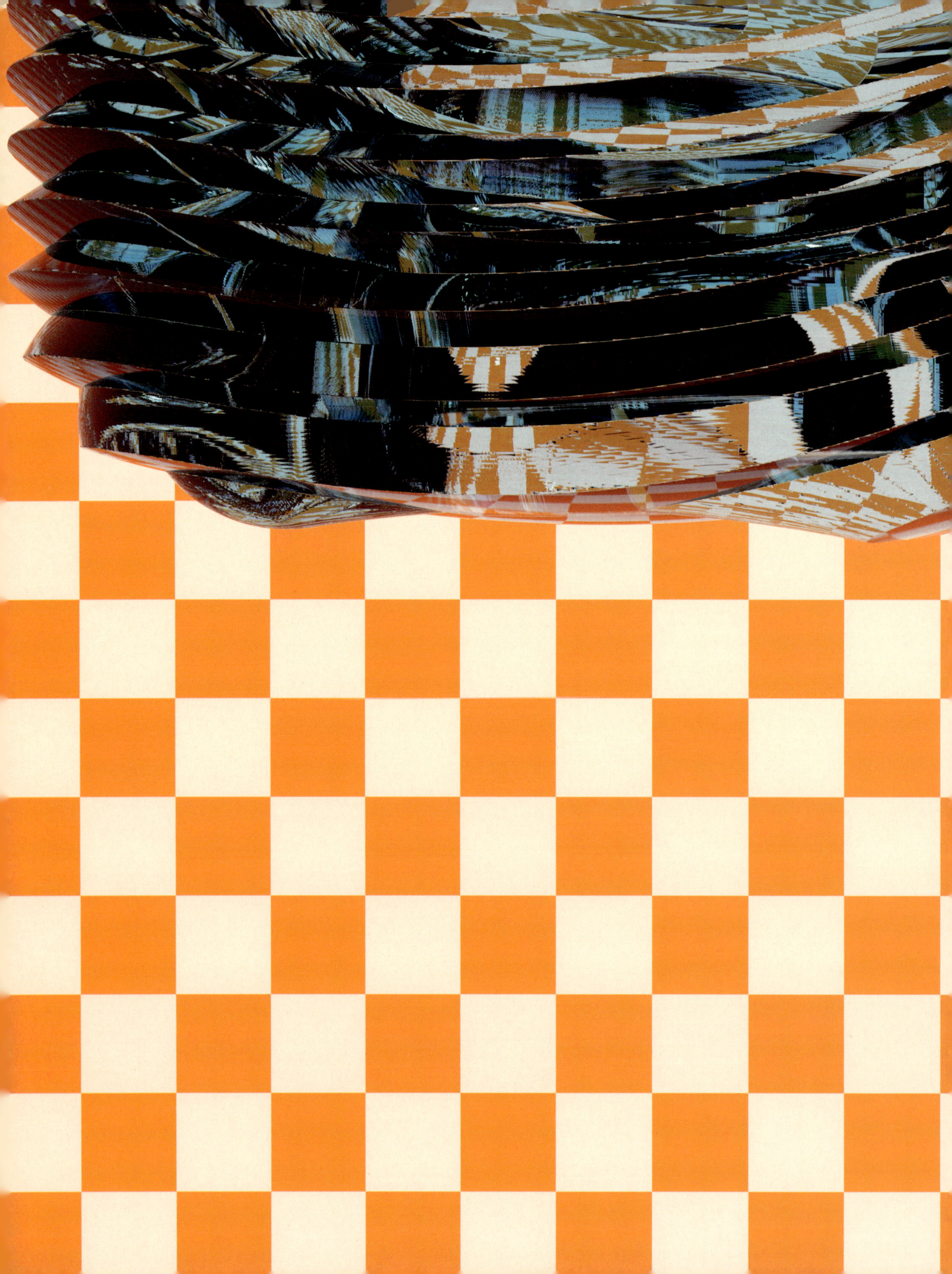

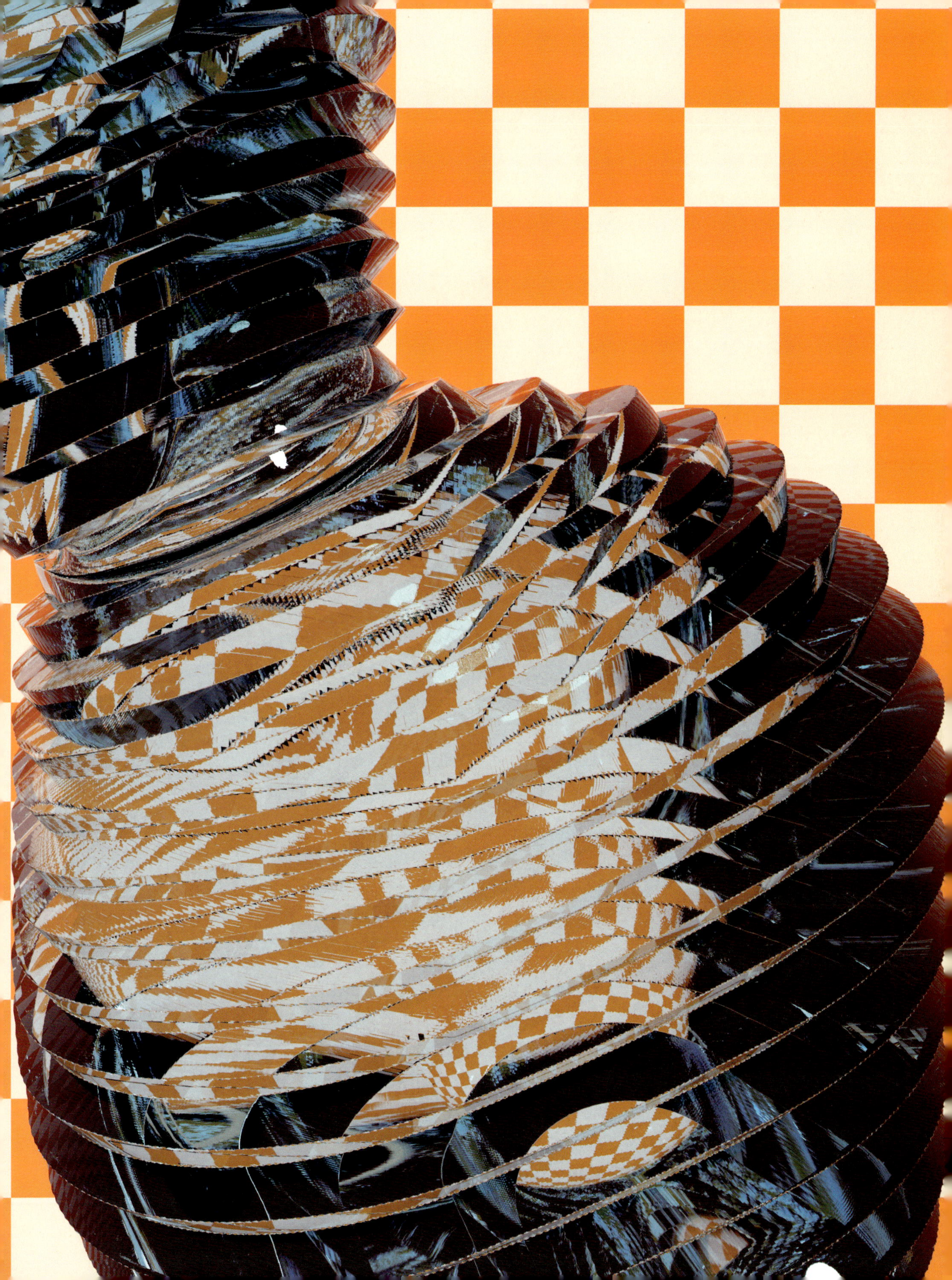

Geometry of the Surface

We've already noted how the digital material made up of algorithms (as opposed to mapped images) doesn't take form and reduce it into an image but generates new form relative to the existing form and other information. Our discussion of the hatched surface is similar. One might assume that hatches are deployed after projection of outline geometry onto a picture plane and fill in the shapes like a coloring book. But the hatch need not remain confined to the picture plane. It can—and must—manifest in the picture plane, but its length, color, and speed are a function of 3-D geometry. Specifically, the geometry of an undulating corner-less and seamless surface participates in promotion of hatch into elemental status.

The hatch also affects the geometry of the surface. The hatch—which is now possible to consider as both door and line simultaneously—is designed to deny curvature. Each element is therefore a negotiation between geometries that moves back and forth between drawing and model. Again, it's important to note that the hatch is not merely a compromised (lower res, lower fidelity) version of the surface. The flat hatch imposes itself onto the surface changing the equations that describe the surface and therefore influencing the other nearby hatches. We can also, in what by now must be a recognizable pattern, conclude that the surface has become inseparable from that which represents it. There is no more a surface rendered with hatches, only hatches that constitute a surface.

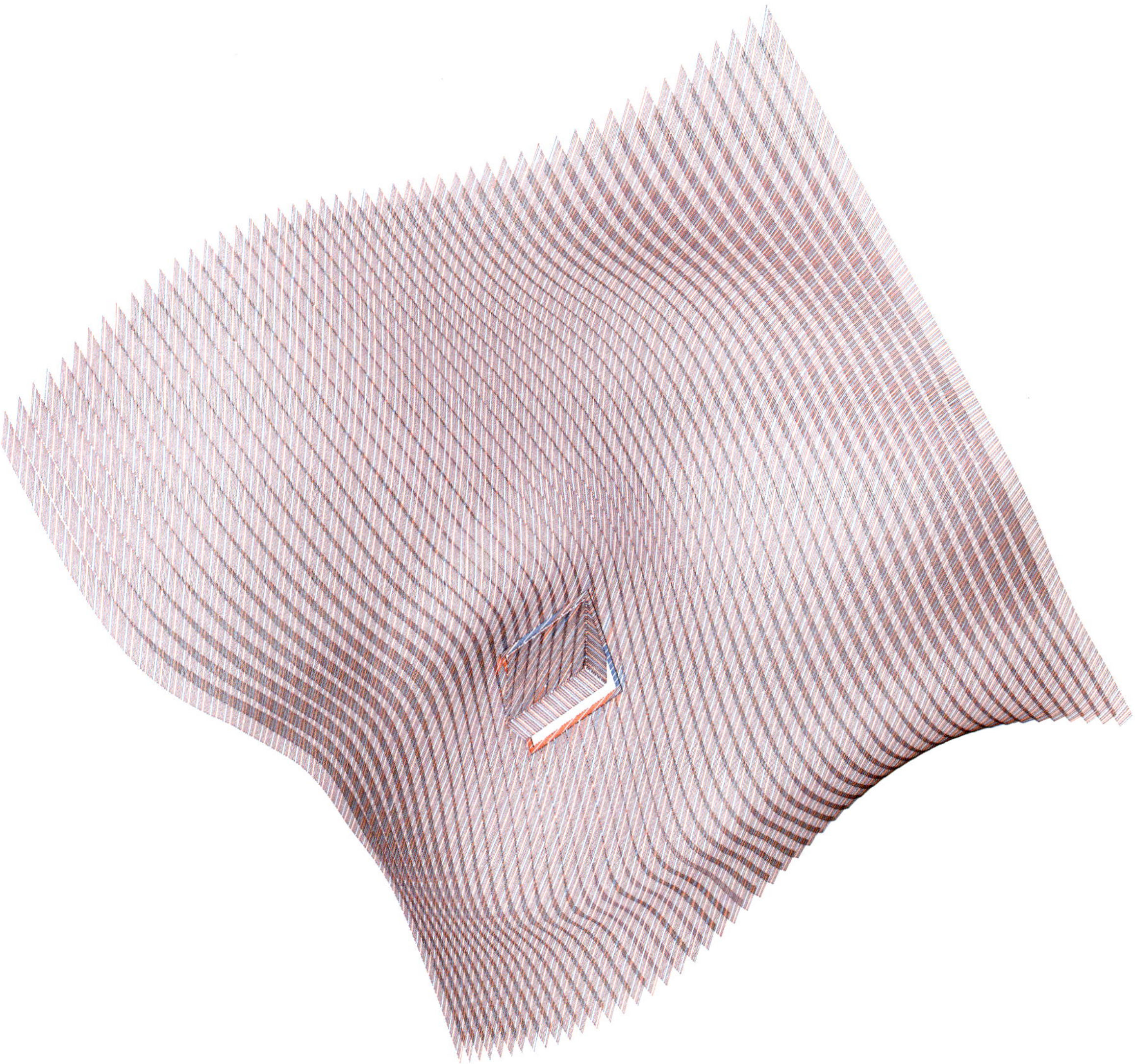

The hatched hatch
resides within a surface
and insists on a form
of continuity even
as it imposes itself
on the geometry.

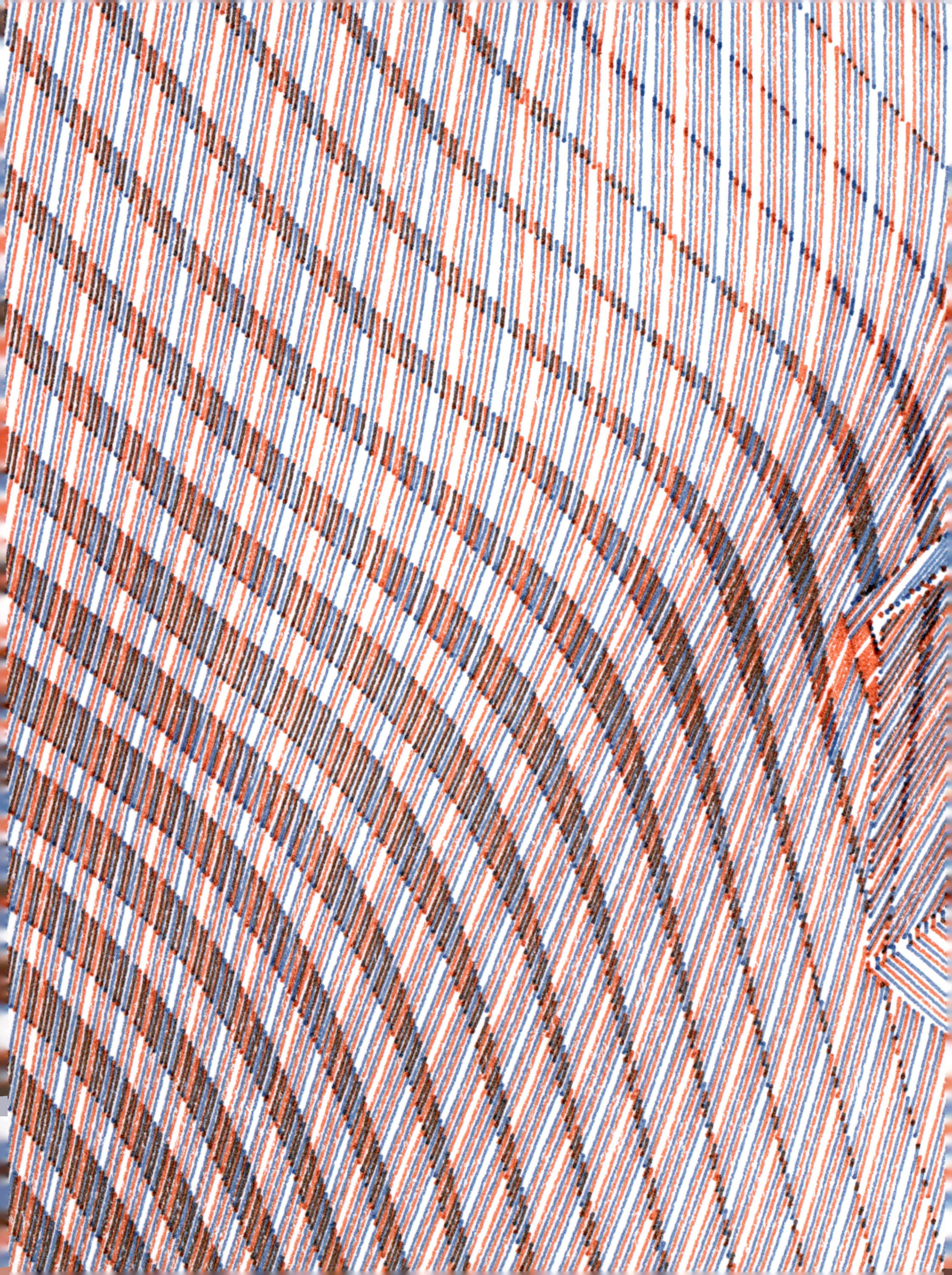

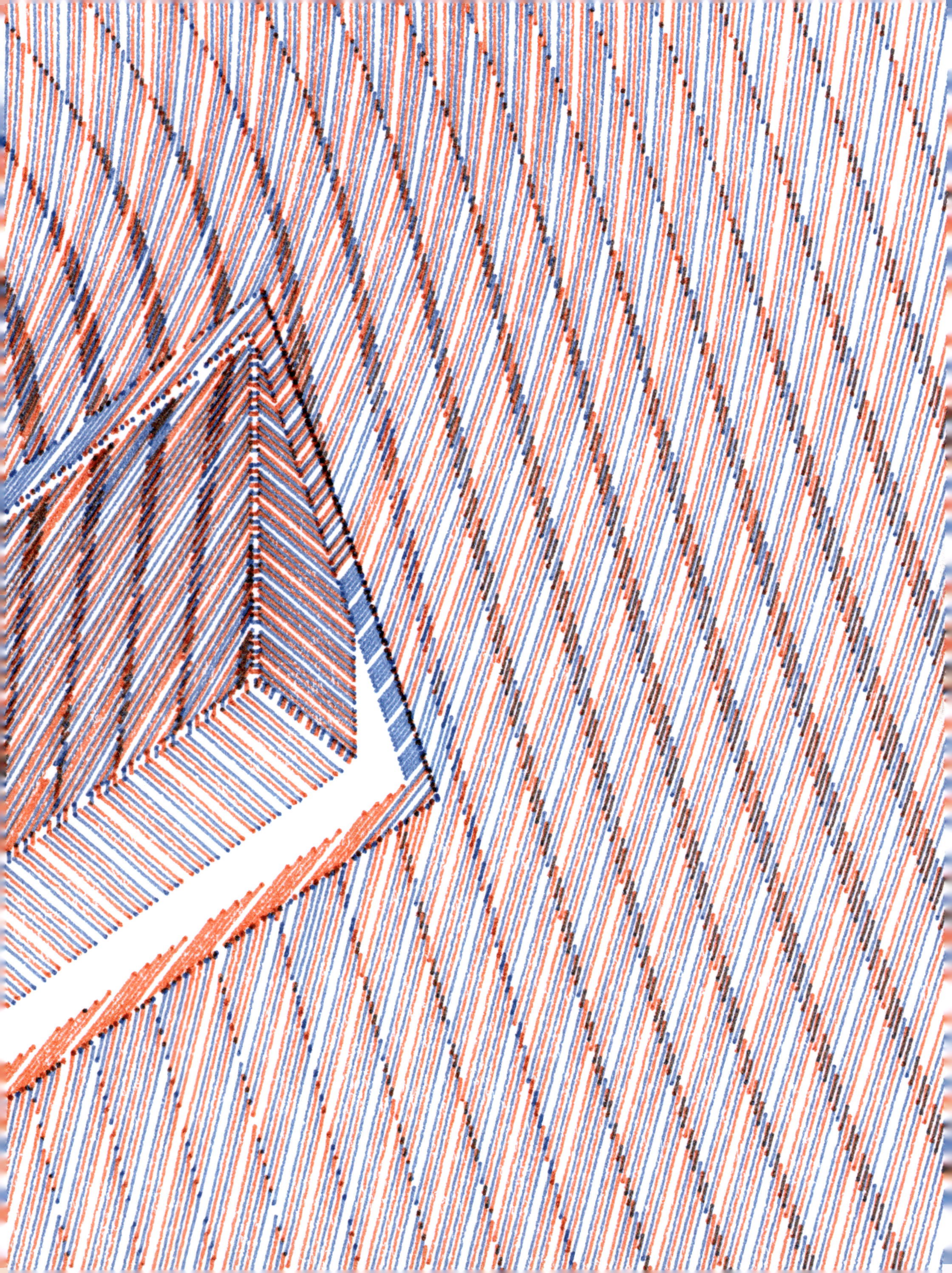

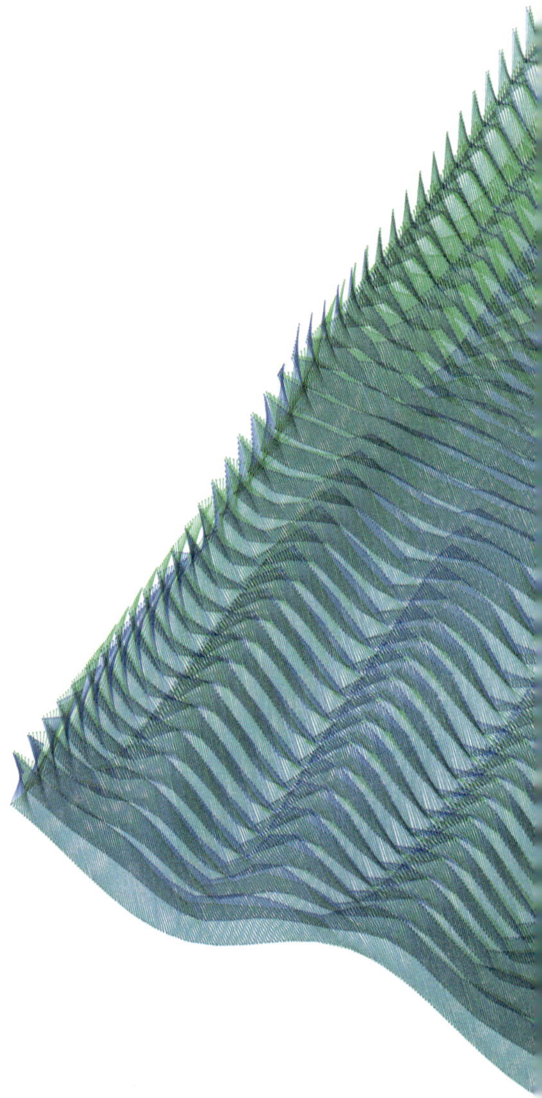

When multiple hatches are rendered with many hatches, the hatch takes on the role of medium and subject.

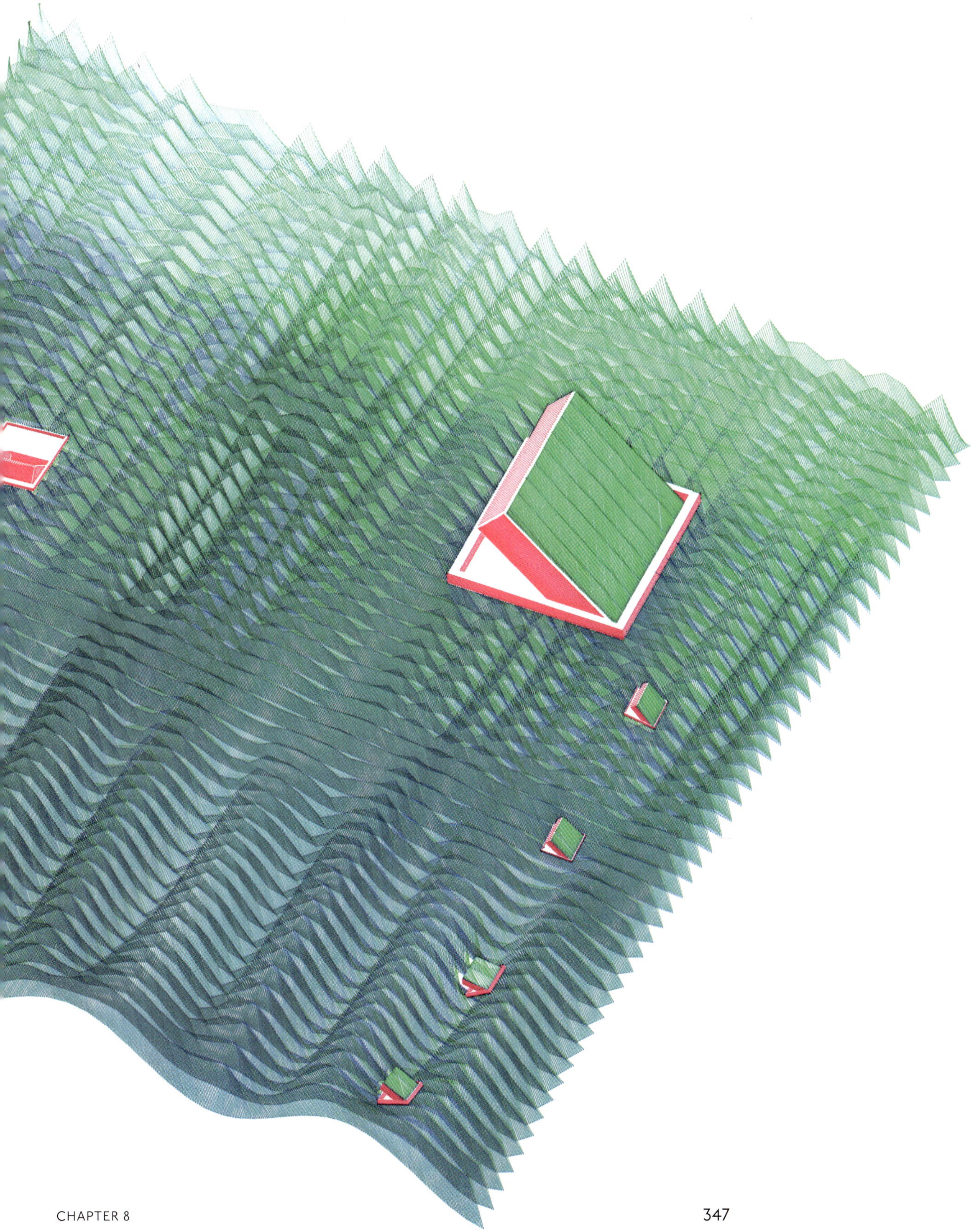

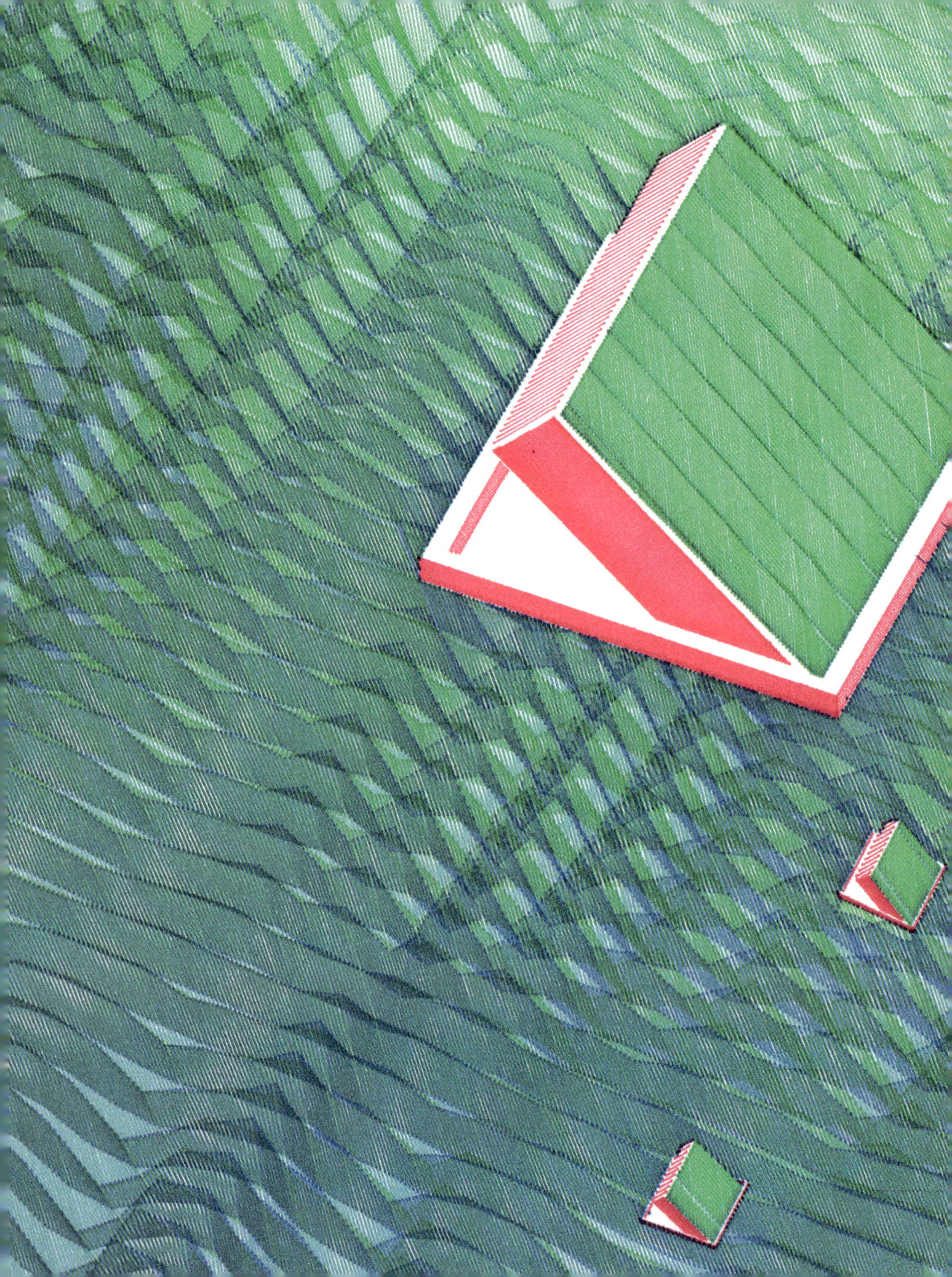

Words and Reality

The "hatched hatch" is pun in the same vein as the "curtain wall." These word plays are silly, yes, but their implications potentially are serious. Words participate in realism and the labeling of these elements furthers their transition from normal to uncanny on the way to impossible. William Empson, literary scholar and ambiguity savant, helpfully identifies most (but not all!) puns as the "third" out of his seven types of ambiguity: "An ambiguity of the third type...occurs when two ideas which are connected only by being both relevant in the context, can be given in one word simultaneously."[2] "Hatch," for example, has two meanings, both of which apply to the element. Arguably, the two meanings for "curtain wall," are also relevant in the broad disciplinary context of this work though only one definition, that the wall is flowing in the wind, is relevant in the context of the drawing. An important observation is possible at this juncture with respect to the curtain wall: the ambiguity is created only when the scope of the work expands to include both drawing and verbal description. Again, we see that which describes the element (where it was previously lines, now it is words) subsumed into the concept of element.

The line between Empson's third and fourth types is a bit labored. Within his lexicon, many literary examples can be debated as to their appropriate categorization—third verses fourth type. To clarify, in Empson's words, the fourth type involves "alternative meanings combine to make a complicated state of mind of the author."[3] This might at first seem to intersect significantly with the third type. The subtle difference, which is relevant to our discourse, lies in the relationship between the two meanings and the subject. Empson's attempt to clarify sheds light on our pursuits of reality. Third-type puns involve two meanings form "more than one universe of discourse."[4] We might say, more than one reality. If the reader's focus is invited to oscillate between those two distinct universes, we are dealing with the third type of ambiguity. If, however, those universes clearly converge in the mind of the author into one reality, we've ventured into Empson's fourth type. To conclude, we can note that our transitional elements are of multiple media: drawings, renderings, and words. The labels of the elements do not merely describe them but participate with the drawings in the oscillation between types. When these types converge into one element, a new reality forms.

Rather than confer superiority on either the third or fourth type, we can instead reflect on the direct relevance of literary ambiguity on the opportunities inherent to architectural representation. An autonomous image or drawing independent of a building is not a new concept in the discipline of architecture, but autonomous representation, which contends with internally constructed and coherent content is an important disciplinary shift. The existential contradictions of that approach require ambiguity.

The hatched hatch, which is planar in its nature, negotiates with and affects the curving geometry of the surface.

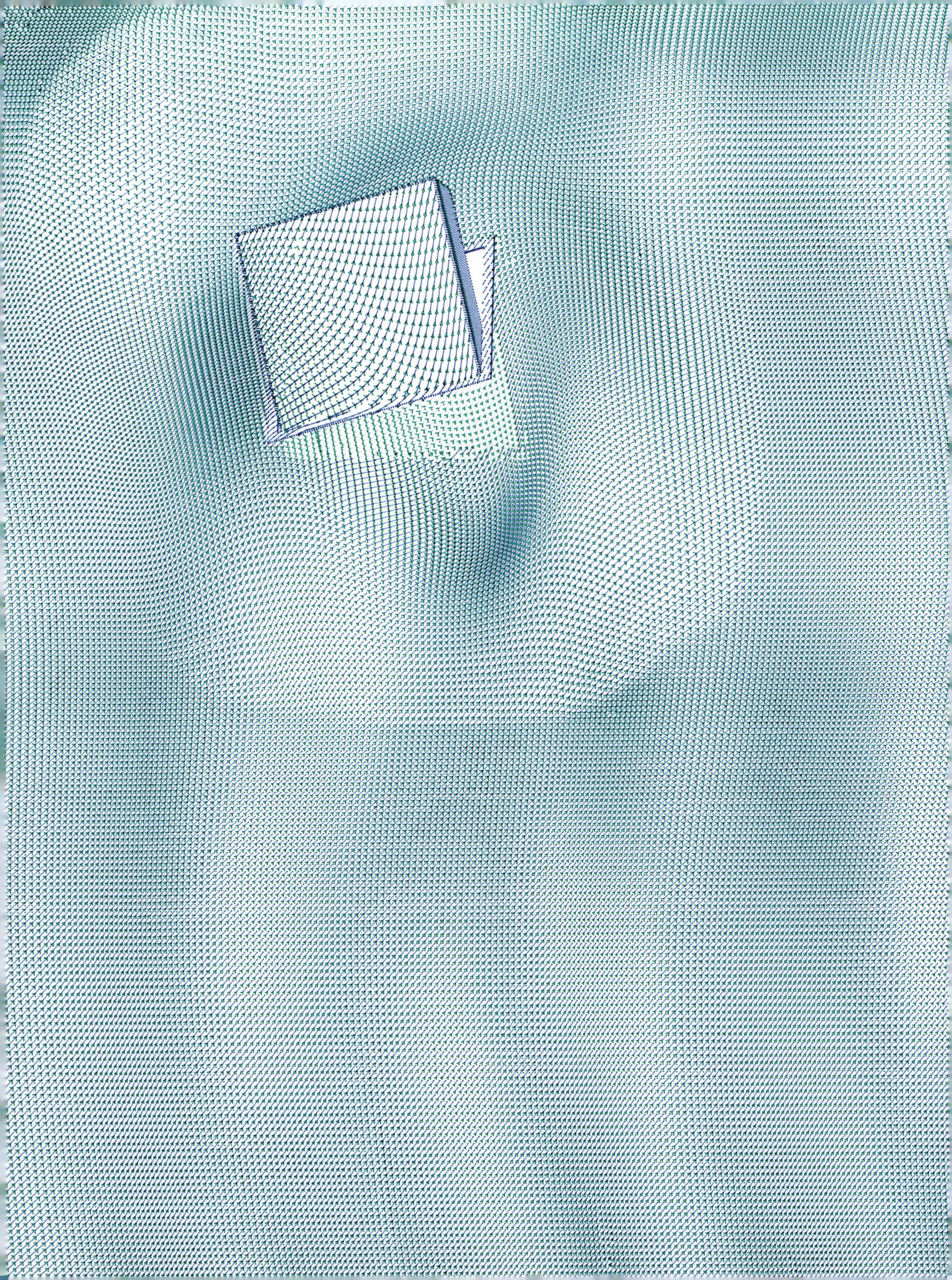

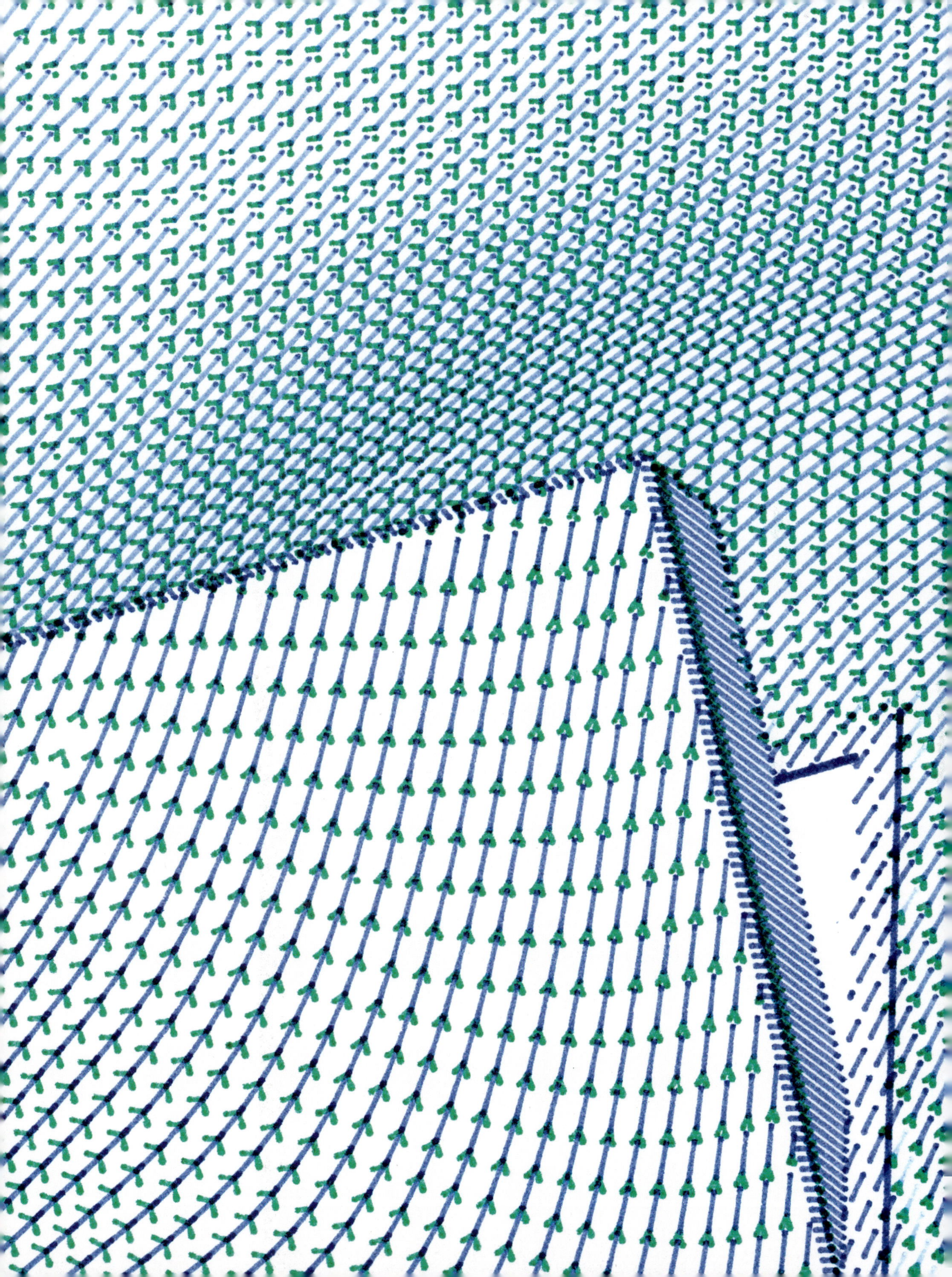

The Curtain Wall is ambivalent with respect to its inherent contradictions.

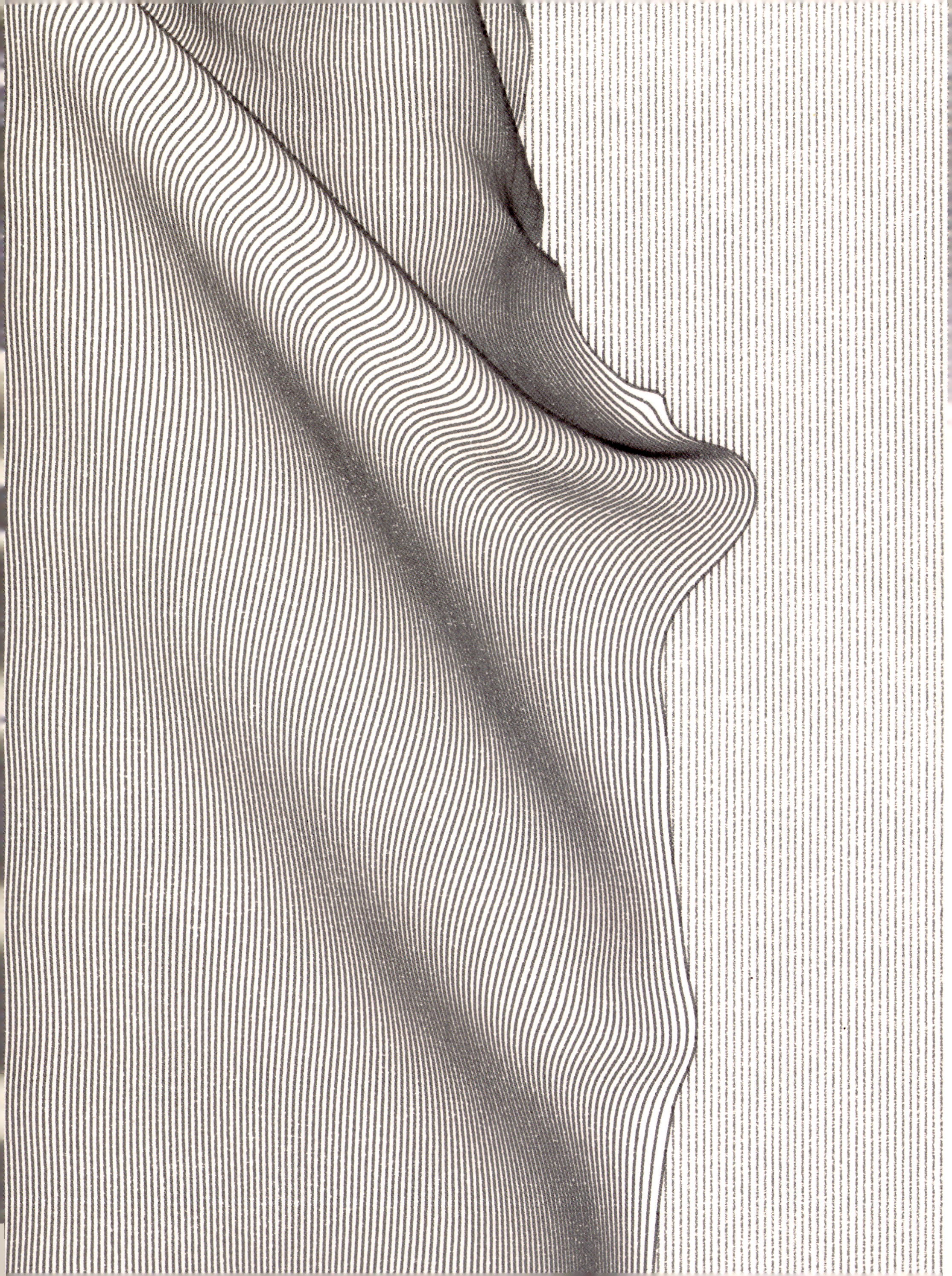

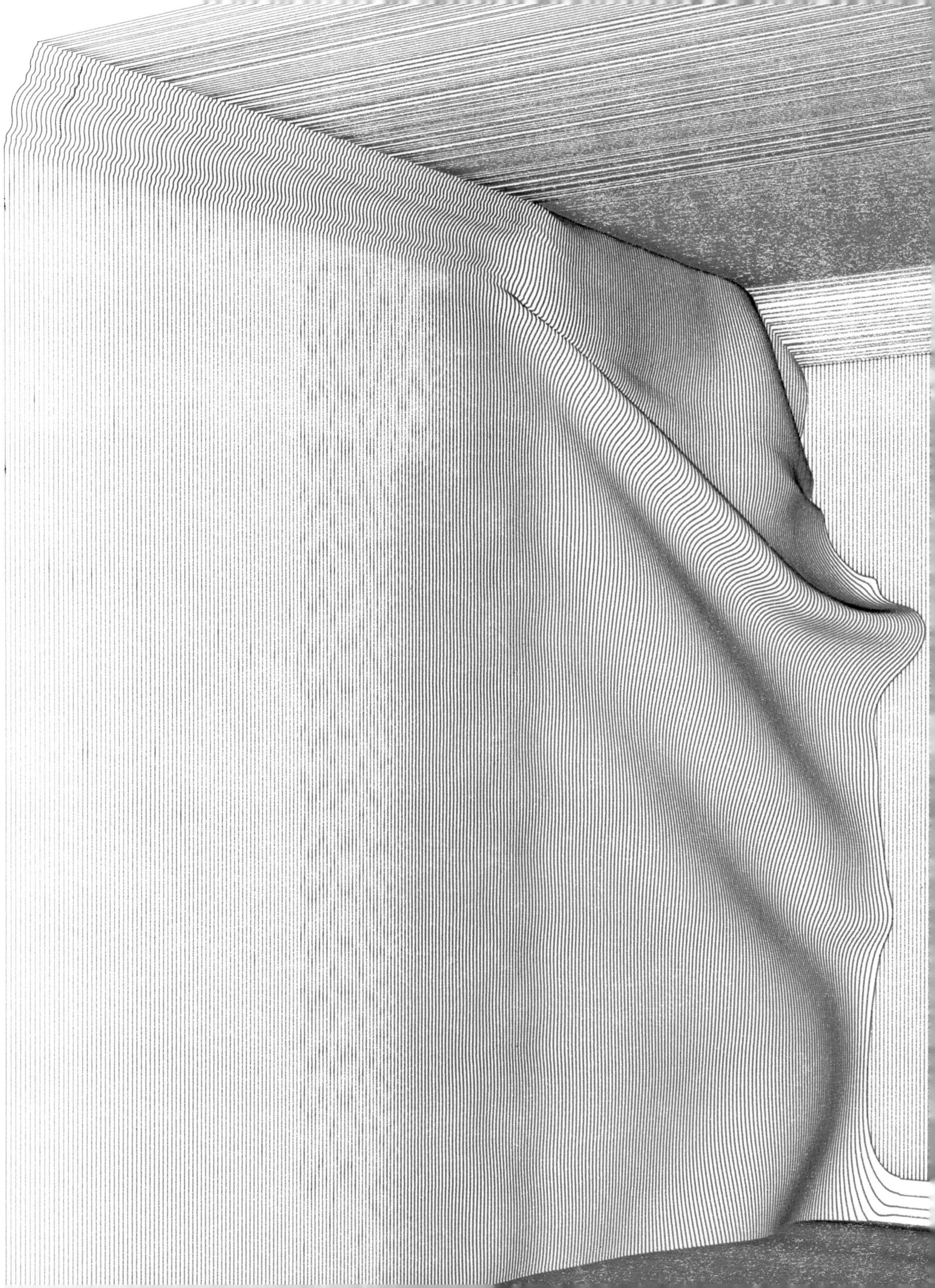

Optics of Material

In most digital rendering software, units and parameters are based on photographic optics. It's then easy, even automatic, to evaluate the output from that software in terms of photorealism. What about the drawing that functions as a rendering? How can optics manifest in a world of lines? More pointedly, we can ask: Without pixels, film, or even paint, how can refraction influence our hatches? As was the case with the hatched hatch, we can note that the qualities inherent to refraction can be rendered, but that does nothing to provoke a new reality, nor does it elevate the element to a position of rhetorical interest. But when the hatches themselves *become* the refracted content, material is inseparable from the methods of rendering. Material mediates between the grid behind the object and the grid drawn by the pen-plotter using material ink. The resulting drawing is far from photo-real but is nonetheless a precise simulation of refraction deployed as a means of rendering.

This suggests that a digital element can disrupt what is usually a clear distinction between digital form—surfaces and meshes—and digital material—texture maps and image outputs. It also suggests that architectural elements can participate in the transition from drawing logics to rendering logics if drawings are released from the expectation that their content resides in the realm of analytic immateriality. Still, we can expect that every drawing—even a drawing that can also be called a rendering—sustains lines that function and perform. In the drawing-as-rendering paradigm, lines relinquish their elemental status and cease to confidently trace the projected outline of modeled form, but they register as more than ink on paper. The line, for example, does its part to place ink where it needs to be on paper, while also responding to the algorithmic representation of refractive material, perspective, and focal blur.

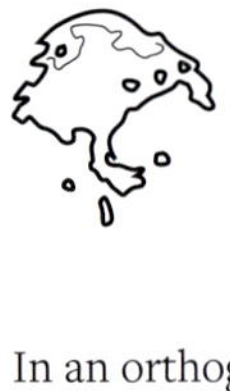

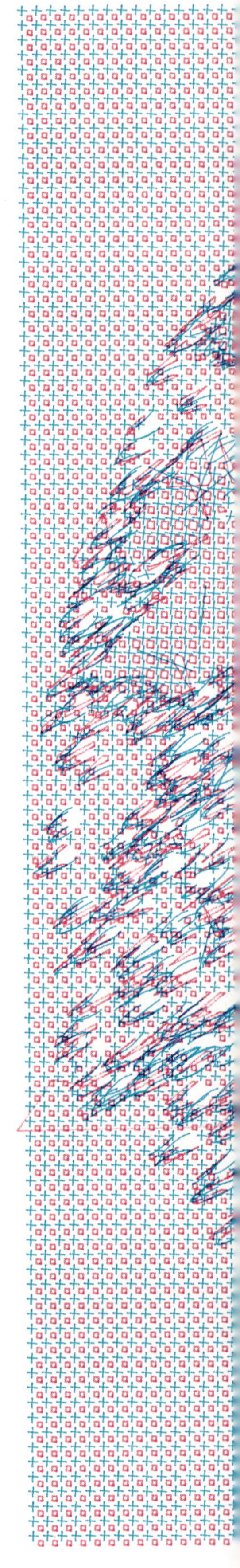

In an orthographic projection of refractivity, the line is a function of light and material rather than aligned to a single form.

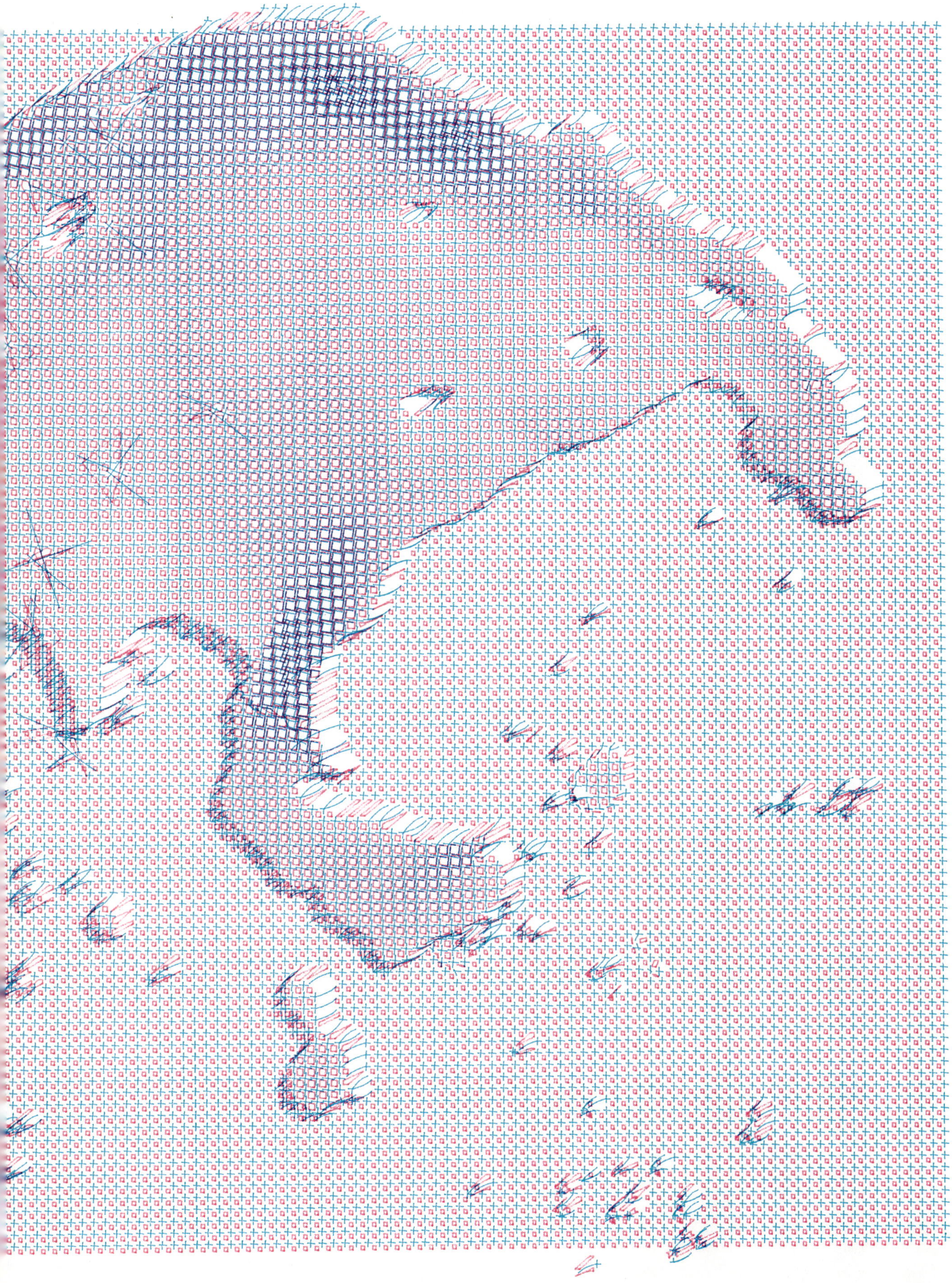

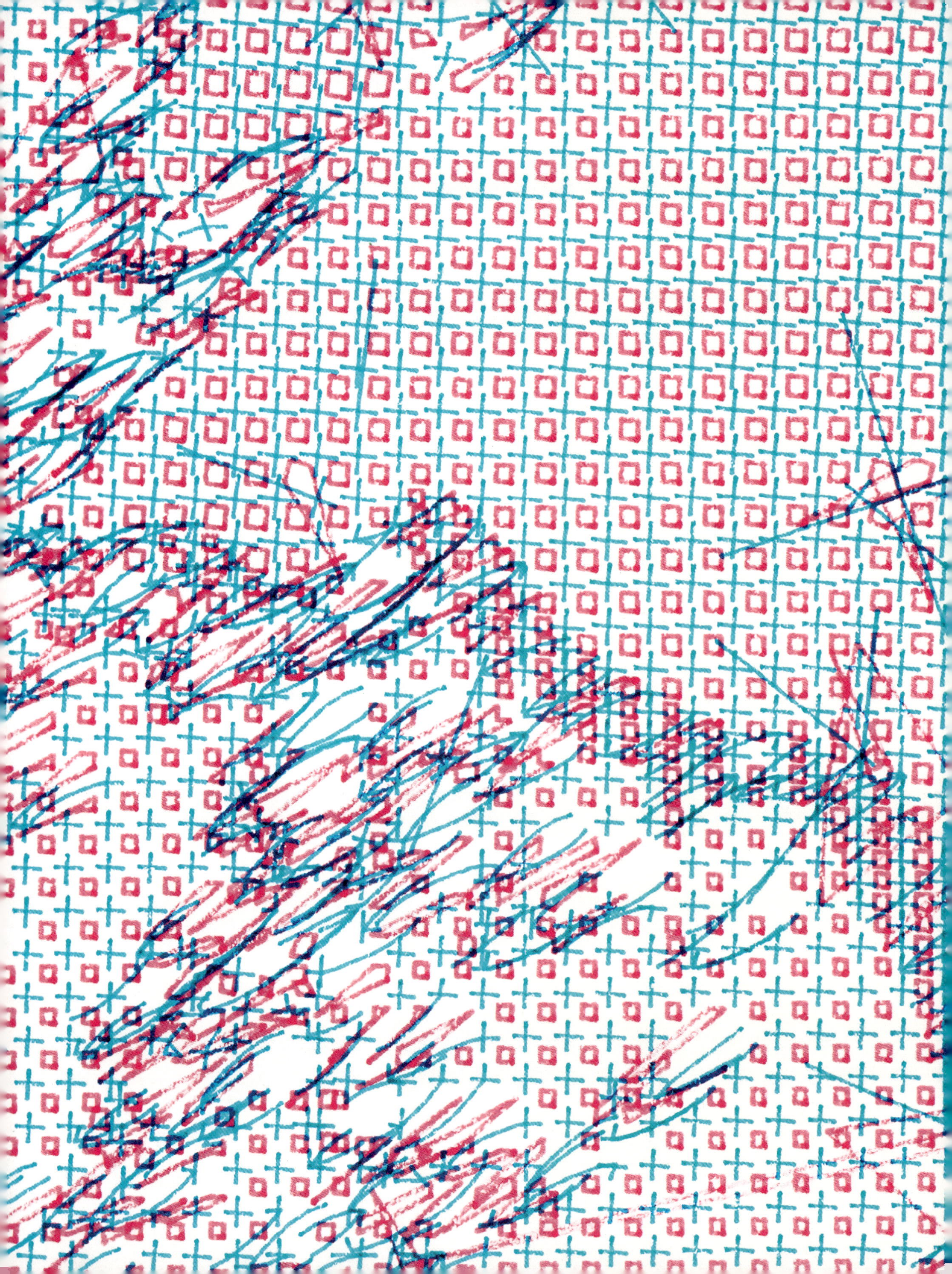

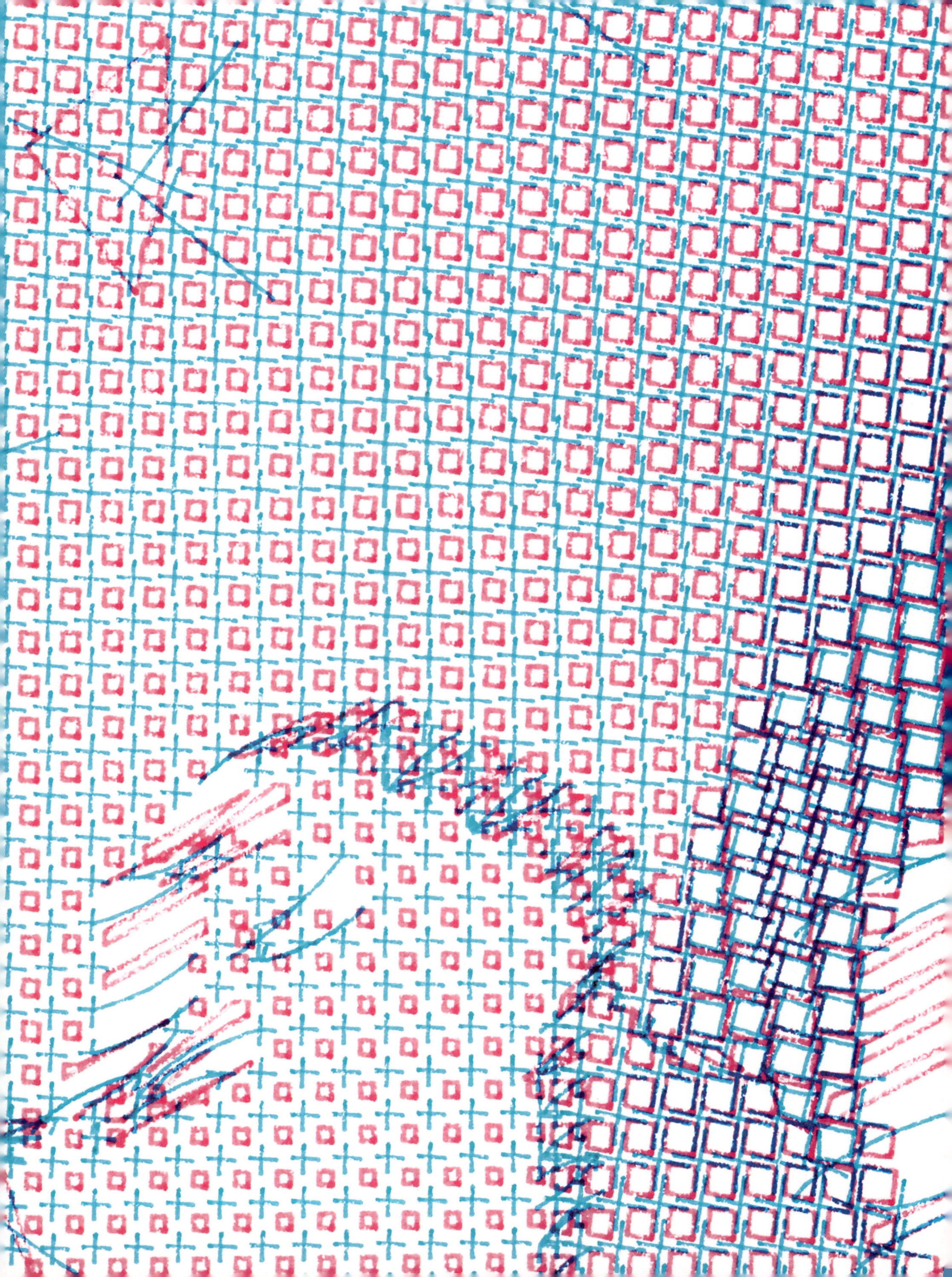

Within this element, the line performs many functions. Its position is related to the optics of focal blur, its color related to geometry, and its shape related to material.

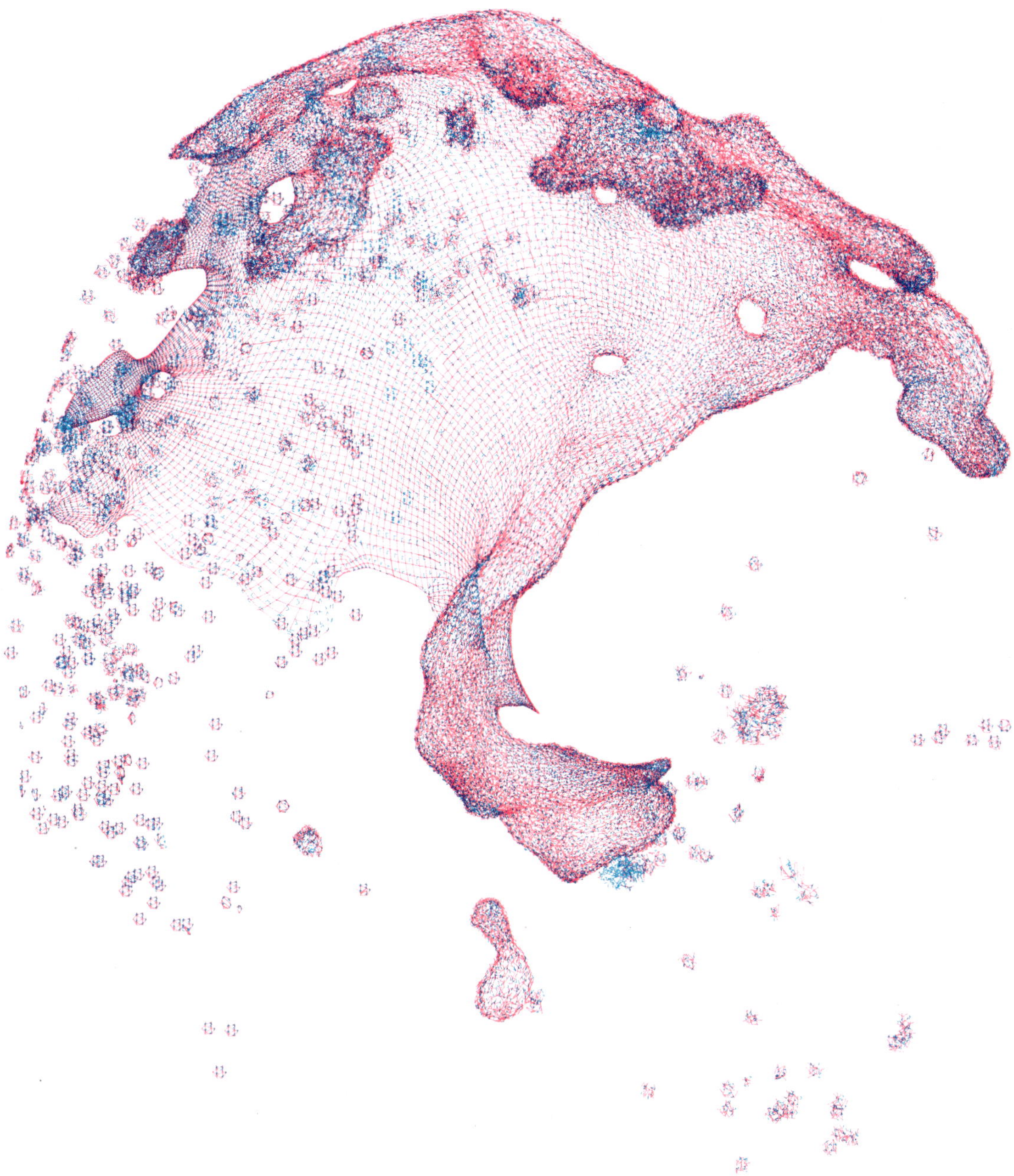

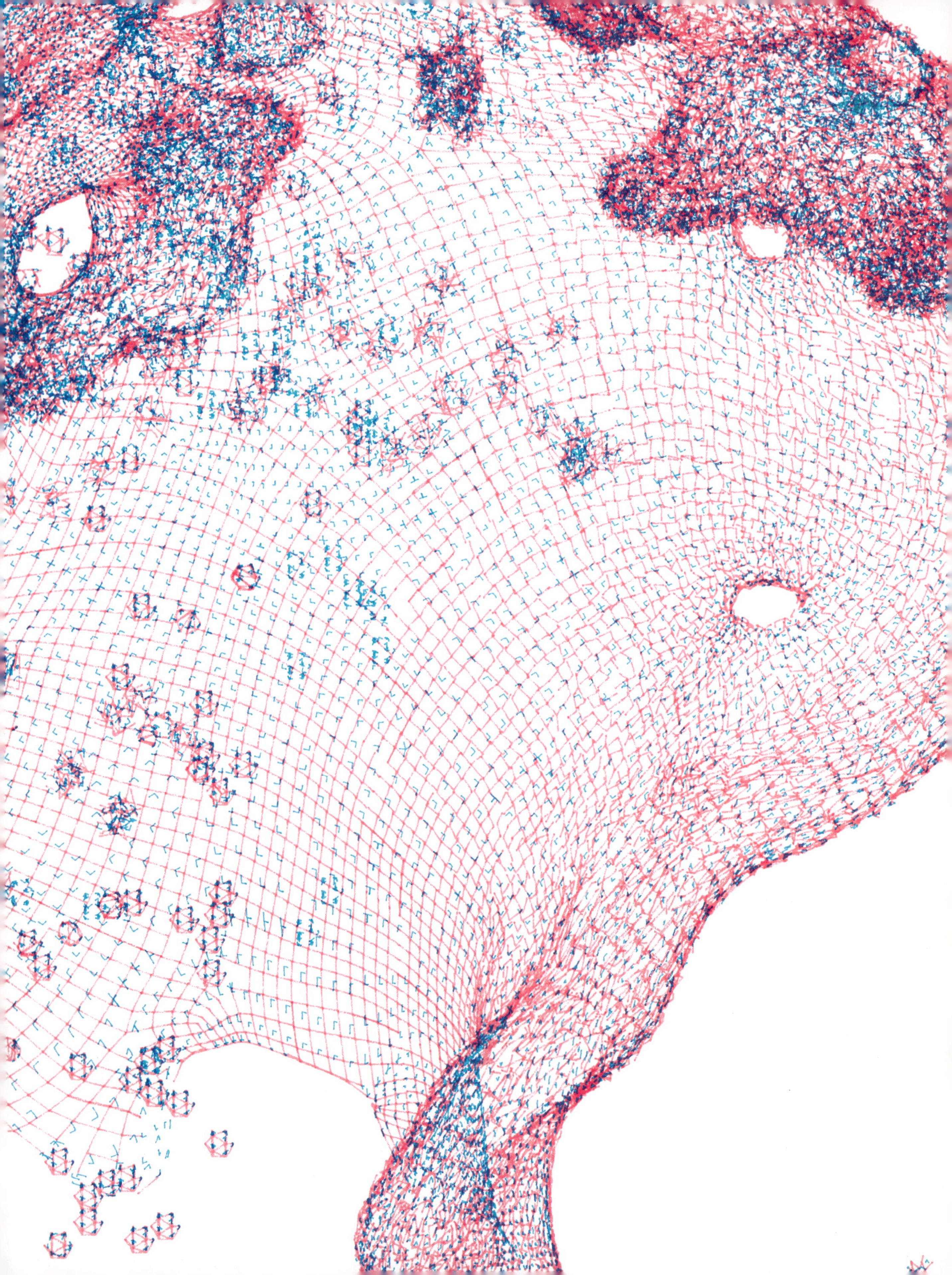

Representation as an Open Loop

The elements in this book exemplify what has been a reoccurring condition: the methods of representation feedback onto—and sometimes become intertwined with—that which is being represented. Rendering, without designed intervention, tends to look like a linear process rather than a loop. The transition elements presented in this final chapter exemplify some ways of deploying the computational line as a rendering, but also within a repeatable loop. These methodologically looping lines bring conventions of drawing and hatching into the act of rendering and modeling. Drawing affects that which is being drawn. However, it's not enough just to loop; loops can be closed systems, constantly growing and evolving, but with respect to themselves and themselves alone. It's easy to fall into this trap when designing elements. They become interesting and provocative on their own to the extent that other elements and contexts seem extraneous. However, an element stuck on a closed loop is irrelevant. Elements must be positioned, tested, linked, or manipulated by forces, information, and form outside themselves. Their autonomy need not be confused for their isolation. The digital bonsai tree, for example, is open to the user's whims and then contends with the diorama as it interfaces with it.[5] Another way to open the representational loop is to invite external content in, as is the case with the refractive hatch. The grid hatches are the element, but the form that could be said to mediate those hatches (and, importantly, is represented by those hatches) is imported from another element, in this case the form resulting from fluid encountering the invisible object inside the diorama.[6]

Rather than asking what an element—especially one that is intertwined with representation such that it distorts reality—wants to be, it's much more productive to ask, "what is it least comfortable encountering?" and then, to construct that encounter.

Our pursuit of the open loop leaves us with one final possible conclusion, which is probably now obvious to the reader: these impossible and hyper-real elements of architecture are nowhere near a complete set. They don't constitute a kit of parts, and they aren't even easy cataloged with shared terminology. Likewise, we offer no polemical argument about what constitutes a good architectural element. Instead, if there is one over-arching contribution this book seeks to make, it is that rendering can be released from prison of the commercialized, commodified image. Architectural representation beyond the digital turn is still rich with possibility and ever-increasing impossibility.

EXERCISE

Represent, Disassociate, Operate, Re-associate with Something Else

Identify something real. Represent it in any medium. When the representation is complete, identify the parts, qualities, and factures of that representation to disassociate them from that which is being represented. Operate on those parts as though the work is the only possible reality and nothing is represented. Exhaustively transform the work while solidifying your understanding of its internal structure. Continue to set aside any concept of representation. Finally, make a new version of the work using the transformed medium that seeks to represent something else entirely. How are these three works, the original representation of the real, the self-referential disassociated real, and the conflicted real, in dialogue with each other? Do the three realities relate?

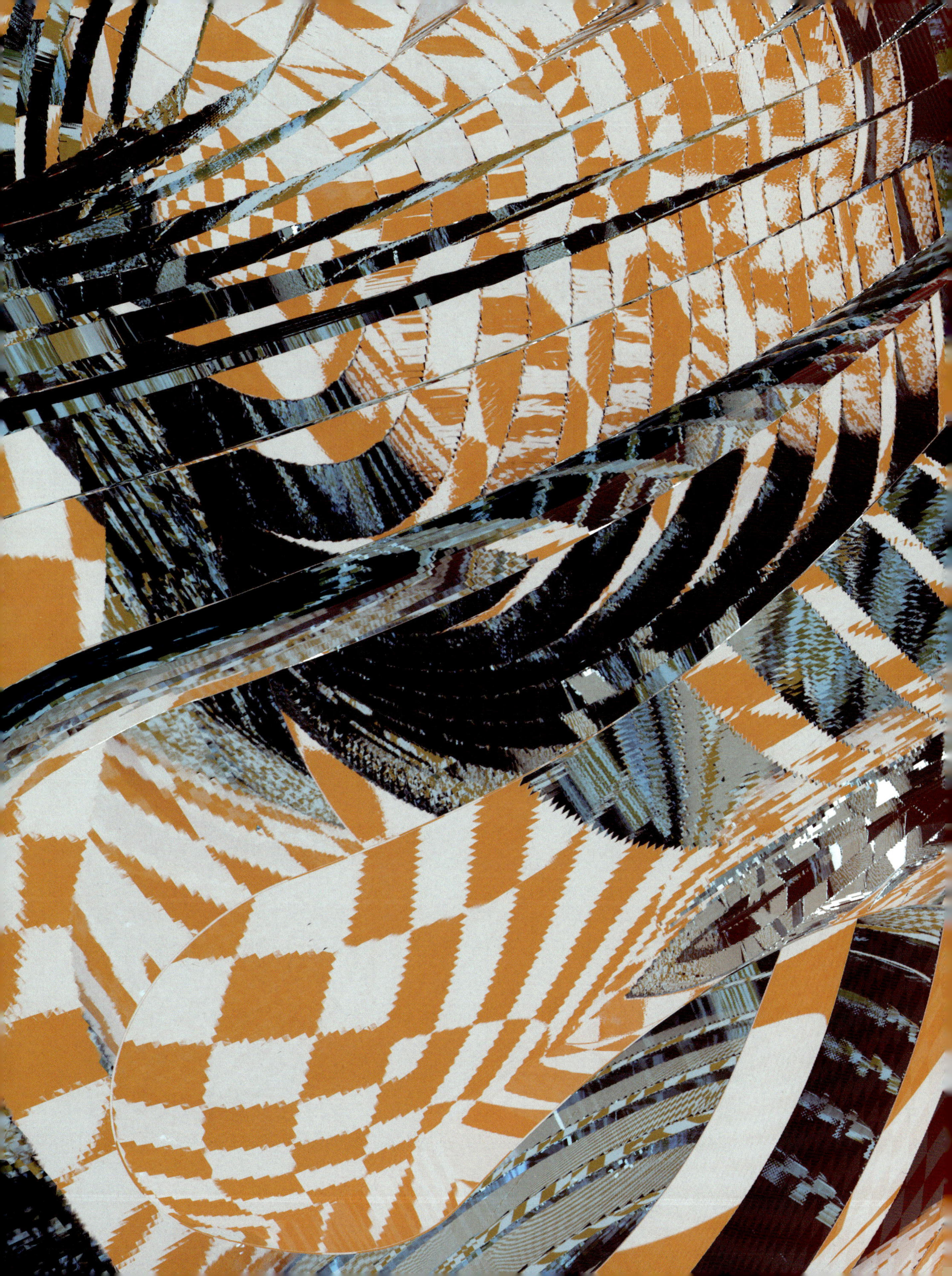

Notes

1. James F Blinn, "A Generalization of Algebraic Surface Drawing," *ACM Transactions on Graphics* 1, no. 3 (July 1982).
2. William Empson, *Seven Types of Ambiguity* (New Directions Books, 1966), 102.
3. Empson, *Seven Types of Ambiguity,* v. The table of contents is especially valuable in Empson's manual given that the line types only become increasingly (and not ironically) ambiguous as the book unfolds.
4. Empson, v.
5. Chapter 3, "Using a Tree to Represent a Tree."
6. Chapter 5, "Rendering the Almost Invisible."

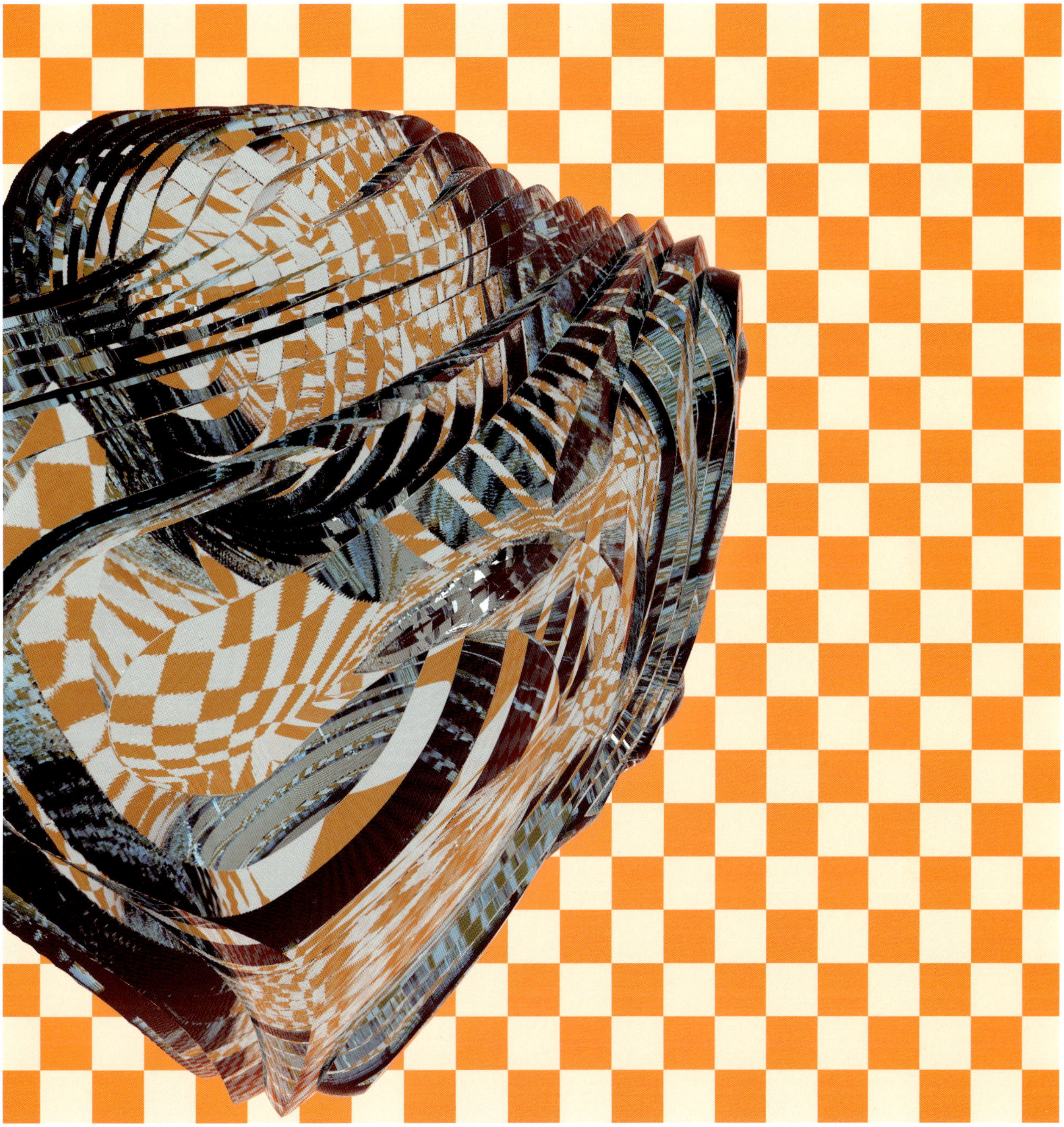

EXERCISE

Structure Discourse around Exercises

Rather than end with a conclusion, this book ends with an exercise, the final and fifteenth of a sequence designed, in part, to give readers open-ended direction in the application of this experimental approach to architectural representation. These exercises assume that you're reading this book because you want to be provoked, informed, and inspired to make new things. These exercises are also meant to be theoretical and meaningful as micro essays, even if your own process is only indirectly influenced by this book. In the full support of the tendency for all representation discourse to drift toward meta-inquiry, this exercise is a prompt for you to prompt yourself. As with almost any ambitious creative project, the pursuit of hyper-realities constructed with representational elements requires the design of prompt. A good exercise prompt is modest. The nature of the outcome should be generally predictable with room for the specific outcome to be unforeseen. The prompt should also be written, for the benefit of you and others.

Image Animation Index

http://impossible-real.how/animations

Chapter 1

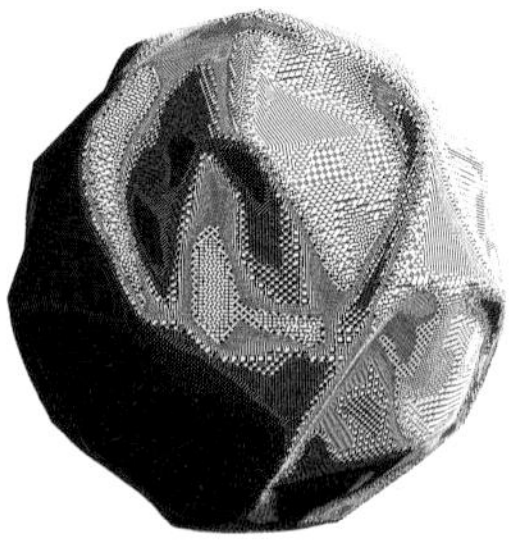

Bitmap Icosphere

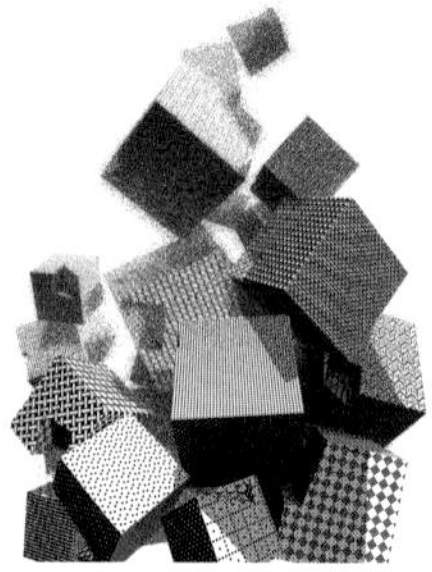

Bitmap Semi-Cubes

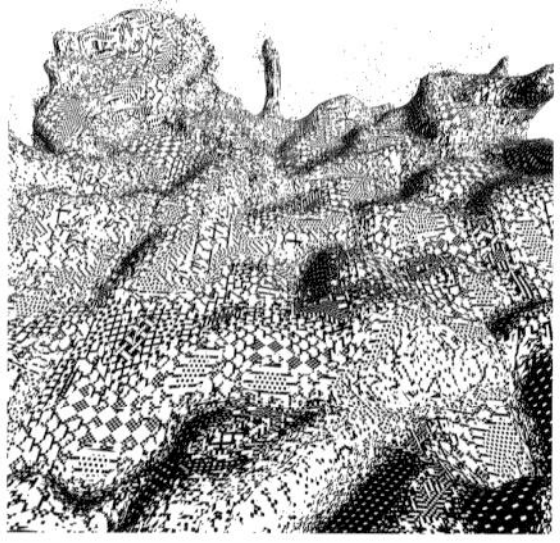

Bitmap Fluid

Chapter 2

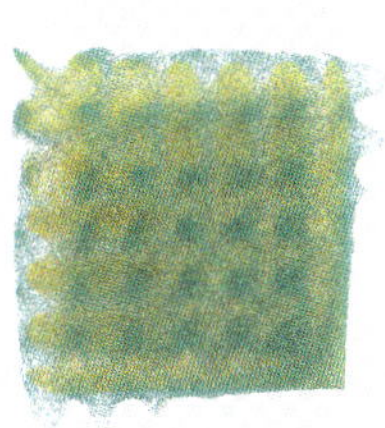

Sandbox

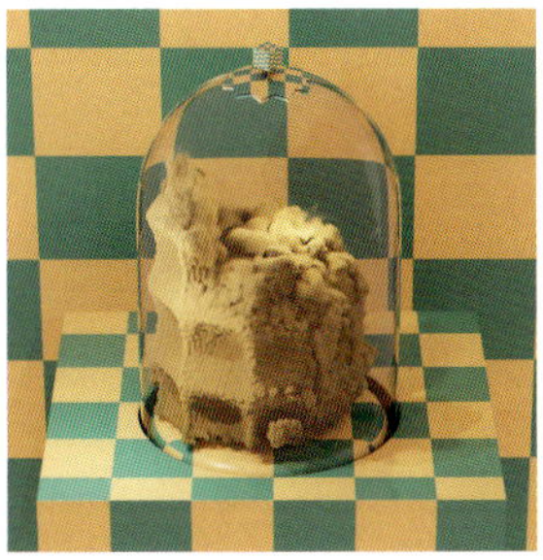

Post-Gridded Smoke

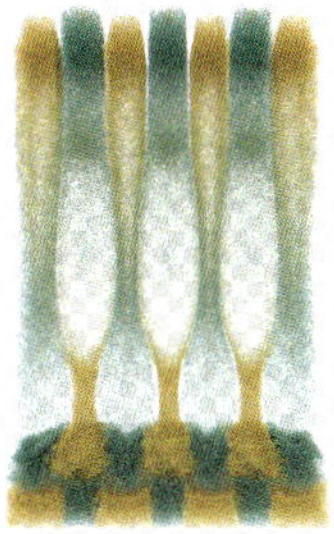

Grid Plop

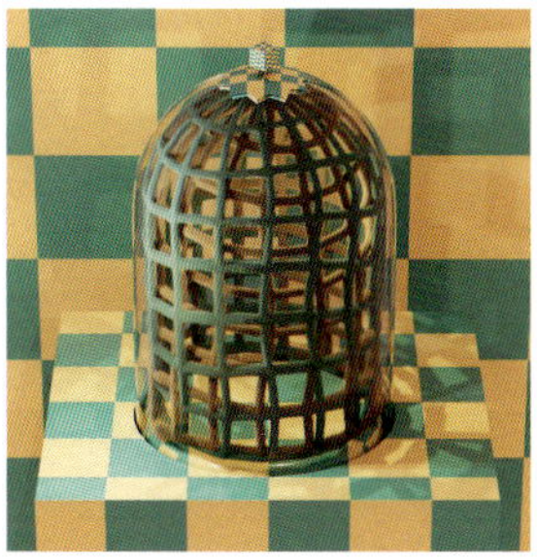

Pre-Gridded Smoke

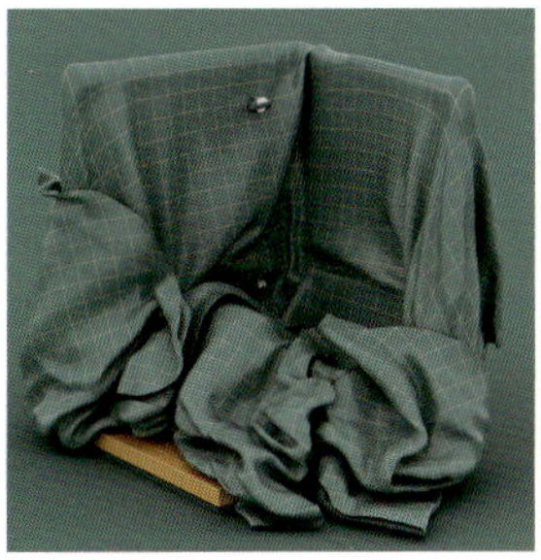

Bathtub Clothed

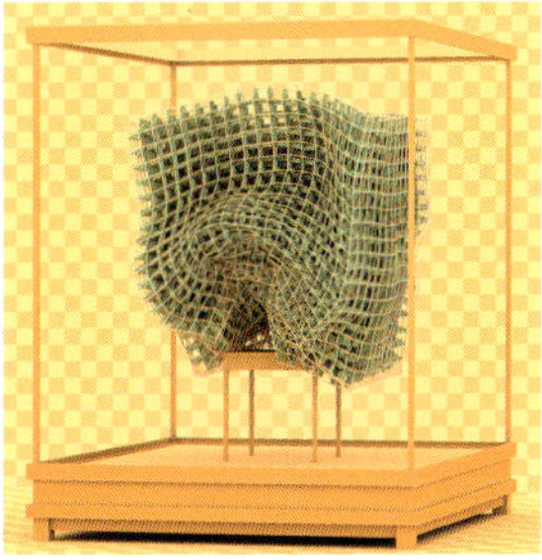

Extra-Dense Scaffold

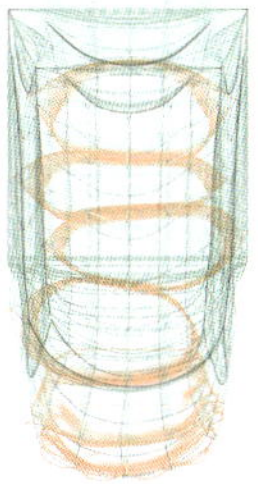

Ambient Lattice

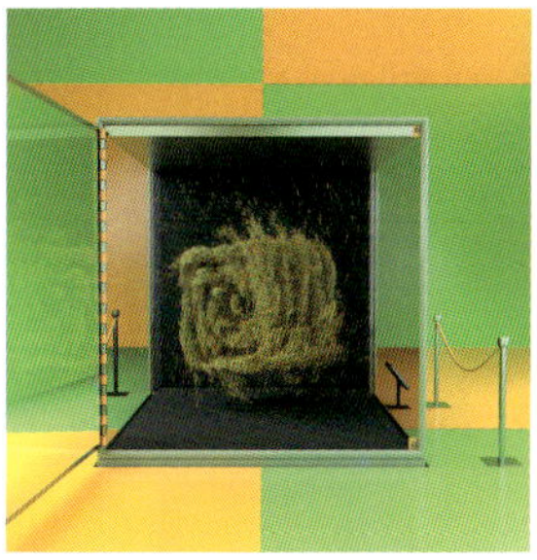

_Symbiotic Scaffold

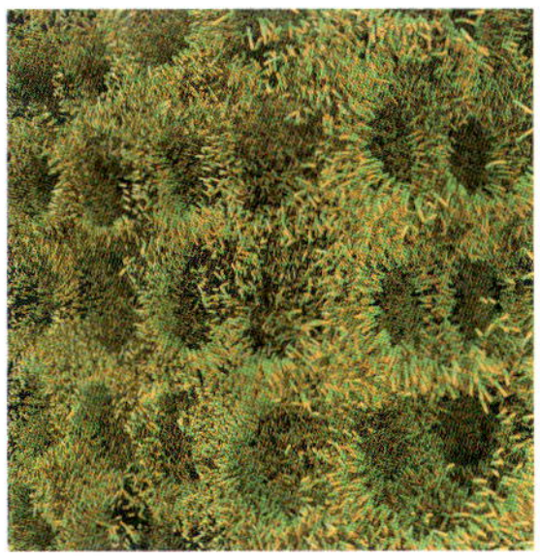

Symbiotic Scaffold

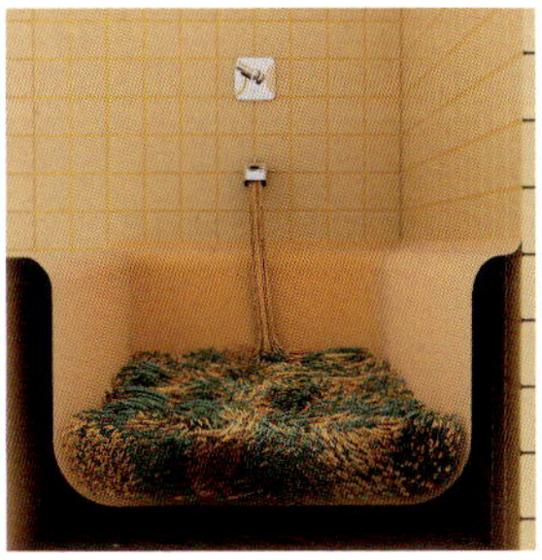

Tiled Bathtub (side)

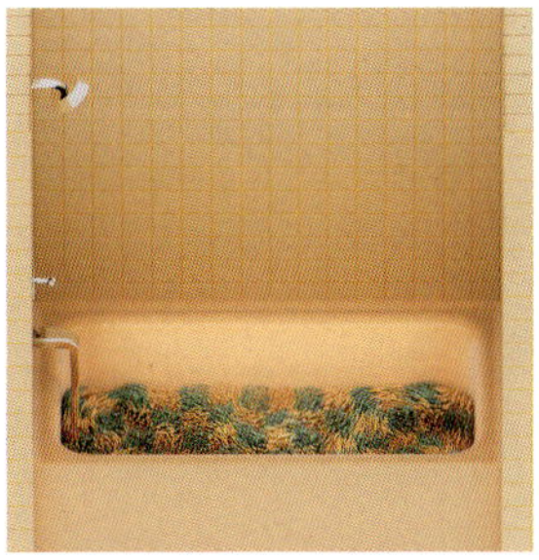

Tiled Bathtub (front)

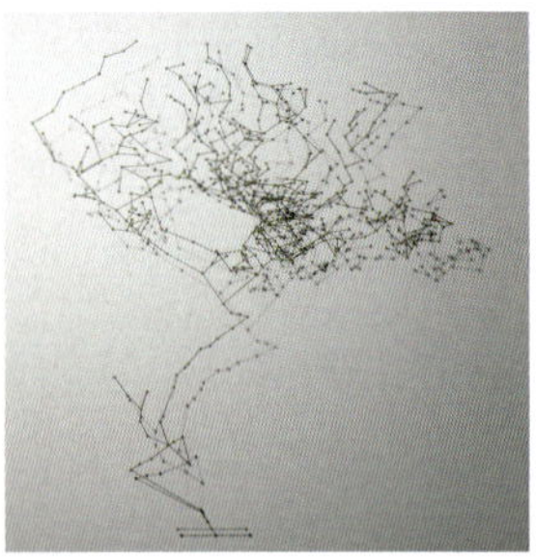
Tree-1 Outline

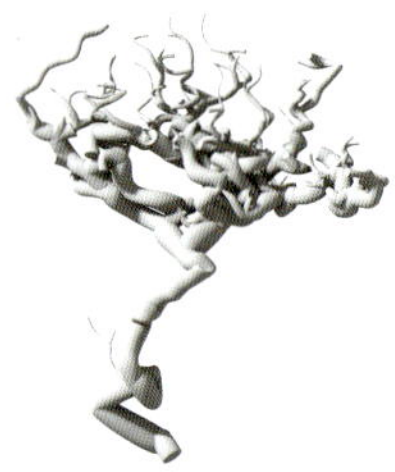
Tree-1 Render

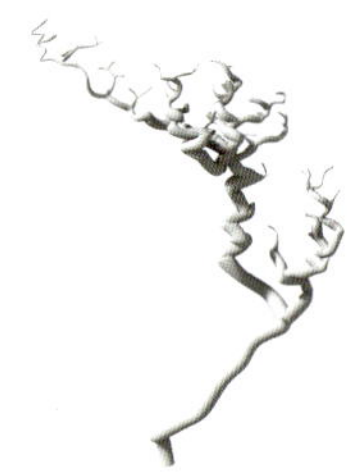
Tree-2 Render

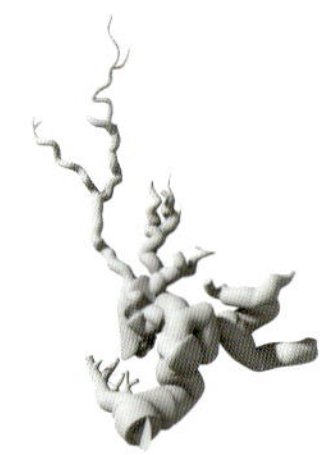
Tree-3 Render

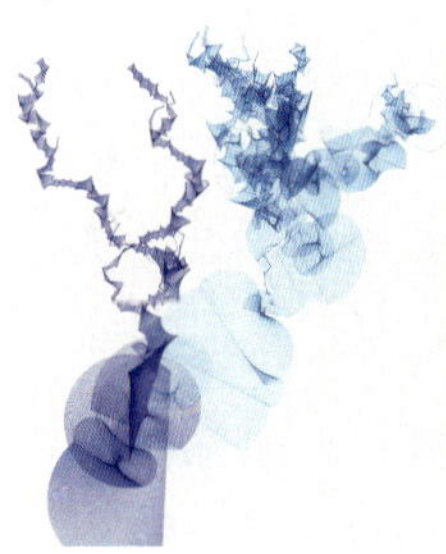
Tree-4 Rendered Differently

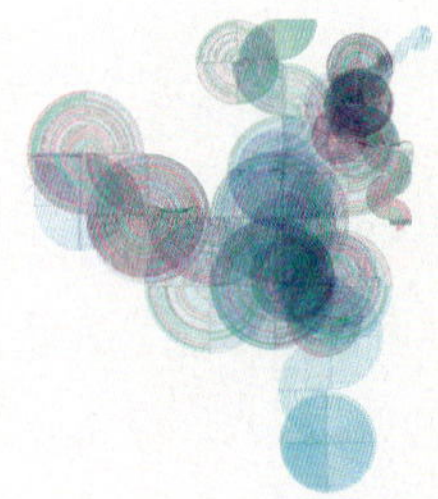
Tree-4 Rendered as Non-Tree

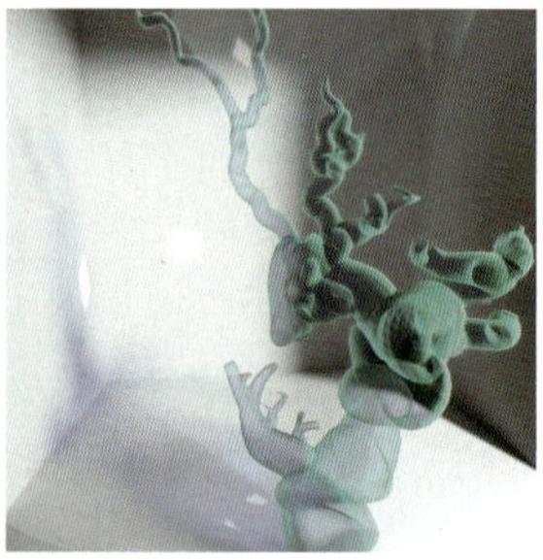
Tree-3 in Diorama

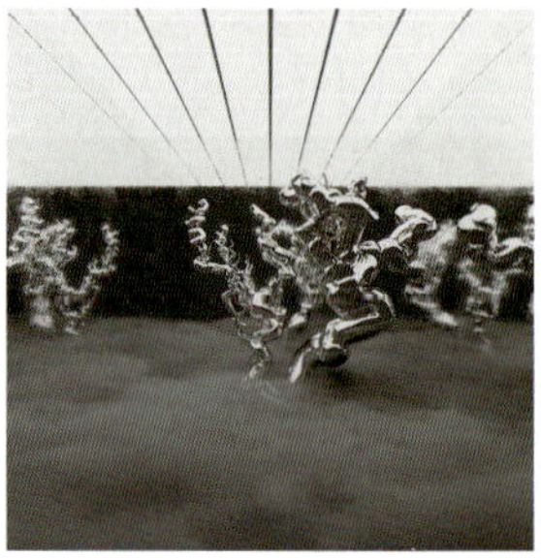
Tree-4 in Diorama

Chapter 4

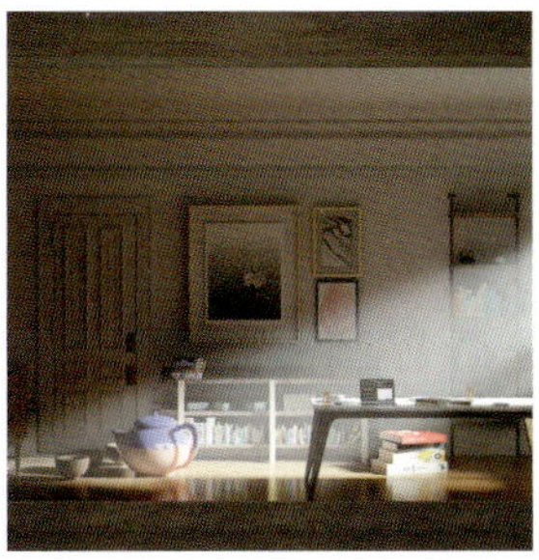

Room Out of Scale

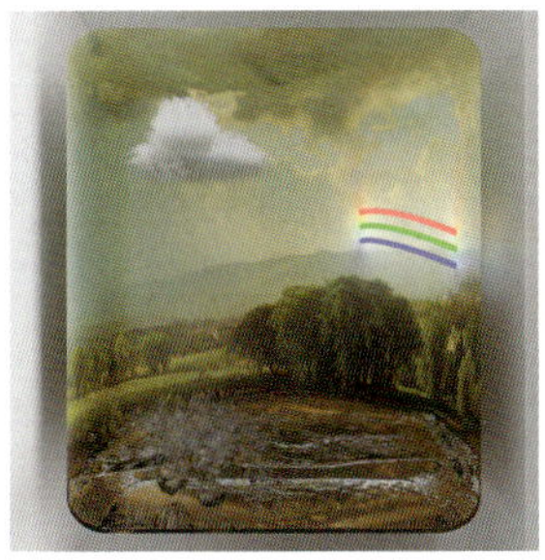

Delaware Valley Diorama

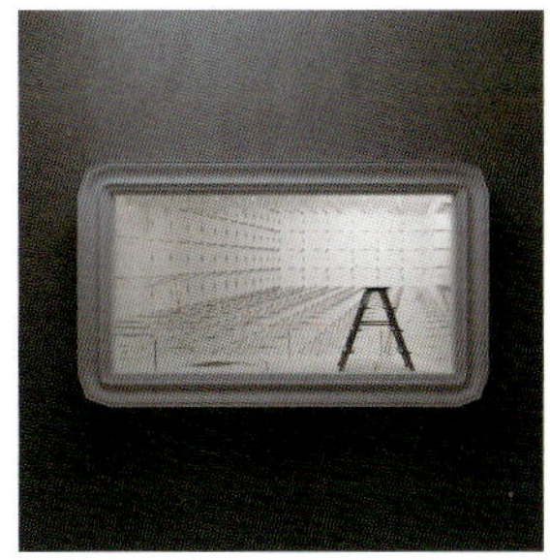

Calibration Diorama Under Construction

Chapter 5

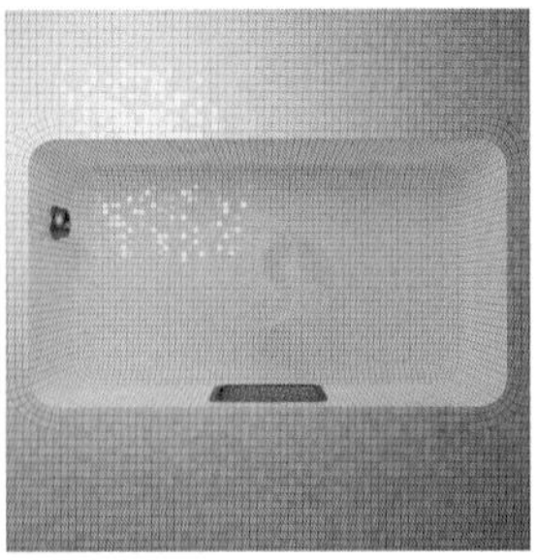

Contingent Material

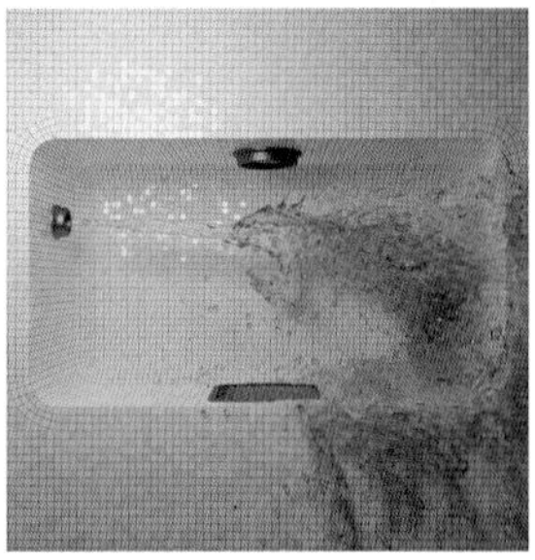

Fluid Spray-over

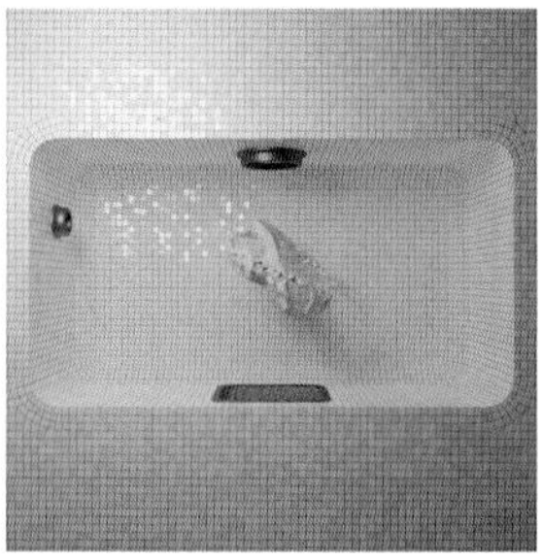

Fluid at Solid

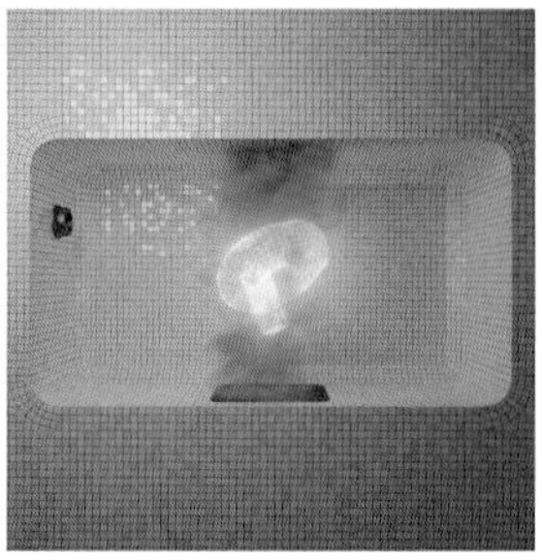

Light-emitting Wireframe within Smoke

Chapter 6

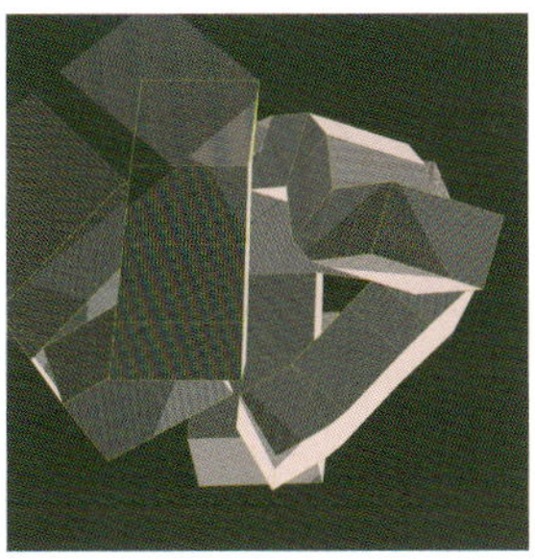

House 2 Framework

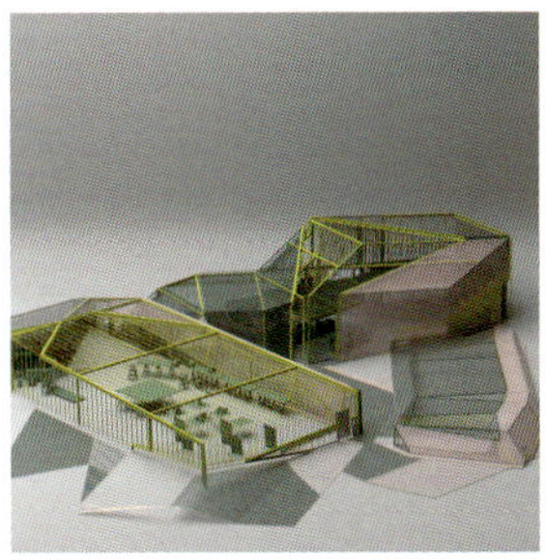

House 2

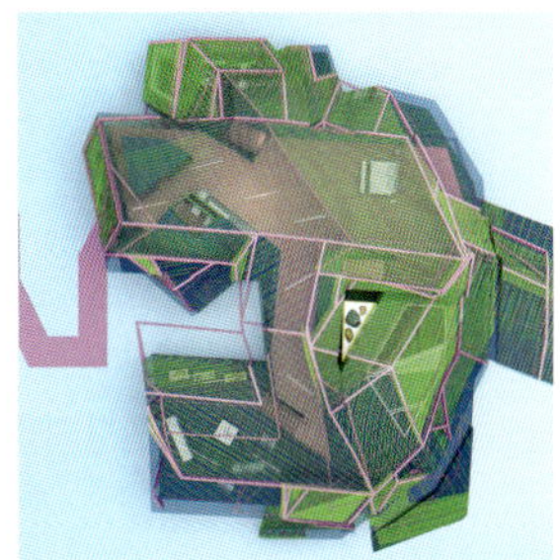

House 3 Top

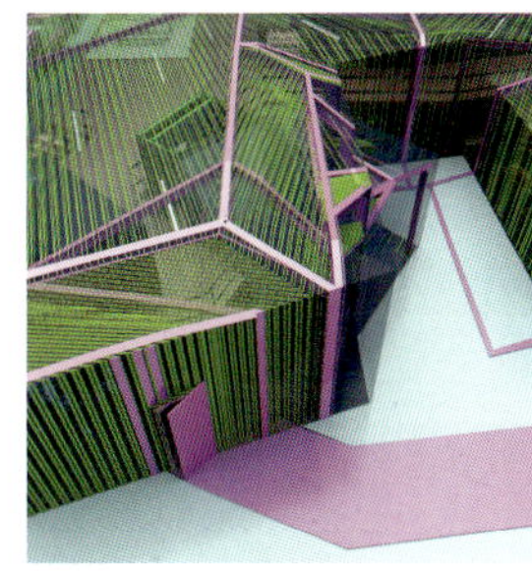

House 3 Perspective

Chapter 7

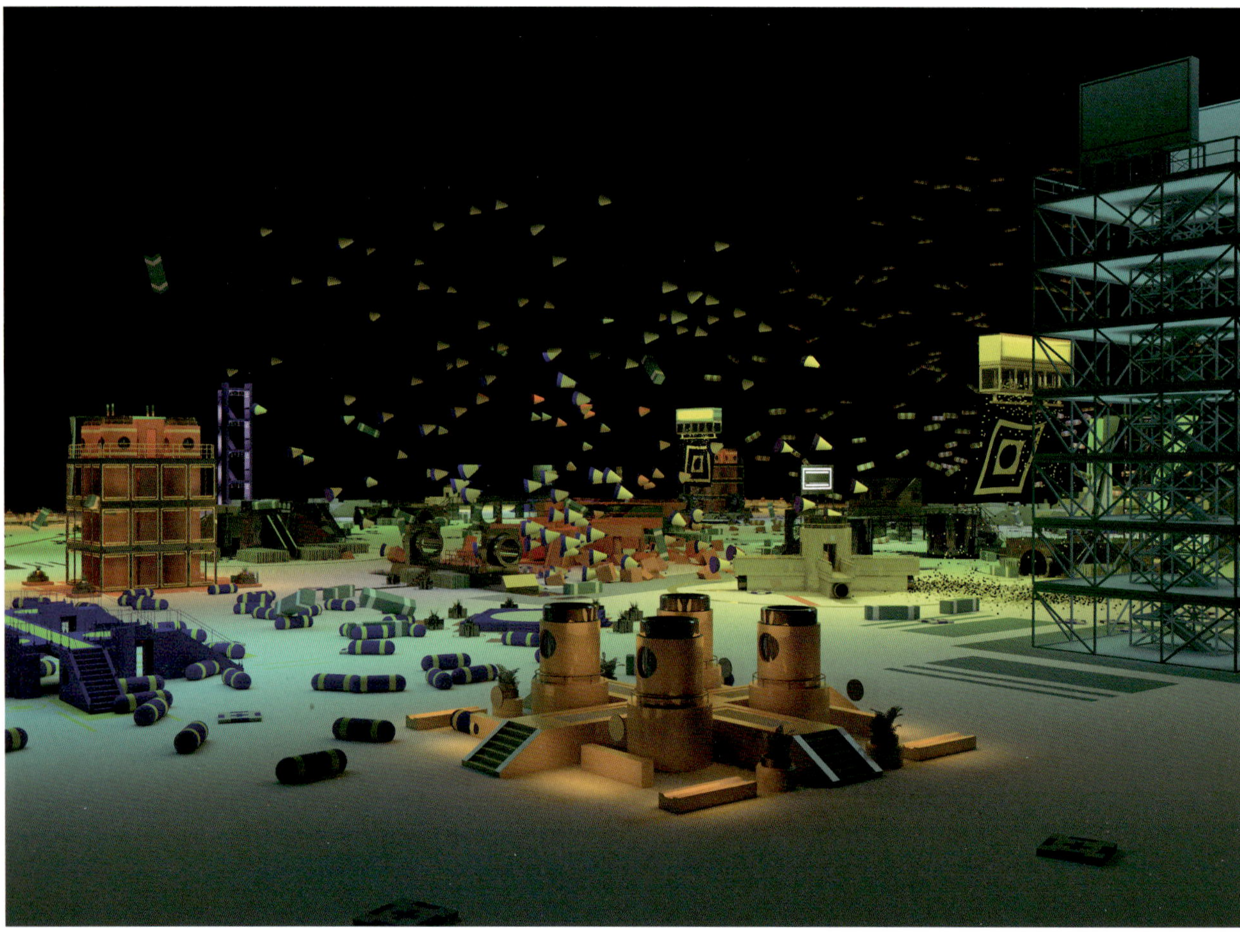

Playing the Complex

Chapter 8

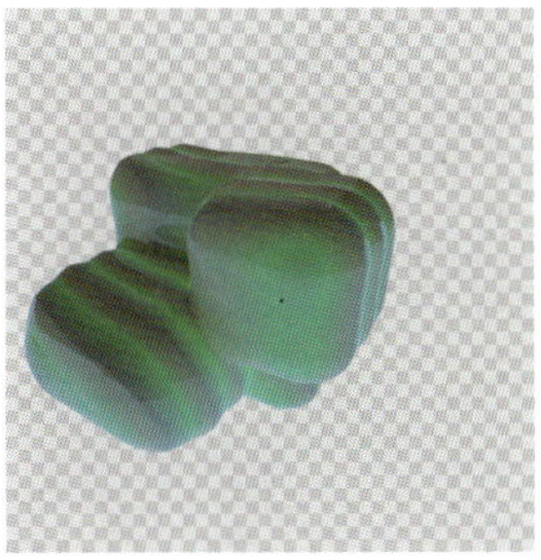

Candied Metaball

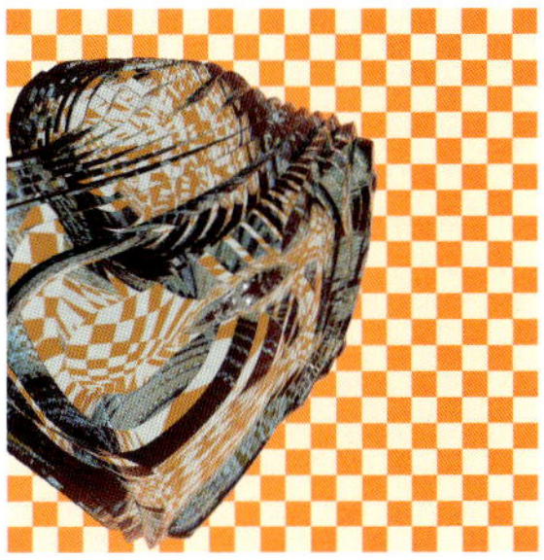

Glassy Metaball

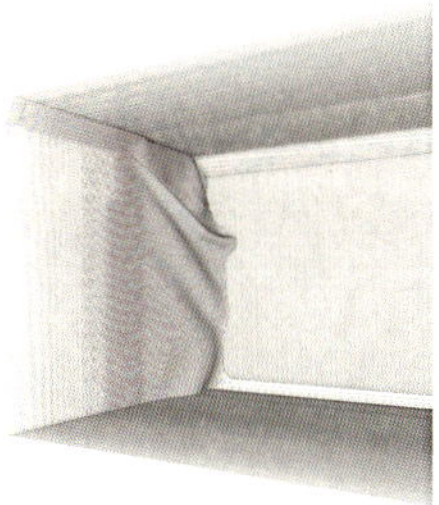

Curtain Wall

Index

Published by Applied Research and Design Publishing,
an imprint of ORO Editions.
Gordon Goff: Publisher

www.appliedresearchanddesign.com
info@appliedresearchanddesign.com

Authors: Carl Lostritto, Viola Ago, Julie Kress and Hans Tursack
Introduction: Carl Lostritto
Book Design: Pablo Mandel / CircularStudio.com
Project Manager: Jake Anderson

10 9 8 7 6 5 4 3 2 1 First Edition

ISBN: 978-1-951541-55-2

Color Separations and Printing: ORO Group Inc.
Printed in China.

AR+D Publishing makes a continuous effort to minimize the overall carbon footprint of its publications. As part of this goal, AR+D, in association with Global ReLeaf, arranges to plant trees to replace those used in the manufacturing of the paper produced for its books. Global ReLeaf is an international campaign run by American Forests, one of the world's oldest nonprofit conservation organizations. Global ReLeaf is American Forests' education and action program that helps individuals, organizations, agencies, and corporations improve the local and global environment by planting and caring for trees.